ETHNIC
CANADIANS
CULTURE AND EDUCATION

edited

by

MARTIN L. KOVACS

CANADIAN PLAINS STUDIES ■ 8

L. G. CROSSMAN, GENERAL EDITOR OF OCCASIONAL PUBLICATIONS

CANADIAN PLAINS RESEARCH CENTER
UNIVERSITY OF REGINA
1978

Copyright 1978 by the Canadian Plains Research Center
ISSN 0317-6290
ISBN 0-88977-009-3

Ethnic Canadians
  (Canadian plains studies; 8 ISSN 0317-6290)

  Papers from a conference held at the
University of Regina, Oct. 1-2, 1976.
  Includes bibliographical references.
  ISBN 0-88977-009-3

  1. Ethnology - Canada - Congresses.
2. Ethnicity - Congresses. 3. Minorities - Educa-
tion - Canada - Congresses. I. Kovacs, Martin
Louis, 1918- II. University of Regina. Canadian
Plains Research Center.
III. Series.
FC104.E84   301.45'1'0971   C77-002248-0
F1035.A1E84

Canadian Plains Research Center
University of Regina
Regina, Saskatchewan
S4S 0A2

Printed and Bound in Canada by Modern Press, Saskatoon.

TABLE OF CONTENTS

Introduction

I Aspects of Ethnicity

II Ethnicity and Solidarity

III Ethnicity and Education

IV Identity and Alienation

V Ethnic Research: Resources and Methodology

VI Ethnic Canadians

INTRODUCTION
MARTIN L. KOVACS

The main objective of this volume is to investigate the cultural-linguistic aspects of ethnic categories, with particular reference to the role and impact of education, and its operationalized instrument, the school, upon the direction and substance of changes in culture, language, and their intangible expression, ethnicity. However, it is not assumed that the respective ethnicities can be segregated in air-tight compartments independently of one another. On the contrary, in most cases two or more ethnicities may be accommodated in the culture of the individual and the group. The term *ethnic Canadian* is meant to imply the position that one may feel and act as a Canadian and be proud of one's Canadian as well as ancestral heritage.

Education, in its wider meaning, is almost coterminous with any cultural change internalized by any individual, irrespective of age and circumstances. In the present context, education is regarded as the process, instrument, and also the result of the socialization of a learner into a society. An essential component of this *formal* education is *enculturation,* implying in the present context "the process and result of conditioning by, adjustment to and integration with the ancestral culture," and *acculturation,* "the process and result of adaptation to an additional culture." It is understood that the formative years of the child within the family are essential in the development of his personality and value system, yet the school can be conceived of as the catalyst and an instrument of socialization into the linguistic idiom and roles of a microcosm erected from the cultural peculiarities and contributions of its members. It is this little world which may create changes in culture, language, emotions, and attachments through frequent and intensive interaction.

It was not the intention of the Conference or of this work to deal with the economic, political, and power aspects of the topic in any length.

The "Culture, Education, and Ethnic Canadians" University-Community Conference, held at the University of Regina on October 1 and 2, 1976, under the auspices of the Canadian Plains Research Center, was supported by the University of Regina, the Canada Council, the Department of the Secretary of State, and the Saskatchewan government, whose assistance — together with the selfless work of the members of the University-Community Group, of the Ethnic Research Section, and the Canadian Plains Research Center — is herewith gratefully acknowledged. The Conference provided the platform for the delivery and discussion of numerous papers on ethnic studies and research. These studies, often revised and greatly expanded, form the bulk of the present book, the publication of which has been greatly helped by the award of a Publication Grant from the Department of Culture and Youth, Regina, Saskatchewan.

The papers constituting this volume are the products of no fewer than thirty-five researchers, representing several disciplines such as sociology, anthropology, education, history, psychology, linguistics, and so on. The papers, presented as chapters on their own, are arranged in six sections in such a way as to deal with a major subject connected with the main theme of the book.

Eleven papers accommodated in the first section deal with such *aspects of ethnicity* as rights, terminological difficulties, folklore, multiculturalism, linguistic trends, image-makers, nation-building, and the nation-state. The second section places emphasis on *solidarity* in respect of *ethnicity* and contains four investigations dealing with ethno-territorial implications concerning Winnipeg, Esterhazy, and Whitehorse respectively, while the fourth addresses itself to the whole of Saskatchewan. The relationship and reciprocal impact between *ethnicity* and *education* forms the subject matter of the third section. Ethnicity and cultural resources, or, expressed differently, the ethnic relatedness and various ramifications up to the present of the *School Question* serves as the common topical denominator for the next eight papers. The consideration of the issue of the role of *identity* and *alienation* is the main subject for the fourth section. Social network and alienation, dual alienation, marginal identity, the alienation of the WASP, and the negative self-image are examined in the five papers of the section. *Ethnic Research: Resources and Methodology,* incorporated in the fifth section, contains a practical model of oral history research as well as an account of ethnic institutes in two papers, in addition to the other two listing and explaining the classes of historical records potentially instrumental for ethnic research, accommodated in the Public Archives of Canada and the Saskatchewan Provincial Archives. The sixth section, entitled *Ethnic Canadians: Synoptic Comments,* attempts the compilation of a tentative synoptic-integrative overview of those findings of the papers which, in the opinion of the editor, have contributed toward the formation of panoramic conclusions.

ASPECTS OF ETHNICITY

THE NATURE OF INDIAN CLAIMS
LLOYD BARBER
PRESIDENT, UNIVERSITY OF REGINA

Considerable attention has been focused on the question of Indian Claims during the past few years. The focus of attention has been heightened by large scale settlements in Alaska and James Bay and, more recently, by the Mackenzie Valley Pipeline hearings being conducted by Mr. Justice Thomas Berger and the Nunavut proposal of the Inuit Tapirisat of Canada.

Indian grievances have been with us in this country since the early stages of European penetration of the North American continent. The various European countries which vied for colonial supremacy in North America had differing policies for dealing with the original inhabitants of the lands they were penetrating. The most significant of these policies for the current Canadian situation was the British policy enunciated in a Royal Proclamation of 1763[1] shortly after the Treaty of Paris. The Proclamation provided for the protection of Indian lands from settlers and others until such time as the Indian rights to the land had been surrendered to the Crown. In effect, it precluded anyone other than the Crown from dealing with Indians for land and laid the basis for the treaty-making process in Canada. This process, which in certain respects is still underway, resulted in the surrender of Indian rights over vast territories, the creation of Indian reserve lands and the establishment of a variety of promises in exchange for native land rights.

Furthermore, the policy enunciated by the Royal Proclamation led to the establishment, within the British North America Act, of Federal rather than Provincial responsibility for Indians and Indian lands.[2] This fact emanating from British colonial policy is the basis for the special status of Indian people within the Canadian federation. No other people is named in the Canadian constitution as being the specific responsibility of either level of government. This special status led to the passage of the Indian Act for the discharge of the Federal responsibility and for various administrative relationships and regulations which have governed the lives of Indian people since Confederation.

Application of the Indian Act and its revisions has created several distinct legal classifications of native people in Canada. First the registered Indians who are Indians for purposes of the Indian Act. These people are sometimes referred to as Status Indians and sometimes as Treaty Indians though many of them do not have a Treaty. Time does not permit a detailed explanation of the basis, in the Act, for Indian status. Those of you who are interested can consult the Indian Act for a more complete exposé. Simply, however, an Indian, under the Indian Act, is one who comes under the jurisdiction of the Act.

In 1867, when the B.N.A. Act made Indians and ˉIndian lands the responsibility of the Federal government and later when the first Indian Act was written, the Inuit were not thought of and no mention was made of them. However, a Supreme Court decision of 1939 defined Eskimos as Indians for purposes of the B.N.A. Act. Thus, Inuit and Inuit lands became the responsibility of the Federal Government, but they did not, at the same time, become Indians for purposes of the Indian Act. The history of administration applied to Eskimos is thus quite different from the administration of Indian affairs. The claims issues arising from this situation are, as a result, different.

There are two other groups of native people in Canada which are not the direct responsibility of the Federal Government, which probably have legitimate claims based on historical treatment and which, to date, have largely been ignored. These are the Metis and the Non-Status Indians. Metis people are a distinct group. They are the descendants of early Scotch and French traders and Indians. They have a history different from the Indian history. While it was early recognized that they had aboriginal rights these rights were treated differently. The story of this treatment and subsequent events is a sorry one indeed. While relatively little has been heard from the Metis in the current discussion about native rights, it is a matter which is far from settled and one which we will hear a great deal more about.

The other group which is in an ambiguous state is the Non-Status Indian. These are people who are not Metis but who have either never achieved status (their ancestors should have been put on the "list" and were not), or who have lost status through the operation of the Indian Act (e.g., Indian women who have married white men).

Broadly speaking, there are three main categories of Indian claims in Canada arising from the various groups described and resulting from the historical circumstances. The first class of claim is the aboriginal rights claims which arise in those areas of the country where Indians have neither had Treaty nor been conquered in war, so that the original rights which they had in the land have not been acquired in accordance with the policy enunciated in the proclamation of 1763 and followed since by various governments of Canada. While the circumstances vary somewhat from area to area in Canada, Indians in British Columbia, the Yukon, Quebec and the Maritimes, Inuit in Quebec and the Northwest Territories and, with some variation, Indians in the Mackenzie region of the N.W.T., all claim that they did not cede their rights as the original inhabitants of their lands and are now demanding settlement.

The process of settlement of aboriginal rights claims is not and will not be easy. The wording of the Quebec Boundaries Extension Act may assist in clarifying why this is so. When the present boundaries of Quebec were established in 1912, the Quebec Boundaries Extension Act obliged the province as follows:

... the Province of Quebec will recognize the rights of the Indian inhabitants in the territory above described to the same extent, and will obtain *surrenders* of such rights in the same manner, as the Government of Canada has heretofore recognized such rights and has obtained *surrender* thereof, and the said province shall bear and satisfy all charges and expenditure in connection with or arising out of such *surrenders* (italics by author).[3]

Indians were, and see themselves as having been, sovereign in this vast land. The idea of *surrendering* sovereignty in one's homeland is anathema to any "nation." A nation does not sell its territory nor does it voluntarily surrender it to anyone except under extreme circumstances. Available historical records tend to indicate that Indians believed, rightly or wrongly, that they were not surrendering their sovereignty when they entered into liaisons with the white intruders into their lands, but rather that they were sharing nature's bounty with the newcomers. Much later, even after it became obvious that the newcomer was more numerous and more powerful than even the wisest Indian leaders had imagined, the idea that he should "surrender" his sovereignty was a foreign idea.

Even now, a hundred or more years after treaties were done on the Prairies, we see a desire on the part of Indians to enshrine their rights in modern settlements rather than surrender them in exchange for money and whatever else may be offered within the terms of modern settlement. The fundamental problem in contemplation of modern aboriginal rights' settlements is both simple and very complex. Europeans tend to see land as a commodity to be held individually and to be bought, sold or hypothecated at the will of the individual holder of the land. In contrast, aboriginal peoples tend to see land as a part of the total life experience. Land is life, life is land. It is something to be used and left much as it was found. It is something of the soul as well as the means for sustaining the body while it dwells on the land.

The James Bay settlement which is to be regularized through the passage of legislation both in the Quebec National Assembly and in the Canadian Parliament appears to satisfy the requirements of a majority of the Inuit and Cree of northern Quebec. Indians in other parts of Canada have voiced concerns that it is a "sell out" and, because it extinguishes rights rather than preserving them, it would not be acceptable as a settlement in their part of the country.

In the Northwest Territories, where because of the proposal to build a pipeline down the Mackenzie River, among other reasons, discussions about settlement have proceeded further than in other aboriginal rights areas of Canada, the complexity of the problem of achieving equitable settlements is readily apparent. The Northwest Territories is a case different from all others. In the first place the vast bulk of the Territories, a million square miles or more, is Inuit country. The Inuit have no treaty. They presented their position paper, Nunavut, and discussions for clarification of the paper were underway between the Government of Canada and the Inuit Tapirisat of Canada. The process was moving well when I.T.C. decided to take the proposal back to their Arctic communities for further consideration. This process is still underway. For purposes of this paper it should be noted that one of the major recommendations in the position paper called for the creation of a separate territory, Nunavut, which would be largely Inuit in population and would be governed through structures reflecting this cultural bias. The concept of sovereignty, while not explicit, is woven throughout the proposal.

The Mackenzie River area, including Great Slave and Great Bear Lakes, has traditionally been Indian country. This area, some 450,000 square miles, is covered by two treaties. Treaty #8 was done in 1899 and covers the region south of Great Slave Lake and includes most of the northern half of Alberta, part of northeastern British Columbia and some of northwestern Saskatchewan. Treaty #11, done in 1921, covers the remainder of the Mackenzie River area.

Both treaties 8 and 11 provide for reserve lands of 640 acres per family of five. These reserves were never established in the Northwest Territories and so one of the major provisions of these treaties remains unfulfilled. From time to time, there have been attempts to settle these treaties. In 1959, a Commission under Mr. Justice Nelson of Prince Albert examined this situation and made recommendations. No action was taken.

The Indians of the Northwest Territories claim that Treaties 8 and 11 did not have the effect of removing their native title in the land but were merely treaties of peace and friendship. Mr. Justice William Morrow, in his judgment later reversed by the Supreme Court in the celebrated caveat case, added weight to this view by indicating that he thought the Indians had a sufficient interest in the land to be allowed to file a caveat against the land. Since this judgment came down in the fall of 1973, the Indians of the Northwest Territories have developed their thinking about their claim. This culminated in the presentation of the Dene Declaration to the Government of Canada in 1976. This document rejects the traditional approach to settlements. It asserts continuing ownership of 450,000 square miles of territory and the establishment of a native state or states within Canada but with native institutions to ensure the preservation and development of their culture along lines which they wish.

For its part, the Government was reluctant to become involved in a process which might appear to be renegotiation of a treaty. However, there was recognition of the fact that the treaties in the north which were virtually carbon copies of treaties made much earlier in the south and were based on assumptions that agriculture would substitute for a hunting economy, are not satisfactory for northern conditions. Because the land provisions of Treaties 8 and 11 are unfulfilled, the Government agreed to receive proposals for a comprehensive settlement in the N.W.T. Discussions about the settlement were overshadowed by the Berger hearings on a northern pipeline. Obviously, the outcome of northern pipeline decisions will have a marked impact on the claims process in the Northwest Territories.[4]

In the Maritimes, the Indians claim that title to their land was not extinguished by the few treaties done in the area. As one proof of this, they point to the lack of any compensation as is inherent in other treaties, both pre- and post-Confederation.

While the Maritime region was under French control, the resident Micmac and Malecite Indians were allies of the French. When Acadia was ceded to the British in 1713, the British claimed that the resident Indians thereby became their subjects and that title to their lands fell to the British Crown. Both the French and the Indians denied these assertions. The French maintained that the Indians had been allies, not subjects, of the King of France. The French could not, according to that reasoning, have transferred to Britain a sovereignty and land title which they did not themselves hold.

To date, the issue of aboriginal claim in the Maritimes (and southern Quebec) has been neither acknowledged nor repudiated. The Union of Nova Scotia Indians has advanced a strong position asserting their right to be included within the aboriginal right negotiation process. The Federal Government policy on these issues, enunciated in 1973, is stated thus:

> In all these cases where the traditional interest in land has not been formally dealt with, the Government affirms its willingness to do so and accepts in principle that the loss and relinquishment of that interest ought to be compensated.

> There are other areas of the country where no treaties of surrender were entered into, such as southern Quebec and the Atlantic provinces. The Government's view is that land claims in these areas are of a different character from those referred to earlier in this statement.

In this brief overview of the aboriginal rights class of Indian Claims, an attempt has been made to provide some insight into some of the issues which make the achievement of just and durable settlements very difficult. In the process, developments in some parts of the country have been accorded only passing reference. This does not imply that developments in these parts of the country are not important, but rather that a detailed discussion of all developments is not necessary for overview purposes.

A second major class of claims is the issue of treaty rights. In those areas of the country covered by treaty and particularly in the West, the issues of treaty rights are paramount in the minds of Indian people. Indians claim, in general, that treaty provisions have not been fulfilled; that promises made at treaty time were not recorded in the treaties and have not been adhered to; and that, in general, the spirit of the treaties has not been lived up to by successive governments in Canada. As a result, Indians now find themselves economically, socially, educationally, and worst of all, culturally deprived. The treaties which were the Magna Carta of a new existence in partnership with the Government of Canada have not fulfilled that promise. Indians are increasingly insistent that the spirit of the treaties should be observed and that if it were, they would regain much of what they have lost in their one-sided relationship with us.

One example of the failure of governments to live up to the promise contained in the treaties should suffice to illustrate the point. The need for education was recognized by the Indians and by the Treaty Commissioners alike. The western treaties contain a promise of schoolhouses and teachers for reserve communities. In the light of education systems available to everyone a hundred years ago, it is easy to interpret this promise, particularly in the context of the discussions which led to its inclusion in the treaty documents, as a promise for free education. The Indians interpret it this way.

The problem is that the promise for education has not been fulfilled. The record of Indian participation in the educational systems made available to them over the years has been dismal. They feel, with some justification, that because the systems provided have not fulfilled the expectations that did exist and continue to exist, something new and better is required. The desire for a more effective system to satisfy the spirit of the treaties is now being expressed as a demand for Indian control of Indian education. Indians suggest that education has failed them because it has been conducted within a system alien to them and it has not recognized their basic cultural values. In fact, it has denied and denigrated those values and been an assimilative influence. They believe that only through greater Indian input into the education system can education be made a positive rather than negative influence in the lives of their people. In this way they would hope to achieve a much greater degree of success in educational attainment while at the same time strengthening themselves as a people. In this way the spirit of the treaties, at least in this regard, will be fulfilled.

There are other areas where Indians claim that the spirit of the treaties has been ignored or broken. Some of these are industrial development; hunting, fishing and trapping rights; and Band government. In sum, the treaty rights claims amount to an indictment of the administration of Indian affairs during the past 100 years. The Indians feel that the partnership which they undertook when they ceded their land has been at best unequal and at worst a betrayal of them as a people. Through an assertion of their treaty rights, they hope that they can regain some of their lost cultural identity and move forward toward a new and better day as proud and self-sufficient people.

The third major class of claim exists in all parts of the country to a greater or lesser extent and depends upon the kind of land which Indians have and the extent of Band funds they have had. These claims can be categorized under the term "Specific Band Claims" and are usually for loss of reserve land or relate to the administration of Band funds and Band business. There are a wide variety of claims under this general category of misfeasance, malfeasance or nonfeasance on the part of the Department of Indian Affairs acting in its role as trustee for Indian lands. The issue of lost reserve lands can serve to illustrate the problem in this area.

It is clear that the Indians who negotiated the Treaties were very concerned that they would not understand how to hold on to the lands reserved for them. They realized that their concept of land "ownership" and land use was different from that understood by the people who were intruding upon them. As a result they insisted, and the Treaty Commissioners agreed, that it be made very difficult for Indian reserve land to be surrendered. Indian Acts from the first onward embodied this concept and contained elaborate procedures for alienation of reserve lands.

From time to time, various reserve lands appeared very attractive to white settlers and the politicians who represented them. As a result, many surrenders of reserve lands took place under circumstances that can be described as dubious at best and fraudulent at worst. The Enoch Band is a case in point. This Band occupies a reserve immediately west of Edmonton. Three surrenders of land from their reserve took place at different times. One surrender was made before the turn of the century, one in 1902, and one in 1908. On the existing reserve, they have 35 producing oil wells. They are a relatively well-off band and, because of this, they have been able to research and advance their claim on the 1908 surrender.

The circumstances of the particular surrender, while unique to the Enoch's Band, illustrate well the nature of land surrender cases across Canada. A man named Oliver, who was editor of the Edmonton Bulletin, had, while editor, advocated a policy of opening up Indian reserve land to white farmers. Subsequently, he ran for Parliament, was elected and became minister in charge of Indian Affairs. He was then in a position to implement the policy which he had advocated when involved with the Edmonton Bulletin.[5]

The Enoch Band had, from earlier surrenders, quite a lot of money in its Band account, an amount in excess of a hundred thousand dollars. Oliver instructed officials of his department to obtain a surrender of more land. In the effort to obtain this additional surrender, it appears that duress was used. The Band, since they had money in their coffers, did not need to surrender but because they wanted to use some of this money for agricultural purposes, they were told that they could not have money to do that unless they surrendered more land to obtain money. In the process which followed, it appears highly probable that the provisions of the Indian Act concerning surrender were violated. The matter is now before the courts. Regardless of the outcome of the legal process in this case, the fact remains that the spirit of the Indian Act, which made and makes surrender of Indian lands difficult and which makes the Minister of Indian Affairs a trustee of sorts, was violated. In this regard, the entire story of this and other land surrender cases across Canada makes interesting reading. It is little wonder that Indians feel a deep sense of grievance as a result of these kinds of transactions.

The problems of redress of Indian Claims and grievances is difficult and complex. In Canada, we have recently come to the realization that we must settle these claims fairly and honourably. Appropriate mechanisms for settlement are slow to evolve because of the complexity of the issues and the reluctance of Indian people to get locked into any process which has the capability of providing solutions which to them would be unsatisfactory. The Indians have been engaged in a period of researching their claims and many have now come forward in a well-prepared manner. However, this process will continue for some time. While it is clear that most claims will fall into one of the categories which have been discussed, there are a variety of sub-sets of these classes not all of which have been detailed.

So far negotiation rather than adjudication is the preferred method for dealing with claims of all types. While there have been some notable court cases, the nature of the claims does not readily lend itself to court processes. Frequently, the claims transcend simple contractual disputes and go to the heart of the relationship between Indians and the larger society; and for Indians, this relationship has been unsatisfactory. In this sense, many of the issues are political in nature and tend, therefore, to defy final solution.

To assist in the negotiation process, a joint Indian/Cabinet Committee supported by the Canadian Indian Rights Commission has been established. Assisting the Joint Committee in its deliberations are a number of joint Indian/Government officials working groups. These working groups are tackling a wide variety of problems in Indian affairs, including the difficult matter of revisions to the Indian Act. Thus, it can be seen that the question of claims and grievances gives rise to the broader consideration of the relationship of Indians to the larger society as reflected in the legislation which so completely dominates their lives.

This, then, is a rather brief summary of some of the issues surrounding Indian claims in Canada. The implications of these issues for Indians and for other Canadians are potentially profound. In simple terms, we are faced with a backlog of grievances which go back a hundred or two hundred or even three hundred years in history. Normally, our Governments do not attempt to go back this far in examining and correcting injustices and it is easy to see why this is so as a general rule. The case of Indian grievances, however, is unique and exceptional. The original people of this country have not been in a position to make their case and insist on their unique rights which evolved from their special status within Confederation. Until recently, their grievances have not been part of the national consciousness because of serious weaknesses in communication and the one-sided nature of the relationship between Indians and others in this country. Indian grievances are not new to Indians nor are they new to the Department of Indian Affairs. Our new found consciousness of these matters should lead us to deal with them now in a fair and equitable manner in spite of all the difficulties inherent in this process.

There is an additional and overriding reason why the grievances must be dealt with. Over the years, the relationships between Indians and the Government have been such that strong feelings of distrust have developed. This distrust goes far beyond distrust of government to the entire society which has tried, since day one, to assimilate Indian people. Indians, who once dwelt proud and sovereign in all of Canada, have resisted with stubborn tenacity all efforts to make them just like everybody else. It is from these roots that all of their grievances stem. Indians have constantly insisted, and will continue to insist, that they are a special people who have an inherent right to their special status within Canadian society. They are not like other "ethnic" groups whose forefathers came voluntarily to this land. They have been here since time immemorial. This is not their land of adoption but their historical domain. Unlike the rest of us who are, or whose forefathers were, strangers in a strange land, Indians have come to feel like strangers in their own land. They are determined to overcome this feeling of alienation, and claims and the processes for settling them will be one way through which they will achieve this objective.

Indians are vitally concerned about their future as Indians within a large and powerful society and culture. They are now demanding, in an educated, articulate and forceful way, that past transgressions against their special status and special right be cleared up as a pre-condition to their self-determination about how they will take their position, proud and independent, side by side with us in shaping a new future. They have given up much in this country, and they feel that the assistance they receive from Government to achieve their objectives must be seen as a right in recognition of this loss and not merely as a handout because they are destitute. In short, their grievances are real, the claims arising from them are genuine, and equitable redress must be provided if the Indians of Canada are to occupy their rightful place in the shaping of the future Canadian society.

NOTES

Editor's Note: Dr. Lloyd Barber was Indian Claims Commissioner for Canada between December 1969 and March 1976. For further information on his work as the Commissioner see his *A Report, Commissioner on Indian Claims: Statements and Submissions* (Ottawa, 1977). An extensive list of references is found in (Research Resource Centre, Indian Claims Commission, Ottawa,) *Indian Claims in Canada: An Introductory Essay and Selected List of Library Holdings* (Ottawa, 1975).
[1]The Royal Proclamation, October 7, 1763, practically established what amounts to Indian rights by stating that the Indians under British protection "should not be molested or disturbed in the Possession of such Parts of our Dominions and Territories as, not having been ceded to or purchased by Us, are reserved to them, or any of them, as their Hunting Grounds. . . ." Adam Shortt and Arthur G. Doughty, eds., *Document* relating to the Constitutional History of Canada, 1759-1791*, 2 vols. (Ottawa, 1918), I, 166-67.
[2]The British North America Act, 1867, while enumerating the powers of the Parliament of Canada, mentions among the related classes of subjects "Indians, and Lands reserved for the Indians." *Statutes of Canada* (Ottawa, 1867), VI, 91, 20.
[3]The Quebec Boundaries Extension Act, 1912, (2c), *Acts of the Parliament of the United Kingdom of Great Britain and Ireland* (Ottawa, 1912), chap. 45, 304.
[4]On March 21, 1974, Justice Thomas R. Berger was designated by the Privy Council "to enquire into and report upon the terms and conditions that should be imposed in respect of any right-of-way that might be granted across Crown lands for the purposes of the proposed Mackenzie Valley Pipeline" with particular reference to its probable social, environmental, and economic impact. The first half of the Berger Report, *Northern Frontier, Northern Homeland: The Report of the Mackenzie Valley Pipeline Inquiry: Volume One* (Ottawa, 1977) was already available at the time of the writing of these notes. It constitutes a volume of 213 pages, well-illustrated with photographs, maps, and diagrams.
[5]Frank Oliver (1853-1933) founded the *Edmonton Bulletin* in 1880 and was its publisher until 1923. Between 1905 and 1911 he held the positions of Minister of the Interior and Superintendent General of Indian Affairs. J. K. Johnson, ed., *The Canadian Directory of Parliament 1867-1967* (Ottawa, 1968), 449.

NATIVE INVOLVEMENT IN CURRICULUM DEVELOPMENT: THE NATIVE TEACHER AS CULTURAL BROKER

JUNE WYATT
SIMON FRASER UNIVERSITY

Introduction

Recent studies of North American Indian education strongly recommend recognition of native culture in the school curriculum.[1] In this article difficulties in developing native cultural programs in the B.C. provincial school system will be briefly described and followed by an examination of program development at the Community School in the small rural Indian reserve community of Mt. Currie, B.C. It will be shown that even under optimum conditions, i.e., a high level of native involvement, there are still obstacles to creating a curriculum expressive of native culture. In particular there are aspects of native culture which are not compatible with the culture of schools; two learning styles — that of the school and that of the native-community — will be contrasted. As director of the Simon Fraser University Community Based Native Teacher Education Program I have observed the Mt. Currie school and community over a three year period. Based on these observations I recommend that it is desirable to synthesize these two styles and that accomplishing this synthesis depends in large part on the native teacher acting as a "cultural broker,"[2] one who can communicate effectively in both a school and a community context and can translate knowledge and skills from one to the other. This skill is critical in building a truly native curriculum.

Mount Currie is a "reserve" community of twelve hundred native Indians located about one hundred miles north of Vancouver in the British Columbia Interior. Nearby is the non-Indian town of Pemberton, population 2,400. A locally elected, all Indian school board has administered the Mt. Currie Community School, formerly a Department of Indian Affairs Day School, since August 1973.

In September 1973 the school board approached the Faculty of Education at Simon Fraser University for assistance in preparing native teacher aides to become provincially certified teachers. The following aspects of program design were of central importance to the Board: provision for training teachers to teach the native language (Lillooet)[3] and to incorporate aspects of native culture into the curriculum; operation of the program in the Mt. Currie community and school; and co-sponsorship and direction of the program by the Board and the Simon Fraser University Faculty of Education. As the Faculty of Education representative I served as the Board's consultant on teacher education and liaison with the

University. I worked with Board members in drawing up a program proposal, interviewing and selecting student teachers, designing program content and staffing. Since 1973 I have taught three courses at Mt. Currie to student teachers, I have observed them during their practica and informally interviewed them about their participation in the program. Information and analysis in this paper derives from my personal involvement in all phases of program development and implementation.

Difficulties in Provincial Schools

Many educators are convinced of the importance of native involvement in building native curriculum programs. King's *Survey* catalogues twenty-one sites in British Columbia where public schools and native people jointly sponsored small scale programs.[4] Native language and Native Indian Studies have both been popular. All language courses were taught by a native person. In the elementary school Native Studies programs local resource people and locally generated materials were used quite fully and effectively to demonstrate native technological skills, or to present stories about local native life. Secondary school courses relied heavily on written materials, and participation of local resource people ranged from occasional to none.

The desirability of native participation is generally agreed upon.[5] While historical and ethnographic manuscripts do not require the interpretation of native people to yield useful information their value is greatly enhanced by it. Learning about native culture is even further enriched when native people demonstrate their skills and communicate their knowledge not only through prepared curriculum materials (slides, tapes, video) but first hand in direct contact with learners. None the less, educators are having considerable difficulty in initiating and sustaining joint projects with native people. A number of factors appear to contribute to these difficulties and are illustrated by the Mt. Currie community's dealings with the provincial school system.

First, native people in general have had few opportunities to participate in long range program planning. At Mt. Currie initial requests for presentations of native crafts, songs, and dances were directed by provincial school personnel to individuals in the native community and to the Mt. Currie Education Committee which secured financing for the activities. While programs were well received by students, native and non-native, it became clear after three years of this type of programming that it would not lead to sustained developments. Each new school year necessitated new proposals for funding and the repetition of organizational work of prior years. As members of the committee became aware of these problems they withdrew from participation in the programs.

A second factor which hampers joint planning is that while native people spend a good deal of time in the schools, few teachers spend any time on the reserve. Members of the Mt. Currie community were recently invited to participate in a teachers' professional day on "Issues in Native

Education" held in the provincial High School. The central issue that emerged in the day's discussion was voiced by the native people: "We are always going to the school but people from the schools never come to us." They felt that true involvement could only come when teachers visited the reserve and participated in its activities. A number of teachers were pleased to be invited but the majority, supported by the administrators, felt their proper place was in the classroom, not in the homes.

Thirdly, native people lack experience as teachers and curriculum developers. While the Mt. Currie Education Committee was recruiting resource people, learning activities were planned and directed by the teachers. Although this meant providing native input where previously there had been none, it established no basis for native participation in planning learning activities or in developing their own teaching skills. This difficulty was also reflected in teachers' concern that resource people were unwilling to assume the conventional teacher role, requiring the host teacher to provide basic directions and control students. Teachers interviewed in King's survey expressed concern about this as well as uncertainty about the balance that should be sought between the study of traditional and contemporary life. Training native people as teachers and curriculum developers would be a step in the direction of alleviating these difficulties.

As these difficulties show, continued growth of programming requires that native people be involved as researchers, planners, fieldworkers and teachers in the schools and that school people participate in the activities of the native community (and, as will be seen, commitment from government and the universities is necessary as well). However, pointing this out is not meant to suggest that blame is to be placed solely on local school districts. The Mount Currie School is located in and operated by the native community. It might be expected that the problems so far mentioned would be avoided. However, this is not completely so, as a review of the developments there will show.

Developments at Mt. Currie: Background

In February 1973 the Federal Department of Indian Affairs endorsed the National Indian Brotherhood Policy Paper entitled *Indian Control of Indian Education*. Under the terms of this paper the Mt. Currie band was able to take over the administration of the Federally operated Day School on the reserve. The band Education Committee became the Education Advisory Board (hereafter called "The Board") consisting of eight members responsible, under the direction of a chairman and a secretary-treasurer, to the band council, and having authority to determine curriculum, hire staff, draw up the education budget and make long range plans for the development of the school. All financial support comes from the Federal government; services in native teacher training and curriculum development are provided by the Faculty of Education, Simon Fraser University.

Increasing Involvement — Ensuing Difficulties

A major responsibility of the Board is long range program planning, quite unlike its marginal role in working in this area with the provincial schools. A notable effort is the development of a native language program. Most of the children in the Mt. Currie community are familiar with, but not fluent in the native language. A graded language program from Kindergarten through Grade 12 is beginning to take shape. Establishing a community-based native teacher training program (described below) in conjunction with the Faculty of Education, Simon Fraser University, is another major effort which affects long range planning in curriculum development.

In addition to solving some of the problems in long range planning, native people at Mt. Currie are taking steps to ensure that teachers will be considerably involved in the community. In hiring for the Community School the Board seeks teachers who will live in the community, learn about the experiences of the children they teach, and build on these experiences in developing learning activities.

Training native teachers and curriculum developers from the community is intended to provide a means of broadening the range of educational activities in which native people are involved, thus dealing with the third main difficulty encountered in provincial schools. Developing classroom skills and skills in preparing learning materials makes it possible for native people to initiate and sustain curriculum programs rather than merely providing resources for other people's programs.

It is in this area, in clarifying the role of native people in classrooms, that solutions to difficulties are most complex. At Mt. Currie the complexities in this area became apparent as resource people worked in the community school.

Since 1973, older people from Mt. Currie who are knowledgeable about the community's traditions have played a substantial role in the school. They have instructed in language, crafts, songs, stories, dances and subsistence activities. Basket making, wool weaving, snowshoe manufacture, and fishing are some of the skills they have taught. Although the level of enthusiasm for these activities among children in elementary school has remained high, it is beginning to diminish among students in the secondary grades. Some have complained of the repetitiveness of the sessions, and resource people have complained about student unruliness, lack of interest and lack of respect. Many resource people, after encountering several sessions where students were inattentive or rude, will no longer come to the school. Other difficulties encountered by native resource people were discussed by them and student teachers, parents and teachers at a recent community meeting. It was evident that resource people were dissatisfied with the brief (20-40 minute) periods of time they were allotted and with working within a classroom environment where emphasis is placed on talking about rather than becoming fully involved in an activity. Presenting songs, stories and skills out of their normal context made it difficult to sustain student interest. In contrast, where resource people were involved in field trips which lasted for a full day difficulties in working with students were minimal.

It is clear then that even in a community based and run school, native cultural education focussing on resource people does not proceed entirely smoothly. Both students and resource people are becoming dissatisfied. How could this path be smoothed? One possible approach would be to dismantle the school and turn the entire community into a learning environment, thus making use of the skills of resource people as they are practised in their natural context. Part of the rationale for taking control of the school was to bring educational experiences for native children in touch with community experiences; immersing children in the community would be a way of doing this if "education" were defined in such a way as to exclude literacy skills. But the Board does not see education in this way. They feel that it would be unrealistic to do so. Many parents in the community at large are skeptical when they see their children going on field trips and have communicated this to Board members and to student teachers. They are not sure they are getting the skills necessary for contemporary survival — field trips and learning which takes place outside of the school look to most parents like "fooling around" without much educational value. Making these experiences credible to parents is critical if they are to be part of the learning program.

At this stage in the school's development a learning program centred entirely in the community is not feasible; but this does not mean that valuable learning resources from the community have to be ignored. Rather, it is necessary to find a way to include these resources without distorting their true character, boring the students, discarding literacy skills or losing credibility with parents. I suggest this can only be done as native teachers become cultural brokers. Accomplishing this is the goal of the Simon Fraser University community-based native teacher training program which has been operating in Mount Currie since July 1975.[6]

The difficulties encountered by resource people suggest that there is a conflict between the communication style with which they are familiar and that of the school. A simple description of these two styles will elucidate the conflict. Ways of resolving it are exemplified by evolving teaching styles among native student teachers. The concept of "cultural brokering" as used by John Herzog in "The Anthropologist as Broker in Community Education" best describes the way in which this conflict can be resolved without completely disregarding either the culture of the school or that of the community. While devised to explain a possible role for the applied anthropologist, "cultural brokering" also provides a model for the role of native teacher.

The applied anthropologist as broker accepts these premises: first, that both parties for whom he works — the government agency and the client (usually indigenous group) — are equals: neither is morally or intellectually superior, and neither should be viewed as "the enemy"; secondly, that development projects can and should draw on the resources of both groups; and thirdly, that his/her skills make it possible to go-beyond mediation — encouraging the two parties to devise solutions — to actually synthesizing these solutions.[7]

The native teacher working as a cultural broker similarly does not see either the school or the community as "the enemy." Rather such a teacher proceeds on the following premises: first, that aspects of the culture and communication styles of both school and community are valuable; secondly, that teaching styles and curriculum materials should draw on the resources of both; and thirdly, that his/her skills make it possible to go beyond simply recommending integration of the two approaches, and actually to develop programs and materials which synthesize aspects of both cultural styles.

Cultural Conflict — Community and School Communication Styles

In relying on native resource people to culturally enrich the curriculum the Board did not initially take into account that native culture consists not only of a certain content but a special way of communicating that content. It is not only what is communicated, but how it is communicated that is uniquely native. My observations, reinforced by commentary of native people involved in the program indicate that there is a community learning style and a school learning style. In the community the usual way for a child to learn a skill from an adult is to observe carefully over long periods of time, and then to begin taking part in the activity. Story telling usually takes place in an impromptu fashion at social gatherings and in co-operative work sessions. The way in which a native child learns the technology of fishing exemplifies community learning patterns. By accompanying adults on fishing trips, and by listening and observing the child learns places for fishing, and how to set nets, use a dip net, and prepare the fish for eating. He also learns names of different types of fish, parts of the fish, types of nets and assorted gear, and styles of preparation. All of this is learned by watching and doing with a minimum of verbal preparation or interchange. Similarly it would be unusual for an adult to ask a child to verbalize what he had learned. Whether or not he had taken in and retained the information would be evident on the next fishing trip. Any number of skills — hide tanning, basketry, or carving — could be taught in this way. The child may, of course, ask questions about the skills being performed, and the adult may supplement the actual performance with verbal commentary. However, verbal instruction without demonstration and participation, a recurrent phenomenon in the schools, is rare in a community context. Participation and demonstration in a classroom is almost always accompanied by verbal instructions. In a community setting this may occur but it is not always an integral part of the learning experience.

Story telling in a community setting and in a school setting are also quite different. During a fishing trip a story about other trips or about the history of the area might be told, or one might be told weeks later in a totally different context. In either case, once the story was started, it might go on for hours. It would be considered stifling to limit a story teller to twenty-minute sessions — a frequent occurrence in the school. During story telling sessions in the community children are expected to listen quietly. At the end no one asks them to recite the names of the main characters or to answer questions about plot, motivation and moral. The community learning pattern is thus quite different from what goes on in most classrooms, where the essence of learning is the articulation of information and skills in verbal and written form according to a pre-determined time table.[8]

Conflict Resolution: The Teacher as Cultural Broker

The conflict between community and school learning styles is now being recognized at Mt. Currie. The educational strategies of native student teachers there show that combining assets of school and community learning styles — "cultural brokering" — can be an effective form of native education. Native student teachers at Mt. Currie are developing a variety of ways of integrating school and community resources and learning styles. This is the foundation for developing curriculum which reflects the cultural experiences of the community and provides opportunities for mastery of school skills. The integration may involve teaching a traditional skill largely in a school context or using a traditional teaching style to teach a school skill. It can also involve drawing on the personal community based experiences of students, student teachers and resource people and using these as a medium for developing school skills — reading, writing and discussion as well as understanding of basic, universal issues in human growth and adaptation. A half-dozen examples of the cultural brokering process at the Mt. Currie School will suffice for indicating its defining characteristics.

Basket making is a traditional skill easily taught in a school context. When the skill was taught at Mt. Currie, responsibility for planning and implementation of a series of lessons was shared by a native student teacher, resource people and the classroom teacher. Consultation by the student teacher and the teacher with a resource person in the community gave them the information they needed to prepare children and organize materials. They gathered the equipment necessary for digging the cedar roots used to make baskets. The student teacher brought to class several completed baskets, borrowed from community people. She also prepared a series of photographic slides of baskets from Mt. Currie and from museum collections and brought these to class for viewing. Once the students had background information they began digging roots under the guidance of a resource person. After digging, they visited the woman in her home for instruction in soaking, stripping, splitting and weaving. A special visit was made to the home of an 85 year old woman who is one of the most prominent artisans in the interior region of British Columbia. Throughout these activities slides were taken which can be used for follow up lessons involving discussions and writing about experiences in basket making.

The assistance of a resource person in the activities described above is critical to the children's success in learning complex techniques. The guidance of a teacher who not only has access to resource people and some familiarity with their skills, but is also skilled in preparing students for the lessons and following up on what is learned is also critical. This is the only way of ensuring that the venture is an integral part of an ongoing learning experience rather than merely a temporary diversion or a token recognition of native culture. The approach outlined above avoids the difficulties which occur when resource people are brought into a classroom setting for a brief period of time and are required to conduct their teaching in a style unfamiliar to them. Here resource people's services are used in community or field settings in which they are comfortable. Their skills are complemented by those of the teacher who can use the children's experiences in learning community skills as a basis for developing their abilities in reading, writing and discussion. The sequence of activities in teaching basket making can be used as a model for teaching fishing, snowshoe making, hide tanning and any of the other traditional activities for which the assistance of resource people is vital.

In story telling and story writing one of the student teachers is using traditional teaching styles to teach school skills. She has a unique talent as a storyteller — learned in part by listening to her mother — and usually begins by telling her stories in the traditional fashion, without a written text. Stories about the "wildman" who terrorized residents of Mt. Currie seventy-five years ago are extremely popular with the children. This is part of the folk history of British Columbia which is not recorded in history texts. The wildman was an escaped prisoner who stole horses, abducted girls, roamed the hills and was finally brought to trial. The storyteller always liberally doses the narrative with dramatic gestures and impromptu play acting. Midway through an adventure she stops, turns to a child in the group and says, "The girl I am telling you about in this story is your grandmother," or, "The place where this story happened is where you went fishing last summer." These sessions are used as a starting point for the children to narrate (and eventually record in writing) their own stories — activities which are an integral part of the school's approach to teaching literacy. Students have so enjoyed the Wildman Stories that the student teacher who tells them has worked with her mother (the original teller of the stories) in compiling them into a six-part series of illustrated booklets — a significant departure from the traditional oral approach. This series is heavily in demand when the children have free time for reading. Their high interest in the dramatic tales, related personally to their lives, is a strong motivation for pursuing a school skill — reading. "Brokering" in this instance has effected a blend between traditional and contemporary narrative styles.

In teaching fifth grade mathematics another student teacher has also found a way to teach school skills using a traditional teaching style. She has decided to teach mathematics the same way her mother teaches hide tanning. Instead of beginning lessons with long verbal descriptions which lack concreteness and often bore students, she distributes materials (Cuisinaire rods, exercises, etc.), may demonstrate, using one or two examples, and then assists students individually as necessary by demonstrating how to do problems rather than by talking about how to do them.[9]

The approach to cultural brokering which opens up the widest field for native input into learning experiences is one which draws on the personal, community based experiences (not necessarily formal skills) of students and native instructors and uses these as the foundation for developing school based skills. The standard Grade 5 and 6 Social Studies curriculum which deals with native cultures of North America and cultures of the world is being used by a native student teacher as a framework in which many aspects of life in Mt. Currie are being included. The information about Mt. Currie is not studied as facts to be memorized. Rather, the students and teachers discuss their common experiences. The teacher can remind children of things they have done (fishing, going to potlatches, berry pickings, etc.) and thus stimulate them to narrate their own experiences. These are then compared with similar activities in other parts of the world. Fishing in Mt. Currie has its counterpart in almost every society in the world — as do family patterns, religious beliefs, community activities, and value systems. Children are led to understand these by identifying and articulating their own parallel experiences through discussion and writing.

Another example of this type of cultural brokering is where contemporary issues relating to land claims, education, fishing rights, Indians and the law and the development of contemporary native art and literature become the basis for developing literary skills and an understanding of historical processes. In the summer of 1975 people protested restrictions on fishing rights by blockading a road which runs through the reserve. In the hands of a native teacher attuned to community political sensitivities this action became the basis for research, discussion and writing in a high school social studies class. The drama of the events — roadblock, protest songs, encounter with RCMP, arrests and ensuing trial — could easily have sensational value only. But addressed by a native student teacher committed to protecting native fishing rights and land claims these events are used as an introduction to profound issues affecting the futures of all who live in Mt. Currie. Analysis and critical awareness of the history of Indian/white relations in B.C. and Canada, a standard part of the school curriculum, is made vital and compelling to Mt. Currie students when related to events in their own lives. This process is greatly facilitated when a native student teacher who is intimately familiar with the issues guides the learning process.

The same student teacher has also increased native involvement in education in her teaching of literature. *The Ecstasy of Rita Joe* (a play about a young native woman who faces discrimination and hardship in a world dominated by non-natives) is meaningful to her because of parallels in her own life. Without conveying either futility or despair she has helped students identify possible parallels in their lives and to articulate ways of dealing with problems. The rapport she has with students makes it possible for them to use personal experiences as the basis for the development of competency in expressive and analytic skills.

Conclusions

At Mt. Currie native education does not mean simply placing resource people in classrooms; nor is the school being turned out into the community. But native teachers *are* acting as cultural brokers synthesizing aspects of both community and school learning styles.

The experiences of student teachers in the Mt. Currie program indicate that cultural brokering is essential in developing native cultural programs in the schools and that only native teachers have the background necessary to be effective cultural brokers. Their access to and rapport with resource people ensures a continued input by these individuals. Moreover, student teachers' own experiences of growing up in a native community provide them with an intimate familiarity with the context and style of community life. They can draw on this repertoire of experiences in developing teaching techniques and in helping students to articulate their own experiences. They combine this familiarity with the community with basic teaching competencies — classroom management, lesson planning and organization, knowledge of B.C. curriculum, etc. The preparation for teaching they are receiving provides background appropriate for teaching in the B.C. public school system;[10] this preparation is integrated with the unique cultural resources which they bring to the teacher training program.

Achieving a balance between school and community styles keeps access to community resources open without jettisoning the possibility of developing basic school skills. Achieving a synthesis of these two styles does not compromise either, but strengthens both. Brokering is a critical skill if ongoing native cultural and educational development is to proceed. Native teacher training programs must take cognizance of the unique and valuable knowledge which native teachers bring to the classroom by virtue of their experiences in living in a native community. Recognition of these experiences is crucial if such programs are to do more than train teachers who just happen to be native.

FOOTNOTES

[1]In the U.S. this trend is documented by E. Fuchs and R. Havighurst in *To Live on This Earth: American Indian Education* (Garden City, N.Y., 1973), and in Canada by H. B. Hawthorn in *A Survey of The Contemporary Indians of Canada; A Report on Economic, Political, Educational Needs and Policies* (Ottawa, 1966). The National Indian Brotherhood strongly

recommends in its policy paper, *Indian Control of Indian Education* (Ottawa, 1972) developing native curriculum and refers to ten education papers by provincial Indian organizations which make similar recommendations.

[2]The term "cultural broker" is adopted from John D. Herzog, "The Anthropologist as Broker in Community Education: A Case Study and Some General Propositions," *Council on Anthropology and Education Newsletter,* American Anthropological Association, Washington, D.C., 3 (1972), 9-14.

[3]Lillooet is one of four languages in the Interior Salish language family. It is spoken fluently by most people over 40 years of age and with decreasing fluency by the younger. The first language of the majority of student teachers (ages 19 to 40) is Lillooet but all now use English as their primary language. Almost all of the children attending the Mt. Currie School speak little if any Lillooet.

[4]A. Richard King, *A Survey of Instructional Activities Developed For Native Indian Students in British Columbia as of 1973-74.* Faculty of Education, University of Victoria, Victoria, B.C. May 1974. An unpublished report of a study undertaken with support provided from the Division of Integrated and Supportive Services, Ministry of Education, Victoria, B.C.

[5]Cf. footnote 1 above.

[6]It was not the initial intent of the program to rectify problems of resource people working in the school. Difficulties in this area became apparent after the teacher training program was well underway. Moreover, there are no individuals who have worked as cultural resource people enrolled in the teacher training program. Resource people are all over 50 years of age, knowledgeable and skilled in traditional aspects of native culture. Since none expressed interest in entering the teacher training program there are no direct efforts being made to assist them in adapting their teaching style to a classroom setting. All of the student teachers are from the 20 to 40 age group. They know about some aspects of traditional culture but do not consider themselves expert in this area.

[7]Herzog distinguishes the applied anthropologist (fieldworker) as broker from the fieldworker as extension agent who sides with government agencies in seeing "modern Western ways as rational and desirable and traditional non-Western ways, as ineffectual and expendable," and the fieldworker as development-facilitator who is "indifferent or hostile to the plans or hopes of outside agencies. . . . His faith is in the common sense of 'the people' " (9-10).

[8]The contrast here between school and community learning styles is parallel to a contrast between styles of verbal participation analyzed by Susan U. Phillips in "Participant Structures and Communicative Competence: Warm Springs Children in Community and Classroom," in *Functions of Language in the Classroom,* ed. Courtney Cazden, *et al.* (New York, 1972), 370-94.

[9]Teaching mathematics by direct involvement rather than by lecturing is not a strategy unique to native teachers. However, developing this approach and understanding its validity is for this native teacher a result of her experiences in a native community.

[10]All of the student teachers in the Mt. Currie program will, upon completion of the program, be eligible for provincial certification and will have credentials for teaching in provincial schools.

ETHNICS AND NON-ETHNICS: FACTS AND FADS IN THE STUDY OF INTERGROUP RELATIONS

JOSEPH R. MANYONI
CARLETON UNIVERSITY

> The term "ethnic" is one of the vaguest known to sociology. We use it merely to designate a state of fact, going in no sense into the question of explaining the fact. — Pareto (1935:1837fn).

The purpose of this paper is to draw attention to an apparent need for a critical re-appraisal of the unreflective way in which the twin concepts "ethnicity" and "ethnic group" are used in discussions of intergroup relations. I argue that the concept "ethnicity" as currently used in the study of "ethnic groups" does not have the scientific status generally accorded to it as an analytical tool; and that the attributes it supposedly defines are not sociologically valid delineators of the socio-cultural phenomenon designated "ethnic group." Similarly, the term "ethnic group" does not appropriately define a specific social entity distinguishable from other aggregates by exclusive attributes.

The poor conceptualization of these analytical tools has methodological and empirical implications liable to vitiate research. Empirically valid and methodologically sound research results are dependent upon the precision of the conceptual tools used to generate data. A researcher is therefore impelled to have a clear, unambiguous idea of their meaning and boundaries. The concepts "ethnicity" and "ethnic group" cannot as yet claim analytic clarity in the identification and delineation of the phenomena they describe. This vagueness is attributable in part to the terminological problem that has been for long the bane of social science, particularly sociology and anthropology. It is also due to our unreflective use of poorly defined concepts. The problem is compounded by the largely metaphoric and derivative nature of much of the vocabulary of sociology and anthropology; hence widely divergent definitions of the same concept abound in the literature of intergroup relations. These divergent definitions have aroused less appreciable concern among students of intergroup relations than among some political scientists interested in utilizing "ethnicity" for the analysis of political behaviour and conflict (Plax 1974; Hechter 1974).

The basic premise of my argument is this: that apart from a "gemeinschaft" of the mind among social scientists as to the meaning of ethnicity, it has not yet been established what exactly are the properties that objectively define the sociological category designated "ethnic group." The current usage of ethnicity and ethnic group is more a matter of convention than analytic precision. Neither is it a means for a substantive differentiation among population segments into clearly defined socio-cultural units.

The conceptual categories under which certain social collectivities are subsumed call for close examination.

Ethnicity: Problems of Definition

"Ethnic studies" generally concentrate on descriptive analyses, measurements and quantification of empirical manifestations of intergroup relations rather than on re-examination and refinement of the heuristic devices by which the units of study are conceptualized. Thus certain socio-cultural collectivities are often lumped into "ethnic" categories, or excluded therefrom, on tenuous grounds of questionable sociological validity. As used in the literature, the term "ethnic group" appears to cover a multitudinous variety of socio-cultural units some of which cannot be broken down into ethnic groups by the criteria assumed to define ethnicity. Broad categories such as blacks, Asians, Orientals and West Indians can hardly be called "ethnic groups" on the basis of the attributes that are traditionally included in definitions. Most so-called definitions of ethnicity and ethnic group are not definitions at all. They are merely inventories of characteristics which purport to be attributes that define an amorphous entity designated ethnic group, usually distinguishable from "the larger society" (presumably comprising non-ethnics). In positing the existence of "ethnic group" as a distinct sociological category, we often overlook that this necessarily entails the existence of its antonym, "non-ethnic group(s)."

The core of the problem would seem to be a cognitive one. We need to broaden our conceptual framework, to distinguish between ethnicity as a cognitive concept, and ethnicity as a reified set of structural relations. In other words, we need to treat ethnic *identity* and ethnic *group* separately and thus avoid the error of confusing the concept "ethnic group" with the existence of a corporate entity which it describes. These distinctions are analogous to the way anthropologists now treat "tribalism" as a socio-cultural concept and "tribe" as a socio-structural concept, both being emergent properties abstracted from social behaviour and structural relations of the individuals. I draw attention to the anthropological usage of the concepts tribalism and tribe to illustrate the confusion that appears to reign supreme in our own thinking about, and use of "ethnicity" and "ethnic group" in studies of intergroup relations (*cf.* Mitchell 1974:15-17).

The way in which ethnicity and ethnic group are treated in sociological literature (as illustrated by the wide range of definitions to be cited here) revolves around the following factors:

Biological — common ancestry, racial origin;
Cultural — language, religion, recreation patterns;
Psychological — historical experience, common sentiments, conscious-
        ness of kind;
Nationality — national origin, citizenship.

The selection of these factors as indicators of ethnicity raises the question: what analytical procedures are used to differentiate the set of attributes designated "ethnic" from the totality of characteristics by which other similar collectivities may de defined? In other words, we would want to know what properties make a particular set of attributes peculiarly ethnic and thus to be associated with the notion ethnic group. Current conceptualizations of ethnicity raise doubts as to whether we do in fact *know* exactly what are the phenomena described by the concepts ethnicity and ethnic group. Their use in sociological analyses of empirical data does not appear to be based on firm epistemological grounds. A satisfactory explanation is not provided by the *a priori* assumptions and tautological explanations that are frequently made about the properties of ethnicity and ethnic group. To illustrate the point, let us consider a few examples of efforts which have been made to define ethnicity.

> What then is ethnicity? It is a synthetic term which refers to the fusion of many traits or components that belong to the nature of any ethnic group, thus ethnicity is a composite of shared values, beliefs, norms, tastes, consciousness of kind within the group, shared in group memories and loyalties, certain structured relationships within the group, and a trend toward continuity by preferential endogamy (Schermerhorn 1974:2).[1]

This definition raises more questions than it purports to answer; for example, What is "the nature of any ethnic group"? Are the enumerated "composite" attributes peculiar only to "ethnic group," or do they encompass other social units not subsumed under "ethnic"? The over-inclusiveness of the defining attributes evokes the neglected question: who are non-ethnics? And, what are the attributes that distinguish them? The view presented by Shils (1968:112) in an attempt to grapple with this conceptual problem underscores the vagueness surrounding this concept.

> Ethnicity does not refer to a genetic link with a particular person or persons. It is a link with a collectivity in which a vital, charismatic quality is diffused. It is thought to represent the possession of some quality inherent in the ethnic aggregate and shared by all its members. Indeed, the possession of that "essential" quality as manifested in certain external features such as skin color, hair form, physiognomy and physique constitutes membership in the aggregate.[2]

Could this "essential quality" be what Enloe (1973:15) calls "a peculiar bond among persons that causes them to consider themselves a group distinguished from others"?[3] Or, is ethnicity "what a person is born with or acquires at birth" but "distinct from all other multiple and secondary identities people acquire" as claimed by Isaacs (1975:30)?[4] These mystic qualities call for further explication if our perception of ethnicity is to be clarified.

In most definitions, biological descent or common ancestry stands out as a pervasive attribute of ethnicity. In Parsons' (1975:53-54) words, "Ethnicity . . . has very generally been interpreted as having a biological base sometimes explicitly stated in terms of racial distinctiveness."[5] This view is expressly shared, among others, by Williams (1947:27); Gordon (1964:27); Schermerhorn (1970:12); Greeley (1971:4). In a recent major

Canadian publication edited by Forcese and Richer (1975), what is otherwise a carefully considered definition of ethnicity tends to be weakened by being too narrowly predicated on the biological criterion: "In our usage, ethnicity refers to descent from ancestors who shared a *common culture or sub-culture manifested in distinctive ways of speaking and/or acting*" (italics original). Where a concession is made for the cultural criterion, it is the biological that is emphasized: ". . . the *kinship networks are crucial bearers of the culture*" (Vallee 1975:165-6, italics original).[6] Biological descent is also given prominence in another major Canadian work, Blishen *et al.* (1968:594), where the element of kinship is stressed: "Thus we can say that the ethnicity of a group refers to descent from ancestors who shared a common culture based on national origin, language, religion, or race, or a combination of these."[7] This bio-deterministic view of ethnicity is too constricting an approach to account for collectivities not predicated on "common ancestry," e.g., Metis and blacks in Canada.

The conceptualization of ethnicity in primarily cultural terms leads to undue emphasis being placed on cultural attributes which are treated as if they were *exclusively* "ethnic." The non-biological indices of ethnicity suggested by Berry (1958:54) eloquently illustrate the point I am making. Berry's repertoire includes: "a high degree of loyalty and adherence to certain basic institutions, such as family patterns, religion and language, distinctive folkways and mores, customs of dress, art and ornamentation, moral codes and value systems, and patterns of recreation."[8] In similar vein Martin and Franklin (1973:85), while noting the variations in definitions, conclude rather prematurely that "there is general agreement that the principal identifying characteristic of ethnic group is culture."[9] The cultural bonds they list in descending order are "language, religion, mores and folkways, style of dress, occupational specialization, esthetic standards, social values and personality models, in short various components of culture" (p. 86). This accretion of attributes makes it difficult to isolate with certainty the specific traits that are unique to this phenomenon, and by which it can be distinguished from other socio-cultural aggregates; (for further inventories of cultural attributes, see also De Vos and Romanucci-Ross 1975:9).

The tendency to confuse conceptual categories with an assumed social reality is implicit in many discussions about ethnicity and ethnic groups. Part of the problem lies in the failure to recognize that such discussions are often based on abstractions derived from quite different levels of analysis. Similarly inadequate is the tendency to extrapolate from situational analyses to more general pronouncements about the nature of the phenomena in question. "Ethnicity" and "ethnic group" are often treated in the literature as if both concepts belong to the same analytical level. A few examples will illustrate how some sociologists write about the way in which they conceptualize ethnicity and ethnic group. Berger and Berger (1972:119) limit the concept to specific situations of migration and suggest that ". . . ethnicity . . . is a term coined by American sociologists and peculiarly applicable to American society only. It refers to those cultural traits retained by immigrant groups to this country from their original home culture."[10] This view of ethnicity has of late been given popular currency by the protagonists of the "White Ethnics" or "New Ethnicity" school such as Novak (1971); Ryan (1973); Weed (1973); Greeley (1971, 1974). In his qualified definition, Greeley says " 'Ethnicity' in the narrow sense refers to the descendants of the European immigrants. 'Ethnicity' in the wider sense refers to any differentiation based on nationality, race, religion or language" (1974:291).[11]

The view of ethnicity represented in these works suggests that we do not yet have a reliable definition of ethnicity from which generalizations about ethnic groups can be made. As an analytic concept, "ethnic" does not have that essential scientific virtue of precision upon which the quality and validity of research conclusions depend. It does not appear that there is at present a satisfactory answer to the question: Who are ethnics? Recent attempts to answer this question have been less than illuminating; they appear to confuse categories and processes of entirely different orders, that is, *ethnicity* and *migration*. In Creeley's view, "One is not an ethnic in one's native village, but only when one has left that village for the city or left one's country for the New World. . . ." (1970:487).[12] This view is shared by Allen (1975:161 fn.) who says "The 'ethnics' are mainly immigrant groups, especially those from southern and eastern Europe. . . ."[13] Thus ethnics are conceived of as synonymous with immigrants. This perspective of ethnicity has more serious implications for sociological conceptions of "ethnic groups" than at first appears. It implies that every collectivity not native to the New World must be classified as "ethnic"; conversely, similar collectivities within Old World countries are not to be regarded as "ethnic." It is not clear how the conceptual boundaries are drawn by which one social category is distinguished from others of similar kind. The distinction between "ethnic" and "non-ethnic" aggregates is still blurred, and the question, who are non-ethnics, has not been seriously considered, let alone explored.

In the extensive literature on intergroup relations, "ethnic group" is variously contrasted with, and discussed as a substitute for "race" or "racial group" (Montagu 1964:80; Rose 1951:434; Berry 1958:55). One wonders whether the intellectual energy expended in efforts to distinguish between race and ethnicity has contributed much to broaden our understanding of ethnic groups. The problem does not appear to be whether race and ethnicity are confused; it is whether the concept ethnic group sufficiently demarcates a distinct type of aggregate from other collectivities. There is as yet little agreement on how objective boundaries are to be drawn. Witness the following attempt to define the boundary beween "ethnicity" and "race" which utilizes both a geographic criterion and a bio-cultural one. According to Bonacich (1972:48).

The difference between ethnicity and race lies in the size of the locale from which a group stems, races generally coming from continents, and ethnicities [sic!] from national sub-sections of continents.[14]

She goes on, however, to state that the two categories share the same bio-cultural attributes:

Both terms refer to groups defined socially as sharing a common ancestry in which membership is therefore inherited or ascribed whether or not members are currently physically, or culturally, distinctive (*ibid.*).[15]

The boundaries suggested in the first part of the definition are blurred beyond recognition by the addition of attributes common to both phenomena being contrasted.

From a logical point of view, "ethnic" ought to be contrasted with "non-ethnic," and not treated as a residual category of "race" or "racial." We need to have a definition of *non-ethnic* as a category distinguishable from ethnic, (its logical antonym). However, we are not likely to produce a definition of "non-ethnic" by virtue of the over-inclusiveness of the attributes ascribed specifically to "ethnic group." I shall put the argument another way. If "ethnic group" is a "distinct social category set apart from the larger society by unique cultural attributes," then it is logical to expect that what is *not* ethnic must not, and cannot, have the *same* properties of the entity from which it is distinguished. The polarity is one of non-complementary attributes and may be expressed as in the following paradigm:

Diag. 1   ETHNICITY CONTRAPOSED

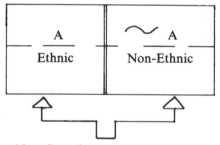

Non-Complementary Attributes

The crux of the problem discussed here appears to lie in the difficulty of separating "ethnic" from "non-ethnic" attributes. This difficulty arises from the fact that standardized criteria and their relative weight necessary to distinguish clearly between these two categories have not been established.

The undifferentiated conceptualization of ethnicity also entails methodological problems about the basis upon which ethnic identity is predicated. The methodological procedures used to deduce the attributes which are deemed to demarcate "ethnic" from "non-ethnic" categories may themselves be faulty. From an empirical point of view, it would seem methodologically appropriate for the researcher to elicit directly from the respondent what ethnicity entails for him, rather than presume the fact.

Subjective self-identification by the respondent would appear to be a more reliable guide for ethnic awareness *and identity* than objective categorization by the observer. The emphasis placed on the "mental states" criteria in definitions of ethnicity leads one to expect that a respondent's conception of his ethnic identity ought to supersede a researcher's preconceptions of that identity. However, there is some evidence in the literature which suggests that self-identification is not always taken as an important guide for establishing ethnic identity in empirical research. As may be inferred from the following research report, objective categorization appears to have superseded self-identification:

> In our research we were not concerned with the explicit awareness of ethnic heritage, that is, that there might be differences between those Irish who were conscious of being Irish and those who are not ... Nor did we concentrate on the decline of ethnic attitudes and behaviors through the generations. When we asked a respondent what his nationality or background was, we assumed that his answer, "Irish" or "Italian", indicated the possible presence of a predisposition to attitudes, values, norms, and behavior that were part of the baggage the immigrant groups brought from their countries of origin and passed on to their children and grandchildren ... (Greeley 1974:91).[16]

One might argue that ascribed identities imposed on individuals provide a less reliable guide than identities elicited from the "structured" behaviour and verbal responses of those individuals. To be sure, ethnic identity is multi-dimensional and is largely dependent upon the actors' perception of their situation within a framework of structured relationships. Thus, which identity is given salience in a particular context is a matter for empirical observation, not what E. K. Francis has labelled "dubious guesswork."

"Ethnic Group" as a Structural Concept

It should be evident by now that there is merit in maintaining an analytical distinction between ethnicity as an *identity* concept and ethnicity as a *structural* concept. As an identity concept, ethnicity may be taken to refer to the quality of "being alike" in the sense that a collectivity of individuals exhibits similar characteristics deemed to be "ethnic." However, "ethnic group" more properly refers to the entity which may emerge when the recognition of "being alike" is transformed into self-conscious cohesive action by the collection of individuals who share the identifying attributes. It cannot be assumed that individuals by merely exhibiting the sum-total of the so-called ethnic attributes thereby constitute an ethnic group. The existence of an ethnic group predicated on the observed similarity of characteristics is a matter for empirical verification rather than theoretical speculation. (See Plax 1974: 296-7; Hechter 1974:1151-2; Mitchell 1974:17-18.)

Definitions of ethnic group are often bedevilled by the common error of mistaking the presence of properties for the existence of the social entity they define. Frequently included in definitions of ethnic group are psychological attributes such as: consciousness of kind, shared sentiments, shared historical experience, and we-feeling. The presence of these mental states as indicators of ethnic *identity* do not *ipso facto* entail the existence of an ethnic *group*. Empirical data have to be adduced to substantiate conclusions to the effect that a collectivity of individuals not only shares a consciousness of kind, but does *in fact* function as an organized community or group. It is not sufficient to resort to mystic bonds as evidence of a presumed existence of a group. Groups are functional entities which operate within some normative framework recognized by their members; it is this factor that distinguishes groups from mere collectivities. An "ethnic association" *is* an ethnic group, yet not all individuals who share ethnic identity constitute membership. Ethnic associations are thus clearly defined *groups,* not to be confused with the abstract entity described as "ethnic group." To the point here is the distinction Weber draws between ethnic group and kinship group — the first being a hypothetical, and the second, an actual community. In Weber's sense then, "ethnic membership does not constitute a group; it only facilitates group formation of any kind ..." (1968:389).[17] In short, it is a structural concept.

The literature is replete with implicit assumptions about the existence of "ethnic group" as a "real" social entity, or as Rose (1968:71) puts it, "a community one could 'feel' if not 'touch.' "[18] These assumptions are largely based on psychological factors which are themselves often not established. Consider the following definition of ethnic *group* based on psychological attributes: Novak (1971:47) asked the right question but gives an elusive answer:

> What is an ethnic group? It is a group with historical memory, real or imaginary. . . . Ethnic memory is not a set of events remembered, but rather a set of instincts, feelings, intimacies, expectations, patterns of emotions and behavior. . . .[19]

Does not this inventory of mental states imply *identity* rather than *group*? It is apparent that the conceptual status of the two terms become confused in the process of definition. Although both are emergent properties they are abstracted from different levels of social relationships. The confusion could well be avoided if the two concepts were *analytically* treated separately. In this way it would be possible to show that there is no necessary connection between a people's perception of its identity, and the existence of a group based on that perception. Ethnic *identity* is an abstraction of the cognitive level, while ethnic *group* is a property of the *structural* level of analysis. The distinction between the various conceptual categories of ethnicity is expressed in the following diagram.

It is apparent from this paradigm that ethnic *group* is a resultant transformation of ethnic *identity* through consciously organized action of the participants, and is a function of their structural relations. At this stage, it would be legitimate to speak of "ethnic group" as distinct from ethnic category or collectivity (see Williams 1964:18; Hughes and Kallen 1974:87; Singer 1962:420).

Diag. 2   CONCEPTUAL CATEGORIES OF ETHNICITY

Conceptual/Cognitive level	Empirical/Structural level
ETHNIC IDENTITY	ETHNIC GROUP
Psycho-socio-cultural attributes	Action/Behavioural indicators

In most definitions of ethnic group there is a tendency to ignore the distinction between the *conceptual* and the *structural* levels. The sum-total of "ethnic" attributes and the confluence of shared characteristics are treated as synonymous with ethnic group and with membership in it. According to Chinoy (1967:45),

> Ethnic groups are made up of persons who share a common cultural tradition which unites them in a single social entity.[20]

The image thus conjured up is one of a consciously organized social entity, but most ethnic categories are not organized into groups in the manner suggested. The frame in which definitions of ethnic group are cast suggests that the social entity is assumed to exist without its properties being first established. Some examples will clarify the point: Bailey and Katz (1969:viii) state that they view ethnic group "as a generic term to cover racial, religious or nationality groups . . . *who are assumed to possess certain traits,* real or affective, distinctive from those of the larger population" (italics added).[21] Similarly Foltz (1974:103) points out that ". . . an ethnic group is assumed to be distinguished by virtue of its sharing of certain properties not shared . . . by members of other groups."[22] A careful reading of Weber suggests that in his original definition of "ethnic group" the use of the words "belief" and "presumed" referred to claims of (putative) common ancestry made by the individuals themselves, not to the analyst's categorization of that self-perception. In Weber's words, "Ethnic membership differs from the kinship group precisely by being a presumed identity, not a group with concrete social action, like the latter."[23]

Another problem entailed in current perspectives of ethnicity is the way it is viewed as an organizational principle at variance with principles of organization in modern complex societies. The current interest in the so-called problem of the resurgence of ethnicity suggests that this phenomenon is somewhat deviant and thus a sociological problem to be investigated and explained. Ethnicity and ethnic groups are thus viewed as particularistic but transient phenomena in a process of development towards a universalistic form of organization — the Nation State. This view is influenced by the dualistic typologies of social forms based on the theories of Durkheim, Weber, Tonnies and Parsons which assume social organization to be an evolution from simple primordial forms to complex universalistic types. Ethnicity is therefore perceived as one of the forms of *Gemeinschaft* that has survived in a rationalized, bureaucratized society (Greeley 1974:27).[24] This model is based on the thesis that:

> ... the ethnic collectivity represents an attempt on the part of men to keep alive during their pilgrimage from *Gemeinschaft* to *Gesellschaft*, from peasant communities to industrial metropolis, some of the diffuse, ascriptive, particularistic modes of behavior that were common to their past (Greeley 1971:4).[25]

It is probably this view of ethnicity that has led to the selective perception of otherwise universal attributes as peculiarly "ethnic" characteristics.

The difficulty involved in attempts to select distinctive characteristics unique to ethnic group was noted some thirty years ago by E. K. Francis in his celebrated essay on "The Nature of the Ethnic Group." The essay is widely cited but its caveat is not always heeded. Francis, like Weber, treats "ethnic group" as a hypothetical category which is not a race or a nation or a kinship group precisely because none of these elements are sufficient delineators of the ethnic group from other aggregates. More specially, Francis states that ". . . we cannot define the ethnic group as a plurality pattern which is characterized by a distinct language, culture, territory, [or] religion . . ." (1947:397).[26] The problem is one of finding distinctive attributes not shared by other social aggregates from which ethnic group is demarcated. Current definitions either encompass too wide a range of social categories by being over-inclusive, or they exclude some collectivities of similar kind by being too narrow.

Schermerhorn (1970), like Gordon (1964) and Berry (1958), has posited one of the most comprehensive definitions of ethnic groups which is at once an eloquent illustration of over-inclusiveness and elusiveness of this concept:

> An ethnic group is defined here as a collectivity within a larger society having real or putative common ancestry, memories of a shared historical past, and a cultural focus on one or more symbolic elements defined as the epitome of their peoplehood. Examples of such symbolic elements are: kinship patterns, physical contiguity . . ., religious affiliation, language or dialect forms, tribal affiliation, nationality, phenotypical features, or any combination of these. A necessary accompaniment is some consciousness of kind among members of the group (1970:12).[27]

Although Schermerhorn does not suggest that the 'collectivity within a larger society' is necessarily a minority (a claim made in most definitions), he does imply that an ethnic group is something distinct from the rest of a society. The problem with Schermerhorn's definition lies in its overinclusiveness. Is the inventory of the 'symbolic elements' he cites as "the epitome of [the group's] peoplehood" unique to ethnic groups? The listed criteria are broad enough to define all other component units of "the larger society." The phrase "kinship patterns" as a defining characteristic of "ethnic group" is vague. It could refer to patterns of tracing descent, or the range of collaterality, or socialization practices purely within the domestic domain, or to sex roles and authority patterns. It is difficult to isolate the uniquely "ethnic" patterns from this phrase. Collectivities often designated "ethnic group" are rarely physically contiguous, or religiously homogeneous, and though they may speak the same language, they are rarely identifiable by phenotypical features from the populace with whom they share the same nationality. "Consciousness of kind" is a less readily established characteristic than "consciousness of *status*" which would be a more appropriate phrase to cover all types of social grouping.

Anthropologists in Kroeber's and Malinowski's day were careful to emphasize the universal imperatives shared by all human societies to serve biological and social needs which each culture then impresses with its own unique imprint. Yet in studies of intergroup relations only "ethnic groups" appear to be singled out for this special quality of uniqueness. According to Rose (1974:13), "Groups whose members share a unique social and cultural heritage passed on from one generation to the next are known as *ethnic groups.*"[28] Apart from the difficulty of locating any culture that (at least in modern complex societies) is passed on from generation to generation as a unique form, this view is contradicted by the general theory of acculturation. Glazer and Moynihan (1970:162) appear to recognize the problem posed by the attribution of uniqueness to ethnic culture: "Ethnic groups, then, even after distinctive language, customs, and culture are lost, . . . are continually recreated by new experiences in America."[29] Rose (1951:7) is even more specific that "By the third and subsequent generations, the language and culture patterns tend to be predominantly those of the dominant group."[30] But the more crucial question relates to the problem of distinguishing between what is an "ethnic culture" and what is a sub-culture within a complex multi-cultural society such as Canada or the United States.

In Canadian studies, ancestry, language, and culture are often closely linked as critical indices of ethnic grouping. This practice has led to the error of confusing biological descent with cultural transmission. One source of this confusion is the census practice of classifying individuals by language. A great many non-empirical sociological analyses of "ethnic groups" are drawn from census tracts. It requires little imagination to contemplate the consequences of the following census definition of "ethnic group":

> Ethnic group refers to ethnic or cultural background *traced through the father's side.* . . . Language spoken by the person or by his paternal ancestor on first coming to this continent was a guide to the determination of ethnic or cultural group in some cases (italics original).[31]

This exclusively patrilineal rule of descent invoked by the Canadian Census is too restricted a guide to one's perceived ethnic identity. The definition also treats culture as synonymous with language and nativity. It ignores the dynamics of culture which involve cumulative accretion of elements from the surrounding society. As a dynamic process, culture is not inexorably tied to a person's ancestral or national origin.

The Metis and blacks in Canada are respectively the kind of collectivities that are not amenable to a classification based on ancestral origin and language. These collectivities cannot be legitimately defined as ethnic groups according to the usual criteria of ethnicity: common ancestry, distinctive language, national origin, distinctive religion or a unique culture transmitted from generation to generation. However, there is an ironic twist inherent in the apparently narrow criterion of classification based on paternal ancestry and linguistic mode used by the Census of Canada. It has broad ramifications when applied to the Metis. It is possible that one might identify as many Metis ethnic groups as the number of individuals who may care to claim identities based on their polyglot paternal ancestry. The criteria of national origin and paternal ancestry have similar implications for the blacks as for Metis. It is legitimate to ask: to what degree is the *skinship* of the blacks predicated upon *kinship* on the basis of common ancestry, or, on the language of paternal ancestors when they first came to this continent? Perhaps hardly. The Metis and blacks do not fit into the ethnic group framework defined by common ancestry and culture. This problem appears to have been recognized by Talcott Parsons in his definition of ethnic group which stresses biological relatedness. Parsons starts by defining an ethnic group as:

> ... an aggregate of kinship units, the members of which either trace their origin in terms of descent from a common ancestor or in terms of descent from ancestors who all belonged to the same categorized ethnic group (1951:172).[32]

He ends up by excluding blacks: "In the case of the Negro color as a visibility symbol in a sense takes the place of a distinctive culture" (*ibid.* fn.). Parsons is thus impelled to shift the emphasis from kinship and culture to "skinship" in an attempt to resolve the definitional dilemma.

What is the Solution?

In a critical review of this nature it would be quite legitimate to argue the case against the existing state of conceptualization of ethnicity without necessarily being impelled to offer a solution to the problem. The argument presented in this paper can be evaluated objectively, not only in relation to the representative examples adduced here, but also the whole body of literature on the subject. As was stated at the beginning of this paper, the purpose of the review is to open up critical dialogue among concerned students of intergroup relations, rather than to offer prescriptions as to how the dilemma could be resolved. However, it may be felt that, if one has the audacity to question widely accepted terminological usage, one has an obligation to offer alternative and better terminology. Consequently, some alternative (and hopefully more appropriate) designations of social categories currently subsumed under "ethnic" are suggested below without the presumption that they are the only possible resolution to our difficulties.

The underlying assumption in most discussions of ethnicity and ethnic group is the implicit (sometimes explicit) notion that ethnic identification is synonymous with minority status. Thus "ethnic" is traditionally employed to refer to individuals and collectivities *not* associated with dominant or majority status; it is a designation applied to socio-cultural aggregates of subordinate, immigrant, and/or peripheral status in situations of power relations. *Status relationship* rather than primordial sentiments of identity would seem to be the universally most distinguishing criterion among population aggregates. Individual and collective identities could thus be seen primarily as a function of common status positions particular segments occupy within a given society. These segments can then be identified by their particular salient distinguishing feature from other component societal entities.

I suggest we would do well to reconsider the time-tested, conceptually unambiguous but now neglected term "minority group." The analytical value of "minority" as a definition of status relations is unassailable; its sociological *meaning* is well established in the literature.* I thus propose that the vague term "ethnic" can be more appropriately replaced by the explicit and specific compound terms: racial minority, cultural minority, religious minority, and linguistic minority. These compound terms are sufficiently comprehensive in reference, specific as to boundaries, and denotative of the salient symbolic nexus of the collectivity. Objections may be raised against "racial" because of its scientific ambiguity, but in intergroup relations the scientific definition of race has long been abandoned in favour of its social definition which is the only relevant one in social perception, interaction and attitude formation. In societies where colour/physique constitutes a salient factor of social distinctions, individuals tend to react to socially perceived "racial" features, and not to scientific definitions of bio-physical characteristics. "Racial minority" thus has relevance at the macro-level of intergroup relations in complex societies in which bio-physical features have primary salience.

"Cultural minority" has the major advantage of being totally embracive of virtually all collectivities currently subsumed under "ethnic" with its attendant ambiguous definitions. "Cultural minority" naturally accommodates such diverse collectivities as Metis, Indian sub-groups, Inuit, blacks (currently arbitrarily designated "West Indian" *and* "Negro" in Canada), Asian sub-groups and various "Latin" Americans. This term implicates far more population aggregates than "ethnic" presumes. A cultural minority may consist of individuals of diverse "racial" backgrounds, bio-physical features, national origins; or it may share a language not native to any of its constituent parts (*vide* Spanish in Latin America,

---

*The term "ethnic" is rarely applied to "majority" or "dominant" segment of society. The latter two are synonymous with "mainstream" and thus often excluded from the designation "ethnic group." The exclusion is unwarranted either on sociological or logical grounds.

French in the Antilles and English in the West Indies). The analytical probity of "cultural minority" becomes even more evident when one considers the respective status positions of "Coloured" in South Africa and the West Indies, Eurasians in India and Indonesia, Mulatré in (former) Portuguese Africa, and many other marginal groups of this nature. A cultural minority may also be a religious minority as is the case with Hutterites and Doukhobors where national origin, language, culture, and religion overlap.

In Canada, it will be noted, the criteria for ethnic distinctions are arbitrary, categorical, and not infrequently devoid of logic. Categorical (ethnic) boundaries may be determined on language, unilineal descent, colour, national and geographical origins. The categorical classification of the population by "ethnic group" in the Census of Canada 1971 population tables bespeaks the imprecision by which group boundaries are selected.

Ethnic Group	1971
Indian and Eskimo	312,760
Negro	34,445
East Indian	75,725
Indo Pakistani	52,100
West Indian	28,025

Source: Extracted from Tables 1.5 and 1.6 *Immigration and Population Statistics* (4), pp. 9-12, Manpower and Immigration, Ottawa 1975.

It will be noted that no mention is made of Metis, and that "West Indian" is treated *as an ethnic group* without regard to whether the subject is a white, black, coloured, Chinese, Portuguese, East Indian native of a particular territory in the region. It would be presumptuous nonsense to suggest that all these different components from the West Indies feel, act, behave and function as "an ethnic group" either at a macro-level or micro-level.

Conclusion

The thrust of the discussion in this paper has been to draw attention to some unconsidered implications of the conceptual tools currently used in studies of intergroup relations. I hope the discussion has shown how the undifferentiated conceptualization of ethnicity leads to unjustified assumptions about ethnic groups. The widely divergent definitions of ethnicity and ethnic group not only suggest uncertainty about the phenomena they describe, they also lead to sociological conclusions which are assailable on epistemological grounds. The definitions comprise criteria that are either too broad, or too narrow to be a reliable guide for delineating specific social categories. The psychological and biological factors posited as indicators of ethnicity tend to be uncertain; the cultural indices are as "elusive and contradictory as the concept of ethnic group itself."[33] The so-called ethnic attributes are no more than ascriptive symbolic elements of identity not necessarily entailing membership in an ethnic group.

Post Script

Three highly relevant papers to this discussion published since my paper was completed have come to my notice. Since they have a direct bearing on the legitimacy of my own argument I wish to direct attention to their conceptualization of the problem of ethnic definiton only by citation (Yancey *et al.* 1976; Brass, 1976; Keyes 1976)*.

---

*William Yancey *et al.*, "Emergent Ethnicity", *ASR*, 41, 3, June 1976, 391-403.
Paul R. Brass, "Ethnicity and National Formation", *Ethnicity*, 3, 3, Sept. 1976, 225-241.
Charles F. Keyes, "Towards a New Formulation of the Concept of Ethnic Group", *Ethnicity*, 3, 3, Sept. 1976, 202-213.

FOOTNOTES

[1]R. A. Schermerhorn, "Ethnicity in the Perspective of the Sociology of Knowledge," *Ethnicity*, 1 (1974), 1-14.
[2]E. A. Shils, "Deference," in J. A. Jackson, ed., *Social Stratification* (Cambridge, 1968), 104-32.
[3]Cynthia Enloe, *Ethnic Conflict and Political Development* (Boston, Mass., 1973).
[4]Harold A. Isaacs, "Basic Group Identity: The Idols of the Tribe," in N. Glazer and D. P. Moynihan, eds., *Ethnicity: Theory and Experience* (Cambridge, Mass., 1975), 29-52.
[5]Talcott Parsons, "Some Theoretical Considerations on the Nature and Trends of Ethnic Change," in N. Glazer and D. P. Moynihan, eds., *op. cit.*, 53-83.
[6]Frank G. Vallee, "Multi-ethnic Societies: Issues of Identity and Inequality," in D. Forcese and S. Richer, eds., *Issues in Canadian Society* (Prentice Hall, Scarborough, 1975), 162-202.
[7]Bernard Blishen *et al.*, eds., *Canadian Society* (Toronto, 1968).
[8]Brewton Berry, *Race and Ethnic Relations* (Boston, 1958).
[9]James Martin and C. W. Franklin, *Minority Group Relations* (Columbus, Ohio, 1973).
[10]P. L. Berger and B. Berger, *Sociology: A Biographical Approach* (New York, 1972).
[11]Andrew M. Greeley, *Ethnicity in the United States* (New York, 1974).
[12]Andrew M. Greeley, "Ethnicity as an Influence on Behaviour," in P. I. Rose, ed., *The Study of Society* (New York, 1970), 486-98.
[13]Irving L. Allen, "WASP — From Sociological Concept to Epithet," in *Ethnicity*, 2 (1975), 153-62.
[14]Edna Bonacich, "A Theory of Ethnic Antagonism: The Split Labour Market," *American Sociological Review*, 37 (1972), 547-59.
[15]Edna Bonacich, *op. cit.*, 548.
[16]Andrew M. Greeley, *Ethnicity in the United States.*
[17]Max Weber, *Economy and Society*, vol. 1, G. Roth and C. Wittich, eds., (New York, 1968).
[18]Peter I. Rose, *The Subject is Race* (New York, 1968).
[19]Michael Novak, *The Rise of the Unmeltable Ethnics* (New York, 1971).
[20]Ely Chinoy, *Society: An Introduction to Sociology* (New York, 1967).
[21]Harry A. J. Bailey and E. Katz, ed., *Ethnic Group Politics* (Columbus, Ohio, 1969).
[22]William J. Folz, "Ethnicity, Status and Conflict," in W. Bell and W. Freeman, eds., *Ethnicity and Nation Building* (Beverly Hills, 1974), 103-16.
[23]Max Weber, *op. cit.*, 389.
[24]Andrew M. Greeley, *op. cit.*, (1974), 27.
[25]Andrew M. Greeley, "Ethnicity as an Influence on Behaviour," in Otto Feinstein, ed., *Ethnic Groups in the City* (Lexington, 1971), 3-16.
[26]E. K. Francis, 1947, "The Nature of the Ethnic Group," *American Journal of Sociology*, 52(1947), 393-400.
[27]R. A. Schermerhorn, *Comparative Ethnic Relations* (New York, 1970).
[28]Peter I. Rose, *They and We* (New York, 1974).
[29]N. Glazer and D. P. Moynihan, "Ethnic Groups and the Melting Pot," in M. Steinfield, ed., *Cracks in the Melting Pot* (Beverly Hills, 1970), 157-77.

[30]Arnold Rose, *Race, Prejudice, and Discrimination* (New York, 1951).
[31]Statistics Canada, *Dictionary of the 1971 Census Terms* (Ottawa, 1971), p. 6.
[32]Talcott Parsons, *The Social System* (London, 1951).
[33]E. K. Francis, *op. cit., 395.*

WORKS CITED

Bailey, H. A. J. and E. Katz, ed., *Ethnic Group Politics* (Columbus, 1969).
Berry, B., *Race and Ethnic Relations* (Boston, 1958).
De Vos, G. and L. Romanucci-Ross, eds., *Ethnic Identity* (Palo Alto, 1975).
Forcese, D. and S. Richer, eds., *Issues in Canadian Society* (Scarborough, 1975).
Glazer, N. and D. P. Moynihan, *Ethnicity: Theory and Experience* (Cambridge, Mass., 1975).
Gordon, M. M., *Assimilation in American Life* (New York, 1964).
Greeley, A. M., *Why Can't They Be More Like Us?* (New York, 1971).
Hechter, M., "The Political Economy of Ethnic Change," *American Journal of Sociology,* 79 (1974), 1151-78.
Hughes, D. R. and E. Kallen, *The Anatomy of Racism: Canadian Dimensions* (Montreal, 1974).
Montagu, A., *Man's Most Dangerous Myth* (New York, 1964).
Mitchell, C. J., "Perceptions of Ethnicity and Ethnic Behaviour: an Empirical Exploration," in A. Cohen, ed., *Urban Ethnicity* (London, 1974), 1-35.
Pareto, V., *The Mind and Society* (New York, 1935), vol. 4.
Plax, M., "On Group Behavior and the Ethnic Factor in Politics," *Ethnicity,* 1 (1974), 295-316.
Rose, A., *Race, Prejudice, and Discrimination* (New York, 1951).
Ryan, J. A., *White Ethnics* (Englewood Cliffs, N.J., 1973).
Singer, L. S., "Ethnogenesis and Negro Americans Today," *Social Research,* 29, 419-32.
Schermerhorn, R. A., *Comparative Ethnic Relations* (New York, 1970).
Weed, P. L., *The White Ethnic Movement and Ethnic Politics* (New York, 1973).
Williams, R. M., *The Reduction of Intergroup Tensions* (New York, 1947).
Williams, R. M., *Strangers Next Door* (New Jersey, 1964).

FOLKLORE IN THE INTERCULTURAL CONTEXT: LEGENDS OF THE CALLING RIVER

KLAUS BURMEISTER
UNIVERSITY OF REGINA

The folk arts, in the context of Canadian society, are fulfilling a dual role. Most of the arts, crafts, and traditions which fall into this category are, of course, the contributions of distinct cultural groups rather than of society as a whole, although their appreciation may be universal. Preservation and performance are therefore significant in maintaining cultural individuation. On the other hand, folk arts are acclaimed as a contribution to our total culture, and thus the indigenous cultural envelope of any such 'folk' becomes — pars pro toto — an exponent of national aspirations.

This integrative (rather than assimilative) process which we refer to as our multicultural design in order to distinguish it from the melting pot concept, has been accepted quite readily and within a comparatively short period of time. However, while highly visible ethno-cultural festivals and community folk arts councils have had little difficulty in finding support, research in less established 'folk'-oriented activities has not been as fortunate. The study of folklore, for example, has remained as one of the least explored avenues to an understanding of the people in a multicultural nation. And this in spite of the fact that folklore is inextricably related to a sense of community, and shares in the artistic process of practically every musical, dramatic, visual or kinetic folk art medium. There is also the matter of philosophical orientation. Our artificially stimulated cultural ecology with its emphasis on ethnic heritage and the 'preservation' of cultural values still tends to project folklore as essentially a nostalgia trip for older people, although traditionalism is by no means an intrinsic part of it,[1] instead of encouraging it as a medium of living interaction. We might better be reminded that the mythologies and thus the lore of our complex society cannot be divorced from our daily lives because they

> ... are covert systems of assumptions, values, beliefs, personal wishes socialized and social wishes internalized, which reveal themselves only in the images and metaphors in which they get expressed, in syntactical relationships, in the articulation of incidents, in the fleshing out of archetypal personae and situations.[2]

But what must be of the most immediate concern, because it indicates a regressive attitude in terms of social objectives, is that the study of folklore, where it is pursued, remains compartmentalized, and that its potential as a tool for cross-cultural understanding is still not being explored beyond the respective ethnic bailiwick. We are suffering from esoteric-exoteric imbalance, a condition which Jansen defines like this: "The esoteric applies to what one group thinks of itself and what it supposes others think of it. The exoteric is what one group thinks of another and what it thinks that other group thinks it thinks."[3]

Reducing this definition to its respective propositions, we find that *esoteric* implies shared group identity and activity, and thus folklore is a medium of shared experience within an enclave, be it racial, religious, professional or social; most of the few folkloristic studies which have been completed so far fall within that scope. Conversely, *exoteric* reflects our understanding of parallel cultures in our social matrix with concomitant appreciation and interchange. The significance of such exoteric studies within the framework of our society is obvious, but unfortunately they have not yet received the emphasis they deserve.

Folklore researchers in the United States have urged for years a multilateral approach to the study of folklore, from "synchronic comparative research in ethnic folklore relations"[4] to "the social base of folklore" and to "folklore performance [which] is the key to the real integration between people and lore on the empirical level".[5] But such approaches are dependent on and, therefore, must be preceded by an appreciation of the contributions of other cultures in the first place. This can be a difficult matter for groups whose approachability suffers from two disadvantages: one, their principal orientation is not toward the dominant cultures and, two, their heritage is non-literary.

Thus the documentary record of our Native Indian cultures is fragmentary and superficial. Little comprehension is shown on the part of the immigrant cultures for the special value of the artistic expression of people "outside the pale," and even less sympathy for their way of life. In addition, the lore of the Indian is especially elusive because of the non-recurrent nature of the oral transmission process, and its general inaccessibility. But, speaking with Botkin, to proceed from "cultural history to cultural strategy" requires our study of all cultural components, because only in this way can the folklorist "outgrow the older 'survival' theory of the 'partial uselessness' of folklore and (may) renew the continuity and survival values of folklore as the 'germ-plasm' of society."[6]

In the western provinces the potential for folkloristics has, on the whole, not yet been surveyed, although conditions are particularly favorable. The socio-economic patterns of development, especially during the period 1880 to 1914, such as agricultural block settlements, ethnocultural enclaves, a high rate of mother-tongue retention and, until recently, the absence of broad educational opportunities in the isolated rural settlements, have preserved excellent field conditions for the student of folklore. Even so, time is running out to record our early history and lore. We are today witnessing rapid changes in social systems and cultural norms alike, and although the folkloric continuum adjusts to reflect prevailing conditions, it is the traditional lore which is irretrievably lost. The patterns of acculturation are rapidly enveloping even the remotest area, and in all likelihood this will be the last decade for collecting first-hand oral history of both pioneer and native culture.

In order to explore the potential for cross-cultural appreciation through folklore, we shall attempt to unravel some of the skein of a local legend from Southern Saskatchewan which meanders out of the oral repository of Native Indian myth into the literature of the White Man. A number of versions have been gleaned from oral and literary sources which are presented here without special regard for 'purity' or communicative context since oral texts cross into the domain of written literature and are, in turn, affected by the printed word.

If this approach is heuristic rather than analytic and the whole question of form, context and the application of folkloristic principles is left to future study, it is because first things must come first. The systematic collecting of evidence must be preceded by an indication that something worthy of pursuit is there — just as the established repertory must precede analysis. The emphasis of this paper is on establishing an awareness of the continuity in the evolution of our multicultural stratigraphy. It is only the first step in recognizing "that all of the past that counts for much is contained in myth, which in turn creates the actuality of the future, which becomes myth to recreate another future."[7]

The local legend perhaps more than any other folkloric genre is suited to illustrate the richness of the native folkloric panorama, because it is the end-product of cultural imagination focused on a distinct phenomenon, such as a prominent physiographic feature or an outstanding event. Even more important, this type of legendry is part of the traditional lore which for successive generations, provides cultural continuity and a sense of belonging to the land. Each era contributes new versions to the general corpus of material because the endemic appeal of the locale survives and perpetuates the legend formation process. For a legend to be accepted as such, it must meet three generally accepted criteria: there must be evidence of its erstwhile popularity in a certain place, it must contain some supernatural element to distinguish it from oral history, and it must contain at least one folk motif to establish its kinship with what is essentially folklore. Thus, the legend is stimulated by historicity and myth alike, and appeals to us because of its inherent ethos rather than as a possible factual truth. It serves as a vehicle of significant psychological and social import, first within the originating culture, and then beyond it in those which supplant it. Legends circulate, are re-shaped and syncretized, and they remain unaffected by either veracity or variability because, in a sense, they are never "wrong."

Onomastics (place-name research) is one discipline which has discovered the usefulness of local legendry to its pursuits. The onomatologist wants to know what a particular place-name reveals of the personality of the people, their values, their prejudices and their relations with other people or even cultures. Place-names of the Indian cultures in Saskatchewan would be a fertile field for this type of investigation, especially the many mini-legends (dites) which give us glimpses of a colorful, otherwise unrecorded history. In Cree, for example, Wolseley was known as "Wolf Hide Hanging," the area around Lipton was "where the skunk dens are" and the Standing Buffalo Reserve was "where the enemy was pushed to the extreme," in reference to one of the many skirmishes beween Cree and Blackfoot.[8] Of all place-names, however, none is more colorful than "Qu'Appelle."

Folklorists have frequently commented on the close connection betweeen topography and legendry. In the case of the Qu'Appelle Valley in southern Saskatchewan which extends for nearly three hundred miles from the town of Elbow to the valley of the Assiniboine, it is easy to see why the collective imagination of many generations of Plains Cree, Saulteaux, Ojibway and immigrant settlers should have focused on its striking features. The valley provides a stark contrast to the southern plains and to the rolling bush country extending toward the North. The Fishing Lakes in particular, Katepwa, Mission, Echo and Pasqua, here and there bordered by high banks with fluted folds which refract sound and light in stunning patterns, enhance the charm and mysteriousness of the valley.

'Kahtapwao' — 'Qu'Appelle?' — 'Who Calls?' . . . the name has given rise to many tales in the Native Indian tradition, explaining the echoes and their effects, some embellished for entertainment, others serving as warning of mysterious creatures and as premonitory signs. Most have been forgotten in the continual reshaping of legendry, and only one, an acculturated tale of Cree provenance, is generally known and circulated today. But by piecing together various shards from different sources, one finds that the motif of the Calling River has always been given wide currency and has therefore also emerged in different folkloric genres.[9]

Reaching back into time, the cosmogonic myth is first to attempt an explanation for the Qu'Appelle echo. In the Algonquian tradition the mysteries of creation in the remote past assume mythopoeic form in the tales of *Wesakachak,* a playful trickster, demiurge and brother of all creation. Here is how a recently collected oral myth of the Woodland Cree explains the origins of the valley and its echo:

[A] One day long ago when the world was young, Wesakachak was touring the plains when he came upon a wide split or crack in the earth. Anxious to see what was in the gulley, he saw a green carpet of grass swaying in the breeze.

"Boy," he said to himself, "would I like to dance like that!" In saying so he shouted to the grass "Brothers!"

From the valley came an answer, "Who calls? (or, in the French language, "Qu'Appelle?").

"Brothers, this is Wesakachak. Would you teach me to dance like that?"

The grasses could not stop because Keewatin, the North Wind, was having too much fun with them. They, however, while they danced, managed to agree to let Wesakachak join them. . . .

And Wesakachak danced well into the night, all the while dancing around the edge, stamping out the grass at each round. To this day, the valley has no grass around the edge. At the early dawn, the grasses were so tired that they could not dance anymore. When they were subdued, Wesakachak went up on the sides and said:

"From this day on, don't ever tell anyone of this incident or I'll trample you into the earth like I did to the sides. You will say that I first invented the Grass Dance."

And he danced again around the edge, all the while beating his drum. By this time, he was tired and full of sweat. And the sweat ran down into the valley creating the three pools, or lakes, which remain to this day.[10]

Purging and bowdlerizing of original material by informants, compounded by the inherent problems of transfer from oral tradition to print, remains a vexing problem. Yet the written word, no matter how expurgated, is frequently the only record of the legend still extant. Much is lost because the 'oralness' of oral literature derives from circumstances of its presentation and its variability and not necessarily from the subject matter itself. The skill of the story-teller combined with the receptiveness of the audience to create an intangible mood which was unlike anything required for the appreciation of the literal record. Even so, the quality of 'oralness' remains the ultimate objective of much of written literature today. Therefore, even the adaptation retains something of the essence of the original.

Our legend first enters print in the accounts of explorers and missionaries. Harmon's Journal of 1804 gives a glimpse of a rich narrative tradition of this place [B] "Ca-ta-buy-se-ps or the River that calls [Qu'Appelle], so named by the natives who imagine a Spirit is constantly going up and down the River, and its voice they say they often hear, but it resembles the cry of a human being."[11] Mr. Dickinson of the Hind Red River Expedition some fifty years later amplifies this account with one from an elderly Indian at Fort Ellice which, in fact, was to become the mold for the legend version known widely today:

[C] A solitary Indian was coming down the river in his canoe many summers ago, when one day he heard a loud voice calling to him; he stopped and listened and again heard the same voice as before. He shouted in reply, but there was no answer. He searched everywhere around but could not find the tracks of anyone. So from that time forth it was named the "Who Calls River."[12]

We note that, while [B] has met the criteria for a legend, [C] is more in the nature of an observed phenomenon which leaves the teller baffled, rather than mystified or afraid of a disembodied presence. Nevertheless, this version remains on the periphery of the legend complex, and imputes to it a degree of substantiality which is missing from some of the following, more fanciful legends.

The Qu'Appelle legend was not strictly localized, although Katepwa is frequently cited, but extended to the river *(Katepweosipiy)* and lake *(Katepweosakahigan)* alike, as one of the oblate missionaries recalls. In the 1880's he recorded the following explanatory version of the place-name from Kakijwe (Loud Voice), an old Cree chief and medicine man:

[D] One day, two groups of Indians, one coming from the north, the other from the south, found each other face to face on each side, and since they could not cross the torrent of water because they had no means of navigation, they could only communicate by shouting very loudly, that is, by *s'appelant.* Ever since the place was called *Rivière-où-l'on-appelle,* from which is derived the name Qu'Appelle, which has remained with us to designate the valley itself.[13]

If it were not for the absence of definitive markers in [D] (e.g., identification of the parties or individuals involved, occasion for the meeting), this rendition could well be classified as local history. Here, it is not an echo-effect which is said to make communication difficult, but the physical effort of shouting above the "torrent of water." Mystery has no place in this matter-of-fact observation — thus no legend. Nevertheless, something has been added to our appreciation of the actual legend cycle: confirmation of native awareness of a rational universe as the basis for the lore of the valley.

Most legends are peopled by non-differentiated characters, and the emotions — fear, anger, love, hate — are implied rather than expressed. But even without detailed psychological reflection, the intended moral purpose is clearly and powerfully conveyed. We return to the echo motif in the oral tradition of the Saulteaux, and learn of the consequences of parental neglect:

[E] During the saskatoon season, a young woman with a baby laced in a mossbag attached to a board, called a cradle, went out picking. She leaned the cradle against a tree in plain view of the berry patch. In peering deeper into the bushes she saw larger berries and went after them and repeated this performance until she got out of view of the baby in her greed. When all her containers were brimming full, she emerged from the bluff . . .; she heard its cry down by the lake shore . . .; then she knew it was the watery serpent that took her baby into the lake and she would never see it again. . . . For generations the cry of this infant was heard on the lake by the Salteau Indians to remind them that they must not indulge in greed.[14]

The echo motif as disguised warning in legendary form appears to have been prevalent throughout this region. A similar theme, presumably a caution to be level-headed in desperate situations, is contained in yet another legend of the Cree, this one of Old Wives Lake, southwest of the Qu'Appelle: [F] three old Indian women, pursued by Blackfeet, missed the saving ford across the lake in their terror, and were drowned. On the anniversary of the event, so the legend goes, they may be seen struggling in the shallows and calling for help.[15]

Native Indian folklore, both as knowledge (wisdom and experience of the past) and as art (song, dance and narrative), has either been disregarded by the immigrant cultures or made to conform to our own peculiar tastes. The previously mentioned best known legend of the origins of the valley's name by Pauline Johnson is a case in point. It bears eloquent testimony to the susceptibility of folkloric material, especially in oral tradition, to the vagaries of fashionable literature in general, and to the shortlived apotheosis of Canadian literature of the 1920's in particular.[16] Her lyrical rendition of "The Legend of Qu'Appelle Valley" was based on a legend which Father Hugonard of Lebret Mission had collected from the Cree.[17] In the mellifluous cadence of Victorian tradition it tells of an Indian brave who, while paddling across one of the valley's lakes to visit his bride after a long journey, is haunted by her voice:

[G]   "Qu'Appelle? Qu'Appelle?" No answer,
      and the night
Seemed stiller for the sound, till round me fell
The far-off echoes from the far-off height —
"Qu'Appelle?" my voice came back, "Qu'Appelle?
      Qu'Appelle?"
This — and no more: I called aloud until
I shuddered as the gloom of night increased,
And, like a pallid spectre wan and chill,
The moon arose in silence in the east. . . .[18]

Upon his arrival at the camp, the brave learns that his bride has died during his eerie encounter with the echo on the lake.

This particular sub-variant of the echo legend has its own antecedents in both oral and written lore. Amelia Paget, who grew up in the valley of the Qu'Appelle in the 1870's and had intimate knowledge of Cree language and lore,[19] records having heard the legend against the background of inter-tribal warfare. That version is detailed enough to shift it from the purely mythical to the quasi-historical spectrum of legendry: [H] the young warrior, son of a renowned Cree chief, is identified by name as "First Son." On a scouting expedition his small band is outnumbered and decimated by hostile Blackfeet. "First Son," severely wounded, escapes with a handful of braves, but "one calm night in the month of June, which the Indians called the 'Month of Young Birds'," he dies after having comforted his companions, and assured them that he would be accompanied by his bride on his last journey . . .; at that point the story takes up the thread of the familiar echo tale and the girl's death.[20]

Only one recorded sub-variant imputes to the Qu'Appelle echo a function other than of omen and warning. It is a sinister reversal of the lovers' motif in which the echo as a manifestation of unpredictable fate destroys without provocation: [I] A young woman imagines her lover calling from one of the hills and leaves in her canoe to join him. He returns shortly after her departure, follows, but finds no trace of her. She is never heard from again. "At twilight her canoe would appear for a few minutes upon the surface of one of the many beautiful lakes in the valley, only to disappear again in a soft mist if anyone tried to approach it."[21]

In the continual reshaping of the legend over the years, certain story elements were added or made more elaborate. When it entered written literature, the presence of the immigrant cultures, whose aggressive exploring and trading in the valley had begun during the latter part of the 18th century, was assumed to be an integral part of the legend.

Such a version is the one told by Osborn in his *Greater Canada* (1900),[22] incidentally, also the only one which, at least indirectly, indicates why the appellation should have been changed from native Cree to French rather than English. The fateful adventure on the lake is that of a warrior returning home from the sale of his furs to the *coureurs des bois* [J], whose activities in the 1780's centred on the area around Fort Esperance (near present-day Welwyn). That such legend modifications can even return to the originating tradition is illustrated by a CBC program (1968), in which a native story-teller wove her version of the Qu'Appelle lovers around the figures of the maiden Evening Bird and Blue Cloud, "a guide for the early fur traders."[K][23]

Something of a curiosity is the alleged naming of Lake Katepwa by Robert Balcarres Crawford, "a Hudson's Bay man, later a postmaster at Indian Head." Visiting the lakeshore in the 1880's, a report goes, he and a friend heard someone calling repeatedly. Crawford then "suggested the place be called Katepwa which is 'Who calls?' in Cree."[24] This account, whose kinship with [C] above is evident, is also misleading, at least to the extent that it implies a degree of originality in Crawford's supposed suggestion. More than likely, he merely corroborated an age-old natural phenomenon, or perhaps popularized 'Katepwa' instead of the less pronounceable *Kahtapwao* or *Kah-tap Wai* among the settlers of the area. But true or not, this episode illuminates a frequently overlooked quality of local legendry: its adaptability to the changing social panorama, and therefore its potential for promoting appreciation of intercultural contexts. The fact that one version of the Qu'Appelle legend has also been set to music,[25] and that another has been translated into German[26] only confirms continuing popular interest in knowing and passing on the traditions of the land.

From mere hearsay, to myth, to legend — the process of enfablement is a mirror of cultural activity. It may elude the historian, but not the folklorist. It provides access to questions which must be answered before individual cultural identities will blend smoothly into the larger society of which they are a part. Dundes has suggested that the study of legendry is hampered by doubts concerning its relevance for "understanding the nature of man."[27] Perhaps by exploring the continuum of our native legendry in the context of social interaction, we shall be able to find much which a fledgling multicultural society cannot afford to overlook.

FOOTNOTES

[1]Dan Ben-Amos, "Toward a Definition of Folklore in Context," *Journal of American Folklore* 84 (1971), 13.

[2]Albert B. Friedman, "The Usable Myth: The Legends of Modern Mythmakers," *American Folk Legend: A Symposium* (Berkeley, 1971), 43.

[3]William Hugh Jansen, "The Esoteric-Exoteric Factor in Folklore," *The Study of Folklore* (Englewood Cliffs, N.J., 1965), 46.

[4]Linda Degh, "Approaches to Folklore Research among Immigrant Groups," *Journal of American Folklore* 79 (1966), 556.

[5]Richard Bauman, "Differential Identity and the Social Base of Folklore," *Journal of American Folklore* 84 (1971), 33.

[6]B. A. Botkin, "Applied Folklore: Creating Understanding Through Folklore," *Southern Folklore Quarterly* 17/3 (1953), 204.

[7]Austin E. Fife, "Folklore and Local History," *Utah Historical Quarterly* 31 (1963), 320.

[8]Cf. J. Z. LaRocque, "Legends of the Qu'Appelle," *Centennial of Sacred Heart Parish 1867-1967* (Lebret, Sask., 1967), 26.
[9]The following legends and their variations (A-K in the text) may be grouped within a trichotomic pattern:

THE ECHO MOTIF

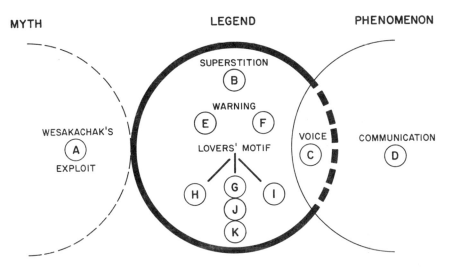

MYTH   LEGEND   PHENOMENON

SUPERSTITION
B

WARNING
E   F

WESAKACHAK'S   VOICE   COMMUNICATION
A   LOVERS' MOTIF   C   D

EXPLOIT

H   G   I
J
K

[10]"Origins of the Qu'Appelle Valley," collected by Jackson Beardy, unpubl. MS. (Island Lake Reserve, Manitoba, 1973). By courtesy of Dr. J. Warner, University of Regina.
[11]W. Kaye Lamb, ed., *Sixteen Years in the Indian Country. The Journal of Daniel Williams Harmon 1800-1816* (Toronto, 1957), 76.
[12]Henry Youle Hind, *Narrative of the Canadian Red River Exploring Expedition of 1857 and of the Assiniboine and Saskatchewan Exploring Expedition of 1858* (Edmonton, 1971), 1, 370.
[13]Gaston Carrière, O.M.I., *L'Apôtre des Prairies* (Montreal, 1967), 19. The quotation was translated from the French. Cf. Amelia M. Paget, *The People of the Plains* (Toronto, 1909), 117.
[14]Eleanor M. Brass, "The Indians' legend of the saskatoons," *Leader Post* (Regina, 8/16/1956), 11.
[15]Cf. Paget, 114.
[16]Cf. Norman Shrive, "What happened to Pauline?" *Canadian Literature* 12 (1962), 37.
[17]See W. Garland Foster, *The Mohawk Princess* (Vancouver, 1931), 80.
[18]E. Pauline Johnson, *Flint and Feather* (Toronto, 1937), 129.
[19]Paget, 12.
[20]*Ibid.,* 112-113.
[21]*Ibid.,* 163.
[22]E. B. Osborn, *Greater Canada* (London, 1900), 140.
[23]Dept. of Education (Sask.) Radio Program "Indian Life I", CBC (4/1/1968). By courtesy of Deanna Christensen, Canadian Plains Research Center, Regina.
[24]E. T. Russell, ed., *What's in a Name?* (Saskatoon, 1973), 161.
[25]See Ella Elizabeth Clark, *Indian Legends of Canada* (Toronto, 1960), 91.
[26]Josef G. Mohl, "Die Sage von Qu'Appelle," *Prisma* (Publ. of the Sask. Assn. of Teachers of German) IV/I (1975), 43-45.
[27]Alan Dundes, "On the Psychology of Legend," *American Folk Legend: A Symposium* (Berkeley, 1971), 21.

ETHNIC ANALYSIS OR POLITICAL ARMOUR: ANALYTICAL PROBLEMS IN THE CANADIAN MOSAIC

PATRICK L. BAKER
MOUNT ALLISON UNIVERSITY, SACKVILLE, N.B.

Two quotations aptly focus on problems which are central to this paper.[1] Despres notes,

Explicit in much of this work ... is the view that the genesis and persistence of ethnic boundaries, the incorporation of ethnic populations, and the organization of inter-ethnic relations are generally related to factors affecting the competition for environmental resources.[2]

Vallee observes,

And so the debates go on, between the 'liberal' assimilationists, that is those who want to but would not force assimilation, and the pluralists. We conclude with a rather trite, but true, observation: whatever the policies are, they have to be implemented in a real world in which much of what happens is beyond the control of planners and policy makers.[3]

The former quotation epitomizes many of the most recent perspectives taken towards ethnicity. The latter pronounces a caveat concerning the niceness of fit between theoretical models and social reality in the sphere of ethnicity and race relations. This paper proposes to explore these questions further in a Canadian context, particularly in the light of assumptions underlying varying models of ethnic relations; their adequacy for analysis; and their role as ideal structures in the light of which policy decisions are made. The central argument of the paper is that there is an implicit contradiction between the existing theoretical formulations of a plural or multicultural society and the ideal structure that is politically envisioned. A Report on *The Black Presence in the Canadian Mosaic*[4] will be used to illustrate the argument.

In discussing Canadian dimensions of racism, Hughes and Kallen refer to the classic model of racial integration: those of "Anglo-conformity, Melting pot, and Cultural pluralism or Multiculturalism."[5] They note that the melting pot model has been considered apposite for an analysis of the American experience, whereas the cultural pluralism model better fits the Canadian context. The concern with both models is an attempt to capture different types of integration of ethnic groups into a broader societal whole. The essential concern was earlier reflected in the typologies of Wirth and Park.[6] The underlying assumptions of these approaches are that society is an organic whole into which individuals and groups are incorporated more or less perfectly. According to Despres:

the substantive and theoretical significance of most sociological investigations derive their intellectual force from the concern that sociologists have shown in a broad range of social problems related to the incorporation of racial and cultural minorities in urban and industrial societies.[7]

Moreover, this model has tended to focus attention on cultural, rather than structural components,[8] and has emphasized the role of values as both integrative and disjunctive in society.[9] One of the implications of this view is that ethnic groups are seen as problematic in the societal quest for harmony and equilibrium. As one commentator puts it, with reference to the blacks,

> The other concepts we use — absorption, acculturation, assimilation, integration — suffer from a similar if less direct bias. No matter how sophisticated their use, these concepts always seem to lead us to focus attention on black people as the problem.[10]

Dawe, among others, has commented on the basic assumptions of this perspective.[11] The sociology of the social system reflects "the doctrine of order . . . . In a nutshell, the central value system is the ultimate source of the moral authority which sets the societal system over its participants in such a way as to impose a common meaning and, therefore, order upon them."[12] It follows from this that, if the problem of order is *the* central problem for sociology, then the doctrine entails "not only a theory of society, but also a characteristic approach to the analysis of society, that is, an equivalent set of propositions about the language and structure of sociology itself."[13] I would argue that this theoretical perspective has imbued much of the conceptualizing and research on ethnic relations, even that which conceives of society in pluralistic terms, both at the academic level and at the overtly political level. The problem with this approach comes when we confront it with reality. As both Hughes and Kallen,[14] and Gordon note, the ideological models of pluralism and assimilation are not consonant with social reality.

What has tended to be left out of these studies are the notions of power, in the more Machiavellian sense, and stratification, in its exploitative sense; in other words elements of the alternative sociological perspective, conflict theory, or what Dawe calls the sociology of "social control." Despres, in his search for "a theory of ethnic phenomena," concludes that "the conceptual framework that emerges suggests that these [ethnic] phenomena might best be understood from the point of view of stratification theory or perhaps more general theories of power" (p. 204). And Gordon reconsiders his earlier position particularly from the stance of "the relationship of assimilation analysis to the concepts of power and conflict which were relatively ignored . . . in [my] previous study."[15] What emerges is a theoretical position that considers former concepts and ideologies of assimilation as utopian and focuses attention on the relationship of ethnic groups to inequality, status and the strategic efficacy of interest groups in attaining certain goals.[16] The alternative societal model that is developed is the plural or pluralistic poly-ethnic society in which the focus of interest is on the differential structural positioning of ethnic groups, either through their participation in the the market situation, or through more general societal institutions.[17]

What is of major importance to note here, is that these pluralistic models are considered by some scholars to be inherently unstable. Society is conceived of as a segmented, not an integrated set of ascribed status groups competing for resources.[18] Rees, for example, argues that societies with cultural pluralism are inherently unstable and that this "must be admitted to have a considerable plausibility, and Canada, Belgium and Northern Ireland are not the only societies which appear to confirm the validity of the thesis."[19] By way of a "solution" he goes on to mention Freedom and Willmott's argument that stability is most likely to be preserved through the balance of power between ethnic groups.[20] If, however, ethnicity is conceived as inherently involving exploitative stratification and power differentials, then the empirical realization of such a balance of power is theoretically tenuous.

The plural society model has been considerably elaborated since its early formulations by Furnivall and M. G. Smith. Smith himself has moved away from a consideration of the plural society to various forms of pluralism.[21] Kuper has made an important distinction between plural and pluralistic societies.[22] The former are associated with a conflict model of society and are primarily the products of colonization and colonial domination. The latter are linked to equilibrium theory and project society in terms of democratic political structures in which integration is achieved through cross-cutting loyalties and a system of constitutional checks and balances. Schermerhorn has further distinguished four types of pluralism.[23] Ideological or normative pluralism refers to an ethnic group's desire to maintain its identity; political pluralism refers to the distinguishing of ethnic groups in terms of cultural criteria such as language, religion, kinship forms; and structural pluralism, which refers to a number of plural structural units where there are distinguishable separate sets of institutions and evinces varying degrees of enclosure.

The importance of this definitional discussion is that there can be, and — I would argue — there often *is* a confusion of these models in our conception of Canadian society. I suggest that the general view of Canadian society reflects Wirth's pluralistic strategy which encourages tolerance from the dominant group towards minority groups such that it will allow them to retain much of their cultural distinctiveness.[24] But this is an ideological model. It reflects, as Schermerhorn mentions, "what *ought to be.*"[25] The assumptions behind this model are versions on the theme of classical equilibrium theory, including the political notion of differential autonomy leading to a balance of forces found in the mechanistic version of pluralism. The problem with this model is that it neither accommodates exploitative stratification, nor the existence of imbalances resulting from powerful interest groups. Thus conflict remains, and is conceived of as problematic. Its existence requires, or rather urges, a solution. So research is undertaken. But the model underlying the research remains the ideal Canadian model of a "harmonious" mosaic, which, as suggested here, is inadequate to capture the social reality.[26] By way of example, I should like to pursue these ideas in relation to a recent report on racial discrimination against blacks in Metropolitan Toronto.

There is laudable concern in and need for research projects designed to study the problems of discrimination in Canadian society. Thus Dr. Wilson A. Head's report, "The Black Presence in the Canadian Mosaic: A Study of Perception and the Practice of Discrimination Against Blacks in Metropolitan Toronto" (henceforth referred to as the *Report*), submitted to the Ontario Human Rights Commission is commendable, both for its evident concern with growing unrest in the Metropolitan area between blacks and other ethnic groups, and for its attempt to meet the need for research into this area. But it will be argued that, though some of the findings are important, and the research is worthwhile, the theoretical perspective limits the adequacy of the findings and the efficacy of the proposed solutions.

The research arose out of a concern with increasing incidents of violent racism in Toronto and aimed "to provide valid information on the basis of which individuals, governmental and voluntary organizations can engage in sound planning for effective action to combat and eradicate discriminatory practices in Canadian life" (p. 5). The kind of information sought related to the areas in which discrimination was experienced; the percentage of the black population who experienced discrimination; their reaction to it and what action they took in response. The study, *de facto,* was of the *perception* of discrimination.

The *Report* is the result of 317 structured interviews conducted by both black and white interviewers between February and October 1974; and 32 non-structured interviews conducted by the Project Director and Research Assistant beween February and April 1974. A truly random sample was not possible because of the exigencies of time and cost.[27] However, a list of some 4,000 names was gathered from membership and clients of many organizations and from this list a sample of 210 adults, as well as sub-samples of 54 youths, 53 non-black, and 32 leadership categories were compiled, totalling 349 interviews.[28] Sixty-one persons refused to be interviewed and 120 could not be located, bringing the total sample to 530. The subsequent analysis falls into four general areas: the experience and perceptions of the Black Leadership Group; the attitudes of the remaining groups toward community institutions; their perception of black identity and relationships; and a section on the general perceptions of and effects on respondents of discrimination.

All black respondents, adult and youth, agreed that discrimination exists, at least in some degree, in Metropolitan Toronto (p. 187). The major areas of perceived discrimination were jobs (87.4%), housing (82.9%), community agencies (60%), and commercial services (61.2%). Interestingly, the *Report* notes that a majority of respondents consider discrimination in these areas to be stable or on the wane rather than increasing (p. 187).

Questions directed towards the perception of discrimination in specific community institutions elicited a wide variety of contradictory responses. Less than 50% of the adult sample felt that there was discrimination in school, though more of the youth and non-black samples thought there was discrimination in this area. Following on from this "most respondents feel only fairly positively about the opportunities available to black graduates from the various academic levels" (p. 95). Attitudes towards the media polarized between black and non-black respondents. The daily press was particularly criticized by the adult black and youth samples (70% thinking it played a negative role), while only 30% of non-black respondents were similarly critical. The black press received moderate support from blacks (56.8% thinking it was a positive force) and less support from non-blacks (37.5% thinking similarly). The police and courts came in for some criticism from the blacks, but less than might have been expected from the statements of black leaders and the black press. "While 50.7% of all respondents believe that the police are unfair in their treatment of blacks, significant differences exist among the minority who believe they are fair" (p. 108). While 40% of Canadian blacks feel they are fair, only 20% of West Indians feel so. These feelings are less apparent towards the courts, possibly because of the lack of experience of them. Regarding the use of community services, 40.2% feel that blacks should use existing community services; relatively few (16.3%) opted for the development of black services, and the majority of these were West Indian. The youth group was more definite about the formation of black social services, 65% believing that blacks should at least have a choice in this matter. Only 2% of the non-blacks felt this way.

The *Report* concludes that there is subtle discrimination against blacks in Toronto, but that black-white relations are viewed with an unexpected degree of satisfaction. The *Report* suggests that this points to the fact that racial harmony can exist in a local community (p. 197), and puts this down to the small size of the black population, its general prosperity, and factors producing a liberal community. But the effects of existing discrimination are that blacks have to work harder at school and even then they meet barriers to economic and social advancement. Their self-image suffers and they have a feeling of marginality (pp. 119-200).

The *Report* finally makes recommendations at two levels: at the level of formal institutions and organizations, and at the level of the black community itself. Recommendations are directed towards schools (11), the police (3), the Courts (1), the Ontario Human Rights Commission (4), other Government Agencies (4), the Media (1), other Community Services (3), and finally towards the Black Community itself (5). A number of these recommendations focus on improving public relations in various domains and some ask for a review of hiring practices. The final word is directed to the blacks to unite, to organize themselves, to select leaders, to obtain government funds and to form coalitions with other ethnic groups, specifically with the Indian and Asian populations; in other words, to organize themselves formally as an interest group.

Certain problems arise in relation to the *Report*. As is evident, there is a concern to restore equilibrium and to integrate the black community into the urban mosaic.[29] Implicitly this is conceived of in terms of value consensus. The *Report* directs itself wholly to the *perception* of discrimination by various groups, and though the author is careful to point this out,[30] there is, nevertheless, some confusion as to the ontological status of his findings. The subtitle of the *Report* is "The Study of Perception and *the Practice* of Discrimination against Blacks in Metropolitan Toronto" (my italics), and the conclusion states: "This study documents *the existence* of a considerable amount of discrimination in Metropolitan Toronto" (p. 229, my italics). The *Report* appears to subscribe to Greene's opinion that "Attitudes, not conditions, determine social problems,"[31] and seems to ignore the Marxian insight into the complex relationship between ideas and social structure. It is undeniable that the attitudes and the world views they express are extremely important in the definition and course of social problems. But, if a central tenet of sociology is that, "things social are not what they *seem* to be," then remaining at the level of perception, to the exclusion of structural considerations, appears to be a questionable omission. The sociologist himself is not free of attitudes and world views that are entrenched in his sociological perspective, as we have briefly noted.[32] If, as Dawe has indicated, the prime trait of much of sociology is a concern for and an understanding of social order, and in the last analysis the desire to maintain or restore it then it is not surprising that the predominant approach to social problems lies along the lines of disorganization and deviance, with their emphases on socialization and values. The black problem is conceived largely in terms of marginality *(Report,* p. 200), and the effect this has on self-identity. If the feeling of discrimination, for the purposes of argument, is placed under the wider and looser term of alienation, the *Report* focuses at the level of feelings of alienation, and is thus consistent with much functional, systems literature. Marx, however, was insistent that "objective" alienation may exist, which may not be felt, nor perceived.[33] It is this objective, structural level of analysis that is missing from the *Report,* but is surely crucial for an adequate assessment of the problem.

It follows from the same systems emphasis that there is a concern with the institutional rather than the interactional order. Man, growing up within society and participating in it, learns its expectations, conforms through his role playing and becomes a more or less good citizen. The *Report,* therefore, focuses on the participation of blacks in formal relationships, particularly in the local mini-society, or community. Thus, as the *Report* states (42-43):

> Membership in voluntary community organizations is often seen as an indication of community participation, acceptance and the successful adaptation of newcomers into the general community life. For this reason we were interested in obtaining some indication of participation by both black newcomers and Canadian born respondents . . . [and] to ascertain how actively our black respondents participate in the

community, we inquired as to their membership in organizations and groups in the city.

But as Hughes and Kallen point out, "participation in the private sphere of primary social relationships" is what is requisite for the structural integration of an ethnic group.[34]

A third area in which the *Report* may be considered problematic is its recommendations. Implicit within the recommendations to the wider society is the ideal model of the Canadian mosaic as an equilibrium, and balanced model of society, comprising a consensus of attitudes and values. Thus recommendations are aimed at the modification of attitudes, as for example in the case of the police, and in the incorporation of blacks into formal institutions. What is omitted from consideration is the element of stratification and power in inter-ethnic relations; and the vested interests on the part of certain groups in *maintaining* certain existing attitudes and values. The recommendations are made in terms of "society," and not in terms of the interactive patterns of social relationships between individuals and groups.

As a result, there are a number of contradictions that appear in the *Report.* One of these has already been alluded to — the status of its findings. Although noting a perceptual focus, it makes statements about the *existence* of discrimination. Thus the *Report* can say that it demonstrates the existence of discrimination (p. 229) and yet states, "it is not our intention to check or attempt to prove whether or not discrimination based upon race or colour actually occurred" (p. 195). There is, moreover, a confusion at the perceptual level itself. At one moment the *Report* uses a dominant group perception of the blacks as an ethnic group who have a collective history (p. 202); at another it clearly indicates and documents the non-collective identity of the blacks among themselves.[35] Likewise in the recommendations there is a presentation of the blacks as culturally different but capable of harmonious integration, given some "understanding" from the wider society; yet elsewhere they are urged to organize as an interest group and fight for their place in Canadian society. Indeed the weight of the solution seems to be placed on black shoulders. Finally the findings of the *Report,* that there is an unexpected harmony between blacks and whites, does not accord with the initial concern that prompted the *Report* — mounting racial violence in the Metropolitan area. I suggest that these contradictions stem from an inadequacy in an ideal model to cope with a complex of structural/attitudinal problems.

The purpose of this discussion has been to indicate an implicit contradiction between on the one hand the ideal model of Canadian society as a mosaic, and its use for an analysis of inter-ethnic relations; and, on the other, the reality of those relations in social life.[36] It is in terms of such discrepancies that more apposite theoretical models develop. If the societal context is perceived to involve unequal power relationships, then ethnic groups may, perhaps, be better conceived of as interest groups.[37] It is along these lines that the "New Ethnicity" theorists are moving.[38] Despres has commented that ethnic analysis may be relegated to an ante-Barth and post-Barth conceptual watershed.[39] However, Barth's subjective approach to ethnic boundary definition and maintainance, while very fruitful, has been criticized by some for its insufficient emphasis on normative constraints.[40] On the other hand, the emphasis on the power dimension of ethnic relations alone has likewise been criticized.[41] Nevertheless, the emerging interactional emphasis on inter-ethnic relations appears to be a fruitful one. What is important to realise is that the adoption of models of ethnicity, themselves, may be related to structural features of the society. As Vincent points out:

> Just as ethnicity may be manipulated by the political actor within the changing situation, so the social science concept may become the tool of a political regime. When we look at the situation, as well as the structure, we can see that the control potential of ethnicity may enhance the position of both ethnic leaders and the leaders of charter groups.[42]

The contradiction between the ideal model of Canadian society as a mosaic, and the reality of major social inequalities (the *Report* gave the modal income for the adult black group as from $6,000 to $8,999), may lead us to ask whether the ideal of a mosaic is not a beneficial model for the two charter groups to espouse.[43] I suggest that a more "realistic" model of a pluralistic society which can serve as *ideal* we have yet to work out.

FOOTNOTES

[1] The title of the paper is polarized for the sake of argument and is not intended to support a theoretical dichotomy. Nor will the paper concern itself with what some consider to be the intrinsically political nature of "underdog research." See, for example, Lee Bridges, "Race Relations Research: From Colonialism to Neo-Colonialism? Some Random Thoughts," *Race,* 14, No. 3 (1973), 331-341.

[2] Leo A. Despres, ed., "Introduction," in *Ethnicity and Resource Competition in Plural Societies* (The Hague, 1975), 2-3.

[3] Frank G. Vallee, "Multi-Ethnic Societies: Issues of Identity and Equality," in *Issues in Canadian Society: An Introduction to Sociology,* eds. Dennis Forcese and Stephen Richer (Scarborough, Ontario, 1975), 198.

[4] Wilson A. Head and Jeri Lee, *The Black Presence in the Canadian Mosaic: A Study of Perception and the Discrimination against Blacks in Metropolitan Toronto,* Report submitted to the Ontario Human Rights Commission (Toronto, 1975). Henceforth referred to as "the *Report.*"

[5] David R. Hughes and Evelyn Kallen, *The Anatomy of Racism: Canadian Dimensions* (Montreal, 1974), 183ff. For a fuller discussion of these concepts see Milton M. Gordon, *Assimilation in American Life: The Role of Race, Religion, and National Origins* (New York, 1964); Milton M. Gordon, "Toward a General Theory of Racial and Ethnic Group Relations," in eds. Nathan Glazer and Daniel P. Moynihan, *Ethnicity: Theory and Experience* (Massachusetts, 1975), 84-110.

[6] Robert E. Park, *Race and Culture* (Glencoe, 1950). For a discussion of his position see Stanford M. Lyman, "The Race Relations Cycle of Robert E. Park," *Pacific Sociological Review,* 11-12 (1968-1969), 16-22. Louis Wirth, "The Problem of Minority Groups," in ed. Ralph Linton, *The Science of Man in the World Crisis* (New York, 1945).

[7] Leo A. Despres, ed., "Toward a Theory of Ethnic Phenomena," in *Ethnicity and Resource Competition in Plural Societies* (The Hague, 1975), 189.

[8] R. A. Schermerhorn, *Comparative Ethnic Relations: A Framework for Theory and Research* (New York, 1970), 80.

[9] See, for example, Frazier's discussion of Sumner's emphasis on mores as racial 'diacritica,' and the later use of this emphasis by Park in his stress on attitudes and social distance as defining the 'stranger.' E. Franklin Frazier, "Sociological Theory and Race Relations," in *E. Franklin Frazier on Race Relations,* ed. G. Franklin Edwards (Chicago, 1968). Banton more

recently places a similar emphasis with his notion of race as a "role sign" and his formulation of the stranger hypothesis. Michael Banton, "Race as a Social Category," *Race,* 8 No. 1 (July 1966), 7-8; "Sociology and Race Relations," *Race,* 1, No. 1 (July 1959), 10; "The Stranger Hypothesis," *Race,* 15, No. 1 (1973), 111-15.

[10]Lee Bridges, "Race Relations: From Colonialism to Neo-Colonialism? Some Random Thoughts," *Race,* 14, No. 3 (1973), 335.

[11]See, for example, John Horton, "Commentary and Debate, Order and Conflict Theories of Social Problems and Competing Ideologies," *American Journal of Sociology,* 71 (1966), 701-713. Alvin Gouldner, *The Coming Crisis of Western Sociology* (New York, 1970). Pierre L. van den Berghe, "Dialectic and Functionalism: Toward a Theoretical Synthesis," *American Sociological Review,* 28 (1963), 695-705.

[12]Alan Dawe, "The Two Sociologies," in Kenneth Thompson and Jeremy Tunstall, *Sociological Perspectives* (Harmondsworth: Penguin Education, 1970), 543.

[13]*Ibid.,* 543. There are important implications derived from the underlying perspective for the *Report* shortly to be discussed: 1. A conception of society and man's relation to "it." 2. A conception of the problems arising from this relationship. 3. A method of investigating social phenomena leading to corresponding solutions. 4. A particular type of conception of ethnic phenomena and problems of inter-ethnic relations.

[14]David R. Hughes and Evelyn Kallen, *The Anatomy of Racism,* 190. Milton M. Gordon, "Toward a General Theory of Racial and Ethnic Group Relations," 88.

[15]Milton M. Gordon, "Toward a General Theory of Racial and Ethnic Group Relations," 86.

[16]Nathan Glazer and Daniel P. Moynihan, eds., "Introduction," in *Ethnicity: Theory and Experience,* 7-14.

[17]J. S. Furnivall, following the Dutch economist Boeke, emphasized the former in his *Netherlands India* (London, 1939) and *Colonial Policy and Practice* (London, 1948). Michael G. Smith developed the latter in his "Ethnic and Cultural Pluralism in the British Caribbean," "A Framework for Caribbean Studies," and "Social and Cultural Pluralism" collected in his *The Plural Society in the British West Indies* (Los Angeles, 1965).

[18]See, for example, T. B. Rees, "Accommodation, Integration, Cultural Pluralism, and Assimilation: Their Place in Equilibrium Theories of Society," *Race,* 11 (1969-70), 487. Leo A. Despres, "Toward a Theory of Ethnic Phenomena," 194ff.

[19]T. B. Rees, "Accommodation, Integration, Cultural Pluralism, and Assimilation," 488-89.

[20]M. Freedman and W. E. Willmott, "South-east Asia, with Special Reference to the Chinese," in UNESCO *International Social Science Journal,* 13, No. 2 (1961), 247.

[21]Michael G. Smith, "Some Developments in the Analytic Framework of Pluralism," in eds. Leo Kuper and M. G. Smith, *Pluralism in Africa* (Berkeley, 1969), 440.

[22]Leo Kuper, "Plural Societies: Perspectives and Problems," in *Pluralism in Africa,* 7ff. Hoetink goes so far as to relegate the utility of the latter concepts to the inception of colonization. H. Hoetink, *The Two Variants in Caribbean Race Relations* (New York, 1966), 93.

[23]R. A. Schermerhorn, *Comparative Ethnic Relations,* 122-25.

[24]Louis Wirth, "The Problem of Minority Groups," *passim.*

[25]R. A. Schermerhorn, *Comparative Ethnic Relations,* 122.

[26]Kuper makes a further criticism of much ethnic research which could be levelled against the *Report.* "Scholars have not studied extensively the reactions of different strata of the subject races to ideologies of cultural superiority. Generalizations are based on research, limited in scope, and not highly sensitive to indications of covert resistance. Our conceptions are certain to change, as scholars probe beyond the apparent acceptance and find the indications of resistance they seek." Leo Kuper, *Race, Class, and Power* (London, 1974), 20.

[27]One of the problems of the *Report* is what level of social reality is being examined. Leach has pointed out that the fieldworker has three distinct levels of social behaviour to study: actual behaviour, average or "normal" behaviour, and ideal behaviour. — See Edmund R. Leach, ed., "Jinghpaw Kinship Terminology," in *Rethinking Anthropology* (London, 1961), 30. See also Max Weber, *The Theory of Social and Economic Organization,* ed. T. Parsons (New York, 1964), 96. Leach further suggested that the fieldworker, pressed for time, often tended to identify normal with ideal behaviour, which was inadmissible (Leach, 51). Obviously a questionnaire can be an apposite tool for determining ideal behaviour in a community. It is, however, more problematic to ascertain normal and actual behaviour in this way. It makes the dubious assumption that what one does and what one says are commensurate. But as the *Report* notes: there are exigencies of time and cost. Nevertheless, the limitations thus imposed should be clearly spelled out.

[28]Detailed characteristics of the groups must be left to a perusal of the *Report.*

[29]The opening paragraph of the *Report* reflects a concern for growing disequilibrium: "This study evolved from a concern of the author that Metropolitan Toronto is beginning to experience increasing discrimination and tension between various racial groups constituting the population of this city" (p. i).

[30]"It should be reiterated that the responses obtained from our interviews are basically attitudes and perceptions of discriminatory treatment. Some questions may be raised, in at least a few instances, as to whether alleged discrimination is actually what it was perceived to

be; other explanations are possible for what may appear to be discrimination. But it is not our intention to check or attempt to prove whether or not discrimination based upon race or colour actually occurred; we are interested in the respondent's perception of discrimination" (p. 195).

[31]Arnold W. Greene, *Social Problems: Arena of Conflict* (Toronto, 1975), 4.

[32]For an interesting discussion of this regarding papers given at a Conference on the subject see: W. T. Jones, "World Views: Their Nature and Their Function," *Current Anthropology*, 13 (1972), 79-109. For a discussion more specifically regarding ethnic analysis see: Leo Kuper, *Race, Class, and Power*, 198.

[33]See, for example: *Marx-Engels Gesamtausgabe*, Section 1, vol. 3, 83-89.

[34]David R. Hughes and Evelyn Kallen, *The Anatomy of Racism*, 166-67.

[35]This has been noted elsewhere. See Harold H. Potter, "Negroes in Canada," *Race*, 13, No. 1 (1969), 40.

[36]Haug notes this confusion: "The term pluralism has been used in political science to describe an 'open society' in which individuals and groups have political freedom and may safely express disparate views and bring diverse pressures to bear on government. This definition is irrelevant to the issues being debated in sociology and anthropology, although it is sometimes confused with them." Marie R. Haug, "Social and Cultural Pluralism as a Concept in Social System Analysis," *American Journal of Sociology*, 73 (1967-1968), 294.

[37]See, for example, Abner Cohen, ed., "Introduction: The Lesson of Ethnicity," in *Urban Ethnicity* (London, 1974), pp. xvi-xvii.

[38]For a resume of some of these views see John W. Bennett, ed., "A Guide to the Collection," in *The New Ethnicity: Perspectives from Ethnology* (New York, 1975).

[39]Leo A. Despres, "Toward a Theory of Ethnic Phenomena," 189.

[40]See Abner Cohen, "Introduction: The Lesson of Ethnicity," p. xv. Also, Robert Paine, *Second Thoughts on Barth's Models,* Royal Anthropological Institute Occasional Paper no. 32 (London, 1974).

[41]See S. R. Charsley, "The Formation of Ethnic Groups," in ed. Abner Cohen, *Urban Ethnicity,* 338.

[42]Joan Vincent, "The Structuring of Ethnicity," *Human Organization*, 33, No. 4 (Winter 1974), 378.

[43]As Kuper observes, "Multi-racialism, instead of being an instrument of domination, may however be a defensive position for a racial group which can no longer maintain its domination." Leo Kuper, *Race, Class, and Power,* 57.

LINGUISTIC TRENDS AMONG SASKATCHEWAN ETHNIC GROUPS

ALAN B. ANDERSON
UNIVERSITY OF SASKATCHEWAN, SASKATOON

Introduction

This paper approaches the topic of "trends in language use among Saskatchewan ethnic groups" from several perspectives. First, the paper discusses, at a general theoretical level, the relationship between the maintenance of traditional languages and the preservation of ethnic identities. One contribution of the paper will be to re-evaluate the notion that retention of a traditional language unique to a particular ethnic group is vital to the preservation of ethnic identities. Second, the paper focuses more specifically on trends in using such traditional languages among the various ethnic groups in Saskatchewan, taking into account urban, heterogeneous rural and homogeneous ethnic bloc settlement contexts for language use, as well as age differences. Third, the paper summarizes pertinent data relating to language use from an extensive field survey conducted among nine ethno-religious groups in eighteen rural bloc settlements situated in the north-central region in Saskatchewan. Finally, in the conclusion an attempt is made to project the trends discerned into the future.

(1) Language and Ethnic Identity

Overview

Numerous sociologists have stressed that language is the most important component of ethnic identity. For example, Freeman has referred to language as "the rough practical test of nationality"; Shibutani and Kwan as "an essential part of culture and at the same time the instrument through which other aspects of culture are organized," as well as — Bram — "a symbol of group identity" through socialization; Park as the keynote to a "common community of purpose"; and Handlin as the main focus of immigrant group identity rather than place of origin. However, as Borrie and others have cautioned, it is possible for an ethnic group to lose its mother-tongue eventually without losing its sense of identity. If the linguistic factor is usually important for most ethnic groups, it is not the only component of ethnic identity.[1] Some ethnic groups or nationalities lay greater stress on folk arts or religious ideologies than on linguistic survival. For example, the vast majority of Scots in Scotland (except in several fairly remote areas in the Highlands and the Hebrides) and of Scottish-Canadians (except, perhaps, in Cape Breton Island) have lost their traditional Gaelic mother tongue, yet retain a considerable pride in Scottish identity and possess a well-defined traditional culture. Some sub-categories within ethno-religious groups, such as General Conference Mennonites or

Reformed Jews, tend to emphasize religious sectarian identity more than ethnic or linguistic distinctiveness. In short, different criteria may be stressed by different ethnic or ethno-religious groups as the primary basis for group identity.

Linguistic Change and Pluralism

Nonetheless, linguistic change in an ethnic group may be to some extent an indication of acculturation and assimilation. The first step may be the alteration of the traditional language of the group, so that an ethnic minority in Canada may after some time be speaking a version of the mother-tongue somewhat different from that now spoken in the mother country. Neologisms may be introduced through adoption of slang by the younger generation, or perhaps through some degree of Anglicization, especially with reference to modern appliances. Or the language of the immigrants may differ from that of members of the same ethnic group back in the "old country" through lack of contact between the former and the latter; the immigrants continue to speak regional dialects, which have become anachronistic (at least in part) in the countries where they originated. Levelling influences break down such distinctions, though, such as the ethnic-oriented media, the importation of reading material from the mother-country, education in an updated, standardized non-English language, interaction in urban as opposed to isolated rural areas, continuing immigration, etc.[2]

Bilingualism may be regarded as a transitional stage between alteration of the mother-tongue and complete loss, although it is not necessarily subsequent to, but would usually be concomitant with, alteration (e.g., bilingualism may lead to Anglicization). The bilingual members of an ethnic group are not easy to classify. They may favour cultural pluralism to the extent that they could speak English easily but prefer to use their mother-tongue as much as possible. Or they could speak both languages poorly, being in a marginal, transitional phase. Or they could prefer to use English much of the time because they are concerned about improving the ability of their group to speak English well. The residents of a segregated bloc settlement may see little reason to learn or use English. And adoption of English may also be retarded by linguistic revival as an important part of ethnic nationalism.[3]

Name Change

Name change is at times closely related to language change as part of ethnic identity change. As linguistic assimilation occurs, some names undergo change and therefore become progressively less reliable indicators of ethnic identity. Name changing is not necessarily a deliberate attempt to obscure one's ethnic origin; rather, it may be a practical attempt to alleviate the embarrassment over people of other ethnic origins not being able to pronounce a name typical of a particular ethnic group. Given names tend to change before surnames. Not infrequently the changing of given names was the result of the arbitrary action of immigration officials at the time of first immigration. Yet either type of name may be altered without being converted entirely into — or exchanged for — an English name; the name may be shortened for conveniece, or the spelling may be changed for easy phonetic pronunciation by English-speakers. However, there has been very little — if any — changing of surnames in the ethnic bloc settlements in Saskatchewan, while significant differences between ethnic groups do exist with reference to changing given names.[4]

(2) Recent Trends in Saskatchewan

Linguistic Assimilation: The Province as a Whole

There has been in recent decades a fairly steady and rapid decrease in the proportion of ethnic group members in Saskatchewan still conversant in their traditional mother tongues (see Table I):

Table 1: Declining Proportion of Ethnic Group Members in Saskatchewan Able to Speak Traditional Mother Tongue, 1941-1971, for Principal Ethnic Groups.

Groups:	1941	1951	1961	1971	1971 At Home*
French	75%	65%	55%	56%	28.4%
German and Dutch combined	72%	54%	38%	40%	9.4%
— German only	73%	58%	51%	42%	10.1%
Major Slavic languages combined (Ukrainian, Polish, Russian)	81%	72%	56%	53%	22.8%
— Ukrainian only	94%	87%	85%	63%	28.9%
Scandinavian languages combined	59%	40%	28%	21%	1.0%

(Approximate percentages based on figures rounded-off to nearest thousand)
*Refers to language most often spoken at home; i.e. proportion of people in each ethnic category primarily speaking relevant traditional mother tongue (instead of English) at home.
Source: 1941, 1951, 1961, 1971 Census of Canada: Bulletins on Ethnic Groups and Mother Tongue.

By 1971 little more than half of the people of Ukrainian, Polish, or Russian origin (combined) could still speak a Slavic language; little more than half of the French Canadians in the province could still speak French; two out of every five people of German or Dutch descent could speak German or Dutch; and only one in five people of Scandinavian descent (traced patrilineally) could speak a Scandinavain language. Moreover, the fact that they *could* speak their traditional mother tongues does not necessarily indicate that they were actually speaking those languages. Thus the 1971 census data informs us that only 28.4% of the French were actually using French more often than English at home, compared to 28.9% of the Ukrainians, 14% of the Russians, 8.2% of the Poles, 9.4% of the Germans and Dutch combined, and only 1.0% of the Scandinavians.

Table 2 furnishes further details on language trends between 1961 and 1971 for a wide variety of ethnic groups in Saskatchewan. It can be noted that out of the 29 ethnic categories listed, only two had more than

Table 2: Population of Saskatchewan by Ethnic Origin and Mother Tongue, 1961 and 1971.

Ethnic Group:	Ethnic Population: (1961)	Speaking Mother Tongue: (1961)	% (1961)	Ethnic Population: (1971)	Speaking Mother Tongue: (1971)	% (1971)
Chinese	3,660	3,073	84.0	4,605	3,595	78.1
Czech	4,591	?	?	4,200	1,460	34.8
Danish	7,303	2,120	29.0	5,220	1,285	24.6
Dutch	29,325[2]	8,054	27.5	19,040[2]	4,695	24.7
Estonian	150	52	34.7	100	55	55.0
Finnish	1,891	1,139	60.2	1,725	745	43.2
French & Belgian	59,824	36,816[1]	61.5	59,755	32,350[1]	54.1
German & Austrian	177,192[2]	89,650	50.6	183,940[2]	75,885	41.3
Greek	809	398	49.2	900	745	82.8
Hungarian	16,059	8,030	50.0	13,830	6,270	45.3
Icelandic	3,405	1,033	30.3	3,095	840	27.1
Indian (Native)	30,630	25,932	84.7	40,475	26,010	64.3
Indo-Pakistani	115	?	?	1,250	695	55.6
Italian	2,413	1,369	56.7	2,865	2,040	71.2
Japanese	280	134	47.9	315	115	36.5
Jewish	2,287[3]	898[3]	39.3	2,195[3]	415[3]	18.9
Latvian	187	78	41.7	235	75	31.9
Lithuanian	644	229	35.6	475	170	35.8
Norwegian	37,204	10,839	29.1	36,160	6,850	18.9
Polish	28,951	10,585	36.6	26,910	7,675	28.5
Rumanian	7,128	2,396	33.6	5,550	1,930	34.8
Russian	22,481[4]	6,868[4]	30.6	10,030[4]	4,255[4]	42.4
Scottish	102,685	384[5]	0.4	?	2,590[5]	?
Slovak	1,263	1,483[6]	117.4	740	430	58.1
Swedish	19,641	5,519	28.1	14,635	3,440	23.5
Syrian/Lebanese	678	259	38.2	595	240	40.3
Ukrainian	78,851	67,087	85.1	85,920	53,385	62.1
Welsh	8,261	243	2.9	?	230	?
Yugoslav	2,420	769	31.8	2,090	955	45.7

Notes:
(1) Includes 653 (1961) and 710 (1971) speaking Flemish, a Dutch dialect.
(2) Almost half of the Mennonites in Saskatchewan claim Dutch origin but traditionally speak a German dialect.
(3) Not all Jews claim Jewish ethnicity. The Jewish language referred to is Yiddish, essentially a German dialect.
(4) Some Mennonites claim Russian origin but speak a German dialect.
(5) The Scottish language referred to is Gaelic.
(6) Could include some Czechs.

three-quarters of their members able to speak the traditional mother tongue by 1971 — Greeks (82.8%) and Chinese (78.1%). In another three ethnic groups approximately two-thirds could speak the mother tongue in 1971 — Italians (71.2%), native Indians (64.3%), and Ukrainians (62.1%). A majority of French Canadians in the province, as well as of the far less numerous, Indo-Pakistanis, and Slovaks, could speak their relevant traditional languages. In most of the other ethnic groups only a minority, between a quarter and half, of the members still retain the mother tongue; among people of Norwegian, Danish, Swedish, Dutch, and Jewish descent the proportion falls below one quarter (the two British groups listed, Scots and Welsh, originally immigrated — directly or indirectly — from countries where the vast majority speak English rather than Gaelic or Welsh). Between 1961 and 1971, in four ethnic groups — Greeks, Italians, Yugoslavs (i.e., mostly Croatians in Saskatchewan), and the few Estonians

— actual increases in the proportion of members able to speak their traditional language could be noted. In several other groups the proportion seemed to be fairly static (e.g., Danes, Dutch, Icelanders, Hungarians, Lithuanians, Rumanians, Swedes, Syrian/Lebanese Arabs, and possibly the French excluding Belgians). But most ethnic groups showed significant declines within this one decade. Loss of the traditional mother tongue was proceeding most rapidly for Finns, native Indians, Jews, Norwegians, Ukrainians, and Slovaks (although, as we have mentioned above, a fairly high proportion of Indians, Ukrainians, and perhaps Slovaks could still speak their mother tongue in 1971).

Urban and Rural Trends

The ethnic group members on farms have been more retentive of traditional language than members in small towns and villages, who in turn have not been as linguistically assimilated as the members in cities and larger towns (see Table 3). Exceptions to this pattern were Scandinavians in 1961 and 1971, and Germans-Dutch in 1971, with the rural non-farm population *less* assimilated than the rural farm; and the Germans-Dutch in

Table 3: *Proportion of Principal Ethnic Groups Able to Speak Mother Tongue, Rural and Urban Areas, Saskatchewan, 1951-1971.*
(rounded off to the nearest percent)

1951:	Urban	Rural Non-farm:	Rural Farm:	Total:
French	46%	71%	72%	65%
German and Dutch combined	44%	50%	59%	54%
Principal Slavic languages combined (Ukrainian, Polish, Russian)	59%	70%	77%	72%
Scandinavian languages	29%	36%	43%	40%
1961:				
French	42%	58%	66%	55%
German and Dutch combined	37%	37%	40%	38%
Principal Slavic languages combined (Ukrainian, Polish, Russian)	49%	47%	62%	56%
Scandinavian languages	24%	32%	30%	28%
1971:				
French	46%	66%	66%	56%
German and Dutch combined	16%	46%	44%	40%
Principal Slavic languages combined (Ukrainian, Polish, Russian)	47%	58%	61%	53%
Scandinavian languages	17%	25%	23%	21%

Source: 1951, 1961, 1971 Census of Canada: Bulletins on Ethnic Groups and Mother Tongue.

1961, with the urban and rural non-farm identical, and the French in 1951 and 1971, with the rural farm and rural non-farm population almost equally retentive. Only the Slavic groups have had a majority proportion in urban areas able to speak the mother tongues. During the 1950s there was a consistent drop in the proportion able to speak a mother tongue in all categories. However, during the 1960s this trend seems to have been reversed for French in urban and rural areas, German-Dutch groups in rural areas, and the Slavic rural non-farm population. While these latter trends (during the 1960s) are most interesting to note, they are at once most difficult to explain without more extensive research.

The North-Central Region

In the north-central region (where our detailed field survey was carried out), as late as 1941 there were still more people speaking German and Ukrainian as mother tongue than there were people of German and Ukrainian origin (Table 4). The German situation can be explained by the fact that many Mennonites were speaking German but considered themselves to be of Dutch origin; and the Ukrainian one by pointing out that many Roman Catholic Poles, as well as "Russian" Baptists (Stundists), from Ukrainian areas in Europe spoke Ukrainian as a mother tongue. All of the groups in the region were more retentive of their traditional languages than in the province as a whole, though only a minority of Scandinavians could still speak their mother tongue as early as 1951. As the figures refer to all members of the ethno-religious groups in the region, regardless of urban or rural residence, it seems likely that there is an even higher retention of traditional languages in the rural bloc settlements.

Table 4: Correlation of Ethnic Group by Population Speaking Mother Tongue, for Principal Ethnic Groups, Census Divisions 15 and 16, Saskatchewan, 1941-1971.

Group:	1941:	1951:	1961:	1971:
French	97.0	79.7	71.5	66.9
— speaking only French	10.7	11.6	8.3	?
German and Dutch combined	71.4	70.7	57.9	50.0
— German	103.3	91.1	72.0	52.4
Principal Slavic languages combined (Ukrainian, Polish, Russian)	95.9	87.7	76.2	61.6
— Ukrainian	107.6	103.6	95.3	70.9
Scandinavian languages	78.4	47.9	35.4	26.8

Source: 1941, 1951, 1961, 1971 Census of Canada: Bulletins on Ethnic Groups and Mother Tongue.

Use of Traditional Languages in Age Categories

The fifth table provides most interesting details on the use of traditional languages in age categories in 1971. Without exception in the five ethnic groups listed (French, Germans, Ukrainians, Poles, and Scandinavians), there is an increase in the proportion of ethnic group members able to speak the relevant traditional mother tongue concomitant with an increase in age level. The table also reveals a general increase in the proportion actually primarily speaking the mother tongue at home (though some exceptions may be noted). Use of the mother tongue at home markedly increases in the older age categories for all of these groups, although the proportion actually using a Scandinavian language remains very low. Older Ukrainians are particularly retentive of their Ukrainian language, in striking contrast to the people of Polish descent (86.9% of Ukrainians over 65 speaking Ukrainian at home, compared to only 33.7% of Poles in that age category speaking Polish).

Table 5: *Proportion of Ethnic Group Members in Saskatchewan (A) Able to Speak Relevant Mother Tongue and (B) Primarily Speaking Mother Tongue at Home, Cross-Classified with Age Categories, for Selected Ethnic Groups, 1971.*

Ethnic Group:	Total:	0-9:	10-19:	20-34:	Age 35-44:	45-64:	65 +:
French							
(A)	56.2	32.8	44.6	53.6	70.6	77.5	89.4
(B)	28.4	20.5	25.9	19.8	28.3	36.4	56.3
German							
(A)	42.1	14.2	18.4	40.3	82.4	73.6	90.1
(B)	10.1	7.3	5.6	7.4	10.2	11.7	36.3
Ukrainian							
(A)	62.6	26.6	39.7	55.5	79.3	89.2	97.1
(B)	28.9	10.8	14.0	13.9	20.1	43.6	86.9
Polish							
(A)	28.2	6.1	9.9	17.7	28.9	50.3	66.0
(B)	8.1	2.5	2.4	2.2	4.0	11.5	33.7
Scandinavian							
(A)	21.3	2.1	3.9	6.5	15.8	38.4	66.9
(B)	1.0	0.2	0.3	0.4	0.2	1.2	4.7

Source: Calculated by the author from the 1971 Census of Canada, Catalogue 92-731, vol. 1, part 4 bulletin 1.4-3 and Catalogue 92-733, vol. 1, part 4, bulletin 1.4-5.

(3) *Field Survey Data*
   Methodology: The Sample

In order more fully to comprehend language trends within the Canadian Prairie region, particularly within the context of ethnic or ethno-religious rural bloc settlements, an extensive field survey was conducted during 1969-71 in eighteen ethno-religious bloc settlements (seven French Catholic, one German Catholic, two Mennonite, two Hutterite, three Ukrainian Orthodox, Ukrainian Catholic, and Polish Catholic, one Russian Doukhobor, and two Scandinavian Lutheran) located in the region between Saskatoon, North Battleford, and Prince Albert (Census Divisions Fifteen and Sixteen).[5] A 2.00% controlled quota sample was stratified by age, generation, and sex to represent as closely as possible the demographic structure of the total population of each settlement. One in every fifty persons of the relevant ethnic and religious category was interviewed in each settlement. Not more than one person was interviewed in a single nuclear or extended family, and no respondent was less than thirteen years of age. The extent of each settlement was statistically determined as the limit beyond which each relevant ethno-religious group

comprised less than a quarter of the total local population, although several
of the communities sampled could be included in two overlapping bloc
settlements. This sampling technique yielded a thousand cases (202 French,
190 German Catholics, 244 Mennonites, 6 Hutterites, 83 Ukrainian
Orthodox, 154 Ukrainian Catholics, 15 Polish Catholics, 20 Doukhobors,
and 86 Scandinavians).* The interviewing procedure employed in the study
was focussed interviewing; instead of designing a strictly structured
questionnaire which would have yielded considerably less information,
each respondent was personally interviewed in depth. Data analysis was
through univariate, bivariate, and trivariate correlations by computer.

Table 6: Population and Sample by Group and Settlement.

Group and Settlement	Ethnic Population	Sample
FRENCH	10,100	202
Prudhomme & St.-Denis	1,100	22
St. Brieux	900	18
Bonne Madone	300	6
St.-Louis, Batoche, & Duck Lake	3,600	72
Albertville	600	12
Marcelin & Coteau	900	18
Leoville & Debden	2,700	54
GERMAN CATHOLIC	9,500	190
St. Peter's Colony	9,500	190
MENNONITE	12,200	244
Rosthern & Saskatchewan Valley	10,700	214
Meeting Lake	1,500	30
HUTTERITE	300	6
Leask Colony	150	3
Riverview Colony	150	3
UKRAINIAN & POLISH	12,600	252
Fish Creek & Yellow Creek	5,500	110
Garden River	2,400	48
Redberry	4,700	94
DOUKHOBOR	1,000	20
Petrofka & Blaine Lake	1,000	20
SCANDINAVIAN	4,300	86
Canwood & Parkside	1,800	36
Birch Hills	2,500	50
TOTAL	50,000	1000

Language Use: Total Sample

Table 7-A indicates the language preferences of the various ethno-
religious groups. The first category applies to respondents familiar only with
a mother tongue (i.e., who cannot speak English at all or who can hardly
speak English); the second to bilingual (in English and mother tongue)
respondents who generally prefer to speak the traditional language both in
home and out; the third to bilingual respondents who generally prefer to
speak their mother tongue at home but English out; the fourth to bilingual
respondents who generally prefer English both in home and out; and the

---

*See Table 6 for the derivation of the sample from the total ethno-religious population in each
settlement.

fifth to respondents familiar only with English (i.e., who have little or no acquaintance with the traditional language of their group).

Table 7-A; Language Preference of Respondents (percentages).

Group:	Category (1)	(2)	(3)	(4)	(5)	Total %	N
French	9.9	48.0	20.3	20.8	1.0	100	(202)
German Catholic	—	13.7	15.3	64.2	6.8	100	(190)
Mennonite	1.6	52.5	14.8	28.3	2.9	100	(244)
Hutterite	—	100.0	—	—	—	100	(6)
Ukrainian Orthodox	6.0	33.7	22.9	37.3	—	100	(83)
Ukrainian Catholic	3.2	44.2	21.4	29.9	1.3	100	(154)
Polish Catholic	6.7	33.3	46.7	13.3	—	100	(15)
Doukhobor	5.0	25.0	40.0	25.0	5.0	100	(20)
Scandinavian	—	25.6	11.6	52.3	10.5	100	(86)
Total Sample	3.6	38.5	18.3	36.2	3.4	100	(Total N = 1,000)

By calculating cumulative frequencies from the above table, we can derive the following information:

Table 7-B; Language Preference of Respondents: Cumulative Frequencies.

Group:	speak only mother-tongue:	use mother-tongue at least fairly often:	can speak mother-tongue:
French	9.9	78.2	99.0
German Catholic	—	29.0	93.2
Mennonite	1.6	68.9	97.2
Hutterite	—	100.0	100.0
Ukrainian Orthodox	6.0	62.6	100.0
Ukrainian Catholic	3.2	68.8	98.7
Polish Catholic	6.7	86.7	100.0
Doukhobor	5.0	70.0	95.0
Scandinavian	—	37.2	89.5
Total Sample	3.6	60.4	96.6

We can note that an extremely high proportion of all respondents can still speak a traditional mother tongue other than English, regardless of group. Virtually all the Hutterite, Ukrainian Orthodox, and Polish Catholic respondents could still speak such a mother tongue as well as almost all French, Ukrainian Catholics, and Mennonites, and a high proportion of Doukhobors, German Catholics and Scandinavians.

Language Use: Specific Ethno-Religious Groups

(a) The French

Let us now examine the mother tongue of each group in some detail, beginning with the French. French-origin minorities in numerous largely French settlements outside Quebec have revealed a devotion to their traditional language; a sizeable proportion of children may reach the age of 10-12 before learning English well because the latter is spoken seldom at home or perhaps even in the separate schools. There have been many forces serving to preserve French identity in general and the French language in particular — the French parishes of the Roman Catholic Church, various organizations, a close connection maintained between the minorities and

Quebec, the mass media in the French language, and the like. French Catholicism and the French language have traditionally been considered inseparable in Quebec as well as among the minorities; in fact, this view has been supported by clergy who have maintained that the language is the guardian of the faith and vice-versa.[6] L'Association Culturelle Franco-Canadienne de la Saskatchewan, formerly L'Association Catholique Franco-Canadiennne (the A.C.F.C.), founded at Duck Lake, has been particularly active in this regard, offering French-language courses in Saskatchewan schools with exams standardized to those of Quebec since 1912. Only about one out of every five French Canadians in the province has taken these courses, but half of the remaining people of French origin are not French-speaking in any case.[7] Of course, restricting this statistic to rural areas which are overwhelmingly French greatly increases our estimate of the influence of the A.C.F.C. as well as of the parishes and homes. But we have noted that while 99.0% of the French respondents in our sample *could* speak French, 78.2% did in fact use this language fairly often. Perhaps an explanation for this discrepancy is forthcoming when we correlate language with generation and age.

It is interesting to note in passing that the French originally came to Saskatchewan from a wide variety of origins reflecting divergent dialects. Probably most came directly from France and Belgium, but these immigrants included Walloons and Flemings from Hainaut and French Flanders (some speaking Flemish, a Dutch dialect), Bretons (many speaking the Breton language, a Celtic language, besides French, notably those who settled in the St. Brieux-Kermaria district), as well as immigrants from a diversity of other regions in France (Poitou, Guyenne, Normandy, Franche-Comté, Burgundy, Maine, Dauphine, etc.). Many French Canadians in Saskatchewan came directly from Quebec due to colonization schemes; some were Acadians from Quebec, while others were Quebecois from American mid-western states. The first Francophone settlers were Métis of mixed French-Indian extraction from Manitoba. However, these various sub-group distinctions and dialect differences have tended to become fused into a common French Canadian identity during several decades of settlement in Saskatchewan.[8]

(b) *The German-speaking Groups*

Undoubtedly the traditionally German-speaking groups generally failed to unite to preserve the German language, not only due to religious differences but also due to the fact that they actually speak distinct dialects so different as to hinder easy communication in the mother tongue. The Hutterites usually speak a Tyrolian dialect, little influenced by Slavic languages (Czech, Slovak, and Russian), Hungarian, and Rumanian admixture; while the language of their own "German school" is Hochdeutsch, High German.[9] The Mennonites, on the other hand, use a variety of dialects. The language of the first Mennonites in the Netherlands of course had been Dutch. By the mid-eighteenth century their Dutch had been gradually transformed into the *Frankische, Niedersachsische,* and *Friesische* dialects of *Niederdeutsch* or *Plattdeutsch* (i.e., Low German). In West Prussia the dialect spoken by most Mennonites was *Westpreussische Plattdeutsch.* With migration to South Russia, a *Schwarzmeer-Deutsch* (Black Sea German) dialect of Low German with Russian admixture was adopted. In Saskatchewan the Old Colony Mennonites used a Low German dialect not only as their daily speech but also in their churches. Other Mennonites, however, tended to look upon this dialect as crude, boorish, corrupted German used only by the uneducated; for their part, they used standard Low German in everyday speech and *Schriftsprache, Bibeldeutsch,* or *Hochdeutsch* ("literary language," Bible German or High German) in their churches and schools.[10]

It is instructive to speculate why the Dutch was lost with migration into Germany but the German was little influenced by Russian admixture with migration into Russia. We may hypothesize that if a sect exists as a minority where the majority is considered by the minority to be more advanced in culture and education, the minority will become linguistically assimilated; whereas they will retain their mother tongue unadulterated if they consider their own culture as superior.[11] In short, German culture and particularly language was more highly valued in eighteenth century Europe than Dutch or Russian. As we have already noted, a feeling of the superiority of German culture also affected the preservation of German identity and language among the German Catholics in Saskatchewan. Until very recently many of the older Mennonites, especially those of the Old Colony sect, spoke English very little and very poorly. The German language was considered a focal point in the avoidance of contact with the larger society, such avoidance being positively valued and backed by xenophobia, and it was considered the only proper language for Mennonite church service.[12]

Although some young people were having trouble with sentence structure in English, using the German structure when talking English, linguistic assimilation of the German groups seemed imminent and inevitable. Gone was much of the German Catholic admiration for German cultural superiority after the world wars. Younger Mennonites, especially in the more liberal sects, were expressing disdain for so much use of the German language.[13] The churches of the liberal sects adopted English, and use of German in public schools was outlawed even earlier. The *Russländer* immigrants expressed their eagerness to learn English, unlike the Old Colony Mennonites who had emigrated from Russia several decades previously.[14] Even among the Hutterites, it became possible that English would replace German due to schooling in the former, though the Hutterites also set up their own schools using the latter.[15] Thus, while the Hutterites interviewed still use German most of the time, little more than two-thirds of the Mennonites and a quarter of the German Catholics use their mother tongue at least fairly often, despite a high proportion being able to speak some German.

(c) *The Slavic Groups*

Of the Slavic groups, the Doukhobors all recognize Russian as their traditional language. However, some of the so-called "Russian" Baptists, having immigrated to the Blaine Lake area from the Ukraine, speak a Ukrainian dialect, as do many people claiming Polish origin. A wide variety of Ukrainian dialects are spoken by people of Ukrainian, and to some extent also of Polish and Russian origin, depending on the precise area from which they or their predecessors emigrated.[16] The Ukrainian language bears a close similarity to Russian; in fact, to emphasize the distinctiveness of Ukrainian, Ukrainian nationalists in Canada replaced letters of the Russian alphabet with new "Ukrainian" ones.[17]

Frequent use of the Ukrainian language — and a corresponding failure to prefer English — was enhanced by the illiteracy of Ukrainian immigrants, by what other non-Ukrainian settlers considered to be their backwardness, by a lack of familiarity with English, reinforcing seclusion from the outside world, by a deep-rooted, nationalistic pride in Ukrainian identity and a love for the mother tongue, by traditional institutions resisting all attempts to tamper with the mother tongue.[18] For example, in the Vonda area in 1917, two decades after the first establishment of the Fish Creek settlement, out of 98 male settlers of Ukrainian and Polish origin, only 16 could speak any English and only eight could also read English; 45 of them were literate in Ukrainian and Polish. Of an equal number of women, only eight could speak English and just one could read English, 31 were literate in Ukrainian or Polish. They had 395 children; of the 175 who were between six and fourteen years of age, 98 could read English, 99 their mother tongue; and of the 86 over fourteen years of age, 52 could read English and 69 their mother tongue. Forty-one families had home libraries in their traditional language; all told these held 659 books (i.e., about 16 books per home), chiefly fiction and Ukrainian history. One family which had lived an isolated existence in a forest in the Ukraine was illiterate but regretted this situation. Another illiterate family, however, was backward in many other respects, farming with oxen, caring little for their children. A similar situation prevailed in the Hafford area in the Redberry Settlement. Out of 56 male Ukrainian and Polish immigrants only 18 spoke some English and nine were literate in English; 36 were literate in their mother tongue. Of an equal number of women, three could speak English, two of whom were also literate in English, compared to 29 literate in their mother tongue. Of 197 children, 94 were from six to fourteen years old, and of these 50 were literate in English and 57 in their mother tongue; of the 30 who were over fourteen years old, 13 could read English and 16 their mother tongue. Thirty-two homes lacked libraries of any sort, while the other homes had books in Ukrainian (including prayer books). In the third Ukrainian-Polish settlement in the north-central region, the Garden River settlement, there were 58 male immigrants, of whom 17 could speak a little English, 11 could read a little English, and 32 could read and write Ukrainian, Polish, or Russian. As for the 52 women, only three could speak any English, one could read a little English, and 32 were literate in their mother tongue. There were 157 children, 49 of them from six to fourteen years old, of whom ten could read and write English and 14 their traditional language; another 21 were over 14 years old, of whom only three were literate in English, compared to eleven in their traditional language. One family had some literature in English; thirty-seven no literature at all; the remainder Ukrainian literature (generally fiction and religious material).[19]

It seems small wonder, then, that such a high proportion of the Slavic people interviewed in our survey could still speak their mother tongue. But some changes in language-use merit mention. Evidently considerable Anglicization of the Ukrainian dialects began to occur at a fairly early date in the bloc settlements of Saskatchewan. Numerous Ukrainian-Canadian words were derived from English, though others actually from the Ukraine were similar to English. English combined with Ukrainian was increasingly adopted, although English verbs were conjugated by the settlers as if they were Ukrainian and Ukrainian sentence structure was imposed when speaking English (this practice became typical of the second generation, whereas the third generation often tended to reverse the process, imposing English structure on Ukrainian).[20] When the first Ukrainians immigrated "en masse" to the Canadian Prairies, an estimated half of them were still illiterate; by 1921 40% of the immigrants were still illiterate; by 1931 almost a third of them in Saskatchewan were probably still unable to speak English.[21] When our interviewing was completed, almost all of the respondents in the Ukrainian-Polish group could still speak their mother tongue, while about two-thirds of the Ukrainians and a higher proportion of the Poles were using their mother tongue fairly often, as we have already noted.

(d) *The Scandinavians*

In contrast, the respondents of Scandinavian origin preferred to speak English much of the time; while almost 90% of them could speak a Scandinavian language, little more than a third of them did fairly often. The Norwegian language was used quite extensively, if not exclusively, in Norwegian Lutheran churches in Saskatchewan during the first couple of decades in this century.[22] But in 1921 only 1.4% of foreign-born Norwegians in Canada were illiterate in English.[23] Possibly the limited extent to which Norwegians could converse in their mother tongue with Swedes or Danes may have created a situation in the Scandinavian bloc settlements where English was readily adopted as a "lingua-franca." Yet Canadians of Norwegian origin undoubtedly predominated in both Scandinavian settlements in north-central Saskatchewan, particularly the Hagan area of the Birch Hills settlement and the Ordale area of the Shellbrook settlement. Consequently the adoption of English as a common language would have been more likely in the Parkside and Canwood areas, where Scandinavians of other national origins were found in greater proportions.

Sample Breakdown

(a) *Age*

The following table gives the breakdown of the sample by age categories:

Table 8-A; Proportion of Respondents in Age Categories, Per Ethno-Religious Group.

Group:	13-19:	20-29:	30-49:	50-69:	70 & Over	Total:	
						%	N
French	14.9	9.4	35.6	26.7	13.4	100	(202)
German Catholic	5.8	15.8	20.5	38.9	18.9	100	(190)
Mennonite	11.5	13.1	23.0	32.0	20.5	100	(244)
Hutterite	16.7	33.3	16.7	16.7	16.7	100	(6)
Ukrainian Orthodox	8.4	10.8	20.5	50.6	9.6	100	(83)
Ukrainian Catholic	13.0	5.8	38.3	27.9	14.9	100	(154)
Polish Catholic	0.0	0.0	26.7	40.0	33.3	100	(15)
Doukhobor	10.0	0.0	45.0	20.0	25.0	100	(20)
Scandinavian	8.1	8.1	34.9	29.1	19.8	100	(86)
Total Sample	10.6	10.8	28.7	32.7	17.2	100	(1000)

It can be readily seen that in the sample respondents in the senior adult and middle aged categories were over-represented, while those in the adolescent, young adult, and elderly categories were under-represented. The uneven distribution is even more apparent when each group is viewed separately. While this departure from giving equal weight to the strata might seem to bias our findings, it was in fact intended to approximate the age structure of the actual population, thereby rendering generalization about the population more significant. Moreover, in sampling, the Ukrainian and Polish groups were considered sub-groups of a single group, accounting for the fact that no young Polish Catholics were interviewed.

The data tend to support the hypothesis that the younger the respondents, the more likely they will be to prefer speaking English rather than their traditional mother tongue. However, the trend is not a steady continuum in certain ethno-religious groups or sub-groups, and no Hutterite respondents preferred to speak English primarily or exclusively, as the following table indicates:

Table 8-B: Proportion of Respondents in Each Age Category Speaking English (Primarily or Exclusively), Per Group.

Group:	13-19:	20-29:	30-49:	50-69:	70 & Over:
French	46.7	31.6	22.2	11.1	7.4
German Catholic	90.9	86.7	92.3	63.6	44.4
Mennonite	39.3	50.0	44.6	30.8	0.0
Hutterite	0.0	0.0	0.0	0.0	0.0
Ukrainian Orthodox	57.1	66.7	47.1	31.0	0.0
Ukrainian Catholic	50.0	55.6	42.4	18.6	0.0
Polish Catholic	—	—	50.0	0.0	0.0
Doukhobor	100.0	—	44.4	0.0	0.0
Scandinavian	100.0	100.0	96.6	44.4	0.0

(b) *Generation*

Given the fact that generation differences do not precisely correspond to age differences, let us now proceed to determine the correlations between generation and language use. The breakdown of the sample by generation is given below:

Table 9-A; Proportion of Respondents in Generation Categories, Per Ethno-Religious Group.

Group:	(1) First Generation	(2) Second Generation	(3) Third or more Generation	Total: %	N
French	19.8	45.5	34.7	100	(202)
German Catholic	19.5	41.1	39.5	100	(190)
Mennonite	17.2	33.6	49.2	100	(244)
Hutterite	0.0	33.3	66.7	100	(6)
Ukrainian Orthodox	26.5	50.6	22.9	100	(83)
Ukrainian Catholic	24.7	57.8	17.5	100	(154)
Polish Catholic	40.0	60.0	0.0	100	(15)
Doukhobor	25.0	50.0	25.0	100	(20)
Scandinavian	15.1	39.5	45.3	100	(86)
Total Sample	20.3	43.8	35.9	100	(1000)

Many sociologists have suggested that the longer the period since immigration (during the first generation, that is) the less will be the emphasis on group identity and on speaking the traditional mother tongue.[24] It is also interesting to note such a suggestion made by the Saskatchewan historian, John Hawkes, back as early as 1924:

> If his [the immigrant's] children, however, and his children's children were to follow in his footsteps and become unintelligent and uninterested citizens, the future would be dark indeed; but the salvation of the situation is with the second and succeeding generations. The Ruthenian, Russian [etc.] child needs no coaxing to become Canadianized. They need only the opportunity which is afforded by contact with Canadian civilization in order to blossom out as enthusiastic Canadians. To them Russia . . . or Sweden or Germany is but a name. What they see of their progenitors, with whom the make comparisons with Canadians, drives them away from the sheepskin coat, the cloth upon the head, the rough footgear, and the hard labour unillumined by social graces. . . . Ask any child born of foreign parents in this country what his or her nationality is, and the answer will not be 'German' or . . . 'Russian' but 'Canadian.'[25]

Presumably, then, such a difference between generations should also be reflected in our data on language. We may hypothesize that the longer the period since immigration, the greater will be the number of group members preferring to use English rather than their traditional mother tongues. The following table illustrates that this was generally the case, excepting the Hutterites and to some extent the Doukhobors.

Table 9-B: Proportion of Respondents in Each Generation Category Speaking English (Primarily or Exclusively), Per Group.

Group:	(1)	(2)	(3)
French	10.0	16.3	35.7
German Catholic	45.9	71.8	82.7
Mennonite	4.8	31.7	40.0
Hutterite	—	0.0	0.0
Ukrainian Orthodox	13.6	38.1	63.2
Ukrainian Catholic	10.5	35.9	44.4
Polish	0.0	22.2	—
Doukhobor	0.0	50.0	20.0
Scandinavian	7.7	44.1	97.4

(c) *Sex*

Let us now examine the possibility of there being different rates of assimilation for each sex. The division of the sample by sex is given in the following table:

Table 10:*Proportion of Respondents in Sex Categories, Per Ethno-Religious Group.*

Group:	Male:	Female:	Total:	
			%	N
French	50.5	49.5	100	(202)
German Catholic	59.5	40.5	100	(190)
Mennonite	54.9	45.1	100	(244)
Hutterite	50.0	50.0	100	(6)
Ukrainian Orthodox	53.0	47.0	100	(83)
Ukrainian Catholic	57.1	42.9	100	(154)
Polish	73.3	26.7	100	(15)
Doukhobor	55.0	45.0	100	(20)
Scandinavian	51.2	48.8	100	(86)
Total Sample	55.0	45.0	100	(1000)

In cross-tabulating language with sex and controlling for group, the hypothesis that more males would prefer English than females was somewhat acceptable in the German Catholic, Mennonite, Ukrainian Orthodox, and Scandinavian cases; but it was not acceptable in the French, Polish, and Doukhobor cases, while the Hutterites and Ukrainian Catholics were balanced.[26]

(d) *Occupation*

Did the occupation of the respondent have anything to do with his attitude toward the preservation of his ethnic identity and traditional mother tongue? Before attempting an answer, we must examine the categorization of our sample by various occupational groupings. Aside from unemployed or retired respondents, the respondents were classified into nine categories: (1) students, (2) full-time farmers, (3) part-time farmers (also holding another job), (4) clergymen, nuns, and the like (excluding ones who were schoolteachers), (5) schoolteachers (including nuns, etc., thus employed), (6) postmasters or postmistresses and other civil servants (rural municipality secretaries, village councillors, etc.), (7) independent owners or proprietors (shopkeepers, innkeepers, etc.), (8) skilled-employed, (9) unskilled-employed. While these categories could not be considered mutually exclusive, they did allow in all but a very few cases easy approximate classification. Housewives, particularly on farms, were classified according to their husbands' occupations, unless they fitted readily into a more specific category, such as postmistresses.

From this table we can note that about half of the sample were engaged in farming, with the Poles and Hutterites, and to a lesser extent the Scandinavians, being overwhelmingly in that occupation.

To proceed, then, with our question concerning a possible relationship between occupation and attitude toward ethnic identity and mother tongue preservation, from our data some very interesting conclusions could be

Table 11: *Proportion of Respondents in Occupation Categories, Per Group.*

Group:	(1)	(2)	(3)	(4)	(5)	(6)	(7)	(8)	(9)	(Other)	Total: %
French	14.9	49.5	1.0	3.5	1.5	3.5	13.9	6.9	4.0	1.5	100
German Catholic	6.8	43.2	1.6	1.6	0.5	3.2	16.8	14.7	0.0	11.6	100
Mennonite	11.5	40.6	3.7	3.7	0.0	4.1	11.9	6.1	6.6	11.9	100
Hutterite	16.7	83.3	0.0	0.0	0.0	0.0	0.0	0.0	0.0	0.0	100
Ukrainian Orthodox	9.6	36.1	2.4	3.6	8.4	7.2	16.9	2.4	2.4	10.8	100
Ukrainian Catholic	13.0	55.2	1.3	1.9	1.3	1.9	14.9	5.8	1.9	2.6	100
Polish	0.0	86.7	0.0	6.7	0.0	0.0	0.0	6.7	0.0	9.9	100
Doukhobor	10.0	50.0	0.0	0.0	0.0	5.0	10.0	5.0	0.0	20.0	100
Scandinavian	9.3	66.3	0.0	0.0	0.0	3.5	3.5	3.5	0.0	14.0	100
Total Sample	11.0	48.1	1.8	2.6	1.3	3.6	13.1	7.3	2.9	8.3	100

drawn. Taking each occupation category in numerical order, first we noted that the students in all groups except the Hutterites were markedly unconcerned about preserving their ethnic identity, especially in the German Catholic, Doukhobor, and Scandinavian cases. Full-time and part-time farmers proved generally conservative, with the exception of more than half of the German Catholic ones. The clergy in general were found to be rather mixed in their attitudes, but breaking down the sample by group revealed that the Ukrainian and Polish priests were all conservative, as were a high proportion of the French clergy and two-thirds of the Mennonite ministers but none of the German Catholic priests and nuns (excluding ones who were also teachers). The French, Ukrainian Catholic, and German Catholic schoolteachers (including many nuns in the French and German cases) were extremely anxious to preserve their group's identities; but this did not hold true for Ukrainian Orthodox teachers. It was found that the Ukrainian Catholic, Scandinavian, and French civil servants interviewed were extremely conservative, the Mennonite ones also very conservative, but only half of the Ukrainian Orthodox and none of the Doukhobor or German Catholic ones. We again encountered a mixed picture for independent owners and proprietors: while those in several groups were on the conservative side — notably the Doukhobors, Ukrainians, Mennonites, and French — those in other groups — the Scandinavians and German Catholics — were not. The skilled-employed Poles, Ukrainian Orthodox, and Doukhobors were found to be very conservative, those in the other groups less so, especially German Catholic ones. A rather different picture emerged in considering the unskilled-employed: only the French in this category were very conservative, while the Ukrainian Catholics and Mennonites were fairly conservative, but the Ukrainian Orthodox not at all.

(e) *Education*

Finally, let us take a look at the relationship between education, ethnic identity, and language use. Again, we must first subdivide the total sample and each group by a number of education categories indicating the various levels of education attained by the respondents. A first category refers to respondents having attained less than high school education (i.e., only grade-school education); a second to those having had some high school, a third to high school graduates who have not had further formal education; and a fourth to respondents having had at least some university education:

Table 12-A: Proportion of Respondents in Education Categories, Per Group*

Group:	(1)	(2)	(3)	(4)	Total: %	N
French	22.3	59.9	11.4	6.4	100	(202)
German Catholic	28.9	47.4	17.9	5.8	100	(190)
Mennonite	36.5	37.2	20.9	3.3	100	(244)
Hutterite	100	0.0	0.0	0.0	100	(6)
Ukrainian Orthodox	41.0	27.7	15.7	15.7	100	(83)
Ukrainian Catholic	32.5	47.4	14.9	5.2	100	(154)
Polish	66.7	20.0	6.7	6.7	100	(15)
Doukhobor	25.0	45.0	25.0	5.0	100	(20)
Scandinavian	10.5	68.6	19.8	1.2	100	(86)
Total Sample	30.3	47.4	16.7	5.6	100	(1000)

*Note that significance of results in some categories may be limited by sample size.

It is interesting to note that in the total sample, almost half of the respondents were in the second category, i.e., had some high school education. Significant group differences could also be noted, such as the disproportionate number of Hutterites, Poles, Ukrainians, and Mennonites with only a grade-school education, compared to the disproportionate number of Ukrainian Orthodox, Poles and French with some university education, or of Doukhobors, Mennonites, Scandinavians, and German Catholics who were high school graduates.[27]

The cross-tabulation of language use with education similarly provided some rather unexpected results, which are summarized in the following table:

Table 12-B: Proportion of Respondents in Each Education Category Speaking English (Primarily or Exclusively), Per Group.

Group:	(1)	(2)	(3)	(4)
French	11.1	23.9	30.4	23.1
German Catholic	43.6	75.6	100.0	81.8
Mennonite	12.4	40.6	39.2	75.0
Hutterite	0.0	—	—	—
Ukrainian Orthodox	23.5	30.4	76.9	46.2
Ukrainian Catholic	12.0	46.5	26.1	25.0
Polish	0.0	33.3	100.0	0.0
Doukhobor	0.0	44.4	40.0	0.0
Scandinavian	0.0	64.5	88.2	100.0

Should we have tested the working hypothesis that the higher the level of education attained, the more likely the respondent will be to prefer English, such a hypothesis would have been clearly verified in the sole case of the Scandinavians, though it would also have been approximated by the Mennonites. What is perhaps more significant is the finding that in four groups — the French, German Catholics, Ukrainian Orthodox, and Poles, loss of mother tongue increases through high school graduates, then

declines for the university-educated, although explanation of this finding
would seem impossible without further research.

Demographic Considerations

(a) Community Size

Does the size of each local community relate to the preservation of
ethnic identity and traditional language? The communities were classified
in a sevenfold manner: (1) larger (officially "urban") towns (population
over 1,000), (2) smaller (officially "rural") towns (incorporated towns with
population under 1,000), (3) major incorporated villages (population over
250), (4) minor incorporated villages (population over 100), (5) unincorporated villages (population over 100), (6) hamlets (population 50-100), (7)
localities (population less than 50).

Table 13-A: Proportion of Interviews Conducted in Communities, by Size of Community, Per
Ethno-Religious Group.

Group:	(1)	(2)	(3)	(4)	(5)	(6)	(7)	Total: %	N
French	0.0	15.3	54.0	0.0	10.4	5.9	14.4	100	(202)
German Catholic	10.0	15.8	21.6	34.7	9.5	8.4	0.0	100	(190)
Mennonite	14.3	8.6	29.9	8.2	16.8	15.6	6.6	100	(244)
Hutterite	0.0	0.0	0.0	0.0	0.0	100.0	0.0	100	(6)
Ukrainian Orthodox	22.9	6.0	18.1	25.3	0.0	7.2	20.5	100	(83)
Ukrainian Catholic	7.1	14.3	24.0	44.8	0.0	1.3	8.4	100	(154)
Polish Catholic	0.0	0.0	53.3	13.3	0.0	0.0	33.3	100	(15)
Doukhobor	100.0	0.0	0.0	0.0	0.0	0.0	0.0	100	(20)
Scandinavian	0.0	7.0	9.3	11.6	0.0	0.0	77.1	100	(86)
Total Sample	10.4	11.5	29.1	18.8	8.0	8.0	14.2	100	(1000)

From our data no correlation was found between community size and
eagerness to preserve ethnic identity for any group. However, to control
such a conclusion, we employed the same technique to examine the
relationship between community size and language, hypothesizing that the
larger the community, the higher would be the proportion of respondents
who prefer to speak English.

Table 13-B: Proportion of Respondents Speaking English (Primarily or Exclusively) in
Communities Categorized by Size, Per Ethno-Religous Group.

Group:	(1)	(2)	(3)	(4)	(5)	(6)	(7)
French	0.0	35.5	22.9	0.0	19.0	0.0	13.7
German Catholic	52.6	60.0	80.4	90.0	38.9	43.8	0.0
Mennonite	40.0	38.1	32.9	40.0	26.9	23.7	12.5
Hutterite	0.0	0.0	0.0	0.0	0.0	0.0	0.0
Ukrainian Orthodox	73.7	60.0	46.7	23.8	0.0	16.7	5.9
Ukrainian Catholic	18.2	18.2	21.6	44.9	0.0	0.0	0.0
Doukhobor	30.0	0.0	0.0	0.0	0.0	0.0	0.0
Scandinavian	0.0	50.0	87.5	10.0	0.0	0.0	69.4

We can see that, on the one hand, our hypothesis must be rejected as a
generalization for most groups, but that, on the other hand, it is clearly
sustained in the French and Ukrainian Orthodox, as well as perhaps the
Mennonite, cases. While this finding is most interesting, however, one
cannot help wondering just how theoretically significant it could be. For it is
curious indeed that the correlation holds for the Orthodox but not the

Catholic Ukrainians, two subtly different groups living together in common communities.

(b) *Community Homogeneity*

The communities in which or near which interviews were conducted were categorized according to the proportion of their population formed by people sharing a relevant ethnic origin. Four categories were designated: (1) 90% and over, (2) 75-89%, (3) 50-74%, (4) approximately 25-49%. The 1961 census was used for the communities incorporated by then, whereas admittedly some guess-work proved necessary for the then unincorporated communities (this was facilitated, though, by the small size of most such communities). The following table indicates the number of interviews obtained in each type of category:

Table 14—A: Proportion of Interviews Conducted in Communities With Various Ethnic Proportions, Per Ethno-Religious Group.

		Ethnic Proportion in Community				
Ethno-Religious Group:	*Under 50%*	*50-74%*	*75-89%*	*Over 90%*	*Total:*	
					%	N
French	9.4	47.0	20.3	23.3	100	(202)
German Catholic	1.6	60.0	18.9	19.5	100	(190)
Mennonite	13.1	18.4	4.5	63.9	100	(244)
Hutterite	0.0	0.0	0.0	100.0	100	(6)
Ukrainian Orthodox	32.5	10.8	30.1	26.5	100	(83)
Ukrainian Catholic	20.8	31.8	14.9	32.5	100	(154)
Polish Catholic	33.3	13.3	46.7	6.7	100	(15)
Doukhobor	100.0	0.0	0.0	0.0	100	(20)
Scandinavian	19.8	8.1	29.1	43.0	100	(86)
Total Sample	15.5	32.1	16.8	35.6	100	(1000)

We can note, fortunately, a fairly even balance between the number of interviews obtained in communities where the relevant ethnic group comprised at least 75% of the communities' total populations, and the number obtained in communities where the relevant ethnic proportion was less than 75%.

We hypothesized that the lower the relevant ethnic proportion in the community, the more likely the ethno-religious group members would be to speak English rather than their traditional mother tongue, primarily if not exclusively, both in and out of their homes.

Table 14-B: Proportion of Respondents Speaking English (Primarily or Exclusively) in Communities Categorized by Ethnic Proportion, Per Ethno-Religious Group.

Ethno-Religious	Ethnic Proportion in Community			
Group:	*Under 50%*	*50-74%*	*75-89%*	*Over 90%*
French	21.1	30.5	14.6	10.6
German Catholic	66.7	75.4	69.4	59.5
Mennonite	43.8	46.7	9.1	25.6
Hutterite	0.0	0.0	0.0	0.0
Ukrainian Orthodox	63.0	44.4	36.0	4.5
Ukrainian Catholic	21.9	28.6	17.4	46.0
Polish Catholic	0.0	50.0	14.3	0.0
Doukhobor	30.0	0.0	0.0	0.0
Scandinavian	64.7	0.0	52.0	81.0

For instance, 21.1% of all the people of French origin, interviewed in communities where people of that origin constituted under 50% of the total community population, spoke English rather than their traditional mother tongue, primarily or excusively, both in and out of their homes. From this table it is apparent that there is little if any correlation per group of community ethnic proportions with language preferences, excepting the case of the Ukrainian Orthodox, who do substantiate our working hypothesis, and possibly the French.

Conclusion: The Future

The first part of this paper reiterated the emphasis found in sociological literature on the close connection between the preservation of ethnic identity and the retention of a traditional mother tongue. But a central question posed by this paper must be whether the ability to speak a traditional mother tongue is necessary for the maintenance of ethnic identity. There can be little doubt that the infrastructure of certain ethno-religious collectivities in Saskatchewan stresses the independence of ethnicity and language. To cite but one example, the Ukrainian Orthodox Church has steadfastly refused to adopt English as the prevalent language of the liturgy. On the other hand, it was noted that some ethnic groups, such as the Scots, Welsh, or perhaps the Scandinavians in Saskatchewan, retain strong advocates of ethnic traditionalism who cannot speak the erstwhile mother tongue. In fact, in the second part of the paper it was pointed out that by 1971, out of the twenty-nine ethnic categories in Saskatchewan listed in Table 2, in only nine do a majority still speak the traditional mother tongue; also that there is very little use of the mother tongue at home among the younger generation in almost every group. This clearly means that in the foreseeable future there will be virtually no use — or extremely little use — of a traditional mother tongue for most ethnic groups in Saskatchewan. But does this necessarily also mean that ethnic distinctiveness — and for that matter multiculturalism — will cease to be stressed? At the very least, the criteria for ethnic identity will progressively become reinterpreted. However, the survey data discussed in the third part of the paper equally clearly suggest that an astonishingly high proportion of residents in rural ethno-religious bloc settlements are still able to converse in their traditional languages, even in the Scandinavian and German Catholic settlements, although use of English is increasingly preferred. But the survey data also indicated that age and generation differences in language use are increasingly becoming evident. Thus, even in the relatively conservative bloc settlement context, linguistic assimilation would seem to be inevitable, if proceeding at a slower pace than in urban and mixed areas.

In sum, even in the rural bloc settlements, the traditional bastions of ethnic cultures, despite a recent re-emphasis of multiculturalism (be it as a national or provincial government policy or as romanticization), many processes of social change doubtless will continue to decrease any use of traditional mother tongues in particular and probably also any emphasis on ethnicity in general. Five principal processes seem particularly worthy of note:

First, widespread intermarriage between people of different ethnic origins.

Second, several decades of discriminatory provincial legislation against use of "foreign" languages in school instruction, a conscious policy of using schools as assimilatory agents to ensure conformity to the dominant Anglo-Canadian mode.

Third, the breakdown of the institutional completeness and segregation of ethnic communities, largely through the consolidation of formerly highly localized and ethnically homogeneous schools and other focal points of local community activity into more heterogeneous units.

Fourth, a steady process of secularization together with a progressive de-emphasis of the one-time close link between ethnicity, language, and religion.

Fifth, very large-scale rural depopulation and the decline of smaller communities, concurrent with rapid urbanization.

REFERENCES AND NOTES

[1] E. A. Freeman, "Language as a Basis of Racial Classification," in E. T. Thompson and E. C. Hughes, eds., *Race: Individual and Collective Behaviour* (Glencoe, Ill., 1958), 34. T. Shibutani and K. M. Kwan, *Ethnic Stratification: A Comparative Approach* (New York, 1965), 59, 75, 479. Joseph Bram, *Language and Society* (New York, 1955), 19, 23. R. E. Park, *Race and Culture* (Glencoe, Ill., 1950), 262. O. Handlin, *The Uprooted* (New York, 1951), 187; cited in Will Herberg, *Protestant, Catholic, Jew* (Garden City, N.Y., 1960), 13. W. D. Borrie ed., *The Culture Integration of Immigrants* (Paris, 1959), 285.
[2] T. Shibutani and K. M. Kwan, *op. cit.*, 285. J. Bram, *op. cit.*, 29-32.
[3] T. Shibutani and K. M. Kwan, *op. cit.*, 446-447, 471-472, 506, 528-529. W. D. Borrie, ed., *op. cit.*, 130. S. Lieberson, *Ethnic Patterns in American Cities* (Glencoe, Ill., 1963), 133-134.
[4] For example, in the French settlements, relatively few English given names are used; there are at least thirty-five frequent French given names among farmers in the settlements (e.g., Pierre, Réné, Emile, Yvonne, Marcel, Antoine, Gaston, Napoleon, etc.). Among the German farmers in St. Peter's Colony and other German Catholic settlements, German given names are numerous; over seventeen varieties may be discerned (e.g., Johannes, Bernard, Ernst, Alois, Reinhold, Otto, etc.). Hungarian Catholics have mixed to some extent with co-religionists of German and French origin in the St. Philippe area near St. Brieux, the St. Benedict and Buda areas near Wakaw, and the St. László-Muskiki Lake area near Prud'homme; yet even in these areas Hungarian given names are still quite numerous (e.g., Nándor, Géza, Béla, etc.). On the other hand, it should be pointed out that probably most third generation people of Hungarian descent in Saskatchewan have been given non-Hungarian Christian names; also that the traditional Hungarian practice of placing the surname before the Christian name has been abandoned in Canada. Among the Mennonite farmers in the Rosthern settlement, German given names are common; more than sixteen varieties may be found (e.g., Waldemar, Johannes, Karl, Helmult, Konrad, Ludwig, etc.). Biblical names used in the German language are also common (e.g., Abram, Isaac, Jacob, etc.), and some English versions of Biblical names are quite common (e.g., Peter, John, etc.). Relatively few of the Ukrainian and Polish farmers have traditional given names, particularly in the second or third generation, although over twenty-four varieties may be detected in the Hafford-Krydor area alone (e.g., Wasyl, Dmytro, Orest, Jaroslav, Bohdan, Slawko, Taras, Metro, etc.). But several English translations of popular saints' names are repeatedly encountered (e.g., Steve, Peter, John, Mike, Paul, Nick). Doukhobor farmers tend to adopt the same few saints' names translated into English; very few have Russian given names (e.g., Malasha, Sergius, Kuzma). Few people of Scandinavian descent retain Scandinavian given names, although the vast majority of Scandinavian farmers in the Hagen area of the Birch Hills settlement retain typically Norwegian names; over forty types may be found in this one area (e.g., Olaf, Einar, Ingvald, Arne, Torbjorn, Ole, Knut, etc.).
[5] A. B. Anderson, "Assimilation in the Bloc Settlements of North-Central Saskatchewan: A Comparative Study of Identity Change Among Seven Ethno-Religious Groups in a

Canadian Prairie Region," unpublished Ph.D. thesis in Sociology, University of Saskatchewan, Saskatoon, 1972. For an abridged and updated paper derived from this study, see A. B. Anderson, "Ethnic Identity in Saskatchewan Bloc Settlements: A Sociological Appraisal," in H. Palmer, ed., *The Settlement of the West* (Calgary, 1977).

[6]See, for example, A. B. Anderson, "Ethnic Identity Retention in French Canadian Communities in Saskatchewan," a paper presented at the session on "Social Organization of Francophone Communities Outside Quebec," at the Annual Meetings of the Canadian Sociology and Anthropology Association, Toronto, August 25, 1974. G. F. G. Stanley, "French and English in Western Canada," in Mason Wade, ed., *Canadian Dualism: Studies of French-English Relations* (Toronto, 1960). T. Sloan, *Quebec: The Not-So-Quiet Revolution* (Toronto, 1965), 101.

[7]W. B. Denis, "Les Canadiens-Francais en Saskatchewan," unpublished research paper in sociology, Collège St. Boniface, Manitoba, November 27, 1967, 17-18.

[8]A. B. Anderson, *op. cit.*, 1974, 2-4.

[9]P. S. Gross, *The Hutterite Way* (Saskatoon, 1965), 91-108.

[10]H. A. Voth, "Mennonites: Languages and Geographic Locations," unpublished research paper in sociology, University of Saskatchewan, February 14, 1970. Leo Driedger, "A Sect in Modern Society: A Case Study of the Old Colony Mennonites of Saskatchewan," unpublished M.A. thesis in sociology, University of Chicago, 1955, 82-85.

[11]L. Driedger, *op. cit.*, 109.

[12]L. Driedger, *op. cit.*, 82-85. C. H. Smith, *The Story of the Mennonites* (Newton, Kansas, 1957), 643.

[13]L. Driedger, *ibid.*

[14]F. H. Epp, *Mennonite Exodus* (Altona, Man., 1962), 207-208.

[15]R. E. DuWors and C. C. Zimmerman, "Memorandum on the Hutterites," appendix in Canadian Mental Health Association, "The Hutterites and Saskatchewan: A Study of Intergroup Relations" (Regina, 1953).

[16]The Sianian dialect is spoken by immigrants and their descendants from the northwest Galicia-Polish frontier area; the Dniester by those from central or east-central Galicia; the Volynian by those from southern Byelorussia, northeast Galicia, and northwest Ukraine proper; the Podolian by those from the western portion of the Ukraine proper; the Pokutian by those from southeast Galicia and eastern Bukovina; the Hutzul by those from the Carpathian mountain area between eastern Transcarpathia, western Bukovina, and southern Galicia; the Boyko by those from southwestern Galicia; the Transcarpathian by those from Podcarpathian Ruthenia; and the Lemko by those from western Galicia and the Polish-Czech frontier area. See A. Royick, "Ukrainian Settlements in Alberta," *Canadian Slavonic Papers*, 10 (1968); partially reprinted as A. Royick and Z. S. Pohorecky, "Ethno-Linguistic Overview of Ukrainian-speaking Communities in the Province of Alberta, Canada," *Napao: A Saskatchewan Anthropology Journal*, 1 (1968), 2-27.

[17]C. H. Young, *The Ukrainian Canadians: A Study in Assimilation* (Toronto, 1931), 32.

[18]C. H. Young, *op. cit.*, 179, 186-190. R. England, *The Central European Immigrant in Canada* (Toronto, 1929), 55-56, 60, 76-77. A. B. Anderson, "Ukrainian Identity Change in Rural Saskatchewan," in W. W. Isajiw, ed., *Ukrainians in American and Canadian Society*, Harvard Ukrainian Research Institute and the Ukrainian Center of Social Research, *Studies*, vol. I (Jersey City, N.J., 1976), 93-121.

[19]These details from the Archives of Saskatchewan, Martin Papers, file no. 168: Ukrainian Rural Communities, 1917: Report of Investigation by Bureau of Social Research, Governments of Manitoba, Saskatchewan, and Alberta (Winnipeg, 25th January, 1917).

[20]Examples of Ukrainian-Canadian words derived from English were the following:

mera — mayor.	dreska — dress.	shusi — shoes.
bossuvati — boss.	halia — hall.	kendi — candy.
parku — park.	shtreeta — street.	farmerstvo — farming.
karu — car.	fornichie — furniture.	plomberstvo — plumbing.
herkot — haircut.	pinatsi — peanuts.	boysik — little boy.

Examples of words from the Ukraine originally similar to English (i.e., not anglicized):

ploohom — plow.	kleric — cleric.	pastyr — pastor.
hoosy — geese.	diakon — deacon.	sestra — sister.
swyni — swine.	eucharistia — eucharist.	sydyt — sit.
rozh — rose.	presveeter — presbyter.	rushila — rush.
struja — stream.	apostol — apostle.	bystra — boisterous.

J. T. M. Anderson, *The Education of the New Canadian* (Toronto, 1918), 62. Vera Lysenko, *Men in Sheepskin Coats: A Study in Assimilation* (Toronto, 1947), 245-246. M. A. Sherbinin, "The Galicians Dwelling in Canada and Their Origin," Historical and Scientific Society of Manitoba, Transaction No. 71, April 19, 1906 (Winnipeg, 1906), 3-4.

[21]A. Milnor, "The New Politics and Ethnic Revolt: 1928-1938," in N. Ward and D. Spafford, eds., *Politics in Saskatchewan* (Lindsay, Ontario, 1968), 172. C. H. Young, *op. cit.*, 172.

[22]"Fiftieth Anniversary of Hanley Evangelical Lutheran Church, 1903-1953," mimeographed commemorative booklet.

[23]C. H. Young, *op. cit.,* 179.
[24]See, for example: T. Shibutani and K. M. Kwan, *op. cit.,* 78, 354, 470, 484-491, 526, 531, 552, 573-574. R. E. Park, *op. cit.,* 50, 263, 363-365. W. D. Borrie, ed., *op. cit.,* 122-123, 286. M. M. Gordon, *Assimilation in American Life: The Role of Race, Religion, and National Origins* (New York, 1964), 244-245. W. Herberg, *op. cit.,* 16-19, 22-23, 27-31. A. B. Anderson, *op. cit.,* 1972, 228-233, and *op. cit.,* 1977.
The reports of the Royal Commission on Bilingualism and Biculturalism have made many interesting suggestions with reference to general conflict and inter-general association among Canadian ethnic groups. For example, while there are some areas, including farming life and religious belief and practice, where the general Canadian society exerts less pressure and permits a wider variety of behaviour, and while many immigrants came from societies in which kin ties were very significant, large kin networks (as opposed to conjugal relationships) have been diminishing since the 1920s and especially since 1945. The Hutterites and some Mennonites have been successful in transmitting unique life styles dependent upon acceptance of total systems of institutions, but most other groups have been less successful, with the result that generation conflict has increased. The school and church may not reinforce norms traditionally inculcated through parental, kin and peer socialization. Report of the Royal Commission on Bilingualism and Biculturalism, Book IV, Part II, Chapter IV (Ottawa, 1967).
[25]John Hawkes, *The Story of Saskatchewan and Its People* (Regina, 1924), vol. 2, 682.
[26]R. M. Williams has suggested that male immigrants are more likely to be exposed to intergroup contacts than female: R. M. Williams, *Strangers Next Door: Ethnic Relations in American Communities* (Englewood Cliffs, N.J., 1964), 144. On the isolation of Doukhobor women see: C. A. Dawson, *Group Settlement: Ethnic Communities in Western Canada* (Toronto, 1936), 17. In 1917 it was reported that in Ukrainian settlements in north-central Saskatchewan the women were consistently less literate and less able to speak English than the men: Archives of Saskatchewan, Martin Papers No. 168.
[27]Details on the educational retardation of Slavic groups, Mennonites and other ethnic groups in western Canada have been provided by: K. A. McLeod, "Politics, Schools and the French Language, 1881-1931," in N. Ward and D. Spafford, eds., *op. cit.* J. T. M. Anderson, *op. cit.,* Chapters 4-5. Report of the Saskatchewan Royal Commission on Immigration and Settlement (Regina, 1930), 195-197. R. England, *op. cit.,* 39-40, 72-76, 108-112. Report of the Royal Commission on Bilingualism and Biculturalism, *op. cit.* C. A. Dawson, *op. cit.,* 20.

WATSON KIRKCONNELL AND THE CULTURAL CREDIBILITY GAP BETWEEN IMMIGRANTS AND THE NATIVE-BORN IN CANADA

N. F. DREISZIGER
THE ROYAL MILITARY COLLEGE OF CANADA

From the late 1920s until his retirement from public life* Watson Kirkconnell was one of the most active and most articulate spokesmen for Canada's immigrant ethnic minorities.[1] The sheer volume of his literary output in this connection testifies to this fact. Several books, dozens of volumes of verse translations, and scores of articles dealing with the literature and culture of the many groups which make up the so-called "third element" of Canada's population, stand as a monument to Kirkconnell's work in the realm of relations between native Canadians and immigrant ethnics. His efforts took on many forms. In the world of scholarship he is known as Canada's most versatile and most prolific verse translator.[2] In the political arena, he had fought for a more enlightened approach to the "enemy alien" problem, particularly during the early phases of the Second World War. The full range of his activities in aid of Canada's immigrant population still awaits analysis, and it will not be examined here. The purpose of this paper is much more modest. It proposes to do no more than to begin a discussion of a narrower subject: Kirkconnell's ideas and work relating to the problem of the cultural credibility gap between native-born Canadians on the one hand, and immigrant ethnics or "New Canadians" on the other. It is hoped that the present exploratory treatment of this interesting and important theme will prompt further discussion and research, and will help to pave the way for a historical assessment of Kirkconnell's role in the harmonization of immigrant ethnic and native Canadian relations which we have witnessed during the past four decades of Canadian national development.[3]

Watson Kirkconnell was born in 1895 in Port Hope, Ontario. His paternal forefathers were mainly Scottish, while his mother had a highly diverse ancestry.[4] The young Watson was brought up in a predominantly English-Canadian environment. He went to high school in Lindsay, the town of Sir Sam Hughes and a stronghold of Ontario Orangeism, and subsequently attended Queen's University in Kingston, another bastion of English-Canadian values and traditions. There was nothing in Kirkconnell's youthful experience which would have foreshadowed or even suggested his later association with Canada's ethnic minorities. Yet it was his education, with its strong emphasis on classics and the study of

---

*Nor did he cease taking great interest in developments in the field of interethnic relations right up to the time of his passing away in Wolfville, Nova Scotia, at the age of 81 on February 27, 1977 [ed.].

languages, combined with his exceptional linguistic talents, which equipped him for the role he was to play later.

Kirkconnell's studies took him to Oxford from where he returned in 1922 to take up a teaching appointment at Wesley (later United) College in Winnipeg. At first it seemed that he would follow a typical academic career which would accord him contact with only certain top layers of Winnipeg's society. Indeed, after a number of promotions in rapid succession, Kirkconnell was about to settle in the comfortable role of a successful academic whose extracurricular public activities remained within the world of the English-Canadian charter group. But fate had other things in store for him. Within a few years of the start of his academic career, he was to come into contact with a different world, one until then almost unknown to him: the world of Canada's immigrant ethnics.

The Canadian West in general and Kirkconnell's Winnipeg in particular had been the great receptacle of European immigrants for much of the first quarter of the Twentieth Century. The trickle of newcomers in the 1870s and 1880s turned into a flood by the late nineties and did not abate until the First World War. It resumed not long after Kirkconnell assumed his professional duties at Wesley College.

The phenomena of immigration and settlement in the Canadian West and the world of immigrant ethnics are vast subjects which defy summarization. They have been treated but never completely exhausted by novelists and scholars alike. The works of such writers as Frederick Philip Grove, Ralph Connor, Nellie McClung and, somewhat more recently, Adele Wiseman, Illia Kiriak, Ruby Wiebe and John Marlyn offer moving portrayals of this world. On a different plain, the studies of J. S. Woodsworth, Robert England, Edmund Bradwin and a host of later generation scholars have traced many aspects of immigrant life from the point of view of the social scientist.

The problem faced by immigrants, especially immigrant ethnics, were enormous and many. The privations of pioneer existence and the lack of adequate social contacts were only two of the hardships that confronted these people. Still another was the problem of acceptance by the host society. It could be argued that, as far as the groups of newcomers were concerned, the question of their relations with native Canadians was one of the most perplexing and often most pernicious problems. Given a strong back, perseverance, ingenuity and good luck, the individual immigrant could reduce the hardships of homestead life and satisfy most of his basic material requirements. Through co-operation, often achieved by close association with his co-nationals, some ethnics could also satisfy their social and cultural needs. But the problem of acceptance by the host society remained one about which the individual newcomers could do very little, and an ethnic group as a whole could do practically nothing.

It is well known that the problem which plagued relations between immigrant ethnics and the native born throughout the years under discussion in this paper was prejudice, persistent and in many ways irrational antagonism by the members of the host society toward newcomers, especially toward those hailing from non-English (and non-French) speaking countries.

Canadian nativism had diverse origins. To some extent it was a phenomenon related to economics. The fear of competition from cheap labour drove many to resent immigrants. But it was not only the fear of reduced wages and fewer employment opportunities for the native born which generated antagonism toward the newcomers. Many in Canada at the time assumed, to use Kirkconnell's own words, that an "alien origin" was the "natural mark of inferiority."[5] These Canadians probably wondered: would the masses of ignorant and uneducated newcomers appreciate the wisdom of Canadian traditions? Would they accept Canadian political institutions? Or would they cling to their uncanadian ways and undemocratic political heritage? Doubts existed in the minds not only of the man on the street but also of the members of the country's elite: churchmen, academics and even leaders in Ottawa.

The anti-alien ravings of clerics such as Bishop G. E. Lloyd of Saskatchewan are familiar to students of the period.[6] A number of university professors also expressed doubts about the advisability of the admission of large numbers of non-British immigrants. Stephen Leacock, for example, was concerned about the future of Canadian Confederation should the West be flooded by peoples who "stand in no hereditary relation to the history of Canada."[7] Politicians also had their reservations. Even before the start of the great influx of immigrants to Canada, Sir John A. Macdonald voiced his fears about the "mass of foreign ignorance and vice" which had poured into the United States and which, presumably, could also threaten Canada.[8] Closer to the period under discussion, and revealing a French-Canadian attitude, is the view of Henri Bourassa toward New Canadians of Central and East European background. In 1904 the French-Canadian M.P. complained that it had never been the intention of the founders of the Dominion to turn this "partly French and partly English country" into a land of refuge for the "scum of all nations."[9]

Such attitudes on the part of the country's elite only served to foster rather than reduce nativistic antagonisms toward immigrant ethnics. The newcomers could do little or nothing to dispel the suspicions of native Canadians. They could not disprove the assumption of many native-born that immigrants were ignorant and uncultured. The masses of underprivileged and often poorly educated peasants and agricultural labourers who had flocked to the Canadian West after the 1880s, were incapable of generating cultural activities on a scale which would have impressed the Canadian public. The few intellectuals among them who had managed to come to Canada despite the government's "farmers only" admission policy, were preoccupied with making ends meet and, when they had time for literary activity, they wrote in their own language. Their works long remained unknown to most Canadians. Clearly, the task of proving these people's cultural worth and equality awaited someone whose impartiality could not be doubted, who would be respected by native Canadians and whose praise for European cultural achievement could not be considered the bragging of a maladjusted newcomer with an inferiority complex. In Kirkconnell the Cànadian West had such a person. Unlike some businessmen, whose interest in the admission of more impoverished immigrants was obvious, Kirkconnell had no material motives for defending New Canadians; he was highly cultured and educated and, most important of all, he was an "English" Canadian. It remained to be seen whether he would assume the role for which he was so ideally suited. And by a strange quirk of fate he did.

Kirkconnell's first encounter with New Canadians came in 1922. On his return trip from a year of post-graduate studies in England he found himself on board the ship a "mess-mate" of many immigrants to Canada. Scattered among this large group of peasants, the young scholar discovered several highly cultured individuals, refugees from the revolutions and civil wars of Eastern Europe.[10] Kirkconnell seems to have taken a keen interest in these people during the voyage but did not keep contacts with them after arrival in Canada. Nor did Kirkconnell's first years of stay in Winnipeg bring him much closer to the world of Canada's European immigrants. The fact that he eventually did come in close contact with them came about in the most unexpected manner.

In the summer of 1925 Kirkconnell's wife died after giving birth to twin sons. To erect a suitable memorial to her, and to cure his own sadness, Kirkconnell embarked on a very time-consuming and attention-demanding project of compiling an anthology of European verse and translating it into English. At the outset this vastly ambitious project had no other purpose, but, in Kirkconnell's own words, first and foremost to "deaden the pain of great bereavement."[11] However, the undertaking soon assumed significance beyond serving as a source of consolation for its originator. As he put it in his memoirs, "it opened doors for me into new worlds of imaginative experience."[12] It also launched Kirkconnell's career as a verse translator. This activity gained him new acquaintances and contacts, at first mainly among the academic and literary elite of several European countries. But in time it also led to his close and life-long association with New Canadians.

The group which Kirkconnell singled out for special attention and which thereafter always remained close to his heart was the Icelandic community of Manitoba. Two of his friends at Wesley College, Skuli Johnson and Olafur Adnerson, were Canadian-Icelanders; so were many of Kirkconnell's students. With the college's library amply offering books on Icelandic grammar, poetry and literature, it is not surprising that the first volume in Kirkconnell's projected series of translations from the national poetries of European peoples was the *North American Book of Icelandic Verse* (New York, 1930). "My anthology," wrote Kirkconnell many years later, "proved to be a key to the hearts of the Canadian Icelanders."[13] Soon, ties were developed with other groups of New Canadians as well, and life-long friendships were forged with many "ethnics." Perhaps the most notable among these friends were Joe Thorson, the young Icelandic-Canadian Rhodes scholar, and Béla Bácskai Payerle, the hard-working and talented editor of the largest Hungarian weekly in Canada at the time.[14] Still another early contact was Frederick Philip Grove, the brilliant novelist of immigrant experience, whose work Kirkconnell aided as much as he could, especially with access to his diverse and growing library collection.[15]

Closer association with the world of immigrant ethnics brought about a change in Kirkconnell's method of popularizing European cultural achievement. As has been mentioned, his first work in the field of verse translation was undertaken for purely personal reasons. That the resulting volume, published after many delays under the title *European Elegies* (Ottawa, 1928), also had a potential for serving the literary interests of Canadians of European background, had not been the original intention of Kirkconnell. But this does not seem characteristic of the then young scholar's subsequent publications. In his next general work, *The European Heritage* (London and Toronto, 1930), Kirkconnell deliberately set out to combat ignorance, the "mother of intolerance," as he put it in the volume's preface. He wrote further:

> Saxon and Slav, Norseman and Celt, all have gifts that have been proven great in the annals of civilization; but sincere co-operation, whether in the New World or in the Old, becomes humanly possible only as men realize the worth of their fellow men.[16]

The volume, some two hundred pages of appreciative comments about the cultural achievements of the nations of Europe, may not have been a definitive piece of historical scholarship, but owing to its complex nature the work could have required the Herculean effort of decades of dedicated research. Yet Kirkconnell's book probably succeeded in generating warm respect for things European in the hearts of its readers. Canada's European immigrants stood only to benefit from such feelings.

In addition to writing a survey of the history of European culture, Kirkconnell began drawing attention to the works of New Canadian poets through articles written for literary and other scholarly journals and in addresses before Canadian learned societies.[17] Still more importantly for the general reputation of immigrant ethnic groups he began translating items of New-Canadian poetry.

The most substantial of Kirkconnell's publications of this type, the *Canadian Overtones* (Winnipeg, 1935) was an anthology of verse translated from the "Canadian poetry" of Icelandic, Swedish, Norwegian, Hungarian, Italian, Greek and Ukrainian poets. In the preface to the book Kirkconnell plainly stated his purpose: to "reveal to English-speaking Canadians a transient but intensely significant phase" of Canada's national literature. Then he went on to stun his readers by pointing out that, during the past three decades, the published poetry of New Canadians had exceeded in bulk "all Canadian poetry published in French; while in Western Canada, ... this unknown poetry has surpassed that of Anglo-Canadians both in quantity and in quality."[18] In the same preface Kirkconnell disclosed his own views on ethnic-native relations. Concerning the subject of the treatment of immigrants by the native born, Kirkconnell observed that Canadian attitudes toward these people had passed through two "ignorant and discreditable phases." At first immigrants were considered by many as "European coolies," good for back-breaking work that no one else wanted to perform. More recently, Canadians had shown a patronizing interest in the folk-costumes and folk-dances of these newcomers, aspects of their culture which Kirkconnell called "picturesque incidentals which have about as much vital share in their lives as the kilt and the Highland fling have in that of the average Scotch-Canadian." Next, Kirkconnell voiced the hope that, through the knowledge of New Canadian poetry, the native-born would develop a "third and much truer attitude" towards these people as "beings breathing thoughtful breath."[19]

Along with the emergence in Kirkconnell of a deliberate desire to improve relations between immigrant ethnics and native Canadians through the popularization of the literary achievements of the former, the *Canadian Overtones* reveals the development of its author's concept of a Canadian multi-ethnic identity. In the second half of the preface to this work, Kirkconnell expressed the hope that New Canadian poetry would help develop in future generations of Canadians a "Canadianism nourished by pride in the individual's racial past." To Kirkconnell, the person with an awareness of his ancestry and a pride in the achievements of his forebears was a better citizen of his country: "As a Canadian, he is not poorer but richer because he realizes his place in a notable stream of human relationship down through the centuries."[20]

Kirkconnell had nothing but contempt for the man who denied his ancestry. He who claims to be "one hundred per cent" Canadian, "is commonly one who has deliberately suppressed an alien origin in order to reap the material benefits of a well-advertised loyalty." Kirkconnell saw no chance of "noble spiritual issues from such a prostituted patriotism." He expressed regret that this type of behaviour was encouraged by the "ignorant assumption" of many English-Canadians that an alien origin was the "mark of inferiority." "He who thinks thus," Kirkconnell continued, "is a mental hooligan."[21]

Kirkconnell's fight against nativistic prejudices, his attempts to transform native Canadian attitudes toward immigrant ethnics into one of understanding and respect, was carried on also in ways other than the praising of European and New Canadian cultural achievement. The then young scholar also tried to dispel his compatriots' fear about the possible undesirable political consequences of the preservation of the respective languages and cultures of immigrant ethnics. He often took pains to refute the charge, frequently voiced at the time, that the retaining of the separate identity of immigrant groups would endanger the unity of Canada. In his preface to *Canadian Overtones* he emphasized, "regretfully," that the phenomenon of flourishing New Canadian literature was a distinctly "transitory" phase in Canadian national development. He explained that the experience of schools in the West showed that the grandchildren of most immigrant ethnics became unilingual and spoke only English:

> Failing continuous reinforcements of new immigrant stock, or a change in the Canadian attitude towards the non-Anglo-Saxon traditions, the impulse towards creative expression in a variety of European tongues will inevitably languish and die.[22]

Three years later he put these views even more bluntly. He told a radio audience that the danger of the "linguistic Balkanization of Canada" was "infinitesimal." He added that immigrant groups posed less of a threat to Canadian unity than quarrelsome and parochial provincial politicans. "In the long perspective of history," he prognosticated, "the New-Canadian literatures will appear only as intensely interesting (and sometimes invaluable) revelation of the soul of an emergent Canadian nation."[23]

Kirkconnell's campaign to achieve better relations between New Canadians and the native born was not conducted solely in tomes of scholarly publications and addresses to learned societies. The above-quoted statements, for example, are taken from a nationwide radio broadcast Kirkconnell made in 1938 over the (air) waves of the young Canadian Broadcasting Corporation. Occasionally, he also took his views on to the pages of popular journals. The best known of his press statements is probably the one he made in July of 1928 in *The Canadian Forum.* In this instance of his spirited defence of the immigrant ethnics of the West, Kirkconnell attacked one of Bishop Lloyd's calls for the closing to most European immigrants of Canada's doors. The cleric had singled out Scandinavians, the Dutch, Germans, Czechoslovaks, Belgians, Hungarians, Poles and Ukrainians as undesirable newcomers. Kirkconnell defended each of these groups:

> Scandinavia has led the world in the literature of the twentieth century. The Dutch reputation for law, government, sobriety, and honesty is unsurpassed. Germany has for a century been pre-eminent in science and music. The Czecho-Slovaks, again, are one of the most notable of modern peoples, with a rich culture extending back to the Middle Ages; . . . Belgians and Hungarians need no apologies on the prairies. Poles and Ruthenians have shouldered most of the heavy construction work of the West. . . . These Slavic peoples are, moreover, born lovers of the soil, industrious, patient and progressive. It is hard to see where the alarmist can find fuel for his fire, except in low ignorance.[24]

Kirkconnell next anticipated the counter-argument, often made by nativists, that the cultural achievement of European nations mattered little when assessing the value of immigrants because it was the "crude unfit types" who came to Canada. He admitted that most of Canada's European immigrants were poorly schooled, but he argued that it did not follow that they were of inferior quality. The social and political institutions of their native lands had denied them educational opportunities and had prevented them from rising to the top. But the European immigrants had great possible assets. "They bring to us," he argued, "the undeveloped potentialities of virgin stock, and their true quality is not evident until the second generation."[25]

It is interesting to speculate whom Kirkconnell had in mind when he wrote these words. Was it his Rhodes scholar Icelandic-Canadian friend at Wesley College? Or, perhaps, it was the poet Guttormur Guttormsson, a Canadian-born Icelander who grew up amidst such poverty and deprivation that his formal education had to come to an end after three months of school attendance.[26] But it does not matter whom the author of this spirited defence of New Canadians had in mind. The important point is that Kirkconnell's extensive interest in and subsequent familiarity with European poetry and literature, which later also encompassed the culture of the ethnic immigrant communities of Canada, convinced him of the cultural worth of Europeans. Finding this fact unrecognized by most of his fellow Canadians, and seeing European immigrants despised or, at best, patronized as people whose intelligence was inherently inferior, Kirkconnell embarked on a deliberate and to a large extent single-handed campaign to bring the achievement of European civilization and European immigrant ethnics before his English-Canadian audiences. By doing so he wished to narrow down that cultural credibility gap which he saw dividing these two groups.

During his efforts in this direction, Kirkconnell developed his own, and at the time probably unique concept of Canadian identity. This was the idea of the citizen being the member of a multi-ethnic community, proud of the achievement of his immigrant forebears. And he went even further. In his preface to *Canadian Overtones,* he described his ideal of the multi-ethnic Canadian nationhood:

> Our nation could not do better than to take "confederation" as its motto in the culture and education. Our national holidays might well be given over to such pageantry (including, perhaps festivals of drama, poetry, and music) as would emphasize the co-operative existence of the distinct racial groups in our population. Our schools might give ample recognition to their history and culture. Our universities might foster their languages and literatures. . . .[27]

But it was not only schools that Kirkconnell saw as possible tools in the effort to preserve the cultures of immigrant groups. He also envisaged, though never defined clearly, a positive role for the state in such efforts. In doing so he anticipated the concept of government-supported multicultural programmes by some four decades. He felt that in the struggle for the preservation of the "full potentialities of our several peoples" certain "fundamentals" had to be kept in mind. One of these was the fact that the state existed not as an "end" in itself," but for the purpose of making possible the "good life" for the people. This "good life," Kirkconnell argued,

> involves far more than economic competence, the possession of some of the toys of modern science, and the pedagogic inculcation of standardized factual information or professional skill; it rather goes on to seek the highest possible realization of personality. This realization of

personality in the individual is closely linked up with the national character which racial constitution and historical experience have wrought out in the group from which he comes.[28]

These then were the concepts for the achievement of which Kirkconnell began to work in the late 1920s. That he was instrumental in the rise of a new approach to ethnic affairs in Canada during the following decades, is indicated by his growing personal reputation and influence after the 1930s. His association with the respected *University of Toronto Quarterly* where for many years he reviewed New Canadian literature, his role in the formulation of the Mackenzie King government's war-time policies toward European groups, his close association with the establishment and early activities of what later became the Citizenship Branch of the Department of the Secretary of State,[29] all attest to his historical significance for the coming of a new age in the relationship of immigrant ethnics and the native born in Canada.

Kirkconnell's struggle was a difficult one. Like all efforts to educate a nation, it brought gradual and at times only meagre results. It was largely a one-man war against a sea of prejudice derived from ignorance. Being such, it was especially vulnerable to changes in political and economic circumstances. In fact, Kirkconnell's work in verse translation, the chief medium of his campaign, was abruptly though not permanently interrupted at the time of the outbreak of the Second World War. The war just brought to an end the first phase of Kirkconnell's fight to achieve better relations between New Canadians and the native born. During the next phase, lasting to about 1945, Kirkconnell devoted his time and energies to the task of convincing his fellow native Canadians of the loyalty of the vast majority of immigrant ethnics to the country and its government. But that is another story which must await investigation on some future occasion.

FOOTNOTES

[1]Other contemporary authors who displayed a great deal of sympathy towards immigrant ethnics included J. S. Woodworth, especially in his *Strangers Within Our Gates: or, Coming Canadians* (Toronto, 1909), reprinted with an introduction by Marilyn Barber (Toronto, 1972); Robert England, the author of *The Central European Immigrant in Canada* (Toronto, 1928) and *The Colonization of Western Canada* (London, 1936); and J. M. Gibbon, *The Canadian Mosaic* (Toronto, 1938). A friend of Canadians of Oriental background was H. F. Angus. See his articles "Underprivileged Canadians." *Queen's Quarterly*, 38 (1931) and "A Contribution to International Ill-Will," *Dalhousie Review*, 13 (1933-34).

[2]J. M. R. Beveridge, "Watson Kirkconnell: A Biographical Sketch," in J. R. C. Perkin, ed., *The Undoing of Babel: Watson Kirkconnell, The Man and His Work* (Toronto, 1975),11-13.

[3]Until Kirkconnell's papers (which, along with his valuable personal library, have been willed to Acadia University) become open to researchers, the student of his activities will have limited evidence to go by. Kirkconnell believed in demonstrating the cultural worth of New Canadians not so much by praising them and philosophizing about their value, but by translating their poetry into English for everyone in English Canada to read and estimate as cultural contribution. Kirkconnell's own appreciative statements about immigrants are infrequent and often short. Most of his ideas on the subject were expressed in the prefaces to his books.

[4]Watson Kirkconnell, *A Slice of Canada: Memoirs* (Toronto, 1967), Chapter I. On his mother's side, Kirkconnell's ancestors included persons of Welsh, German, Spanish and other nationalities. See also, Watson Kirkconnell, *Climbing the Green Tree and Some Other*

Branches (Wolfville, 1976). A letter by Professor Kirkconnell linking the "green branch" to the ancient house of Árpád of Hungary is in my possession.

⁵Watson Kirkconnell, *Canadian Overtones* (Winnipeg, 1935), 4.

⁶See, for example, George Exton Lloyd, "Immigration and Nation Building," *Empire Review*, February 1929, 105-106, as abstracted in Howard Palmer, ed., *Immigration and the Rise of Multiculturalism* (Toronto, 1975), 55-56. For a discussion of some of Lloyd's pronouncements in 1927-28 see the *Canadian Annual Review*, 27 (1927-29), 188.

⁷Stephen Leacock, "Canada and the Immigration Problem," *National and English Review*, April, 1911, 316-27, as abstracted in Palmer, *op. cit.*, 46-51. Other academics unsympathetic to immigrants and immigration were W. B. Hurd — see "The Case for a Quota," *Queen's Quarterly*, 36 (1929), and A. R. M. Lower — see "The Case Against Immigration," *Ibid.*, 37 (1930).

⁸Toronto *Empire*, 2 October 1890, cited in Carl Berger, *The Sense of Power: Studies in the Ideas of Canadian Imperialism, 1867-1914* (Toronto, 1970), 164.

⁹Quoted in Robert Craig Brown and Ramsay Cook, *Canada 1896-1921: A Nation Transformed* (Toronto, 1974), 74.

¹⁰Kirkconnell, *A Slice of Canada*, 259.

¹¹Watson Kirkconnell, *European Elegies* (Ottawa, 1928), [9].

¹²Watson Kirkconnell, *A Slice of Canada*, 59.

¹³*Ibid.*, 263.

¹⁴*Ibid.*, Chapter 20. For further details of Kirkconnell's Hungarian connections see his article "A Canadian Meets the Magyars," *Canadian-American Review of Hungarian Studies*, 1 (1974), 1-11.

¹⁵Margaret R. Stobie, *Frederick Philip Grove* (New York, 1973), 89. Kirkconnell, *A Slice of Canada*, 350-52.

¹⁶Watson Kirkconnell, *The European Heritage: A Synopsis of European Cultural Achievement* (London and Toronto, 1930), v.

¹⁷Kirkconnell's addresses relating to new Canadian themes included his lecture "A Skald in Canada," and "The European-Canadians in their Press" read before meetings of the Royal Society of Canada and the Canadian Historical Association respectively. Also in the present context belongs his article "Canada's Leading Poet, Stephen G. Stephanson, 1853-1927," *University of Toronto Quarterly*, 2 (1936).

¹⁸Kirkconnell, *Canadian Overtones*, 3.

¹⁹*Ibid.*, 4.

²⁰*Ibid.*, 5.

²¹*Ibid.*, 4.

²²*Ibid.*, 3.

²³Watson Kirkconnell, "The Literature of New Canadians," in *Canadian Literature Today* (Toronto, 1938), 64.

²⁴Watson Kirkconnell, "Western Immigration," *The Canadian Forum*, 9 (1928), 706-707, as abstracted by Palmer, *op. cit.*, 56-58. That Kirkconnell was not alone in finding Lloyd's views repugnant is illustrated by the fact that even the editors of the Toronto *Globe* found the Bishop's opinions unreasonable. See the Toronto *Globe*, 9 May 1928.

²⁵Kirkconnell, "Western Immigration," *loc. cit.*

²⁶On Guttormsson see Watson Kirkconnell, "A Skald in Canada," *Transactions of the Royal Society of Canada*, Series 3, 33 (1939), Section II, 107-21.

²⁷Kirkconnell, *Canadian Overtones*, 6.

²⁸*Ibid.*

²⁹Kirkconnell, "A Canadian Meets the Magyars," 8. Also, see Kirkconnell's comments on the draft of my manuscript: "Watson Kirkconnell, a Friend of the Magyars."

FROM RINGSAKER TO INSTOW: A NORWEGIAN RADICAL'S SASKATCHEWAN ODYSSEY

JORGEN DAHLIE
UNIVERSITY OF BRITISH COLUMBIA

In a timely bibliographical essay on historical scholarship in western Canada, Hartwell Bowsfield has noted that "one of the themes in writings on the West is that the West was invaded by an eastern culture."[1] Parenthetically, one should add that the invasion has been partly of European origin as well. Bowsfield continues: "Studies of the cultural carriers — the newspaper editors, the clergymen, the professional class, the agrarian and political leaders — are needed to represent both the process of Canadianization of the West as well as the regionalization of its people."[2] Until very recent times, studies made of those who spearheaded the cultural invasion, have almost entirely neglected the "ethnic Canadians."[3] J. Donald Wilson's recent perceptive discussion of the Finnish-Canadian intellectual, Matti Kurikka,[4] is a welcome exception to established historiography. His essay underscores how little is known of the educational and cultural influence of spokesmen from outside the dominant Anglophone and Francophone groups. Wilson contends that "in addition to our traditional emphasis on Canadian political history to the exclusion of other types of history, there is also this large missing link ... in intellectual and social history, namely the work of Canadian intellectuals who did not write in French or English."[5]

The history of Matti Kurrika — who fits Bowsfield's categories of newspaperman, editor, professional, and political leader — strongly suggests that scholars in the field of ethnic studies should turn more often to the non-English and non-French sources if they hope to redress the imbalance to which Wilson refers. In my own research, a cursory check of some early editions of the Norwegian-language periodical *Nordmanns-Forbundet*[6] led to a chance encounter with an unusual prairie homesteader, Ole Hjelt. This unorthodox newcomer kept the western Canadian Scandinavian community in an "intellectual" uproar for almost two decades. From his bastion near Instow, Saskatchewan, where he had settled in 1908, Ole Hjelt cultivated the land and exercised his own considerable intelligence until tragedy in 1925 caused him to return to his native Norway. A steady flow of words issued from Instow: books, pamphlets, travel accounts, letters, and above all hundreds of pages of articles to the Norwegian and Swedish-language newspapers of Winnipeg and Chicago.[7] Dedicated, zealous, almost fanatically loyal to the cause of socialism, Hjelt sparked heated controversy and prolonged, partisan debate among his Scandinavian readers and the farmers or workers who came to hear his stump speeches. No one could remain neutral toward the man; still his espousal of radical political action was always infused with a compassionate concern for his fellow man, an enlightened academic bent, and a piquant sense of humour. In detailing the salient facts of Hjelt's Canadian experience, I propose to examine his origins and background, to discuss representative selections from his writings, and to assess the views of some of his contemporaries. Hjelt recounts much of the story himself, which is wholly in character for one who kept writing for a cause well into his ninetieth year.[8]

In November 1918, Nils Brown, then the editor of *Svenska Canada-Tidningen,* asked Hjelt to publish his book entitled *Farmers and Socialism* in the Swedish weekly.[9] Hjelt readily agreed. Brown was a political and ideological colleague; furthermore, Hjelt, by now an established radical spokesman, saw another opportunity to place his views before an audience of Swedish Canadians. In the opening instalment he wrote:

> In response to his [Brown's] request, I should be permitted to record a few brief episodes from my life which I find to have had a significant effect on my own development. This is not to have you believe that my life has been of such great importance, since, through the study of history and science, I have been made aware of the extremely limited role that even the greatest . . . individuals play in the evolving historical process, not to speak of their insignificant impact on cosmic evolution.

> But this is not the same as saying we live to no purpose. I believe that each moment is worth living. . . . I am not at all in accord with August Strindberg when he says: 'Just this, that you live your life as well as you can is an heroic achievement; and each one who drags himself forward to a natural death is a hero; each dead man earns a monument, so bleak and wearisome it is just to live.' That is a despairing, hopeless, self-destructive philosophy. . . . It is a sad fact that we live our lives under a system where a great part of mankind must 'drag their lives through to a natural death' but that is one of the things that can be changed.[10]

Here we have a typical Hjelt pronouncement — optimistic but self-deprecatory, authoritative, yet somewhat consciously academic. We will find time and again in this man's prolific output many references to Goethe, Georg Brandes, Ibsen, Proudhon, and, most frequently, Karl Marx.[11] There are clear indications in his writings of a conviction that the written and spoken word could work a political and social transformation, given perseverance and dedication to one's belief. "I had not studied socialism in Norway," wrote Hjelt, "but followed with a great deal of interest the parliamentary debates as reported in the daily press and took the views of Dr. Alfred Ericksen and Johan Castberg . . ." who were socialist and democratic-labour spokesmen in the Ringsaker region.[12] To another query as to why he became a socialist, Hjelt replied: "Not because I was hungry, I have never been on the shady side in society. But I have studied the question and been convinced through reading."[13]

Hjelt's conversion to the socialist cause was actually attributable to both his education and early work experience. One of six children born to the well-established Peder and Antonette Hjelt family in Hedmark's Ringsaker parish, Ole graduated in 1904 from the Jønsberg Landbrukskole (an agricultural, forest, and technical college) as a forester.[14] As a professionally educated twenty-year old, he was hired for supervisory duties with a number of timber firms in the eastern river valleys of Norway. He describes his position as one where he was expected to do his best for the company:

> Here I had my first lesson in the class struggle. . . . I was the one who should maintain 'harmony' between capital and labour. . . . During the log drives in the summer, the workers wanted high hourly wages and many extra hours, the company wanted few hours and low pay. . . . I was hired by the company to get the most work possible out of the workers for the least possible wage. . . . I understood that I had found myself on the wrong track and set my course for America. Here life's reality taught me what the theories of the international workingman's movement would teach me from books.[15]

Hjelt arrived in New York City on New Year's Day 1907, then travelled westward to Wisconsin, where an aunt had settled some years before. After almost two years of what he called a "proletarian existence" in the United States, Ole and his brother Andrew (Andreas) headed for Canada. An unscheduled meeting with a Danish-Canadian colonization agent had persuaded the Hjelts to go to Saskatchewan rather than Minnesota.[16] Ole Hjelt took up a half-section of "free" land thirty miles south of Gull Lake:

> I hadn't lived here too long before I understood that land was not all that free and the same capitalistic system existed here as well. I was not blind either to what a new country offered in comparison to an older, more densely populated country. . . . Here in addition to doing what a pioneer must do to survive in the loneliness of the prairie, I found ample time, with the burning of considerable midnight oil, to continue my various studies: sociology, history, science, and foreign languages. Here also in later years I engaged in a good deal of agitation and organizational work for the Social Democratic Party of Canada and the Socialist Party of America.[17]

Hjelt has left a book-length account, *Pioneer Life on the Prairie,* as well as several articles describing how the Norwegian immigrants coped with the difficulties of establishing themselves in Canada.[18] There is considerable evidence that he augmented his own income in the first years by trapping, fishing, and working for other farmers. At any rate, by 1915 Hjelt had his farm on a productive basis, sufficiently so in fact that he was able to devote increasingly more time to what he saw as his real mission — bringing about the socialist revolution and a transformed order in the New World. In the introduction to *Socialism,* written at Bellingham, Washington in December 1916, Hjelt spelled out his conviction:

> When people learn to think historically and scientifically, they will soon come to realize that society is not static . . ., but is constantly undergoing evolution, and is therefore in harmony with all else in the universe. . . . Man can as soon try to stop the earth turning on its axis, or

stop the evolving revolution in the universe, as to try to prevent the coming social revolution. Our cause is holy since it conforms to the universe's eternal law. Socialism will triumph since socialism stands for truth.[19]

In one way or another, Hjelt's books all carried variations on this theme. But it was in the quintessential immigrant forum — the foreign-language press — where this writer's call for action sounded most incessantly, and incidentally, where it could be challenged. In this respect, Hjelt was well served by such people as Peter Martin Dahl, Ingver Olsen and Nils Brown. These editors did not necessarily share Hjelt's views, but their newspapers, *Norrøna* and *Svenska Canada-Tidningen,* were exceptionally free and open for discussion on any issue.[20] Much as Matti Kurikka had used the *Aika* (Time) as a sounding board in the Sointula Finnish colony,[21] so did Hjelt fill the columns of the Scandinavian weeklies which were circulated widely throughout the prairie settlements. The immigrant press, as has been noted elsewhere, was a "powerful agent of adult education"[22] but it was more — a place where educated adults matched wits and learning, uninhibited by language difficulty or unfamiliarity with the culture.

For a man of Hjelt's temperament and background, the ethnic press was made to order. To list only a few of his articles will quickly suggest something of the man's political bias but perhaps as important, indicate his involvement in what he called the day's "burning issues." With facile pen and serene equanimity he wrote about such diverse topics as "Catholics and World War," "Stable Wheat Prices," "Anarchism," "A Non-Political Fishing Trip," "Norwegian Society," "America and Revolution," "History and Economic Determinism," "A Memorial to Karl Liebknecht," "From Canada to Glasgow," and "Farmers and Cooperation."[23] But it was his regular column entitled "Ole's Hand Grenades," with its unsettling verbal explosions, which aroused the most controversy and made his name a by-word for radicalism among the Norwegians and Swedes. In a typical "Hand Grenade" column Hjelt wrote:

> Indeed, it is no wonder that pastors will not discuss issues with socialists; in the first instance they have no arguments, and in the other, find themselves opposed by the ideology of the times and historical inevitability; therefore it is prudent to remain home by the comfort of the fireside, and not venture out to do battle against people who have all the arguments, the ability, the significant literature, science, historical currents, and the whole spirit of the times with them.[24]

This is not the first or last time that Hjelt attacked the church, which he saw as essentially a reactionary institution standing in the way of the revolution. In an earlier response to a pastor who had cancelled his subscription to *Norrøna* because of its "socialistic" leanings, Hjelt replied:

> If I understand Pastor Kjøs correctly, he would have *Norrøna* forego handling the time's most burning issues and events, and those ideas which underly these questions and events. But such an injunction the newspaper can hardly follow when it is opposed to what is synonymous

with the responsibility of the press. . . . It is the newspaper's mission to
record contemporary history. . . . Cardinal Begin wrote in *La Croix*
several months ago a lead editorial under the title: 'Après la guerre — le
socialism.' . . . In this article and similar ones the cardinal discusses
socialism and all the possibilities for socialism's triumph after the
war.[25]

Hjelt goes on to point out that if the "most sensational and most reactionary
press in all Canada" can discuss socialism to keep its "readers à jour with
the time's major events," then *Norrøna* can do no less.[26]

On the same theme, publication of *Pioneer Life on the Prairie* (1920)
allowed Hjelt, rather poorly disguised as Olaf Hagen in the book, to go on
the attack again. When Hagen is approached by two churchmen for money
to help build a church he replies: "It is too late to build churches. Had it
been a 100 years ago, I would have thought about it. We live in a scientific
and rational era, not in an age of superstition and miracles."[27] When the
counter-argument was raised that the church was not opposed to education
(and the examples Lutheran Colleges at Decorah, Iowa, and Outlook were
pointed out), Hagen insisted that "church schools are built to keep . . .
young people away from the universities and public schools where they
would learn scientific truths and learn how to think instead of using blind
faith. This is not Olaf Hagen's theory, my friends. This is a theory advanced
by the church's leaders in print and speech."[28]

Hjelt's book and his writings in the "Hand Grenade" columns did not
go unchallenged. Because *Pioneer Life on the Prairie* referred rather
obviously to actual people in the Shaunavon area, it was denigrated or
praised, depending on the reader's political or religious persuasion. One
angry reader from nearby Scotsguard claimed that Hjelt had a "fifteen year
old boy working like a slave while he sits around the fire studying
socialism." Because of the book's scurrilous character, he adds, it is no
wonder that Hjelt had to have it published himself.[29] A more typical
statement, perhaps, was that of one of Hjelt's more consistent opponents, Ed
Hermanson:

> If *Norrøna* had opened its columns only to the socialist viewpoint and
> denied other views a chance for expression, that would have been quite
> another matter. . . . My own view is that P. M. Dahl and Editor Olsen
> have done us a great favour in permitting Mr. Ole Hjelt to cast his
> radicalism out in the open instead of having it lurk in the shadow. . . . I
> believe that P. M. Dahl is as far from being a socialist as anyone, but he
> wants to see reform in our graft-ridden and profiteering society, the
> same thing that Olsen wants. . . .[30]

The editors, of course, were quite aware of Hjelt's ideological stance,
but they insisted that "the Norwegian people in Canada are a mature people
who do not need a nursemaid to watch over what they shall or shall not
read."[31] Olsen conceded that he often found himself *mellom barken og veden*
(between the bark and the wood):

> One day we get a letter which damns us as unreasonable because we
> allow Ole Hjelt to write in *Norrøna*. The next day there is an equally

vehement and well-intentioned diatribe because we allow the pastors to get their pronouncements in the press. . . . An angry subscriber writes to say he will cancel his subscription if Ole Hjelt has more to say, while others complain of the "priestly drivel" which takes up valuable space.[32]

Some Swedish editors appeared to view Hjelt more favourably than their Norwegian colleagues and it may be because they sympathized with his radicalism. For example, Rudolph Einhardt, editor of the Swedish-language *Forum* in Winnipeg, was strongly impressed after meeting the man whom he had only known previously through his writings:

Hjelt is a very sympathetic man . . . [who] has a large library which he hasn't collected simply for show.. . . I have never on a farm, and seldom at a professional man's place seen . . . such a rich, representative collection of books. It is a mistake to say that the socialistic literature has a place of prominence on his book shelf. No matter how many try to type him as a one-sided individual, he is definitely not that. On his bookshelf were books in five modern languages representing — apart from romantic literature — the best that man's intelligence has brought forward.[33]

In a similar vein was Nils Brown's review of *Pioneer Life on the Prairie* which he had read in manuscript. Brown said, in part: "Ole Hjelt had documented himself as a realistic writer of considerable stature. His characters are clearly drawn. Here are individuals that one can relate to, types that one can easily recognize." Brown cites figures to show that of Hjelt's three books, all have sold more copies in the Swedish edition than the Norwegian ones.[34]

As for Hjelt, criticism — whether informed or otherwise — simply worked on him as a spur to even more writing. He could be devastating — and often unfair — in replying to his critics, but he took a delight in responding. For years, he exchanged verbal blows with a man named Lone, who came from a conservative Norwegian family which valued education and religious orthodoxy. Once when Lone wrote in praise of democratic freedoms in Canada, Hjelt reacted vehemently: "There exists a law in Canada called 'The Wartimes Election Act.' Are you familiar with that Law, Mr. Lone? There exists two socialist parties here in Canada with official press organs, these are all legal but it is forbidden to belong to them. If a man possesses certain books he can get up to 5 years of hard labour and a fine of $5,000. . . . Is all this unknown to you, Mr. Lone?"[35] Hjelt's own *Farmers and Socialism* was among those books which were held to be subversive and this fact no doubt accounted for some of his anger.[36]

Other responses to Lone were somewhat more temperate, although Hjelt claimed he tended

to preach a morality that has no roots in reality, to criticize that which he had no understanding of beforehand, and as a literary critic to serve out banal phrases — for example, 'that Ibsen has taught the Norwegian people to think in a big way,' a phrase that is a half-century old and one which all people who know Ibsen's name already know.[37]

Other questioners were handled more kindly, at least in the initial response. One reader complained that the author had not been explicit enough in defining two chapters, "Capital" and "Ownership of Wealth" in *Farmers and Socialism*. Hjelt informed him that the chapters in question had been reprinted in Swedish and Finnish-language newspapers in Canada and the United States, and concluded that it must have been easily understood by all workers to get such wide dissemination.[38] Another frequent correspondent to *Norrøna* faulted Hjelt for quoting from French, then using additional valuable space for translation that could be used for discussion, in which context Hjelt said:

> If Alexander has learned something from what I have written, he will also have learned that I do not quote only from French.. . . I often quote English and Swedish in the original without translating and when I don't translate . . . it's because most readers understood . . . and when I translate French and other languages and leave the passages side by side, it is to guard myself against the doubting Thomases.

He concluded his remarks with a prescient statement on the use of languages in Canada:

> One should not point a finger at a person because he understands several languages, and it especially ill behoves one Canadian to point the finger at another 'British subject' because he understands French: for as is well known, there are two official languages in Canada, English and French.[39]

When Hjelt was not engaged in verbal jousting with editors and correspondents, he would deal at some length with a number of serious topics, in which he attempted to educate farmers and workers to the harsher realities of the political and economic system. He would point out to farmers, for example, that it was the free enterprise system of "devilish speculation" which placed farmers in debt, and he argued that it was only through co-operation that they would be assured a just price for wheat.[40] In another article entitled "Political and Industrial Democracy," he argued since "Saskatchewan is farming" it should be represented by farmers — not farmer politicians, but people with both practical and theoretical knowledge of land, livestock, the economics of importing farm machinery.[41] In a chapter "The Farmer and Industrial Capitalism" (from *Farmers and Socialism)* he reported on his visits to such farm-related firms as Armour, Swift, McCormick and Deering; the gist of his message was that farmers and workers alike were being exploited, primarily because they had not taken time to organize and because they were willing to accept discredited capitalist theory, especially the myth of free enterprise.[42]

Another facet of Hjelt's educational work took the form of speaking engagements "among the Western Reds," as he put it. On these journeys he found that "a socialist lecturer experiences a little bit of everything as far as questions are concerned. One is often asked dumb questions which have nothing to do with the issues.. . . Some come to . . . meetings with the understanding if a socialist . . . cannot with mathematical precision give the age of the earth or the actual distance between the so-called canals on Mars, then socialism cannot be accepted."[43] He said he could measure the intelligence level of an audience by the calibre of the questions. If he was asked "Why did the bolsheviks abolish marriage and establish free love?" it would be a dumb audience. Fortunately, he added, the farmers who attended the Scandia school did not believe in such "black lies"! Hjelt addressed his audiences in English or Norwegian as the occasion warranted. One of his tours went as far as Prince Albert (Hjelt was critical of the penitentiary), others included such communities as Spring Grove, Birch Hills, Weldon, Russborough, and Horse Butte. A socialist colleague, Harold Melbo, was the mayor of Horse Butte and had to overcome local opposition to allowing a "flaming radical" like Hjelt to speak in the schoolhouse. Nevertheless, permission was granted and Hjelt afterwards declared:

> I have sold more socialistic literature at these two meetings than I have ... any other single day in my travels in Canada.... When I sell books at the meetings I usually always hold them up in front of the assembly and say a few words about the contents. I did the same this time for the book *Farmers and Socialism,* except that I didn't say anything about its contents, only this: 'This book was banned by the press censor; if you had owned it in Canada a few months ago it would have cost you 1,000 dollars cash and two years behind iron bars, now you can have the book for 25 cents.' And believe me, the book went like hot cakes.[44]

Although Hjelt had strong ties with Saskatchewan's Scandinavian farmers, he was no parochial, concerned only with the issues which affected the prairie settlers. From his writings and reports of travel throughout western Canada and the major industrial states of America, not to mention Europe, it is evident that he saw himself as vitally involved in various issues with international ramifications. He tells of visits to Wall Street, an address to Swedish and Finnish workers at a New York Socialist Party rally, a meeting with the influential Martin Tranmael in Oslo (who had been prominently involved in labour organizations in the U.S. as well as Norway), files commentaries on the abortive strikes of railway workers in Norway, the Peace of Brest-Litovsk (and its implications for the working-man): and the coming to power of Hjalmar Branting in Sweden.[45] Branting's alleged "success" did not sit too well with Hjelt, who claimed that so-called "right wing" socialists are merely liberals in disguise who usually hold well paid positions in the system:

> The latest news ... comes from Sweden where it was stated that the king had asked the 'socialist' Hjalmar Branting to form a 'socialist government.' Can one think of anything more absurd and contradictory in the use of language? No, when the socialists come to power in Sweden, the king will have nothing to say ...; the announcement in the daily press will read approximately as follows: 'The Socialists have taken over in Sweden. They have established a workers' government and started their work with an order to the king for him to pack his suitcase and leave Stockholm and Sweden within 48 hours....'[46]

Needless to say, the king is still on the Swedish throne, and even Hjelt, given his next five decades' support for the Norwegian Labour Party, would probably have agreed that the socialists, left and right, have made progress. In summing up the Canadian career of Ole Hjelt, it would seem that much of what he said and wrote were expressions of an impatient idealist, infused with the natural ebullience and enthusiasm of youth. No doubt Hjelt saw himself as a crusader with a cause, but there is just enough evidence here and there — particularly when he spoke to a European audience — to suggest that he was rather less sanguine about the prospects of socialist revolution than the rhetoric proclaimed. When asked almost sixty years ago about the coming "revolution" in America, Hjelt expressed that on which Louis Hartz was to build *his* academic reputation with *The Liberal Tradition in America.* There not having been a feudal tradition in the New World and with America being a new nation, its living standard was high compared with that of Europe; it had no homogeneous population, and, indeed, the New World still offered economic opportunity to the individual.[47]

Ingvar Olsen, who did so much to encourage open debate in the columns of *Norrøna,* was not far off the mark in his assessment of Hjelt's role:

> He is not a man who can be dismissed with a wave of the hand. . . . He is too gifted and knowledgeable a man, and finally, has too great an impact on thousands of his countrymen that he can be relegated to oblivion without further ado. There has been from time to time many . . . rather bitter battles in *Norrøna's* columns about Ole Hjelt the man. Many people have attempted to reduce the man to a zero. . . . But Ole Hjelt and *løvetanden* — better known as the dandelion — have the same characteristic, the more one tramps on them, the more they grow. Ole Hjelt is today . . . despite all attempts to tear him to ribbons . . . the acknowledged leader of the Norwegian socialists in Canada. And in this respect we should note the Norwegian socialists . . . are not some kind of wild animal; neither do they belong to some modern bogeyman class of blood-dripping bolsheviks. . . . The Norwegian socialists . . . represent a solid, well-founded impact in today's political discussion. Whenever we say, therefore, that Ole Hjelt is leader of the Norwegian Socialists . . . , we have then said he has a respectable position in society in general and among our countrymen in particular.[48]

Hjelt's subsequent career in Norway, in detail, does not concern us here. He returned home in 1925 following the tragic death of his wife in childbirth. For a while he farmed in Hedmark but was soon involved in politics: first, on the executive of the Norwegian Labour Party in Akerhus, later as a long-time editor of the labour journal, *Follo.* Always an avid sportsman — he had won medals in markmanship, skiing, gymnastics and swimming — he dedicated much of his spare time to training young people in sport shooting and participated himself in competition up to a year before he died in 1974. In keeping with a lifelong enthusiasm for learning, he began the study of Russian when he was eighty.[49] It is obvious that Hjelt, despite personal tragedy, never succumbed to Strindberg's philosophy of despair. As he noted in a letter to *Norrøna,* prior to leaving Instow to Ringsaker, "each moment of life is worthwhile . . . in spite of all the obstacles. The only thing that gives life meaning is to live it fully."[50] There is no question that this Norwegian-Canadian radical, who had enlivened the political scene in the New World for so many years, did just that over the next half century in his native land.

FOOTNOTES

[1]Hartwell Bowsfield, *"The West" in Canada Since 1867, A Bibliographical Guide,* eds. J. L. Granatstein and Paul Stevens (Toronto, 1975), 116.

[2]*Ibid.*

[3]I have referred elsewhere to reasons why the ethnic Canadian voice has been heard infrequently. See Jorgen Dahlie, "Learning on the Frontier: Scandinavian Immigrants and Education in Western Canada," *Canadian and International Education* (December 1972), 56-66. Howard Palmer's unpublished paper, "Reluctant Hosts: Anglo-Canadian Views of Multiculturalism in the Twentieth Century," (available in mimeograph), provides useful background information to related aspects of this issue (Ottawa, 1976).

[4]J. Donald Wilson, "Matti Kurrika: Finnish-Canadian Intellectual," *B.C. Studies,* No. 20 (Winter 1973-74), 50-65.

[5]*Ibid.,* 50-51.

[6]*Nordmanns-Forbundet,* 14 (1921), 24-25. Translations of all excerpts from Norwegian and Swedish sources are mine. *Nordmanns-Forbundet,* founded in 1907, is the official organ of the worldwide Norsemen's Association; it has had an important function for Norwegians in maintaining cultural ties with the Old Country.

[7]Information on Ole Hjelt's arrival in Instow has been excerpted from Hamar *Arbeiderblad,* May 10, 1974, *Svenska Canada-Tidningen,* November 14, 1918 and interviews with Andreas Hjelt, September 20 and 21, 1975 in Shaunavon, Saskatchewan. Additional information on the first years of settlement was provided in letters to the writer from Andreas Hjelt, December 20, 1973, and March 21, 1974. Ole Hjelt wrote primarily for *Norrøna,* a Norwegian language weekly started by Peter Martin Dahl and Ingvar Olsen in Winnipeg in 1910. It is still being published in Vancouver as a bi-weekly, edited by a recent Norwegian immigrant, Gunnar Warolin. Hjelt also contributed to the short-lived Swedish periodical *Forum,* edited by Rudolph Einhardt in Winnipeg, and to *Svenska Canada-Tidningen,* another Winnipeg-based weekly which was the successor to *Skandinaviske Canadiensaren,* first published in Winnipeg in 1887. Some of Hjelt's articles were reprinted in *Svenska Socialisten* and *Social-Demokraten,* two Chicago Scandinavian newspapers.

[8]Hamar *Arbeiderblad,* May 10, 1974. Additional information on Hjelt's activities in Norway after his return is recorded in *Arbeiderens Leksikon,* III (1933), 917-918.

[9]Nils Frederiksson Brown, editor of *Svenska Canada-Tidningen* from 1913 to 1919 (?), took his *examen artium* and studied law for some years at Uppsala University. He was born in Bro parish, Upland, in 1886 and arrived in the U.S. in 1910, taking a position as associate editor of *Svenska Amerikanska Posten* of Minneapolis until he moved to the Winnipeg paper. See *Svenska Canada-Tidningen,* December 19, 1917, for further details.

[10]*Svenska Canada-Tidningen,* November 14, 1918. Hjelt adds that "in a well-ordered socialist society, the suffering and distress which now predominates, can be reduced to a minimum." He then concludes with a verse from Henrik Ibsen: "Where law sits on knife point/And right on the gallow lives/the day's victory is nearer and assured/than there where there is murder with words." The book *Farmers and Socialism* was serialized (in Swedish) through various issues with the final chapter printed July 3, 1919.

[11]The preface to *Pioneer Life on the Prairie* contains a verse from Goethe but Hjelt has also cited Canadian Robert C. J. Stead's poem "My Beloved" in the first chapter, and has subsequent references in this book to the Swedish writer Ellen Key, to Schiller (in a chapter on the lack of women on the prairie) and Henrik Ibsen, whose poem "En Kirke" (A Church) introduced the chapter "Social Life on the Prairie." Almost all of Hjelt's extended articles on socialism, co-operatives, revolution, and related topics contain interpretations of Marx, Proudhon or the Danish reformer George Brandes. For example, see *Norrøna,* November 16, 1918, article entitled "Wealth." Further evidence of the breadth of Hjelt's reading can be gathered from articles in which he quotes from Louis Machlin, Vince Grassi, and D. Cureau. See *Norrøna,* April 21 and 28, and September 23, 1920.

[12]*Svenska Canada-Tidningen,* November 14, 1918.

[13]*Nordmanns-Forbundet,* 14 (1921), 26.

[14]Hjelt's family was by no means rich; however, they managed to put two sons through Jønsberg. In the April 10, 1976 edition of *Ringsaker Blad/Brummuncolen* (Moelv, Norway) there is a 1905 photograph of Andreas Hjelt and six of his classmates from Ringsaker who attended Jønsberg Landbrukskole. Even though Norway had by then an enviable literacy rate, it was still noteworthy to have two from one family completing fourteen years of schooling as the Hjelts had done.

[15]*Svenska Canada-Tidningen,* November 14, 1918.

[16]Interview with Andreas Hjelt, September 21, 1975, Shaunavon, Saskatchewan and Ole Hjelt, *Nybyggeriliv Paa Praerien [Pioneer Life on the Prairie]* (Winnipeg, 1920), *passim.*

[17]*Svenska Canada-Tidningen,* November 14, 1918.

[18]See fn. 16 and Ole Hjelt, "Nybyggerliv i Kanada," *Nordmanns-Forbundet,* 14 (1921), 170-76.

[19]Ole Hjelt, *Socialismen* (Socialism) (Chicago, 1916), 4. This book was the published version of an address given by Hjelt to several meetings in Canada and the United States. After Hjelt's presentation to the Lake View Socialist Association in Chicago in the fall of 1916, Henry Bengston, editor of *Svenska Socialisten,* and Bengston, suggesting a close relationship between Scandinavians in Canada and the United States engaged in radical political activity.

One report is that Hjelt was for a time involved in the Mesabi strike but that as a non-violent socialist, he broke with the union leaders over tactics. See Hamar *Arbeiderblad,* May, 1974.

[20]Peter Martin Dahl was born in Ørkedalen, Norway in 1869, moved to Sweden in 1882 and remained there until 1896. He attended business college in Trondhjem in 1898, worked briefly for a timber firm before emigrating in 1902 to Canada. An industrial accident in Winnipeg led to newspaper work, first with *Canada Posten,* a Swedish weekly with a strong religious orientation. He started *Norrøns* in 1910 with Ingvar Olsen, also from Trondhjem, where he had been a lawyer. Dahl became a director of both *Norrøna* and *Svenska-Canada-Tidningen.* Olsen was editor of *Norrøna* from 1910-1911, 1913-1917, and from 1918 to 1924. He has written a memoir, *Vor Flyvende Smaahistorier Fra Canada-Praerien* (Winnipeg, 1916), which recounts in a humourous vein, some of Olsen's experiences as an immigrant to Canada. Olsen could give Hjelt a spirited battle in *Norrøna* and did, on occasion, whenever he thought his countryman had been too sweeping or caustic in his statements.

[21]Wilson, *op. cit.,* 59-62.

[22]Jorgen Dahlie and J. Donald Wilson, "Negroes, Finns, Sikhs: Education and Community Experience in British Columbia," in *Sounds Canadian, Languages and Cultures in Multi-Ethnic Societies,* ed. Paul Migus (Toronto, 1975), 81.

[23]*Norrøna,* January 2, April 17, July 10, and August 14, 1919, December 18, 1920; and January 6, and November 17, 1921.

[24]*Norrøna,* May 15, 1919.

[25]*Norrøna,* February 27, 1919. Hjelt notes that he is currently reading seventeen different newspapers, including *La Presse* and *Le Devoir* in addition *La Croix,* as well as several European papers, and others from his socialist colleagues in the United States.

[26]*Ibid.*

[27]Hjelt, *Pioneer Life on the Prairie,* 174.

[28]*Ibid.,* 175.

[29]*Norrøna,* November 24, 1921. The charge that Hjelt did not work the farm himself was rejected by Rudolph Einhardt, who is amazed to find him doing both the farm labour and his writing. *Norrøna,* June 15, 1922.

[30]*Norrøna,* August 28, 1916.

[31]*Ibid.,* February 19, 1920.

[32]*Ibid.*

[33]*Ibid.,* June 15, 1922.

[34]*Svenska Canada-Tidningen,* March 23, 1922. Einhardt gives the following figures: of 1000 copies in Norwegian and 2000 in Swedish of *Farmers and Socialism,* there were sales of 750 and 1100 respectively of 2000 copies in Norwegian and 4000 in Swedish of *Socialism,* there were sales of 1000 and 3100 respectively. He adds: "I hope *Pioneer Life on the Prairie,* which is Hjelt's most literary effort, does as well."

[35]*Norrøna,* May 8, 1919.

[36]*Ibid.*

[37]*Ibid.,* April 8, 1920.

[38]*Ibid.,* November 4, 1920.

[39]*Ibid.,* April 15, 1920.

[40]*Ibid.,* April 17, 1919.

[41]*Svenska Canada-Tidningen,* March 29, 1919 and *Norrøna,* December 19, 1919.

[42]*Svenska Canada-Tidningen,* January 23, 1919 and March 29, 1919. Hjelt reports on visits to the four western provinces, and the states of Indiana, Illinois, Wisconsin, Minnesota, North Dakota, Montana, Idaho, Washington, Oregon, and California.

[43]*Norrøna,* November 27, 1919.

[44]*Ibid.,* July 29, 1920.

[45]*Ibid.,* January 6 and January 20, 1921. Hjelt likes Tranmael, whom he describes as "un homme d'action." Tranmael was a leading Labour Party functionary; born in 1879, he spent almost five years in the United States and helped to organize unions in Los Angeles.

[46]*Norrøna,* November 3, 1921.

[47]*Ibid.,* November 17, 1921; *Nordmanns-Forbundet,* 14 (1921), 25.

[48] *Norrøna,* January 29,1920.

[49]Hamar *Arbeiderblad,* May 10, 1974. The tribute to Hjelt reads in part: "Throughout all his life he has worked to promote sport shooting, and in the later years he has tried hard to keep the young people interested. There are hundreds who have learned to shoot under his knowledgeable instruction.... Right up to this winter he was a reporter for the rifle association in Brummunddal, and is truly the country's oldest active sports journalist. Last year he won a gold medal in shooting and two years ago one recalls a record that commands respect: 34 of 50 possible standing at a distance of 300 meters! ... He is a shining example for today's pensioners on how one should take care of body and mind. The daily gymnastic program on the radio he followed strictly right up to this winter."

[50]*Norrøna,* May 1, 1924. Hjelt left the following year.

THE BEGINNINGS OF UKRAINIAN SCHOLARSHIP IN CANADA

VICTOR BUYNIAK
UNIVERSITY OF SASKATCHEWAN, SASKATOON

The first wave of Ukrainian settlers in Canada — those land-hungry peasants whom economic conditions forced to emigrate from their native land — could only dream that, one day, their grand-children or great-grandchildren would occupy responsible positions in Canadian education and would contribute to the development of Canada's intellectual and scholarly life. However, subconsciously they felt that in order to prepare their children for an easier and richer life it was imperative to provide them with *some* education — a most important tool which they themselves lacked. On festive occasions, Sundays and holidays, the pioneers would gather together and discuss the possibilities, however remote at the moment, of having their native tongue taught in Canadian public schools, collegiates and even universities.

Although the reality of the time required hard physical labour to ensure their own and their children's immediate economic survival in the new land, they never ceased to dream about a better and more fulfilling future. And in those early years over the century no one could have foreseen the shape of this future: two world wars, a failure to establish independence in their homeland, revolutionary movements, a severe intervening depression, startling technological changes, and the emergence of new worldwide political forms. All these events were instrumental in shaping the Canadian and Ukrainian communities on this continent, both economically and culturally.

The educational, cultural and community needs of those early settlers who were able to maintain contacts with the outside world were supplied to some degree by the Ukrainian language daily "Svoboda," published in the U.S.A. In 1903, the first Ukrainian newspaper in Canada appeared — "The Canadian Farmer."[1] The following year saw the publication of the first Ukrainian book in Canada.[2] The year 1905 marked three culturally significant events: the opening of the first Ukrainian bookstore in Winnipeg; the foundation in that city of the first "Prosvita" society; and the establishment of a "Ruthenian Training School" for teachers.[3]

The so-called "Laurier-Greenway Act of 1897" provided for the implementation of bilingual schools in those districts of Manitoba which had a certain percentage of schoolchildren whose mother tongue was other than English.[4] The Ukrainian settlers in the Prairies were quick to avail themselves of this cultural opportunity, and soon training schools or seminaries for Ukrainian teachers were opened in several centres in western Canada. The first conference of such teachers took place in Winnipeg in 1907.[5] 37 persons attended it.[6] The following year already boasted the first

Ukrainian school in that city.[7] In order to provide qualified instructors for the training centres, teachers and scholars were invited from the Old Country. Among them was the Ukrainian poet Petro Karmans'ky, one of the first of the scholar-intellectuals who were to arrive at intervals during subsequent decades.[8]

With the graduation of the first class from the Ruthenian Training School in 1906, one could designate roughly the beginning of Ukrainian scholarship in Canada. Almost all the future Ukrainian leaders, professionalists, and intellectuals passed through these seminaries and started their careers in teaching Ukrainian children in various districts of the Prairie Provinces.[9] A cultural pattern was established which was to last for several decades among the Ukrainians in Canada: educated Ukrainians, whatever their field, interest, profession or calling, felt morally obligated to help educate their countrymen who did not have the same opportunities. The trend produced many dedicated nationally-conscious community leaders in Canada.

The existence of these training schools encouraged young people with some secondary education to enrol in them, to live in residences during the period of instruction and to form clubs which, in time, became the nuclei of Ukrainian student societies. Students attending schools in cities stayed at the so-called "Institutes," communal student residences, which not only provided an atmosphere conducive to learning the regular subjects required by schools but also stimulated the students to examine the Ukrainian language, history and various aspects of Ukrainian culture. The first such student residence was established in St. Boniface in 1910. Then came the Adam Kotsko residence in Winnipeg in 1915, the Institute in Saskatoon, 1916, and in Edmonton in 1926.[10] The Ukrainian settlers quickly grasped the importance of higher education. Already in 1902 the first immigrants to Canada and the U.S.A. sent contributions from their modest earnings to assist Ukrainian students at L'viv University in the Western Ukraine.[11]

Those who were unable to attend schools themselves derived cultural and intellectual enrichment through a variety of educational organizations, societies, clubs and institutions which were established for this purpose through church and lay initiative. The two traditional Old Country societies for the dissemination of education to large segments of population were the already mentioned Prosvita and the Taras Shevchenko Society. They were transplanted to Canada shortly after the arrival of the first Ukrainian settlers. The first branch of the Shevchenko Society was already active in Winnipeg in the early 1900s.[12] Another institution, the so-called "National Homes," played a very important role as cultural and social community centres where members could read newspapers and books, listen to lectures by prominent speakers or specialists, see a play, sing and dance, or take part in the celebration of an important anniversary or event. These Homes were also favourite meeting places for social activities in the community. By the early 1920s most of the larger centres in Canada populated by Ukrainians had such institutions. One of the first scholars from the Ukraine to visit

Canada and to speak at public gatherings in these institutions was Dr. Julius Bachynsky, who arrived in June 1906.[13] These societies and clubs filled the need temporarily until a more elaborate and more sophisticated structure could be established.

Even before the first Ukrainians graduated from Canadian universities, some immigrants with qualifications acquired in the Old Country or in the U.S.A. tried to fill temporarily the gaps in various professions among their countrymen in Canada. To this category belonged D. M. Svoboda, the first notary of Ukrainian origin, who opened his office in Winnipeg in 1909.[14] T. K. Pazdriy, a medical doctor who was educated in the U.S.A., arrived from Chicago in 1915 to establish a practice in Winnipeg.[15]

In the meantime, more and more young people passed through the training schools. The year 1910 saw the first conference of Ukrainian teachers in Saskatchewan.[16] In January 1911 the first official demand to introduce teaching of the Ukrainian language in Winnipeg public schools was recorded.[17] The same year the first Ukrainian primer (a direct translation from an English language version) was published for use in Ukrainian schools in Canada.[18] In 1912 there were already seven Ukrainian students enrolled at the University of Manitoba.[19] The same year a Ukrainian students' club was organized at Manitoba College.[20] This club grew into the regular Ukrainian University Club in 1916 at the University of Manitoba.[21]

The distinction of becoming the first graduate of Ukrainian origin from a Canadian university belongs to Orest Zherebko, B.A., 1913, University of Manitoba.[22] Not only was he active in Ukrainian students' associations during his university years, but he continued his interest in community affairs throughout his life. He was one of the first organizers of the Ukrainian Publishing Company "The Ukrainian Voice," one of the founders of the National Home in Winnipeg, and the first MLA of Ukrainian origin in Saskatchewan.[23] Zherebko arrived in Canada at the age of 13 to join his brother in 1903, learned English, taught in Ukrainian-speaking districts and then prepared himself for university entrance.[24] He was not content with the first degree but went to Europe to broaden his knowledge and studied at universities in Vienna and L'viv. Zherebko died in 1940.

The first woman of Ukrainian origin to graduate in Canada was Maria Sawchak-Dyma, B.A., 1923, University of Manitoba. She came to Canada with her parents in 1920.[25] Like Zherebko, she became a well-known community worker, woman organizer and leader among Ukrainians in Canada.

It should be emphasized at this point that economic circumstances among the Ukrainian settlers in Canada until World War I were such that only a very few individuals could attend any schools past the elementary grades. Many talented and eager students who wanted to go to school were unable to do so as their parents could not afford the expense. This fact helps to explain that at first university students formed the élite of a select few among the Ukrainians in Canada. As in every beginning, this one also was difficult, but a start had been made. This limited number of students of Ukrainian origin encouraged other young people to go to school, to learn and to set up libraries and develop various aspects of their native culture.

Thus, already in 1912, a plan was advanced to organize a three-month course in Ukrainian studies on a higher level.[26] It was the first such attempt to establish some sort of college or university for Ukrainians in Canada. Steps were also taken in 1914 to initiate an official demand for the creation of a Ukrainian chair at the University of Manitoba.[27] Plans to expand the teaching of Ukrainian studies were discussed during World War I, although conditions for national minorities were not favourable at that time in Canada. One such plan was to try to found a Ukrainian college.[28] The other was to announce that A. Kryzhanovsky, one of the instructors in the Ukrainian-English Seminaries, was to begin reading lectures on Ukrainian history at the University of Saskatchewan in 1915.[29] In February 1916, a representation was made by a Ukrainian delegation to the Manitoba Legislature for the retention of the bilingual school system in that Province.[30] The spokesman of the delegation, J. W. Arsenych, also expressed the desirability of establishing a Ukrainian chair at the University of Manitoba and appointing a Ukrainian teacher at the Brandon Teachers' Seminary.[31] In August 1916, a Ukrainian rally in Saskatoon appealed to the Saskatchewan Legislature to introduce Ukrainian at the University of Saskatchewan.[32]

All these representations were, however, of no avail. The war in Europe had a detrimental effect on the liberalization of education on the Prairies. The Legislative Assemblies of both Manitoba and Saskatchewan had revoked the Bilingual School Act in 1916.[33] These events and the general attitude of the Anglo-Saxon group toward any concessions to alien minority groups during the war had the effect of suppressing all ideas and plans regarding education among Ukrainians in Canada. This situation continued until the 1920s.

There were, however, no limitations on Canadians of Ukrainian origin enrolling in universities. The Manitoba Agricultural College had two Ukrainian students in 1916.[34] The University of Saskatchewan graduated its first Ukrainian student, Joseph Megas, B.A., in 1917.[35] In the University of Alberta the first Ukrainian graduate was Harry Kostash, B.A., 1921.[36] The 1918 year was a most successful one for the Winnipeggers. Of the three Ukrainian students at the Manitoba Agricultural College, C. S. Prodan was awarded the Governor General's Gold Medal.[37] Four Ukrainian students graduated from the University of Manitoba, one of whom was S. Swystun, B.A., who was to play a prominent role in Ukrainian community life in Canada in the next five decades.[38]

These years gave Ukrainians a number of "firsts" in the professional fields as well. J. W. Arsenych, who so eloquently presented the Ukrainian position in the Manitoba Legislature in 1916, became the first Ukrainian lawyer in Canada in 1917, and was the first Ukrainian awarded the title of

K.C. in 1935. The first dentist was Dr. Manoly Mihaychuk, University of Toronto, 1922; the first pharmacist — Michael Lazechko, University of Manitoba, 1922; the first physician — Dr. Hryhory Novak. The distinction of the first appointment to a university faculty for a Ukrainian, not only in Canada but on the whole North American Continent, belongs to Dr. John Orobko. A graduate of McGill University, he became a staff member in the College of Medicine at the University of Alberta in 1921.[39]

The career of Cyril S. Prodan, the first agronomist of Ukrainian origin in Canada, is of interest. He may serve as an outstanding example of the research worker, scholar and community leader, a typical first-generation Ukrainian Canadian who made a great contribution in his field. Prodan was born in 1891 in the Eastern Ukraine. He came to Canada in 1907, learned English, and, when the opportunity came, enrolled in a B.S.A. program which he completed with distinction in 1921.[40] He was also the first B.S.A. graduate of Ukrainian origin on the North American Continent. All his life (he died in 1969) he dedicated himself to professional and public service in his chosen country. He published hundreds of articles on agriculture in Ukrainian newspapers and almanacs. His contribution to advanced farming in Canada was unique.[41]

Some scholarly activity, predominantly in the field of Ukrainian literature, in original and in English translation, and in the compilation of Ukrainian-English and English-Ukrainian dictionaries, is also attested to during this early period. A great service in this field was rendered by such non-Ukrainians as Florence Randall Livesay, A. J. Hunter, Percival Cundy, Edward W. Thompson and others. They were active during the first two decades of this century. Dr. Hunter and Percival Cundy were Presbyterian ministers in the Prairies working chiefly among newly-arrived Ukrainian settlers to Canada. In addition to works in translation, they also published various educational and informative articles in English and Ukrainian-language newspapers and journals on the North American Continent. Individuals like these, through their dedicated work, helped greatly to pave the way for an understanding of Ukrainians and their spiritual culture on the part of their Canadian compatriots of other ethnic backgrounds.[42] All these were pioneering efforts in literary scholarship. Great progress has since been made in these areas.

The years 1917-1921 in the Ukraine were a period of war, revolution, national reawakening, great expectations and, subsequently, disillusionment for many. When the goals of the Ukrainian proclamation of independence could not be realized, many a Ukrainian patriot, member of the Ukrainian national armed forces, or refugee from political and economic oppression emigrated abroad. Since a large number of these nationally conscious emigrants were intellectuals with higher education, they saw fit to organize free Ukrainian institutions of learning in exile, particularly in the newly-created Czechoslovak Republic.[43] These institutions became centres of dissemination for knowledge and scholarship among the Ukrainian exiles in Europe. In time, educated immigrants began arriving on the North American continent. This new contingent gave a boost to the already budding crop of Ukrainian Canadian intellectuals and scholars.

The new political immigration brought with it fresh ideas on how to educate Ukrainian Canadians in their original language and culture. Many an institution and organization was established in the 1920's and 1930's by these highly motivated émigrés to ensure the preservation of Ukrainian nationality. In addition to activity in the political sphere they also initiated such cultural and educational projects as founding schools for children and adults, organizing community centres, drama, music and dance clubs, establishing libraries, giving lectures and talks and promoting a variety of other activities. Their efforts helped to spark political, national, cultural and educational consciousness among the Ukrainians in Canada, especially among the youth.

In the 1920's more and more students of Ukrainian origin enrolled in Canadian universities. Some of them were already born here while others, born in the Old Country, resumed their education on this continent. The graduates of this decade, imbued with the national spirit, turned out to be among the most dedicated to the Ukrainian cause and culture: they worked as national leaders, youth educators, teachers and school inspectors, instructors in universities, organizers, writers, journalists, researchers, etc. Most of these "men of the hour" have already passed away after a long and laborious life: the Stechishin brothers — Michael, Myroslav and Julius — Honore Ewach, Ilya Kyriak, F. T. Hawryliuk, Michael Luchkovich, to name only a few.

Also this decade gave Ukrainians in Canada some "firsts." The youngest B.A. to graduate was Yakiv Stan'ko, University of Manitoba, 1925 — he was only 18.[44] Ilya Shklanka, a teacher from Saskatchewan, was the first to obtain the M.A. degree, also in 1925.[45] The first school inspector of Ukrainian origin to be appointed in Canada, 1925, was the above mentioned F. T. Hawryliuk.[46] The first B.Mus., Taras Hubitsky from Winnipeg, graduated in 1926.[47] The first Doctor of Law, Ivan Yatsiv, born in Winnipeg, was awarded this degree in 1926.[48]

Numerically, the ranks of university graduates became increasingly stronger as the years passed by. If by the end of 1921 there were only about twenty of them,[49] by 1925 Ukrainian Canadians who had completed university studies in Canada or the United States numbered seventy-two.[50] In the academic year 1928-1929, in the three Prairie universities there were over 130 Ukrainian students enrolled — sixty-seven of them at the University of Manitoba, whose total enrolment was 2700.[51]

The Ukrainian teachers' associations were re-established as soon as the restrictions imposed by World War I were removed. Winnipeg hosted a convention of teachers in July 1921.[52] A new Association of Ukrainian Teachers of Saskatchewan was formed in 1929.[53] Along with this renewed teaching activity went the establishment and development of various students' clubs, organizations and journals in the 1920's. Thus in 1920 a

Ukrainian students club came into existence in Winnipeg.[54] A similar club, for students and teachers, made its appearance in Saskatoon in 1921.[55] The first Ukrainian students' journal, the *Kameniari* (Stone Cutters), was established at the Mohyla Institute in Saskatoon in 1920.[56]

Practically all publishing activity in Ukrainian during these two first decades of the century had been connected with Ukrainian printing establishments and newspapers. As in every other field, the beginning was modest. The intellectual and scholarly level of the publications had to be adjusted to the level of the readers. Early works published in Canada consisted chiefly of popular Ukrainian literature, translations, dictionaries, works of religious and generally informative character. The first Ukrainian book published in Canada was consequently a collection of folk songs from the Old and New Country.[57] Almanacs, popular works in history, memoirs, jubilee books and other such items were common fare for the reader of the day.

In this short survey the author has tried to show the pioneering stage of development of Ukrainian scholarship in Canada. Through individual and group endeavours and through assiduous and dedicated work, it became possible to lay a strong groundwork for future growth. These labours brought fruit in a very brief period of time. The older generation of pioneers in many cases saw their dreams come true: their children and grandchildren became educated and played an important role in professional, intellectual and scholarly life of the country in which they settled. In this case the Ukrainian ethnic group can serve as a good example of how uneducated, politically and economically oppressed peasants from Eastern Europe, when given an equal opportunity in Canada, developed their full potential and became in a short time a viable and responsible element contributing to the well-being of their new fatherland.

FOOTNOTES

[1]Olha Voycenko, *The Annals of Ukrainian Life in Canada* (Winnipeg, 1961), vol. 1, 5.
[2]Voycenko, *op. cit.,* 5.
[3]*Ibid.*
[4]W. T. Zyla, *Contribution to the History of Ukrainian and Other Slavic Studies in Canada* (Winnipeg, 1961), 13.
[5]Voycenko, *op. cit.,* 6.
[6]I. H. Syrnyk, "*Ukrains'kyi Holos* v pershykh rokakh," in *Jubilee Almanac to Commemorate the Fiftieth Anniversary of Ukrainian Voice, 1910-1960* (Winnipeg, 1961), 39.
[7]Voycenko, *op. cit.,* 6.
[8]Voycenko, *op. cit.,* 64.
[9]D. Doroshenko, ed., *Propamiatna Knyha Ukrains'koho Narodnoho Domu u Vinnipegu* (Winnipeg, 1949), 90.
[10]*Ibid.,* 92
[11]Michael H. Marunchak, *The Ukrainian-Canadians: A History* (Winnipeg, 1970), 321.
[12]Paul Yuzyk, *The Ukrainians in Manitoba. A Social History* (Toronto, 1953), 81.
[13]Marunchak, *op. cit.,* 321.
[14]*Ibid.,* 235.
[15]Voycenko, *op. cit.,* 125.
[16]*Ibid.,* 11.
[17]Voycenko, *op. cit.,* 16.
[18]J. W. Stechishin, *Twenty-Five Years of the P. Mohyla Ukrainian Institute in Saskatoon, 1915-1941* (Saskatoon, 1945), 39-40.
[19]Marunchak, *op. cit.,* 187.
[20]Voycenko, *op. cit.,* 32.

[21]Marunchak, *op. cit.*, 235.
[22]Voycenko, *op. cit.*, 53.
[23]Doroshenko, *op. cit.*, 415.
[24]*Ibid.*, 57.
[25]Voycenko, *The Annals of Ukrainian Life in Canada*, vol. 2 (1963), 297.
[26]Voycenko, *op. cit.*, vol. 1, 50.
[27]*Ibid.*, 87; Zyla, *op. cit.*, 13.
[28]Voycenko, *op. cit.*, vol. 1, 117.
[29]*Ibid.*, 103.
[30]Zyla, *op. cit.*, 15.
[31]Voycenko, *op. cit.*, vol. 1, 148.
[32]*Ibid.*, 178.
[33]O. Buyniak, "Ukrains'ka mova v Saskachevani", in *Northern Lights: An Almanac in Ukrainian* (Edmonton, 1964), 133.
[34]Voycenko, *op. cit.*, vol. 1, 146.
[35]*Ibid.*, 212.
[36]J. G. MacGregor, *Vilni Zemli: The Ukrainian Settlement of Alberta* (Toronto, 1969), 257.
[37]Voycenko, vol 1, 256.
[38]Voycenko, vol. 1, 258.
[39]Voycenko, vol. 2, 189.
[40]Doroshenko, *op. cit.*, 58-59.
[41]Olha Voycenko, *The Ukrainians in Canada* (Ottawa-Winnipeg, 1967), 41. Charles H. Young, *The Ukrainian Canadians: A Study in Assimilation* (Toronto, 1931), 207.
[42]Marunchak, *op. cit.*, 535-536.
[43]*Ukrainian Free University: Short Review* (Munich, 1958), 13-15.
[44]Voycenko, *The Annals of Ukrainian Life in Canada*, vol. 3 (1965), 55.
[45]*Ibid.*, 34.
[46]*Ibid.*, 51.
[47]*Ibid.*, 67.
[48]*Ibid.*, 249.
[49]Voycenko, vol. 2, 244; Doroshenko, *op. cit.*, 62.
[50]Voycenko, vol. 3, 39.
[51]Young, *op. cit.*, 205-208.
[52]Marunchak, *op. cit.*, 442.
[53]*Ibid.*, 444.
[54]Voycenko, vol. 2, 83.
[55]*Ibid.*, 188.
[56]*Ibid.*, 84.
[57]M. I. Mandryka, *History of Ukrainian Literature in Canada* (Winnipeg-Ottawa, 1968), 32.

ASPECTS OF UKRAINIAN OPINION IN MANITOBA DURING WORLD WAR I

Nadia O. M. Kazymyra
Public Archives of Canada, Ottawa

Introduction

By the turn of the century, the deep and heated religious strife between the Roman Catholics and the Protestant denominations in Eastern Canada had spread and taken root on the Prairies. The French Canadians attempted to preserve their political influence in the area to ensure religious expression and cultural survival, but above all, to extend their presence outside Quebec. In contrast, the mainly Protestant Anglo-Canadian sector hoped to implant the tenets of British tradition in the minds and to shape the West in the image of Ontario. Thus incompatibility of interests led to tension and conflict.

The need to develop the West and bring the National Dream to completion required people, able-bodied sources of energy, for grain production, mineral extraction and transportation expansion. It was almost inevitable that the frenzy accompanying the drive for economic stability would expose many settlers to religious confrontation, political manipulation and economic exploitation.

The coming of Central and Eastern Europeans to settle the Prairies added an additional dimension to the existing cultural and religious complexity. As more nationalities came to the West and as the cultural gap between the resident population and the new settlers widened, problems in creating a homogeneous society increased. The realization of this fact led to deep anxiety among members of the Canadian leadership.

In the case of Ukrainians, the majority had come in search of free, fertile land away from autocratic rule. Being simple peasants, many were prone to conform to pressures, at least to a certain extent. In spite of the bewilderment and apathy that arose among many Ukrainians, a handful of young students who had been among the first settlers found the Prairie setting conducive to abstract theorization. They had not been attracted by the call of free land and its material benefits propagated by the campaigns encouraging immigration. Imbued with populist ideas, critical of church authority, and swayed by the credo of the Ukrainian Radical Party and the Ukrainian Social Democratic Party, the idealistic youths were preoccupied with the question of how to build a unique nation. The position of the Ukrainian as seen by the idealists depended intrinsically on the advancement of human pride, self-respect, and personal improvement. Indeed, Winnipeg was to emerge as a haven for socialist activities, a source of unorthodox ideas and the embryo of a new, more optimistic life.

Within a short span of fifteen years the socialists separated, forming distinct enclaves along political and religious lines. It is not surprising that the students, being interested in political thought and a new social order, should have become concerned with novel and often tantalizing social concepts. For this reason and in view of the strong propagation of the supremacy of British legal institutions and the Anglo-Saxon tradition, groups which saw little that seemed attractive in their own cultural institutions and political structure, aspired to benefit from the opportunities in Canada which tended to lend support to conformity. Thus, initially politicized in Galicia, then falling prey to the cross-currents of Protestantism and Roman Catholicism within the wider framework of Liberal and Conservative warfare, the Ukrainian socialists separated, forming five general groupings.

The moderate students, products of the Ruthenian training schools, formed a new class of "semi-Canadianized" Ukrainian liberal professionals. A second group formed around Bishop Nykyta Budka, the Ukrainian Catholic emissary, and developed into the conservative-oriented right wing. The more radical socialists, reinforced by new members who had been affected by the events of the 1905 revolution in Russia, became founders of several socialist parties in Canada.* Ukrainian support also arose in favour of the Presbyterian Church in opposition to the ritualism, spiritualism and a lack of progressiveness in the Ukrainian Catholic Church. As well, under the influence of the Liberal Party a number of Ukrainians chose, perhaps also owing to patronage and indoctrination, the Canadian way of life.

By 1914, noticeable social tension existed in western Canada. In consequence of religious conflicts, the economic pressure, and cultural heterogeneity, the period of the Great War witnessed an outburst of open social discontent.

During World War I, Ukrainian opinion in Manitoba was vocalized by a small group of individuals who acted as leaders and spokesmen for the Ukrainian community. These leaders who resided in Winnipeg established the major Ukrainian newspapers there, strictly for the purpose of guiding and educating their public. Rightly or wrongly, the press came to look upon the problems encountered in North Winnipeg as indicators of the social and economic malaise affecting Ukrainians throughout the Prairies. Numerous visitations made to Ukrainian settlements tended to reinforce the leadership's views that the existing inequality, both social and economic, had to be rectified. Thus, owing to their related activities members of this core of intellectuals came to resemble a type of Ukrainian political and economic elite.

The dissemination of ideas through the Ukrainian press of the time well reflects the scope of contemporary Ukrainian activities. Yet the degree of the leadership's comprehension of the problems of the Ukrainian farmer and labourer cannot be ascertained on the basis of newspaper research alone. It is impossible, moreover, to assess accurately the extent of the

---

*These political parties became known as the Ukrainian Social Democratic Party, the Federation of Ukrainian Social Democrats, the Socialist Party of Canada, and the Social Democratic Party of Canada.

newspaper's influence upon the Ukrainian public, for neither sufficient feedback from the readership nor reliable figures exist indicating the circulation of each newspaper.

The examination of the contents and underlying opinions of three newspapers provides most of the subject matter of the present study. Therefore, the *Ukrainian Voice,* the *Canadian Ruthenian* and *The Working People* will serve as respective sources of "liberal" professional, Catholic and Socialist views. Because of the unavailability of two other sources, *The Canadian Farmer* and *The Dawn,* this essay does not attempt to investigate the roles in the context of the Liberal Party and the Presbyterian Church, both major forces behind the drive to sway Ukrainian opinion.

The three conspicuous concerns were connected with language rights, economic security, and the status of the Ukraine. All three problems appeared to the contributors as being mutually compatible and not infringing on the question of Canadian identity or British loyalty. In fact, a section of the Ukrainian leadership became energetic supporters of the British political system, not only owing to the prestige of the Empire but also because some of the tenets underlying the British order could be interpreted as supportive of Ukrainian aspirations. This very obvious weakness of political perception among Ukrainians can be attributed, on the one hand, to lack of political experience and, on the other, to the vagueness of the relationship between Canadianism and British imperialism. The issue of dual loyalty existed partly because of the inability of the Anglo-Canadian leadership to provide political and cultural concessions regarded as adequate by Ukrainians, and partly because of the existence of Ukraine-orientedness among Ukrainians. Therefore, the Ukrainian leadership miscalculated the limits of compromise; on some issues they were unable to modify their position sufficiently in order to obliterate dual loyalty. Thus the great degree of uncertainty prevailing in the leadership's attitudes towards Canada, Great Britain and the Ukraine came to reflect itself in the ambivalence of their policies.

The year 1914 proved most important towards the formation of cultural and political awareness among Ukrainians, not only in Europe but also in Canada. Having resulted from a sequence of events, from the scope of Ukrainian awakening and the European situation, the reaction of the Ukrainians to the war is best understood in the context of European developments. It would seem logical that the war effort should have received primary press coverage; however, the issues at stake were not reported at great length. Blame for the imposition of censorship — with specific written and implicit restrictions — rests amongst others, on the Ukrainian press. Also, internal bickering within the Ukrainian elite and the employment of Ukrainian translators (converts to Presbyterianism) by the Chief Press Censor, tended both to hinder accurate reporting and to obscure the main issues. Accusations of disloyalty, in many instances, overshadowed all the events, thus hindering consistent reporting of the war. Furthermore, the Ukrainian leadership failed to take a firm stand on the British war policy and so did *not* dissociate the war effort and the need for outward manifestations of loyalty from domestic issues, such as job discrimination, registration and internment. Most Ukrainians could not meet the requirements for enlistment in the armed forces to demonstrate their loyalty to the British cause in this manner; yet in Canada they were obstructed in their attempts to prove their claims of loyalty in other ways. The issues immediately affecting them, first the grave injustice committed against Ukrainians and the war on Ukrainian territory, despite numerous threats by the censors of suppressing the Ukrainian newspapers, received broader coverage. Since the articles were scrutinized by the censors after publication, the editors gambled with the future of their newspapers in every such case.

At times the issue of the war was obscured by the struggle for the maintenance of the bilingual school system. Protection of language rights was viewed by Ukrainains as an extension of the fight for cultural survival in Europe. Indeed, Ukrainian political awareness in Europe had gathered great momentum since 1914, and led to the formation of a united Ukrainian National Republic in 1919. Both the *Ukrainian Voice* and the *Canadian Ruthenian* expended much energy in defending the bilingual schools. These two newspapers tended to interpret any criticism of bilingual teaching as a specific attack on the Ukrainian language and, consequently, the Ukrainian ethnicity and culture. As the opposition to language rights became more vocal, the matter of language preservation moved for Ukrainians into the category of cultural survival. The abrogation of cultural rights in connection with the introduction of uniformity in education was perceived by the Ukrainian press as the first step toward forcible assimilation to Protestantism and the Anglo-Saxon culture.

The schools question was complicated by the position of the censors, who associated the matter of language rights with Catholicism and concluded that both the controversy and the stance on it of Catholics constituted external signs of disloyalty towards the war effort. There were numerous attempts by the censors to constrain the Ukrainian newspapers from voicing their opinions on this matter; indeed, the prospect that the Catholic publication *Canadian Ruthenian* would be suppressed appeared imminent. Thus the attitudes to the bilingual schools issue, to the war and the independence of the Ukraine became a type of test of allegiance to Canada.

The Press And World War I

Discontent and apprehension were in the air on the eve of 1914; yet few individuals could have foreseen that the assassination of the Austrian Archduke Francis Ferdinand would trigger a world war. To most Canadians, initially at least, it seemed that 1914 would be remembered only for the state of the national economy. By 1912, the tide of rapid expansion had exhausted itself, and as a result there had been massive cutbacks of industrial production and urban development. There had also been a rise in unemployment.

The young, socially-conscious contributors of *The Working People* had continually warned the Ukrainian immigrant against zealous agrarian and business interests. Even the organ of the Canadian-educated bilingual teachers, *The Ukrainian Voice,* and the tabloid of the Ukrainian Catholic Church, *The Canadian Ruthenian,* published occasional articles on the economic question; however, they were more concerned with the problem of progress via enlightenment and the need for a strong Ukrainian leadership. In many cases there was little if any questioning of the dominant values at the base of Canadian society in the first years of publication of these newspapers.

> Today we see that this is a country of work and freedom. People are more cultured here than those who discouraged us or forbade us from coming to Canada. . . . [Above all] we must [and we can] study, think and develop our minds in Canada without letting them fall asleep. Of what worth is a tall, strong and beautiful human being if he is not educated?[1]

Regardless of the individual emphasis of each of the newspapers, 1914 was heralded by the Ukrainian press in Canada as "the great year for the Ukrainian people."[2] The rapidly rising surge of nationalist rebirth in Western Ukraine, shifting from the cultural to the political arena, had gained momentum since the turn of the century. The jubilant celebrations commemorating the centenary of Shevchenko's birth bear witness to this fact. Acclaimed as the national poet of the Ukraine, Shevchenko seemed the symbol of victory over political oppression. Ukrainians in western Canada viewed Shevchenko as a heroic figure, the leader of a struggling nation against ominous odds. Specifically, the socialists ranked Shevchenko with Karl Marx and radicalism leading eventually to the revolt of the proletariat, while the liberal nationalists saw Shevchenko as the messiah of enlightenment and the martyr for Ukrainian nationalist aspirations.

The "liberals" contended that the dissemination of Shevchenko's written "word" was most important:

> . . . we must spread his Kobzar [the poet's first volume of poetry named after a wandering minstrel] and popular brochures about his life and literary work . . . so that . . . they appear in every Ukrainian home; we must give talks about him at every possible occasion . . . [for] it is important that not only the adults but also every Ukrainian child know who and what Shevchenko is for us. . . .[3]

The purpose of popularizing Shevchenko's message was to impress upon the Ukrainian pioneer that Shevchenko's own relentless search for truth to quench his thirst for knowledge was the only means to shed ignorance and servitude. The Ukrainian teachers would refer to Shevchenko as the greatest advocate of education. In this way they sought to encourage the immigrant to study and raise himself from the depths of illiteracy. Naively, the teachers believed that through acquaintance with the Ukrainian historical tradition and the Canadian ways, Ukrainians would be accepted as welcome and respected Canadians. For the above reasons, 1914 was seen as signalling the breaking point with the past "Dark Ages" and the introduction to a new era for Ukrainians in Canada.

> The centenary celebrations must become the turning point in the life of the Ukrainian people in Canada from which a new and better era will spring forward — an era blossoming in a multi-faceted rebirth in cultural life, rejuvenation of power of the nation ... and in material wealth of the people.[4]

The socialists had been the most nationalistically conscious element among the first Ukrainian settlers. They did not oppose the concern of the "liberals" for education as a means to alleviate economic servitude of the Ukrainian peasantry. What they objected to, however, was the peasants' strange sense of inferiority and submissiveness to authority. Furthermore, it seemed pointless to create a sense of a Ukrainian identity over and above narrow regionalism (i.e., identification with Galicia, Bukovina or the archaic generic name of "Ruthenia") if the Ukrainian conscience "liberals" could not rescue themselves from political submissiveness. Ukrainians had to become more critical of authority, whether it be Austrian, British or Canadian.[5]

Up to 1914 the nationalist rebirth in Western Ukraine had received steady coverage in Canada because of the ties maintained with Galicia and Bukovina. On arrival, Ukrainian settlers were compelled to attain a degree of economic security; yet, from the earliest days of settlement, numerous "penny" campaigns were conducted to aid schools, orphanages, churches, and reading halls in Western Ukraine. With the appearance of the Ukrainian press and a more organized cultural life on the Prairies, the leadership, despite fragmentation, effectively influenced the development of the Ukrainian nationalist sentiment in Canada. This factor, coupled with numerous requests and visits made by dignitaries from Western Ukraine, tended to unify Ukrainians on certain issues and furnished a base for a common aim.

In spite of growing nationalist sentiment, the intelligentsia in Western Ukraine remained loyal supporters of the Habsburgs. All forms of injustice there were blamed primarily on the local Polish or Polonized nobility. Since the incorporation of Galicia and Bukovina into the Habsburg Empire in 1772, special favours and special status had been granted to the Ukrainian clergy and to the lay intelligentsia, most often of clerical origin. The concessions allowed for language and cultural rights, economic benefits and political representation in the Austrian parliament.[6] It is not surprising, therefore, that the Ukrainian intelligentsia supported the Habsburgs when Austria-Hungary declared war on Serbia (July 29, 1914) and subsequently fought as an ally with Germany against Russia. The Ukrainian Catholic Church in Western Ukraine and in Canada were opposed vehemently to Russian interference in the political and religious spheres. From this follows their support of an autonomous Ukraine within the boundaries of Austria-Hungary as a counterbalance against Russia and as a viable method of sustaining Ukrainian identity. Thus the Austrians were able to use Ukrainian dislike of the Russian government and insure their loyalty by making promises for greater political autonomy.

Already on July 27, 1914 Bishop Nykyta Budka, approached by the Austro-Hungarian consulate, echoed their appeal for the mobilization of all Austrian subjects against Serbia. Budka's "Pastoral Letter,"[7] addressed to all Ukrainians and printed in all the Ukrainian newspapers, provides ample proof of the Ukrainian intelligentsia's sympathies.

Criticism of Budka's position was heard immediately. John W. Dafoe, editor of the *Manitoba Free Press* and Budka's greatest opponent, viewed the statement as an instance of the jeopardizing by alien elements of the national security of Canada. At a time of war, a pluralistic society hampering national unity was detrimental. The Bishop's stand reinforced Dafoe's view that quick assimilation was imperative for all non-Anglo-Canadians:

> The episcopal proclamation of Bishop Budka is a striking manifestation of the danger that this country may become a land inhabited by different peoples, speaking foreign tongues and cherishing divergent national ideals.[8]

The Ukrainian social democrats contested both Budka's position and the right of the Austrian consulate to call upon all reservists to fight Serbia. As early as November 5, 1912, the Ukrainian social democrats in Canada and in Galicia had protested against Austrian intervention in the Balkans.[9] In the summer of 1914, Budka was seen as a "spineless, social parasite," all too eagerly responding to the beck and call of authority, all too willing to compromise principles.

> Only those Ukrainians will go who dream of an independent Ukraine; they will butcher the Serbs because they desire an independent Serbia. Ukrainians should remember — he who oppresses others is not worthy of his own freedom.[10]

The socialists were vehemently opposed to rearmament and war for the sake of furthering imperialist causes or defending capitalism, both of which were tools of oppression against the common man. *The Working People* was equally critical of Borden's allocation of $35 million for building war ships, and of the liberals' proposed naval policy.[11]

In spite of the socialists' position against capitalist warfare and their concern for the welfare of the labourer, the question of Ukrainian nationalism produced severe division among the ranks. The vocal leader of the socialists, Pavlo Krat, editor of *The Working People* and sympathizer with the Presbyterian Church, was responsible in part for disuniting the movement. Not only were his religious beliefs unacceptable but his support of the "Society for an Independent Ukraine" identified both the paper and the SD Party with Krat's schismatic position. The "Society" announced, much to the consternation of the RNWMP:

> Sons and daughters of Ukraine, here in these far away prairies, stir up your heart from its deep slumber, inflame your spirit, with your burning love for your forlorn fatherland. . . .

Down with the Czar! Organize into rifle associations! Through struggle
we will get our freedom![12]

Krat's impassioned rhetoric on the pages of *The Working People* — "out of
the flames of fire and blood, like the unvanquished Phoenix will rise a free
and independent Ukrainian republic from the river Sian to the Kuban"[13] —
advertising the "Society" was clearly seen as a substitute for the voice of the
branches of the Ukrainian Social Democratic Party.

Krat was on his way out, to be replaced by younger men, Matviy
(Matthew) Popowich and Ivan Navisivsky (John Navis), who fell under the
sway of Bolshevism. Still the social democrats would have to grapple with
the question of the Ukraine with or without Krat. Up to 1916, the socialists
contended that national consciousness was compatible with proletarian
internationalism, for the former did not obliterate the latter.[14] For the time
being, it was not by an imperialist war based upon political expediency, but
by revolution based on internal will power and strength of the Ukrainians
themselves.

> The fate of Ukraine rests in revolution. And he whose heart pains
> for our oppressed people, he who has not lowered himself to the ranks
> of the aristocratic mutt, let him stand in the ranks of the revolution
> against the entire black reaction. Let us lay our heads for Ukraine, for a
> democratic Ukraine, for land and freedom but not for our own
> hooligans and the Austrian bums![15]

Britain's declaration of war on Austria drastically altered the
Ukrainians' status in Canada, particularly in light of their Austrian
citizenship and Austrian sympathies. Bishop Budka quickly repudiated his
statements made in his "Pastoral Letter," realizing the possibility of
repercussions. His agility at switching allegiance showed the political
immaturity of the then Ukrainian mainstream in Canada. Soon thereafter,
numerous demonstrations of loyalty to the British Empire were staged by
Ukrainians on the prairies.[16]

The social democrats could hardly believe the Ukrainians' humbleness,
but above all Budka's opportunism. Intolerant of co-operation with any
power leading to compromise and promulgation of "tyranny," the social
democrats were most critical of Budka's action:

> Budka at first called upon Ukrainians to fight against Serbia and
> Russia. Now the same Budka turned the cat by its tail and is calling all
> to fight against Austria. The Winnipeg clerics, which at the Shevchenko
> celebrations wished for an independent Ukraine and the demise of
> Russia now are liberating Ukraine so that they can help Great Britain
> which is defending Russia. Alas! How they love their brother's hide and
> sell it to anyone they can.[17]

Yet, in spite of their righteousness, the socialists would become entangled in
matters of Ukrainian status, unable to decide whether Ukrainians should
seek total independence or become an autonomous state in the Russian
federation, or under Austria.

Despite Budka's recantation, neither he nor Ukrainians in general were
spared suspicion. After Canada entered the war, all persons of "enemy-

alien" birth or nationality or speaking an alien language were viewed as major threats to Canadian security and unity. The Canadian government identified Ukrainians from Galicia and Bukovina with the enemy, Austrians or Germans, even if they had been naturalized citizens of Canada. Strangely, the small number of Ukrainians from the Russian Empire were not considered dangerous, despite the fact that many of them were political refugees who had been involved in clandestine revolutionary activities. This position was temporary, however, for the existing standards collapsed once the Russian subjects became suspect, following the political upheaval commencing in February 1917.

Alongside numerous Orders-in-Council and the introduction of the "War Aliens' Act" (August 2, 1914), the first expression of impending repercussions upon the alien enemy was the "British Nationality and Status of Aliens Bill" (May 1914).[18] The purpose of the "Naturalization Act," as it was commonly called, was to establish uniform criteria for British nationality throughout the empire. For Ukrainians, the change in regulations was seen as a threat to their acceptance as Canadians and conjured visions of rejection.

The introduction of registration created much confusion. Many a Ukrainian farmer associating registration with police and military conscription in Austria, failed to comply with the regulation and was sent to an internment camp. About 1500 Ukrainians were interned during the war for failing to report for registration or to demonstrate their loyalty to the Allied cause.*

Incredible as it seemed to the social democrats, the "liberals" and the "right-wing conservatives" did not object to the restriction of movement imposed upon the Ukrainians, and their press urged its readers to comply with the wartime regulations. Perhaps they did not link the matter of registration with the all-enveloping question of alien status in Canada. One writer claimed that if Ukrainians were discriminated against, it was only because they deserved it; despite great potential, they were culturally inferior, and had to raise themselves beyond the level of the "stupid Galician."[19] The answer lay in confirming Ukrainian loyalty to Canada by emphasizing devotion to the country and by seeking education.

The social democrats did not believe in throwing laurel wreaths of thanks to Canada. To them Canada appeared as barbaric and despotic as the Russian Empire. They felt Canadian endorsement of Russia plus half-hearted and insincere guarantees of freedom made Canadian attestations of liberty and democracy a joke.

> As for Canada, the government appealed to us, guaranteed work and freedom from conscription. We fled from the tsarist detachments and the Austrian regiments, cursed the tsar and kaiser and made our way to the 'free' Canadian soil, to build with settlers from all the other nations

---

*The figure of 1500 Ukrainians interned was an estimate reached by members of the Ukrainian committee formed in Winnipeg by Fred J. Livesay to discuss the question of internment. See P.A.C., *Records of the Chief Press Censor*, R.G. 6 E 1, vol. 28 file 144C.

who had settled here, a single, mighty, new Canadian nation. And how
have we been received? . . . Why as 'enemies of the Empire.' . . . Having
entered into an alliance with Russia, the Canadian government has
become an accomplice of the Russian Black Hundred gangs.[20]

There was little thought given on the part of the average Ukrainian as
to why he was termed an "enemy" and why this led to abuse and
discrimination. But the effects of hostility were evident and this was at the
base of the Ukrainians' distress. In some cases the internee had not realized
that his lack of knowledge of English had been the reason for his sudden
arrival at the camps. Upon being asked whether he was pro-German, the
Ukrainian thought "pro" was a short form of the Ukrainian word "proty,"
meaning "against," and answered in the affirmative. Regardless of the
reasons for internment, the plight of the internee was even more deplorable
once it became evident that no provisions existed for appeal. One internee
only seeing his own misery gave vent to his helplessness and bitterness in
this sweeping generalization:

> . . . who levelled the mountains from sea to sea? . . . who built the
> railroads and cultivated this wasteland where formerly only the wind
> howled? We, the victims, who today are being tortured in a manner
> reminiscent of the Christian captives held by the Turks 500 years ago
> . . . make our case known so that all Ukrainians and all the nations of
> the world may see how the blind, "civilized", English chauvinists and
> their Canadian hangers-on treat foreigners.[21]

From August 1914 to June 1915, the Ukrainian newspapers regularly
printed items on the political and economic conditions in Western Ukraine
and to a lesser degree in Eastern Ukraine. News was obtained from
newspapers and contacts in the Ukraine and the United States. Translations
from local Canadian newspapers were also reprinted. Needless to say,
information about the war, particularly on the eastern front, was scarce and
vague. There were many complaints about the lack of news, inconsistencies
of the reports and indulgence in hypothesizing. By 1914, in order to boost
the nationalist spirit among Ukrainians in Canada, their newspapers had
printed instalments on the general history of the Ukraine, on the
exploitations of the Muscovites, on the rise of Ukrainian political
consciousness, and also excerpts from books by social critics Ivan Franko,
Vasyl Stefanyk, and Mykhailo Pawlyk were published.

By mid-1915, reaction towards the "alien" in Canada reached its
zenith, only to be sharpened by the red scare in 1918 and 1919. In
particular, newspapers printing in an "alien" language appeared as a threat
to Canadian solidarity, supposedly carrying news of a disloyal nature. The
need to institute conformity in audio-visual communications was met on
June 10, 1915 (Order-in-Council, P.C. #1330). Censorship remained in
effect until January 1, 1920 (Order-in-Council, P.C. #2465).[22]

The belief that some alien residents in Canada were involved in
conspiratorial action and presented a serious threat to Canadian stability
has become a recorded fact. For this particular purpose, the office of press
censorship was established to work in the capacity of a "watch-dog." In the

case of Ukrainians in western Canada, there is sufficient evidence to prove that the main issues which concerned the majority of them — namely, Ukrainian independence and the maintenance of bilingual schools — were categorized by the censors under the same rubric. The advocacy of Austrian co-operation by the "right wing" and the "liberals" to obtain Ukrainian independence and the public assertion of Ukrainian language rights were seen by the censors as instances of excessive Catholic power, and of the incitement of ignorant Ukrainians to conspire and threaten Canadian strength and unity.[23]

Ukrainian hatred of Russia was not permissible perhaps because it reflected negatively on the good judgement of the leaders of Great Britain. With the imposition of censorship, criticism of Russia in the Ukrainian press was curtailed but not eliminated. On the issue of Russian autocratic domination, Ukrainians were practically unanimous. The Ukrainian editors tried to justify their anti-Russian articles but in the final analysis were forced to remain silent. The Russian question solved itself with the outburst of revolutionary unrest in March 1917. By October 1917 the Canadian government sided with the politically "moderate" Ukrainians on the Russian matter; the Ukrainians, however, were still viewed on other matters as enemy aliens.

At the time when Ukrainian reactions to the war were being tested, the question of bilingual schools added another dimension to the problem. Furthermore, the question of Ukrainian nationalism in the process of being decided upon in Europe and supported in principle by Ukrainians on the prairies came to be reinforced by the presence of the bilingual schools issue.

From its founding in 1910, the *Ukrainian Voice* had as its purpose "to educate Ukrainian people in Canada about political, economic and social conditions which affect them."[24] Founded mainly by young, idealistic teachers educated at the Ruthenian Training School in Winnipeg (1905-1907) and Brandon (1907-16), the self-imposed although readily accepted leaders became a crucial element in the Ukrainian community. They filled the vacuum created by the absence of the Ukrainian Catholic clergy who in Western Ukraine had exerted a great influence and held the positions of leadership.

Yet leadership in itself was inadequate. The effective mobilization of a powerful community commanding respect required an educated base. For this reason, article upon article called on Ukrainians to study and to prepare themselves to take the reins of leadership.[25]

The Ukrainians had taken advantage of legislative grants to operate their own language schools. By granting concessions to the Ukrainians in education, the Conservative party in Manitoba was able to manipulate the Ukrainian vote.[26] Both the *Ukrainian Voice* and the *Canadian Ruthenian* carried reports on school activities and various teachers' congresses to emphasize the need for active and positive interest in bilingual education.

However, not all Ukrainian newspapers were in favour of supporting the school issue. *The Working People* was in favour of language retention but contended that the rectification of the economic position of labourers was more pressing.[27] When the matter went before the legislature, however, the socialists supported the school issue. Adamant in its opposition to bilingual schools was the *Canadian Farmer*, which toed the line laid down by the liberals.

By 1914, particularly in view of the alien threat and the need to Canadianize the foreigner, the Liberal party accelerated its attempts to consolidate its hold in Manitoba and to curtail multilingual instruction. The victory of the Manitoba Liberal party in 1915 enabled them to abolish the bilingual schools, but not before Ukrainians, the French and Poles raised opposition.

A peculiar twist was given to the school question. For many an Anglo-Canadian, the language struggle was ample proof of conspiratorial activities among the aliens. The agitation which arose over this issue augmented the likelihood of alien threat to the point that the existence of "a danger to national security" was claimed.[28] This could result, it was maintained, in the internment of Bishop Budka, alleged to be a spy for the Austrian army, and in the suppression of the *Ukrainian Voice*.[29]

Both the *Ukrainian Voice* and the *Canadian Ruthenian* led a vigorous campaign against the attacks on the bilingual school system. The chief spokesman for the *Ukrainian Voice* was T. Ferley, the MLA for Gimli, who was particularly vocal on this issue in the Manitoba legislature. Bishop Budka was already under suspicion for his support of the Austrian war effort. His loyalty had been in doubt since August 1914, and his advocacy of bilingualism seemed to reinforce the views of the *Manitoba Free Press* and the Orangemen that it was his religious beliefs which were at the root of his views on the school issue. Understandably, there is little evidence, indeed, in the *Canadian Ruthenian* that would substantiate such accusations. Budka, it would appear, separated his quest for consolidating his position among Ukrainian Catholics from his support of the school issue. Yet Budka's stance did not mean, of course, his disavowal of the abolition of bilingual schools as an attempt by the Protestants to assimilate Ukrainians.

Soon the suspicion of disloyalty towards the war effort was associated with those who supported bilingualism. The newspapers do not clarify the reason for the entanglement of religion and loyalty with bilingualism; rather, they show the scope and the complexity of the matter.

From the pages of the *Canadian Ruthenian* and the *Ukrainian Voice*, a challenge was launched based on the premise that every individual possessed innate legal and natural rights, as guaranteed by the British legal tradition. Indeed, the years of the experiencing of the superiority of Canadian political and social institutions espousing Canada's great and promising future had left an effect upon the Ukrainian elite. The "moderates" ("liberal" and Catholic) viewed the drive towards fulfilling the Canadian dream, rounded off and molded to perfection in the malleable

West, as a plausible process. Furthermore, strongly adhering to this principle, the "moderate" Ukrainians contended that they were a necessary and integral part of this development. It was precisely this belief and the actions to support it that weakened the Ukrainian method of attack, making it ineffective. By joining in the emphasis of the dominant theme of realizing the Canadian vision, the Ukrainians proved to the Anglo-Canadian that quick assimilation was feasible and necessary.

It was the socialist press which stood to raise the challenge from a different perspective. It demanded the curtailment of the process of asking for, and providing proofs of, Ukrainian integrity and visible gratefulness. It asserted that Ukrainians had nothing for which to be thankful. What few benefits they had received, they had more than repaid. They were urged not to spend their time and energy defending their rights, but to direct their assault at the bigotry underlying the social and political system. One's rights were synonymous with obligations. Surely Canada had an obligation to its citizens.[30]

In a final futile protest, the editors portrayed the schools question as a continued struggle by Ukrainians against intolerance and oppression which had existed in Europe and which they had not escaped in Canada.[31] The Ukrainians were a strong people, who had successfully withstood the Tartars, Muscovites, Poles, Turks and Germans.[32] Canada would not overwhelm them with the abolition of the bilingual school system. It was alleged that

> The abolition of our schools is a trick of the "Canadians" to engulf us. Should they succeed they would go farther on; that is to say, they would forbid us to read our own newspapers and books; they would molest us by sending to our farms their female importuners to Canadianize our children by forcing us to accept in our churches the Protestant "preachers"; to give ... money to the "Salvation Army" or to the YMCA for the upkeep of Protestant "Sunday schools" and for every kind of political and sectarian fund, and we, being so laden with all these burdens, will not see the sun and will become foreign beasts of burden.[33]

Once the heat from the bilingual schools question had abated, Ukrainians rose in protest over the implementation of conscription in 1917, an issue tied strongly to the electoral status of enemy aliens. The once sympathetic conservatives were jeered on the pages of the Ukrainian press[34] for their "sleaziness" and "backhandedness" for switching allegiance and leading the campaign to disenfranchise enemy aliens. Ukrainians were left fuming but convinced that indeed the Canadian government was working for the interest of the well-to-do class who could profit from investing their money in the war Victory Loans at 3 per cent annually.[35] Having prophesied the institution of conscription, *The Working People* stressed that the Prime Minister's promise to Great Britain, shallow as it was, overrode concerns at home.[36] Canada was in the midst of grave economic difficulties.

The rising wave of discrimination against Ukrainians peaked with the verbal and physical assault of the Orangemen and war veterans supporting the conscription of labour and the internment of all "laggards and vagrants." Why should the foreign-born labourer receive higher wages while the Canadian soldier was risking his life overseas for a mere $1.10 per day.[37]

The situation on the home front was not promising. The revolution in Russia further complicated the issue of aliens. Pandemonium seemed to reign as frantic officials tried to grapple with the dire problem which was, to a large extent, a creation of their own imagination.

As of September 25, 1918, publications in enemy languages were banned. The law was modified, however, since special provisions by the Secretary of State allowed for the publication of the same matter in parallel columns, one being in English.[38] *The Working People,* because of its socialist bias, was banned. The regulation was removed for Ukrainian publication on April 9, 1919 in view of the fact that the Paris Peace Conference recognized the independence of the Ukrainian Republic.[39] Nor could Ukrainians be regarded any longer as enemy aliens.

Hostile attitudes towards Ukrainians in Canada did not seem to interfere with their growing interest in the fate of Western and Eastern Ukraine. The series of events which led finally on January 22, 1919 to the unification of the Ukrainian National Republic (established in November 1917) with the Western Ukrainian National Republic (established in November 1918), capitalized on political conditions and common sentiment and occurred in a spontaneous fashion. The chronology of events in both territories published in all Ukrainian newspapers on the Prairies owing to the inconsistency and vagueness of the accounts cannot be established. Blame can be placed partly on Canadian censorship regulations but even more on the lack of information.

The news of the outbreak of the Russian Revolution in March 1917 — an event which made possible the establishment of a Ukrainian government in Kiev — was received enthusiastically not only in Western Ukraine (still subordinate to Austria) but also in Canada. With the proclamation of the Ukrainian National Republic, momentum accelerated for unification with the western lands. The Ukrainians on the prairies urged the creation of one united country. The press stressed the determination of all Ukrainians not to be satisfied until unification had been achieved.

Problems immediately arose with the revolution. The central *Rada* (Committee) which negotiated with the Provisional Government in Petrograd for more rights for Eastern Ukraine was unable to maintain control once Lenin seized power on November 7, 1917. Criticism was voiced in all Ukrainian newspapers on the conclusion and terms of the Treaty of Brest-Litovsk (February 8, 1918) between the *Rada,* the Soviet delegation and the Central Power. The signing of the Treaty not only led to the recognition of the Ukraine but also allowed for German intervention against the Bolshevik invasion. Kiev was liberated on March 1, 1918. The

Canadian Ruthenian and the *Ukrainian Voice* supported the action of the *Rada* while *The Working People* condemned the *Rada* for their attitude toward the Bolsheviks and particularly for the separate peace treaty. The transfer of power to the Germans was seen by the paper as favouring capitalism and militarism.[40]

The end of the war and the subsequent fall of the Austrian Empire allowed for the formation of the Western Ukrainian National Republic (November 1918) in Galicia and Bukovina, where agitation for greater political rights had increased since 1914. Simultaneously, war broke out between Poland and the Republic. Yet the move towards unification was initiated, in spite of the numerous counter-forces discouraging it. The complexities of political negotiations and development need not be elaborated. What is of major importance is how Ukrainians on the Prairies reacted towards unification once the process was initiated.

Up to November 1918, Ukrainians did not have a co-ordinating body of all groups. In order to achieve a semblance of unity at a time of urgency, the Ukrainian Canadian Citizen's League was founded in Winnipeg. The League, however, was never able to act as a united body. Regardless of this fact, two delegates were chosen for the purpose of representation at the Paris Peace Conference. Here the fate of the Ukraine would be decided and Ukrainians on the prairies contended that they must become involved. The significance of 1919 to the press lay in the forecast of the ebbing of the tide of hostility in Canada and in Europe against Ukrainians. Indeed, the 1920s were to be a time of reconciliation, but to be tested by the onslaught of the Great Depression.

Conclusions

The activities of the Ukrainian elite during the war years would be misunderstood if their concern for the creation of a prosperous and harmonious Prairie society were underestimated or overlooked. There was just as little disagreement among them as among other Canadians that the establishment of a firm economic base was a necessary component in realizing the Canadian dream by building a unified nation. These common goals represented by the entrepreneur, evangelist and politician spurred men to action. Initially, social repercussions generated from rapid industrialization and haphazard settlement were few, and the Ukrainians responded with readiness, in general, to the call for the building up of Canada. Even their leaders rarely objected to this endeavour. However, once attention was diverted from economic concerns, the problem of how to deal with socio-cultural tensions began to loom large.

Confrontation with the problem of cultural heterogeneity would inevitably lead to political fermentation. Discussion, in most cases extremely strained, failed to lead to significant understanding among various cultural groups. During the war years, government controls had been imposed to contain dissent rather than alleviate tension and eradicate areas of contention. Sophistication was lacking in the political apparatus to perceive problems, to analyze their origins and propose rational solutions. The announcement of war had caught the Canadian government totally unprepared to deal either with the international malaise or with domestic concerns. On many occasions the governing bodies shirked responsibility and hoped time would resolve the problems.

The Ukrainian leadership was not familiar with the art of political finesse. According to our survey of their press the leaders lacked insight on such matters as the long-standing racial and religious conflict in Canada and seemed incapable of perceiving the problems of the Ukrainians within a broader spectrum. Consequently, owing to their insufficient understanding of the underlying reasons for social tension the leadership tended to refuse overtures to compromise as the method for achieving unity within the Canadian framework. It was not that they were incapable of compromise; rather, the available course appeared from their perspective to tip the balance unduly in favour of the Anglo-Canadian at their expense. For example, the schools issue as fought on the pages of the Ukrainian press was based on a hard line policy — that cultural survival was dependent on language rights. No compromise could exist on this issue. By contending that cultural development was an innate right, the object of compromise was obscured. Obstinacy led to further tensions.

On the issue of Ukrainian culture and political independence, the leadership was capable of compromise — first supporting Austria and then Great Britain. Such action did not mean that their views had altered considerably; rather, being caught in an extremely difficult position, the leadership was forced to choose the most expedient route leading, so it seemed to them, to long term benefits. No doubt political immaturity lay at the base of such actions, but they went to prove the existence of a dilemma indicative of the Ukrainians' insecure position on the Prairies. Inability to find an acceptable solution to this issue resulted in hesitancy and vacillation, with consequent dissatisfaction to all.

The experience of the Ukrainians during the war years was similar to that of other Central and Eastern Europeans classified as "enemy aliens." The inability of the governing body to deal effectively with sensitive domestic issues stemmed from its overwhelming concern for security and a successful war effort. Soon it became glaringly apparent that the Canadian bureaucracy and military apparatus lacked, to a large degree, the expertise and sensitivity essential for dealing with delicate domestic problems. The imposition of censorship was intrinsically connected with the question of loyalty. The conflict between clashing loyalties for the Ukrainian and some other Central Eastern European Canadians was exacerbated by the war measures. On the other hand, the introduction of censorship and other measures of safety with concomitant hardships for some groups of people proved simply inevitable for the government under the extraordinary circumstances of world-wide war. However, the resulting human suffering and anxiety left, in many cases, psychic scars and ethno-cultural tensions in their wake and contributed to subsequent demands for the re-evaluation of Canada's relationship to the Empire.

FOOTNOTES

[1] *Ukrainian Voice* (hereafter *U.V.*), April 13, 1910, 5. The purpose of the *Ukrainian Voice* in 1914 remained as it had been when the paper was launched in 1910 — "to free the people from the bonds of darkness, to spread self-consciousness among the masses of our people and to defend our rights in this vast country.. .." *U.V.*, January 7, 1914, 3. For this purpose the paper increased its size from eight to twelve pages.
The *Canadian Ruthenian* (hereafter *C.R.*), much more conservative than the *Ukrainian Voice* and more concerned with the religious question than any other, adhered to "the preservation of the Greek [Ukrainian] Catholic faith, the propagation of our language and literature and the founding of our churches, schools and societies.. .." *C.R.*, May 27, 1911, 2.

[2] *U.V.*, January 21, 1914, 4.

[3] *Ibid.*

[4] *Ibid.*, February 18, 1914, 1.

[5] See *U.V.*, March 29, 1911; January 5, 1912; October 30, 1912; April 29, 1914.

[6] Volodymyr Kubijovic, ed., *Ukraine: A Concise Encyclopedia* (Toronto, 1963) I, 698-706.

[7] See *C.R.*, August 1, 1914, 1 and *U.V.*, August 5, 1914, 1. A copy of the letter is also found in the Chief Press Censors Records. See Public Archives of Canada, Secretary of State, *Chief Press Censor*, 1915-20, RG 6 E1, Vol. 28, file 144-F.

[8] *Manitoba Free Press*, August 5, 1914, editorial cited by D. H. Avery, "Canadian Immigration Policy and the Enemy Alien, 1896-1919: the Anglo-Canadian Perspective," unpublished Ph.D. thesis, University of Western Ontario (London, 1973), 379.

[9] *The Working People*, December 4, 1912, 1. Hereafter *WP*.

[10] *Ibid.*, August 12, 1914, 1.

[11] *Ibid.*, January 8, 1913, editorial.

[12] P.A.C. *Borden Papers*, MG 26H 106235.

[13] *W.P.* September 9, 1914, 2.

[14] *Ibid.*, November 19, 1914,2.

[15] *Ibid.*, November 25, 1915, 2, editorial.

[16] *C.R.*, August 8, 1914, 1; *U.V.*, August 12, 1914, 4 and September 16, 1914, 1. Newspaper clipping found in *Chief Press Censor*, RE 6 E 1, vol. 28, file 144C. No title.

[17] *W.P.*, August 12, 1914, 1. See also August 26, 1914, 4.

[18] *U.V.*, July 10, 1914, 6. The "British Nationality and Status of Aliens Bill" (May 1914) repudiated the law of 1868. New provisions were introduced for a uniform procedure throughout the Empire, a five-year residence requirement instead of three, the transferral of administering naturalization from individual judges to the Secretary of State in Ottawa.

[19] *U.V.*, December 2, 1914, 4.

[20] *W.P.*, May 5, 1915.

[21] *Ibid.*, August 28, 1915. Nevertheless, credit must be given to the Censors for not having suppressed this statement, despite the heated atmosphere caused by the war.

[22] Peter Rider, "The Administrative Policy of the Chief Press Censor for Canada," unpublished honours essay, Carleton University, Ottawa, 1966, 4.

[23] *Chief Press Censor*, vol. 43 file 196-1. Livesay to E. J. Boag, Press censor, April 7, 1916. See also, *Department of National Defense*, vol. 2847 HQC 3281. Chambers to Assistant director of military intelligence; final report, March 31, 1920, 99. Acute consternation was raised in the censorship office by the participation of Ukrainians from Canada at the First Ukrainian Congress in New York (October 1915), where it was resolved to support the Central Powers. It should be noted, however, that the proclaiming of an independent Poland with jurisdiction over Galicia in November 1916 by Germany and Austria created strong opposition among Ukrainians. The General Ukrainian Council *(Rada)* discontinued its action and support of both Germany and Austria.

[24] *U.V.*, March 16, 1910, editorial, 4.

[25] *Ibid.*, August 26, 1914, 4.

[26] See Cornelius Jaenen, "Ruthenian Schools in Western Canada, 1897-1919," *Paedogogica Historica*, 10 (1970), 517-41.

[27] *W.P.*, October 23, 1912 and March 5, 1913, editorial.

[28] *Chief Press Censor*, vol. 27 file 144-A-1, Chambers to Livesay, January 3, 1916.

[29] *Ibid.*, vol. 43 file 196-1.

[30] *W.P.*, September 5, 1917, 2 and *U.V.*, April 4, 1916, 6.

[31] *C.R.*, March 17, 1915.

[32] *Ibid.*, February 23, 1916.

[33] *Chief Press Censor*, vol. 28 file 144-C. Editorial in *Manitoba Free Press*, June 20, 1916, 9.

[34] *C.R.*, see October 1917 issues.

[35] *W.P.,* March 9, 1917, 2, editorial.
[36] *Ibid.,* May 23, 1917, 2, editorial.
[37] *C.R.,* April 3, 1918 and May 1, 1918, 4.
[38] *Borden Papers,* MG 26, vol. 92, no. 48164. Borden to P. H. Woycenko, October 28, 1918.
[39] *C.R.,* March 21, 1919, 1.
[40] See separate issues of all three newspapers for March and April, 1918.

THE RESURGENCE OF CULTURAL PLURALISM AND THE PROBLEM OF THE NATION-STATE: LORD ACTON REVISITED

JOEL NOVEK
UNIVERSITY OF WINNIPEG

The Relevance of Lord Acton's Thinking

More than a century has passed since Lord Acton first published his celebrated essay on the national question in 1862.[1] Despite the Victorian style and dense elliptical phrases, the essay retains a contemporary ring for anyone concerned with the evident resurgence in ethnic and cultural pluralism in Canada and other industrialized nations these last few years. Perhaps more than any other Victorian writer, Acton championed the cause of those states formed through a political union of two or more national or cultural groups. He argued that the unity in diversity resulting from the combination of two or more nationalities is a superior principle of political organization to the virulent nationalism which accords citizenship rights only on the basis of membership in a particular national or cultural group:

> The coexistence of several nations under the same state is a test, as well as the best security of its freedom. It is also one of the chief instruments of civilization; and as such, it is in the natural and providential order, and indicates a state of greater advancement than the national unity which is the ideal of modern liberalism.[2]

The idea of judging a political state by the degree of tolerance and autonomy it extends to its constituent ethnic and cultural communities is well in line with the recent policies pursued by many French-Canadian, native and "third-force" groups in Canada. Lord Acton's use of the word "nation" would be especially pleasing to those French-Canadians and natives who claim national status within (or outside of) the larger Canadian Confederation. Likewise, they would be cheered by his rejection of the modern nation-state which made entry into the political community conditional on membership in a single dominant ethnic or cultural group. He feared that the denial of political rights to minority cultures would open the way for their oppression or absorption at the hands of an aggressive majority backed by the full power of the state.

> By making the State and the nation commensurate with each other in history, it [the nation-state] reduces practically to a subject condition all other nationalities that may be within the boundary. It cannot admit them to an equality within the ruling nation which constitutes the State, because the State would then cease to be national, which would be a contradiction of the principle of its existence. According, therefore, to the degree of humanity and civilization in that dominant body which

claims all the rights of the community, the inferior races are exterminated, or reduced to servitude, or outlawed, or put in a condition of dependence.[3]

There is something arresting in the prophetic accuracy of these words which so clearly anticipate the oppressive and even genocidal activities of the late nineteenth and twentieth centuries. Indeed, the last sentence could serve as a most apt description of the sorry history of the Canadian native peoples. Yet Lord Acton's clear prophecies and reasoned judgment appeared to have little impact in his own day, which witnessed the decay of old culturally plural empires throughout Europe and the rise of nation-states in France, Italy and Germany. Later on, the Austro-Hungarian Empire would be dismembered and the new states of Austria, Hungary and Czechoslovakia created.

In the United States, a new culture, assimilating and expansionist, was pushing inexorably across the continent to the detriment of the many indigenous cultures it overwhelmed. To the north, a newly activated English-Canadian nation was also moving west at the expense of native, Metis and French-Canadian groups previously established in the prairie region. The reasons for the rise of the nation-state and the flight from cultural pluralism lay in the profound social and economic changes sweeping Europe and North America during the nineteenth century, and it is to these that we must turn.

The Promise of the Nation-State: Lord Acton Rejected

The rise of the nation-state at the expense of cultural pluralism within its frontiers was aided by four distinct but interrelated factors arising out of both the Industrial and French Revolutions and providing the impetus for major changes in Western societies. These four factors consisted of two structural factors of great importance — the development of capitalist industrialization and the growth of state bureaucracies — as well as two concomitant ideological factors also of major significance — the spread of both liberalism and socialism. The effects of each of these factors will now be briefly examined.

Capitalist industrialization and the spread of the market economy[4] played a key role in aiding and abetting the emergence of major nation-states in Europe and North America. Industrialization brought a new and aggressive class of capitalists to power, often at the expense of local aristocracies or regional, tribal or clan authorities. These new economic managers fostered change, strove toward national unification and worked to smooth over local customs and traditions.[5] The tentacles of the market economy grew rapidly outward from a metropolitan centre to incorporate various regional, colonial and ethnic minorities into one burgeoning economic system.[6] Thus the fur trade played a leading role in the early process of nation-building in Canada by establishing an economic system in which English settlers, French settlers and native people could all participate in the same enterprise. Later on, a transcontinental railway and the prairie wheat economy would prove decisive in establishing Confederation.

Industrialization and the market economy also helped to disrupt traditional relationships based on feudal ties and replace them with new ties based on purely economic power or the "cash nexus." Other related consequences were an increase in social mobility at the expense of regional or group ties and a rapid increase in urbanization. A trend toward centralization, standardization and homogeneity resulted from the emergence of mass education, mass consumer markets and, eventually, mass communications.[7] Such a "great transformation" of all aspects of economic life served to establish the economic infrastructure in which the modern nation-state could develop.

The replacement of old ties of community and locality by new ones based on economic power and the marketplace was both widely noted and decried by the sociologists of the time. In the Communist Manifesto, for example, Karl Marx argued that capitalism

> has put an end to all feudal, patriarchal, idyllic relations . . . ; it has drowned the most heavenly ecstasies of religious fervor, of chivalrous enthusiasm, of philistine sentimentalism in the icy waters of egotistical calculation. . . ."[8]

Other more conservative sociologists worried about the erosion of the primary ties of family and community and their replacement by structures more impersonal, more alienating and less satisfying to the individual. Tonnies outlined the transition from *Gemeinschaft* to *Gesellschaft* in pessimistic terms. Durkheim wrote about the change from simple mechanical solidarity to more complex organic solidarity and expressed concern about the degree of *anomie* or normlessness found in the latter type of society. Perhaps the most pessimistic sociologist of all, Max Weber, agonized over the rationalization and disenchantment of the modern world.

It is instructive to note that while these sociologists expressed grave concern over the effects of the transition to the modern nation-state, few if any felt that a reversal of these changes was possible. Indeed, so pervasive was the belief in the inevitability of the transition from simple to complex forms of social life that it remains a powerful dominant image or domain assumption[9] of modern sociology.

A second and related factor in the rise of the nation-state was the emergence of the modern centralized government bureaucracy. In early modern Europe, both the English and French monarchies encouraged the growth of the state bureaucracy at the expense of feudal lords and regional authorities.[10] During the Industrial Revolution the growth of government activity was clearly related to burgeoning capitalist industrialization. One of the major tasks of government during the early period of industrialization was to build up the infrastructure necessary to make industrialization possible. Government provided defence and security for industrial development, lent or guaranteed money to entrepreneurs, and charter companies, and overrode opposition to new developments. As industrialization progressed, government was called upon to supply or subsidize an expanding number of services to sustain continued growth. These included transportation and communications, educational and vocational training, energy supplies and research activity.

Finally, in situations of advanced industrialization the state began to furnish a growing number of welfare services in order to mitigate the negative effects of fluctuating and turbulent industrial expansion. These services included unemployment insurance, old age pensions and workmen's compensation. Also important was the massive volume of regulations concerning hours and conditions of work, minimum wage levels and consumer protection. The effect of all this was to shift the responsibility for social welfare and individual protection from local communities, kinship and ethnic groups to the state, which spawned a huge bureaucracy to meet all these services. Inevitably, local communities, kinship and ethnic groups suffered a corresponding decline in authority and autonomy.

As Akzin states, "The groups that are most directly interested in a state-wide ethnic integration of the inhabitants are the groups personally connected with the state machinery in a dominant capacity ". . . [and] successful integration means . . . the strengthening of the state for whatever tasks may be set to it."[11] This process can be seen in Canada where many ethnic groups have entered into client relationships with the federal government. Indeed, so pervasive is the federal control over native communities that a good definition of a status Indian is an individual involved in an official relationship with the Indian Affairs Branch of the Department of Indian Affairs and Northern Development.

In addition to the effects of industrialization and the growth of government, the rise of the nation-state was aided by two ideologies which focused attention on the central government at the expense of regional, ethnic or kinship loyalties. Liberalism is often associated with both a market economy and political democracy. Liberalism tends to view the individual as a rational and solitary being, a citizen, free of all family, ethnic and religious ties, owing his loyalty solely to the political state.[12] Glazer and Moynihan have argued that liberal ideology becomes transformed into

> the expectation that the kinds of features which distinguish one group from another would inevitably lose their weight and sharpness in modern and modernizing societies, that there would be increasing emphasis on achievement rather than ascription, that common systems of education and communications would wipe out group differences, that nationally uniform economic and political systems would have the same effect.[13]

The liberal expectancy anticipates that the individual will free himself from the primordial and irrational ties of the old social order to play a new role as a citizen in a democratic polity.

In the twentieth century the liberal ideology has come under increasing attack from a second ideology, that of socialism. The increasing influence of socialist ideology is related, both as consequence and as cause, to the growing role of the state in the economy and social welfare. Like liberalism, socialism anticipates the erosion of primordial family, ethnic, and religious ties among men.[14] Unlike liberalism, socialism looks to social class and economic interest, rather than individual free choice, as the prime motive force in political history. Glazer and Moynihan argue that socialism represents a radical expectancy "that class would become the main line of division between people, erasing the earlier lines of tribe, language, religion, national origin, and that these class divisions would themselves, after the Revolution disappear."[15] Thus socialism anticipates a society in which men's chief ties would be formed in the political and economic arenas, with all other ties secondary.

The influence of the preceding four factors on the rise of the nation-state did not occur in any mechanical or inevitable way. Rather, each of these factors inspired a set of popular expectations — a promise, really — that the transformations which were occurring and their eventual realization would be both positive and beneficial. The promise of industrialization was the belief that industrialization would result in new and unprecedented levels of wealth, comfort and material progress. The growth in the scope of government activity was largely based on the promise of social justice through political solutions to complex social and economic problems. Liberalism promised the extension of political democracy, legal equality and civil rights to all citizens. Finally, socialism promised a radical collectivism, a levelling of inherited differences and, perhaps most enticing of all, a sense of purpose and commitment in life.

Together, these expectations constituted the promise of the nation-state, for the growth of nation-states was bound up, at least to some extent with a popular belief that they would be more prosperous, more just, more egalitarian and more purposeful than previous forms of political organization. In short, there was a belief that the nation-state would be able to deliver on its promises, the very promises which the emerging nation-state itself had come to inspire among its citizens. In the euphoria over expanding economic development and political centralization, the glowing promise of the modern nation-state easily outshone Lord Acton's warnings about its inherent contradictions and instability.

The Problem of the Nation State: A Reprieve for Lord Acton?

Today industrialization, state bureaucracies, liberalism and, especially, socialism have developed to an unprecedented degree and spread throughout many parts of the world. The promises associated with these trends have likewise spread to become an integral part of the modern age. "Nevertheless," as Lloyd Fallers has indicated, "today the nation-state is in trouble virtually everywhere."[16] The mounting problems facing nation-states are not confined to the poly-ethnic societies of North America nor to the emerging states of the third world. We are all aware of the tensions in our own society between English and French, European and native, citizen and immigrant. What is truly remarkable is the upsurge in cultural pluralism and the challenge to centralized authority in Great Britain, Spain, France and other nations formerly thought to be relatively homogeneous.

The problems faced by modern nation states in maintaining cultural unity and centralized political authority are too evident and too widespread to be attributed purely to local issues or unique cases. The evidence points to some aspect of the structure and development of nation-states which is itself problematic. In my view, a key problem of modern nation-states has been their failure to deliver on their promises. The same promises which played such a major role in establishing modern nation-states now stand in the way of their consolidation.

Industrialization and technological development promised universal prosperity. However, the uneven and inequitable outcome of those processes has seriously undermined that claim. Not only has industrialization failed to dissolve ethnic and cultural divisions,[17] but in many cases it has actually increased them. The industrialization of Quebec did not terminate the existence of a separate French-speaking society in North America. Instead, ethnic differences became compounded by class differences as French-speaking workers found themselves confronting a largely English-speaking management. Scottish nationalism has been greatly exacerbated by the uneven pattern of industrial development in Great Britain, with the technologically stagnant heavy industries of Scotland languishing in contrast to the more dynamic light manufacturing and service industries of southern England. The North Sea oil potential has only stiffened Scottish resolve for greater autonomy.

The march of advanced extractive and pipeline technology in the Canadian north has heightened the militancy of native people and led to demands for greater cultural and political autonomy. Indeed, the relationship between cultural pluralism and economic inequality has become so marked that Glazer and Moynihan now argue that the ethnic group has largely come to behave as an economic interest group.[18] However, the growing relationship between ethnicity and economic interest is not merely the result of the failure of industrialization to eradicate ethnic differences. It is also the result of the failure of the other three key promises associated with the modern nation-state.

The growth of centralized state bureaucracies promised social justice through political solutions to social problems. However, these solutions have not been forthcoming and the political solution has, in many cases, become the political illusion.[19] The federal government's costly bilingualism programs have not significantly altered the basic cleavages between French and English Canada and have been pursued at the cost of considerable opposition in English Canada, especially in the western provinces. There are few more monumental failures than the federal government's policy toward native people. Over one hundred years of administration of Indian affairs by Ottawa has resulted in widespread poverty, dependency, alcoholism and alienation. Native people are increasingly frustrated by bureaucratic delays and lack of control of their own communities.

Outside Canada the picture is much the same. We have only to examine the failure of American anti-poverty programs in the black ghettos or the ineptitude of British policy in Northern Ireland to see a similar pattern emerge. Given such results, it is little wonder that modern nation-states have great difficulty retaining the loyalty of ethnic minorities who are so often forced to fall back on their own resources in defence of their interests.

The broken promises and failed hopes associated with industrialization and political centralization have also been the fate of such ideologies as liberalism and socialism. Liberalism promised universalism and democracy, but the two concepts were often contradictory and their union problematic. There is no necessary connection between political democracy and universal rights, and majorities soon learned to use democratic methods to subjugate minorities. Thus, English-speaking majorities in various parts of Canada have used their voting strength to deny educational rights to French-Canadians who are trying to do the same thing in Quebec where they are the majority. Native people who, until recently, were denied the franchise have been almost completely at the mercy of the electoral process. Far from fostering universalism, democratic politics have proven highly amenable to ethnic bloc voting and the maintenance of pluralism.

Despite expectations to the contrary, socialism has likewise proven unable to dissolve ethnic differences and replace them with new forms of affiliation based on class interest and collective action. Early calls for international proletarian unity have been tempered by a more pragmatic strategy which implicitly recognizes group differences. The principle of "National liberation" has been put forward as one which attempts to embrace aspirations for both nationalism and socialism. Mature state socialist societies like the Soviet Union have attempted to allocate resources among contending ethnic groups, pursuing punitive policies against some, such as Jews, while consolidating the position of the Russian-speaking majority.

The failure of liberalism and socialism to eradicate ethnic pluralism is by no means a historical accident. What proponents of both ideologies did not realize was that both are based on the assumption of common sentiments and values and a common cultural and political community which are the preconditions for either democratic civility or socialist collectivization. When cultural pluralism prevails, the achievement of either democracy or socialism is rendered that much more difficult. It is instructive to note that the one nation, Sweden, which has most successfully combined the principles of both democracy and socialism is also among the most culturally homogeneous of all advanced industrial societies.

The failures associated with industrialization, political centralization, liberalism and socialism have vindicated Lord Acton's warnings on the essentially problematic nature of modern nation-states. The problems are deep and serious but nation-states are still too strong and the pressures toward centralization too great for them to be easily dismembered. More likely, growing countertrends against centralized power will emerge in the near future, perhaps along Actonian lines stressing cultural pluralism and political decentralization. In the field of industrialization and technological development, this would mean heightened local initiative in determining which level of technology and economic development is most suitable for particular communities and regions. The goal here would be something approaching Illich's "convivial" technology[20] or Schumacher's "economics as if people mattered."[21] The efforts of northern natives to have a say in the pipeline developments that will affect their lives is a step, but only a step, in this direction.

The growth of national power will be countered by increasing demands for local autonomy and political decentralization. There is evidence that local governments often allow minorities a greater role in decision making than governments further removed from local needs. The fact that municipal and provincial governments have recently begun to grow at a much more rapid rate than the federal government may in itself be a portent of this trend. Finally, cultural pluralism will require an attenuation of the role of ideology in social life and a growing toleration of human differences. We are coming to realize the distortions and sacrifices[22] of human life and decency involved in attempting to live according to the dictates of some ideology. We must re-learn Lord Acton's lesson that the effort to force everyone to live the same way can be far more divisive than the acceptance of whatever differences do exist.

FOOTNOTES

[1]Lord Acton, "Nationality." Reprinted in Lord Acton, *Essays on Freedom and Power*, Gertrude Himmelfarb, ed. (Glencoe, Illinois, 1948).
[2]*Ibid.*, 185.
[3]*Ibid.*, 192-93.
[4]The impact of industrialization and the market economy on developing nation-states has been extensively discussed in modern social science. See, among others, Guy Hunter, ed., *Industrialization and Race Relations* (London, 1965). Clark Kerr et al., *Industrialism and Industrial Man* (New York, 1964). Wilbert Moore, *The Impact of Industry* (Englewood Cliffs, N.J., 1965). Barry Turner, *Industrialism* (Essex, 1975).
[5]C. A. Macartney, *National States and National Minorities* (New York, 1968), 38.
[6]Ibid., 44.
[7]Kerr, et al., *op. cit.*, 78-79 and 226-31.
[8]Karl Marx and Friedrich Engels, "Manifesto of the Communist Party," in Lewis Feuer, ed., *Karl Marx and Friedrich Engels: Basic Writings on Politics and Philosophy* (Garden City, New York, 1959), 9.
[9]Alvin Gouldner, *The Coming Crisis of Western Sociology* (New York, 1970).
[10]Macartney, *op. cit.*, 39.
[11]Benjamin Akzin, *State and Nation* (London, 1964), 87.
[12]*Ibid.*, 88.
[13]Nathan Glazer and Daniel P. Moynihan, "Why Ethnicity?" *Commentary*, October, 1974, 33.
[14]*Ibid.*
[15]*Ibid.*
[16]Lloyd Fallers, *The Social Anthropology of the Nation State* (Chicago, 1974), 2.
[17]Striking confirmation of this fact is provided by Herbert Blumer, "Industrialization and Race Relations," in Hunter, *op. cit.*, 220-54.
[18]Glazer and Moynihan, *op. cit.*, 34.

[19]The problem is extensively discussed in a brilliant book by Jacques Ellul. See Jacques Ellul, *The Political Illusion,* Konrad Kellen, Translator (New York, 1972).
[20]Ivan Illich, *Tools for Conviviality* (New York, 1973).
[21]Ernest Schumacher, *Small is Beautiful* (London, 1973).
[22]The problem of the sacrifices men must make in attempting to achieve ideological goals is well discussed by Peter Berger, *Pyramids of Sacrifice* (New York, 1974).

ETHNICITY AND SOLIDARITY

UKRAINIAN IDENTITY IN WINNIPEG*
LEO DRIEDGER
UNIVERSITY OF MANITOBA

Some scholars (Joy, 1973; Vallee, 1969; Lieberson, 1970) tend to be optimistic about the potential for maintenance of ethnic group identity when such a group has political and economic control over an ecological territory, within which the population can be nationalized into a cohesive group. They tend to have less hope for ethnic communities who seek to build identity by socialization, voluntary social relations, ethnic culture and institutions. Others like Moynihan and Glazer (1970) and Barth (1969) seem to be much more optimistic about the ability of groups to change and still retain an identity of their own, without assimilation into the larger society. In this paper we plan to explore the extent to which Ukrainians in Winnipeg employ: 1) macro-structures to maintain ethnic boundaries, 2) ethnic enclavic community boundaries, and 3) symbolic social psychological means of identification.

The Ukrainians came relatively late to Manitoba, when many other ethnic groups were already in control of the economic and political structures. Thus, they were much more dependent on building mini-structures in rural communities, which acted as ethnic enclaves where the Ukrainian language, culture and institutions could be maintained. Now that they are moving rapidly into Winnipeg and other cities, they are leaving these rural enclaves for a more heterogeneous environment. In this paper we wish to see whether they are able to transplant their Ukrainian communities into the city as ethnic urban villagers (Gans, 1962); to what extent they are also active in the macro political and economic structures of Winnipeg; and to what extent they employ social psychological means of identification.

I. *Ukrainian Macro-structures: Regions of Power and Influence*

Since the Ukrainians have seldom been in political control of their national territory in the Ukraine, they did not come to Canada with great visions of power and influence in this country. They came to organize ethnic communities in the West patterned after their homeland which was centered around a rural religious and ethnic peasant community. In part one we will sketch the historical development of the ecological, demographic, political, and economic setting into which they came and see to what extent these macro-structures were an important factor in their quest for survival.

*This research was made possible by Grants S69-1445 and S72-0331 received from the Canada Council, which are gratefully acknowledged. The author wishes to thank J. B. Rudnyckyj and John Lehr for helpful comments.

Ecological Territory

The Ukrainians were latecomers to western Canada when they arrived during the turn of the century. Much of the better land in the southern prairies had been claimed by the British, French, Germans, Scandinavians and others. The majority of the first Ukrainian settlers in Canada were illiterate peasants seeking free land and they settled in large blocks in the aspen parkland belt of the Canadian West. This block settlement belt extended from the Manitoba Interlake and Dauphin areas north of Winnipeg, northwest through Yorkton and north of Saskatoon, into the Edmonton region. The land was not as fertile as the southern parts of the prairies, so that their economic base for successful farming was somewhat less promising. The settlement belt bordered on the urban centers of Winnipeg, Saskatoon, and Edmonton, so that when the rural-urban shift took place, there was a fairly natural continuity between their rural and urban communities.

When the Ukrainians moved into the Northend of Winnipeg, they were among some of the first to settle in that territory together with the Poles and Jews who came from eastern Europe as well. These three groups had often been in contact with each other in the old country and felt some affinity to each other. The Northend was isolated from the rest of Winnipeg by the Red River on the east, separating them from the Kildonans, and in the south by the Canadian Pacific railroad which acted as an iron curtain with few outlets to southern Winnipeg. To the north and west were the Ukrainian settlements in the interlake, a natural extension of rural Ukrainian community influence and support. This Northend territory was dominated by the East Europeans, of which the Ukrainians were a substantial part, and this has been the case almost to this day (Driedger and Church, 1974). East Europeans (Jews and Ukrainians) have been moving northward out of the Northend for several decades now, so that their dominant influence is fading although they are still influential.

Demographic Trends

In 1971 the 580,655 Ukrainians were the fifth largest ethnic group in Canada, representing only 2.7 percent of the total Canadian population (Census of Canada, 1974). Nationally, they are a small minority, but they are a much larger proportion of the population in the West, where the 114,410 Ukrainians in Manitoba represent 11.6 percent of the population of that Province, being the third largest ethnic group. The Ukrainians have remained about twelve percent of Manitoba for the past thirty-five years. They are a significant force in the West.

Until recently a majority of the Ukrainians were rural, but in 1971 over half (64,305) lived in Winnipeg as shown in Table 1. They tended first to settle in the Northend of Winnipeg and until 1951 about half (20,144) still resided in the Northend. Increasingly they are moving to other parts of the city so that by 1971 only about one fourth (27.5 per cent) remained in the

Table 1. Ukrainian demographic trends in Canada, Manitoba, Winnipeg, and the Northend.[c]

	1901	1911	1921	1931
Ukrainians in Census Tracts (4,11,12)				
Ukrainians in the Northend (CTs 1-13)				
Ukrainians in Metro Winnipeg			7,001 (3.1)	21,459 (7.3)
Ukrainians in Manitoba	3,894 (1.5)	31,053 (6.7)	44,129 (7.2)	73,606 (10.5)
Ukrainians in Canada	5,682 (.5)	75,432 (1.1)	106,721 (1.2)	225,113 (2.2)

	1941	1951	1961	1971
Ukrainians in Census Tracts (4,11,12)		5,135 (52.4)[a]	3,700 (53.9)	2,490[b] (33.5)
Ukrainians in the Northend (CTs 1-13)		20,144 (31.3)	21,054 (29.7)	17,380[b] (27.5)
Ukrainians in Metro Winnipeg	28,162 (9.3)	41,437 (11.6)	53,918 (11.3)	64,305 (11.9)
Ukrainians in Manitoba	89,762 (12.3)	98,753 (12.7)	105,372 (11.4)	114,410 (11.6)
Ukrainians in Canada	305,929 (2.7)	395,043 (2.8)	473,337 (2.5)	580,655 (2.7)

[a]All numbers in parentheses are percentages.
[b]Census Tracts 1-13 were renumbered 34-36, 41-49, in 1971.
[c]1901-1971 are Census of Canada figures.

Northend. Whereas the Ukrainians were a majority in some of the southerly Northend census tracts (4, 11, and 12) until 1961, by 1971 they represented only one third of the population in those areas.

While the Northend during the early 1900s was occupied largely by the Jews, Ukrainians and Poles, this has changed drastically. The Jews have moved almost entirely out of the Northend, and the Ukrainians are increasingly leaving this segregated East European stronghold (Driedger and Church, 1974). The Poles are still fairly concentrated in the Northend, but increasingly more recent immigrants from Yugoslavia and Southern Europe, plus many Native Indians are coming into this old part of the Northend. The Ukrainians are shifting north into West Kildonan, and northeastward into North and East Kildonan where they are less segregated, and where they represent a small proportion of the total population. Demographically they have become more diffused, and they have moved into other areas where they have fewer political allies who will support them in their quest for multiculturalism.

Political Dominance

In a democracy an ethnic group must dominate an ecological area demographically in order to gain control of the political decisions in the area. Since the Ukrainians in the Ukraine were often dominated politically by others, they seem to have devised ways and means of working within a political context where they were not the dominant group. In contrast to the French, who hoped to gain dominance in Manitoba in the 1800s, the Ukrainians seem never to have had such high hopes. When they arrived in Manitoba, the British and French were much more numerous and powerful than they, so there was no hope of becoming a political majority.

In Winnipeg too, the Northend was not a separate suburb with political powers over the Northend territory as the French in St. Boniface enjoyed in the early days. The Northend was always a part of the city of Winnipeg. The East Europeans did send representatives from their Northend wards which were often Ukrainian, who represented multicultural views in the city council. Mayor Juba, who is himself of Ukrainian origin, has been the mayor for many years now, and gives Ukrainians a fair hearing.

There is however some ingroup political polarization within the Ukrainian community. This is seen most readily in the organizational structure of Ukrainian non-ecclesiastic organizations. The communist organizations are grouped under the Association of United Ukrainian Canadians while non-communist organizations belong to the nationalist and anti-communist Ukrainian Canadian Committee. The latter organization coordinates the activities of all Ukrainian societies which have a national membership and apart from pursuing a mildly nationalist policy is essentially a non-political organization. Thus, Ukrainian political influence in Manitoba is minimal; in Winnipeg it is largely localized to the municipal level.

Economic Influence

As illustrated by our discussion of control over an ecological territory, demographic trends, and political influence, the Ukrainians have not been a major factor in the macro-structures of the province and the city. They are very much an entrance group (Porter, 1965) who have not been very influential nor very powerful. The same is true for Ukrainian influence economically.

Since the Ukrainians were latecomers, they were not able to settle on the best land, so they have remained less affluent than many of the other groups. The Northend of Winnipeg, being a part of the city of Winnipeg, did not develop into an important industrial area, nor did it become a residential area for the elite. In many ways the Northend was perceived by those living in southern Winnipeg as the other side of the tracks.

We conclude that the Ukrainians never were able to dominate the ecological, demographic, political and economic macro-social structures in Manitoba, therefore they were not able to use state means of power and force to perpetuate the Ukrainian way of life, as was the case a few brief times in the Ukraine. If this is the only means of maintaining ethnic boundaries, then scholars like Joy, Vallee, and Lieberson are right that Ukrainian identity is doomed outside of a sphere of political control. We suggest however, that there are social and community means of building minority mini-structures available to ethnic groups, which, promoted by socialization within ethnic enclaves, are not as dependent on external force, as upon voluntary identification.

In part two we wish to explore to what extent the Ukrainians in the Northend of Winnipeg have adopted such minority means of survival, and whether they seem to be effective.

II. *The Ukrainian Ethnic Enclave: Social Factors Related to Boundary Maintenance*

Another option of maintenance of ethnic boundaries seems to be the ethnic enclavic community. When minorities wish to develop means of control over a population in a specific area, they cannot rely on legislative majorities, and military force; they are left with the option of creating ethnic enclaves which their offspring will need to perpetuate through means of socialization and voluntary identification.

There were a sufficient number of minorities who assimilated as Park (1950) predicted, to keep American researchers preoccupied with documenting the progress of their assimilation. For fifty years, these scholars tended to ignore groups which retained a separate identity and to regard their separateness as a relatively insignificant factor in the total pattern of minority-majority relations (Newman, 1973).

The multivariate approach of Gordon (1964) forced scholars out of the assimilationist unilinear rut. However, each of the seven stages or types of assimilation he established (cultural, structural, marital, identificational, attitude and behavior receptional, and civic) tended to be oriented toward either an assimilationist or amalgam target. On the other hand, Gordon did point out that while structural assimilation usually takes place in economic, political, and educational institutions, religious, family and recreational institutions encourage minority pluralism (Newman, 1973).

Glazer and Moynihan (1970) maintain that all groups change, but those which are able to shift from traditional cultural identities to new interest foci maintain their distinctive identities while they change. This formulation recognizes change; maintains that identification can be shifted; suggests that some groups may change more than others; and infers that the outcome may be a pluralist mixture with a non-anglo-conformity target. Indeed, Glazer and Moynihan contend that traumatic experiences, such as conflict, encourage the development of a sense of identity among minorities.

A new enclavic perspective can embrace elements of Gordon's multivariate approach and Glazer and Moynihan's beyond the melting theory, both of which encourage pluralist assumptions. Enclavic cultural pluralism seems to be a model which can be implemented into the city, in the form of an ethnic village, as rural-urban migration occurs (Gans, 1962). The Hutterites are one of the best examples of rural enclavic pluralism, characterized by extensive boundary maintenance and controlled systemic linkage with outsiders (Hostetler, 1974). Most minorities cannot maintain such exclusive enclaves; however, it is a model to which many minority groups seem to aspire.

In part two we will explore factors related to social variables involved in enclavic boundary maintenance. The basic assumption is that in order for the Ukrainians to maintain any separate identity, they will need to build and maintain ethnic cultural enclaves or communities if they cannot dominate a national territory. In attempting to find social variables influential in the maintenance of the Ukrainian enclave in the Northend of Winnipeg, we shall examine territorial segregation, institutional completeness, cultural identity, and social distance (Driedger, 1977). The Ukrainians will be compared with six other groups in greater Winnipeg to see how they fare in comparison.

Residential Segregation

Both Joy (1972) and Lieberson (1970) argue that the maintenance of an ethnic language in Canada is not possible unless there are a sufficiently large number of citizens speaking that language concentrated in a given territory. Joy demonstrates how in Quebec the French were in control of the provincial territory, thus perpetuating their language through religious, educational, and political institutions. French Canadians within the Soo-Moncton belt, surrounding the Quebec French block, seemed to be able to maintain their language because of the support from Quebec nearby. Driedger and Church (1974) found that segregation of the Ukrainians in the Winnipeg Northend seemed to operate the same way.

Ukrainian immigrants began coming to Canada and Manitoba in 1896 (Marunchak, 1970). Since they came to the West, and since Winnipeg was the main center from which they fanned out into their rural communities, some stayed in Winnipeg. From the beginning, Ukrainians have been highly concentrated in the Northend of Winnipeg. Winnipeg became the stronghold of Ukrainian activity. By 1941 the 28,000 Ukrainians in Winnipeg represented 10 percent of the metropolitan population as shown in Table 1. About half (20,144) of the 41,437 who lived in Winnipeg in 1951 lived in the Northend (census tracts 1-13); within the Northend they represented about one third (31.3 percent) of the population. In some of the southerly Northend census tracts they represented over half (52.4 percent in tracts 4, 11, 12) of the total population in 1951.

While the Ukrainian segment has continued to increase both in numbers and proportion within the population of Winnipeg (64,350 and 11.9 percent) in 1971, the concentration in the Northend has declined somewhat. As shown in Table 1 the Ukrainians declined from about one third to about one fourth (27.5 percent) in the Northend by 1971, and they declined from over one half to about one third of the residents in the most highly concentrated area (Census Tracts 4, 11, 12). The Ukrainians, as they become somewhat more upwardly mobile, are moving increasingly north into West and North Kildonan into newer housing in the suburbs. Although the Ukrainians are still heavily concentrated in the Northend, they are, as indicated by their declining Shevky-Bell-type isolation and segregation index scores in Table 2, becoming less isolated and somewhat less segregated (Driedger and Church, 1974).

Table 2. *A comparison of ethnic group isolation and segregation in Winnipeg, by 1941, 1951 and 1961 decades with 1971 estimates.*[a]

ETHNIC GROUPS	ISOLATION				SEGREGATION			
	1941	1951	1961	1971 (Estimated)	1941	1951	1961	1971 (Estimated)
Jewish	.31	.21	.18	.15	.71	.64	.62	.60
French	.19	.20	.18	.18	.43	.52	.57	.60
Ukrainian	.23	.16	.12	.10	.64	.58	.56	.53
Polish	.05	.04	.02	.02	.61	.60	.59	.58
German	.08	.04	.04	.03	.48	.47	.48	.45
Scandinavian	.02	.01	.00	.00	.26	.37	.47	.44

[a]Driedger and Church, 1974.

In comparison to the other six ethnic groups shown in Table 2, Ukrainian isolation is somewhat less than that of the Jews and French in Winnipeg. However, they are substantially more isolated than the Poles, Germans and Scandinavians.[1] With regard to segregation, the Ukrainians tend to fall between the Jews and French who are somewhat more segregated.[2] The Ukrainian decline in isolation is considerable (from .23 to .10 on the Shevky and Bell isolation index). The Ukrainian decline in residential segregation (from .64 to .53) is moderate. We conclude that as the Ukrainians begin to become socio-economically mobile, they will increasingly move out of the older Northend into other parts of northern Winnipeg which will make them less isolated and segregated.[3]

Institutional Completeness

In addition to Ukrainian residential segregation as one indicator of boundary maintenance, we wish to evaluate the ethnic institutional completeness of the Ukrainians in the Northend (Lieberson, 1970; Driedger and Church, 1974).[4] Breton (1964) argues that "The direction of the immigrants' integration will to a large extent result from the forces of attraction (positive and negative) stemming from three communities: the community of his ethnicity, the native (receiving) community, and the other ethnic communities." These forces are generated by the social organization of ethnic communities and their capacity to attract and hold members within their social boundaries. Ukrainian integration into their own ethnic community, supported by the institutional completeness of their group would reinforce solidarity.

The rationale for institutional completeness is that when a minority can develop a social system of its own with control over its institutions, then the patterned social interaction of the group will take place largely within the system. Breton (1964) suggests that religious, educational, and welfare institutions are crucial, while Joy (1972) adds the importance of political and economic institutions. Vallee (1969) confirmed Breton's claims by summarizing the need for organization of group structures and institutions which influence socialization and ethnic community decision-making.

As illustrated in Table 3, the Ukrainians have 27 Greek Orthodox and Ukrainian Catholic churches in metropolitan Winnipeg (Driedger and Church, 1974). The eastern architecture of the churches makes them easily distinguishable from other churches. The religious institutions seem to be as well developed as any of the other groups in Winnipeg. The Ukrainians support more voluntary institutions than any of the other groups including the Jews and French; so they are strong in voluntary support. Many of these organizations are well integrated into the church, such as immigration agencies, bingo organizations and the like. Many of these organizations are united under the Ukrainian Canadian Committee which is a major force in teaching the Ukrainian language (Marunchak, 1970). The Ukrainians are the weakest in ethnic schools. They do have Saturday classes in many churches, but have fewer other schools. St. Andrews College on the campus of the University of Manitoba serves many in the West. Other schools, however, receive less than sufficient support, and they, not like elementary and high schools would do, reach very few students for more extended periods of time. The several Ukrainian newspapers which are published in the city may make up in some measure for the lack of schools.

We conclude that Ukrainian institutions are strong in the areas of religion and voluntary organization, but weak in parochial education. Compared to other ethnic groups in Winnipeg their institutions are not as complete as those of the Jews and the French, but much more complete than those of the Poles and Scandinavians. Many of these institutions are also located in the Northend where they are more highly concentrated.

Cultural Identity

Kurt Lewin (1948) proposed that the individual needs to achieve a firm clear sense of identification with the heritage and culture of the ingroup in order to find a secure "ground" for a sense of well being. We assume that a minority culture can be better groomed and nourished within the territorial enclave where an ethnic group can build a concentration of ethnic institutions. Ukrainian territorial segregation and institutional development in the Northend would suggest that they have laid important ground for their Ukrainian culture.

A multidimensional measure of ethnic identity is needed to distinguish the components that different individuals and groups stress (Lazerwitz, 1953). Our studies (Driedger, 1975) of cultural identity by comparing seven ethnic groups in Winnipeg indicated that Ukrainian university students

Table 3. A comparison of institutional completeness (religion, parochial education, voluntary associations) by ethnic groups.

ETHNIC GROUPS (Population, 1961 Census)	SOCIAL INSTITUTIONS								ASSOCIATIONS	
	RELIGION				EDUCATION					
	Members Per Capita	(No.)	Churches/ Synagogues Per 1000 Population	(No.)	Students Per 10 Population	(No.)	Schools Per 1000 Population	(No.)	Per 1000 Population	(No.)
Jewish (19,375)	.36	(7000)	.42	(8)	.70	(1365)	.20	(4)	1.18	(23)
French (39,777)	.27	(10,700)	.22	(9)	1.08	(4300)	.25	(10)	.56	(22)
Ukrainian (53,918)	.23	(12,500)	.50	(27)	.07	(200)	.04	(2)	.58	(31)
German (50,206)	.26	(13,200)	.68	(34)	.18	(900)	.10	(5)	.18	(9)
Polish (24,904)	.16	(4000)	.12	(3)	.00	(0)	.00	(0)	.24	(6)
Scandinavian (17,834)	.04	(800)	.11	(2)	.00	(0)	.00	(0)	.39	(7)

scored moderately high in comparison with other ethnic groups on many of the six cultural identity factors (language use, endogamy, choice of friends, and participation in religion, parochial schools, and voluntary organizations).[5] As indicated in Table 4, Ukrainian university students did not rank highest on any of the six factors but three fourths (75.6 percent) indicated only endogamy in their family, and almost half (43.6 percent) attended Ukrainian religious services twice a month or more. The overall identification of Ukrainian students with their culture is greater than that of the Scandinavians but less than that of the French and the Jews. Ukrainian cultural identity was moderately strong. It is interesting to note that while many members of the Ukrainian elite emphasize the need to learn the Ukrainian language, only about one fifth (21.8 percent) spoke Ukrainian to their parents at home; three times as many (60.5 percent) French students did so.

Table 4. Comparison of ethnic group behavioral rankings by composite mean scores, and six identity factors (religion, endogamy, language, organizations, parochial education, friends).

COMPOSITE MEAN BEHAVIORAL IDENTITY RANK		BEHAVIORAL IDENTITY FACTORS (Means)					
		F_R	F_E	F_L	F_O	F_{PE}	F_F
1 French (F)	55.0	55.6(G)	91.3(J)	60.5(F)	28.6(J)	79.1(F)	62.5(J)
2 Jewish (J)	44.2	53.5(F)	75.6(U)	29.4(G)	22.9(U)	74.0(J)	48.8(F)
3 German (G)	40.8	46.4(P)	72.0(B)	21.8(U)	22.6(F)	57.1(P)	44.6(B)
4 Ukrainian (U)	36.8	43.6(U)	65.4(F)	14.3(P)	16.3(G)	44.3(G)	36.3(G)
5 Polish (P)	31.5	22.9(B)	62.8(G)	1.8(J)	12.7(P)	41.1(U)	15.9(U)
6 British (B)	29.3	14.7(S)	57.1(S)	0(S)	10.0(B)	27.4(B)	5.4(P)
7 Scandinavian (S)	16.4	7.2(J)	53.2(P)	0(B)	2.0(S)	24.5(S)	0(S)

Social Distance

Cultural identity supported by ethnic institutions in a specific territory will tend to hold the individual within an ingroup orbit where much time and social interaction will take place. We would expect, as Simmel (1955) predicted, that a high degree of ingroup solidarity and identity will place social distance between the ingroup and other groups (Driedger and Peters, 1977). Little time and effort is spent in relating to others because much of the individual's activity is confined to the ingroup.

We found, using Bogardus's social distance scale, that the Ukrainians who were moderate cultural identifiers also indicated moderate social distance scores compared with those of the others. As indicated in Table 5 (Driedger and Peters, 1977), Jewish and French social distance scores tended to be high. The Scandinavians, who are not highly segregated, whose institutional completeness is greatly lacking, and who score low on cultural identity, also indicated the lowest social distance from others.

Table 5. Comparison of ethnic social distance (SD) rankings by Ukrainian and six ethnic groups (Jewish, German, French, Polish, British, and Scandinavian).

SOCIAL DISTANCE RANKINGS OF ETHNIC GROUPS (Means)

Ethnic Groups (N = 763-774)	Composite Mean SD Rank	French (N = 72-74)	Jewish (107-110)	Ukrainian (176-181)	Polish (50)	British (151-153)	German (80-84)	Scandinavian (53-56)
Ingroup		1.32(F)	1.05(J)	1.17(U)	1.16(P)	1.13(B)	1.17(G)	1.11(S)
British (B)	1.33	1.59	1.38	1.41	1.54	—	1.20	1.16
American (A)	1.46	1.64	1.33	1.58	1.62	1.43	1.34	1.36
Scandinavian (S)	1.52	1.73	1.74	1.53	1.58	1.35	1.35	—
Dutch (D)	1.55	1.86	1.64	1.67	1.70	1.41	1.23	1.34
German (G)	1.62	1.69	2.36	1.67	1.56	1.48	—	1.36
Ukrainian (U)	1.65	2.00	2.09	—	1.68	1.67	1.61	1.30
French (F)	1.69	—	1.69	1.84	1.66	1.73	1.43	1.44
Polish (P)	1.78	2.15	1.89	1.63	—	1.79	1.62	1.50
Italian (I)	1.94	1.99	1.84	1.88	2.00	1.88	2.06	1.71
Russian (R)	1.95	2.29	2.07	1.81	1.80	1.97	1.63	1.82
Jewish (J)	2.01	2.31	—	2.32	2.10	2.10	2.17	1.71

It is interesting to also note how other university students tended to perceive the Ukrainians in greater Winnipeg. Table 5 shows that the total student sample tended to rank the Ukrainians in the middle with regard to social distance. The Ukrainians (SD mean of 1.65) tended to rank with the French and Germans, well below student acceptance of the British and Americans, and more accepted than the Jews, Russians, and Italians. Simmel's prediction that segregation, ethnic institutions, and ethnic identity would correlate with greater social distance seems to be the case for the Ukrainians in the Northend.

When the four dimensions of Ukrainian enclavic boundary maintenance (territory, institutions, culture, and distance) are examined in Winnipeg, we conclude that most of the variables generally show that Ukrainian identification is moderately strong in comparison. All in all the four dimensions discussed seem to best explain rural ethnic society and appear to be helpful in describing some ethnic villagers in the city. However, we sense increasingly in our research that more dynamic components must be studied, and these are factors which we wish to examine in part three.

III. *Ukrainian Self-Identification: Maintenance of Symbolic Factors*

Although Ukrainian enclavic pluralism may have flourished in rural and small town environments, it seems increasingly more difficult to maintain the boundaries of the minority ethnos in the urban environment. Where are the "urban Hutterites" of the metropolis, if indeed it is possible to maintain a pluralist ethnos in greater Winnipeg? It is our opinion that the Jewish model bears examination because Jews are highly urban, and have had a long urban experience with a considerable degree of identity (Driedger and Church, 1974; Driedger, 1975; Driedger, 1977). Is residential segregation, institutional completeness, cultural identity, and social distance sufficient support for urban ethnic pluralism? We suspect that these factors alone are not enough because the dynamic metropolis will eventually lure the offspring of minorities into its orbit, as Park predicted. How, then, have minorities such as the Jews maintained their long history of urban pluralism, and to what extent are the Ukrainians in the Northend following their pattern?

The enclavic factors seem essential for any rural or lower status group to gain a foothold of identity in the city. During the span of several generations, however, we think they must, as Glazer and Moynihan (1970) suggest, shift from an enclavic ethnic orientation to a more dynamic orientation (Driedger, 1977). An ideological vision, historical symbols, charismatic leadership, and social status seem to be essential social psychological factors and bear examination. Research into how the Ukrainians in the Northend are creating these factors has hardly begun, but we shall discuss them briefly.

Ideological Vision

Although both political and religious ideology may rally followers to a goal beyond (Glazer and Moynihan, 1970) cultural and institutional values, Ukrainian historical success in the political arena has been brief and spotty. In Europe they were continually sandwiched between the Austro-Hungarian, Polish, and Russian powers who controlled them politically. Their brief state of independence in 1917-21, however, is still very fresh in their memories, which tends to spur on many Ukrainians to maintain their identity in Canada. In Canada they have never been able to control a province politically, but they have been in the majority in some of the rural municipalities, and in some of the census tracts in Winnipeg. This has resulted in successful election of Ukrainian representatives such as Mayor Juba in Winnipeg, and representatives to municipal boards, city councils, provincial legislatures and the Federal parliament. These tend to act as symbols for a multicultural political vision at least in the West. Their political ideology, however, has not been unified, since a fairly large minority have supported communism, while a majority are very anti-communist. Thus their political ideologies have been fragmented.

Religiously too the Ukrainians have been fragmented into the two dominant Ukrainian Catholic and Ukrainian Greek Orthodox faiths. Their Eastern Greek or Byzantine rites, however, tend to act as a separation factor from the rest of western Christians. Their struggle for survival between the influences of Constantinople and Rome, between the Orthodox and Catholic churches, has both strengthened their determination to survive, and set serious conflict between the two Ukrainian religious ideologies. The eastern religious influence is evident in the church architecture which acts as a distinct religious symbol, quite evident in the Northend, including the Ukrainian Orthodox cross. The Ukrainian Catholics have had since 1956 their own Ukrainian archdiocese which is directly responsible to the Pope and which plays a major role in retaining a separate Ukrainian religious identity.

Historical Symbols

Minority urban villagers may perpetuate their social structures and community as an end in itself, without much reference to where they came from and their future purpose. A knowledge of their origins and a pride in their heritage seem essential for a sense of purpose and direction among Ukrainian Northend urbanites (Driedger, 1977). Without such pride and knowledge the desire to perpetuate tradition rapidly diminishes. The Ukrainians in greater Winnipeg have developed some historical symbols which should stand them in good stead. Ukrainian historical interests and Ukrainian societies seem to be flourishing.

Although much Ukrainian history in the Ukraine is tragic, their many conflicts and struggles can be a reminder of their identity (Glazer and Moynihan, 1970; Coser, 1956). A comparison of the identity of seven ethnic groups, using Worchel-type questions, indicated that Ukrainian ingroup affirmation was not as strong as that of the Jews and French, but stronger than the rest (Driedger, 1976). Ukrainian students were moderately proud of their ingroup, felt bound to it, wished to remember it, and contributed to it. Their ingroup was a positive symbol for many, but they indicated high ingroup denial (Driedger, 1976). Many tried to hide their ethnicity and some felt inferior about their ethnicity. On the average they were moderately annoyed and felt somewhat restricted by their Ukrainian identity. Such attitudes of Ukrainian university students seem to indicate that they have a discrepancy between ingroup affirmation and denial which is not as positive as that of the Jews and French.

Charismatic Leadership

The importance of charisma is demonstrated in a variety of new minority movements including Martin Luther King and Malcolm X among the Blacks in the United States; the leadership of Rene Levesque among the Quebecois, and Harold Cardinal's Indian movement in Alberta — to name a few. Individuals with a sense of mission often adapt an ideology to a current situation, linking it symbolically with the past, and using the media to effectively transform the present into a vision of the future. The Ukrainians have the additional problem that until 1917 the Ukrainian national state did not exist, and as a result many who were ethnically Ukrainian were content to regard themselves as citizens of the country responsible for the administration of their homeland provinces. This meant that when Ukrainians came to Canada they were often recorded as Ruthenians, Little Russians, Austrians, Galicians, Bukovinans, Poles, Ukrainians or Russians (Wangenheim, 1971). Thus, from the very beginning the Ukrainians in Canada had problems of a feeling of unity. Usually charismatic leaders can be a unifying factor in such circumstances of diversity.

Of the three major Ukrainian migrations into Canada, the first consisted heavily of peasants who settled on farms. As pioneers with limited education they were too preoccupied with eking out a living from the land to spend time and effort in unification. Religious leaders nucleated among the Ukrainian Greek Orthodox and Ukrainian Catholics respectively, have emerged from among those who came in the second and third migrations, which included more educated persons, and many of these settled in cities also augmenting the number of professionals. A monument of the poet Shevchenko was raised on the legislative grounds in Winnipeg as a symbol of his writings and leadership and a museum was opened in his honor. Franko's writings have also been influential since he favoured Ukrainian nationalism.

A number of outstanding intellectuals have become prominent in both the Ukrainian and Canadian communities. Senator Paul Yuzyk, a former professor who is now in the Canadian Senate, has written extensively, and

Table 6. Comparison of Real Ethnic Ingroup Affirmation by Seven Ethnic Groups (Tukey's HSD and Analysis of Variance).

Ethnic Groups	Real Affirmation Means	Differences of Means by Ethnic Groups						
		Jewish (N=112)	French (N=85)	Ukrainian (N=188)	German (N=160)	Polish (N=55)	British (N=157)	Scandinavian (N=61)
Jewish	3.42							
French	3.37	.05						
Ukrainian	3.01	.41*	.36*					
German	2.94	.48*	.43*	.07				
Polish	2.89	.53*	.49*	.12	.05			
British	2.89	.53*	.49*	.12	.05	.00		
Scandinavian	2.77	.65**	.60**	.24	.17	.12	.12	

Anova Summary

Source of Variance	SS	df	MS	F
Treatment	37	6	6.17	5.71***
Error	875	811	1.08	
TOTAL	922	817		

*P<.05   **P<.01   ***P<.001

has spoken across Canada representing the need for Canadian multiculturalism (Yuzyk, 1953, 1964, 1967). Professor J. B. Rudnyckyj, one of the members of the Bilingual and Bicultural Commission, advanced multiculturalism also with his minority report on the need to promote the cultures of members of non-British and non-French origin (Royal Commission on Bilingualism and Biculturalism, 1969). Rudnyckyj who founded the Department of Slavic Studies at the University of Manitoba has published extensively, and has tirelessly furthered the Ukrainian cause. The leaders mentioned above are but a few charismatic representatives of the emergence of a well trained elite who have done much to promote Ukrainian identity.

Social Status

John Porter (1964) suggests that social class is a more important factor for consideration than is ethnic origin. Urban minorities of lower status, such as the Canadian Indian, will be powerless to influence their surroundings, while the Jews, who are of higher socio-economic status than the British in Winnipeg, will find urban minority life much more manageable. The fact that the Jews, who are, on the average, of the highest socio-economic status in Winnipeg, also indicate high residential segregation, cultural identity, and institutional completeness, would seem to challenge the view that status is correlated with a decline in ethnic identity (Driedger, 1976).

Our findings suggest that if the Ukrainians can maintain an enclavic foothold in the Northend long enough to groom several generations of urban Ukrainian identifiers, their socio-economic status can be raised so that they will be able to compete on an equal footing with other groups in the city, and maintain pride in their Ukrainian identity (Driedger, 1975, and 1976). The Ukrainians came somewhat later to Manitoba when most of the best rural land had been settled, so they took land in the interlake and Dauphin regions. These rural areas have been less prosperous, so that rural Ukrainians coming to Winnipeg on the average are not as well to do as some of the other ethnic groups. From our studies of Ukrainians in Winnipeg, we found that Ukrainians on the average were of somewhat lower education and income, and also were more heavily located in the lower status occupations (Census, 1971). This, it would seem, is one of the reasons why they have settled in the older southerly parts of the Northend, and many of them are still located there. It is true, also, that some are beginning to move to the newer suburbs in the Kildonans faster than the Poles, but much more slowly than the Jews.

The average non-agricultural Ukrainian male in Canada in 1961 (Royal Commission on Bilingualism and Biculturalism, 1969, Volume 4) earned $4,128 which was lower than the earnings of the Jews, British, and Germans, but higher than the earnings of the French and Italians. The Ukrainians also ranked the same in the cities of Montreal, Toronto and Ottawa in 1961. Our thesis is that as members of an ethnic group rise in socio-economic status and still maintain their ethnic identity, that they will then be able to compete better in an urban environment and also raise the status of their group, and will therefore be able to compete on an equal basis with other groups without inferiority. This will make the group more attractive to its own ingroup members so that they will remain more attracted to their own ethnic group. This is happening with the Jews especially. It is not yet clear whether the Ukrainians will be able to rise fast enough socio-economically, before assimilationist influences make severe inroads on their identity.

Although Ukrainian self identification with social psychological factors needs to be studied more, it would appear that Ukrainians have a strong religious ideological base, surrounded by numerous voluntary organizations, supported by a growing number of influential leaders. On the other hand their parochial educational institutions are weaker than those of some other groups, politically they are more fragmented in their ideology, and their historical symbols are based on brief national successes, reinforced by only moderate socio-economic status. The Ukrainians in Winnipeg affirm their ingroup moderately, but have high ingroup denial, which is not a sign of an integrated ethnic self-concept. Ukrainian self identity factors which are needed in the urban environment could be stronger than they are to assure continued survival.

Conclusions

The Ukrainians never did have a chance at majority dominance in Manitoba. Ecologically, demographically, politically and economically, they are one of the minorities of the province. Those who believe that ethnic boundaries can be maintained only by directing macro-social structures, are indeed correct, that the Ukrainians in Winnipeg cannot avoid assimilation.

It is our contention, however, that many minorities in Canada can maintain ethnic enclaves especially in rural areas by means of residential segregation, institutional completeness, cultural identity, and social distance, which can also to some extent be transferred by urban villagers into the city. The Ukrainians have maintained such a mini-structure in the Northend of Winnipeg, and although there is evidence that they will continue to maintain such an enclave it is not as strong as that of the French and the Jews. This enclave is changing and it is not clear whether this change will lead to new forms of identity as Glazer and Moynihan (1970) suggest, or whether it is assimilation setting in.

For an ethnic group to compete effectively in an urban environment, we suggest that social psychological factors must reinforce enclavic factors to keep the enclave dynamic, and relevant to the changing urban patterns. The Ukrainians in Winnipeg support a strong religious ideology, heavily located in the Northend. Charismatic leaders from their status elite have led this community into a vision of a future. Historical symbols such as national independence in 1917-21, plus writers, institutions and newspapers add to this hope of a future. Nevertheless the future for Ukrainians in Winnipeg does not look as bright as it does for the French and the Jews.

We agree with Barth (1969) that the view that geographical and social isolation are the critical factors in sustaining cultural diversity is too simplistic. "Boundaries persist despite a flow of personnel across them, so that categorical ethnic distinctions do not depend on an absence of mobility, contact and information, but do entail social processes of exclusion and incorporation whereby discrete categories are maintained despite changing participation and membership in the course of individual life histories" (Barth, 1969). Self-ascription and ascription by others is certainly important. Common to all is the principle that ethnic identity implies a series of constraints on the kinds of roles an individual is allowed to play, and the partners he may choose for different kinds of transactions (Barth, 1969).

FOOTNOTES

[1]See Shevky and Bell (1955:44) and Driedger and Church (1974) for more details on the formulae used to calculate the isolation index.
[2]See Shevky and Bell (1955:47) and Driedger and Church (1974) for more details on the formulae used to calculate the segregation index.
[3]For more details on how the samples were selected and how mobility patterns were established see Driedger and Church (1974).
[4]On the method by which the ethnic institutions were calculated see Driedger and Church (1974) for more details.
[5]As to the Driedger Ethnic Cultural Behavioral Identity (ECBI) Index, see Driedger (1975) for more methodological information.

REFERENCES

Barth, Fredrik, *Ethnic Groups and Boundaries* (Boston, 1969).
Breton, Raymond, "Institutional Completeness of Ethnic Communities and Personal Relations to Immigrants," *American Journal of Sociology*, 70(1964), 193-205.
Coser, Lewis, *The Functions of Social Conflict* (Glencoe, Illinois, 1956).
Driedger, Leo, "Native Rebellion and Mennonite Invasion: An Examination of Two River Valleys," *Mennonite Quarterly Review* 46(1972), 290-300.
Driedger, Leo, "Doctrinal Belief: A Major Factor in the Differential Perception of Social Issues," *Sociological Quarterly* 15(1974), 60-80.
Driedger, Leo, "In Search of Cultural Identity Factors: A Comparison of Ethnic Students," *Canadian Review of Sociology and Anthropology*, 12(1975), 50-162.
Driedger, Leo, "Ethnic Self Identity: A Comparison of Ingroup Evaluations," *Sociometry*, 39(1976), 131-141.
Driedger, Leo, "Toward a Perspective on Canadian Pluralism: Ethnic Identity in Winnipeg," *Canadian Journal of Sociology*, 2(1977), 77-95.
Driedger, Leo and Glenn Church, "Residential Segregation and Institutional Completeness: A Comparison of Ethnic Minorities," *Canadian Review of Sociology and Anthropology*, 11(1974), 30-52.
Driedger, Leo and Jacob Peters, "Ethnic Identity and Social Distance: A Comparison of Ethnic Groups," *Canadian Review of Sociology and Anthropology*, 14(1977), 158-73.
Gans, Herbert J., *The Urban Dwellers: Group and Class in the Life of Italian Americans* (New York, 1962).
Glazer, Nathan and Daniel P. Moynihan, *Beyond the Melting Pot* (Cambridge, Mass., 1970).
Gordon, Milton M., *Assimilation in American Life* (New York, 1964).
Gregorovich, Andrew, *The Ukrainians in Canada* (Toronto, 1964).
Hobart, C. W., "Adjustment of Ukrainians in Alberta: Alienation and Integration," in B. R. Bociurkiw, ed., *Slavs in Canada* (Edmonton, 1966), vol. 1.
Hostetler, John A., *Hutterite Society* (Baltimore, 1974).
Isajiw, W. W. and N. J. Hartman, "Changes in the Occupational Structure of Ukrainians in Canada," in W. E. Mann, *Social and Cultural Changes in Canada* (Toronto, 1970).
Joy, Richard J., *Languages in Conflict* (Toronto, 1972).

Kalbach, W. E., "Some Demographic Aspects of Ukrainian Population in Canada," in B. R. Bociurkiw, ed., *Slavs in Canada* (Edmonton, 1966), vol. 1.

Kaye, Vladimir, *Early Ukrainian Settlements in Canada* (Toronto, 1964).

Kirkconnell, Watson, *The Ukrainian Canadians and the War* (Toronto, 1940).

Lazerwitz, Bernard, "Some Factors in Jewish Identification," *Jewish Social Studies*, 15(1953), 24.

Lewin, Kurt, *Resolving Social Conflict* (New York, 1948).

Lieberson, Stanley, *Language and Ethnic Relations in Canada* (New York, 1970).

Marunchak, Michael H., *The Ukrainian Canadians: A History* (Ottawa, 1970).

Millet, David, "The Orthodox Church: Ukrainian, Greek and Syrian," in Jean Leonard Elliott, *Immigrants in Canada* (Scarborough, 1971).

Newman, William H., *American Pluralism: A Study of Minority Groups and Social Theory* (New York, 1973).

Nicholson, T. G. and M. H. Yeates, "The Ecological and Spatial Structure of the Socio-Economic Characteristics of Winnipeg, 1961," *Canadian Review of Sociology and Anthropology*, 6(1969), 162-178.

Porter, John, *The Vertical Mosaic* (Toronto, 1965).

Royal Commission on Bilingualism and Biculturalism, *The Cultural Contribution of the Other Ethnic Groups,* Book IV (Ottawa, 1969).

Simmel, Georg, *Conflict.* Trans. Kurt Wolff (Glencoe, Illinois, 1955).

Statistics Canada, *Population: Specified Ethnic Groups,* Catalogue 92-774 (SP-4) (Ottawa, 1974).

Statistics Canada, *Winnipeg: Population and Housing Characteristics,* Catalogue 95-753 (CT-23B) (Ottawa, 1974).

Vallee, Frank G., "Regionalism and Ethnicity: The French-Canadian Case," in B. Y. Card. ed., *Perspectives on Regions and Regionalism* (Edmonton, 1969), 19-25.

Wangenheim, Elizabeth D., "The Ukrainians: A Case Study of the 'Third Force,' " in W. E. Mann, ed., *Canada: A Sociological Profile* (Toronto, 1971).

Woychenko, Ol'Ha, *The Ukrainians in Canada,* Canada Ethnica IV (Winnipeg, 1967).

Yuzyk, P., *Ukrainians in Manitoba* (Toronto, 1953).

Yuzyk, P., "Ukrainian Catholic Church," in *Encyclopedia Canadiana* (Ottawa, 1966), vol. 10, 166-168.

Yuzyk, P., *Ukrainian Canadians: Their Place and Role in Canadian Life* (Toronto, 1967).

ETHNIC SOLIDARITY IN THE ESTERHAZY AREA, 1882-1940

DONALD E. WILLMOTT
YORK UNIVERSITY, DOWNSVIEW

The purpose of this paper is to describe some "colonies" around Esterhazy, a town in southeastern Saskatchewan, and to account for the strength of ethnic solidarity in each.

In 1902, when the railroad reached the Esterhazy area and the station was built in open fields, the countryside was already populated by farmers. Beginning in 1882, English immigrants had settled a few miles north of where the town was to be. Irish and Scots settlers had also taken up homesteads in the area. This nucleus of fifteen to twenty English-speaking families came to be known as the "Sumner Colony." In 1885 they established the area's first Post Office, and two years later they built a hall which was to serve for both church services and dances. They held toboggan and skating parties in the winters, and community fairs in the summers. When Esterhazy was established in 1903, a number of Sumner settlers, and others also mainly of British origin, became the merchants, doctors, and lawyers of the town. They provided Esterhazy with its prominent leaders, with Tories and Socialists, with Anglican, Presbyterian, and Methodist churches, and with an excellent weekly newspaper, the *Esterhazy Observer and Pheasant Hills Advertiser.*

The town was named after an immigrant agent who called himself "Count Paul O. Esterhazy." Although he had only a dubious claim to the title he assumed, his colourful military career in Hungary, England, South Africa, India, and the West Indies showed him to be a man of considerable ability, impressive leadership qualities, and high culture.[1] He conceived a plan to establish a large Hungarian colony in the Northwest Territories and won the support of the highest officials of the railroads and of the governments in Ottawa, Winnipeg, and Regina.

In 1886, Esterhazy conducted thirty-five Hungarian families[2] from Pennsylvania to what was later to be called the "Esterhaz," then the "Kaposvar" area, a few miles south of the future townsite. In spite of very considerable material assistance from the CPR, about two-thirds of these families went back to the United States, discouraged mainly by the very severe prairie winter. Undaunted, Esterhazy continued his colonization efforts. By 1889, at least twenty new families had arrived from Hungary, and others followed, both from Hungary and from the United States. By 1902 the Roman Catholic priest of the Kaposvar Parish claimed to have "800 souls" under his care.[3] In that year "Count" Esterhazy was commissioned to write a promotional pamphlet to encourage further Hungarian immigration.[4] A few years later, the parish priest, himself of

Belgian origin, described the loyalties of his parishioners in the following terms:

> The Hungarians have scrupulously preserved their ancient customs: a deep-seated respect for authority, civil and religious.. . . It is usual with the Hungarians when the priest comes, for nearly all of them to go to confession, so that every Sunday the whole year round, owing to confessions, mass, sermons, baptisms, etc., we cannot take breakfast before two or three o'clock in the afternoon.[5]

Not all of the Hungarian colonists were Roman Catholics, however. Some forty families of the Reformed Church of Hungary were ministered to by the minister of their place of worship at Bekevar (later Kipling), sixty miles to the south. This man, in a testimonial written for Esterhazy's immigration pamphlet, well expressed the devotion of both Catholics and Protestants to their former land and their language:

> Whenever we meet in prayer we offer our grateful hearts to Almighty God for having brought us here to this blessed land and given us our new homes. We shall never forget, however, our own dear fatherland, nor the glorious history of our illustrious compatriot Louis Kossuth, nor the beautiful capital of Hungary, Buda-Pesth, and we shall ever cultivate the sweet language of our forefathers, even in this far away land, and we will sing and worship by prayers to the glory of our God and Saviour also in the true vernacular tongue of our native land, Hungary.[6]

There is no doubt that the early colonists were determined to maintain the Hungarian language, but a conflict arose over the question of whether this should or could be done through the public schools. In 1910, a Winnipeg-based nation-wide, or rather prairie, Hungarian organization began to advocate employment of Hungarian teachers in predominantly Hungarian school districts like Kaposvar. In its journal, the *Canadian Hungarian Farmer,* letters began to appear which also demanded Hungarian priests for Hungarian parishes. It was not long before the controversy became as much a matter of religious as of ethnic politics.

Prominent in the leadership of the Hungarian Brotherhood in Winnipeg were several Protestants, and also a Hungarian Catholic priest sided with them, who was only later recognized by the French Canadian archbishop in St. Boniface. Father Pirot, resident priest of the Kaposvar Colony, feared not only that the members of the Brotherhood would isolate Hungarians from the rest of the society, but that they would wean Catholics away from their "Mother Church." Throughout the latter half of 1910, what Pirot called "open warfare" raged in the pages of the Hungarian press, in the Winnipeg *Free Press,* and in the churches and meeting halls of Hungarian settlements. Father Pirot travelled to Hungarian colonies near and far to warn them against the "enemies" of Canada and his church.[7]

In August 1910, the Hungarian Consul in Winnipeg was quoted in the *Free Press* as saying that the Hungarians of Kaposvar had come to him with the complaint that they were not allowed to have a priest of their own nationality, a Frenchman being forced upon them instead. He also charged that the "French bishop" was imposing French priests on Ruthenians (Ukrainians), who might therefore become "one-sided and prejudiced supporters of the French idea in Western Canada." According to the *Free Press,* he argued further that Hungarian immigrants "are of a different stock from the half-breeds of Louis Riel."[8]

In reply to this appeal to the prejudices of English readers, Father Pirot pointed out that not one of the priests serving Hungarian parishes was of French origin. He himself was a Belgian, and furthermore, he had made and was continuing to make strenuous efforts to get a Hungarian priest for the Kaposvar parish. Father Pirot also instigated supporting letters to the *Free Press* from his parishioners, including one from an Irish Catholic who affirmed that the Kaposvar priests had constantly used their influence to have the Hungarian settlers "send their children to school and acquire the English language."[9]

In September, Archbishop Langevin addressed a circular letter to the Hungarian Catholics of western Canada. In it he threatened excommunication for any Catholic receiving the *Canadian Hungarian Farmer.*[10] Thus the full authority of the Church was thrown against the Hungarian Brotherhood and the newspaper. The campaign to obtain Hungarian teachers seems to have ended thereafter, and no nationalistic organization was established in the Kaposvar colony. Ironically, however, pressure to obtain a Hungarian priest remained high, and Father Pirot was replaced by a Hungarian in 1915.

The events of 1910 highlight the basis of solidarity in the Kaposvar Colony. The fact that most of the colonists were not involved in any formal ethnic organization and were not reading the major Canadian Hungarian newspaper of the time suggests that Hungarian nationalism was not overly strong among them. Yet language was an important social bond among the older settlers; Hungarian was even used to a great extent among the young. But as Father Pirot pointed out, the people of the colony "had a deep-seated respect for authority," and were greatly devoted to their church. It seems clear that, at least after the turn of the century, the high level of group solidarity among them stemmed in a great degree from a common religious commitment and the active community life centred in the church. The faithful are attracted in large numbers to the beautiful stone church and to Our Lady's Shrine at Kaposvar as the locale of an annual midsummer pilgrimage.[11]

The once thriving Hungarian community is now mainly a memory. Its people are dispersed and few of them now speak the mother tongue. An elderly pioneer, who had returned to Esterhazy to retire after farming elsewhere for many years, told the author of his disappointment in discovering that the "old Hungarian community" no longer existed. He complained that the younger generation could not speak Hungarian and considered themselves "only Canadians."

It is clear that through the years, the heart of the Hungarian Colony was the stone church on the hill. It was the centre of the community's social life and the basis of its solidarity. By contrast, the development of a vigorous Czech community was based mainly upon secular organizations.

Three families of Czech origin had arrived in the area south of Esterhazy in 1886, probably a month or two after the first Hungarian colonists. They homesteaded in what became known as the Kolin District, which is credited with being the first Czech settlement in the West.[12] By 1889 four or five more families had arrived, and dozens followed in the last decade of the century. Some of the Czechs were Catholics, but most were Protestant or claimed no church at all. In 1890 they established a Protestant school, known as "Kolin School" after 1902. The nearby Esterhaz School of the Kaposvar Colony, which also served some Czech families, was a Catholic school.

Unlike the early Hungarian colonists, the Czech and some of the Slovak pioneers came on an individual basis. Hence many of their homesteads were scattered throughout the area and their neighbours were Swedes, Hungarians, English, Welsh, or Germans. Some settled near the present hamlets of Hazelcliffe, Yarbo and Atwater. After 1898, there were concentrations of Czechs around Gerald, to the east of Esterhazy, and in the district of Dovedale to the northeast. After Esterhazy was established, in 1903, many Czechs moved into the village as workmen, businessmen, and retired or commuter farmers.

Thus Esterhazy became the centre of what was claimed to be the largest "Czech and Slovak settlement" in the West. In those days the Czechs were known as "Bohemians." As early as 1904, the Bohemian Brass Band was playing at sports days, community picnics, dances, and Saturday night town gatherings. The Bohemian Hall in Esterhazy was in constant use for meetings, social gatherings, dances, weddings, concerts, and plays.

A history of the Czechs and Slovaks in Canada declares that the first of their ethnic organizations was established in Winnipeg in April 1913, with 54 charter members.[13] Yet the following item appeared in the *Esterhazy Observer* in May 1912:

> The Bohemians of Esterhazy and district are the first to form a fraternal society. The objects are — help for the sick or needy, and dramatic, library and education work in their own language. The attempt is quite in its infancy, but if generally taken up — as it deserves to be — the society will get incorporated. Sixty members now belong to the society and a very successful dance was held in the Bohemian Hall on Mon. preceded by a historical farce entitled "NaSkripci" in which Mesdames Fila, Hermansky and Kreck and Messrs. T. Sayner, F. Sayner and K. Nusl took part.[14]

During World War I, many Czech men from the Esterhazy area enlisted in the army, chiefly in the "Bohemian Detachment" of the 223rd Battalion of the Canadian Expeditionary Force. Referring to the double nationalism which motivated the Czech and Slovak volunteers, Gellner and Smerek say: "We may suppose that the men of ... the 'Bohemian Detachment' ... fought with half their hearts filled with loyalty to their new homeland and half with the desire to win a better future for their old."[15]

Between the two wars, Czech nationalism in the Esterhazy area received a boost from an unexpected source. A local chronicler gives the following account in the Esterhazy paper:

From the year 1932 to 1936, services were held in Kolin School, conducted in the Czech language. The Reverend Vaclavik, who was in charge of Esterhazy United Church, preached at Kolin in the Czech language. Those services were especially well attended by the elderly pioneers. He brought Czech people from Toronto to teach the Czech culture and songs to the younger generation, who had organized themselves into a service club called "The Kolin Good Companions."

Under the direction of Reverend Vaclavik, the young people staged a play called "V Cerven im Mlenem" (In the Red Mill). All the dialogue was in Czech. The costuming and presentation were excellent. It was staged in an open air theatre on the farm of Louis Hendrich, during a Czech picnic.[16]

Soon after Czechoslovakia was overrun by the German armies in March 1939, a Czechoslovak National Alliance was established in Toronto. By the end of 1942, it had some 6500 members in 86 branches from Springhill, Nova Scotia, to Tupper Creek, B.C. During the course of the war, it collected $331,000 "for various causes connected with the war and the drive for the liberation of Czechoslovakia."[17] It got off to an early start in Esterhazy, as the following item from the December 14, 1939, *Esterhazy Observer* indicates:

Rev. Joseph Zayicek of Winnipeg, on invitation of the local Czechoslovakian National Alliance, arrived from Winnipeg on Sat. and addressed a meeting, in the Czech language which was greatly enjoyed by a large number attending.

The main purpose of the meeting was to weld the Czech people of Canada into one org. in order to help rebuild when peace is declared, the country of Czechoslovakia to its original position as an independent nation.

Mr. Karl Kulovany was chairman of the meeting. Rev. Zayicek also held U.C. service at Kolin.

The Alliance organized fund-raising bazaars and dances throughout the war and did much to maintain both Canadian and Czech nationalism at a high level. The following report from the *Esterhazy Observer* in October 1941 indicates a high point in the activities of the local Alliance:

Almost 400 people, principally of Czech and Slovak parentage from Esterhazy and nearby points, greeted the Czechoslovakian War Mission at Esterhazy Community Hall. The Mission was headed by Senator V. Benes, brother of President Edward Benes of the Czechoslovakian government-in-exile in Britain.

There was a short address by Mr. W. H. Blyth, overseer of the village, welcoming the honored guests to Esterhazy. The main address of the afternoon was given by Senator Benes. An address was given in both English and Czech by Karel Buzek, sec.-treas. of the Czechoslovakian National Alliance, Toronto, and other addresses by the Czech ace flyer, Lieut. Col. John Ambrash, and Capt. John Nekola of the Czech army in England.[18]

Since the end of World War II, Czech nationalism and ethnic identification appear to have declined steadily. A Czech Club, the only ethnic organization in Esterhazy, continues in existence. But it is largely a social and charitable group, and its members are all elderly. Like the Hungarians, then, the Czechs of Esterhazy have passed through periods of high group consciousness, but are now rapidly losing interest in the language, culture, and politics of their "homelands." The same can be said of the Swedes, Welsh, Germans, and other Europeans who settled in the area. In each case, the initial strength of ethnic solidarity can be accounted for by three factors: ecological settlement patterns, organizational development, and cultural commitments. Let us examine these factors in turn.

In the Esterhazy area, a large proportion of the land — perhaps more than half — was settled in a random fashion, with homesteads being chosen for the appearance of the land rather than the ethnic identity of neighbours. In these ethnically mixed areas, the school system, neighbourhood interdependence, and sociability speeded the process of assimilation. A comparable situation in Alberta has been described by Burnet:

> All the settlers mingled freely, except the Chinese. No group, not even the large Anglo-Saxon one, was isolated enough to maintain its own set of community institutions. Economic and social pressures promoted full co-operation. Neighbouring, in the rich sense in which that word is used in many rural societies, was practiced without regard to ethnic lines. Farm women tell how members of different ethnic groups exchanged recipes with them, and helped feed threshing-crews and guests at bees, weddings, and dances. Men speak of work and of informal social relationships with members of different groups. It was not long before cultural differences disappeared.[19]

This "melting pot" process was occurring in a sea which nevertheless also included important cultural islands, or "colonies." The term "colony" was applied to grouping which varied from the more or less accidental clustering of congenial neighbours of one ethnic group (as in the case of the British "Sumner Colony" north of Esterhazy) to the relatively dense and homogeneous settlement created by an ethnic colonization project (as in the case of "Count" Esterhazy's Hungarians, many of whom arrived in organized groups). The Czech pattern lay between these two extremes. Starting from an original cluster in the Kolin area, new arrivals scattered rather widely throughout the district, some in ethnic concentrations and some in mixed areas. It happened, therefore, that the focus of Czech group life was not primarily in rural neighbourhoods but in the Bohemian Hall, with its brass band and its social life, in the town of Esterhazy.

The Hungarian colonists appeared to be much more committed to building close-knit rural communities. A local priest-chronicler wrote:

> The immigrants from Hungary had been living in villages before coming to this country. It was very difficult for them at the start to live on scattered farms. But this change was made comparatively easy under the circumstances, as the inhabitants on farms were connected by many common ties.... The whole colony seemed to be practically one family.[20]

The first Hungarians made unusual efforts to live close together. Kovacs found evidence that in the first few years they built the houses of the four homesteaders within each section "in a foursome at the center of the section."[21] This practice, however, was soon abandoned because it placed the houses too far from the nearest roads.

Esterhazy himself worked assiduously to assure a densely settled Hungarian colony. In prolonged negotiations with the railway and government authorities, he succeeded in having certain homestead areas "reserved" for his colonists, at least for short periods. In this way he forestalled the "encroachment" of the adjacent Swedish colony.[22] He also persuaded the CPR to forego its proprietary right to withhold the odd-numbered sections until they could be sold for $300 or more per quarter section. In the usual case, this practice meant that only half the land was taken up by homesteaders in the first five or ten years of settlement. For example, in the area between the Kaposvar colony and the future townsite of Esterhazy, the CPR-owned odd-numbered sections were still vacant in 1902. In the original colony itself, however, both even- and odd-numbered sections were taken up, with result that a "solid" rather than a "checkerboard" pattern of settlement was formed.[23] An analysis of homestead information given in Kovacs' study of the early colony[24] indicates that settlers arriving after 1887 had either to homestead on even-numbered sections or purchase land from the CPR. Few new settlers could afford to purchase land, but by 1902 the early settlers had saved enough money to buy up most of the CPR land contiguous to the original colony, in order to expand their own farms or to settle their sons close by.

This review of ethnic settlement patterns reveals two polar types: 1) areas of mixed settlement, which provided the conditions for rapid assimilation, and 2) areas of ethnic concentration, in which proximity, mutual dependence, and a common culture and "mother tongue" encouraged ethnic solidarity. In his 1936 study of ethnic and religious group settlements in western Canada, Dawson summarized the characteristics of homogeneous colonies as follows:

> The cultural factors which conditioned the productive efficiency of these ethnic groups also facilitated their social contacts and the establishment of their own institutional services. The loneliness of the pioneering period was lessened in an atmosphere of sympathy and understanding which made neighbourly visits so frequent. In these homogeneous groups, too, more formal institutional services sprang into being quickly. Religious leadership, church buildings, and varied forms of religious organization emerged at the outset. Schools also were soon established among most of these groups upon their own insistence and very often through their own provision. . . . To these basic services the members of these colonies soon added a system of social and recreational organization.[25]

It is significant that even though these observations are based on the study of ethnic colonization schemes and religious communities such as the

Doukhobors, they seem to apply equally well to such loose groupings as the British "Sumner Colony" and the Czechs clustered at Kolin. This is because the economic and ecological conditions of pioneer life on the prairies led to the formation of rural neighbourhoods as social units based upon schools, churches, organizations, mutual aid, and sociability.[26] Where these rural neighbourhoods were ethnically mixed, they constituted a strong pressure against ethnic consciousness. But where they comprised people of one language and culture, they intensified ethnic solidarity at the local level. Hence, in each case, the Sumner English, the Kolin Czechs, and the Kaposvar Hungarians were held together not only by tradition and culture, but also by local conditions which created loyalty to the neighbourhood group.

Dawson also argued that, in addition to the factors outlined above, prejudice and conflict contributed to ethnic isolation:

> It was to be expected that these separatist communities would arouse the antagonism of those settlers who belonged to neighbouring communities in which a more secular pattern of life prevailed. Many of the social and economic movements which had received the ready support of other settlers were met with stout opposition in these colonies. The politics of the latter were uncertain; they seemed to be opposed in some instances, to public schools, to avoid the official language of the region and, in certain groups, to be antagonistic to the nationalistic sentiments of the linguistic majority.[27]

This degree of ethnic or religious group antagonism probably never occurred in the Esterhazy area, yet prejudice and tension did exist for some of the same reasons. When we asked about ethnic group conflict, Esterhazy people were reluctant to discuss it. One person replied: "There was no conflict, and if there was I wouldn't tell you." Another said: "It's better to let sleeping dogs lie." Still others, however, gave instances of hostility or tension, though emphasizing that no such problems exist today. Before Saskatchewan became a province in 1905, there was much controversy as to whether separate schools should be publicly financed. Later there were conflicts or resentments over religion and language in the schools. Over the years, members of other ethnic groups often accused the Hungarians of failure to support the various co-operative and protest organizations of the prairie farm movement.

World War I created divided loyalties for many Hungarians, whose countrymen in Europe were to be found among the ranks of the "enemy." They therefore supported Laurier against the Union Government, and generally opposed conscription. An Esterhazy citizen who had been Returning Officer in the Kaposvar poll for the election of 1917 told the author that the vote there was 65 for the Liberals, one for the Union Government. He interpreted this as an anti-war vote. The inter-ethnic animosities surrounding this election may be judged from the following "news item" in the *Esterhazy Observer* of December 14, 1917:

> Esterhazy on Tuesday last was treated to an exposition of the views of the Laurierites of the West. There was no slinging of neck yokes, but

Gardiner, M.L.A. for North Qu'Appelle by grace of foreign vote, was distinctly disloyal to the British race in Canada. His address was one long diatribe why the Alien should have full citizenship and why neither he nor anyone else in Canada should be conscripted.... Gardiner warned his British speaking listeners that after the war they would have to reckon with the foreigner, particularly those of North Qu'Appelle who were the gallery to which the speaker pandered.

Most of the Czechs, on the other hand, were Protestant or, at least, had a more secular outlook. They were also more oriented toward English Canada. When the war broke out the interests of their homeland were with the Allies. They were therefore doubly motivated to support the war effort, and, as we have seen, they did so enthusiastically. The fact that some Esterhazy Hungarians did serve in the armed forces did not prevent the Czechs (and, of course, the English too) from resenting the generally anti-war attitudes of "the" Hungarians. A delegation of Czechs went to the local newspaper editor to urge him to join them in a campaign to have the name of the town changed from Esterhazy to Sumner. No doubt they represented only a minority of the Czech community. But differences of language and outlook did create certain ethnic tensions during the first four or five decades of settlement.

In the early days, we were told, many of the people of British origins looked down upon the European immigrants, and often discriminated against them with regard to employment and other matters. The following statement is typical of the testimony of both British and European pioneers who were interviewed by us about the early years in February 1960:

For a long time the English-speaking people looked down on the Czechs and Hungarians. They called them "dirty farmers" and "foreigners." They had their own social groups. At community dances or other affairs, the English got together in their own groups.... Gradually, however, the English snob attitude disappeared altogether.

There can be no doubt, then, that among many of the early settlers ethnic prejudices and animosities tended to create social barriers and to augment "in-group" solidarity based on the other factors discussed above. On the other hand, we have found evidence that there was a considerable degree of inter-ethnic co-operation and harmony in the Esterhazy area, beginning from the first days of settlement. In fact, the balance of ecological, organizational, and social forces gradually shifted against ethnic solidarity, as I plan to show in a subsequent article. Today, among the young and middle-aged, at least, ethnic origins and national languages are usually forgotten or disregarded. Most people consider themselves simply as "Canadians," and some insist upon it. There seem to exist considerably fewer ethnic lines in friendship, employment, or marriage. The outlines of the once distinct cultural mosaic in the Esterhazy area are much less visible today.

FOOTNOTES

*The material upon which this study is based was gathered while the author was a research officer of the Centre for Community Studies at the University of Saskatchewan in Saskatoon. As project director of a team-study of the town and district of Esterhazy, the author visited the community regularly during 1959-61. More general information about the town and its history will be found in the following source: Donald E. Willmott, *Industry Comes to a Prairie Town* (Saskatoon, 1962), a monograph published by the Centre for Community Studies.

[1] Dojcsak, G. V., "The Mysterious Count Esterhazy," *Saskatchewan History*, vol. 26 (1973), 63-72.

[2] In their book *The Czechs and Slovaks in Canada* (Toronto, 1968), 64, John Gellner and John Smerek claim that about half of the original "Hungarian" settlers were actually Slovaks. However, evidence from the research of M. L. Kovacs, as reported in *Esterhazy and Early Hungarian Immigration to Canada* (Regina, 1971, pp. 138, 143, 145), suggests that the linguistic and cultural identity of many settlers with Slovak names was definitely Hungarian. Undoubtedly there were Slovaks in the population, and perhaps also among the "Bohemians," but since they did not emerge as a distinct ethnic or linguistic group in the Esterhazy area, we have been unable to gain any precise knowledge of them.

[3] Kovacs, *op. cit.*, 78-79.

[4] *Ibid.*, 6-12.

[5] Pirot, Reverend Father, *One Year's Fight for the True Faith in Saskatchewan, or The Hungarian Question in Canada in 1910* (Toronto, 1911).

[6] Kovacs, *op. cit.*, 83-84.

[7] Pirot, *op. cit.*, *passim.*

[8] *Manitoba Free Press*, Aug. 30, 1910.

[9] Pirot, *op. cit.*, 12.

[10] *Ibid.*, 16.

[11] *The Miner*, June 22, 1961.

[12] Gellner and Smerek, 61.

[13] *Ibid.*, 98.

[14] *Esterhazy Observer*, May 30, 1912.

[15] Gellner and Smerek, 71.

[16] *The Potashville Miner-Journal*, July 10, 1974.

[17] Gellner and Smerek, 105-106.

[18] *Esterhazy Observer*, October 9, 1941.

[19] Jean Burnet, *Next Year Country: A Study of Rural Social Organization in Alberta* (Toronto, 1951).

[20] Paul Santha, D. D., *Three Generations, 1901-1957: The Hungarian Colony at Stockholm, Saskatchewan, Canada* (n.p., 1958).

[21] Kovacs, *op. cit.*, 19.

[22] *Ibid.*, 22-23.

[23] *Ibid.*, 19.

[24] *Ibid.*, *passim.*

[25] C. A. Dawson, *Group Settlement: Ethnic Communities in Western Canada* (Toronto, 1936), 379.

[26] The nature of these rural neighbourhoods is elaborated in Donald E. Willmott, *Organizations and Social Life of Farm Families in a Prairie Municipality* (Saskatoon, 1964). The ecological, economic and cultural conditions which brought about the active organizational life in rural neighbourhoods are elaborated in: Donald E. Willmott, "The Formal Organizations of Saskatchewan Farmers, 1900-1965," in Anthony W. Rasporich, ed., *Western Canada: Past and Present* (Calgary, 1975).

[27] Dawson, *op. cit.*, 379.

TO BE OR NOT TO BE INDIAN: A QUESTION CONCERNING CULTURAL IDENTITY IN WHITEHORSE, YUKON

CARMEN LAMBERT
McGILL UNIVERSITY, MONTREAL

The problem of cultural identity persistence and change among North American Indians had been the subject of a large number of studies. But this problem has been usually treated in terms of acculturation and assimilation into the dominant white culture. The persistence of particular cultural traits, the retention of a native language as well as other ethnic manifestations, were often used as indicators of the maintenance of an Indian cultural identity.

These studies had shown for example that life on reservations is an important factor in the maintenance of an ethnic identity based on ancestry and cultural heritage. It had been argued in the case of Canadian Indians that the ones who still retain some of their cultural identity are the ones who live on reserves.[1] Nagata had also concluded in a study of Hopi Indians that urban migration "entails the abandonment of the Indian identity when the migrants submit to the domination of the White American culture and economy."[2] Urban migration is thus seen as leading to a lessening sense of cultural identity because migration to the city results in greater assimilation.

However, urban Indians seem to have adopted a new sense of Indianness, a neo-Indian identity. Pan-Indianism was described as the expression of this new identity as well as an attempt to create a new ethnic group.[3] The development of this complex social phenomenon is related to the disappearance of local aboriginal traits, to a developing commonality among Indians in an urban environment, and to a growing recognition among Indians that they have common interests and problems regardless of their tribal or cultural affiliations.[4] Nagler had argued that this general Indian identity is being imposed upon Native people "partly through their own awareness of how they are viewed by others, but mainly through the pressures of the larger society on them to see themselves as a different and separate group."[5] This new conception of Indianness is thus closely related to the common social, economic, and political situation of the Native people in the North American society. Continued conflict between the larger society and the Indians was critical in the development of this neo-Indian identity.[6] New symbols of Indianness had had to be created in order to unify all Indians into a single ethnic group.

In this paper data from a small northern town in the Yukon are presented to illustrate the formation and maintenance of one example of contemporary Indian identity. Our purpose is to analyse the development of this general Indian identity in a town where many Indian cultural groups cohabit, as well as the maintenance of a cultural identity. The focus is on the symbolic identifications and not on ethnic manifestations. Focussing on behaviour or group formation could be misleading because it implies a direct correspondence between the manifestations of an ethnic identity and the components of that identity. An identity system could be best analyzed in terms of the set of identity symbols used by people to demonstrate distinctiveness and commonality.[7]

Any sociocultural element may be exploited as an identity symbol at any given historical moment. Signs and symbols of identity change through time and from place to place.[8] Moreover, the referents of ethnicity may vary with age, sex, social classes; various segments of an ethnic group may have different conceptions of their ethnic identity. However, the set of cultural elements utilized forms a code which permits the persistence of the identity system. The analysis of the identity components and the symbolic code used by Indians in Whitehorse[9] to express their ethnic identity may have general implications for understanding the whole process of cultural identity maintenance and change.

First a brief note on the Indian population of Whitehorse. In 1971, about 40% of the Yukon Indians were settled in this main population centre of the territory. The Indian community in Whitehorse, composed of status and non-status Indians, numbered approximatively 1,000 persons. More than half were living in the unserviced parts of this small town of 11,220 people — the squatter areas and the Indian village located at the periphery of the city centre. The more wealthy Indians or the middle-class Indians[10] lived in various serviced sectors of the town.

Formal and informal interviews were conducted with a total of 157 Indians on the components of their Indian identity. Many informants were able to expand upon what it means to be an Indian and upon what keeps them "Indians" in an urban environment. Moreover, many were very explicit in describing the components and the symbols of Indianness and usually volunteered to list these components in a scale of importance.

Identity Components and Symbols

As shown in Table 1, Indians in Whitehorse have a number of diverse cultural identity bases. There is thus a wide range of sociocultural elements that may be utilized as identity symbols in any given situation. However, a selection is made among these sociocultural elements forming a code or language system. But before analysing this system or the interrelationships between elements of this code, we have first to examine the meaning of each specific component.

Racial origin is described by a great majority of our informants (83.4%) as the principal element of Indian identity. The political struggle prevailing in the Yukon at that time over aboriginal rights may explain in part why so many individuals listed racial origin as the most significant element of

TABLE 1

Percentage distribution of Identity components by social classes

Identity Components	Lower-class N=82	Middle-class N=75	Total N=157
Racial Origin	81.7	84.0	83.4
Regional Origin	75.6	65.3	69.4
Indian Status	67.0	54.6	61.8
Cultural Traits	86.5	69.3	79.0
Cultural Values	97.5	93.3	96.1

group definition. In the land claim issue, racial origin was an important symbol manipulated by both whites and Indians. While government representatives claimed that only status Indians were entitled to become part of any land settlement, the Indian representatives argued that the definition of Indian should be based on racial origin rather than on a legal distinction. Thus, the Yukon Native Brotherhood stated in 1973 that all individuals over 18 years of age who can prove that they have one-fourth of Indian blood and that they were born in the Yukon should be entitled to become part of this land settlement.

It is clear though that racial differences as such have no intrinsic significance when detached from the historical context or when detached from the land referent. Statements like this one were quite common: "The color of my skin is the only thing that proves that I am an Indian and that my ancestors owned this country." There is symbolization of racial origin by connotation along two axes: vertical (descent) and horizontal (land ownership or occupancy).

The legal Indian status was also listed by our informants as an important sociocultural element. However, it was listed less as a component of Indian identity than as a symbol of Indianness. A majority (86.2%) of status Indians interviewed stressed the fact that non-status Indians should be regarded as "Indians" by the larger society. The mere fact of having this legal status recognized by the Canadian society does not make one more Indian. Yet these same individuals argue that the Indian status must be maintained in order to protect the territorial and political rights of Indian people in Canada. In this context, the legal status in its symbolic meaning connotes descent as well as land ownership or occupancy. Thus, the Indian legal status is closely linked to racial origin as interdependent elements of identity, and in certain situations, as interchangeable symbols.

The racial origin and the Indian status symbolizing the particular sociopolitical situation of Indian people in Canada are important elements of a general Indian identity. These symbols are used to minimize traditional cultural differences among Indian groups and to foster group solidarity in various social and political contexts. We may, then, argue with Cohen[11] that ethnicity is a political, not a cultural phenomenon. Another example of this would be the recent political division between two important segments of the Indian population in the Yukon which led to the development of two separate Indian political organizations. In the present land claim negotiations, the Yukon Indian Council created recently represents only the

Indians whose ancestors inhabited the Yukon from time immemorial. On the other hand, a former association still existing, the Yukon Native Brotherhood, does now represent only the Indians whose ancestors migrated to the Yukon either from the Northwest Territories or the Northwest coast of Canada and the United States.

However, the identification with a particular regional or tribal group is still very strong and it does not only manifest itself on the political scene. Individuals first defined themselves as Tlingit or Kutchin or Loucheux and not as Indians. They almost never use the generic term "Indian" in categorizing themselves. They do so not only within the context of the Indian community, but also within the context of the larger society even though white people in Whitehorse never make any distinction between Indians from different regional or tribal groups. This identification is not so much based on cultural differences as on the particular history of the different regional or tribal groups.

Evidently, the political situation as well as the urbanization process had helped in creating a general Indian identity by stressing elements of commonality among Indians. Nevertheless, a tribal identification did persist. However, the tribal or regional history is used both as a symbol of differentiation among Indian groups and as a symbol of commonality in its connotation of common descent and land occupancy in front of the Euro-Canadian population.

Ethnicity for the Whitehorse Indian people is also tied to a set of cultural elements which includes language, institutions, and values. These elements may be utilized as symbols of both commonality and distinctiveness among Yukon Indian groups and among Canadian Indian groups. Table 2 describes in detail the cultural elements mentioned by our informants as identity referents. Among these cultural elements, traditional institutions such as the potlatch and the clan system seem to be the most significant ones. However, these institutions are especially referred to by the poor-class segment of the Indian population; only 33.3% of the middle-class Indians interviewed mentioned the clan system as opposed to 65.8% of our lower class informants. It should also be noted that within the middle class segment, men put more emphasis on this institution than women, especially women married to white men. This seems to be related to the fact that class stratification is becoming more important than the clan system in regulating marriages.

For old people, the clan system is still in some way linked to the traditional beliefs, but the young adults and the middle-class people define the clan system only in its social characteristics. In fact, the traditional religion has become a minor element of cultural identity. Only 8.7% of young people and 12.0% of middle-class people mentioned traditional religious beliefs; it is however referred to by 32.9% of lower-class people and by 31.0% of older people. Despite an increasing disillusionment towards Christian religion, there is no evidence of a strong revival of interest in native religious beliefs. It is interesting to note that even young people stress

TABLE 2
Percentage distribution of cultural elements by social classes

Cultural Traits and Values	Lower-class N=82	Middle-class N=75	Total N=157
Potlach	68.3	58.6	63.6
Clan System	65.8	33.3	50.3
Native Art	65.8	42.6	54.7
Language	12.1	60.0	35.0
Religion	32.9	12.0	22.9
Values:			
Individualism	90.2	90.6	90.4
Independence	91.4	88.8	89.8
Freedom	95.1	28.0	63.0
Community spirit	76.8	69.3	73.2

the necessity to perpetuate certain customs related to the traditional religion: a potlatch after a funeral with or without a Christian ceremony, a burial in the Indian cemetery, etc. It does not necessarily follow that traditional beliefs are a significant force serving to perpetuate a sense of Indianness. Yet traditional religious rituals may be used in certain situations as ideological symbols.

Native art work was also referred to by 54.7% of the informants. It seems that if lower-class people put a certain emphasis on this element, it is because many still make various pieces of clothing from caribou skin or moose skin for the family or for sale as a financial supplement. But still, 45.6% of young adults and 42.6% of middle-class people listed native art before native religion and clan system; it should be noted that many among them had renewed their interest in native art as well as in other cultural practices.

TABLE 3
Percentage distribution of cultural elements by age groups

Cultural Traits and Values	-35 years old N=57	+35 years old N=100	Total N=157
Potlach	52.6	70.0	63.6
Clan System	31.5	61.0	50.3
Native Art	45.6	60.0	54.7
Language	43.8	30.0	35.0
Religion	8.7	31.0	22.9
Values:			
Individualism	89.4	91.0	90.4
Independence	84.2	93.0	89.8
Freedom	45.6	73.0	63.0
Community Spirit	56.1	82.0	73.2

Young people often stress the fact that being Indian does not entail following traditional customs. However, these young people emphasize the need for a basic knowledge of these customs. They all regret not having been able to get a better knowledge of their fathers' culture because of the boarding school system. They criticize this system for its constant devaluation of the Indian culture and history. This is one of the reasons why many of them are now trying to learn their native language or dialect, and teach it to their children and why they tend to valorize the language as a symbol of attachment to the group of origin. They also believe that in an industrialized urban world language is more likely to survive than the clan system. Language while not limiting integration will act, they argue, as a barrier to complete cultural assimilation; language, moreover, will assure the maintenance of a particular philosophy and a particular "mode of thought." Language may then become one of the major elements of cultural identity for young middle-class Indians.[12] For example, within the middle-class segment, all the male informants and 60.0% of the female informants mentioned language as a significant element while only 12.5% of lower-class informants listed this element.

All or some of these cultural traits could be used at any time as symbols of distinction in any social or political context. These cultural elements are valorized in their functions of maintaining solidarity and unity among Indians and, more important, as vehicles of cultural and social values. The potlach, the clan system, and the religion stress to various degrees reciprocity and sharing as well as respect for nature and one's fellow men. Language and art are expressions of a world view, of a way of thinking about the relationships between people and between man and nature; they also serve as vehicles of cultural values.

Indians themselves do insist on a specific value orientation which they often describe as "community spirit." This expression refers to whole sets of values: co-operation, reciprocity, sharing, generosity, and solidarity. Other important values are individualism and personal independence. All these values are very often emphasized in contrast to what is perceived as being Euro-Canadian values, with regard to individual competition, social status, and money. Whitemen are often considered as persons who always strive for more and more money, who characterize others on the basis of their material possessions instead of on their personal intrinsic qualities, and as persons who would do almost anything to get a higher social status.

In this context, the emphasis on independence and individualism reflects a desire to be able to "succeed" within the dominant society without a complete overthrow of traditional customs and values, and then without conforming to all the norms of behaviour or accepting all the values of the dominant society. It also reflects a strong resistance to collective assimilation.

Personal freedom is another value referred to by 63.0% of the informants. This element is less important or significant for young people and middle-class Indians than for the others. This difference seems to be related to the degree of adaptation to the urban environment and to the wage labour market. Lower-class Indians often define freedom as the possibility of linking work and pleasure; the possibility of continuing trapping and hunting while taking only occasional or seasonal wage labour jobs if necessary; the possibility of organizing their time as they wish. Middle-class Indians on the other hand speak of freedom almost exclusively in political terms as the possibility of self-government for native people. While one segment stresses personal freedom, the other puts the emphasis on collective freedom. Thus, the connotation may be different from one segment to another, from one individual to another, and could consequently be used in various ways for different purposes.

Norms of Behaviour

This set of values which may indicate a cultural continuity is one of the most important referents of ethnicity. Moreover, these values do have some influence on social behaviour; they are used independently in some situations as standards of evaluation of one's behaviour.

For example, each individual is expected to keep close ties with the community as a whole and to co-operate with every segment of this group. The pattern of relationship shows in fact that there is maintenance of community ties by frequent visits to former communities; maintenance also of extended family relationships; assistance among individual relatives; and active participation in collective activities like potlatches and the "Yukon Indian Days."[13]

This seems to correspond to Barth's argument that ethnic identity is being associated with a cluster of expectations and that membership in an ethnic category implies adherence to certain norms.[14] However, a much more detailed study would be necessary to define the extent to which this pattern of behaviour is tied to a specific value orientation associated with behavioural norms. We might argue for example that this type of behaviour is basically a response to kinship demands. Assistance, co-operation and the sharing of one's property are in fact restricted to family relatives. Also, even if some friendship ties cut across social classes, social interaction tends to be restricted to one's social class. A certain social distance is maintained between the two class segments. (For example, middle-class Indians never go to taverns where lower class Indians always gather.)

Generosity, sharing, and reciprocity may be used as criteria of evaluation of one's behaviour at the level of the extended family. But the evidence suggests that at the community level, there is no single set of standards of evaluation and judgement of one's performance or one's socio-economic behaviour. This means that there is no single cluster of expectations and no single set of norms of behaviour. Let us now consider more attentively these norms and standards of evaluation in relation to social classes.

A certain group of Indians, mostly lower-class Indians, chose in Whitehorse a certain way of life which could be compared to a skid row life style characterized by part-time jobs, welfare dependency, begging, heavy drinking, and daily life in and around taverns and street corners.[15] This life style is also similar in many respects to what Honigmann and Honigmann described as a "frontier culture" characterized by outdoor-type activities, unconventionality, individual independence, personal freedom, heavy drinking, and welfare dependency.[16] Dosman argues that skid row "permits community life outside the norms of the larger society."[17] Honigmann and Honigmann (1970:63) also argued the same point with reference to the frontier culture which "sets the native population off from the dominant middle-class culture . . . but also serves as a means of repudiating firm commitment to certain of that culture's norms and values which people find spurious and restrictive."[18] This life style could act, according to Honigmann and Honigmann, "as a nativistic brake controlling further assimilation and as a symbol of native group identity."[19]

Evidence presented in this paper shows that the sense of Indianness for skid row Indians in Whitehorse is primarily based on Indian cultural traditions and values, and not on superficial characteristics of life style. There is no particular value put on this way of life even if it could be used in certain circumstances as a symbol of ethnicity because it connotes independence, individualism, and freedom. This sense of Indianness is thus only indirectly related to their conditions of poverty and their consequent life style. However, because of their economic position, they share a set of expectations and aspirations different from that of the middle-class Indians. Consequently, they respond to different norms of behaviour and different criteria of evaluation of performance.

The middle-class Indians in Whitehorse who chose to accept a competitive life style had adopted many middle-class values as their own: steady employment, social and economic competition, individual promotion, power and prestige. They had also accepted the corresponding standards of evaluation and judgement of performance. It is worth pointing out also that they tend to share the Whites' negative view of the poor Indian people being stereotyped as drunken, lazy, and irresponsible people.[20]

These Indians are often called "white Indians" because of their drive for money, power, and prestige within the dominant society. They reject this label, however, in that they want to "succeed" in the dominant society as "Indians". They aspire to preserve their Indian heritage while adapting to urban life and to the dominant free-enterprise society. They have a number of reference groups which are relevant simultaneously, alternatively, or situationally. But the Indian group seems to remain the prime identification group. A middle-class informant told us for example: "If I ever have to choose between whites and Indians, I will definitely choose my own people." Many other informants made clear to us that being well adapted to an urban industrialized situation does not mean being or becoming "whitemen." In fact, there is no strong evidence of an identity crisis; very few showed ambivalence about their native ancestry and none of the informants showed signs of rejection of their Indian heritage. Furthermore, they do not see that heritage as a hindrance to urban adjustment or social mobility. Dosman in his study of the Indian population in Saskatoon also showed that "Affluent Indians" have a strong sense and a consciousness of Indianness.[21] These data suggest that social mobility, like urban migration, does not entail the decline of ethnic identity, and they tend to contradict Cohen's hypothesis about such a decline following the growth of inequality within an ethnic group.[22] But, because this identity does not always lead, as exemplified in Whitehorse, to participation in native associations or to active involvement in promoting interest in native traditions, it would be misleading to try to evaluate the importance of ethnicity on the basis of behavioural patterns and ethnic manifestations.

The content of ethnicity is influenced by and reflects class stratification. Social classes could be viewed as cultural units exhibiting specific customs, norms of behaviour, standards of evaluation, and value orientations. Social class does very often constitute an identification group — hence the need for an adjustment in the content of ethnicity to the social position. But behavioural constraints imposed by class membership do not necessarily lead to a change of identity, even if another identity is available, but only to changes in the referents of ethnicity.

In summary, Barth's arguments about a shared value system and shared criteria of evaluation associated with adherence to a set of norms may be relevant for small non-stratified ethnic groups but the problem is much more complex when one is dealing with an urban stratified group. Individuals from different social strata do not necessarily share a common set of expectations and do not necessarily follow common behaviour and performance norms. We may argue that within the Indian group in Whitehorse, there is a shared value orientation based on sharing, co-operation, and reciprocity, even though this represents an "ideal" model. However, we must take into account the fact that the middle-class segment put much less emphasis than the lower-class segment on these values (Table 2). Also, the obligations of sharing and reciprocity are counter-balanced by the need for personal independence. The emphasis on individualism and personal independence which reflects cultural and socio-economic heterogeneity within the Indian group, allows for the possibility of non-sharing and non-cooperation. These values allow individuals to manipulate their cultural background and their class position to maximize their own personal options. They allow then, variability of behaviour, standards of evaluation, and even value orientations.

Indian people in Whitehorse do share a common general identity as Indians which could be described as pan-Indian in its orientation. The racial concept plays down cultural, social, and economic differences by affirming a common descent. It could thus be used as a major symbol of Indianness in the urban context. The Indian status in the Canadian society may also be used as a symbol of a general Indian identity because this reference like the racial origin connotes descent and land occupancy from time immemorial. The emphasis on values such as individualism and personal independence reinforces the sense of a general identity. Thus the identity at the group level vis-à-vis other groups which transcends situational adjustments, may be a response to the urban environment, to racial discrimination, and to the power structure. It is the expression of a common conflict with the dominant society and a reflection of political relations. The power structure and the class structure by imposing such an identity on Indian people prohibited the emergence of a shared "northerner" identity between Indians and long-time white residents in the north.

The Indian identity seems nevertheless to be based on cultural heritage. Even young Indians stress the necessity to maintain a certain cultural continuity or at least some cultural differences not only between Indians and whites but also between Indian groups. Another dimension of this identity is tied to strong feelings of group obligations — hence, the emphasis on values such as sharing and co-operation, and on traditional institutions like the potlatch and the clan system.

What are the relationships between all these referents? In order to answer this question one must look at the different dimensions or levels of symbolization. Referents such as the racial origin, the tribal or regional origin, and the Indian status in the Canadian society are tied to a social and political reality. They may connote the cultural heritage of particular Indian groups as well as common descent among all Canadian or North American Indian groups. Traditional institutions or cultural traits also connote both aspects or dimensions: particular/general. They may be used in the context of the larger society as symbols of common group affiliation vis-à-vis the Euro-Canadian group; they symbolize a set of common traditional values including individualism, co-operation, reciprocity, and sharing. As described before, the norms of behaviour followed by members of the Indian group are not directly tied to these values because of age group membership or class affiliation. This set of values refers to an "Indian ideal model" vis-à-vis the Euro-Canadian model.

Referents of ethnicity do not have real meaning as isolates but only as parts of sets which are responsive to changing situations. Race and language do not have real significance when considered in isolation. Their meaning is based on their articulation with other referents such as territoriality or certain cultural values. The symbolic value attributed to the referents is more important than the referents themselves in defining the content of ethnicity. The sets form a code of symbolization which permits the persistence of cultural identity despite structural changes in the culture.

FOOTNOTES

[1]M. Nagler, *Indians in the City* (Ottawa, 1970) and *Natives without a Home* (Don Mills, 1975).
[2]S. Nagata, "The Reservation Community and the Urban Community: Hopi Indians in Moenkopi," in J. O. Waddell and O. M. Watson, eds., *The American Indian in Urban Society* (Boston, 1971), 148.
[3]R. K. Thomas, "Pan-Indianism," in D. E. Walker Jr., ed. *The Emergent Native Americans* (Boston, 1972), 739.
[4]J. Ablon, "Relocated American Indians in the San Francisco Bay Area: Social Interaction and Indian Identity," *Human Organizations,* 24 (1964), 296-305. See also Thomas, "Pan-Indianism," in D. E. Walker Jr., ed., *The Emergent Native Americans* (Boston, 1972).
[5]M. Nagler, *Natives without a Home* (Don Mills, 1975), 9.
[6]See E. H. Spicer who discusses the importance of the oppositional process in the formation and development of a persistent identity system: "Persistent Cultural Systems," *Science,* 174 (1971), 795-800.
[7]P. Mercier had argued some time ago that the study of ethnicity "must be to a large degree at the level of symbols and justifications;" "On the Meaning of 'Tribalism' in Black Africa," in P. Van den Berghe, ed., *Africa, Social Problems of Change and Conflict* (San Francisco, 1965), 485.

[8]See F. Barth, "Pathan Identity and its Maintenance," in F. Barth, ed., *Ethnic Groups and Boundaries* (Boston, 1969); A. Cohen, "Introduction. The Lesson of Ethnicity," in A. Cohen, ed., *Urban Ethnicity* (London, 1974); H. Eidheim, "When Ethnic Identity is a Social Stigma," in Barth, ed., *op. cit.;* U. Hannerz, "Ethnicity and Opportunity in Urban America," in Cohen, ed., *op. cit.*

[9]The data for this paper are drawn from long-term research for a Ph.D. thesis in 1970-1971 in Whitehorse. This research was funded by the Department of Indian Affairs and Northern Development, Ottawa.

[10]For the purposes of this study, Indian people were classified into two sub-groups, the middle class group and the lower class group, on the basis of education, income, and professional activities. This classification, however arbitrary in many respects, permitted us to verify variations in ethnic identity referents with regard to class membership.

[11]A. Cohen, *Custom and Politics in Urban Africa: A Study of Hausa Migrants in Yoruba Towns* (London, 1969) and "The Lesson of Ethnicity" (1974).

[12]W. L. Leap's analysis of Indian English showed the importance of a shared language in the definition and development of cultural identity for American Indians; "Ethnics, Emics, and the New Ideology: The Identity Potential of Indian English," in T. K. Fitzgerald, ed., *Social and Cultural Identity* (Athens, U.S.A., 1974), 51-62.

[13]The "Yukon Indian Days" are a three-day Indian festival organized each year since 1970.

[14]Barth, "Introduction" in F. Barth, ed., *Ethnic Groups and Boundaries,* 15-19.

[15]See H. Brody, *Indians on Skid Row* (Ottawa, 1971); E. J. Dosman, *Indians: The Urban Dilemma* (Toronto, 1972).

[16]J. J. Honigmann and I. Honigmann, *Arctic Townsmen* (Ottawa, 1970).

[17]Dosman, *op. cit.,* 15.

[18]Honigmann and Honigmann, *op. cit.,* 63.

[19]*Ibid.,* 15.

[20]Carmen Lambert, "Identification et Integration Ethnique à l'Intérieur d'une Ville Nordique, Whitehorse, Yukon," Thèse de doctorat, Université McGill (Montreal, 1974).

[21]Dosman, *op. cit.*

[22]Cohen, "Introduction. The Lesson of Ethnicity," xxii.

THE CHANGING ROLE OF ETHNOCULTURAL ORGANIZATIONS IN SASKATCHEWAN: CASE STUDIES WITH STATISTICAL DATA CAST IN HISTORICAL PERSPECTIVE

ZENON POHORECKY
UNIVERSITY OF SASKATCHEWAN

A major reason for the existence of any ethnocultural organization in Saskatchewan since the turn of the 20th century has been the ethnic group's concern, not only for the welfare of its individual members, but also for the survival of its unique cultural identity, which is based on traditional values rooted firmly in language and religion.

The pressure of institutionalized discrimination against ethnic groups in Saskatchewan has recently been greatly reduced by the official federal and provincial policies in regard to multiculturalism. The Canadian government's multicultural policy was announced in Parliament on October 8, 1971. The Saskatchewan government, on May 10, 1974, not only enacted the Saskatchewan Multicultural Act, which was the first of its kind in Canada, but also repealed, after 55 years, that section (209) of the School Act which had forbidden the use of any language but English for purposes of instruction.

The initial question must be whether the many ethnocultural organizations in Saskatchewan must eventually vanish, since their initial reason for being founded seems to be vanishing in the warm new climate of tolerance. This question is easily answered. No. The reason is, not just a cautious mistrust of politicians who promise a new era of peace in our time, but also a desire to participate more effectively in the development of a Canadian lifestyle that is compatible with the ethnic group's basic values and traditional ways.

In addition, taking into account the great diversity that already exists among the various kinds of ethnocultural organizations in the province, it is apparent that the key to any ethnocultural organization's survival lies in its ability to adapt to unexpected and even drastic changes in the Canadian milieu.

The ultimate purpose of this brief paper, then, is to suggest, not only any detectable trends, but also possible future directions for ethnocultural organizations in Saskatchewan. These rather general and modest suggestions will be based on the most recent statistical information available in regard to the ethnocultural organizations of Saskatchewan (Pohorecky 1977b), analyzed rather selectively in a historical perspective.

Which Organizations are Ethnocultural

Stereotypes may be useful for identifying members of groups, but they usually mislead, because they tend to caricature the group in negative terms.

For instance, a very common stereotype of the ethnocultural organization assumes that it must a kind of mini-Mafia, whose main goal is to herd all members of an ethnic community into a ghetto of immigrants. It is also sometimes assumed that the ethnocultural organization must hide its seamy aspect with a bright and happy mask, which seems to sing out with lusty folk tunes, while feet go dancing and hands go cooking exotic dishes and producing beautiful arts and crafts. This rather patronizing view of an ethnocultural organization's "good points" expects its members to be costumed appropriately on certain ceremonial occasions.

Such demeaning stereotypes tend to restrict the wide range of positive roles that ethnocultural organizations could (and usually do) play by defining their major role rather narrowly in the performing arts, and, at best, in digging up and making available some archival information about the historical or cultural significance of its folkloric activities.

If one is committed to such a wrong impression of what ethnocultural organizations are all about, or should be like, then one would never classify as "ethnocultural" such real organizations as: Ukrainian parish organizations, German Catholic church organizations, Jewish community organizations, Mennonite congregations, Hutterite colonies, Doukhobor prayer homes, or Indian reserves. Some of these might be dismissed as strictly religious institutions, in spite of the fund-raising, cultural and educational activities that are conducted in their halls, church basements and summer camps. They might not be classified as ethnocultural, although they are essential to any meaningful definition of the ethnic group itself. Nor might such real organizations wish to be stereotyped as "ethnocultural" in view of the poor image that has become associated with the term, which currently connotes a kind of frivolous superficiality. No wonder some have even felt insulted at being classified as ethnocultural.

Still, such essentially religious organizations must be classified as truly ethnocultural, because it is only through them and their ministers that many ethnic communities have managed to survive at all in western Canada, by using their own language and preserving their cultural traditions through the celebration of certain religious events in ways that are distinctively cultural, and not strictly or only religious. So much is history and fact.

For instance, it is a fact that Ukrainians feel most "Ukrainian" (rather than Christian) when they celebrate Christmas and Easter with traditions that predate Christianity. Moreover, Ukrainians celebrate these events pretty well the same way everywhere, whether they are of the Orthodox or Catholic persuasion, or neither (or in between). Significantly, they also celebrate these religious events very differently from their fellow Christians of different cultural roots. Clearly, then, the cultural (and pagan) aspects of these religious celebrations are vital to the members of Ukrainian churches anywhere in the world.

It is apparent from this example that any meaningful definition of an ethnocultural organization must allow for inclusion of such "parish" organizations. This inclusion may have to be made over the objections of some devout member (like the pastor, priest or minister) who may argue that religious institutions should be classified separately from ethnocultural ones, especially if the religious institutions are open to members of all ethnic groups, hence aspiring to congregate a multicultural community. This argument would be most compelling in Saskatchewan in those religious institutions that use English only as the sole working language. Understandably, young people, influenced by schools and media, would use English. However, it is the rare religious institution that would insist that its older members use broken English in church activities.

A valid role of the church has been to reflect and support the most profound cultural values of an ethnic community. This has resulted, of course, in the church basement often becoming a kind of "underground" meeting place, where parents could conduct Saturday morning language classes for children, while a funeral was being conducted overhead. Such activities might even have been termed "subversive" by those who noted that such language classes were not permitted in public schools.

Having thus extended the criteria to be used for including hitherto excluded organizations (mainly religious ones) in a category called "ethnocultural," it is now necessary to exclude other kinds of organizations from our definition, in order to make it very clear as to what is not an ethnocultural organization. Obviously, the public school in Saskatchewan is not even a multicultural organization, although it has students of various ethnic backgrounds. It is not an ethnocultural organization, even if it has certainly tended to use the English language exclusively for the purpose of instruction since 1919.

The school may be viewed more accurately as anti-cultural, especially from the viewpoint of the non-English student who may feel that his own language and historic background has been threatened by institutionalized discrimination, which may be defined here as the unfair treatment that is given to specific ethnic groups by publicly supported institutions, like the school system and the civil service. By discriminating against every language except English, and by rejecting every bias of history except the British one, the school has acted as a major force in taking away culture from a child rather than as a force in giving the child more culture. That is, it has actually robbed the child of its pride in its cultural identity by alienating the child from its parents. This subversion of ethnic values by teachers and texts, that have neglected or rejected those who were not British by birth, has resulted in a great social pathology which has affected the mental and spiritual health of almost everybody in the community.

There are other publicly supported institutions that should not be confused with ethnocultural or multicultural organizations. For example, the community concert hall or the local art gallery is not usually ethnocultural, unless it is owned and operated by some ethnic group for the promotion and development of its own arts. Some museums do fall into this ethnocultural category, and others may tend to be multicultural. Therefore, it may be best to consider each individual institution on its own merits before rejecting it from our classification. That is what has been done here; so if some questionable ones have been subsumed under the category of multicultural, it is due to lack of adequate data to the contrary, because the benefit of the doubt has been given to the organization which took the time to fill out the questionnaire.

Privately owned institutions like banks have not been regarded as ethnocultural organizations, and this may be a correct assessment, but the failure of such financial institutions to provide adequate credit to members of certain ethnic groups has prompted some ethnic groups to establish their own financial institutions. Therefore, it is not unusual to find ethnic groups with their own co-operatives, foundations, benevolent societies, nursing homes, old age homes, and student residences, catering mainly to their own people, but also doing business with others. Such ethnocultural organizations may not stage concerts or bake sales, as a rule, but this should not serve to exclude them from our classification.

In summary, then, an ethnocultural organization may be described as any formally constituted group that protects the cultural values of an ethnic community from the kind of de-culturating milieu that our constantly modernizing and technologically biased society mass-produces with its emphasis on economic goals, like "getting a job" to know what and who you are. This is its ghetto function and its humanizing function. Any organization that performs such functions for an ethnic community is classified here as ethnocultural.

The Statistical Story

The census of 1971 lists the population of Saskatchewan at 926,245. All population figures in this section are based on the 1971 census. It has been possible to identify all, except 2,447, according to ethnic background. These 2,447 have been excluded from the computations here.

The original research material has been gathered during the past three years through the Saskatchewan Association on Human Rights, assisted by the Canadian Department of the Secretary of State, for the Saskatchewan Department of Culture and Youth, and sponsored for publication by the Saskatchewan Multicultural Advisory Council. The list of ethnocultural organizations in Saskatchewan is certainly not yet exhaustive. However, it is still the best single source currently available, based on continuing original research. Since the list is incomplete, it is apparent that the available figures may somewhat warp the precise proportions between ethnic groups, but such skewing may be assumed to be of minimal relevance to the rather general and tentative kinds of conclusions that are reached here.

There are 753 ethnocultural organizations, which have responded to questionnaires, listed so far in Saskatchewan. These are listed in Appendix I, where it will be seen that they represent about 40 ethnic groups in the province. The unequal distribution of organizations, between the various ethnic groups, is at once striking and significant, especially when the ethnic groups are themselves grouped into eight major units, each based on linguistic and/or cultural affinities, as well as on more general geographic considerations in regard to the original homelands of the groups. Organizations that involve unrelated ethnic groups in special activities or events have been classified separately in a ninth category called multicultural.

These nine groupings have been ranked, more or less, in terms of which has more ethnocultural organizations, so that the one ranked first would tend to have the most, and the one ranked last would have the least. The precise figures are listed in Appendix 2. It will be seen that, in actual rank order, the nine groupings would be: (a) Eastern Europeans (mostly Slavic people); (b) Central Europeans (mostly Germanic people); (c) Multicultural; (d) Native (Indians and Metis); (e) French; (f) Non-European (outside Europe and America); (g) British (English-speaking people); (h) Southern Europeans and (i) Northern European (Scandinavian people).

(a) *Eastern Europeans*

Ukrainians constitute just over nine per cent of the population of Saskatchewan, but they alone have established and maintained, sometimes for over 60 years, a full 36 per cent of all ethnocultural organizations in the province today. This statistic may astonish some. It does represent the highest per capita rate of organization formation, with, in terms of gross averages, one Ukrainian organization for every 316 Ukrainians in the province. Also, Ukrainians have over 86 per cent of all Slavic organizations in the province today.

Over 41 per cent of all Ukrainian organizations in Saskatchewan are Orthodox, and about 28 per cent are Catholic, although there are many times more Ukrainian Catholics than Ukrainian Orthodox persons in the province. This suggests, of course, that Ukrainian Catholic organizations tend to be larger and far less numerous than the Ukrainian Orthodox ones. Over 30 per cent of all Ukrainian organizations crosscut religious affiliations.

Significantly, strictly women's organizations (83) account for over 30 per cent of all Ukrainian organizations in Saskatchewan. When it is also noted that most Ukrainian schools and dancing schools are conducted by women, it is impossible to escape the conclusion that Ukrainian women play a leading role in preserving those aspects of the Ukrainian culture that may be of particular concern to women — language, embroidery, singing, culinary arts, and dancing. This leading role played by women also reflects the traditional matriarchal family in Ukraine, where the man, often divested of his freedom, particularly in Eastern Ukraine, was a kind of benevolent patriarch at home, where his wife really ruled.

Women's organizations are particularly prevalent in the smaller communities outside Saskatoon and Regina, usually associated with church parish groups, where the women's organizations account for over 49 per cent of the Catholic community groups, and almost 48 per cent of the Orthodox community groups. Interestingly, there are no women's organizations outside Saskatoon and Regina that are *not* associated with either a Catholic or Orthodox group, although there are a great number of language school and dancing school organizations that are virtually run by the women. The role of the Ukrainian woman in Ukrainian organizations in Saskatchewan is perhaps even more vital than that of the Ukrainian man, whose own organizations tend to be concerned more with political and economic concerns than strictly folkloric or archival activities.

Regina has seven per cent of all Ukrainian organizations in the province. Almost 58 per cent are non-denominational. Significantly, there are almost twice as many Ukrainian Orthodox organizations as Ukrainian Catholic ones in Regina (actually 26 per cent compared to 16 per cent). The reason for this difference is not clear, but it may reflect in a general way the level of cultural activity conducted by members of the two denominations in a capital city where there are about 5,000 Ukrainians. It may also reflect, on the other hand, more concern with religious matters by the larger Catholic segment of the Ukrainian population. In any case, the reason is not too apparent.

Saskatoon has over 20 per cent of all Ukrainian organizations in Saskatchewan. This figure is three times that of Regina. This ratio is consistent with the fact that there are about three times as many Ukrainians in Saskatoon as there are in Regina. About 52 per cent of these Ukrainian organizations in Saskatoon are non-denominational. About 34 per cent are Ukrainian Catholic, and about fourteen per cent are Ukrainian Orthodox, reversing the proportion that is true in Regina, and confirming the observation that Ukrainian Catholic organizations tend to be more active and more concentrated in centres of high Ukrainian population. For instance, the national executive of the Ukrainian Catholic organization that had been founded in Saskatoon over 40 years ago was situated in Saskatoon until quite recently. Also, the Ukrainian Catholic organizations in Saskatoon are all very active in the educational and cultural fields, conducting language schools, dancing schools, and even a museum.

Over 72 per cent of all Ukrainian organizations in Saskatchewan, however, are actually outside such high population density centres as Saskatoon and Regina. Only about 22 per cent of these are non-denominational, and this dramatic figure indicates that non-denominational Ukrainian organizations tend to be associated with large urban centres, where this kind of "specialization" (not just dividing into women's and youth's groups, but also into dancing, choir, Ukrainian language schools, and professional or business associations) may actually be more unifying and integrative of the socially stratified Ukrainian community than the usual segregation of a more egalitarian Ukrainian population into either a Catholic or an Orthodox parish.

In rural areas generally, outside Saskatoon and Regina, about 28 per cent of the Ukrainian organizations are Ukrainian Catholic, and of these, 49 per cent are strictly women's organizations. An astounding 50 per cent of all Ukrainian organizations outside Saskatoon and Regina are Ukrainian Orthodox, of which almost 48 per cent are strictly women's organizations. These statistics tend to support the impression that Ukrainian Orthodox organizations are inclined to be smaller in size than Ukrainian Catholic ones, and seem to flourish mainly in rural and smaller population centres (like Regina as opposed to Saskatoon, which has about eighteen per cent of all Ukrainians in Saskatchewan).

In summary, Ukrainian organizations seem to be based essentially on the "three-part" system, which would involve the formation of not one single organization, but usually three — one for men, one for women, and another for the youth. Although the men's group is formally at the top of this three-rung ladder, with the youth at the bottom of the scale, it is apparent that the women's group, formally in-between, in actual fact is the most important. It is the women's group that usually sponsors the activities of the youth, caters to the events produced by the men, and conducts many activities which sometimes call for separate organizations: dancing groups, Ukrainian language schools, and choral groups. The women also run Ukrainian museums. For women, their organizations are community projections of the home, where the concern is with raising the young and with caring for "the master" of the house, even in church parish organizations. Ukrainian women, almost singlehandedly in many cases, have been most instrumental, not only in the formation and maintenance of most Ukrainian organizations in Saskatchewan, but also in the preservation and development of the Ukrainian language and major Ukrainian arts and crafts in the province.

No wonder Mother's Day is among the most important Ukrainian holidays in Saskatchewan. Women are shown respect, on that day, for the role that they continue to play, not just in the home, but in the cultural community where there are a number of activities that could not get along without the women's contribution. For instance, Ukrainian Easter would not be Ukrainian without the women's contribution of beautifully decorated pysanky, many special foods (like paska and baba), embroidered cloths, songs (hahilky) and traditional customs (with blessed candles). The costumes worn by Ukrainian dancers are almost invariably designed, sewn and decorated by Ukrainian women, sometimes working together as groups in sewing bees.

Women are also active in commemorating the lyrical contribution of Ukrainian poet Taras Shevchenko to Ukraine's continuing struggle for freedom. Every year during March, the women help to stage a concert in the great bard's honor, teaching the young to recite the poet's immortal words in Ukrainian, and encouraging choral singing of the poetry written by Shevchenko. It is interesting that Ukrainian poets like Taras Shevchenko, Ivan Franko and Lesia Ukrainka are regarded by the Ukrainian people, not as aesthetes in some ivory tower, but as real and vibrant political symbols and forceful spokesmen.

Besides Ukrainians (and their very active women), there are seven other Eastern European groups in Saskatchewan. These would include the Doukhobors (and Russians), Czechs, Polish, Roumanians, Hungarians, Serbians and Croatians. They have established about 16 per cent of all

Eastern European organizations in the province. This would be equivalent to almost six per cent of all ethnocultural organizations in Saskatchewan.

It is noteworthy that 42 per cent of the eighteen Eastern European groups in the province have ethnocultural organizations, and that these eight "organized" groups (including Ukrainians) represent over 97 per cent of the total Eastern European population in Saskatchewan. These eight groups represent almost sixteen per cent of the province's total population, and have almost 42 per cent of all ethnocultural organizations in Saskatchewan.

This high percentage is about two and a half times more than the population of these eight groups may seem to warrant. Several reasons for this high percentage may be identified here. First, of course, is the so-called "Ukrainian fact" which has already been discussed briefly in a general way, and which will be examined in greater detail further in this presentation (as a case study). The essential point, however, is that Ukrainians have the highest per capita rate of organization formation in Saskatchewan, which means that they have over 86 per cent of all Eastern European organizations in the province today, and 36 per cent of all ethnocultural organizations in Saskatchewan.

Second, the Eastern European people as a group seem to have been subjected to considerable discrimination from the time that they came to this province at the turn of the century, prompting them to form ghettos for survival, especially immediately after the outbreak of the first world war, when intolerance seems to have peaked in Saskatchewan. There is a possible correlation between the intensity of such discrimination and the number of ethnocultural organizations that may be founded to protect discriminated members of Canadian society.

On the average, very roughly, every Slavic organization in Saskatchewan would have about 452 persons to service. Not all would be members, of course, and many individuals may be members of several organizations simultaneously. Still, the Slavic groups do seem to have enough ethnocultural organizations to service their needs.

Taken individually, it is significant that Doukhobor and Russian organizations, when combined, are tied for second place with the number of Polish organizations in the province (each with about five per cent of all Slavic organizations in Saskatchewan), although there are over twice as many Polish people as Doukhobors and Russians in the province. An obvious reason would seem to be, following up on what has already been mentioned, that the Doukhobors have been subjected to more discrimination than the Polish people. This is, in fact, true, as is documented further in this presentation (as a case study). However, it is not quite that simple, because the Polish people in Saskatchewan are just beginning to organize on their own after having been virtually assimilated by the overwhelmingly more numerous Ukrainians in many parts of the province. The kind of discrimination that the Polish may have felt most intensely was not the hostile kind that might have been directed against all Slavic groups by non-Slavs in Saskatchewan, but the assimilative kind that virtually swallowed the Polish language and culture and substituted the Ukrainian language and culture.

Roumanian (or Romanian) organizations come next, accounting for almost three per cent of all Eastern European organizations in Saskatchewan. Roumanians are very close to the Hungarians, who have almost two per cent, but who are almost three times as numerous. It would seem that Hungarians have tended to assimilate more readily with the anglophone urban community (where they seem to have gravitated) through professionalization and intermarriage than the Roumanians have, but the reasons for this are not clear.

A clue may be found in the ugly racist epithet "bohunk" which may have derived from two words, contracted: "Bo" for Bohemian, and "Hunk" for Hungarian (or "Hunky"). The derogatory term was applied indiscriminately as well to all Slavic peoples who had come from the Austro-Hungarian Empire prior to the first world war. This indicates that Hungarians, who had come to Saskatchewan long before the first massive Slavic migrations began, were also subjected to intense discrimination, especially after the outbreak of the first world war.

Such bigotry may have been ameliorated somewhat after the second world war, especially after the Hungarian uprising in 1956 when the Saskatchewan community of Esterhazy welcomed many political refugees. In spite of this recent rejuvenation, the Hungarians seem to have drifted slowly away from much of their cultural heritage, perhaps more than Roumanians who were never really subject to the same intense pressure, and who constituted a "safely small" pocket of people clustered mainly around Regina, or else assimilated with Ukrainians, like the Polish, in some of the rural areas.

Czechs, Serbians and Croatians are last here, with only one known organization for each. Ten other Eastern European groups have had no ethnocultural organizations listed so far. The largest of these groups is Yugoslav (excluding Croatians and Serbians). Nine of the groups (Bulgarian, Byelorussian, Estonian, Gypsy, Kuban Cossack, Latvian, Lithuanian, Slovak, and Slovene) number less than 1,000, averaging about 300 each. Their small numbers (only 3,917 in all) may help to explain their lack of ethnocultural organizations, especially when coupled with the fact that some are scattered throughout the province, rather than concentrated in some single community.

(b) *Central European*

Three quarters of the groups from Central Europe have ethnocultural organizations in Saskatchewan. Still, these six "organized" groups represent over 97 per cent of the respective population in the province. In terms of gross averages again, there is one "Germanic" organization for every 1,221 "Germanic" people in the province.

Overall averages also indicate that just about 22 per cent of the total population of Saskatchewan is Central European, and these people have about 22 per cent of all ethnocultural organizations in the province. This is an interesting correlation of percentages. It is repeated twice more here — for the Native and for the French groupings — although its precise significance is not honed in more than to suggest generally that this may be some indication of the "normal" number of organizations that may be expected from ethnic groups in Saskatchewan.

Far above "normal" here is the Mennonite group, which constitutes about 45 per cent of the "Germanic" population of the province, and has almost 62 per cent of all "German" organizations in Saskatchewan. It is for this reason that the Mennonites have also been singled out here for special examination further in this presentation (as a case study). Again, the basic reason for this great number of religiously defined organizations, many of which still retain a very strong ethnocultural flavour in some community activities, is the intensity of discrimination felt by the Mennonites, especially after the first world war, when they were lumped indiscriminately with other "foreigners" whose homelands were at war with Britain in Europe. The more conservative Mennonites simply left Canada, leaving behind those who were willing to endure the bigotry or to bend towards economic assimilation with other anglophones.

Hutterites come second here, with about eighteen per cent of all "Germanic" organizations in the province. They are very recent arrivals in Saskatchewan, having migrated from Alberta only after the second world war, as a direct result of the discriminatory legislation passed by the Alberta legislature, in response to the political pressure exerted by a lobby spearheaded by returned war veterans, who did not sympathize with the pacifist Hutterites who did not believe in war. The discriminatory Alberta law prohibited Hutterites from buying land wherever they chose. The Saskatchewan government has accommodated the Hutterites, because it was the first province in Canada to have adopted a Bill of Rights, shortly after the second world war, and it could not violate its own proclaimed Bill of Rights.

The Hutterite mode of organization is in colonies of about 100 persons, each related to the others in some way, so that they live on what may be described essentially as "extended family" farms, which are run like corporations, efficiently, and like rural communities, humanely. They prosper with fewer acres per person than most other individualist farmers, because their organization is superior. They are also very hard working. Their profits are usually reinvested in a new daughter colony. Over the past 20 years, 30 Hutterian Brethren colony organizations have been founded in Saskatchewan, mainly in the south-western quarter of the province.

Jews are in third place, with about nine per cent, while Germans and German Catholics are fourth, with over seven per cent, although German Catholics and other German groups outnumber Jews in Saskatchewan by about 44 to 1. One cannot invoke discrimination to explain this situation, although discrimination is certainly involved, because the situation is complex enough to merit more detailed examination further in this presentation (as a case study). The major point that emerges from the more detailed analysis is that, although Jews have always been subject to anti-Semitism, they have made a successful adjustment to combatting the racism by forming a great number of active organizations (like Ukrainians). However, German Catholics were subjected to rather sudden and unexpectedly virulent discrimination during the two world wars. Their response was to withdraw into the religious dimension of their church organizations, and to disclaim any genuine concern for their language or culture, at least in public. In short, the cultural component of the German Catholic group seems to have withered under the hot blast of intolerance directed against it during the two world wars, so that very little seems to have survived.

The Dutch and the Austrians have the smallest number of Central European organizations, with less than two per cent each, although the Dutch outnumber Austrians by a ratio of over 5-to-1. The reasons for this interesting situation are perhaps obvious. The Austrians were certainly subject to discrimination during the first world war, after which time many Slavic groups that had been classified as Austrian or Hungarian had themselves re-classified, partly to avoid the flak that Austrians were still getting in Saskatchewan. On the other hand, the Dutch have never been discriminated against in Saskatchewan. In fact, the powerful anglophone elite, supported by such representative community organizations as the Ku Klux Klan in the late 1920's, classified the Dutch, along with other Scandinavian groups, as preferred as Anglo-Saxons in the province (Swanson, 1930). Therefore, the Dutch probably never felt that they needed any ethnocultural organizations for the survival of their language or culture, or for the protection of their members against discrimination.

(c) *Multicultural*

Only eleven per cent of all ethnocultural organizations in Saskatchewan are devoted to the activities of more than one unrelated ethnic group; so they have been called multicultural. About 6,000 identifiable Americans in Saskatchewan have been placed in this category, although members of many ethnic groups participate, particularly in the co-ordination of some special community events.

(d) *Native*

This group may be considered to be 100 per cent "organized." Because Indians have been forced to live on reserves since 1885, they identify as much with their bands as with their tribes. Only in 1951 was the Indian Act relaxed enough to "emancipate" Indians from their reserves, allowing Indians to wander freely from their reserves to "whiteman" Saskatchewan without having to obtain permits to travel from the Indian agent. The Metis (or halfbreed) segment of the native population has been organized only since about 1965. Although Metis organizations are now quite numerous, their offices have been so slow in replying to the questionnaires that none except one (concerned with housing) have been returned for listing in the directory. Special government funds are available to these organizations.

In spite of this apparent reluctance to respond, native organizations (including 67 reserve bands in the province) constitute eleven per cent of all ethnocultural organizations in Saskatchewan. As with the Germanic group, there is an interesting correlation of percentages, so that thirteen per cent of the population of Saskatchewan here has eleven per cent of all ethnocultural organizations in the province. Very grossly, this averages to about 1,452 persons for every native organization in Saskatchewan.

These are not the usual middle-class ethnocultural organization, because native people in Saskatchewan (which has the highest per capita native population of any province in Canada) have been among the most economically impoverished, subject to the most restrictive and oppressive legislation affecting any group in Canada. The institutionalized discrimination that was also directed against the Metis has prevented the native people generally from being able to participate fully in the political and economic life of Canada. Their reserves and settlements are the closest thing to rural ghettos that Saskatchewan has yet produced.

(e) *French*

The French constitute about five per cent of the population of Saskatchewan. Like the Germanic and Native peoples, their percentage of the population coincides closely with the percentage of French organizations in the province — almost six per cent. Very grossly again, there is one French organization for every 1,070 French persons.

The 43 French organizations in Saskatchewan are dispersed over almost 20 localities. The Association Culturelle Franco-Canadienne (ACFC), which is represented in almost half of these places, is the dominant French organization in the province. However, there are also a great number of very local French organizations, whose purpose is to service local community needs. For instance, in one small community, it was found that the only way to keep more culturally oriented activities alive at all was to form a separate curling and hockey club, in order to attract French people from their television sets and get them to interact with each other again.

(f) *Non-Europeans*

Less than one per cent of Saskatchewan's population consists of persons from outside Europe and America. Still, these have over three per cent of all ethnocultural organizations in the province. Very grossly, this averages to about 345 persons per organization. This is a very high percentage of organizations for such a "minor minority" as this, suggestive of possible discriminatory practices having been directed against it perhaps more intensely than some other groups in Saskatchewan.

East Indians and Pakistani, combined, represent about one third of these non-European people in Saskatchewan. They also have 44 per cent of all non-European organizations in the province, and almost two per cent of all ethnocultural organizations in Saskatchewan. They are also the targets of the most violent and recent racist attacks and slurs, parading as "humour."

No wonder the East Indian and Pakistani ethnocultural organizations are concerned, not only with the preservation of their arts, but also with a very grim struggle against the racism that has been directed against them by bigots in our midst.

Arab groups have eight per cent and Filipino groups have 12 per cent of all non-European organizations, followed by Egyptians and Koreans, each of whom has four per cent. Three groups (Black, Japanese and West Indian) have no formal organizations listed. These three groups number only about 850 persons, with none having more than 360 individuals, so the small numbers may account for the apparent lack of formal organization.

There are twice as many Chinese as East Indians and Pakistani people in Saskatchewan. However, the Chinese actually have fewer, and perhaps larger, organizations than the East Indians and Pakistani people. There appear to be several reasons for this. First, the discrimination against the Chinese, once very intense, has abated over the past generation, since the Chinese have worked their way up into the middle-class, in spite of many obstacles not encountered by other groups. Second, the Chinese have traditionally been dispersed over rural Saskatchewan, usually operating the only restaurant and laundry in the small prairie town, rather than concentrated enough in urban centres to form strong formal organizations. Third, the Chinese organizations that do exist seem to be strong and viable, whereas some of the East Indian ones may actually exist "only on paper" at this time, while the energies of the members are expended fighting intolerance.

(g) British

It may be somewhat surprising to some, in view of the traditional "majority" stance of the British in Saskatchewan (where they have never really been in the majority), that the British, who constitute less than 35 per cent of the population of Saskatchewan, have less than three per cent of the ethnocultural organizations in the province. There is certainly no "normal" coincidence of percentages here, as with the French, Native and Germanic peoples. On the contrary, there is almost a, reversal of the lop-sided percentages that marked the Ukrainians, for instance, suggesting some rather significant inferences, particularly in regard to the felt need of these two groups (Ukrainians and British) for cultural survival in Saskatchewan.

In terms of gross averages, there is only one "British" organization for every 15,238 Britons. What is perhaps more significant here is that the Scottish group alone accounts for over 57 per cent of all British organizations in the province. This suggests a somewhat special status that may be felt by some Scottish people in Saskatchewan, as opposed to the English (almost 24 per cent) and the other two British groups (the Irish and the Welsh, each of whom has almost ten per cent of all British organizations in Saskatchewan, in spite of the great disparity in numbers between them). It is noteworthy that the English are about 30 times more numerous than the Welsh, and at least twice as numerous as the Irish. Still, the English have only twice as many British organizations run by them in Saskatchewan as either Irish or Welsh. The English obviously feel that they have little use for any such ethnocultural organizations. They certainly seem to have less need or use for such ethnocultural organizations than even such British groups as the Welsh, and especially the Scots, who do not seem to identify as much with the British institutions (which have been supported by "Canadian" institutions) as the English may wish.

(h) *Southern European*

Southern Europeans constitute less than half of one per cent of the population of Saskatchewan. They have little over one per cent of the ethnocultural organizations in the province. Grossly, this averages to about 500 Southern Europeans for every Southern European organization in Saskatchewan.

Greeks make up about one quarter of the population of Southern Europeans in the province, but have over 62 per cent of all Southern European organizations in the province. The actual numbers involved are now so small that it is unwise to try to read too much into such figures, but it is fairly apparent that generally the Greeks in this province are supportive of one another in the business world; it is therefore not surprising to find that they socialize in their own community organizations, which tend to be middle-class. This is even less surprising when one knows that most Greeks in Saskatchewan come from a particular region around Peloponnesus in southern Greece.

Italians are over three times more numerous than the Greeks, but have only about a quarter of the organizations, and the Spanish-speaking people, whose number is one-fifteenth of that of the Italians have half as many organizations. Only the Portuguese have no organizations listed in the province.

(i) *Northern European*

Northern Europeans constitute almost seven per cent of the population of Saskatchewan, but have only one per cent of the ethnocultural organizations in the province. Norwegians have about twelve times as many people in the province as the Icelandic people. Still, the Icelandic people have formed an Icelandic society, while the far more numerous Norwegians have managed to form only two (both in Swift Current). However, both Icelandic and Norwegian groups have pooled their resources with Swedes (who are half as numerous as Norwegians) and Danes (who are seven times less numerous than Norwegians) to form three Scandinavian organizations.

The Finnish community in Saskatchewan is the smallest Scandinavian community. It may have some viable organizations around Lucky Lake and Whitewood, but these have been difficult to identify. At one time, there were three Finnish settlement areas in the province: *Southeastern* (around Tantallon, Esterhazy and Spy Hill); *Central* (around Outlook, Dunblane, Dinsmore, Birsay and Lucky Lake); and *Western* (around Biggar, Kerrobert, Kindersley, Elrose and Eston). About 1910, some 200 families came from Minnesota to the central area. About 70, some with Marxist orientations, settled in the King George Settlement north of Lucky Lake. About 130, opposed to Marxism, and very religious (Lutheran Evangelical Lestadean), settled in the Rock Point Settlement near Dunblane and Birsay. Their land was dry, rocky, hilly and poor for farming, so, in the 1930s, some Marxist families in the King George Settlement moved to the Soviet Union and settled in Karelia. Their land was even worse than it was in Canada, and since Russian hostility was also very strong many returned to Saskatchewan, where they were the subjects of numerous RCMP witch hunts for communists. The repression resulted in the loss of Finnish identity and culture among the King George people, while the Rock Point settlement became an informal culture centre of the Finnish community in Saskatchewan.

In terms of gross averages, every Scandinavian organization would have to accommodate about 7,604 persons. This figure tends to underline the relative paucity of Scandinavian organizations in Saskatchewan, perhaps due to the fact that most Scandinavians arrived in Canada from the United States, where they had been urged to "melt" into the anglophone consumer society of the New World.

Summary of Statistics

The statistics and comments here would suggest at least a few significant hypotheses, which could be formulated more precisely perhaps near the end of this presentation, after the following examination of some basic historical data available on at least four major groups, if not all 40 groups discussed here. Of course, there is an abundance of information, some of questionable value, pertaining to almost all the ethnic groups in Saskatchewan. A number of authors have written about the people in Saskatchewan generally (Archer, 1965; Dawson, 1935; England, 1936; Hawkes, 1924; Morton, 1938; Oliver, 1926 & 1935; Pohorecky, 1975, 1977a, 1977b; Swanson, 1930; Wright, 1955).

Most authors, however, have tended to concentrate on some particular ethnic group in Saskatchewan, so that we have books about native peoples (Howard, 1965; Pohorecky, 1970), the French (Hughes, 1943), the English (Reynolds, 1935; Shepperson, 1957), the Scots (Bryce, 1911; Gibbon, 1938), the Welsh (Brynmor-Jones & Rhys, 1902), the Dutch (Lucas, 1955), the

German Catholics (Becker, 1967; Doerffler, 1956; England, 1929; The
Humboldt Story, 1954; Stemp, 1956; Wendshiegle, 1953), the Hutterites
(Gross, 1965; Lobb, 1963), the Jews (Hart, 1926; Kage, 1962; Sack, 1965),
the Mennonites (Epp, 1962 & 1974; Horsch, 1942; Hostetler, 1968;
Mennonite Encyclopedia, 1957; Redekop, 1969; Smith, 1957), the Doukho-
bors (Popore, 1971; Tarasoff, 1969; Wright, 1940), the Hungarians (Kosa,
1957; Timar, 1957), the Polish (Makowski, 1967; Turek, 1960), the
Roumanians (Johnson, 1961), the Ukrainians (Darkovitch, 1967; Kaye,
1964; Pohorecky & Royick, 1969; Yuzyk, 1967), the Finns (Heinonen,
1930), the Icelandic (Lindal, 1955), the Norwegians (Blegen, 1940), the
Greeks (Vlassis, 1942), the Italians (Barzini, 1964), the Chinese (Luk, 1971;
Osterhout, 1929; Sinclair, 1962), and the Blacks (Potter, 1964).

Rather than deal with each of these 40 groups in this brief presentation,
it should suffice, as has already been indicated, to concentrate here on just
four major groups — the Ukrainians, the German Catholics, the
Mennonites, and, especially at the turn of the century, the Doukhobors.

Historical Overview

One important reason for the existence of any ethnocultural organization in Saskatchewan has been to combat the institutionalized discrimination that had been directed against the ethnic group forming the
organization. In this province, it was not uncommon for "desirable" persons
(of British ancestry) to obtain positions in the civil service and the school
system at levels above that of the school janitor or street cleaner, which
involved menial labour at minimum wages, and which were usually
reserved for the "white niggers who had just come off the boat" from
eastern Europe (rather than Britain). Positions of authority were rarely
allotted to such "undesirables" as Ukrainians, Doukhobors or Mennonites
prior to the first world war.

The first schools in the province were usually bilingual, providing
instruction in English and either Ukrainian, German, Plattdeutsch, or
Russian. This freedom was severely restricted towards the end of the first
world war, when a war hysteria combined with open bigotry to suppress all
languages but English for purposes of instruction in the schools of
Saskatchewan. This repressive tendency caused great unrest and resentment
among members of the four major ethnic communities being considered
here.

These four ethnic groups did not see the related legislation as an
innocent attempt to get all immigrants to learn the English language and
thus become better Canadianized, as the British understood it at that time,
when their imperial power was swiftly waning in colonies around the
world.

Each group reacted very differently, in a manner consistent with that
group's own-history and traditional way of responding to such challenges.

Four Case Studies

(1) *Doukhobors*

Doukhobors are members of a Christian sect whose origin can be traced to the eighteenth century. The term "Doukhobor" can be translated roughly as "spirit wrestler" or "spirit fighter" in Russian. This sect had its roots in Russia, where its members believed that divinity could be transmitted to all people, because mankind was naturally and inherently good, making the intercession of a religious specialist or organization quite unnecessary and irrelevant to believers. Therefore, Doukhobors reject churches, scriptures (including the bible), and elaborate ritual, while preaching that everyone has to discover the divinity within oneself, and follow its direction as a sacred duty.

Logically, then, they argue that they should not be subject to any human authority, and that refers to governments, too. They yearn for perfection in personal character and conduct, and believe that this is both attainable and real. Doukhobors tend to be mystical, and thus their interests are not strictly intellectual. Bread, salt and water are the only symbols of their faith. They call themselves "People of God" and are dedicated to a life of toil and peace, rejecting self-seeking motivation in favour of communal living. The famous "Sons of Freedom" in British Columbia are a very rigorous branch of this sect which had originally settled in Saskatchewan.

Historically, the Doukhobors first sought refuge in the Crimea, where their group assumed very definite cultural forms, based largely on their opposition, not only to the established clergy in Russia, but also to bearing arms for the Tsar. The Russian Tsar and Russian Church reacted by unleashing terrible retaliations against the Doukhobors, who were uprooted and banished to the barren lands of Georgia. Despite the poor soil, severe climate, and stark differences with the neighbouring peoples (who regarded the group as intrusive), the Doukhobor colonies prospered. Even growing constrictions, imposed by hostile government officials, could not crush the Doukhobors.

Then a conflict erupted over succession and the principle of communal living. Members of the stricter wing were spurred to leave Russia. With the help of Leo Tolstoy, the Quakers of England, and others, like Aylmer, this minority portion of the Doukhobor group sent an exploratory mission to Canada in the spring of 1898. The following year, 7,427 Doukhobors completed their long journey to the District of Saskatchewan, which was still part of the Northwest Territories. They settled in large blocs, each consisting of many townships, around Yorkton, Kamsack and Blaine Lake (which did not even exist as settlements yet). Religious freedom was promised. Their pacifism was recognized by an Order-in-Council. Financial assistance was secured from American Quakers, and they had some funds of their own. By winter, the great majority were housed. To help buy what they needed for farming, especially oxen and horses, the men went to work for the railway company, engaged in construction, and returned with enough savings to help make the colony financially secure. The first crops had already been put away in community barns during the first winter, after both men and women had helped to pull the ploughs.

The Homestead Act of 1872 also required an oath of allegiance before the 160 acres permitted to each man could be granted. The Doukhobors were exempt from this requirement, they thought, by the Order-in-Council that did not require them to bear arms. Government officials thought otherwise.

Other issues also aroused disagreements. A minority within the group favoured private ownership of land, but felt compelled, especially after the arrival of their exiled leader Peter Verigin in 1902, to join in the opposition to the private ownership of land. This small minority's opposition weakened as government policy hardened against community ownership. As a consequence, the majority of the Doukhobors did not complete their claims in a manner that was acceptable to the bureaucrats, and more than half of their land reverted to the government. Only about a thousand Doukhobors agreed to government terms and received their homesteads. Doukhobors also resisted attempts by Quakers and others to introduce education to the children that differed from their traditional way of raising children. The registering of births, deaths and marriages took place only when an outsider was willing to do it, because the Doukhobors were not. In 1903, 29 extremists were arrested for their first parades of protest against unbending government policies. The protest had involved undressing in public near Yorkton. What had begun as a simple split between those who had wanted private ownership of land and those who had insisted on communal ownership soon resulted in three groupings, based on the degree to which each opposed the policies of the federal government. The "Sons of Freedom" rejected any compromise with the requirements imposed by the remote government. The "Independents" had begun to be tempted by the materialistic standards and educational "subversion" that supported individual titles to land. The "Orthodox Doukhobors" tried to tread an uncertain but peaceful path between them.

During both wars, conflict arose between Doukhobors and non-Doukhobors over the issue of service in the armed forces. This conflict only added to the difficulties that they encountered during the depression in drought-ravaged Saskatchewan. Thus, the Doukhobors reacted to discrimination in Saskatchewan in much the same way as they had in Russia. The more militant and stricter wing left for elsewhere, in the first instance, from Russia to Canada, and in the second case, from Saskatchewan to British Columbia. Those who remained gradually adjusted to the ways and laws of their neighbours, in spite of continuing discrimination against them for their firm beliefs in such ideals as peace, and for their alien origin. Many old prayer homes lie abandoned in the area around Kamsack. Only memories of those first bitter years remain to haunt the living. The role of the various Doukhobor societies in Saskatchewan has been redefined over the years, so that much time and effort is expended, sometimes on strictly cultural events, in order to raise funds for worthy service organizations which have goals consistent with Doukhobor ideals. By supporting charitable institutions, the Doukhobors have looked beyond their own group towards persons of goodwill everywhere. Their concept of sharing has extended their horizons.

(2) *Ukrainians*

The Ukrainians are the largest ethnic group in Canada, after the British, French, German, and most recently Italian (in that order). The Ukrainians number over half a million in Canada. The 1971 census listed 85,920 in Saskatchewan, making Ukrainians a major ethnic group in this province. Today, about three-quarters of all Ukrainians in Canada were born in Canada, with most of these being third or fourth generation Canadian-born.

The massive immigration of Ukrainians began shortly after 1895, although nine Ukrainian families had arrived and settled at Star in Alberta during 1894. The continuous flow began in 1896. A professor at Lwiw in Western Ukraine (Dr. Josef Oleskiw) helped to organize the first big wave of Ukrainian migration to the three prairie provinces, supported by an immigration policy which had been initiated by Clifford Sifton of Winnipeg for Prime Minister Wilfrid Laurier's Liberal Government at Ottawa. The new policy no longer discriminated against Eastern Europeans, as Sir John A. Macdonald's Conservative Government's policy had. As a result, Sifton had to defend Ukrainian immigrants who were being attacked mercilessly in the press and in Parliament after the turn of the century. The main reason for the migration of Western Ukrainians to western Canada was a situation in the Old Country that had become intolerable. Over-population, excessive land subdivision, hopeless economic conditions, as well as severe social, political, linguistic, cultural and religious oppression, particularly in those parts of Ukraine that were ruled by the Tsar of Russia, all contributed to the dissatisfaction that prompted many to try their luck in Canada. The cultural and linguistic situation in that part of Ukraine which was ruled by Emperor Franz Josef for Austro-Hungary was more tolerable, but the economic poverty was just as harsh.

A second wave came to Canada after the first world war, and continued into the depression years. These Ukrainian immigrants were mainly political refugees who had witnessed the rise and overthrow of independent Ukraine by the Bolsheviks of Russia and later its partition among Roumanians and the newly formed nations of Poland and Czechoslovakia.

A third wave came after the second world war, beginning about 1949. These were persons who had refused to return to their homeland, because it had been taken over by the communist regime which they felt threatened their lives if they returned, because many had fought against the Soviets during the war. Most of these "Displaced Persons" (DP's) came from Western Ukraine, which had been part of Poland, and which had been invaded by the Soviets in 1939. A very high percentage of these political refugees were highly educated. These encountered some discrimination, sometimes from fellow Ukrainians who were upset by the refugee's concern with Old World Politics rather than with the problems encountered by Ukrainians in Canada.

When the use of the Ukrainian language was banned from the public school system in Saskatchewan during 1919, the Ukrainians reacted predictably, as they had in the Old Country, by going "underground" into their church basements, where they taught their children about Ukrainian culture and history in the Ukrainian language, after regular school hours at the "English School." The Ukrainian community throughout the province rallied to build educational residences and institutes, like the Mohyla Institute in Saskatoon. The discrimination probably spurred Ukrainians to fight even more tenaciously to preserve and develop their Ukrainian language and cultural identity. They resolved to do this with the help of their churches, whose ministers helped the people resist the cultural and linguistic pressure that was being inflicted on them by a bad law (Section 209 of the School Act) which was finally repealed in 1974.

After the second world war, many Ukrainian veterans decided that they were entitled to have their language and culture, not hidden away in church basements, but out in the open, on the street, in the media, and especially in the schools and universities. This struggle of Ukrainians to maintain their cultural identity in Canada can now serve as an example for other Canadians, who may take heart in the fact that Ukrainian culture has indeed, not only survived, but also flourished, especially in western Canada, where it is now part of what being a western Canadian is all about. Even non-Ukrainians in Saskatchewan now share in enjoying such Ukrainian cultural items, produced by Ukrainian women, as babushky, perohy, holubtsi, Ukrainian Easter eggs (pysanky), Ukrainian embroidery, and Ukrainian dancing. Ukrainian culture seems to be secure in Saskatchewan.

Still, Ukrainians do not trust governments, especially the ones that had taken away their language rights in public schools and not returned them for over 55 years. The role of the ethnocultural organization, then, is practically unchanged owing to the bureaucrat's apparent unwillingness or inability to implement a policy that has been approved by the politicians, especially in regard to the use of the Ukrainian language for purposes of instruction in the public school system. Nor is the role of the Ukrainian organization likely to relax enough to shed its defensive stance and boxing gloves until the Ukrainian language is firmly entrenched in the public school system. This is perhaps as it should be.

(3) *German Catholics*

German Catholics (or "Russland Deutsche") originally came from a group of German-speaking people who had settled in Roumania and Russian-ruled Ukraine, before fleeing to the United States, and finally to

Saskatchewan. Because the Germans in the midwestern states had begun to "talk American" rather than German, they were already Americanized enough to have lost a good deal of their German language when the Benedictine monks decided that they should all move into Saskatchewan, in order to save both the German language and the German Catholic religion. The involvement of the clergy always made it appear that these people were more Catholic than German, and this may indeed be so, but the German cultural component, no matter how eroded or tattered it may appear, especially in terms of the loss of the German language, was also very important.

The German Catholics were unhappy about having to live on expensive and scarce farmlands, which were scattered throughout Minnesota and North Dakota, so they sold their individual land plots at high prices, and bought very good Saskatchewan land very cheaply, and in very large blocs containing fifty townships (and even ninety townships later) which were suitably immense for homogeneous colonies to develop within them. The first huge colony was established about 75 years ago around Humboldt.

The war years were bad years for the Germans in Saskatchewan, but the discrimination against them eased after the war was over, especially since the Germans had been very careful not to expose their German origin by speaking German in public. The second world war also took its toll of Germans in Saskatchewan. The German language was virtually wiped out among German Catholics, who had been admonished even for using such German words as "sauerkraut" in English sentences when, it was pointed out, there were perfectly good English equivalents, like "pickled cabbage." The pettiness of some of the attacks against the Germans in Saskatchewan now appear ridiculous, but it helped to crush the German language almost completely. Very little of it has survived in the years since the second world war, even in such large German Catholic colonies as the ones around Humboldt and Tramping Lake. It is apparent that the German Catholics did not effectively resist the onslaught against their language and cultural identity. The German language simply could not survive in a social climate where one dared not admit to being of German origin.

It should not be surprising, then, that German Catholics in particular, and Germans generally in Saskatchewan have so very few ethnocultural organizations. With the greater acceptance of ethnocultural heritages in Saskatchewan, it is likely that the attitudes of the Germans may change enough to result in the formation of many more German ethnocultural organizations than exist today. A good place to start may be within existing church structures.

(4) *Mennonites*

There are an estimated 86,000 Mennonites in Saskatchewan, although official figures may acknowledge only a quarter of this estimate, while the census counts absolutely none, because all tend to be lumped with

Germans. Actually, the Mennonites speak a form of low Dutch, which sounds very much like low German, and which reveals their origin in the Netherlands in 1515 as a Protestant (Anabaptist) movement which denounced war and violence as sinful. Menno Simons was their leader in Holland, where many were persecuted so harshly that they died. Under Swiss leaders, they fled to Austria and Germany, where they were known for their emphasis on plain ways of living, worshipping and dressing.

Mennonites base their beliefs on the bible, especially the New Testament. Their creed, or statement of beliefs, is based on the Sermon on the Mount (Matthew 5-7). They believe that this sermon forbids people from going to war, swearing oaths, or holding offices that require the use of force. Mennonites keep to their own family groups, and are divided into many branches, based partly on family groupings.

In 1786, Catherine the Great granted them asylum in Russia, provided they agreed to work on the barren steppes of Ukraine. They agreed, and prospered until 1870, when the Tsar began a policy of complete russification.

The more "liberal" Mennonites succumbed to the use of the Russian language, and remained in Ukraine. However, the more conservative "Old Colony" (Kanadier) people emigrated to the United States, where they settled among the "Pennsylvania Dutch" who had come about 350 years before them. Some even came to Canada, and settled in Manitoba. In 1891, the first five families to move from southern Manitoba to the District of Saskatchewan arrived at Rosthern. Many more Mennonites came from Manitoba between 1901 and 1911. These settled around Hague and Osler, and Rosthern became the Mennonite capital in Saskatchewan.

The school language law, which made English the sole language of instruction in the schools, was passed in 1919. The Mennonites decided to open their own bilingual schools, which taught both English and "Plattdeutsch" to their children, while still supporting with their tax dollars the teachers and school buildings which they did not even intend to use. They also paid for their teachers, while the "government teacher" in the English School sat all day in front of empty seats and desks, and collected his monthly pay for this.

The provincial government was not pleased with this peaceful resistance to its unfair law, so it fined the Mennonites $10 a month for each child that was kept out of school by the parents who were protesting the bad school law. Several poor families had to pay over $700 a year. Still, some schools stood vacant for the entire term. In cases of actual hardship, the whole Mennonite community pitched in to help pay the fines. Finally many gave up in disgust. About 900 Mennonites then moved from Hague in Saskatchewan to Durango in Mexico, where they bought 35,000 acres of land, and ran their own schools.

It is apparent that the Mennonites' traditional response to official discrimination and persecution had always been to move away to some other place, where there might be less oppression. This was why they had come to western Canada from Russian-ruled Ukraine. This was why they had left Saskatchewan and Manitoba to move to Mexico and Paraguay.

The bad school law, which had the direct effect of driving thousands of Mennonites from this province shortly after the first world war, was finally repealed in 1974. This was about 55 years too late for thousands of Mennonites, but still welcome to some who may yet return.

The more "liberal" Mennonites accepted the anglicizing schools while retaining their church congregation organizations for religious pursuits rather than ethnocultural activities. Still, many did form more worldly institutions, like fire insurance companies or trust companies and foundations, in order to help Mennonites cope in the economic milieu of Canada. Other Mennonites formed a central committee to co-ordinate a number of service organizations for the elderly, the sick, and the retarded, while raising funds, through annual auctions, for charitable purposes. Some churches are sponsoring summer bible camps, which provide family outings, and choirs that perform at a high level of competence. Thus, the role of the Mennonite organizations seems to have been humanized enough in many instances to permit distinctively ethnocultural activities.

Conclusions

It is evident from the foregoing that four major ethnocultural groups in western Canada reacted very differently to the socio-cultural environment. It is also evident that correlations with numbers of ethnocultural organizations are implicit in these differences. Whatever changes have occurred in the roles played by their ethnocultural organizations reflect, not only the apparent decline in discriminatory practices against these minority groups, but also the group's own traditional methods of serving the best interests of its members.

When Mennonites were discriminated against, their traditional form of defence was essentially the same as they had used in Russia, and before that in Germany. The more militant and conservative wing simply left the country, and went to Mexico or Paraguay, when they found Canada unbearable. Less militant, more flexible individuals accepted the new ways, usually for economic reasons. Still another group tried to effect a compromise by living according to their religious beliefs, but adapting them to existing conditions. In effect, the group splintered in at least three ways, as it had in the past.

On the other hand, the German Catholics were almost wiped out completely as a culturally identifiable unit. They were made to feel ashamed of their mother country, which had been involved in two great wars with the British. A complete rebuilding of ethnocultural organizations, possibly using the church as a base, would seem to be needed here.

Doukhobors reacted in a way very much like the Mennonites, except that their most militant group simply moved to another province, where their difficulties continued. Some ended up in prison as a result of their protests. The more flexible individuals remained in Saskatchewan, where their ethnocultural organizations have reached out, beyond themselves, to help service organizations.

Ukrainians seem to be the only ones who anticipated what was coming in 1919, because they had experienced similar pressures in Russia, and were ready to go "underground" into their church basements, where they would preserve and develop their language, their history, their literature, and their many cultural traditions under classic ghetto conditions known to all people who had to work out their own formula for survival under the most hostile conditions.

It will be recalled that Ukrainians formed hundreds of ethnocultural organizations throughout Saskatchewan, for men, for women, for the young, and even for non-Ukrainians. In this way, the Ukrainians have saved their language and culture from extinction, or the virtual extinction which may be felt now, for example, by some German Catholics in Saskatchewan, who have among the fewest ethnocultural organizations per capita in the entire province (with the possible exception of the English, who may feel that they do not need any to survive in Saskatchewan).

It seems that, with the relaxation of the pressure of discrimination, there may be more ethnocultural organizations forming among German Catholics, for instance, in order to achieve during relatively good times what the Ukrainians had to achieve during some quite bad times. The changing role, then, of an ethnocultural organization, would seem to be aimed currently, not just at survival (since even those ethnic groups who enjoy a strong cultural-language identity are still wary of the recent thaw), but also at the development of even more cultural and linguistic diversity among the other groups in the province. This will require more, rather than fewer ethnocultural organizations, except perhaps among the Ukrainians.

REFERENCES

John H. Archer and Charles B. Koester, *Footprints in Time* (Toronto, 1965).
Luigi Barzini, *The Italians* (Toronto, 1964).
A. Becker, "St. Joseph's Colony, Balgonie," *Saskatchewan History,* 20 (1967), 1-18.
Theodore C. Blegen, *Norwegian Migration to America* (Northfield, Minnesota, 1940).
George Bryce, *The Scotsman in Canada: Western Canada* (Toronto, 1911), vols. 1 and 2.
David Brynmor-Jones and John Rhys, *The Welsh People* (London, 1902).
W. Darcovich, *The Ukrainians in Canada* (Ottawa, 1967).
C. A. Dawson, *Group Settlement and Ethnic Communities in Western Canada* (Toronto, 1939), vol. 6.
Bruno Doerffler, "Father Bruno's Narrative Across the Boundary," *Saskatchewan History,* 9 (1956).
Robert England, *The Colonization of Western Canada* (London, 1936).
Frank H. Epp, *Mennonite Exodus* (Altona, Manitoba, 1962).
Frank H. Epp, *Mennonites in Canada* (Toronto, 1974).
John M. Gibbon, *Scots in Canada* (Toronto, 1911).
Paul S. Gross, *The Hutterite Way* (Saskatoon, 1965).
Arthur Daniel Hart, *The Jew in Canada* (Toronto, 1926).
J. Hawkes, *The Story of Saskatchewan and Its People* (Chicago, 1924).
Aroi I. Heinonen, *Finnish Friends in Canada* (Toronto, 1930).
John Horsch, *Mennonite History* (Scottsdale, Pennsylvania, 1942).
J. A. Hostetler, *Amish Society* (Baltimore, 1968).
Joseph Kinsey Howard, *Strange Empire* (Toronto, 1965).
E. C. Hughes, *French Canada in Transition* (Toronto, 1943).
"The Humboldt Story, 1903-55," *Humboldt Journal,* 49 (1954).

Gilbert Johnson, "The Roumanians in Western Canada," *Saskatchewan History,* 14 (1961).
J. Kage, *Immigration and Integration in Canada* (Montreal, 1962).
Vlademir Kaye, *Early Ukrainian Settlements in Canada, 1895-1900* (Toronto, 1964).
John Kosa, *Land of Choice: The Hungarians of Canada* (Toronto, 1957).
W. J. Lindal, *The Saskatchewan Icelanders, a Strand of the Canadian Mosaic* (Winnipeg, 1955).
Harold O. Lobb and Neil McKagnew, *The Hutterites and Saskatchewan* (Saskatoon, 1963).
H. S. Lucas, *Netherlanders in America* (Ann Arbor, 1955).
L. W. Luk, "The Assimilation of Chinese in Saskatoon," M.A. Thesis, University of Saskatchewan, Saskatoon, unpublished, 1971.
W. B. Makowski, *History and Integration of Poles in Canada* (St. Catherines, Ontario, 1967).
The Mennonite Encyclopedia (Scottsdale, Pennsylvania, 1957).
Arthur S. Morton, *History of Prairie Settlement* (Toronto, 1938).
E. H. Oliver, "The Settlement of Saskatchewan to 1914," *Royal Society of Canada Transactions,* Third Series, vol. 20 (1926).
E. H. Oliver, "The Beginnings of Agriculture in Saskatchewan," *Royal Society of Canada Transactions,* Third Series, vol. 29 (1935).
S. S. Osterhout, *Orientals in Canada* (Toronto, 1929).
Zenon S. Pohorecky and Alexander Royick, "Anglicization of Ukrainians in Canada between 1895 and 1900," Canadian Ethnic Studies, I (1969), 141-219.
Zenon Pohorecky, *Saskatchewan Indian Heritage* (Saskatoon, 1970).
Zenon Pohorecky, *Illustrated Guide to the Ethnocultures of Saskatchewan People* (Regina, 1975).
Zenon Pohorecky, *Saskatchewan People* (Saskatoon, 1977).
Zenon Pohorecky, *Saskatchewan Ethnic Organizations* (Saskatoon, 1977).
W. Popore, *The Doukhobor Saga* (British Columbia Centennial Committee, 1971).
M. Potter, *Negroes in Canada* (Montreal, 1964).
Calvin Wall Redekop, *The Old Colony Mennonites* (Baltimore, 1969).
L. C. Reynolds, *The English Immigrant* (Toronto, 1935).
B. G. Sack, *History of the Jews in Canada* (Montreal, 1965).
W. S. Shepperson, *British Emigration to North America* (Oxford, 1957).
A. C. Sinclair, *Facts Regarding the Chinese Mission in Moose Jaw,* unpublished manuscript, 1962.
H. C. Smith, *The Story of the Mennonites* (Newton, Kansas, 1957).
Karl Stemp, *The German Russians* (Freilassing, West Germany, 1966).
W. W. Swanson, *Saskatchewan Royal Commission on Immigration and Settlement* (Regina, 1930).
K. Tarasoff, *Pictorial History of the Doukhobors* (Saskatoon, 1969).
L. J. Timar, *A Short History of the Hungarian People in Canada* (Toronto, 1957).
Victor Turek, *The Polish Past in Canada* (Toronto, 1960).
G. D. Vlassis, *The Greeks in Canada* (Ottawa, 1942).
Peter Wendschiegle, *Fifty Golden Years, 1903-1955* (Munster, 1953).
J. F. C. Wright, *Saskatchewan* (Toronto, 1955).
Paul Yuzyk, *Ukrainian Canadians* (Toronto, 1967).

APPENDIX I

List Of Ethnocultural Organizations in Saskatchewan

83* *Native*

Ottawa: National Indian Brotherhood.
Prince Albert: Federation of Saskatchewan Indians.
          Prince Albert Indian and Metis Friendship Centre.
Regina: Regina Friendship Centre.
          Saskatchewan Association of Indian and Metis Friendship Centres.
          Saskatchewan Indian Federated College, University of Regina.
Saskatoon: Indian Homemaking Program, Saskatoon Indian Women's Association.
          Indian Teaching Education Program, University of Saskatchewan.
          Metis Housing Group.
          Native Court Workers.
          Saskatoon Indian Friendship Centre.
          Saskatoon Intertribal Celebrations Committee.
          Saskatoon Native Follow-Up Program.
          Saskatchewan Indian Community College.

---

*Numbers in headings and subheadings refer to organizations within the respective groups.

Reserves (67)

Yorkton District:

    Cote Band, Kamsack.
    Cowessess Band, Broadview.
    Keeseekoose Band, Kamsack.
    Key Band, Norquay.
    Kahkewistahaw Band, Broadview.
    Ochapowace Band, Broadview.
    Sakimay Band, Grenfell.
    White Bear Band, Carlyle.

Fort Qu'Appelle District:

    Carry the Kettle Band, Sintaluta.
    Day Star Band, Punnichy.
    Fishing Lake Band, Wadena.
    Gordon Band, Punnichy.
    GORDON INDIAN POW-WOW DANCERS.
    Little Black Bear Band, Goodeve.
    Muskowekwan Band, Lestock.
    Muscowpetung Band, Edenwold.
    Nekaneet Band, Maple Creek.
    Okanese Band, Lorlie.
    Pasqua Band, Muscow.
    Peepeekisis Band, Lorlie.
    Piapot Band, Craven.
    Poorman Band, Quinton.
    Standing Buffalo Band, Fort Qu'Appelle.
    Starblanket Band, Balcarres.
    Wood Mountain Band, Wood Mountain.

Meadow Lake District:

    Joseph Bighead Band, Pierceland.
    Canoe Lake Band, Canoe Narrows.
    English River Band, Patuanak.
    Meadow Lake Band, Meadow Lake.
    Peter Pond Lake Band, Peter Pond Lake.
    Portage la Loche Band, La Loche.
    Turnor Lake Band, Turnor Lake.
    Waterhen Lake Band, Waterhen Lake.

Prince Albert District:

    Peter Ballantyne Band, Pelican Narrows.
    Cumberland House Band, Cumberland House.
    Fond du Lac Band, Fond du Lac.
    Lac La Hache Band, Wollaston Lake.
    Lac La Ronge Band, La Ronge.
    Montreal Lake Band, Montreal Lake.
    Red Earth Band, Red Earth.
    Shoal Lake Band, Pakwaw Lake.
    Stoney Rapids Band, Black Lake.
    Sturgeon Lake Band, Spruce Home.
    Wahpeton Band, Prince Albert.

Saskatoon District:

    Beardy and Okemasis Band, Duck Lake.
    Big River Band, Debden.
    James Smith Band, Kinistino.
    John Smith Band, Prince Albert.
    Kinistino Band, Chagoness.
    Mistawasis Band, Leask.
    Moose Woods Band, Saskatoon.
    MOOSE WOODS DAKOTA SIOUX POW-POW, Saskatoon.
    Muskeg Lake Band, Leask.
    Nut Lake Band, Rose Valley.
    One Arrow Band, Rosthern.
    Pelican Lake Band, Chitek Lake.
    Sandy Lake Band, Canwood.
    Witchekan Lake, Spiritwood.

North Battleford District:
Island Lake Band, Pierceland.
Little Pine Band, Paynton.
Loon Lake Band, Loon Lake.
Lucky Man Band, Paynton.
Moosomin Band, Cochin.
Mosquito Grizzly Bear's Head Band, Cando.
Onion Lake Band, Onion Lake.
Poundmaker Band, Cutknife.
Red Pheasant Band, Cando.
Saulteaux Band, Cochin.
Sweetgrass Band, Gallivan.
Thunderchild Band, Turtleford.

43 *French*

Bellevue: L'Association Culturelle Franco-Canadienne (ACFC), Bellevue Branch.
Club Age d'Or.
Jeunesse en Action, Bellevue.
Fédération des Femmes Canadiennes Françaises, Bellevue Branch.
Club Culturel de Bellevue.
Cabri: Classe Française de Cabri.
Coderre: L'Association Culturelle Franco-Canadienne (ACFC), Coderre Branch.
Delmas: Association Culturelle Franco-Canadienne (ACFC), Delmas.
Debden: Comité des Activités Culturelles, ACFC, Debden Branch.
Comité de Camp Feu, Debden.
Domremy: L'Association Culturelle Franco-Canadienne (ACFC), Domremy Branch.
Ferland: Fédération des Femmes Canadiennes Françaises, Provincial Executive.
Fédération des Femmes Canadiennes Françaises, Ferland Branch.
Institut Culturel de Ferland.
Gravelbourg: L'Association Culturelle Franco-Canadienne (ACFC), Gravelbourg Branch.
Le Collège Mathieu, Gravelbourg.
Le Mat, Gravelbourg.
Guernsey: La Famille Gilles Doray, French Performing Group.
North Battleford: France-Canada Association de la Saskatchewan, North Battleford.
L'Association des Loisirs et Centre Culturel.
Ponteix: Centre Culturel de Ponteix.
Prince Albert: La Commission Culturelle de la Saskatchewan.
La Societe Française de Prince Albert.
Regina: Association Culturelle Franco-Canadienne de la Saskatchewan (ACFC).
Association Culturelle Franco-Canadienne de la Saskatchewan Summer Camps.
Greenhouse Society.
Apprendre et Jouer.
Théâtre Fransaskois.
Bilingual Centre, University of Regina.
L'Alliance Française de Regina.
St. Denis: Club Culturel de St. Denis.
St. Front: L'Association Culturelle Franco-Canadienne (ACFC), St. Front.
Curling and Hockey Club, St. Front.
St. Victor: Le Centre Sylvain.
L'Association Culturelle Franco-Canadienne (ACFC), St. Victor.
La Fédération des Femmes Canadiennes-Françaises, St. Victor.
Saskatoon: Les Voix du Printemps.
Saskatchewan Association of Teachers of French.
The Saskatoon French School.
Willow Bunch: Willowbunch Museum Society.
Zenon Park: Association Jeunesse Fransaskoise (Nord), Zenon Park.
Citizens Committee for the Saskabec Project U.9, Zenon Park.
Centre de Culture et de Loisirs.

5 *English*

Grenfell: Grenfell Museum Association.
Milden: Milden Community Museum.
North Battleford: Grand Guardian Council of Saskatchewan, International Order of Job's
Daughters.
Regina: Imperial Order of the Daughters of the Empire (IODE), Provincial Executive.
Saskatoon: Order of the Eastern Star, Grand Chapter of Saskatchewan.

2 *Irish*

Saskatoon: Saskatoon Association for the Promotion of Irish Culture.
Yorkton: Yorkton Irish Community.

12 *Scottish*

Estevan: Estevan Elks Army Cadet Pipe and Drum Band.
Moose Jaw: Prairie Pipe Band Association.
              Moose Jaw Scottish Society.
Prince Albert: Prince Albert Highland Dancing and Piping Association.
Regina: Regina Highland Dancing Association.
              Fraser Pipe Band, Regina.
              Sons of Scotland Benevolent Association, Balmoral Camp No. 177, Regina.
              Regina Scottish Country Dance Group.
Saskatoon: Bonnie Bluebell Pipe Band, Saskatoon.
              Saskatoon Highland Dancing Association.
Swift Current: Swift Current Pipe and Drum Association (Green Braes Pipe Band).
Yorkton: Yorkton Scottish Cultural Association.

2 *Welsh*

Bangor: Morris Lodge Society.
Regina: St. David's Welsh Society of Regina.

3 *Austrian*

Regina: Austrian Canadian Edelweiss Club of Regina.
              Gentlemen's Fish and Hunting Club (Austrian Canadian Edelweiss Club).
              Ladies Edelweiss Auxiliary.

3 *Dutch*

Saskatoon: Netherlands Canada Society, Saskatoon.
Yorkton: Let's Dance and Sing, Yorkton Dutch Language School.
              Dutch Cultural Society, Yorkton.

4 *German Catholic*

Muenster: St. Peter's Orchestra.
              St. Peter's Adult Chorus.
              St. Peter's College Museum.
              The Catholic Women's League of Canada.

8 *German*

Neudorf: Neudorf Historical Museum.
Regina: German Canadian Harmonie Club Ltd.
              Saskatchewan Teachers of German.
              German Language School.
Saskatoon: German Canadian Club Concordia of Saskatoon.
              German Folk Dance Group.
              German Club, University of Saskatchewan.
Yorkton: Parkland German-Canadian Cultural Society.

30 *Hutterite*

Abbey Hutterite Community, Abbey.
Bailden Hutteren Brethren, Moose Jaw.
Bench Hutteren Brethren, Shaunavon.
Hutterian Brethren Church of Box Elder, Walsh.
Clear Spring Hutterian Brethren, Kenaston.
Cypress Hutterian Brethren Colony, Maple Creek.
Estuary Hutterian Brethren, Leader.
Fort Pitt Hutterian Brethren, Lloydminster.
Glidden Hutterian Brethren, Glidden.
Haven Hutterian Brethren, Fox Valley.
Hutterian Brethren Church of Hillcrest, Dundurn.
Hodgeville Hutterian Brethren, Hodgeville.
Kyle Hutterian Brethren, Kyle.
Leask Hutterite Brethren, Leask.
Main Centre Hutterite Colony, Rush Lake.
Riverview Colony, Saskatoon.
Rosetown Hutterian Brethren, Rosetown.
Tompkins Hutterite Community, Tompkins.

Sand Lake Hutterite Community, Masefield.
Simmie Colony, Admiral.
Spring Creek Hutterite Community, Walsh.
Smiley Hutterite Community, Smiley.
Waldeck Hutterite Community, Swift Current.
West Bench Colony, Eastend.
Arm River Hutterian Brethren, Lumsden.
Hillsvale Hutterian Brethren, Baldwinton.
Huron Hutterian Brethren, Brownlees.
New Wolf Hutterian Brethren, Maple Creek.
Ponteix Hutterian Brethren, Ponteix.
Scott Hutterian Brethren, Scott.

15 *Jewish*

Melfort: B'nai B'rith Lodge # 1888.
Melville: B'nai B'rith Lodge # 1846.
Moose Jaw: Moose Jaw Hebrew Community.
          B'nai Brith Lodge # 1251.
Regina: Beth Jacob Synagogue.
Saskatoon: Agudas Israel Sisterhood.
          B'nai B'rith Lodge # 739.
          B'nai B'rith Youth Organization.
          Hadassah-Wizo Organization of Canada.
          Canadian Friends of the Hebrew University.
          Histadrut.
          Jewish University Students Organization.
          Western Jewish Historical Society.
          Canadian Jewish Congress.
          Congregation Agudas Israel, Jewish Community Centre.

102 *Mennonite*

       11 *Inter-Mennonite Institutions*
       Winnipeg: Mennonite Historical Society of Canada.
                Mennonite Historical Society of Saskatchewan and Alberta.
       Herbert: Herbert Nursing Home.
       Rosthern: Saskatchewan Valley News.
       Saskatoon: Mennonite Central Committee (Saskatchewan).
       Winnipeg: Mennonite Foundation of Canada.
       Saskatoon: The David Toews Memorial Festival of Sacred Music.
                Saskatoon Mennonite Relief Auction Sale.
       Waldheim: Mennonite Mutual Fire Insurance Company.
                Mennonite Trust Limited.
                Menno Home of Saskatchewan.

       40 *General Conference Mennonite*
       Borden: Great Deer Bethel Mennonite Church.
       Drake: North Star Mennonite Church.
       Fiske: Fiske Mennonite Church.
       Duck Lake: Horse Lake Mennonite Church.
       Eyebrow: Eyebrow First Mennonite Church.
       Glenbush: Hoffnungsfelder Mennonite Church.
       Gouldtown: Gouldtown Mennonite Church.
       Hague: Neuanlage Grace Mennonite Church.
       Hanley: Hanley Mennonite Church.
       Kerrobert: Superb Mennonite Church.
       Laird Mennonite Church.
       Laird: Tiefengrund Rosenort Mennonite Church.
       Langham: Zoar Mennonite Church.
       Meadow Lake: Grace Mennonite Mission Church.
                   Immanuel Beaverdale Mennonite Church.
       Osler: Osler Mennonite Church.
       Mayfair: Hoffnungsfelder Mennonite Church.
       Prince Albert: Grace Mennonite Church.
                M-2 "Person to Person" Rehabilitation of Offenders.
       Regina: Grace Mennonite Church.

Rosthern: Mennonite Home for the Aged.
          Mennonite Nursing Home.
          Mennonite Youth Farm.
          Eigenheim Mennonite Church.
          Rosthern Junior College.
Saskatoon: Der Bote.
           College Park Mennonite Fellowship.
           First Mennonite Church.
           Mayfair Mennonite Church.
           Mount Royal Mennonite Church.
           Nutana Park Mennonite Church.
           Pleasant Hill Mennonite Church.
Swift Current: Swift Current Bible Institute.
                                    Lac Pelletier: Camp Elim.
Swift Current: Swift Current Bible Institute Motel.
               Zion Mennonite Church.
Waldheim: Zoar Mennonite Church.
          Grace Mennonite Mission Church.
Warman: Warman Mennonite Church.
Watrous: Bethany Mennonite Church.
Mennonite Institution: Canadian Mennonite Bible College, Winnipeg.

27 *Mennonite Brethren*

Beechy: Beechy Mennonite Brethren Church.
Brotherfield: Brotherfield Mennonite Brethren Church.
Carrot River: Carrot River Mennonite Brethren Church.
Dalmeny: Mennonite Brethren Church.
         Dalmeny Home for the Aged.
Elbow: Elbow Mennonite Brethren Church.
Glenbush: Mennonite Brethren Church.
Hepburn: Mennonite Brethren Church.
         Bethany Bible Institute.
Herbert: Herbert Mennonite Brethren Church.
Langham: Langham Emmanuel Mennonite Brethren Church.
Lanigan: Philadelphia Mennonite Brethren Choir.
Lucky Lake: Lucky Lake Mennonite Brethren Church.
Main Centre: Main Centre Mennonite Brethren Church.
McMahon: McMahon Mennonite Brethren Church.
Meadow Lake: Mennonite Brethren Church.
North Battleford: Mennonite Brethren Church.
                  Mennonite Conference Church.
Regina: Parliament Community Church.
Saskatoon: Central Mennonite Brethren Church.
           Nutana Mennonite Brethren Church.
           West Portal Mennonite Brethren Church.
Swift Current: Swift Current Mennonite Brethren Church.
Waldheim: Waldheim Mennonite Brethren Church.
Warman: Warman Mennonite Brethren Church.
Watrous: The Philadelphia Mennonite Brethren Church.
Woodrow: Woodrow Gospel Church.

Old Colony Mennonite (3 still open) (+1 Old Age Home).

• Kronsthal (now at Martensville).
• Neuanlage.
• Neuhorst.
Warman: Warman Mennoniten Altenheim.

9 *Evangelical Mennonite Conference*

Arabella Fellowship Chapel.
Endeavour Fellowship Chapel.
Heron Evangelical Mennonite Chapel.
Kamsack Fellowship Chapel.
Northern Fellowship Chapel.
Pelly Fellowship Chapel.
Swift Current Evangelical Mennonite Church.
Weeks.
Wymark Evangelical Mennonite Church.

6 *Evangelical Mennonite Mission Conference*
Blumenhof: Blumenhof Gospel Church.
Hague: Hague Gospel Church.
Hepburn: Hepburn Gospel Church.
Saskatoon: Westmount Evangelical Church.
Warman: Warman Gospel Church.
Wynyard: Wynyard Gospel Church.

4 *Other Mennonite Groups*
Osler: Osler Mission Chapel (Chortitzer Mennonite Conference, Steinbach).
Guernsey: Sharon Mennonite Church (Northwest Conference Mennonite).
Gruenthal: Gruenthal Church (Independent).
Waldheim: Grace Mennonite Mission Church (Waldheim Mission Conference).

1 *Czech*
Esterhazy: Polka Festival Association of Esterhazy and District.

14 *Doukhobor (+ Russian)*
Blaine Lake: Doukhobor Society of Blaine Lake.
             Doukhobor Ladies Club.
             Doukhobor Choir of Blaine Lake and Saskatoon.
Kamsack: Doukhobor Prayer Home.
Saskatoon: Doukhobor Society of Saskatoon.
           Doukhobor Society of Saskatoon Ladies Auxiliary.
           Russian Circle, University of Saskatchewan.
           Association of Canadians of Russian Descent.
           Russian-Ukrainian Baptist Church.
           Atamanenko Russian Trio.
Verigin: Doukhobor Society of Verigin.
         History Museum of the Society of Doukhobors.
Watson: Doukhobor Society of Watson.
Yorkton: Doukhobor Society of Yorkton.

5 *Hungarian*
Regina: Regina Hungarian Cultural and Social Club.
        Balaton Dancers.
        Hungarian Language School.
Stockholm: St. Elizabeth's Church.
Yorkton: Hungarian Physical Culture Group.

14 *Polish*
Moose Jaw: Polish Cultural Society (disbanded).
Prince Albert: Prince Albert Polish Association.
               Polish Cultural Society of Prince Albert.
               Polish Language Class, Prince Albert.
               Ladies Polish Cultural Society.
Regina: Polish School of St. Anthony's Parish.
        Regina Polish Choir.
        Polonia Dance Ensemble.
Saskatoon: Polish Catholic Association (Polish Language School).
           Ladies Altar Society, Polish Catholic Association.
           Polish Catholic Youth Organization.
           Gniezno Dancers.
           Polish University Club, University of Saskatchewan.
Zenon Park: Christ the King Multicultural Youth Camp at Morean Lake.

7 *Roumanian*
Kayville: Cana'Roma Roumanian Dancers.
Moose Jaw: Roumanian Canadian Club.
Regina: Eminescu Roumanian Dancers.
        Roumanian Canadian Cultural Club "Mihail Eminescu."
        Daughters of the Canadian Roumanian Club.
        St. Nicholas Reroy.
        Orthodox Brotherhood of Canada.

1 *Croatian*
Regina: Croatian Canadian Club "Jadran."

1 *Serbian*
Regina: Serbian Parish Hall.

272 *Ukrainian*
19 *Regina*

11 *General*
Poltava Ensemble.
Association of United Ukrainian Canadians, Saskatchewan Committee.
Association of United Ukrainian Canadians, Regina Branch.
Society of Prosvita.
Ukrainian Professional and Businessmen's Club.
Ukrainian National Federation.
Ukrainian Women's Organization.
Ukrainian National Youth Federation.
Chaban Ukrainian Dance Ensemble.
Alpha Omega, University of Regina.
Ukrainian Canadian Committee, Regina.

3 *Catholic*
Ukrainian Catholic Brotherhood.
St. Basil Ukrainian Catholic Parish Ukrainian School.
Ukrainian Catholic Women's League.

5 *Orthodox*
Ukrainian Self-Reliance League, Saskatchewan Provincial Executive.
Ukrainian Self-Reliance Association.
Canadian Ukrainian Youth Association.
Ukrainian Women's Association of Canada.
Ukrainian School.

56 *Saskatoon*

29 *General*
Rushnychok Ukrainian Dancing Association.
Vesnyanka Ukrainian Dance Company.
Yevshan Ukrainian Folk Ballet Ensemble.
Ukrainian Culture and Folk Art Series Radio Program.
Saskatoon Society of Ukrainian Artists.
Association of United Ukrainian Canadians, Saskatoon Branch.
Ukrainian National Federation.
Ukrainian War Veterans Association.
Ukrainian Women's Organization.
League for the Liberation of Ukraine.
Ukrainian Youth Association of Canada.
Women's Association, Canadian League for the Liberation of Ukraine.
Pavlychenko Folklorique Ensemble.
Saskatoon School of Ballet.
Ukrainian Canadian Foundation of Taras Shevchenko, Saskatchewan Rep.
Ukrainian Circle, University of Saskatchewan.
Ukrainian Credit Union.
Ukrainian Professional and Business Club.
Ukrainian Language Immersion Summer Camp at Green Grove (Orthodox).
Ukrainian Baptist Church.
Ukrainian Missionary and Bible Society, Inc.
Ukrainian Gospel Hour.
Gospel Press.
Vesna Chorus.
Vesna Festival.
Ukrainian Canadian Committee, Saskatoon Branch.
Women's Section, Ukrainian Canadian Committee, Saskatoon Branch.
Ukrainian Educational Council.
Saskatchewan Teachers of Ukrainian.

19 *Catholic*

St. George's Ukrainian School.
Ukrainian Catholic Youth, National Executive (Past).
Boyan Ukrainian Dance Association.
Sts. Peter and Paul Ukrainian Catholic Church Parish Council.
Ukrainian Catholic Women's League.
Ukrainian Catholic Youth Association.
Fides, Ukrainian Catholic Businessmen's Club.
Museum of Ukrainian Culture.
Obnova, University of Saskatchewan.
Sts. Peter and Paul Ukrainian School.
St. George's Sadochok.
Sheptycky Institute.
Ukrainian Catholic Brotherhood.
Ukrainian Catholic Council of Saskatchewan.
Ukrainian Catholic Women's League, St. George's Branch.
Ukrainian Catholic Women's League, Branch # 3.
Ukrainian Sadochok (Ukrainian language kindergarten).
Ukrainian Catholic Brotherhood, National Executive (Past).
Ukrainian Catholic Youth of Saskatchewan.

8 *Orthodox*

Ukrainian Self-Reliance Association.
All Saints Parish Ukrainian School.
Ukrainian Women's Association of Canada.
Kameniari, University of Saskatchewan.
Mohyla Institute.
Ukrainian Orthodox School.
Ukrainian Arts and Crafts Museum.
Canadian Ukrainian Youth Association.

197 *Outside Regina and Saskatoon*

43 *General*

Alvena: Alvena Ukrainian Dancing.
   Alvena Taras Shevchenko Group.
   Alvena Ukrainian Sadochok.
Blaine Lake: Blaine Lake Ukrainian Dancing Club.
   Blaine Lake Ukrainian Language Study.
Candiac: Arkan Ukrainian Dance Group.
Canora: General organizations in the area.
   Ukrainian Canadian Committee.
   Ukrainian Dancing School.
Carrot River: Franko Hall District Ukrainian School (Orthodox).
Donwell: Ukrainian Hall Association.
Foam Lake: Inactive groups.
Hafford: Ukrainian Arts Festival.
   Multicultural Association Ukrainian Language School.
   Ukrainian Tradition Society.
   Ukrainian Dancing Association.
Hyas: Senior Citizens Centre.
Lloydminster: Ukrainian Language School.
   Ukrainian Organization.
   Ukrainian Cultural and Educational Association.
Montmartre: Montmartre Ukrainian Dancing Group.
Moose Jaw: Ukrainian Canadian Committee.
North Battleford: Ukrainian Canadian Cultural Council.
   Ukrainian Svoboda Dancing School.
   Ukrainian Historical Society.
   Canadian League for the Liberation of Ukraine.
Prince Albert: Ukrainian Cultural Group Representatives.
Prud'homme: Ukrainian Dancing Club.
Richard: Ukrainian National Hall.
Stenen: Senior Citizens.
Swift Current: Southwest Ukrainian Cultural Council.
Swan Plain: Ukrainian Peoples Home.
Theodore and District: Ukrainian Dance Club.

Wadena: Ukrainian Organization.
Yorkton: Ukrainian Canadian Professional and Business Association.
Ukrainian Dancing.
Yorkton Ukrainian Chorus.
Canadian League for the Liberation of Ukraine.
St. Mary's School "Culture Day."
Provincial Executive, Saskatchewan Council, Ukrainian Canadian Committee.

55 *Catholic*

Alvena: Ukrainian Catholic Women's League.
Bankend: Ukrainian Greek Catholic Parish Organization.
Borden: Ukrainian Catholic Women's League.
Brooksby and Marysville: Ukrainian Catholic Church Parish.
Buchanan: Ukrainian Catholic Women's League.
Men's Church Committee.
Canora: Ukrainian Catholic Women's League.
Sts. Peter and Paul Ukrainian School.
Ukrainian Catholic Brotherhood.
Ukrainian Catholic Youth.
Cudworth: Ukrainian Catholic Women's League.
Glentworth: Ukrainian Catholic Women's League.
Glidden: Ukrainian Catholic Church Parish Organization.
Gronlid: Ukrainian Catholic Brotherhood.
Hafford: Ukrainian Catholic Youth.
Ukrainian Catholic Women's League.
Humboldt: Ukrainian Catholic Women's League.
Hyas: Ukrainian Greek Catholic Church.
Ituna: Ituna and District Ukrainian Program.
Ukrainian Catholic Women's League.
Camp Chaban.
Ukrainian Catholic Youth.
Sacred Heart Parish Men's Club.
Kamsack: Ukrainian Catholic Women's League.
Krydor: Sacred Heart Ukrainian Catholic Church.
Ukrainian Catholic Women's League.
Kuroki: Ukrainian Catholic Women's League
Lanigan: Ukrainian Catholic Women's League.
Meacham: Ukrainian Catholic Women's League.
Meath Park: Ukrainian Catholic Women's League.
Melfort: Ukrainian Catholic Brotherhood.
Ukrainian School.
Moose Jaw: Ukrainian Catholic Women's League.
Montmartre: Ukrainian Catholic Women's League.
Norquay: Ukrainian Greek Catholic Parish at Swan Plain.
North Battleford: Ukrainian Catholic Women's League.
Porcupine Plain: Ukrainian Catholic Women's League.
St. Olga's Catholic Ladies Club.
Prince Albert: Ukrainian Catholic Women's League.
St. George's Ukrainian Catholic Parish School.
Wakaw: Ukrainian Catholic Women's League.
Watson: Ukrainian St. George's Church.
Speers: Ukrainian Catholic Women's League.
Stenen: Ukrainian Catholic Church.
Wadena: Ukrainian Catholic Ladies Organization.
Weyburn: Ukrainian Catholic Women's League.
Ukrainian Catholic Church Ladies Aid.
Wynyard: Ukrainian Catholic Women's League.
Yellow Creek: Ukrainian Catholic Brotherhood.
Yorkton: Ukrainian Catholic Women's League # 1.
Ukrainian Catholic Women's League # 2.
Knights of Columbus.
St. Mary's Ukrainian Catholic Youth.
Ukrainian Catholic Youth, Junior.
St. Joseph's College.

99 *Orthodox*

Alvena: All Saints Ukrainian Greek Orthodox Church.

Arran: Ukrainian Women's Association of Canada, dissolved.
Ukrainian Orthodox Association.
Aylsham-Cadet: Ukrainian Women's Association of Canada.
Bankhead: Ukrainian Orthodox Organization.
Borden: Ukrainian Women's Association of Canada.
Ukrainian Greek Orthodox Parish, Assumption of St. Mary.
Brooksby: Ukrainian Women's Association of Canada.
Ukrainian Greek Orthodox Parish, Sts. Peter and Paul.
Buchanan: Ukrainian Women's Association of Canada.
Candiac: Ukrainian Women's Association of Canada.
Canora: Canadian Ukrainian Youth Association.
Ukrainian Self-Reliance Association.
Ukrainian Orthodox Trident Church and Language Camp.
Ukrainian Women's Association of Canada.
Cudworth: Canadian Ukrainian Youth Association.
Ukrainian Women's Association of Canada.
Cudworth/Wakaw/Prince Albert Branch of the Ukrainian Self Reliance League.
Danbury: Ukrainian Greek Orthodox Church Parish.
Donwell: Ukrainian Women's Association of Canada.
Ukrainian Hall Association.
Eatonia: Ukrainian Women's Association of Canada.
Ukrainian Greek Orthodox Church Parish.
Endeavor: Ukrainian Women's Association of Canada.
Ukrainian Greek Orthodox Parish Organization.
Foam Lake: Ukrainian Women's Association of Canada.
Fosston: Ukrainian Greek Orthodox Parish, Holy Trinity.
Glaslyn: Ukrainian Women's Association of Canada.
Gronlid: Ukrainian Women's Association of Canada.
Gorlitz: Ukrainian Women's Association of Canada.
Hafford: Canadian Ukrainian Youth Association.
Ukrainian Women's Association of Canada.
Honeymoon: Ukrainian Women's Association of Canada.
Hubbard: Ukrainian Women's Association of Canada.
Hudson Bay: Ukrainian Women's Association of Canada.
Ukrainian Language School.
Ukrainian Greek Orthodox Ladies Association.
Hyas: Ukrainian Greek Orthodox Parish Organization.
Church Women's Association of St. Ann.
Central Committee of eleven Ukrainian Orthodox parishes.
Senior Citizens Centre.
Ituna: St. Ilarion's Ukrainian Greek Orthodox Women's Association.
St. Olga's Ukrainian Greek Orthodox Women's Association.
Holy Trinity Ukrainian Greek Orthodox Church Parish.
Kamsack: Ukrainian Women's Association of Canada.
Ukrainian Community Centre.
All Saints Ukrainian Greek Orthodox Church Parish.
Kindersley: Ukrainian Greek Orthodox Church.
Ukrainian Women's Association of Canada.
Krydor: Sts. Peter and Paul Ukrainian Greek Orthodox Church Parish.
Krydor and Blaine Lake: Ukrainian Women's Association of Canada.
MacNutt: Ukrainian Orthodox Organization.
Mazeppa: Ukrainian Women's Association of Canada.
Melfort: Ukrainian Women's Association of Canada.
Melville: Ukrainian Women's Association of Canada.
Moose Jaw: Ukrainian Women's Association of Canada.
Ukrainian Greek Orthodox Church. St. Vladimir Parish.
Nipawin: Ukrainian Women's Association of Canada.
Ukrainian Self-Reliance Association.
North Battleford: Ukrainian Women's Association of Canada.
Canadian Ukrainian Youth Association.
Prince Albert: Ukrainian Women's Association of Canada.
Ukrainian Men's Greek Orthodox Church Group.
Ukrainian Adult Mixed Choir.
Richard: Ukrainian Greek Orthodox Church.
Canadian Ukrainian Youth Association.
Ukrainian Women's Association of Canada.

St. Julien: Ukrainian Women's Association of Canada.
Sheho: Ukrainian Women's Association of Canada.
Stenen: Ukrainian Greek Orthodox Parish.
Ukrainian Women's Association of Canada.
Ukrainian Choral Group.
Ukrainian Language School.
Sturgis: Ukrainian Women's Association of Canada.
Holy Trinity Ukrainian Greek Orthodox Church Parish.
Swan Plain: Ukrainian Greek Orthodox Parish.
Tarnopol: Ukrainian Self-Reliance Association.
Ukrainian Women's Association of Canada.
Theodore: Ukrainian Women's Association of Canada.
Wadena: Ukrainian Women's Association of Canada.
Ukrainian Greek Orthodox Church Organization.
Wakaw: Ukrainian Women's Association of Canada.
Watson: Ukrainian Women's Association of Canada.
St. Michael's Ukrainian Greek Orthodox Church Parish.
Ukrainian Ladies Association.
Weirdale: Ukrainian Women's Association of Canada.
Ukrainian National Home, Taras Shevchenko.
Ukrainian Greek Orthodox Church, St. John's Parish.
Whitkow: Canadian Ukrainian Youth Association.
Winmer: Ukrainian Women's Association of Canada.
Wynyard: Ukrainian Women's Association of Canada, disbanded.
St. Mary's Ukrainian Greek Orthodox Church Parish.
Yellow Creek: Ukrainian Women's Association of Canada.
Ukrainian Greek Orthodox Church Parish.
Ukrainian National Hall Association.
Yorkton: Ukrainian Women's Association of Canada.
Ukrainian Self-Reliance Association.
Ukrainian Orthodox Youth and Culture Committee.

2 Finnish
Lucky Lake: Rock Point, East Finn and Laestadion.
Whitewood: Uusi Suomi (New Finland).

2 Norwegian
Swift Current: Swift Current Norwegian Ethnic Group.
Norwegian Singers.

4 Scandinavian
Birch Hills: Scandinavian Cultural Society (Scandia Club).
Moose Jaw: Moose Jaw Scandinavian Club.
Saskatoon: Saskatoon Scandinavian Club.
Wynyard: Icelandic Cultural Society.

5 Greek
Regina: Greek Orthodox Community of Regina.
Greek Language School.
AHEPA, Daughters of Penelope.
Saskatoon: Hellenic Community of Saskatoon, and Greek Language School.
AHEPA, Daughters of Penelope.

2 Italian
Saskatoon: Coascit Saskatchewan, Italian Language School.
Saskatoon Club Italia.

1 Spanish
Saskatoon: Circulo Hispanico.

8 Chinese
Moose Jaw: Chinese Children's Group.
Regina: Chinese Cultural Society of Saskatchewan.
Chinese Language School of Regina.
Regina Chinese Benevolent Association.

Saskatoon: Saskatoon Chinese Benevolent Association.
Saskatoon Chinese Culture Retention School.
Saskatoon Chinese School.
Chinese Freemasons, Saskatoon.
Saskatoon Chinese Mandarin School.

11 *East Indian*

Moose Jaw: Moose Jaw East Indian Cultural Association.
Prince Albert: No-Sask. Asian Cultural Association.
Regina: The Third World Ethnocultural Community.
India Canada Association of Saskatchewan.
India Canada Cultural Association.
Islamic Association of Saskatchewan.
India Association Saskatchewan.
Gajarati Samaj.
Saskatoon: Pakistan Canada Cultural Association.
India Canada Cultural Association.
East Indian Navbahar Club.

1 *Arab*

Swift Current: Arab Cultural Club.

1 *Egyptian*

Saskatoon: Egyptian Dancing.

1 *Korean*

Regina: Regina Korean Association.

3 *Filipino*

Prince Albert: Filipino Cultural Group, Prince Albert Region.
Regina: Philippine Association of Saskatchewan, Regina and Moose Jaw Districts.
Saskatoon: Filipino Canadian Association.

85 *Multicultural*

Annaheim: Project Mosaic.
Arcola: Arcola Museum.
Batoche: Batoche National Historic Site.
Battleford: Saskatchewan Drama Association.
Battleford National Historic Site.
Biggar: Biggar and District Museum.
Blaine Lake: Blaine Lake Community Band Association.
Babushka Folk and Country Club Society.
Bulyea: Lakeside Museum.
Candiac: Arkan Ukrainian Dance Group.
Carrot River: Carrot River Old Time Fiddlers Club.
Craik: Prairie Pioneer Museum.
Donwell: Donwell Community Museum.
Elbow: Elbow Museum.
Esterhazy: Esterhazy Community Museum.
Esterhazy Arts Council.
Estevan: Estevan Arts Council.
Eston: Eston Music Festival and Arts Council.
Fort Qu'Appelle: The Valley Dance Association.
Fort Qu'Appelle and Lebret Historical Society.
Glen Ewen: Glen Ewen Community Antique Centre.
Glentworth: Glentworth Historical Museum.
Grenfell: Grenfell Con-Chord Singers.
Ituna: Ituna Museum.
Kamsack: Kamsack Dance Association.
Kerrobert: Kerrobert and District Museum.
Kinistino: Kinistino District Pioneer Museum.
Kindersley: Kindersley Plains Museum.
Kronau: Kronau Arts and Crafts Club.
Langenburg: Langenburg Senior Band.
Lashburn: Lashburn Centennial Museum.
Lloydminster: Lloydminster Arts Council.
Loon Lake: Loon Lake Museum.

McCord: McCord Grassland Fair.
Melfort: Melfort Agricultural Society.
           Melfort Arts Council.
Melville: Melville Senior Citizens Club: Community Crafts and Social Centre.
Moose Jaw: Palliser Regional Library.
           Saddlebag Ministry and Support Committee.
           International Band Festival.
Nipawin: Nipawin and District Museum.
Prince Albert: Prince Albert Arts Council.
           Saskatchewan History and Folklore Society.
North Battleford: Western Development Museum.
           Battleford Allied Arts Council.
Quill Plains: Quill Plains Regional Association.
           Quill Plains Arts Council.
Regina: Provincial Library.
           Canada-China Friendship Society.
           Regina Public Library: Prairie History Room.
           Saskatchewan Museum of Natural History.
           "Telerama."
           National Conference on Ethnic Studies and Research.
           Multicultural Council of Saskatchewan.
           Regina Multicultural Council.
           Betty and Her Brothers Five.
Riverhurst: Fred T. Hill Museum.
Saskatoon: Organization of Saskatchewan Arts Councils.
           Saskatchewan Elks Association.
           Saskatchewan International Folk Dancers.
           One Sky.
           Saskatchewan Craft Council.
           Western Development Museum.
           Riverside Players.
           Alliance of Youth and Elderly Society.
           Saskatoon Folk Arts Council.
           Saskatchewan Dance Theatre, disbanded.
           Wowk Enterprise Limited.
           Saskatchewan Teachers Federation.
Strasbourg: Strasbourg Marionettes.
Swift Current: Swift Current Multicultural Council.
           The Meistersingers (high school choir).
           Swift Current Square Dance Club.
           Old Tyme Fiddlers.
           Swift Current Allied Arts Council.
Weyburn:
           Weyburn Arts Council.
           Soo Line Historical Museum.
Wynyard: Wynyard Museum.
Yorkton: Yorkton and District Multicultural Council.
           Willowbrook and District Ethnic Society.
           Yorkton International Film Festival.
           Yorkton Arts Council.
           Yorkton Western Development Museum.
Zenon Park: Citizens Committee for the Saskabec Project U.9 (French).

APPENDIX II

Some Statistical Data On Ethnocultural Organizations in Saskatchewan

All figures are from 1971 census.
Total provincial population (identified by ethnic group) = 926,798.
Total number of organizations (replying by April 14, 1977) = 753.

Nine Categories
(1) *Eastern Europeans (Slavic)*
      18 groups = 150,757 (16.3% of total population).
      8 groups (42% of 18), constituting 97.4% of the Eastern European population (and 15.8% of

the total population) in Saskatchewan, have 315 organizations (41.8% of all in the province).

Average = 452 persons per organization (for these 8 groups).

(a) Ukrainians (85,920 or 9.3% of the Saskatchewan population) have 272 organizations (36% of all in the province, and 86.3% of all Eastern European ones).

Types of Organizations: General = 30.5% (83)
Catholic = 28.3% (77)
Orthodox = 41.2% (112)

Regina has 7% (19) of all Ukrainian organizations:
General = 57.9% (11)
Catholic = 15.8% (3)
Orthodox = 26.3% (5)

Saskatoon has 20.6% (56) of all Ukrainian organizations:
General = 51.8% (29)
Catholic = 33.9% (19)
Orthodox = 14.3% (8)

Places outside Saskatoon and Regina have 72.4% (197) of all Ukrainian organizations:
General = 21.8% (43)
Catholic = 27.9% (55)
Orthodox = 50.3% (99)

(b) Seven other groups (60,465 or 6.5% of the Saskatchewan population) have 43 organizations (5.7% of all in the province, and 15.8% of all Eastern European ones).

Of all Eastern European organizations:

1. Czechs (4,200) have 0.4% (1).
2. Doukhobors (9,425) and Russians (300) (TOTAL 9,725) have 5.1% (14).
3. Poles (26,910) also have 5.1% (14).
4. Roumanians (5,550) have 2.6% (7).
5. Hungarians (13,825) have 1.8% (5).
6. Serbians (255) and
7. Croatians (455) each have 0.4% (1).

(c) Ten Eastern European groups (nine with populations under 1,000) have no organizations listed. They number 3,917:

Yugoslav =   1,280
Bulgarian =   592
Byelorussian =   50
Estonian =   100
Gypsy =   50
Kuban Cossack =   300
Latvian =   235
Lithuanian =   475
Slovak =   740
Slovene =   95

(2) *Native (Indian and Metis)*

5 Indian tribes (Cree, Assiniboine, Dakota, Ojibwa, Chipewyan) = 40,500.

Metis = 80,000 est.

13% (120,500) of Saskatchewan population have 83 organizations (11% of all in the province).

Average = 1,452 persons per organization (for these six major groupings).

(3) *Multicultural* (may include 6,000 Americans):

85 multicultural organizations = 11.3% of all organizations in Saskatchewan.

(4) *Central European (Germanic)*

8 groups = 206,981. 6 groups (75% of 8), constituting 97.4% of the Germanic population (and 21.7% of the total population) have 165 organizations (21.9% of all in the province).

Average = 1,221 persons per organizations (for the six groups). Of all Germanic organizations:

(1) Mennonites (86,000) have 102 organizations, 13.5% of all in the province, and 61.8%.
(2) Hutterites (2,346) have 18.2% (30).
(3) Jews (2,195) have 9.1% (15).
(4) Germans (88,000) have 7.3% (12).
(5) Dutch (19,040) have 1.8% (3).
(6) Austrians (3,845) have 1.8% (3).

Two Central European groups have no organizations listed (Belgian = 3,555, and Swiss = 2,000. TOTAL = 5,555).

(5) *French*

46,000 = 5% of the total population.
43 organizations = 5.7% of all in the province.
Average = 1,070 persons per organization.

(6) *Non-European*

10 groups = 9,480. 7 groups (70% of 10) have 8,630 persons (0.9% of the total population) and 25 organizations (3.3% of all in the province). Average = 345 persons per organization.

(1) East Indians (1,625) plus
(2) Pakistani (1,250) = 2,875, which have 1.5% (11) of all organizations in the province (and 44% of all non-European ones).
(3) Chinese (4,605) have 32% (8) of all non-European organizations.
(4) Arabs (950) have 8% (2) of all non-European organizations.
(5) Filipinos (+50) have 12% (3) of all non-European organizations.
(6) Egyptians (+100) have 4% (1) of all non-European organizations.
(7) Koreans (+50) have 4% (1) of all non-European organizations.
Three non-European groups have no organizations listed:

Blacks = 360
Japanese = 310
West Indians = 180

(7) *British*

320,000 (34.6% of the total population) have 21 organizations (2.8% of all in the province). Average = 15,238 persons per organizations.
(1) Scottish (95,000) have 1.6% (12) of all organizations in Saskatchewan (and 57.1% of all British organizations).
(2) Irish (70,000) have 9.5% (2) of all British organizations.
(3) English (150,000) have 23.8% (5) of all British organizations.
(4) Welsh (5,000) have 9.5% (2) of all British organizations.

(8) *Northern European*

60,835 = 6.6% of the total population. 5 groups have 1.1% of all organizations in the province. Average = 7,604 persons per organization.
(1) Icelandic (3,095) have 1 organization.
(2) Finnish (1,725) have 2 organizations.
(3) Norwegians (36,160) have 2 organizations.
(4) Scandinavians have three organizations.
Scandinavians include SWEDISH (14,635) and DANISH (5,220).

(9) *Southern European*

4 groups = 4,250. 3 groups (75% of 4) have 3,970 persons (0.4% of the total population) and 8 organizations (1.3% of all in Saskatchewan). Average = 500 persons per organization.
(1) Greeks (900) have 0.7% (5) of all organizations in Saskatchewan (and 62.5% of all Southern European ones).
(2) Italians (2,860) have 25% (2) of all Southern European organizations.
(3) Spanish (210) have 12.5% (1) of all Southern European organizations.
One Southern European group has no organizations listed.

Portuguese = 275.

ETHNICITY AND EDUCATION

THE RELATIONSHIP BETWEEN ETHNICITY AND EDUCATIONAL ASPIRATIONS OF POST-SECONDARY STUDENTS IN TORONTO AND MONTREAL

ANN B. DENIS
UNIVERSITY OF OTTAWA, ONTARIO

Introduction

The purpose of this paper is to examine the relationship that may exist between ethnic origin and one's aspirations to obtain tertiary-level education. Analyses of the relation between ethnicity and education encounter two major conceptual problems. The first concerns the content of the concept ethnicity and its "operationalisation" measurement while the second relates to the explanation of the observed relations. Are these due to cultural differences among ethnic groups or to differences in socio-economic composition? This paper compares the results obtained while using two alternative operationalisations of ethnicity in the analyses of educational aspirations. Controls for attitudinal variables are also introduced as a first step in the explanation of the observed relations.

We will follow Vallee[1] in proposing that "ethnicity refers to descent from ancestors who share a common culture or subculture manifested in distinctive ways of speaking and/or acting."[2] An ethnic category refers to a statistical aggregate composed of those sharing the same ethnicity, while ethnic group refers to those who define themselves and are defined by others as belonging to a social group made up of those sharing a common ethnicity and defining themselves in terms of it.[3] Such a definition of ethnic group entails objective factors (birth in a particular group), subjective ones (one defines oneself and is defined by others as being a member of the group) and behavioural ones. However the operationalisation of these concepts in empirical research is not always complete or explicit insofar as their referents are concerned. In studies of the relationship of ethnicity or ethnic groups and education in Canadian society as a whole the census definition of ethnic group is frequently used.[4] This has the advantage of permitting extensive analyses of educational attainment in relation to a number of socio-economic variables, including ethnicity. There is a potentially severe, but as yet not greatly investigated, problem about the sociological meaningfulness of the census ethnic origin question. Respondents particularly among those whose families have been in North America for several generations, may be unsure of their origin or deny the relevance of having one other than as "Canadian." Moreover, it is not obvious that in exogamous unions the children's ethnic reference group is that of the father. Further research is needed here, but one could argue intuitively that, given woman's predominating responsibility up to now for early socialization, it is more likely that her values and patterns of behaviour than her husband's will be transmitted to the children. Research on language use in mixed marriages suggests that structural factors also have an important influence on what language is adopted by both parents and children.[5] The validity of ethnic origin as a measure of anything other than a statistical category is thus open to question. Differences in educational attainment do, however, exist among ethnic origin categories, which raises the question of what is causing these differences in attainment. Commonly cited factors include socio-economic background and cultural differences independent of social class and patterns of immigration.

Language is a behavioural indicator of ethnicity that has had some currency in Canadian studies of educational aspiration and attainment. King,[6] for instance, found that the retention rate in Ontario secondary schools between grade 9 (the base year) and grade 13 varied considerably by the child's mother tongue, with French-speaking children having the lowest retention rate (3.2), Hebrew children the highest (40.6) and others clustered together between 13.2 (British) and 18.8 (Hungarian). At the same time (mid 1960), although French language instruction was available up to grade 9, none was available in the state system thereafter. The very great loss of French students during the first grade of secondary school (which no other language group exhibited) suggested that the fact of changing language of instruction (particularly a change into a second language) part way through school could be a definite handicap. The other language groups had presumably made a similar transition at the beginning of their schooling, but during high school were succeeding better than the English students.

In a more recent study of the educational aspirations of grade 12 Ontario students, Anisef[7] found that the state of being Canadian-born males of Canadian-born parents, was associated with lower levels of educational aspiration than was that of being Canadian born of foreign-born parents or being first-generation foreign born. The boys' educational aspirations were not inconsistent with their school results. There were no significant differences for the girls. Thus, for successful achievers within the high school system, descent from a cultural or language background different from that which is predominant in the school system does not necessarily result in lower aspirations or success rates than membership in the dominant cultural group. King's results for francophones suggest, however, that for a more complete understanding of the relationship between ethnicity and education one would need to consider also whether there had been differential retention rates at earlier levels of study. The latter consideration may help in understanding the seeming paradox between the King and Anisef findings and the more general observation that the greater the difference between the home and the school cultures (whether for class or ethnic reasons) the greater the likelihood of failure and of low educational aspirations.[8]

The Study

In order to ascertain whether ethnic origin, with all its conceptual imperfections, did discriminate in relation to attitudes (a contextual variable) and to educational aspirations (the dependent variable) the distributions of educational aspirations were examined. An additional independent variable, a scale composed of items distinguishing those of Canadian background and English mother tongue was constructed, and the analyses were repeated using it in place of ethnic origin. Separate analyses were made for each sex.

The Data

The present study compares the educational aspirations of a random sample of 1318 students in their first year at university or college of applied arts and technology (C.A.A.T.) in Toronto and at the English language college of general and professional education (Cegep) in Montreal. Only anglophone institutions in Montreal were studied since that is where the students of non-French ethnic origins are very highly concentrated. Responses to the question "If you had your choice, how far *would you like* to go in school?" were grouped into the following categories for analysis here: not complete a post-secondary degree or diploma; complete a technology programme (the usual response of the CAAT and Cegep technology students); complete a university programme (the usual response of the university and Cegep pre-university students). Students who planned only to finish the pre-university Cegep programme without completing a university programme as well were included in the incomplete post-secondary category since pre-university Cegep is primarily a preparation for university. Whereas technology programmes provide training that is more explicitly related to particular jobs, university degrees are prerequisite for most higher status occupations. The university programmes also tend to be longer and to include more courses intended to provide a general education. The technology programmes on the other hand are largely made up of courses which have direct vocational reference. Thus, although at the end of his or her course a technology graduate may be more likely to have clear cut certification for a job, the long term possibilities for high status occupations are greater with a university degree. Students demonstrated their awareness of these distinctions elsewhere in the questionnaire in that technology students were much more likely than university students to give an instrumental reason (to secure vocational training or to earn a higher salary) as the most important reason for their current studies, rather than a more expressive one (to develop my mind and intellectual abilities, or to work out my life's goals). We will therefore argue that in absolute terms hoping to complete a university degree represents a higher level of educational aspiration than hoping to complete a technology diploma, while not planning to complete any post-secondary programme represents the lowest level of aspiration. We wish to examine here whether differences in aspiration exist among ethnic categories. The larger study of which this paper is a part will also consider whether differences exist when the level of aspiration is measured relative to the student's socio-economic background, and it will also examine other behavioural and subjective indicators of ethnic identification.

Measures of Ethnicity

With regard to ethnic background, two types of measure are used, ethnic origin as defined in the census[9] and a scale of degree of difference from the dominant Canadian model, based on the answers to five questions about birthplace and language use. Six ethnic origin categories are analysed: British; French; German and other north-western European; Italian and other southern European; Jewish; Ukrainian and other eastern European. Seven per cent of the sample does not fall into these categories and is excluded from analyses in terms of ethnic origin. As we have noted the census ethnic origin question has the attraction of allowing for comparison with data collected nationally by the census, but potentially has conceptual limitations as a sociological variable.

The components of the scale of difference from the dominant cultural model included five items: the birthplace of the respondent and of each of his or her parents, the respondent's mother tongue, and the language he or she usually used in conversation with parents. Language of instruction had also been considered, but was not included since over ninety per cent of the respondents had received their instruction in English. Use of English and birth in Canada were taken as indicators of no difference from the dominant cultural model, on the basis that English was the language of instruction in the institutions studied and that the school system is informed by the values, language, and behaviour patterns of Canadian society, notably middle class Canadian society.[10] We are arguing here that those whose socialization has occurred in a milieu most similar to that of the educational system will, other things being equal, have been able to adapt most easily to the educational system. Comparing the degree of difference from this dominant model, we find that the distributions for males and females are similar. Sixty-nine per cent of the British, 43% of the Jews and 38% of the French are not at all different from this model, while for the other three groups, the percentages range from 26% for the Germans to 6% for the Italians. Conversely the Italians have the highest proportion who differ from the dominant model on all 5 of the variables (i.e. are very different), but it is the French who have this high degree of difference least often. Moreover, whereas language most often distinguishes the French from the dominant model, for all the other groups parental birthplaces function in the same manner. Thus if the state of being similar to the dominant cultural model of the schools and society is associated with high educational aspirations, one would predict that the proportions of British, Jews and French with high aspirations would be greater than those of the Germans and especially of the Ukrainians and Italians. On the other hand, Anisef's findings would lead us to predict the reverse order for males and no significant variation for females.

We will first compare the distribution of educational aspirations for those of different ethnic origins and for the various levels of difference from the dominant model. Some analysts[11] have argued that education differences among ethnic origin groups are due to the degree to which the cultural values of the group result in attitudes favouring achievement, particularly occupational achievement, individualism and an orientation toward the future. Such attitudes, it is contended,[12] are associated with high levels of educational and occupational aspiration. We consider four of these clusterings of attitudes here: occupational primacy; individualism (in contrast to a strong family orientation); future orientation and achievement orientation.[13] High values on each have been associated in the American literature with high levels of educational and occupational aspiration. Following from our analysis of the occupational opportunities open to technology and university graduates we predict that high values on the future and achievement orientation clusterings will be associated with a preference for university programmes. This was the case for the sample as a whole. The relationship of occupational primacy to educational aspiration is more difficult to predict, since on the one hand it could entail primary emphasis on the instrumental function of education, the provision of precise job training, which as we have seen is not necessarily associated with university education. On the other hand, if it implies entering higher status occupations, then extended university education is entailed. High occupational primacy is associated with plans to complete technology programmes for the sample as a whole. It was not immediately obvious whether independence (low family orientation) would be associated with preferences for university or technology. In fact, for the sample as a whole there was a mild association between a high level of independence and a preference for technology programmes. If observed differences in level of educational attainment among ethnic groups are due primarily to differences in values, we could predict that the rank order of the ethnic origin categories on achievement and future orientations will be the same as the rank order that can be derived from Kalbach's[14] analysis of level of educational attainment for the Canadian population. Considering only the ethnic categories included in our study, the ranking on the basis of percentage having completed some university would be Italian, French, German, Ukrainian, British, Jewish, with the Italian favouring these attitudes the least and the Jews the most. We would further predict that the rank order on occupational primacy will be the reverse. If differences in educational aspirations between ethnic groups are due to attitudinal differences, when the attitude variables are controlled for, the relationship between ethnic origin and educational aspirations should disappear. As we said earlier, if difference from the dominant group is a disadvantage we would expect that the Italians and the Ukrainians would be least likely to aspire to a university degree, followed by the Germans, French, Jews and British. Again if attitudes are the determining factor we would expect the differences to decrease when the attitudinal controls are introduced.

Findings

Only 2% of the total sample did not plan to complete some post-secondary studies, so our major contrast refers to those intending to complete university and technology programmes, and the results will be presented in terms of the percentage wanting to undertake university training. Virtually all the remainder hope to qualify for a technology diploma. Overall 65% of the sample wanted to complete university education, a finding that reflects the fact that about 10% of the students in technology programmes, especially in Cegep, also hoped to graduate from a university.

When the attitude clusterings were broken down by ethnicity, the results were significant (F from .05 to .001) on each. For men, only occupational primacy, independence and achievement orientation produced significant differences (F from .05 to .001), with Germans, British and Ukrainians tending to favour these attitudes more strongly than the French, Jews and Italians. For the women there were only significant differences on achievement orientation, though general trend was for German, British and Italians to favour the various attitudes more strongly than the other ethnic categories. The differences on the scale of favouring work were also significant, with the Italians, Jews and Ukrainians being most in favour. There is, then, variation among the attitudes of ethnic categories, but it is not consistent across either attitudes or sex.

With regard to the degree of difference from the dominant model, apart from achievement orientation, which steadily and significantly declines as difference increases for each sex, most relations are curvilinear. They peak at a moderate level of difference and then decline, but the relation is statistically significant only for occupational primacy for males and independence for females.

From Tables 1 and 2 (which summarize the relationship between ethnicity and educational aspirations for men and women), we see that overall a slightly higher proportion of men hope to complete a university degree, and that the percentage of different ethnicities hoping to do so ranges from 58.9% to 80.0% for men and from 48.6% to 74.6% for women. For both the percentage is lowest for the Italians and highest for the Jews and Ukrainians. However, the rank ordering of ethnic categories from lowest to highest does differ and in the case of the Germans a higher percentage of women than men hope to complete university education.

When each of the attitudinal variables, dichotomised at its median, is introduced as a control variable we continue to observe considerable variations among the percentages hoping to attend university, for both sexes. It is, furthermore, obvious that the effect of the control variables differs both by ethnicity and by sex. Of the men, it is only in the case of the Jews that those expressing a high level of occupational primacy wanted to complete university. For all other groups the relation was inverse, suggesting that occupational primacy for them was associated with wanting to complete fairly specific vocational training. When independence vs. family orientation was controlled, for the Italian, German and French men, favouring independence was associated with a greater tendency to aspire to university, while the reverse was true for the British, Ukrainians and Jews. For all except the Italian males, the more students were future oriented, the more likely they were to aspire to university. Finally, in all cases greater achievement orientation was associated with being more likely to hope to complete a university degree. The amount of variation in aspiration was only reduced by the control variable in two cases, low occupational primacy and high independence. Occupational primacy seems to have vocational connotations for all but the Jews, while it is only for Italians that future orientations seems to have this connotation. It is possible that with their low socio-economic status the technology programmes are perceived as representing more realistic choices for economic mobility. Within this relatively selected group of those already in post-secondary studies there remain considerable differences in the proportion planning to complete a university degree, with fewer Italians, Germans and French, and more British, Jews and Ukrainians planning to do so. These variations persist and in fact become accentuated at times when the selected attitudinal variables are held constant. The major contrast between men and women is the

Table 1

Ethnicity and educational aspirations, controlling for attitudinal variables. Men.

	Italian	French	British	German	Jewish	Uk-rainian	Total
% hoping to complete university	58.9	62.1	71.0	60.0	80.0	75.9	68.2
(N)	(95)	(66)	(238)	(45)	(50)	(54)	(548)
% hoping to complete university controlling for:							
Occupational primacy							
Low	67.9	69.0	75.2	76.5	72.2	76.7	73.7
(N)	(28)	(29)	(133)	(17)	(18)	(30)	(255)
High	55.2	56.8	65.7	50.0	84.4	75.0	63.5
(N)	(67)	(37)	(105)	(28)	(32)	(24)	(293)
Independence							
Low	54.7	61.5	77.3	50.0	85.3	80.6	70.5
(N)	(53)	(39)	(119)	(24)	(34)	(36)	(305)
High	64.3	63.0	64.7	71.4	68.8	66.7	65.4
(N)	(42)	(27)	(119)	(21)	(16)	(18)	(243)
Future orientation							
Low	61.8	53.2	67.7	33.3	66.7	65.6	61.7
(N)	(55)	(47)	(127)	(21)	(21)	(32)	(303)
High	55.0	84.2	74.8	83.3	89.7	90.9	76.3
(N)	(40)	(19)	(111)	(24)	(29)	(22)	(245)
Achievement orientation							
Low	56.3	46.4	64.9	50.0	73.1	73.9	61.0
(N)	(64)	(28)	(94)	(24)	(26)	(23)	(259)
High	64.5	73.7	75.0	71.4	87.5	77.4	74.7
(N)	(31)	(38)	(144)	(21)	(24)	(31)	(289)

Table 2

Ethnicity and educational aspirations, controlling
for attitudinal variables. Women.

	Italian	French	British	German	Jewish	Uk-rainian	Total
% hoping to complete university	48.6	51.5	61.7	71.4	70.1	74.6	62.0
(N)	(72)	(66)	(264)	(49)	(67)	(59)	(577)
% hoping to complete university controlling for:							
Occupational primacy							
Low	47.6	48.6	63.5	69.0	73.8	78.1	63.0
(N)	(42)	(37)	(156)	(29)	(42)	(32)	(338)
High	50.0	55.2	59.3	75.0	64.0	70.4	60.7
(N)	(30)	(29)	(108)	(20)	(25)	(27)	(239)
Independence							
Low	61.1	40.0	62.7	75.0	59.4	70.4	62.2
(N)	(36)	(20)	(110)	(24)	(32)	(27)	(249)
High	36.1	56.5	61.0	68.0	80.0	78.1	61.9
(N)	(36)	(46)	(154)	(25)	(35)	(32)	(328)
Future orientation							
Low	50.0	42.9	61.6	62.1	75.0	77.5	61.7
(N)	(42)	(35)	(138)	(29)	(40)	(40)	(324)
High	46.7	61.3	61.9	85.0	63.0	68.4	62.5
(N)	(30)	(31)	(126)	(20)	(27)	(19)	(158)
Achievement orientation							
Low	51.9	46.2	65.1	80.0	62.5	69.7	62.3
(N)	(52)	(26)	(126)	(20)	(32)	(33)	(289)
High	40.0	55.0	58.7	65.5	77.1	80.8	61.8
(N)	(20)	(40)	(138)	(29)	(35)	(26)	(288)
Pro Women Working							
Low	43.1	48.1	60.2	69.0	63.2	70.3	58.3
(N)	(51)	(52)	(196)	(29)	(38)	(37)	(403)
High	68.4	77.8	75.6	75.0	78.9	78.9	75.6
(N)	(19)	(9)	(41)	(12)	(19)	(19)	(119)

likelihood of German men to be among the lower three and the German women the upper three. For the women, the relationships are somewhat different. The same overall ordering of ethnicities obtains, but the control variables do not have the same effects. High occupational primacy is associated with a greater likelihood to aspire to university for the Italians, French and Germans. For the other three groups, the reverse is the case. There is a positive relationship between favouring independence and university aspirations for the French, the Jews and the Ukrainians, and a negative one for the other ethnic categories. The same applies to achievement orientation. On the other hand for the Italians, Jews and Ukrainians high future orientation is associated with lower likelihood of aspiring to university. It is only for the additional scale of attitudes favouring women's working that the same relationship obtains for all ethnicities: the more this is favoured, the greater the likelihood of aspiring to university. This in fact, seems to be the most significant variable for predicting women's educational aspirations. The fact that the intervening variables do not affect men's and women's aspirations in the same way suggests that comparative analyses of sex role concepts and socialization within and between the various ethnic groups would be fruitful.

The second measure relating to ethnicity was the degree of difference from the dominant societal model. The relation of this variable to educational aspirations is summarized for men and women in tables 3 and 4. The relationship is not linear and is different for the two sexes. In general those of both sexes who differ the most are the least likely to aspire to attend university, while for the males, those who differ on at least three characteristics are the most likely to. Regardless of the degree of difference, the men who express less occupational primacy, less independence, greater future orientation and achievement orientation are more likely to want to complete a university degree. For the women such a consistent pattern only obtains for the favouring of women working. Occupational primacy does not differentiate level of aspiration at all, while the other attitudinal variables do so through complex curvilinear relations. Since for all but the French the most frequent variants from the dominant model are parental birthplace, these results are congruent with Anisef's[15], that Canadian born males of Canadian born parents have lower levels of aspiration than other males, whereas for females there is no significant (here, consistent) difference.

Table 3

Difference from dominant model and educational aspirations,
controlling for attitudinal variables. Men.

	0	1	2	3	4	5	Total
% hoping to complete university	70.7	66.2	60.5	74.1	73.4	63.5	68.5
(N)	(242)	(74)	(76)	(58)	(64)	(74)	(588)
% hoping to complete university controlling for:							
Occupational primacy							
Low	69.6	75.7	68.8	76.9	78.9	77.1	72.6
(N)	(125)	(37)	(32)	(26)	(19)	(35)	(274)
High	71.8	56.8	54.5	71.9	71.1	51.3	65.0
(N)	(117)	(37)	(44)	(32)	(45)	(39)	(314)
Independence							
Low	75.6	68.3	64.4	78.6	72.5	68.6	72.0
(N)	(123)	(41)	(45)	(28)	(40)	(51)	(328)
High	65.5	63.6	54.8	70.0	75.0	52.2	64.2
(N)	(119)	(33)	(31)	(30)	(24)	(23)	(260)
Future orientation							
Low	66.4	52.3	52.0	72.4	65.7	57.9	61.7
(N)	(125)	(44)	(50)	(29)	(35)	(38)	(321)
High	75.2	86.7	76.9	75.9	82.8	69.4	76.8
(N)	(117)	(30)	(26)	(29)	(29)	(36)	(267)
Achievement orientation							
Low	62.7	62.5	56.3	65.4	66.7	62.5	62.7
(N)	(102)	(32)	(32)	(26)	(39)	(56)	(287)
High	76.4	69.0	63.6	81.3	84.0	66.7	74.1
(N)	(140)	(42)	(44)	(32)	(25)	(18)	(301)

Table 4

Difference from dominant model and educational aspirations,
controlling for attitudinal variables. Women.

	0	1	2	3	4	5	Total
% hoping to complete university	63.1	64.0	65.9	64.2	63.2	56.5	63.0
(N)	(274)	(75)	(82)	(67)	(57)	(69)	(624)
% hoping to complete university controlling for:							
Occupational primacy							
Low	63.2	64.7	67.3	63.2	57.1	58.3	63.1
(N)	(155)	(51)	(52)	(38)	(28)	(36)	(360)
High	63.0	62.5	63.3	65.5	69.0	54.5	62.9
(N)	(119	(24)	(30)	(29)	(29)	(33)	(264)
Independence							
Low	63.4	52.6	70.6	61.8	70.0	64.1	64.2
(N)	(112)	(19)	(34)	(34)	(30)	(39)	(268)
High	63.0	67.9	62.5	66.7	55.6	46.7	62.1
(N)	(162)	(56)	(48)	(33)	(27)	(30)	(356)
Future orientation							
Low	64.2	59.1	63.3	66.7	59.5	55.6	62.1
(N)	(151)	(44)	(49)	(30)	(37)	(45)	(356)
High	61.8	71.0	69.7	62.2	70.0	58.3	64.2
(N)	(123)	(31)	(33)	(37)	(20)	(24)	(268)
Achievement orientation							
Low	67.2	54.3	74.4	59.5	64.7	48.9	62.8
(N)	(122)	(35)	(39)	(37)	(34)	(45)	(312)
High	59.9	72.5	58.1	70.0	60.9	70.8	63.1
(N)	(152)	(40)	(43)	(30)	(23)	(24)	(312)
Pro Women Working							
Low	59.6	64.8	62.7	56.8	57.1	48.6	59.3
(N)	(198)	(54)	(59)	(44)	(35)	(37)	(427)
High	80.4	69.2	81.3	71.4	75.0	66.7	75.6
(N)	(51)	(13)	(16)	(14)	(16)	(21)	(131)

Conclusions:

The fact that so few students had received any instruction in a language other than English suggests that having to change one's language of instruction to a less familiar language during school years can militate against entry into post-secondary institutions. This would be consonant with King's observation of the low retention rate for francophone students in Ontario from the point when many changed from French to English instruction. On the other hand, students of other mother tongues (whose earlier instruction had probably been in English) did not display lower retention rates at the high school level than the English. It also seems from our results, however, that a combination of foreign birth, a mother tongue other than English and not using English with one's parents resulted in a greater tendency to aspire to technology programmes, where it is likely that there is less emphasis in verbal skills. Particularly for men, however, some difference from the dominant model was associated with higher levels of university aspiration. Further analysis will reveal whether this is an artifact of socio-economic status or whether it merits further investigation in its own right. The results of this initial analysis show that even controlling for selected attitudinal variables ethnic origin still exhibits a relationship with aspiration to attend university which is similar to the patterns of university attainment documented in Kalbach, though somewhat different from the high school retention rates King has analysed in Ontario. Further, the intervening variables do not affect all ethnic categories in the same way, nor are the patterns the same for both sexes. This indicates that differences among ethnic categories persist even in this educationally highly selected group, and raises further questions about their basis. One step will be to determine from additional information on behavioural and subjective identification, how strong an association exists between ethnic origin and ethnic identity. It will also be necessary to ascertain whether the ethnic differences persist when socio-economic status is controlled. A structural variable that will also be introduced into the analysis is the post-secondary educational structure in each province. Unlike the Ontario institutions, the Quebec pre-university and technology streams in Cegeps are tuition-free, share common facilities and some common courses of study. As the data for this study were collected before Bill 22 was passed in Quebec, there is no difference between respondents from the two cities insofar as their legal choices of language orientation are concerned.

FOOTNOTES

[1] Frank Vallee, "Multi-Ethnic Societies" in D. Forcese and S. Richer, *Issues in Canadian Society* (Toronto, 1975), 162-202. Vallee's distinctions are informed by R. Schermerhorn's analysis in *Comparative Ethnic Relations* (New York, 1970), but provide in addition useful distinctions between ethnicity, ethnic category and ethnic group.

[2] *Ibid.*, 165-66.

[3] *Ibid.*, 166-67.

[4] The 1961 Census question (definition), "To what ethnic or cultural group did you or your ancestor (on the male side) belong on coming to this continent?" was used, for example, in John Porter, *The Vertical Mosaic*, (Toronto, 1965) and in W. Kalbach, *The Impact of Immigration on the Canadian Population* (Ottawa, 1970).

[5] Colette Carisse, "Orientations Culturelles dans les mariages biethniques," *Sociologie et Sociétés*, 1(1969), 39-52.

[6] A. King, "Ethnicity and School Adjustment," *Canadian Review of Sociology and Anthropology*, 5 (1968), 84-91.

[7] Paul Anisef, "Congruence of Ethnicity for Educational Plans Among Grade 12 Students," in A. Wolfgang, ed., *Education of Immigrant Children* (Toronto, 1975), 122-36.

[8] R. Breton, *Social and Academic Factors in the Career Decisions of Canadian Youth* (Ottawa, 1972).

[9] The question asked here is: "What is your ethnic origin? That is, what is the cultural or ethnic origin of the first male ancestor on your *father's* side to come to North America (or what is *your* cultural origin if you migrated to North America)?

[10] A. Wolfgang, *Education of Immigrant Children* (Toronto, 1975).

[11] For example: B. Rosen, "Race, Ethnicity and the Achievement Syndrome," *American Sociological Review*, 24 (1959), 47-60.
J. Kahl, "Some Measurements of Achievement Orientation," *American Journal of Sociology*, 70 (1965), 669-81.
K. Marjoribanks, "Achievement Orientation of Canadian Ethnic Groups," *Alberta Journal of Educational Research*, 18 (1972), 162-73.

[12] R. Breton, *op. cit.*

[13] a) For *Occupational Primacy* the questions were:
  1) The job should come first even if it means sacrificing time from recreation.
  2) The best way to judge a man is by his success in his occupation.
  3) Education should provide the student with skills necessary to obtain a job.

b) For *Independence* the questions were:
1) When looking for a job, a person ought to find a position in a place located near his parents even if it means losing a good opportunity elsewhere.
2) If you have a chance to hire someone it is always better to hire a relative instead of a stranger.
3) When you are in trouble only a relative can be depended on to help you out.

c) For *Future Orientation* the questions were:
1) Making plans only brings unhappiness because plans are hard to fulfill.
2) It is very important to make plans in life and not be satisfied with what comes along.
3) With things as they are today, an intelligent person ought to think only about the present, without worrying about what is going to happen tomorrow.

d) For *Achievement Orientation*, the questions were:
1) A person needs good connections to get ahead in the occupational world.
2) The son of a working man does not have a very good chance of rising into the professions.
3) All I want out of life in the way of a career is a secure, not too difficult job with enough pay to afford a nice car and eventually a house of my own.

In each case the questions were coded so that high values indicated strong occupational primacy, independence (as against strong family orientation), etc.

For women only, an additional scale of favourableness to women working was used. The questions were:

If you were married, indicate for each of the situations described below, whether you *would prefer* to work full-time, to work part-time, or not to have a job outside the home.
1) As long as we have no children.
2) While the children are small.
3) Once the children are in school.

Indicate how close each one comes to describing what you would like to do later on:
4) To have a satisfying job outside the home.
5) To have the necessary qualifications to get a job that will provide some security and independence.

[14]Kalbach, *op. cit.,* Table 4.15.

THE EDUCATION OF BLACK STUDENTS IN MONTREAL SCHOOLS: AN EMERGING ANGLOPHONE PROBLEM, A NON-EXISTENT FRANCOPHONE PREOCCUPATION

MICHEL LAFERRIÈRE
MCGILL UNIVERSITY

The formal education of black children in North America has often constituted a "problem," differently defined by the different groups involved and in different times and places. In the United States, certainly the most studied and best documented case, the problem, for many whites, had been first to prevent blacks, by law or by custom, from getting any kind of education at all; after the abolition of slavery, the problem became one of finding ways of avoiding equal contacts between the two races and of reserving a better education for white children. On the other side, the problem had been first one of simple access to basic literacy; at the end of the nineteenth century, it bore on the type of segregated education which would best promote the social uplift of blacks, with the majority of black and white educators and philanthropists supporting Booker T. Washington's idea that a practical vocational education would prepare blacks better for the only jobs open to them, while a minority, led by W. E. DuBois, argued that blacks should receive the same type of education as whites in order to come out of their social inferiority and show the unfairness of segregation. Only in the second half of the twentieth century did both the segregated aspect and the low quality of the education most black children were receiving in the United States become a major concern for groups other than blacks and their allies.[1] The education of black children has now become a manifest social problem — a problem, according to Robert K. Merton, widely recognized in society, the first and basic ingredient of which "consists of a substantial discrepancy between widely shared social standards and actual conditions of social life."[2] The 1954 Supreme Court Decision and numerous social intervention programs, for instance, indicate a recognition of the discrepancy between the official ideology of equality of opportunity and the actual limitations encountered by black students in segregated school systems.

When one turns to Canada, one realizes that the education of black children in the public schools gave birth to problems and debates often akin to those of the United States, although locally limited and generally less known and less documented by contemporary research. There is no comprehensive study of the education of blacks in Canada, but information has been gathered for areas where black communities have been numerically important for a long time, such as Ontario and Nova Scotia. Robert Winks, in his very detailed account of the history and present position of blacks in Canada,[3] stresses the fact that local school laws or educational practices very strongly contradicted the Canadians' traditional feeling of moral superiority over their Southern neighbors and their "self-congratulatory attitude towards their position on the negro."[4] Thus Winks gives numerous examples of de facto school segregation in Canada West, of creation by local school administrations of segregated schools for black children, of white citizens' petitions or comments requesting that the black children of the community be separated from their own children, for such varied reasons as their odors or the risks of intermarriage, or for no reason at all. Winks also stresses the fact that the school law of 1859, which made possible the creation of separate Negro schools, remained on the statutes of the Ontario Ministry of Education until 1964, or that, in Nova Scotia, in 1918 an Education Act permitted the establishment of separate buildings to avoid the mixing of sexes or races.[5] Social discrimination and de facto school segregation also affected the small isolated black settlement of Amber Valley, Alberta.[6] Most research dealt with Nova Scotia, where "By 1970 the Negro . . . — one tenth the population of the province — was one of the most overstudied, underprivileged minorities in Canada."[7] In the Toronto area, however, where West Indian immigrants have been arriving in greater numbers since the late 1960's, the education of the black newcomers has been defined, both by active West Indian groups and by the schools as "making a problem" — a problem more of acceptance and adjustment than of segregation.[8] But in both Nova Scotia and Ontario the blacks are in predominantly anglophone societies and school systems; thus it seems that an examination of the ways in which the schools in predominantly francophone Quebec have been treating black children, and the reasons for this treatment, might provide interesting comparative elements towards a refinement of race relations theory.

In order to examine the education of blacks in Quebec, we considered three types of sources: one official source at the provincial level, the reports of the Superintendent or Minister of Education;[9] official sources for the City of Montreal, where most blacks have always been concentrated,[10] the annual reports and accessible committee reports of the two public school commissions, the predominantly anglophone Protestant School Board of Greater Montreal (P.S.B.G.M.) and its predecessors, and the francophone Commission des Ecoles Catholiques de Montrèal;[11] and finally various published sources giving historical or sociological accounts of blacks in Quebec or in Canada. By selecting official sources and published research we consciously and intentionally rejected writings and documents by groups or individuals which were not stressed in published works or annexed to official documents. Groups or individuals might have been in the past, or might be now, aware of educational "problems" of blacks, but might not be influential enough to leave traces. We did not try to find especially aware or insightful "precursors"; on the contrary, we decided to stress the manifest (i.e., recognized) aspect of possible "problems" for people involved in educational institutions serving black children in Quebec. Following C.

Wright Mills' distinction, we shall consider the private troubles of individuals only if and when they become "public issues."[12] We are not aiming at giving an account of the actual educational experience of blacks in Quebec, but are attempting to examine the way the education of blacks has been considered by public school administrators or educators. The first period, up to the late 1960's, when there were very few blacks in Quebec, could be called the time of the unnoticed presence; the second period, which could be dated as starting with race incidents in the schools in 1968, could be termed the present emergence of a problem.

Blacks in the Schools of Quebec: The Unnoticed Presence

As Winks points out, "Negroes lived in Canada for nearly as long as in the present United States,"[13] but one cannot help noticing the dearth of historical or sociological studies concerning them, especially in Quebec. In addition to the comparatively small number of the Negroes in Canada, one could attempt to explain this dearth by the retardation and specificities of the Social Sciences in Canada. It has often been said that social science research in Canada has only recently begun, and has been staffed by foreigners or Canadians educated abroad whose main concerns lay more with Europe or the United States than with Canada.[14] One could also consider that the main Canadian "race problem" (so called) has been the conflict between the two founding peoples, the English and the French. One could argue further that some of the *real* race problems existing in Canada have been obscured by the great numbers of American academics in Canadian universities, as well as by the tendency of Canadians to adopt a self-righteous and self-congratulatory stand as they observe the highly complex racial problems just below their southern border.[15]

In the case of Quebec, the characteristics of its black population made its study still less likely: most blacks were anglophone in a predominantly francophone province, their number has always been, up to the last decade, very small, and many of them were quite transient, either because they moved to anglophone provinces, or because, as in the case of sleeping car porters since the end of the nineteenth century, they have been residing in other cities and have been coming to Montreal only for work, or because, as might have been the case for the few black slaves of New France, they might have intermarried and lost, after a few generations, their distinctive physical characteristics.[16] Thus it cannot be said that blacks in Quebec have been, until recent years, consciously or unconsciously rejected outside the realm of historical or sociological studies because of the use of a dominant "white" paradigm, as recent writers have suggested has been the case for black Americans.[17]

In Quebec, the history of blacks has perhaps been most studied for the period of the French colonization. One can find several reasons for this: first, New France has been one of the favorite fields for French Canadian historians, often for ideological motives, because it allowed them to ascertain the specificity and the French and Catholic character of the province, in opposition to the rest of Canada and the English ruling class of Quebec, but also because the French administration and the Catholic Church provided them with numerous administrative documents they could use as data;[18] New France also offered American (and especially black American) historians a field of comparison for the study of slavery.[19] Thus, tucked away in studies on slavery or society in France, one finds some indications relating to the education of blacks. According to Trudel, who attempted to trace all the slaves from whom he could find documents, there were only 1132 slaves between 1686 and 1802 in what is now Quebec, most of them being house slaves and often better educated than the other slaves, the Indians or "Panis."[20] If one believes the relations of the Jesuits, "little savages" (i.e., Indians), "little Negroes" and "little settlers" were taught together,[21] and it does not seem that there were conscious attempts to prevent slaves from getting an education; moreover, Lapalice suggests that:

> Dans ce pays, et surtout à Montréal, les maîtres d'esclaves prodiguèrent à ceux ci les bienfaits de la civilisation et leur apprirent qu'un noir est un être raisonnable, créé à l'image de Dieu.[22]

It does not seem that black slaves were purposefully deprived of an education in New France; nowhere in what is now Quebec were special schools for "African" children created by missionaries, or segregated schools for "colored" pupils established because white parents objected to having their children go to schools with blacks. A cultural explanation of this absence of segregated schooling for blacks in Quebec could be attempted: Quebec being predominantly francophone and Catholic would hold different values than anglo-Protestant parts of North America and would have treated differently its slaves and non-white people. This type of explanation implies that religion and values condition attitudes and behavior, and assumes that Catholicism treats all human beings as persons, while Protestantism could lead to a treatment of slaves and their descendants as things. Such an interpretation might be supported by the actions of the Catholic clergy, which attempted to convert black slaves and "savages," but it is contradicted by the often noted request of the French settlers, who petitioned the King in order to have the right to import and own slaves.[23] The limited and paternalistic character of slavery in New France was more likely due to climatic conditions and economic and historical circumstances which prevented the creation of a manpower-incentive plantation economy. The attitudes of French settlers in the West Indies towards their black slaves and the numerous black rebellions there — or a yet unwritten history of the attitudes and behavior of Quebecers from the seventeenth century to the present — seems to prove that economic demands might have been quite often more determinant than religious values.[24]

The fact that blacks were very few, that slavery had never been very much debated nor numerically important, and that most of Quebec was rural explains why no segregated educational institution for blacks was created in Quebec. Up to the 1960's, most of the few blacks in Quebec were of Canadian or American origin, or, more rarely, of West Indian backgrounds.[25] Nearly all of them were English-speaking and Protestant and did not create institutional problems as did other groups (the Jews, for instance, encountered legal and financial difficulties when they tried to benefit by the schools, owing to the religious basis of public education in Quebec and also to French and English anti-Semitism).[26] Nor did they create major language problems, as did the children of many immigrant groups who spoke neither of the two official languages.

Besides not creating institutional or linguistic problems, the education of blacks never created, up to the recent years, a problem of quality, for education was considered in Quebec more like a privilege than like a right. The notion of equality of educational opportunities, and still much less of the quality of educational results, does not seem to have played an important role in Quebec. Education became compulsory only in 1943, and if access to secondary and higher education had always been much easier in the Protestant than in the Catholic part of the public school system, it might have been because the Protestant system had generally been serving a wealthier and more prominent segment of the population.[27] As for blacks, and although "hard" data are difficult to come by, it seems that they were achieving educational results similar to those of whites of the same socio-economic backgrounds. For over half a century, the very few studies devoted to blacks in Quebec have dealt with the Saint Antoine area of Montreal, where most noticeable blacks (i.e., lower class blacks) had been concentrated until recent years, surrounded by lower class anglophone Canadians of English or Irish origin and by lower class French Canadians. There is no indication that they fared worse or better in school than their white lower class fellow students.[28]

The Education of Blacks in Montreal as an Emerging Problem

During the last decade, several indicators drawn from the P.S.B.G.M. reports and implemented or discussed policies seem to signify that the predominantly anglophone board has been made aware of problems in the education of blacks, while no equivalent indicators can be found for the Catholic board; moreover, it seems that different internal and external definitions of what the problem might be and of remedial policies have been competing.

When one looks at the annual reports of the two school commissions of Montreal, one hardly notices the fact that these commissions might have been serving black children. Blacks are never mentioned in the CECM reports. In its 1969-70 annual report, the P.S.B.G.M. presented pictures including a few black faces, while the practice of including pictures of school activities, students, and personnel had started more than ten years before; from then on, most annual reports have been including at least a few black faces. Attention has been given to the problems of the inner city by the two school commissions, the School Council of the Island of Montreal and the Quebec Ministry of Education. The P.S.B.G.M. has formed an inner city school committee, and has instituted a position of inner city co-ordinator and several remedial programs. The CECM launched in 1970 "Operation Renouveau," an inner city intervention program, and the newly created School Council has had the education of disadvantaged students as one of its two mandates, along with the reform of the structures of education on the Island of Montreal; the Ministry of Education has subsidized remedial programs and research, and has published working documents stating its educational philosophy in relation to the disadvantaged.[29] One should note, however, that "inner city" or "disadvantaged" is not, in Montreal, a euphemism for "black," as it is in many school systems in the northern United States. Thus, for the CECM, nearly all of the disadvantaged are poor French Canadians, and for the P.S.B.G.M. they are generally immigrant children in schools where blacks very rarely constitute more than 50% of the student body.[30]

The P.S.B.G.M. has also started policies which indicate that special attention is now being given to black students. Although they are only briefly mentioned in the annual report, there are now a black psychologist, a black social worker, and a Black Liaison Officer. This last position was created in 1969, along with the Greek Liaison Officer.[31] (There are many more students of Greek origin and schools with a majority of Greek students than there are black students or black schools in the P.S.B.G.M.)[32] The function of the Black Liaison Officer, who is from Trinidad, is to serve as a link between the black community and the school, to place newly arrived black students, and to make sure that they adjust to the schools. He works with teachers and outside social welfare agencies. The Black Liaison Officer has also created a library on the black experience and is developing a curriculum for social studies on the West Indies.[33] The P.S.B.G.M. created in 1974 an Ad Hoc Committee on Personnel Practices as They Relate to Racial and Minority Peoples' Issues; this Committee submitted a report in March 1975 stressing the need for more black and Greek teachers, for the teaching of courses in modern ethnic studies, for better communication and services for minority children, and for a committee evaluation of principals (although the evaluating committee would be made up of representatives of the school committee, commissioners, senior officers of the Board and teachers, which means that ethnic communities served by the Board might be represented but will most likely not constitute the majority of the Committee).[34] The P.S.B.G.M. also created three welcoming classes in the fall of 1976 in an area of heavy anglophone immigration. It is estimated that, in that area, 95% of the anglophone immigrant children come from the West Indies, so that these classes will be primarily for black immigrant children and will attempt to help them to adjust to Canadian schools, to overcome any retardation or differences in their educational backgrounds, and to get used to the Canadian dialect of English.[35] Finally the P.S.B.G.M. has been supporting remedial programs for black students, run either during the summer or during the school year by the Quebec Board of Black

Educators, the Da Costa Hall Program and the Bana program. These programs emphasize academic skills.[36]

The programs offered by the P.S.B.G.M. seem to emphasize two elements: the adjustment of black students in the schools and an eventual compensatory education. It is interesting to examine one program that the Ad Hoc Committee on Personnel Practices did not examine, for not being part of its mandate, i.e., the Black Community Central Administration of Quebec proposal for an Institute of Primary Education under its administrative control. This document was annexed to the Ad Hoc Committee on Personnel Practices report to the Chairman of the P.S.B.G.M. The proposal, termed a working paper, suggested the creation of an institute of primary education which would be part of the P.S.B.G.M., would have a staff with an 80:20 ratio of black to white teachers, selected in consultation with the Black Community Central Administration of Quebec, and chosen for their sensitivity to the problems encountered by black children as well as for their professionalism; its program would emphasize the Three R's, French, and discipline, and the work of the teaching staff would be helped by extended psychological and social services to students. Such a proposal was felt necessary because of the failure of the P.S.B.G.M. schools to motivate and educate black students, and because the black community had been denied the right to administer and participate in the decision-making process. It was hoped that such an institute would foster self-worth, positive self-identification, cultural growth, creativity and motivation among black students, thus bettering their academic results.[37] Although very sketchy, this proposal reminds one of some parts of programs of American or West Indian black cultural nationalist groups. It referred to self-identity as black, without mentioning the national origins of the students, or their social class. Thus the proposal assumed that mere blackness sets them apart from others and makes of them a unified group, that, as anti-Semitism creates the Jew, white racism creates the black,[38] and that blackness becomes the most salient attribute of an individual. The proposal could also be interpreted as leading to a de facto segregated school and as preventing the free choice of schools of "integrationist" blacks, for it was not mentioned whether the program would be compulsory for all black pupils, or whether white disadvantaged students would also be admitted. The proposal apparently encountered strong opposition from blacks' and whites alike and was never accepted or implemented by the Board. The Ad Hoc Committee on Personnel Practices as They Relate to Racial and Minority Peoples' "Issues" suggested that the concept of "administrative control" as elaborated in the proposal be considered on an experimental basis, for staffing the schools where the majority of the children belong to a specific ethnic group, but stressed that "No one on this Committee wants to see quota systems, ghetto schools or practices which discriminate."[39] Thus one could say that there was no passage from a concept of the education of blacks to a concept of black education, stressing racial specificity, and perhaps superiority.

If one turns towards the Catholic sector of the Montreal public school system, one realizes that blacks are very rarely mentioned. Statistics for the whole system indicate that in 1938, there were 21 blacks for the whole system, 15 in the francophone and 6 in the anglophone section out of a total of respectively 106,925 and 16,733 pupils;[40] in 1960, there were 12 black students, out of 145,744 francophone students, and 38 out of 30,015 anglophones! One wonders, however, how these figures were arrived at, for there was no way of racially categorizing the students from the CECM register. It seems that we encounter there one of the common difficulties in counting blacks in Montreal (or for that matter in Canada in general).[41] The CECM has had since 1934 a Comité des Néo-canadiens (New Canadians' Committee); this committee has been publishing annual reports since 1944, which comprise few statistics and mostly stress the role of New Canadian groups, activities and from 1948 on, classes, to keep the Catholic faith. The few published statistics show the great number of Italian, Polish, Lithuanian, Hungarian, German and Ukrainian children in the New Canadian group of the CECM. Moreover, immigrant blacks would not have been considered as an important category, for few among them were Catholic, and most of the Catholics spoke either French or English. The CECM created in 1973 welcoming classes, the goal of which has been to teach children French and to prevent them from losing an academic year, while the previous New Canadian classes were mostly for adults; the main goal of these classes is to integrate the children as quickly as possible into regular schools through a total immersion in French. Statistics on enrolment are only available for the July 1st 1974 to the June 30th 1975 period; they indicate that out of a total number of 1533 students who went through welcoming classes, 80 were Creole speakers, all Haitians.[42] But these statistics give a very wrong image of the black enrolment of the CECM. First, the schools of the CECM may enrol blacks from other countries than Haiti, such as the other West Indian countries, the United States, or African countries. Then, even if all of the black students of the CECM were Haitians, most of them would not be found in the welcoming classes, because, up to very recent years, most Haitains who came to Canada were qualified members of the elite, which means completely bilingual in French and Creole. Even if no precise statistics are available, the exact number of Haitian children in the schools of the CECM is certainly more than 80, for between 1969 and 1974, 10,737 Haitians immigrated legally to Quebec. In 1974 alone, 4,856 Haitians, of whom 4,555 spoke only French (which most likely means that they were fully francophone but were also creole speakers) and of whom only ten spoke neither French nor English, immigrated to la Belle Province.[43] These figures do not take into account the important illegal Haitian immigration; it is obvious that the Haitian population of Montreal, including legal and illegal immigrants and Montreal-born persons of Haitian origin, would provide much more than 80 students to the francophone school commission.

One could wonder why Haitians, who are recent black immigrants, have not been seen as a "problem" by the commission which serves them, the CECM, except for the few students who have been directed towards welcoming classes and have been treated as other immigrant students. One of the first answers which comes to mind is that, even if Haitain children, the bulk of black children in the CECM, number several hundreds, they are lost among the 141,694 francophone students of the commission, most of whom are French Canadians. Haitians might also be less concentrated residentially, and thus form, within the whole commission and within each of its schools where they are present, only a very small minority compared to a homogeneous large group. The P.S.B.G.M., on the contrary, has many students from minority ethnic groups in its anglophone schools, including over 6,000 Greek students and 4,000 black students, out of a total population of 51,570 anglophone students.[44]

One of the other reasons for the absence of a "Haitian" or "black" problem might be that these students were, up to the recent increase in immigration,[45] the children of the elite. Several proofs can be given of this assertion. First, Canadian immigration laws have always been quite discriminatory against non-white groups, and Haitians had to be professionally qualified in order to enter the country; then only the elite could afford the fare between Montreal and Port au Prince, for it is higher than the average yearly Haitian income. Moreover, only 10% of all Haitians speak French (this percentage corresponding roughly to the literate population of the country),[46] and previously quoted Quebec immigration statistics indicate that nearly all of the *immigrants* from Haiti speak French. Thus Haitians in Montreal schools would have few language problems or academic problems because of their educated elite status in their country of origin. Recent changes in the type of immigration from Haiti might, in a few years, create a "Haitian" school problem of adjustment to the culture of French Canadian schools, to Canadian French, and to a more advanced educational system.[47]

The last explanation of the difference between the Haitians and the West Indians in the two school commissions might deal with the groups involved in defining educational problems. Glick suggested that, in New York City, a Haitian community was "created" by the demands of the larger society. Thus because the schools and different social welfare agencies needed to have interlocutors, Haitians had to form groups.[48] Similarly, the P.S.B.G.M. in Montreal sought the advice of anglophone black groups; some members of these groups also wanted to influence the Board, and to stress a militant Black Power ideology, as some interpretations of the proposal for the creation of an Institute of Primary Education for blacks might suggest. On the contrary, the CECM never formally consulted the black community, perhaps because it never had to; the two main social service agencies of the Haitian community have dealt mainly with the economic conditions and the legal immigration harassment of the newly arrived poor Haitian immigrants.[49] The intellectual backgrounds of West Indians and Haitians are also quite different, and the two groups have very rarely a common language for communicating, reproducing on that account the linguistic division of Montreal. Haitian intellectuals are very much concerned with the political fight in their country, and very often, to use a Marxist analysis, much akin to French and French Canadian trends; thus their approach to education might be a structural one, emphasizing the role of the school for different social classes.[50] Because Haiti has been independent for over a century and a half, and because Haitian intellectuals have had many ties with francophone black and white intellectuals,[51] they do not have to ascertain their identity in the same manner as anglophone blacks and are less close than they, for linguistic and cultural reasons, to an American or West-Indian-inspired Black Power ideology. For the different concepts and ideals found among the works of francophone blacks are never the equivalents of the Black Power ideology. Whether one looks at Senghor's concept of Negritude, Jacques Roumain's poetry, or Fanon's books, one finds closer ties to French existentialist, phenomenological, or Marxist writings than to Carmichael's and Hamilton's Black Power.[52]

From this brief examination of the Montreal case, one can attempt to sort out the different factors which might enter the definition of the educational problems a certain group might present for a public school system; it appears that, in addition to the ideology of members of the public school bureaucracy, the needs of the group, but also and perhaps in a large measure the ideologies of the different groups of problem definers, might be the determining element. In the case of West Indian anglophone blacks, the problem of their education was defined in relationship to a model of psychological remedial education: thus it was assumed that better personnel practices would increase the pride of the children and that a better self-concept would have as a consequence better motivation. Such a model could be easily traced to many American experiments in urban education; it also includes, however, elements linked to a traditional model of immigrant education, such as the provision for welcoming classes. On the other side, the francophone school commission treats black immigrant children as it treats any other immigrant group, because no "problem definer" has defined Haitian children as being first and foremost black. It is suggested that Haitian culture, as well as the position of Haitian children within the school commission, might explain why no problem definer from the Haitian community came forward stressing the racial factor. Thus it appears that Haitian children requesting special attention are either in welcoming classes or in regular remedial programs of the francophone Catholic school commission, and that the trend one finds in the anglophone Protestant board from a problem of an education of blacks to a problem of Black education has not yet occurred at the CECM. It may, however, occur soon, for more and more Haitians come into contact with Haitians settled in the United States, who sometimes identify with American blacks, and because Haitians, and particularly lower class Haitians, experience covert or overt racial discrimination in Montreal.[53]

FOOTNOTES

[1]There are numerous books covering the history or the present problems of the education of blacks in the United States. Cf., for instance, Henry Allen Bullock, *A History of Negro Education in the South* (New York, 1967), *passim.*

[2]Robert K. Merton and Robert A. Nisbet, *Contemporary Social Problems* (New York, 1966), 10.

[3]Robin W. Winks, *The Blacks in Canada* (New Haven, 1971).

[4]Robin W. Winks, "The Canadian Negro: A Historical Assessment," in *Black Society in the New World,* ed. Richard Fruch, *et al.* (New York, 1971), 233.

[5]Robin W. Winks, *The Blacks in Canada*, 362-89.

[6]*Ibid.*, 381 and Stewart Grow, "The Blacks of Amber Valley — Negro Pioneering in Northern Alberta," *Canadian Ethnic Studies*, VI (1974), 28 and 37.

[7]Robin W. Winks, *The Blacks in Canada*, 384.

[8]Cf., for instance, Jan Edward Schreiber, *In the Course of Discovery: West Indian Immigrant Children in Toronto Schools* (Toronto, 1971).

[9]The name of the principal officer for education at the provincial level and his type of function changed several times since the beginning of the nineteenth century. See, for instance, Louis-Philippe Audet, *Histoire de l'Éducation au Québec* (Montreal, 1971), *passim.*

[10]For studies of the demography and ecology of blacks in Montreal, see: Ida Greaves, *The Negro in Canada* (Montreal: McGill University Economic Study No. 16, 1930); Robin W. Winks, *The Blacks in Canada;* Wilfred Emerson Israel, "The Montreal Negro Community," M.A. Thesis, McGill 1928; Harold Herbert Potter, "The Occupational Adjustment of Montreal Negroes," M.A. Thesis, McGill University, 1949.

[11]The Conseil Scolaire de l'Ile de Montréal was created in 1971 to prepare a restructuring of the school organization for the island of Montreal and programs for schools in "grey", i.e., poor areas of the island. See for instance the different issues of *The School Council of the Island of Montreal Newsletter* since 1972.

[12]C. Wright Mills, *The Sociological Imagination* (New York, 1959), 9.

[13]Robin W. Winks, *The Blacks in Canada*, ix.

[14]This complaint is fairly frequent in professional bulletins such as *University Affairs* or *Social Sciences in Canada;* it is also the theme of books such as Robin Mathews and James Steele, ed., *The Struggle For Canadian Universities* (Toronto, 1970).

[15]For instance in J. Cleland Hamilton, "Slavery in Canada," *Magazine of American History,* 25, 3(1891), 238. Winks often criticizes this Canadian self-righteousness: Robin W. Winks, *op. cit., passim.*

[16]Marcel Trudel, *L'Esclavage au Canada Français* (Quebec, 1960), 97.

[17]Joyce A. Ladner, ed., *The Death of White Sociology* (New York, 1973) or Stanford M. Lyman, *The Black American in Sociological Thought: A Failure of Perspective* (New York, 1972).

[18]One could attempt a history of French historiography in Canada by showing, in accordance with its different periods, its nationalistic purposes with people such as Lionel Groux or its modern empirical and scientific trend, with the young social historians of the present who are often influenced by the French École des Annales and the Paris École Pratique des Hautes Études.

[19]The *Negro Journal of History* published articles on slavery in Canada: Fred Landon, "Negro Migration to Canada," *Journal of Negro History,* V (1920); William R. Riddell, "Notes on Slavery in Canada," *Journal of Negro History,* VII, 3 (1922), 396-411 and "Notes on the Slaves in Nouvelle France," *J.N.H.,* VIII, 3 (1923), 316-30 and "Further Notes on the Slave Trade in Canada," *J.N.H.,* IX, 1 (1924), 26-33 and "Le 'Code Noir' in Canada," *J.N.H.,* X, 3 (1925), 321-29.

[20]Trudel, *op. cit.,* chapter 11.

[21]The well known quote by Father Le Jeune "J'avais l'autre jour un petit sauvage d'un côté et un petit nègre ou maure de l'autre, auxquels j'apprenais à connaitre les lettres" ("I had the other day a little savage on one side, and a little negro or moor on the other, whom I was teaching how to recognize letters") has even been reproduced in satirical books such as Eloi de Grandmont *et al., Un Bill 60 du Tonnerre* (Montreal, 1964).

[22]"In this country, and particularly in Montréal, masters gave their slaves the benefits of civilization and taught them that a black person is a reasonable being created in God's image." O. Lapalice, "Les Esclaves Noirs à Montréal Sous le Régime Français," *Canadian Antiquarian and Numismatic Journal,* XII, 3 (1915), 158.

[23]Guy Frégault, *La Civilisation de la Nouvelle France 1713-1744* (Montreal, 1944), 83-84.

[24]Toynbee, *A Study of History* (London), 223-225; Frank Tannenbaum, *Slave and Citizen: The Negro in the Américas* (New York, 1946), 49-50; and Stanley M. Elkins, *Slavery: A Problem in American Institutional and Intellectual Life* (Chicago, 1959), *passim,* support the idea that catholic slavery was different from Anglo-Saxon protestant slavery. François Girod, *La Vie Quotidienne de la Société Créole* (Paris, 1972), 182 and Chapter IV, and Michael Banton, *Race Relations* (London, 1972), 113 suggest on the contrary that slavery in catholic countries was often very harsh.

[25]Potter, *op. cit., passim;* Greaves, *op. cit., passim;* and Israel, *op. cit., passim.*

[26]For an account of Jewish education in Montreal, see Joseph Kaye, "The Education of a Minority — Jewish Children in Greater Montréal" in Paul M. Mingus, *Sounds Canadian. Languages and Cultures in Multi-Ethnic Society* (Toronto, 1975), 93-104.

[27]*Canadian Royal Commission on Bilingualism and Biculturalism Report* (Ottawa, 1967), Book III, part 1.

[28]Potter suggested, in a private interview in 1975, that in his youth West Indian children often came from strict and achievement-oriented families, and succeeded better than their white neighbors.

[29]Gouvernement du Québec. Ministère de l'Éducation, *Éducation et Développement. Une approche aux interventions d'éducation en milieux défavorisés* (April 1975).

[30]In a list of schools of particular concern to the Greek and black minority groups annexed to the "Report of the Ad Hoc Committee on Personnel Practices as They Relate to Racial and Minority People's Issues," March 18, 1974, one notes that out of the 20 schools listed, only 2 have slightly more than half of their enrolment black while 11 schools have more than half of their enrolment Greek; for 3 of these 11 schools, more than 75% of their enrolment is Greek.

[31]Interview with the Black Liaison Officer, March 1975. I would like to take this opportunity to thank Mr. Winston Williams, the P.S.B.G.M. Black Liaison Officer for his cooperation.

[32]Greek students have also been seen as problems. They often speak a poor English, have a high drop out rate and present discipline problems. Perhaps because lower class Greek parents do not speak English, or because they do not stress education, has the problem of the low achievements of students been less emphasized by the Greek community than by the black community.

[33]Interview with the Black Liaison Officer, March 1975.

[34]*Report of the Ad Hoc Committee on Personnel Practices ...* , March 18, 1974, 4, V.

[35]Interview with the Black Liaison Officer, March 1975.

[36]The Québec Board of Black Educators groups teachers at every level; it is linked to the Black Community Central Administration of Québec, a broader organization. Although no study of the membership of those two organizations is available, my impression is that they are mostly made up of educated West Indian immigrants.

[37]"Towards Black Community Administrative Control of An Institute of Primary Education," presented to the "Committee on Ethnic Affairs" of the Protestant School Board of Greater Montreal by Black Community Central Administration of Québec on November 5, 1974, 2.

[38]This Sartrian position that one finds in his *Reflexions sur la question juive* has been followed by many other writers.

[39]Letter of the Ad Hoc Committee on Personnel Practices ... to Rev. John A. Simms, Chairman of the P.S.B.G.M., March 10, 1975, 1.

[40]Statistics from the "Statistics" files of the Archives of the CECM. I would like to take this opportunity to thank the librarians and the Archival Librarian of the CECM. No definition of the words "nègres" or "noirs" is given in these archival documents.

[41]Winks, *The Blacks in Canada,* 484-496, devotes a thorough appendix to this problem: "How Many Negroes in Canada?"

[42]These statistics on the "Nombre d'élèves inscrits aux classes d'accueil" were given to me by Mr. Attar of the CECM.

[43]Gouvernement du Québec. Ministère de l'Immigration. Direction de la Recherche, "L'Immigration au Québec Bulletin statistique annuel," vol. 2 (1974), 20, tableau 10.

[44]The 4,000 figure was given to me by the Black Liaison Officer of the P.S.B.G.M. The figure for the anglophone students in the P.S.B.G.M. is taken from a table in *Unisson,* vol. 3, No. 3 (Juin 1975), 5. *Unisson* is the Bulletin of the Conseil Scolaire de l'Ile de Montréal.

[45]Gouvernement du Québec. Ministère de l'Immigration, *op. cit.,* 16-17.

[46]François Latortue, "Haiti et sa main d'oeuvre. Perspectives d'avenir" and Max Chancy, "Education et développement en Haiti," in *Culture et Développement en Haiti,* Publié sous la direction du professeur Emerson Douyon (Montreal, 1972), respectively 39-50 and 135-55.

[47]This problem is now present in New York City. The Board of Education has opened several classes in French for Haitian children under the provisions of the Bilingual Education Act. Interview with Ms. Michelle Auguste, Board of Education of the City of New York, November 1975. I would like to take this opportunity to thank Ms. Auguste and many other Haitian teachers for their cooperation.

[48]Nina Barnett Glick, "The Formation of a Haitian Ethnic Group," Ph.D. Thesis, Columbia University, 1975.

[49]1,500 Haitians were threatened with deportation in the fall of 1974. Quebecers were quite prompt to remark that the Federal Minister of Immigration was persecuting immigrants who happened to be poor, black and francophone.

[50]*Culture et Développement en Haiti, passim* is an example of this trend.

[51]*Culture et Développement en Haiti,* 163-86, and, for literature, Lilyan Kesteloot, *Les Écrivains Noirs de Langue Française: Naissance d'une Littérature* (Bruxelles, 1963).

[52]See, for instance, Kesteloot, *op. cit.*, Frantz Fanon, *Peau Noire, Masques Blancs* (Paris, 1952) and *Les Damnes de la Terre* (Paris, 1961) and Stokely Carmichael and Charles Hamilton, *Black Power* (New York, 1967).

[53]The linguistic legislation proposed in April 1977 by the government of the Parti Quebecois elected on November 15, 1976, might increase contacts between Haitians and anglophone West Indians in the schools, for it would send all immigrant children to French schools, allowing entrance to English schools only for children whose father or mother attended English elementary school in Quebec or who have a brother or a sister in an English school at the time the legislation was promulgated.

CULTURE, EDUCATION AND ETHNICITY: A CASE STUDY OF THE CANADIAN NORTH

JAMES S. FRIDERES
UNIVERSITY OF CALGARY

The thesis of the present paper is that education has had differing influence upon the major ethnic groups in the North.[1] While the general impact has been one of cultural destruction for Native people, it has, at the same time, provided them with basic skills to play a powerful role in mediating the development now taking place in the North. As a consequence of education for the white, they emerged as agents for the facilitation of migration from the South so that it can take place easily and with minimal difficulty.

The impact of education on whites has been one which guarantees an education to them, comparable to that received in Southern Canada. Thus the migration of whites both in and out of the North is facilitated.

Before we discuss the impact of education on the three major ethnic groups in the North, a brief historical review seems in order so as to enable us to evaluate the present day education in its proper cultural context. Hence we will begin by discussing the history of the Yukon and the Northwest Territories. Since they developed in different circumstances, the initial discussion will be made in separate sections.

The Yukon

Before 1898, formal education was virtually non-existent in the Yukon. However, in that year, a number of white residents petitioned the Yukon Commissioner in Council for a school. The results of this request set a precedent in the Yukon so that the founding and maintenance of public schools came to be regarded as a territorial responsibility. The Commissioner, at that time, organized a number of people interested in establishing nonsectarian schools, and the outcome was the creation of public schools financed and controlled by the Territorial government. The only dissent was voiced by representatives of the Roman Catholics, who wanted government-assisted separate schools. However, the conflict between separate schools and public schools never developed into a serious rift, because two years later the council agreed to fund *any* school in existence so that it might continue its activities. As a result, both public and separate schools were maintained through grants from the council. It is estimated that enrolment in schools at the turn of the century in the Yukon was about 500.[2]

However, by the end of World War I (and after the decline of the mining industry) the population of the Yukon decreased; what remained became more "urbanized" (centralized) and as a result most of the smaller schools were closed. At this time fewer than 320 students were enrolled in six different schools.

By the beginning of World War II, the territory was still maintaining these six schools with a total enrolment of less than 300 pupils in ten classrooms. At the same time, the federal government set up and maintained a number of schools for Indian children, operated by religious orders. It has been estimated that at this time less than 50 per cent of all children between the ages of five and nineteen were attending school. During the war there was again an influx of whites into the Yukon. The result again was an expansion of school facilities. By 1950 there were eleven schools operated by the Territorial government, two separate schools, six full-time Indian schools (as well as a number of seasonal Indian schools), and one Indian residential school. However, only two schools had high school departments providing an education leading to university entrance.[3] Since 1950, the Territorial government has slowly taken over the responsibility for education.[4] At the same time, Indian schools have been phased out with the result that the Indian students have been taken into the Territorial schools. The general outcome has been a steady increase of students in school attendance. Presently it is estimated that about 85 per cent of school-age children (five to nineteen) now attend school.[5] In 1960 a school district was organized in the Yukon with a full-time superintendent who supervised Indian education throughout the district. Besides, Grade 12 is now available in four areas, and in Whitehorse it is possible to proceed to Grade 13. Currently, there are over twenty schools in operation in the Yukon with a net enrolment of over 3,500 students. In addition, there is a vocational training school (completed in 1964) which provides vocational training to over 200 students. The above discussion illustrates clearly that increases in educational opportunities correspond with increases in the white population of the Yukon.

Northwest Territories (N.W.T.)

As the N.W.T. did not experience the large influx of southern whites, education there has evolved quite differently than in the Yukon. Education in the N.W.T. until after World War II was ignored by all levels of government. In fact, the entire N.W.T. was virtually overlooked by the federal government. As Fumoleau pointed out:

> The Canadian Government did not feel it has any obligation toward a people [Natives in the North] with whom it did not have a formal agreement, nor did the government see any purpose in making a treaty with Indians whose land was apparently of such little value.[6]

The Hudson's Bay Company (H.B.C.) had always traded with the Indians; and although the H.B.C.'s interest in the country was transferred in 1870 to the Dominion of Canada, the federal government argued that responsibility for the native peoples remained with the H.B.C.

The rationale provided was that because no white settlement had occurred after the transfer, because there had been no disruption in the Native's traditional occupational activities (hunting and trapping), and because the H.B.C. had experienced no loss — had, in fact, realized substantial gains in money and land grants —, the native peoples should therefore remain the Company's responsibility.

This policy of "no help" by the federal government was opposed by the missionaries, and because H.B.C. felt no obligation towards the native peoples, missionaries took complete control of the field of education. As early as 1867 the Roman Catholics began to set up schools, and in 1894 Anglicans followed suit. Until the signing of Treaty Eight (wherein the provision of schools was laid down) the federal government totally absolved itself of any responsibility for education. Even after 1899, the federal government found it expedient to leave the job of education to missionaries. Before this time, one Roman Catholic residential school and two day schools were in full yearly operation. By 1920, there were fewer than ten schools, all of them church-sponsored.[7] The churches were most willing to take on the job of educating the "heathens" because the students would become good Christians and the churches themselves would benefit financially. As Chance points out:

> Nineteenth century Christian missionaries viewed Alaskan and Canadian Natives as heathen. Uncivilized, dirty, and uninhibited, these people [natives] were frequently considered inferior creatures of Divine creation.[8]

By the 1920s, when oil was first discovered and whites began to enter the North in large numbers for the first time, demands for educational opportunity increased. While this population influx was short lived, it did point up the fact that the existing school system was inadequate. Local people asked the Territorial government for funds to build a public school, but they were told to rely upon the correspondence courses out of Alberta.

It was not until the late thirties, when mining development once again increased, that the "restructuring" of the educational system in the N.W.T. began. It was, in fact, in 1937 that the first public school was opened in Fort Smith. By the beginning of World War II there were thirteen day schools and five residential schools. Nine of the schools were Roman Catholic, and the remainder were operated by the Church of England.

With the advent of World War II, interest and activity were deflected toward the war effort, and little thought was given to education. When changes did take place, they came as a direct result of the military developments as well as the pressure created by the great expansion of the white population in the N.W.T. For example, in 1921, about 8,000 people were in the N.W.T.; over 75 per cent of these were native people.[9] By 1941 the population had increased by 4,000; and although the proportion of whites to non-whites remained about the same, the absolute number of whites increased substantially. In 1971, Indians made up 21 per cent of the total population, and Inuits 33 per cent. In 1955, through an agreement with the Indian Affairs Branch, the Northern Administration and Land Branch accepted the entire responsibility for education of all Indian children in the N.W.T. It should be noted, however, that the government policy of this period (which has continued until the present day) stressed education as the strategy for achieving rapid economic and cultural assimilation for Natives.

The result was that prior to 1969 there was no Territorial Department of Education. When a Department was established at this time, it covered only the Mackenzie District. A year later, however, the eastern Arctic was incorporated into the purview of this organization. Since the mid-sixties, several experimental educational programmes have been developed with limited success. For example, in 1968 the "teacher education programme for native students" was launched. This programme has given fifteen students one year of professional training and academic enrichment in Yellowknife.[10]

Education and Ideology

The impact of education on the North must be seen in its theoretical and political context. First of all, in the political context, it must be made clear that concern over education for Native people was not evident until a sizable white population resided in the area. Only from that time on was it deemed politically expedient to channel manpower and money into this institutional sphere. In addition, it became clear that the cultural-geographic context of education would not be taken into consideration because even though there were large numbers of Euro-white Canadians in the North, they would always return to the South.[11] Hence, educational instruction had to be gauged according to southern Canadian standards. This educational ideology was made easier when racist bureaucrats began to control the Department of Indian Affairs and Northern Development. These individuals (generally authoritarian and unable to "make it" in the South) soon found their way to the North. Here they were able to achieve and maintain positions of power, but always holding southern values. All these values and ideologies were firmly and legally buttressed by the federal government.

It has long been one of the major suppositions of whites in Canada that social progress is best achieved (and stimulated) by education. If the proportion of school-age children attending school is taken as a measuring instrument, then the conclusion is that social progress in the North is a smashing success. As the figures in Table 1 show, nearly all school-age children in the Yukon and the N.W.T. attend school.[12]

If the above claim is true, then as Fisher points out, we should find that there has been an improvement in the social and economic position of natives.[13] However, our data show that 50 per cent of Indians and 30 per cent of Inuits (compared to three per cent of whites) have never attended school. Only 11 per cent of Indians and 18 per cent of Inuits have achieved secondary schooling (compared to 80 per cent of whites in the North). The impact of education upon income can be seen when one discovers that the average income of whites in the North (1971) is $8,387, while for Inuits and Indians it is $2,663 and $1,301 respectively. As Kuo[14] points out, formal education in elementary and secondary school has a significant influence on

Table 1

Growth of Pupil Enrolment, by Ethnic Group,
Northwest Territories Schools, 1959-60 to 1973-74

School Year	Total Enrolment	Change from Previous Year	Indians		Eskimos		Other	
			Enrolment	Change from Previous Year	Enrolment	Change from Previous Year	Enrolment	Change from Previous Year
	No.	%	No.	%	No.	%	No.	%
1959-60	4,197		1,066		1,425		1,706	
1960-61	5,029	19.8	1,130	6.0	1,710	20.0	2,189	28.3
1961-62	5,512	9.6	1,198	6.0	2,052	20.0	2,262	3.3
1962-63	6,004	8.9	1,221	1.9	2,399	16.9	2,384	5.4
1963-64	6,241	4.0	1,187	-2.8	2,494	4.0	2,560	7.4
1964-65	6,730	7.8	1,283	8.1	2,765	10.9	2,682	4.8
1965-66	7,196	6.9	1,285	0.2	2,987	8.0	2,924	9.0
1966-67	7,767	7.9	1,347	4.8	3,343	11.9	3,077	5.2
1967-68	7,820	0.7	1,495	11.0	2,975	-11.0	3,350	8.9
1968-69	8,474	8.4	1,512	1.1	3,342	12.3	3,620	8.1
1969-70	9,032	6.6	1,524	0.8	3,400	1.7	4,108	13.5
1970-71	10,334	14.4	1,629	6.9	4,128	21.4	4,577	11.4
1971-72	11,184	8.2	1,796	10.3	4,365	5.7	5,023	9.7
1972-73	11,772	5.3	1,944	8.2	4,493	2.9	5,285	5.2
1973-74	11,992	1.9	1,768	10.0	4,600	2.4	5,624	6.4

Source: Annual Report of the Commissioner of the Northwest Territories 1973, Department of Information, Government of the Northwest Territories, Yellowknife.

earnings for Indians but not for Inuits and whites. Only university or vocational training of these latter groups will be significant.

In the Mackenzie Corridor, fewer than five per cent have a Grade Ten education — the minimum needed for entering vocational programmes. As of 1970, slightly over 1,000 Northerners (mostly white) were enrolled in a vocational training programme. The result is that few Native people presently have education and vocational skills necessary to participate in the mining or petroleum industry in the North.

It is clear, then, that education in the North has had a differential impact on the three groups under study. The major impact of the educational system stems from the 1900-1950 era. During this era, while there was no basic change in educational philosophy, new ideas began to emerge which would provide the basis for the new policy that was implemented in the 1950s.[15] The result has been that the older generation of Natives are ill equipped to participate in the development of the North. However, in 1955 the federal government decided that education in the North should be structured, and that in order to ensure a considerable degree of universality, stability, and continuity, an ethnically integrated school system would be established.[16]

Natives have had the least benefit of education as at present (and historically) constituted. Because of their unwillingness to accept Anglo education,[17] they have been forced to send their children to federal boarding schools normally controlled by religious organizations. This, of course, has meant that the children would have to remain in the school ten months of the year. The social problems — both cultural and personal — that have resulted are now evident in the high rates of alcoholism, mental illness, suicide and family breakdowns.

To illustrate the process, let us first discuss the macro impact. To begin with, Natives in the North were trappers and hunters. They trapped individually and hunted in small groups. The result was that while some would separately produce furs, and thereby income, few would go hungry since sharing of the meat acquired by hunting was an accepted cultural practice. Because the trading posts in the area were concerned with producing furs for the South, it was to their advantage to keep Natives in the bush to increase productivity of furs and maintain subsistence levels for all native community members. However, when the federal government insisted upon education for all Natives (in the 1950s), several direct and indirect results could be observed. The children were first removed to boarding schools. This meant that the trap lines would have to be reduced, since fewer people would be looking after them. It also meant that children would become culturally alienated from their parents and community. Since the language of instruction was English and values inculcated by the young student were "southern," the result was the production of "marginal man."

As the children moved into the schools, communities which had school facilities began to grow. This was a result of maintaining the educational systems. Parents of native children wanted to be with their children and thus followed them to the communities. The migration of Natives to villages and towns began at this time and has not stopped.[18] However, once in town, they found they did not have the skills nor the education to enter the small "wage" labour force. Moreover, it was then impossible to maintain trap lines. As a result, these people became dependent (and still are) upon public assistance. In 1971 it was estimated that 50 per cent of the income of Natives was a result of "welfare." In a short period, the culture of Natives has been destroyed. Young people have no knowledge of their parents' culture, and they are unable to adapt themselves to the lifestyles of the older generation.[19]

One result of the above phenomena has been an overuse of alcohol, which allows native people to bear the frustrations imposed upon them. Those few Natives who achieve a fairly high standard of education find that they cannot find employment in the larger industrial economy. Commercial enterprise will not hire Natives because there is the feeling that they will attract other Natives to the business and thereby reduce the sales. Construction firms do not hire Natives because, as one person put it, "while they have the 'book' education, they lack the experience." In other words, while they may theoretically know how to fix a motor or drive a caterpillar, they could not actually do it. As a result, Natives find themselves the victims of "bitter betrayal." All along they have been told to get an education so as to become employable. However, once they have achieved this, they are unable to get jobs. This bitter experience reflects the basic colour bar (institutional racism) that exists in the North.[20]

One further complicating fact of the Tri-ethnic structure of the North is that Indians have to compete with Inuits if the area encompasses the two groups. Because of stereotypes and myths that have emerged out of the past, Inuits are defined as more capable than Indians. Hence if a job opens and an Indian and an Inuit apply, the Inuit is much more likely to get it. This of course produces conflict between these two groups and reduces the possibility of a coalition between them.

The end result is that native culture has been defined consistently as "worthless." Natives have been forced to attend an institutional setting (the school) which has reinforced this definition. The school which the Native attends was not (and still is not) conceptualized as mediating between two cultures but rather, as Fisher pointed out, ". . . as an institution teaching and imposing an alien culture upon a subject (and possibly inferior) people."[21] The institution produced (and still produces) an individual who is poorly suited to either industrial labour or traditional activities of hunting and trapping.[22]

Only female natives have been able to participate in the educational process with any degree of "success." However, they have not yet been able to become recognized as leaders within their own culture and cannot participate outside because of the effective colour bar. To date, their participation in the economy has largely been in small, short-term experimental projects — for example, crafts.

Inuits in specific areas of the Arctic have participated in the educational systems with a great deal of vigor and zeal. The impact upon them has been similar to that upon the Indians, although they have an additional impediment. After having received an education, they find that because of the lack of economic opportunities in the area, they cannot find any use for it. The building of the D.E.W. line demonstrated to them the need for education, yet twenty years later it questioned that basic premise.

Adding to the complexity of the situation is the conflict between private industry and the official position of the federal government. Until recently (and this will probably hold true for the near future, at least), the low educational achievements of native people have been considered economically beneficial by private industry to development in the North. Perhaps a bit of explanation is in order. Each country has a primary labour resource pool of skilled and professional workers as well as a secondary labour resource pool of unskilled workers. Development currently in the North requires both skilled and unskilled workers — skilled to provide the technical know-how, unskilled to clear land, and do other low-paying jobs. The actual installation and maintenance of mining or petroleum related activities requires highly skilled (but few) workers. This means, of course, that Natives (who are in the area and living at a subsistence level) can be hired cheaply to engage in jobs for short periods.[23] When these low skilled jobs are completed, these individuals (Natives) are then returned to the secondary labour resource pool and go on welfare (i.e., federal government subsidy). For example, only two per cent of the income of whites comes from "unearned" sources (family allowance, old age pension, government transfer payments) while for Indians it is 25 per cent and 11 per cent for ·Inuit. This means, of course, that private enterprise does not have to keep these people on the payroll nor pay for their acquisition of skills. Highly skilled workers can be brought in from the South (for short periods of time), paid high wages, and then returned to the South. Clearly, then, private enterprise has every incentive to maintain the status quo.

Education Today

The impact of education on the North and the native culture can be best placed in context when one understands that all educational aims, policies, curricula, and staff recruitment are provided from within a bureaucratic hierarchy, controlled by administrators outside the North. For example, the N.W.T. uses an educational curriculum programme patterned closely on the Alberta programme. Natives have been unable to participate in the decision-making process. All of this is underscored by the absence of teachers of indigenous background.[24]

This means that since nearly all children of age six are attending school,[25] the young native students are most affected by the southern educational curriculum without being able to resist. Even the new proposed educational ordinance would only allow the community education committee to provide for non-English instruction at kindergarten and Grade 1 (and then only treating the native tongue as a second language). After Grade 1, the superintendent of education determines the school programme (with English as the language of instruction), construction of new facilities, and appointment of staff.

As Gourdeau[26] points out, perhaps nowhere does the present northern educational system impinge in a more damaging way on the native sense of identity than in the field of language. Only in the high Arctic and eastern Arctic Inuit communities have substantial strides been taken in the language question.[27] This charge is made in view of the fact that it has been well documented that language functions as a means of providing group identification and social solidarity. Because the northern educational system fails to provide this, one can only view this failure as denigration of native culture.

Beyond the elementary level, only five communities in the North (Frobisher Bay, Inuvik, Yellowknife, Fort Smith and Whitehorse) have a vocational, trade, and secondary school. This means, of course, that if parents wish to send their child to a secondary school but do not live in these communities (which are heavily populated by whites), they must be housed in one of these communities. Since most native people live outside these heavily populated areas (for the North), a decision (and one involving financial cosiderations) must be made by the parents as to whether or not the child takes on additional "education." This fact, coupled with the government policy of forbidding vocational training in Indian schools before Grade 9,[28] and ensuring that post-secondary education can only be achieved outside the North,[29] means that few Natives become educated beyond the elementary level.[30]

The formal criteria usually set forth to evaluate educational standards generally centre on student-teacher ratios, quality of teacher, general expenditures, and curriculum. In all these formal aspects, one could argue that the criteria are met. The student-teacher ratio is 1:18 (comparable to that in the South); sixty per cent of the teachers have at least one university degree (with an ongoing programme to "upgrade" those with no degrees); and there is a budget in excess of 30 million dollars a year for an enrolment of about 12,000 students in the N.W.T.

From these facts one might conclude that the quality of northern education is on a par with that in the South. These formal criteria, however, omit other factors relevant to the educational process. First of all, the overall teaching experience of northern teachers is quite low. The average age of the teacher is about thirty years, and a large percentage have fewer than eight years of teaching experience. Perhaps more important is the fact that well over half have had only two years of experience in the North, and 75 per cent have had less than three years' experience in the North. In fact, the overall average for all teachers in the North is less than three years.[31]

Secondly, the teachers, because of their lack of mingling in the communities, have few personal relations with community people.[32] As a result parents have no involvement in the educational process and become alienated from those people controlling it. The teachers concurrently feel frustrated in that they have few opportunities to introduce innovative or context-specific programs which they feel would benefit the community.[33]

Tied closely to the above is the fact that few northern learning materials have been created. While one could argue that well over 100 northern books, filmstrips, and related educational materials have been developed in English and specific northern languages, it would be incorrect to suggest that they have had any beneficial impact on students. The department of education has not encouraged the use of these materials, and in most cases they are applied as secondary materials. At best, these northern learning materials have been used as "window dressing," not as something to be integrated into the child's programme of study.[34]

Conclusions

Whites, whether native to the North or from the South — and whether they plan to stay or are transient — all insist that their children be provided with an education which parallels their southern and provincial practices and customs. This attachment to the South permeates the whites' entire outlook for themselves and their children. There is always the feeling that if they leave the North, they must have educational training similar to that offered in the South. As a result, neither northern culture nor native culture is taken into consideration in the planning or execution of education in the North.

As Gourdeau states, the consequence is that "cultural conflict and the resulting *anomie* within the community, as well as the loss of personal (and group) identity and self esteem among individual participants are inevitable."[35] Part of this inevitability is a direct result of an educational system which provides temporal discontinuity to two quite different but competing ways of life.

While the educational accomplishments of Natives in the North are relatively low, a small number have been able to attain sound, advanced educational achievements.[36] This small educated group is now in a position to understand the more global problems facing native people and, consequently is able to research the issues at hand and evaluate the results.[37] This small group is now challenging the white Euro-Canadian influence in the North.

The result is that many young Natives are becoming disillusioned with the existing social climate in the North. Their choices are to further assimilate and deny their heritage (while at the same time maintaining their unique phenotypical traits) or to return to the old ways with certain modifications. They are now at the crossroads in choosing their destiny, for whatever choice they make, it will not be easy to return. This small Native, Euro-Canadian educated group is now able to provide the expertise and leadership necessary to coalesce Native people into a political force capable of controlling their own destiny. The emergence of such pressure groups as The Committee for Original Peoples Entitlement, The Inuit Tapirisat, and The Council of Yukon Indians gives evidence that their presence is now being felt. To this extent, education has had a powerful influence on Native peoples.

Only time will tell the degree of acceptance or rejection of the wishes and desires of Native people by white society. Education is only one sphere of influence that is now being challenged by Native people and it is imperative to keep in mind that its interrelationships with other institutional spheres (political, economic, etc.) is complex. For as Smith[38] points out, Native students in the North have high occupational aspirations and are beginning to have very similar occupational preferences to whites. To date, southern whites (as well as teachers in the North) have grossly underrated the preferences of Native students to achieve high status positions in Canadian society.

FOOTNOTES

[1]The North will be defined (for purposes of this paper) as the area comprising the Northwest Territories and the Yukon.
[2]Three major schools were in existence at this time which made up a major proportion of this population: Dawson (public); Whitehorse (public) and St. Mary's (separate). See K. J. Rea, *The Political Economy of the Canadian North* (Toronto, 1968), 285.
[3]J. Gherson, "Education in The Yukon," *Reference Studies on Social Services and Resource Industries* (Ottawa, 1968), 4, 13-14.

4In the matter of funding, all schools in the Yukon (including Roman Catholic denominational) were treated as part of the public school system.

5*Annual Report of the Commissioner of the Northwest Territories,* Department of Information (Yellowknife, 1975), 36.

6R. Fumoleau, *As Long as This Land Shall Last* (Toronto, 1975), 38.

7The language of instruction was English. See K. J. Rea, *The Political Economy of the Canadian North* (Toronto, 1968), 276-77.

8N. Chance, "Premises, Policies and Practices: A Cross Cultural Study of Education in the Circumpolar North," in F. Darnell, ed., *Education in the North* (Montreal, 1972), 4.

9It should be noted that prior to 1940 the *official* responsibility for education in the N.W.T. rested with the Territorial *and* Federal governments.

10Personal correspondence with Mr. Brian Lewis, Chief, Programme Development Division, Department of Education. Letter dated July 14, 1976, Yellowknife.

11Northwest Territory Government, *Survey of Education* (Yellowknife, 1972), 16.

12At present it is estimated that Indian and Inuit children are between one and two years behind their white counterparts in terms of age-grade position. That is, if one normally starts Grade One at age six, then by age ten one should be in Grade Five. For Native children, one would find that a student in Grade Five would be between eleven and twelve years old. See A. Berger and J. Das, *A Report on Indian Education* (Edmonton, 1972), 69.

13A. Fisher, "White Rites Versus Indian Rights," *Transaction,* 7 (1969), 29-33.

14Chun-yau Kuo, *The Effect of Education on Earnings in The Mackenzie District of Northern Canada* (Ottawa, 1972), 4-16.

15F. Vallee, "Eskimos of Canada as a Minority Group: Social and Cultural Perspectives," in F. Darnell, ed., *Education in the North* (Montreal, 1972), 24-43.

16Canada Superintendent, *Education North of 60* (Toronto, 1963), 1-6.

17A. Fisher, "White Rites versus Indian Rights," *Transaction,* 7 (1969), 30.

18The reader should bear in mind that at present the North has a very small "rural" population.

19For a further elaboration of this, see F. Vallee, "Eskimos of Canada as a Minority Group: Social and Cultural Perspectives," in F. Darnell, ed., *Education in the North* (Montreal, 1972), 29-34.

20Each community in the North is physically and socially segregated between whites and Natives. White sectors of the town are usually serviced (sewers, electricity, water) and are usually near a school and commercial establishments. The Native sector has few (if any) of these amenities.

21A. Fisher, "Education and Social Progress," *Alberta Journal of Educational Research,* 12 (1966), 265.

22D. Born Omar, *Eskimo Education and the Trauma of Social Change* (Ottawa, 1970), 12-13, 15.

23This means they will be hired as casual labour and thus receive minimum wages and will not be eligible for other various benefits, e.g., unemployment insurance, pension.

24In addition to this is the fact that no substantial pre-service training for teachers who are new to the area is performed.

25In 1960, about fifteen per cent of all school-age children were attending elementary school on a continuous basis. By 1971 this figure had increased to 95-98 per cent.

26E. Gourdeau, "The People of the Canadian North," in P. Pimlott, K. Vincent and C. McKnight, eds., *Arctic Alternatives* (Ottawa, 1973), 71-85.

27P. Robinson, "A View of Education in the N.W.T.," *Canadian Association in Support of the Native People,* 16 (1975), 4-7.

28P. Sindell and R. Wintrob, "Cross Cultural Education in the North and Its Implications for Personal Identity," in F. Darnell, ed., *Education in the North* (Montreal, 1972), 55-59.

29The N.W.T. grants for education are based on the following criteria: you must have resided (with parents) for two years and have not been out of school for more than three. If you meet these requirements, you are entitled to your tuition, student fees (for nearest school offering the degree sought), one return air fare annually, allowance for books and eight dollars a day for room and board. If you are not eligible for the grant, you can apply for the $1,600 a year bursary.

30Eight students from the North graduated from a degree-granting institution in 1975, all of them with teaching certificates.

31See Arctic Institute of North America, *Education in the Canadian North* (Montreal, 1973), 42-49.

32Part of the problem lies in the fact that teachers lack the Native language necessary to carry on social interaction.

33J. Hodgkinson, "Is Northern Education Meaningful?," *The Western Canadian Journal of Anthropology,* 12 (1970), 156-64.

34P. Robinson, "A View of Education in the N.W.T.," *Canadian Association in Support of the Native People,* 16 (1975), 4-5.

35E. Gourdeau, "The People of The Canadian North," in D. Pimlott, K. Vincent and C. McKnight, eds., *Arctic Alternatives* (Ottawa, 1973), 73-76.

³⁶Less than one per cent of Indians and Inuit (compared to twenty-five per cent of whites) have
attended university, college or training school.

³⁷D. Ahenakew, "Task Force in Education," *The Journal of the Canadian College of Teachers,*
14 (1971), 37-46.

³⁸D. Smith, "Occupational Preferences of Northern Students," *Social Science Notes,* 5
(Ottawa, 1974), 30-34.

ETHNICITY AND CANADIAN EDUCATION
JOHN R. MALLEA
QUEEN'S UNIVERSITY, KINGSTON

Introduction

To observe that a resurgence of interest in ethnicity has occurred in recent years has become commonplace. In both industrial and non-industrialised nations alike, ethnicity is becoming an increasingly important factor in determining the shape of social, political and economic change. Part of its significance, of course, derives from the nature of ethnicity's relationship to the process of modernization, and the question of whether there exists a basic incompatibility between the universalizing forces of modernity and the distinctive cultural norms of minority ethnic groups.

The boundaries of this relationship are only now being explored, and that this is so can clearly be seen in the variety of positions taken on the question. "At one extreme is the presumption that development is synonymous with modernization, which in turn so pervades men's lives that peculiarities defining ethnic groups necessarily vanish. At the other extreme is the conviction that development can be encouraged in such a way that modernity does not infringe on cherished ethnic distinctiveness."[1]

Some commentators believe that democratic societies have tended to place themselves towards the latter end of this continuum, and that this helps explain the difficulties they are experiencing in dealing with the challenges associated with ethnic revitalization. As Professor Enloe has observed:

> Democratic ideology goes undisturbed as long as ethnic communities are intent upon assimilation or as long as they are too politically underdeveloped to make their existence forcefully known to the obvious majority. While this blissful condition lasts, democrats can sing the praises of individualism and pluralism simultaneously. The conceptual trick is to acknowledge diversity of cultures within the society but assume that culture deals mainly with styles and cooking recipes and has relatively little impact on ambitions, moral judgements and public goals. If ethnicity is this shallow, then things that really matter to individuals will hardly be affected, and it will not impinge on important national decisions. In other words, the discrepancy between democratic ideology and ethnic reality is resolved by reducing ethnicity to style.[2]

When the values of assimilation are thrown into question, however, and when ethnic communities engage in their own political development, this comfortable premise is harder to maintain.[3]

Conscious of a renewed interest in ethnicity within its own borders, and not unmindful of its international dimensions, Canada is trying to come to grips with issues that draw much of their intensity from perceived ethnic differences and the aspirations to which they give rise. Some of these, like the aboriginal rights of the Native Peoples, and the cultural sovereignty of

Quebec are clearly contentious and long-standing issues. But they are not alone in testing the will of the Canadian people to face up to the cultural and linguistic divisions of their society. As Freda Hawkins has pointed out, the collective size of the non-British and non-French groups is now approaching the Francophone presence in Canada's population and will probably overtake it by 1977.[4] Moreover, the assimilationist approach to social cohesion is being rejected, the discussion of ethnic identity and diversity is enjoying a renaissance, and the traditional relationship between subordinate and superordinate groups in Canadian society is undergoing reappraisal and challenge.

All this is perhaps familiar. It will be hardly surprising, therefore, to learn that issues of language and culture are receiving much greater attention in both the press and the electronic media. Less well known perhaps is that a similar development can be observed in the world of scholarship, where a flood of articles, books and reports dealing with topics of the same type threatens to overwhelm even the most selective and persistent reader. Even within an applied field of study, like education, it is becoming increasingly difficult to keep afloat, much less keep pace.

A number of scholars have attempted to explain the "surprising vitality" of ethnicity in modern societies and most stress the exploratory nature of their efforts. One acute observer, for example, suggests we may have overestimated the extent of modernization in nations such as Canada, the Soviet Union, and the U.S.A. While these countries may be developed on the whole, they may also contain pockets of traditionalism that social scientists (concerned in the main with nation-level analysis) have overlooked. And the explanation for this could be that communal man needs social relationships which are more enduring and less instrumental than occupation, status and legal right. One kind of collectivity that meets these needs, perhaps, is the ethnic group, and ethnicity therefore survives long after its traditional functions have been assumed by more impersonal, secular groups and institutions.[5]

The educational system is a case in point. In most societies, the agency formally charged with the systematic transmission of culture from one generation to the next is the school. And in most societies, too, the school has been seen as a major agency of assimilation. This assumption, however, is currently undergoing scrutiny and re-evaluation. In the United States, for example, the notion that the common school was the crucible of the American melting-pot has recently come under attack.[6] In Britain, the role of the school in the assimilation of immigrant children is undergoing re-examination, and similar developments can be observed in Israel and Australia.[7] In Canada, meanwhile, committees, commissions and work groups are busy scrutinising the education of ethnic and linguistic minorities.[8] As they do so, they are asking timely questions regarding the effective co-ordination of national and educational goals.

An examination of the co-ordination of these goals is the focus of the present essay. After a necessarily brief look at definitional concerns, the statement of national goals in Canada's policy of multi-culturalism within a bilingual framework is examined. Educational goals are discussed next, to be followed by a discussion of the past performance of the school in reflecting and appreciating cultural diversity. A final section comments on the school's role in achieving a more effective integration of educational and national goals.

Definitional Concerns

A number of difficulties hinder our understanding of the relationship between education and ethnicity. Conceptual and definitional problems, for example, frustrate the construction of clear theoretical frameworks, and their continued absence obstructs the task of both analysis and interpretation.[9] Little wonder, then, that attempts to establish coherent and responsive educational policy and practice reflect a certain confusion over aims and objectives. Little wonder, too, that when the nation cannot agree about its policies of ethnic pluralism, education and educators reflect the basic tension and uncertainties of this disagreement.[10]

Another reason discussions of ethnicity often seem to lack direction is that definitions of the terms "culture" and "ethnic group" have failed to achieve any widespread acceptance.[11] The term "pluralism" is also plagued with multiple meanings. And when we place the terms culture and pluralism together, we may simply be compounding our difficulties.[12] A fourth concept, federalism, is also subject to varying interpretations. It has, however, the advantage of having been subjected to rigorous analysis by Canadian scholars. It is therefore a useful point from which to begin our attempt to clarify pertinent conceptual and definitional issues.

In his comparative study of federalism in multicultural societies, R. L. Watts writes that federalism is "the principle of political organization by which concurrent desires for territorial integration and diversity within a society are accommodated by the establishment of a single political system...."[13] And according to E. R. Black, this accommodation of diversity "includes the idea that institutions and social forces affect each other, that neither is wholly dependent as an effect of the other, and that modern society is both dynamic and diversified."[14] Thus Canada's form of government not only reflects the need to take account of diversity, it also reflects the belief that society's institutions are affected by diversity and in turn affect it.

Useful analytical distinctions have also been made regarding culture and pluralism. R. A. Schermerhorn, for example, distinguishes between culture and social structure in the following way. Culture, he argues, signifies the ways of action learned through socialization based on norms and values that serve as guides or standards for behaviour. Social structure, on the other hand, refers to

> the set of crystalized social relationships which its [the society's] members have with each other which places them in groups, large or small, permanent or temporary, formally organized or unorganized and

which relates them to the major institutional activities of the society, such as economic and occupational life, religion, marriage and the family, education, government and recreation.[15]

Culture, then, has to do with standards or "designs for living" while social structure refers to the clustering of men in patterned ways.[16]

Definitions of ethnicity, while underlining the complexity of this concept, at the same time help us identify some of its chief features. For example, Vallee and his colleagues believe that ethnicity refers primarily to descent from ancestors who shared a common culture based on national origin, language, religion or race, or a combination of these.[17] Enloe, on the other hand, considers that ethnicity depends primarily on self-identification, that ethnic groups share clusters of beliefs and values (which find expression through associational forms), and that they are networks of regular communication and interaction.[18] Both definitions are regularly employed in discussions of Canadian ethnicity and, taken apart or together, help us understand what is meant when we speak of an ethnic group.

Definitions of education are notorious for their lack of shared meaning. It has been suggested, for example, and not entirely facetiously, that the definition of terms should be banned if one wishes to engage in any discussion of the intellectual, moral, physical and emotional development of individuals young and old. Here again, however, a number of useful points can be made. First, we can limit our interpretation of education to those activities that go on within the formal institutions of learning: schools, colleges and universities. Second, we can recognize that the school differs from other agencies of socialization in that society has consciously chosen it to formally and systematically socialize its young.[19] Third, we can recall and agree with John Dewey's observation that as a society becomes more enlightened, it realizes that its responsibility is not to try to transmit and conserve the whole of its existing achievements, but only those which make for an improved society in the future.[20]

National Goals

The fundamental question lying at the heart of any and all discussions dealing with the relationship between minorities and the dominant society is one of cohesion. Thus, ideally, a federal system assures some degree of autonomy to the varied linguistic, racial and religious communities within a society.[21] Moreover, a federal society which adopts a pluralistic rather than a universalistic stance, has as one of its major goals an equilibrium which "provides significant cultural minorities with an enduring sense of security for their distinctiveness, and which, at the same time, continues to generate a sense of community among all its diverse groups."[22] Contemporary Canadian society has adopted a number of approaches in this regard; three major sets of governmental initiatives can be identified, and each has been the source of controversy and acrimonious debate. They are, briefly, the policies and programs associated with the Native Peoples, Bilingualism, and Multiculturalism.[23]

The third of these, Multiculturalism, is perhaps the most all-embracing and certainly the least widely known or understood. On October 8, 1971, Prime Minister Trudeau presented a new state policy of multiculturalism in the House of Commons where it won overwhelming support from all parties. In his presentation he expressed the view that the Canadian government did not support a "melting pot" approach to the realities of Canada's cultural diversity. On the contrary, it considered assimilation to be both an undesirable and unacceptable goal for Canadian society. Moreover, according to the Prime Minister, the time was "overdue for the people of Canada to become more aware of the rich tradition of the many cultures we have in Canada."[24] The new policy aimed at ensuring the continuation of this tradition and expanding the appreciation of its contribution to Canadian society. In the words of the then Secretary of State, Gerard Pelletier, it called into being a new vision of Canadian society, which refused to sacrifice diversity in the name of unity, and which placed the cultures of Canada's many groups on an equal footing.[25]

A closer examination of the Trudeau government's policy of multiculturalism is instructive, for it outlines a set of national goals based on the recognition of Canada's cultural heterogeneity. Briefly, the policy is concerned with the preservation of basic human rights, the development of Canadian identity, the strengthening of citizen participation, the reinforcement of Canadian unity, the encouragement of cultural diversification, and the elimination of discrimination.[26] It reaffirms the principle of individual freedom of choice, and takes pains to point out that membership in an ethnic group should not place constraints on this freedom. Membership in an ethnic group is, furthermore, considered of great importance in that it helps combat the alienating effects of mass society "in which mass produced culture and entertainment and large impersonal institutions threaten to denature and depersonalize man."[27] The policy also reflected a belief that confidence in one's individual identity, strengthened by a sense of belonging, provided an acceptable and necessary base for national unity.

> The more secure we feel in one particular social context, the more we are free to explore our identity beyond it. Ethnic groups often provide people with a sense of belonging which can make them better able to cope with the rest of society than they would as isolated individuals. Ethnic loyalties need not, and usually do not, detract from wider loyalties to community and country.[28]

Given this interpretation of the benefits of ethnic group membership, the viewpoint "that there cannot be one cultural policy for Canadians of British and French origin, another for the original peoples, and yet a third for all others" seems both logical and persuasive. Its corollary, moreover, appears equally clear. That is, if the many cultures in Canada are seen as a heritage to treasure, then the attempt to ensure their continuance and development should help in the breakdown of discriminatory attitudes and cultural jealousies.[29]

These broadly stated goals are replete with implications for education. Schools have been accorded a significant part to play in the formation of political values. And, as David Easton has pointed out, they can and do contribute to the effective integration of a political system by helping "develop and transmit certain basic political orientations that must be shared, within a certain range of variation, by most members of any ongoing system."[30]

Educational Goals

In general terms, there appears to be a remarkable degree of agreement among educators over the *broad* goals of education for a pluralistic Canada. In a recent survey of the purposes of education, for example, carried out by the Canadian Education Society, a questionnaire was circulated to each of two selected boards of education in each of the ten provinces and one in the Yukon Territory. A total of 1,680 copies were circulated and 1,540 were completed (an unusually high return of 92 per cent). The questionnaires were then analysed and interpreted by Dr. J. Lauwerys who concluded that

> The over-riding concern in Canada about educational aims and policies is the protection of the individual against the powerful influences of state and society. Nothing is to be imposed. The rights of all must be cherished and protected whatever their religion, or mother tongue or individual gifts. Complete and genuine respect for diversity and individuality is, indeed, the necessary condition for the maintenance of national unity.[31]

Consensus is much less likely to occur on a local level, however. Here fundamental disagreements can and clearly do occur. The Work Group on Multicultural Programs of the Toronto Board of Education, for example, discovered that a basic disagreement existed between the professional educator and the community at large over the school's role in the maintenance of language and culture.

> On the one hand, the community felt that the school system has a responsibility to contribute directly to the "maintenance" of cultures and languages other than English and French. The schools, on the other hand, supported the idea that all ethnic communities have a natural right to maintain their linguistic and cultural heritage but that "maintenance" itself was the community's responsibility rather than the school's.[32]

The Chairman of the Work Group, D. Leckie, went to the heart of the matter when he asked whether educators considered previous cultural and linguistic experience in terms of differences or deficiencies:

> If differences, then the school's programs and the teacher's response should build on the learner's past education, language and cultural experience as a wealthy base for learning. If we approach the needs of non-Anglo-Saxon children as deficiencies, then we impose on them an expectation of becoming someone new and different, of cutting out the old personality.[33]

For his part, he rejected the latter approach and argued that the goal of education is to help develop the personality of the learner, and that this personality is clearly shaped in part by ethnic background.

The Work Group itself came down in support of multiculturalism. It concluded that schools should assist children to think of themselves as possessing a cultural identity that drew on the riches of their ancestral heritage and anticipated the role their culture could play "in discovering a Canadian identity in cultural diversity itself."[34] A similar view is taken by C. Michalski, Chairperson of the Ontario Ministry of Education's Seminar on Multiculturalism. In her definition of the education needed for a multicultural Canada, she stresses the potentially enriching qualities of diversity:

> It is an education in which the child of whatever origin finds not mere acceptance or tolerance but respect and understanding. It is an education in which cultural diversity is seen and used as a valuable resource to enrich the lives of all. It is an education in which differences and similarities are used for positive ends. It is an education in which every child has the chance to benefit from the cultural heritage of others as well as his or her own. It is an education for all who hope to live in the Canada of the future.[35]

The Gap Between Promises and Reality

Aspirations inevitably contain the unspoken acknowledgement that what is envisaged for the future is not widely available in the present. And this is particularly true of education's efforts to respond to Canada's ethnic pluralism. Indeed, far from adopting a positive stance towards differences in language and culture in the schools, Canadian society has until recently gone out of its way to eradicate them.[36] Assimilation, not appreciation of differences, has been its policy; conformity, not diversity, its goal.[37]

Some years ago A. B. Hodgetts pointed out that despite "continuing criticism and the persistent evidence of deep dissatisfaction with the state of Canadian studies in our schools" no major reforms had occurred.[38] At the same time he reminded us that "Although we laugh at ourselves for doing so, and perhaps have convinced each other that today things are different, in actual fact we are continuing to teach a white, Anglo-Saxon, Protestant political and constitutional history of Canada."[39] His remarks, unfortunately, appear to have retained their accuracy. Professor Lupul, for example, tells us that the portrayal of Canada's ethnic groups, other than English or French, in Alberta's senior high school textbooks is woefully inadequate.[40] And the co-author of *Teaching Prejudice*,[41] D. Pratt, has recently concluded that school textbooks do not generally represent a pluralist model of Canadian culture, but continue to portray a consensus, non-controversial view of society.[42]

Clearly much remains to be done if we are to improve the co-ordination of national and educational goals. And if confirmation were needed, it is to be found in a variety of current publications. Thus, in a report that could easily be applied to the other provinces, the Ontario

Advisory Council on Multiculturalism confirms the amount of work to be accomplished in the development of resource materials, teacher sensitization, and curriculum.[43] The Second Canadian Conference on Multiculturalism, held in February 1976, also confirmed the distance we have to travel before ethnic heterogeneity becomes a welcome feature of Canadian life in all its facets.[44] And, finally, Volumes I and II of the Report of the Commission on Canadian Studies, published in late 1975, confirm the widespread neglect of Canadian issues and problems in our colleges and universities.[45]

Conclusions

Perhaps the federal government's adoption of a policy of multiculturalism is best viewed as an attempt to reduce the impact in Canadian development of secular, universal and material values. In eschewing uniformity and rejecting assimilation, it seems to be trying to counterbalance the effects of these values, suggesting that progress also be measured against the distinctive cultural norms of Canada's ethnic groups. Seen in this way, controversy and disagreement are to be expected; they not only precede unity but are a necessary prelude to it. And if this appears contradictory, contradictions may be essential for social cohesion and the preservation of society. For as R. A. Schermerhorn has pointed out, not only do some functional requirements in a society contradict others, but they can also engender antagonistic processes that actually uphold the system.[46]

In dealing with these contradictions it will be necessary for Canadians, both individually and collectively, to develop tolerance for ambiguity and paradox. Governments and institutions will have to create and apply a variety of policies, if they are to respond humanely and effectively to the legitimate aspirations of the diverse ethnic groups that participate and take pride in the evolving Canadian identity. They will have to devise developmental strategies that are based on a much wider and fuller participation in the decision-making process than presently conceived, if these are to be more responsive and appropriate to the communities they serve. For their part, ethnic groups will have to establish more informed and tolerant relationships with groups whose culture and aspirations are shaped by different criteria than their own.

The challenge, of course, is for the schools to help students appreciate contradiction, ambiguity and paradox. The task will not be easy. As we shall see in the pages that follow, interpretations of the reality and appropriate image of Canadian ethnic pluralism vary considerably. This means that schools, colleges and universities not only experience the tensions of having to both reflect and help shape the community's normative attitudes and standards, they also face the potentially explosive situation of which languages to teach and which culture to transmit.[47]

The St. Léonard *Affaire* illustrates this last point very well, and underlines the fact that the schools are so often the arena in which political struggles over cultural diversity occur. In November 1967, in the north-east section of Montreal, a proposal to phase out bilingual education in the St. Léonard School Commission, which enrolled large numbers of children of Italian immigrants, gave rise to a conflict which led to street demonstrations and ultimately to violence.[48]

Following hotly contested school elections, the School Commission (now controlled by members committed to French as the sole language of instruction), passed a resolution phasing out the French-English bilingual programme. The immigrant and English-speaking communities responded angrily to what they saw as overt discrimination; they organized themselves and launched a counter-attack with the aim of reversing the decision. The conflict soon spilled over its local boundaries and became a provincial political issue of some intensity. It also rapidly became clear that the issue could not be resolved by the opposing parties in St. Léonard. The Quebec provincial government was reluctantly drawn into the dispute and eventually promised legislative action to help resolve it. This only seemed to exacerbate matters and, after one legislative initiative (Bill 85) was withdrawn, the rancorous debate continued throughout 1968 and 1969. Even after the passage of Bill 63, which gave parents freedom of choice over the language of instruction for their children, the basic issue of French cultural sovereignty (in particular the primacy of the French language) continued to dominate the Quebec political scene. Thus, in mid-1974, the passage of Quebec's Official Language Act (Bill 22), which stated that French was the official language of Quebec, evoked a furious response from the province's Anglophone community. With repeal of the legislation in view, an opposition radio campaign was launched, a mass petition circulated, and a number of legal challenges initiated. To date, actions in the courts have proved unsuccessful, but the implications of the issue are far from played out. And, in addition to their broader ramifications for politics and economics, they are likely to have important and far-reaching effects in the schools.[49]

Whether one views the fact with enthusiasm or not, we are now much less confident about the potential of the school to reform society and alter its basic structures. Experience has also taught us to be sceptical of the power of any one institution, acting in isolation, to effect significant social change. This is far from saying, however, that schools cannot help promote social cohesion, foster an appreciation of diversity, contribute to attitudinal change, and teach that the freedom to maintain one's language, values, and customs is an essential and distinguishing feature of Canadian life.

Schools can unquestionably further these ends. They can make their students more aware of the challenges and complexities of contemporary society. They can help young Canadians understand the source of their differences, and ensure their emotional and intellectual commitment to preserving their common heritage. They can contribute to a social climate in which ambiguity and paradox are recognized as characteristic, not unusual, features of human relations. Moreover, while recognizing the validity of jurisdictional boundaries and concerns, and appreciating the powerful needs and aspirations of Canada's minority ethnic groups, schoolmen and women might agree with A. B. Hodgetts when he writes:

> Let is be re-emphasized that these national interests can be served without infringing on provincial rights, without perverting the educational system to the cause of any political establishment or extremes of nationalism, without distorting history for any kind of propaganda purposes and without detracting from a deep concern for the universal problems of mankind.[50]

Finally, educators of all persuasions can recognize that constitutional change is part and parcel of our system of government, and that many informed Canadians currently see the need for such change.

REFERENCES

[1]Cynthia H. Enloe, *Ethnic Conflict and Political Development* (Boston, 1973), 4.

[2]*Ibid.*, 60-61.

[3]This, it has been argued, is precisely what is occurring in Canada. See, for example, Harold Cardinal, *The Unjust Society: The Tragedy of Canada's Indians* (Edmonton, Alberta, 1969).

[4]Freda Hawkins, "Destination Unknown: Difficult Decisions in Immigration Policy," *Queen's Quarterly*, 82 (1975), 598.

[5]Cynthia E. Enloe, *op. cit.*, 268.

[6]See, for example, Colin Greer, *The Great School Legend, A Revisionist Interpretation of American Public Education* (New York, 1972).

[7]N. Hawkes, *Immigrant Children in British Schools* (London, 1966); R. Oakley, ed., *New Backgrounds* (London, 1968); H. E. R. Townsend, *Immigrant Pupils in England: The L. E. A. Response* (Windsor, 1971); H. E. R. Townsend and E. M. Buttan, *Multiracial Education: Need and Innovation,* School Council Working Paper 50 (London, 1973); Chaim Adler, "Education and the Integration of Immigrants in Israel," *International Migration Review*, 3 (1969), 3-19; The Hon. A. J. Grassby, Minister for Immigration, "Migrant Education Programme: Financial Year 1972-73" (Canberra, 1973); and the Hon. A. J. Grassby, "A Multi-Cultural Society for the Society" (Canberra, 1973).

[8]The list is now quite long and growing longer. A number of the key sources are cited in the footnotes to this essay. For a general introduction, however, see Book IV, *The Cultural Contribution of the Other Ethnic Groups,* Report of the Royal Commission on Bilingualism and Biculturalism (Ottawa, 1970); and Book III, *The Ethnic Groups,* Report of the Commission of Inquiry on the Position of the French Language and on Language Rights in Quebec (Quebec, 1972).

[9]R. A. Schermerhorn, *Comparative Ethnic Relations: A Framework for Theory and Research* (New York, 1970), 15, 16 and 235.

[10]There are important differences of perception with respect to ethnic pluralism which appear to be influenced by region as well as group membership. In the western Provinces, for example, there is much greater support for multiculturalism than there is, say, in Quebec.

[11]Howard Palmer and Harold Troper, "Canadian Ethnic Studies: Historical Perspectives and Contemporary Implications," *Interchange*, 4 (1973), 15.

[12]See R. A. Schermerhorn, *op. cit.*, 122-27.

[13]Ronald L. Watts, *Multicultural Societies and Federalism* (Ottawa, 1970), 11.

[14]Edwin R. Black, *Divided Loyalties, Canadian Concepts of Federalism* (Montreal, 1975), 9.

[15]R. A. Schermerhorn, *op. cit.*, 80.

[16]The same author takes the position that "The structural dimension of pluralism prevents the investigator from taking the cultural factor by itself as though it were the whole picture; this has been done uncritically in the past by anthropologists who placed the entire emphasis on acculturation or cultural borrowing . . . or the sociologists who conceptualized assimilation in much the same way.. . . This approach has played down the features of power and conflict which appear in societies whose structural features have been maximally different." *Ibid.*, 127-28.

[17]F. G. Vallee *et al*, "Ethnic Assimilation and Differentiation in Canada," *The Canadian Journal of Economics and Political Science*, 23 (1957), 541.

[18]Cynthia H. Enloe, *op. cit.*, 15-19.

[19]This point is made very neatly in David Pratt's chapter "The Social Role of School Textbooks in Canada," in *Socialization and Values in Canadian Society*, E. Zureik and P. M. Pike, eds. (Toronto, 1975), 100-26.

[20]John Dewey, "Education as a Social Function," in *The School in Society,* Sam D. Sieber and David E. Wilder, eds. (New York, 1973), 33.

[21]Ronald L. Watts, *op. cit.,* 1.

[22]*Ibid.,* 28.

[23]The present essay draws primarily on the policy of multiculturalism. However, either or both of the other two areas might just as appropriately be chosen as the window through which to examine the response of Canadian society and education to cultural diversity.

[24]Canada, Federal Government's Response to Book IV of the Report of the Royal Commission on Bilingualism and Biculturalism, Document tabled in the House of Commons on October 8, 1971 by the Prime Minister, 2.

[25]Elements of a Speech by The Honourable Gerard Pelletier in Vancouver, March 6, 1972, Press Release, Department of the Secretary of State.

[26]Richard Stock, "Multiculturalism as a Community Development Program," Unpublished M.A. thesis, McGill University, 1973, 41.

[27]Federal Government's Response to Book IV, *op. cit.,* 2-3.

[28]*Ibid.,* 3.

[29]Statement of the Prime Minister, *op. cit.,* 1 and 2.

[30]David Easton, "The Function of Formal Education in a Political System," *The School Review,* 65 (1957), 311, 314-15. Easton considered that among the numerous institutions that contribute "to the stabilization and transformation of political systems, education looms large." However, he also took care to point out that, even if they do loom large, a number of basic questions remained unanswered. Many of them remain so to this day. For example, we are still scratching the surface of questions such as the following: What types of orientations find their way into the school system, not only via instructional materials but via the informal instruction that depends on the knowledge and experiences of the school staff? Do they differ, and in what ways, according to the socio-economic characteristics, ethnicity, religion, political views of the teachers? And to what extent is there a disparity between the perceived image and the desired image (of basic political orientations) in the minds of the students?

[31]Joseph Lauwerys, *The Purposes of Education: Results of a CEA Survey* (Toronto, 1973), 47.

[32]*Final Report of the Work Group on Multicultural Programs* (Toronto, 1976), 21.

[33]"Report on Proceedings," Working Draft II (mimeographed), Seminar on Multiculturalism, Toronto: Ministry of Education, December 16, 1975.

[34]*Final Report of the Work Group, op. cit.,* p. 25. The Work Group noted, at this point in the report, that it had mistakenly referred to "maintenance" of cultures when its intent was to refer to their development.

[35]C. Michalski, "Report on Proceedings," Provincial Seminar on Multiculturalism, Toronto: Ministry of Education, 3-4.

[36]See, for example, C. J. Jaenen, "An Introduction to Education and Ethnicity," in *Sounds Canadian,* Paul M. Migus, ed., (Toronto, 1975), 71-75.

[37]H. Palmer, ed., "Social Adjustment," *Immigration and the Rise of Multiculturalism* (Toronto, 1975), 112-18.

[38]A. B. Hodgetts, *What Culture? What Heritage?* (Toronto, 1968), 6.

[39]*Ibid.,* 20.

[40]Manoly Lupul, "The Portrayal of Canada's 'Other' Peoples in Senior High School History and Social Studies Textbooks in Alberta, 1905 to the Present," Paper presented to the 54th Annual Meeting of the Canadian Historical Association, University of Alberta, Edmonton, June 6, 1975, 31.

[41]Garnet McDiarmid and David Pratt, *Teaching Prejudice* (Toronto, 1971). The techniques in this pioneering study have been employed in a number of subsequent analyses of textbooks. See, for example, *Bias in Textbooks Regarding the Aged, Labour Unions, and Political Minorities,* Final Report to The Ontario Ministry of Education (Principal Investigator: Patrick Babin; Research Officer, Robert Knoop), Faculty of Education, University of Ottawa, 1975; and *The Shocking Truth About Indians in Textbooks* (Winnipeg, 1974).

[42]David Pratt, *op. cit.,* 120-22.

[43]"Chairman's Remarks," *Annual Report of the Ontario Advisory Council on Multiculturalism 1975* (Toronto, 1975), 1.

[44]"Multiculturalism as State Policy," Second Canadian Conference on Multiculturalism (Ottawa, 1976).

[45]T. H. B. Symons, *To Know Ourselves,* The Report of the Commission on Canadian Studies (Ottawa, 1975).

[46]R. A. Schermerhorn, *op. cit.,* 38.

[47]Again, what follows is just one illustration. A number of others (drawn from other major metropolitan areas in Canada) could easily be cited. It is probably appropriate to add, though, that they have not led to the seemingly complete breakdown in communications which occurred for a time in the St. Léonard district of Montreal.

[48]Two theses have been written in English on the controversy. They are John Parisella, "Pressure Group Politics: Case Study of the St. Leonard Schools Crisis," Unpublished M.A.

thesis, McGill University, 1971; and Robert Issenman, "Contemporary French Canadian Nationalism and the M.I.S.," Unpublished B.A. thesis, Harvard University, 1968.

[49]For a full discussion of the major factors bearing on this situation, see John R. Mallea, ed., *Quebec's Language Policies: Background and Response*, Quebec: Laval University Press (in press).

[50]A. B. Hodgetts, *op. cit.*, 86.

CANADIANIZATION THROUGH THE SCHOOLS OF T.. PRAIRIE PROVINCES BEFORE WORLD WAR I: THE ATTITUDES AND AIMS OF THE ENGLISH-SPEAKING MAJORITY

MARILYN BARBER
CARLETON UNIVERSITY, OTTAWA

A combination of pride in national development, a sense of human drama, and simple curiosity made western Canada the focus of much attention in the early twentieth century. For the first time since Confederation, Canada was receiving a major influx of immigrants, and large numbers of these were directed by government and railway propaganda, or by encouragement from relatives and friends, to the sparsely settled territory of the Canadian prairies. For the first time since the territory from the Great Lakes to the Rockies was acquired by the Dominion of Canada in 1870, the population of the region was rapidly increasing. Hopes for the future of the prairie frontier were high and many confidently expected that the West would grow to dominate the Canadian nation.

Such rapid growth did create problems, especially since it was produced to a large extent by the arrival of new immigrants from overseas and from the United States. In the decade between 1901 and 1911, immigration to Canada for the first time since Confederation exceeded emigration from Canada, and the number of immigrant arrivals grew from 21,000 in 1897 to reach a peak of over 400,000 in the fiscal year 1912-13. Much of the increase consisted of immigrants from the British Isles and the United States, and smaller numbers arrived from north-western Europe, from Scandinavia, Germany, France, Belgium and Holland. These immigrants most Canadians believed could be rapidly absorbed. However, the majority of continental European immigrants, and a significant proportion of the total immigration to western Canada, came from eastern Europe, from areas which previously had contributed little to Canadian immigration and which appeared to be separated from Canada by vast cultural as well as geographical distances. These were the immigrants who attracted most attention, because they not only were observed to be "more foreign" but also were frequently considered to be inferior.

The nation receiving the immigrants was already composed of two dominant cultures, English Canadian and French Canadian, but by the beginning of the twentieth century, the English Canadian influence had become dominant in western Canada, reinforcing the majority position of English Canadians in the country. English Canadians believed that Canada could survive only as a homogeneous British nation, at least outside the province of Quebec which most regarded as regrettably a special case. The presence of a large group of French Canadians in the country only confirmed their conviction that homogeneity was vital, and by contrast and conflict helped English Canadians to define more precisely what they considered to be essential values of their own culture and thus of the nation — the English, not the French language; Protestantism, not Roman Catholicism; and the British connection. Because of their previous experience, most English Canadians when confronted with the influx of immigrants stressed these particular values.

Not all English Canadians were disturbed by the polyglot character of the immigrants settling in western Canada. Many were preoccupied with the work of economic growth and either had no time for other issues or else regarded the immigrants to be primarily and properly an economic resource. While there was some opposition to immigrants who competed with Canadian workers, especially in urban areas, sturdy agricultural immigrants were considered particularly desirable. In the optimism of the pre-war period, most assumed that such immigrants would be assimilated with time, and few thought carefully about the meaning of assimilation. For most English Canadians, assimilation simply meant that the immigrants would become Canadians by adopting the language, cultural patterns, and institutions of English Canada. The society itself would not change but the immigrants would be absorbed. Although not well defined, the process which they envisaged was definitely that described by later analysts as "Anglo-conformity." In addition, English Canadians were equally vague in their understanding of how assimilation could be accomplished in practice. Most frequently they simply assumed that the two agencies of the church and the school would undertake the work. Such an assumption was natural since these were two major institutions considered responsible for preserving and transmitting the values of the country. Whether the churches and the schools could successfully accomplish their appointed task remained an unanswered question in the pre-war period. Only those most directly involved with transforming the rhetoric into action fully realized either the difficulties or the possibilities for success.

Educators in western Canada shared the views of the English-speaking majority of the country and agreed that the schools had a particularly important responsibility for assimilating immigrants. As one Manitoba inspector wrote in 1906:

> The great work of the public school in Canada is the formation and development of a high type of national life. This is particularly true in Western Canada, with its heterogeneous population. Here are to be found people of all countries, from the keen, clever American, with highly developed national ideals, equal to but perhaps somewhat antagonistic to our own, to the ignorant peasantry of central and eastern Europe and Asia. These incongruous elements have to be assimilated, have to be welded into one harmonious whole if Canada is to attain the position that we, who belong here by right of birth and blood, claim for her. The chief instrument in this process of assimilation is the public school.[1]

Educators, therefore, viewed the immigrants as a "challenge and invitation"[2] to Canadian institutions, a challenge which they believed the schools could meet successfully. Indeed, the elementary schools of western Canada, even more than the churches, would decide whether or not Canada could assimilate the immigrants. Because the elementary schools worked with the children, the most adaptable age group, their prospect for success was good. Elementary education, moreover, appeared to the immigrants to be far more necessary for successful life in Canada than did the Protestant religion; therefore educators had an advantage over evangelical Protestants. However, education, like religion, was a divisive issue in western Canada where the homogeneous national school ideal of the English-speaking Protestant majority was challenged, first by the separate schools of the Roman Catholic minority and then by the language issue. Thus, the assimilation of immigrants through the schools was potentially an explosive political issue which could arouse public agitation and angry emotions.

In schools where immigrant children knew no English, educators considered the teaching of the English language to be the first and most important task of the teacher. English was the medium of communication, the practical key for imparting other knowledge, and, in addition, a major symbol of identity. As a Saskatchewan inspector explained in 1913:

> In a province where fifty per cent of the people are of foreign extraction the question of the education of the immigrant must be and is one of the chief duties, if not *the* chief duty of many of our schools. In these schools other subjects are of secondary importance. Teach the children to speak, to read and to write English — this is our first and great educational commandment. Our second commandment is like unto the first — through the common medium of English, within our schools build up a national character.[3]

Thus, in addition to a common language, immigrant children were to acquire a common culture through the schools. The school curricula of western Canada stressed that the schools were not only to teach the fundamental skills of reading, writing and arithmetic, but also to transmit the cultural values of the society. Educators regarded patriotism and loyalty to Canada and the greater British Empire as essential values to be inculcated in the pupils. The British tradition was defined as synonymous with political and personal freedom, so all pupils had to be taught to understand and respect British parliamentary institutions and the basic equality of each individual before the law. In addition, the schools accepted a responsibility for teaching the personal values necessary for daily living. The purpose of education was to build character as well as to train the mind. As the Principal of the Manitoba Provincial Normal School stated:

> There is necessity for urging that our teachers must not forget that tastes, habits and disposition are as real products of education as knowledge and power, and that the prime object of school education is to build up noble and worthy lives.[4]

Manners, morals, and hygiene formed an important part of the school curriculum, and the teachers were instructed to set a good personal example for the pupils. Cleanliness was considered very important and usually rated first under "Duties to Self."[5] At school, pupils were thus expected to learn the central moral values of Canadian Christian civilization — truthfulness, courtesy, courage, pride in work, obedience to parents and to those in authority.[6]

While confident that the schools could and should act as an important agency of assimilation, educators were more aware than most Canadians of the problems involved. Educators were inclined to differentiate among immigrants according to the difficulties which they encountered or expected to encounter in educating them. All immigrants had some values or ideals which differed from those developed by the Canadian experience, and Canadians were still on guard against American encroachment. However, little mention was made of American or British immigrants in the education reports. When educators spoke of the task of assimilating immigrants they usually referred to the non-English-speaking immigrants. All non-English-speaking immigrants, whether from preferred or non-preferred areas, posed similar problems of language teaching. Immigrants who settled in rural colonies also created more problems than those in cities or in mixed communities where the English language was more readily learned through daily contact and English-speaking Canadians could provide leadership. Mennonites in Manitoba and Saskatchewan, Doukhobors and German Catholics in Saskatchewan, Ukrainians, Hungarians and other immigrants across the prairies, all presented a group structure which made assimilation through education more difficult.

Although all non-English-speaking immigrants created similar problems of language teaching, educators were particularly concerned about the immigrants from eastern Europe, most frequently called Galicians.[7] In part, the Galicians attracted more attention simply because they were more important numerically in all three provinces than most other groups of non-English-speaking immigrants. However, numbers are not the only explanation. Most educators, like other English-speaking Canadians, accepted the common division between immigrants from north-western Europe and those from eastern Europe. They perceived the Galicians on arrival as more ignorant and alien. The Scandinavian immigrants also had to learn English but their home environment was better. A Manitoba inspector commented that conditions in Swedish communities were "just as pleasant as in the English-speaking communities,"[8] and a Saskatchewan inspector reported that Icelandic children were progressing satisfactorily at school in spite of poor teaching because they received good training at home and possessed a desire and ability to learn.[9] German Catholics coming from the United States who spoke English as well as German were able to establish private Roman Catholic bilingual schools in their Saskatchewan colonies and escape the assimilating force of the public school without attracting attention from educational authorities or from the public until the First World War. However, the Galicians were considered lower in the scale of civilization; it was therefore believed more important that the public school should reach them. Equally significant, the Galicians were approachable. Many expressed a desire to have their children educated in public schools.[10] Although most were Greek Catholic and thus subject to Roman Catholic influence, they were not Roman Catholic and therefore were more open to accepting public schools than were the German Catholics. Unlike the sects, the Mennonites and the Doukhobors, they had not been promised any educational exemptions by the federal government and they did not view the public school as an unwarranted incursion of the state. The sects, indeed, posed the greatest problem for educational authorities but educators in the pre-war period tended to view them as a special case, which could be solved only very gradually but which did not affect the whole educational system.

Educators believed that it was essential for the welfare of the nation that the immigrants, and especially the Slavic immigrants, be educated, and they knew that recent immigrants required special assistance. Yet at a time of rapid expansion and pioneer settlement it was difficult to provide even a minimal standard of elementary education in many immigrant districts. Each year the annual reports of the Departments of Education documented the major theme of growth and expansion as the number of teachers and pupils doubled and even quadrupled in the three prairie provinces in the pre-war decade.[11] Officials of the Department of Education were occupied with attempting to keep pace with the need for new schools, and inspectors were responsible for the supervision of one-room rural schools scattered over a wide territory. In such conditions, educational officials had little time or energy to devote to the special needs of immigrants. Establishing schools was more difficult for European immigrants who understood neither the English language nor the system of electing three trustees to manage local school affairs. As Inspector Norman Black reported in Saskatchewan:

> In some localities serious difficulties arise from the inability of trustees to read or write English. In these and other districts, exasperating delays and local misunderstanding might be prevented if more official expert assistance were available, especially in the organisation of new districts.[12]

Since the operation of schools depended to a large extent on local initiative and control, education in immigrant districts suffered if the settlers did not receive adequate direction and encouragement.

The most serious problem was the scarcity of teachers. The provincial normal schools did not graduate nearly enough teachers to supply the demand. Some of the vacancies were filled with teachers qualified elsewhere, mainly in Ontario. Nevertheless, each year permits were issued to unqualified persons to augment the supply of teachers, and still some schools had to remain closed because no suitable teachers could be found. First year university students were often hired to teach short-term schools or summer schools open for approximately five months from May to October. This term coincided with the university vacation and was also dictated by climatic conditions in western Canada. Not all the first schools were built to withstand the rigours of a prairie winter, and parents were reluctant to allow their children to walk to school in the winter, particularly if they did not have suitable clothing. Therefore, in some districts the short-term schools were a temporary necessity, but the long gaps between sessions and the frequent changing of teachers impeded the progress of pupils.

The scarcity of teachers affected the immigrant communities the most severely. Teachers tended to shun the strange boarding houses and the cultural isolation of immigrant communities when more familiar and attractive alternatives were readily available. The inspectors' reports chronicled the frustrations and failures involved in obtaining teachers for the "foreign schools." As a Saskatchewan inspector explained:

> Over the rural portion of the district great difficulty was experienced in securing qualified teachers. . . . This was most particularly true with regard to the schools where a language other than English was the language used. Teachers naturally avoid these districts so long as they can secure positions in other districts. I have one school upon my list, the trustees of which secured no less than three teachers at different times during the term but upon arriving in the district and experiencing difficulty in getting suitable boarding places they left for parts unknown without even opening the school.[13]

Thus, the districts with immigrant children, the districts which vitally needed well qualified and enthusiastic teachers, too often were left only with the dregs or with no teachers at all.

Educational progress was also impeded by unsatisfactory school attendance. In a newly developed area even young hands could aid the family, and the result was visible in the irregular attendance figures during the year and the sudden drop of enrolment after Standard III. Manitoba had no compulsory attendance law and in Saskatchewan and Alberta the compulsory attendance ordinance was not adequately enforced. Measures for compulsory attendance only worked when enforced by the school board, and trustees were not willing to fine and thus annoy their neighbours. As a result, in both Saskatchewan and Alberta, the attendance of those enrolled in provincial schools remained within the fifty percentile range.[14] No differentiation was made in the attendance statistics between English-speaking and non-English-speaking communities and, judging from the inspector's reports, the attendance in "foreign districts" was not significantly better or worse than in English-speaking districts.

While the difficulties encountered in providing education in pioneer conditions were similar in the three prairie provinces, the solutions adopted varied. Education was a provincial responsibility, so each province made separate and different provisions for the education of immigrant children. Since education was a political matter, political decisions, subject to public pressure, helped to determine the educational response to immigration. In particular, the training of teachers and the use of language in the schools were key issues which affected the subsequent development of controversy. In all provinces, the successful integration of immigrant children into the existing society was considered important, but only Alberta established procedures which educators and the majority English-speaking population later considered satisfactory.

In Manitoba, a major educational controversy had already occurred before the influx of immigrants from continental Europe began. In the 1890's the English-speaking Protestant majority, becoming more dominant in the province and encouraged by Ontario, demanded that the existing system of Protestant and Roman Catholic schooling be replaced by a uniform national school system with no special rights for Roman Catholics and with English as the language of instruction. The Roman Catholic minority, predominantly French-speaking, led by Archbishop Taché and his successor Archbishop Langevin and supported by Quebec, fought to retain the separate official status of the Roman Catholic schools. The resulting compromise in 1897, known as the Laurier-Greenway Agreement, satisfied neither group. In response to the will of the majority, a uniform nondenominational system was imposed. However, the minority won on the language issue as a bilingual system of education was made mandatory if requested by the parents of ten pupils in a school who spoke French or any language other than English.[15] Thus, an uneasy truce was established but no permanent peace. Many English-speaking Protestants accepted bilingual schools only as a transitional stage leading to unilingual English education. They believed that coercive measures were not necessary because English, the dominant language of the country, would gradually prevail. On the other hand, Archbishop Langevin denounced the agreement as totally unsatisfactory, for "les écoles neutres" could never be accepted as a substitute for Roman Catholic schools.[16] With denominational schools banned, Langevin turned to language as an even more important defence of the faith, using bilingual schools to reinforce a separate group identity.

The bilingual system in Manitoba created serious problems for educators responsible for providing teachers for the schools. Where were teachers to be found who could teach in English and Ukrainian or English and Polish or English and German on the bilingual system? The Manitoba Department of Education chose to solve the problem of bilingual teachers by establishing special training schools and accepting lower qualifications for teachers drawn from the different language groups. There was actually little choice. The bilingual system was established. The political power of the Roman Catholic Church was exerted to maintain it, and English-speaking Protestants, considering they had won a major victory in the 1890's with the destruction of the denominational school system, did not yet perceive the bilingual principle as a major threat to their ideals. Besides, at a time of teacher scarcity when it was very difficult to obtain English-speaking teachers, bilingual teachers, even with lower qualifications, seemed a feasible alternative. Surely education of a lower standard was better than no education at all.

By giving separate teacher training to immigrant students and then sending them to teach in immigrant communities, the Department of Education did help to accentuate the isolation of the immigrant groups. However, the announced intention was not only to find some means of dealing with a critical teacher shortage, but also to assist the assimilation of the immigrants by training some of the brighter young men to serve as leaders in the Canadianization process. Certainly, J. T. Cressey, the Principal of the Ruthenian Training School, was very concerned both to give his students a knowledge of the history and institutions of the British Empire, and also to instill in them the correct moral sentiments needed for citizenship in Canada. In his view, the immigrants would be a danger to the state if they were not educated:

> As the Ruthenians and Poles have been placed in large communities by themselves, where, if allowed to grow up in ignorance, they would eventually become a menace to the state, therefore it seems to me that the state must educate these people for its own self-preservation.[17]

The young men of the training school, therefore, were being prepared as community leaders in the hope that they would educate entire settlements, parents as well as children. Although legal and practical considerations dictated the formation of separate teacher training institutions for bilingual teachers with lower qualifications, the procedure was nevertheless justified on the grounds that it conformed with the general educational aims of acculturation.

Saskatchewan chose to adopt the Manitoba solution to the problem of educating immigrants by establishing in Regina a Training School for Teachers for Foreign Language Communities. In Saskatchewan there was no legal compulsion to follow such a course, since bilingual schools, far from being mandatory, were actually illegal. A primary course might be taught in French and a language other than English might be taught for one hour in the afternoon but otherwise English was to be the language of the school.[18] However, the Saskatchewan government faced many of the same practical difficulties and political pressures as did Manitoba. The Saskatchewan training school, based on the Manitoba model, was intended to accomplish similar purposes — to give the students at least the rudiments of academic and professional preparation in English and to lead them to an appreciation of Canadian values in order that they might then act as agents of assimilation.[19] However, the separate training and lower standards again reinforced the segregation of the immigrant communities, especially since the graduates of the training school were not permitted to teach in areas where there were English-speaking children.

Alberta, although beginning with the same school law as Saskatchewan, diverged from the path followed by the other two provinces. Alberta refused to sanction any segregation in the educational system and demanded that all teachers in the province be qualified in the same manner. Conditions in Alberta made it easier for the government to maintain this position. Alberta did not have large colonies of Mennonites or Doukhobors or German Catholics who were hostile to state education, and the majority of Ruthenian settlers were congregated in one area of the province so the problem of supervision was simplified. Nevertheless, the determination of the Alberta government not to allow any deviation from a single standard of education definitely seems to have arisen from principles and not from demographic conditions. After the creation of the province, the government quickly took action to ensure that the immigrants were provided with education. In Alberta, unlike the other provinces, a Canadian-born Supervisor of Schools for Foreigners was immediately appointed to assist the non-English-speaking settlers in the establishment of school districts, the erection of schools, the employment of teachers, and the levying of taxes.[20] Robert Fletcher devoted his time primarily to the large Ruthenian colony north-east of Edmonton as this was the district in Alberta considered most in need of assistance. He reported that at first he encountered so much distrust and suspicion that progress was extremely slow, but that gradually he was able to overcome the opposition which arose from fear and lack of understanding. Where necessary, he was appointed official trustee to assume the duties ordinarily performed by a board of trustees elected by the ratepayers.

In particular, Robert Fletcher performed a vital function in obtaining qualified teachers for the immigrant schools. There were no more qualified teachers available and willing to teach in the immigrant schools in Alberta than there were in Manitoba and Saskatchewan. However, the Alberta schools were more likely to obtain qualified teachers because of the efforts of Robert Fletcher, and the policy of the Alberta government which refused to grant permits except under exceptional circumstances. With his knowledge and connections, Fletcher was able to secure qualified teachers for the schools more easily than could local trustees, and he had the power to ensure that these were the teachers who were engaged. The Alberta government and the Alberta Department of Education took firm measures to defend their educational policy when it was challenged in 1913 by Ruthenian teachers brought in from Manitoba. As official trustee, Fletcher dismissed the unqualified Ruthenian teachers and appointed qualified teachers whom he was responsible for securing and taking with him when he visited the district. To prevent the "invading" Ruthenian teachers from simply moving to other schools when expelled by Fletcher, the government passed legislation which not only prevented unqualified teachers from receiving payment for services in a court of law but also gave the Minister of Education power to prosecute unqualified teachers.[21] Thus, in spite of opposition, Alberta continued to demand more immediate conformity from the immigrants than did the other prairie provinces.

It is undoubtedly significant that the westward decline in willingness to deal with representatives of immigrant groups or to tolerate delayed conformity was paralleled by the westward decline in influence of the Roman Catholic Church and French-speaking Roman Catholics. Manitoba, the oldest province, was the centre of the conflict in western Canada between the two dominant Canadian cultures and the centre of Roman Catholic influence in western Canada. Therefore, assimilation to English-speaking Protestant standards was more difficult in Manitoba and more politically controversial. Winnipeg was also the strongest centre of immigrant organizations which slowly developed in the pre-war period. The

differences between Saskatchewan and Alberta can be explained partly by
their differing proximity to Manitoba. In addition, however, the Roman
Catholic Church did seem to be politically stronger in Saskatchewan than in
Alberta, although the proportion of Roman Catholics in the population of
the two provinces was not significantly different.[22] Saskatchewan problems
were also more complicated because Saskatchewan had more scattered
group settlements than did Alberta. In the final analysis, however, lack of
evidence makes it impossible to determine whether the difference in
procedure between Saskatchewan and Alberta resulted from a difference in
the English-speaking communities or from different attitudes held and
decisions made by a few key men in the Departments of Education and the
governments of the two provinces. Whatever the reasons for difference in
procedure, the English-speaking majority accepted the methods only so
long as serious doubts were not raised about the success of assimilation.

In the pre-war period, educators were encouraged by evidence that the
schools could perform their task of Canadianization. According to the
inspectors' reports, educational conditions in the immigrant communities
were constantly improving, and it is obvious that the inspectors believed
that the immigrant children, bright, attentive, eager, could definitely be
assimilated. They were not the dregs of a backward civilization, but the
hope of the future, the new generation growing up in a new land, ready and
able to learn and to become valuable Canadian citizens. In addition, the
inspectors rejected another stereotype imposed by the doctrines of Social
Darwinism and Anglo-Saxon supremacy. They observed that the schools in
Ruthenian settlements were clean, not dirty; indeed, in terms of cleanliness,
such schools far surpassed those in English-speaking settlements. As
Inspector Anderson of Yorkton reported in 1912:

> Here again, I must compliment our Ruthenian friends upon their
> superior cleanliness. In all the foreign schools I visited I found that they
> scrubbed the floors at least twice a month, while *twice or even once a
> year* was the general rule in English speaking rural districts.[23]

At the same time, the educators did observe less attractive qualities of
the immigrants. Houses in the Ruthenian districts were generally considered by inspectors and teachers alike as not providing suitable boarding
accommodation for English-speaking teachers. Quarrelling and factious-
ness in immigrant districts sometimes delayed the building of schools or the
hiring of teachers. At first the immigrants often seemed to regard the
intrusion of English-speaking inspectors and teachers with distrust. In these
conditions, it was often difficult to establish schools in the immigrant
districts. Nevertheless, the inspectors and teachers did not use the problems
to build a case against the immigrants. In the inspectors' reports and in
articles in educational periodicals, the positive qualities and contributions
of the immigrants definitely outweighed the negative characteristics.

Inspectors and teachers had many reasons for presenting a favourable
picture of the immigrant settlers. In part, the educators were employees of
the state and therefore were not in a position to criticize government policy.

Most of the inspectors' published comments took the form of official reports to the central educational authority, reports usually written to justify their work. In addition, inspectors and teachers, responsible for supervising the education of all children in the rural schools, wished to avoid rather than foment discord. Inspectors also wanted to encourage, not discourage, English-speaking teachers who might be persuaded to teach in the immigrant communities. However, their comments and observations were not simply designed to serve a purpose. Educators believed that the prospects for success in educational work were good and they were genuinely encouraged by the evidence of intelligence, eagerness, and cleanliness which exceeded their expectations. As the years passed, the progress, though gradual, provided considerable basis for optimism.

All problems, however, had not been solved. The process of assimilation through education had begun but was by no means complete. In the first years of the rapid influx of immigrants, educational authorities were occupied with trying to develop and expand an educational system to supply even the most elementary needs of the settlers. The conviction that all children should receive an education for their own welfare and for the welfare of the country was implicit in their efforts and in their complaints about irregular attendance, even if not explicit in the laws of the provinces. However, pioneer conditions meant that many children, and especially many immigrant children, did not receive an education. In addition, with the scarcity of teachers, it was not possible to be too particular about the qualifications of teachers or the kind of instruction given in the schools. In Manitoba and Saskatchewan, although not in Alberta, Ruthenian and Polish teachers with lower qualifications and an imperfect knowledge of English were sent to teach in immigrant districts. As a result of the difficulties, the theory of education contained in the courses of study was often very imperfectly translated into practice in the classroom. In particular, the vital question of teaching English to immigrant children depended to a large extent on the approach and qualifications of the teacher, as well as on the regulations governing language use in the schools. As the educational systems in the three provinces became better established, progress could be assessed and more demands could be made of the schools. Therefore, even though educational conditions were improving, the education of immigrants began to receive more public criticism.

A movement for reform of the educational system developed with the emergence of western Canada from the pioneer stage of development, and also formed part of a more general reform movement of the period in both Canada and the United States. In 1913, J. W. Dafoe of the *Manitoba Free Press* published a daily series of 64 articles on "The Bilingual Schools of Manitoba"[24] exposing the critical lack of schools in immigrant districts and the low standards of education, and especially of the teaching of English, in the schools which did exist. Similarly, in Saskatchewan a Better Schools Campaign was begun in 1915 to improve the school system, and much of the impetus for reform was directed by Dr. Edmund Oliver to the lack of satisfactory public school education in immigrant districts.[25] The reform impulse thus helps to explain the increased public interest in the type and quality of education being provided in western Canada.

Changes in the theory of language teaching reinforced the demands for reform of immigrant education. Initially, many educators had argued that English was best taught through the medium of the mother tongue. However, as a result of observation and experience, leading Canadian educators refuted the efficacy of the indirect method of language teaching and concluded that immigrant children learned English best in schools where only English was used. Many of the conclusions of the educators were contained in the book *English for the Non-English* written by Norman F. Black, a Regina high school teacher and former Saskatchewan school inspector, and published in the spring of 1913.[26] In spite of the fact that western Canada had been attempting to educate large numbers of non-English-speaking children for more than a decade, Black's book was a pioneer study in the field.

To obtain information, Black wrote to all the provincial education departments in Canada, to many education departments in the United States, and also to authorities in England, Wales, Porto Rico, South Africa, New Zealand, Australia and other areas. Guided by the answers received, he then sent letters to approximately 150 inspectors, superintendents, and directors with suitable experience, and questionnaires to approximately 600 teachers suggested by the supervisors. As a result of his inquiries, supplemented by personal experience, Black came to the conclusion that the key to the correct teaching of English to beginners was the practically exclusive use of that language in the school room. Therefore, in the view of Black and an impressive array of educators who supported him, it was not desirable to have teachers drawn from the immigrant communities teaching in the schools of those communities.

Reformers and educators, seeking to improve education in the immigrant districts, publicized the difficulties in order to dispel public apathy. While they demanded conformity from the immigrants, they also expressed sympathy with them. In their view, if the schools did not succeed in their task of assimilation, it would be the fault of Canadians, not of the immigrants. They accused Canadians of being prejudiced against the strangers within the gates and urged greater acceptance, especially since "our immigrants have shown in countless instances a genuine and somewhat pathetic anxiety to become and to be recognized as our real fellow-citizens."[27] The *Free Press* correspondent cited the example of the Ruthenian father who refused to bring his little girl a Ruthenian story-book from Winnipeg because he was afraid that she would not learn English.[28] Norman Black reported as typical the case of an immigrant child who, when asked whether she was Austrian or Hungarian, replied with dignity, "I am Canadian."[29] However, behind the appeal for sympathy and for an acceptance of social and civic responsibility lay an appeal to English Canadian nationalist sentiments.

The majority of English Canadians were most receptive to the nationalist appeal, and the traditional conflict with French Canadians reinforced their emphasis on the need for assimilation. The reform movement therefore became a vehicle through which the English-speaking Protestant majority attempted to assert the dominance of its ideals for the nation. While educators emphasized the importance of the teacher, the public response concentrated on the language issue. In Manitoba and Saskatchewan, where it could be shown that immigrant communities had not been reached by the assimilating force of the English language school taught by a Canadian-born teacher, the coming of war translated the pressure for educational reform into a hostile demand for immediate and total conformity. In those provinces, administrative procedures similar to the ones which Alberta always had followed were adopted only after controversy had aroused bitter emotions.

FOOTNOTES

[1]*Manitoba, Department of Education Annual Report* (hereafter cited *Manitoba, Report*), 1906, 31. T. M. Maguire.

[2]*Annual Report of the Council of Public Instruction of the North-West Territories*, 1898, 11. D. J. Goggin, Superintendent of Education.

[3]*Saskatchewan, Department of Education Annual Report* (hereafter cited *Saskatchewan, Report*), 1913, 70. W. S. Cram.

[4]*Manitoba, Report*, 1898, 25.

[5]For example, *Province of Saskatchewan, Course of Study for Public Schools*, 1910, 5.

[6]See *Programme of Studies, Manitoba; Course of Study for Public Schools, Saskatchewan; Report of the Council of Public Instruction of the North-West Territories.*

[7]In the paper, I have used the terms "Galician" and "Ruthenian" to follow the original sources. It is not always clear whether "Galician" was intended to mean Ukrainian immigrants from Galicia, or all Ukrainian immigrants, or all eastern European immigrants. "Ruthenian," a term adopted slightly later, generally meant "Ukrainian."

[8]*Manitoba, Report*, 1902, 64. T. M. Maguire.

[9]*Saskatchewan, Report*, 1911, 59.

[10]See V. J. Kaye, *Early Ukrainian Settlements in Canada, 1895-1900* (Toronto, 1964), 221-22, 232, 245.

[11]

	Teachers Employed			Pupils Enrolled		
	1896	1906	1914	1896	1906	1914
Manitoba	1,143	2,365	2,864	37,987	64,123	93,954
Saskatchewan	433	1,017	4,501	12,796	31,275	111,059
Alberta		729	3,978		28,784	89,910

	Schools		School Districts	
	1906	1914	1906	1914
Manitoba	1,270	1,478	1,399	1,784
Saskatchewan	873	3,055	1,190	3,523
Alberta	570	2,027	746	2,360

The Statistics, compiled from the Annual Reports of the Departments of Education, present problems of interpretation because more than one teacher might be employed in the same school in one year and pupils enrolled did not always attend.

[12]*Saskatchewan, Report*, 1908, 50.

[13]*Ibid.*, 1907, 45. John Hewgill.

[14]See attendance figures provided each year in the Annual Reports of the Departments of Education.

[15]Confirmed by an amendment to the Public School Act in 1897. *Canada, Sessional Papers*, XXVI, No. 13, 1897, 1-2.

[16]A constant refrain in *Les Cloches de Saint-Boniface*, organ of the Archbishop.

[17]*Manitoba, Report*, 1908, 107.

[18]*General Ordinances of the North-West Territories*, 1905, 1046-47; *Saskatchewan, Report*, 1906, 77.

[19]Public Archives of Saskatchewan, Saskatoon, Saskatchewan Department of Education Files, 8(b); *Saskatchewan, Report*, 1909, 12.

[20]*Alberta, Department of Education Annual Report* (hereafter cited *Alberta, Report),* 1906, 11-12. Report of the Deputy Minister.

[21]*Ibid.,* 1913, 39-49; 1914, 66-70.

[22]Of course, in absolute numbers there were more Roman Catholics in Saskatchewan than in Alberta. The greater proportion of English-speaking Roman Catholics in Alberta is also undoubtedly significant. The census statistics provide no correlation between religion and language but *Les Cloches,* 1 juillet 1909, 162-63, lists statistics for Roman Catholics as: Diocese of Saint Albert (Alberta), English-speaking 14,290, total 52,100; Diocese of Prince Albert (Saskatchewan), English-speaking 5,000, total 44,000; Diocese of Saint-Boniface (Manitoba), English-speaking 11,181, total 123,073. Statistics were not given for the area of Saskatchewan not yet organized into a diocese.

[23]*Saskatchewan, Report,* 1912, 62.

[24]*Manitoba Free Press,* 1 January - 15 March, 1913.

[25]*Saskatchewan's Great Campaign for Better Schools, 1915-1916* (Regina, 1916); Rev. Edmund H. Oliver, *The Country School in Non-English Speaking Communities in Saskatchewan,* published by the Saskatchewan Public Education League, n.d.

[26]Norman Black, *English for the Non-English* (Regina, 1913).

[27]Norman Black, "Western Canada's Greatest Problem, The Transformation of Aliens into Citizens," *Western School Journal,* May 1914, 92. See also J. T. M. Anderson, "The Education of the Foreigner," *The School,* January 1914.

[28]*Manitoba Free Press,* 22 January 1913.

[29]Black, *Western School Journal,* May 1914, 92.

THE PUBLIC SCHOOL AS A GUARDIAN OF ANGLO-SAXON TRADITIONS: THE SASKATCHEWAN EXPERIENCE, 1913-1918

RAYMOND HUEL
UNIVERSITY OF LETHBRIDGE

The school question has been one of the most contentious and divisive issues in Canadian national life. The essence of this controversy often has been lost sight of as a result of the infusion of other issues, notably politics. The roots of the school question go deep into the very character of Canadian society and reflect the polarization of views concerning the nature of the Canadian identity and the character and extent of cultural duality. There was, within the Dominion's Anglo-Saxon population, a dominant élite which believed that its language, culture and traditions were superior to any other. It was argued that Canada was the legatee of British ideals in North America and that she was "to be the interpreter and reconciler of a new world."[1] If Canada failed to fulfil her pre-ordained rôle in the Empire, the finest language, culture and institutions ever devised by man could not enlighten the world. To these zealous individuals, the Empire was more than a figment of the imagination: it was a precious legacy that had to be cherished, preserved and enhanced at all cost. Thus the attempts of European and French-speaking minorities to preserve their language and culture were viewed as treasonable acts because they threatened Canada's British character and institutions. The Anglo-Saxon élite responded to this "menace" by attempting to compel minorities to adopt norms based on Anglo-Protestant values.

It is within this context that the school question assumes its true proportions. For those who regarded cultural homogeneity and national unity as synonymous, the public school appeared to be the ideal instrument with which to mould the country's ethnic minorities into responsible British subjects and Canadian citizens. The non-sectarian public school and English language instruction were the great solvents that would make the New Canadian lose his foreign characteristics.[2] It was argued that the segregation of children along linguistic and religious lines for educational purposes would undermine the ideal of a united Canada and lead to national disaster. Hence, it was the duty of government to erase racial and religious differences rather than perpetuate and accentuate them by means of separate schools and foreign language instruction.

It was in the West that the worst fears of Anglo-Saxon nativists appeared to be on the verge of being realized. At the turn of the century, that vast area was being populated by individuals whose language, religion and traditions differed significantly from those of the dominant group. It was felt that if the large influx of immigrants continued unabated and if these elements segregated themselves from the larger society and refused to adopt its norms and values, the West would never become a British preserve and the Anglo-Protestant character would disintegrate. The West could take its rightful place in Canada and, for that matter in the Empire, only if cultural conformity were imposed on its polyglot population.

While these fears and anxieties were manifested throughout the West in its formative years, in Saskatchewan they were to assume the status of a unique obsession. Saskatchewan was born in the midst of a controversy involving separate schools. In bringing down legislation to establish and provide for the government of Alberta and Saskatchewan in 1905, Prime Minister Laurier was forced to abandon his attempt to introduce confessional schools in the new provinces. Nevertheless, he was able constitutionally to guarantee the religious minority's right to establish and maintain separate schools.[3] The school question in turn became the dominant issue in Saskatchewan's first election in December, 1905. The Provincial Rights party, under the leadership of F. W. G. Haultain, the former territorial premier, argued that education came under provincial jurisdiction and that the constitutionality of the Saskatchewan Act should be tested in the courts. Haultain also accused the Liberals of having formed a compact with the Catholic Church and he declared himself in favor of a non-denominational public school system. On the other hand, Walter Scott, the Liberal leader, defended the provisions of the Act on the grounds that the federal government was morally bound to guarantee minority rights which existed in 1905.[4]

The Liberals won the election and the political platforms relating to educational matters remained virtually the same for the next quarter of a century. The Liberals, in appealing to the more tolerant and liberally-minded elements in the province, supported the maintenance of separate schools and the granting of minor concessions to the non-English with respect to foreign language instruction. The Provincial Rights party and its successor, the Conservatives, appealed to the nativist element within the Anglo-Saxon population and maintained that in order to forge national unity, Saskatchewan's future citizens should receive instruction in English in non-sectarian public schools.

After the election of 1905, the school question lay dormant for several years as the attention of the province focussed on other issues. It re-emerged in December, 1912, when Premier Scott removed an ambiguity in the School Act by introducing an amendment making it mandatory for the ratepayers of the religious minority to support their separate school.[5] The provisions of the School Assessment Act, dealing with the manner in which corporate property was to be assessed for public or separate school purposes, were also amended. The Reverend Murdock MacKinnon, pastor of Knox Presbyterian Church in Regina, was extremely critical of Scott's amendment, claiming that it would prevent Roman Catholics from sending their children to public schools.[6] Furthermore, MacKinnon viewed the amendment to the Assessment Act as a "lever" to force companies to support separate schools and as a "convenient and legal" means of diverting support to such schools.[7] A few days later, a 40 member delegation representing the Regina and Moose Jaw Public School Boards, Orangemen, and Protestant clergy met with the Premier. In presenting the views of the delegation, MacKinnon declared that the legislation interfered with human liberty and that it was contrary to the principles of "British law and equity."[8] After the legislation had been assented to in January, 1913, MacKinnon advised Scott that the matter had not been dealt with satisfactorily and that he intended to stimulate public opinion by discussing the matter from his pulpit.[9]

Sixteen months later, in May 1914, Knox's pastor made good his promise to preach on the issue. He chose his time well because his sermon was delivered on the eve of the annual convention of the Grand Orange Lodges of British America meeting in Regina. MacKinnon began by referring to separate schools as an ugly question but one which, nevertheless, could not be evaded. He argued that it was the duty of government to unite the people rather than segregate them on the basis of creed. He claimed that the separate school was the greatest enemy of the "unifying movement" and that the government had strengthened that school with its recent amendments. MacKinnon called upon all lovers of "freedom, justice and fair play" to smite hard against legislation which was an insurmountable obstacle to the attainment of national unity.[10] The issue had gone beyond a consideration of the financial status of separate schools and was assuming more significant proportions.

A new dimension was added the following year when Premier Scott introduced an amendment to the language clause of the School Act in an attempt to provide proper support for foreign language instruction in schools. Under existing legislation, languages other than French could be taught for one hour a day and the cost of employing a "competent person" to provide such instruction was borne by a special levy on the parents of the children who took advantage of it. Scott's amendment stipulated that if the regular teacher were competent to provide foreign language instruction, the board would not have to impose and collect the special rate.[11]

In itself, the legislation was innocuous, but Regina's *Evening Province and Standard* 'discovered' that it concealed a sinister plot. In a front page editorial entitled "A Wedge for Bi-Lingualism," the journal declared that the non-English majority in any school district could escape the extra cost of foreign language instruction by engaging a teacher of their own nationality and, consequently, competent under the terms of the legislation. Predicting that pupils would not be exposed to English-speaking teachers, the *Evening Province* asserted that the amendment was a "deliberate" and "dastardly" attack on public schools.[12] Similar accusations were raised in the legislature, and Scott withdrew this controversial clause. Commenting on this 'defeat' the *Evening Province* prided itself on having been instrumental in eliminating bilingualism from the public school system, "the melting-pot from which the second generation may emerge Canadian to the core."[13]

A few days later, on June 22, 1915, the Premier announced that the time had come to overhaul the province's educational system and he asked the members of the Assembly to co-operate in a non-partisan campaign to stir public opinion on the rural school problem. A Citizen's Committee on Public Education was formed shortly after Scott's appeal and an organizing convention in Regina in September 1915 resulted in the establishment of the Saskatchewan Public Education League.[14] The most important address presented at this convention was that of the Reverend E. G. Oliver, a prominent clergyman and educationist. Oliver was keenly interested in the problems and education of "New Canadians," and his address dealt with the highly charged issue of country schools in non-English communities. He reported that in Ruthenian, Doukhobor, German, and French districts there was evidence of private schools, unorganized school districts and instruction in languages other than English.[15] According to Oliver, the language question was the greatest obstacle to educational reform and it had to be settled immediately before Saskatchewan became another polyglot Austria. He argued that linguistic concessions had to be terminated "for the good of the future *Canadian* citizenship of this Province."[16]

The hope that a non-partisan movement could have suggested an objective policy of reform was quickly fading and the school controversy gained momentum with each passing month. On December 26, 1915, MacKinnon again discussed the school question in a 100 minute sermon in which he charged that separate schools were perpetuating "non-Anglo-Saxon ideals and features" in Saskatchewan. He accused non-English groups of using those schools to promote their own sectarian ends and of discriminating against that "great unifying agency," the public school.[17] On January 23, 1916, MacKinnon preached "The Crime of Coercion" — the third, and last, of his pontifications on the separate school question. He maintained that Scott's amendments had subordinated civil liberties to sectarian designs. He claimed that Saskatchewan could not afford to remain a polyglot population, and that the more educational and social ideals were abandoned to accommodate non-Anglo-Saxon elements, "the more confused our future will be."[18]

The publication of the Scott-MacKinnon correspondence in the Regina daily press in January and February 1916 provided the polemic with unprecedented publicity. Although the Privy Council later upheld Scott's arguments in the Bartz case,[19] it was obvious that the matter was not closed because many disciples had emerged to continue and elaborate upon the questions which MacKinnon originally had raised in 1913. By late 1915, the controversy had been transformed into an assault against the teaching of languages other than English. In the heightened agitation that accompanied this transition, the climate of opinion engendered by the war made it extremely difficult for many normally liberally-minded English-speaking Canadians to display a sense of toleration toward French Canadian and European minorities in Saskatchewan or sympathize with their desire to preserve their cultural heritage.

Traditionally susceptible to nativist undercurrents, the Conservative party was quick to trim its sails to capitalize on the patriotic backlash resulting from the war effort. In January 1916, the Conservative leader, W. B. Willoughby, declared, before his party's annual convention, that English should be the only language of instruction in Saskatchewan schools. Two hundred delegates cheered themselves hoarse upon hearing this electrifying pronouncement.[20]

The applause of the Conservatives was an indication of what was to happen when the language question was discussed by other organizations. In March, for example, the influential Saskatchewan School Trustees' Association passed a resolution requesting that the School Act be amended to prohibit the teaching of foreign languages in the first five grades. The resolution was opposed by 150 non-English delegates who asked that a new vote be taken and the original motion be translated into French, Ruthenian, Polish, and German. When presented, this request was greeted by cries of "No" from all corners of the room.[21] Interviewed after the convention, A. J. Sparling, Chairman of the Saskatoon Public School Board, declared that it was scandalous that foreigners should ask British trustees in a British country to translate resolutions into four languages and that foreign delegates be allowed to lead the discussions. He urged his colleagues to organize and fight these elements "as our sons and brothers were fighting them on the continent of Europe."[22]

By 1917, the publicity and agitation surrounding schools and foreign language instruction had not abated. The topic was again taken up by the annual Trustees' convention which passed a resolution requesting that the Department of Education institute a uniform system of English language readers to replace existing French, German, and Catholic readers. This resolution was introduced by A. J. Sparling, who declared that he could not stand to see his sons fighting for British institutions while foreigners were perpetuating their national languages in Saskatchewan schools.[23]

In June, the Methodist Conference of Saskatchewan passed a resolution urging the government fully to enforce the provisions of the School Act regarding the teaching of English in public schools. The Reverend M. Bennett of Swift Current provoked a heated debate when he claimed that hundreds of children were not getting "one bit" of instruction in English. Under these circumstances, Bennett claimed that people could not become British subjects or Canadian citizens and he declared this state of affairs to be tantamount to Prussianism.[24]

Against this background, the language question could not fail to become a major issue for the Conservatives as they prepared for the 1917 provincial election. Longing for power after twelve years in the wilderness the Conservatives campaigned on a nativist platform that reflected war time emotions. The government's educational policy was castigated and, as a patriotic solution, the opposition pledged itself to provide "efficient instruction in reading, writing and speaking" English in every school in Saskatchewan.[25] Conservative rallies heard charges that government members had been driven from English-speaking constituencies and had to take refuge behind "second line trenches" manned by the same foreign elements that had dominated the recent Trustees' convention. Opposition candidates were also assisted by officials of the Grand Orange Lodge.[26]

Despite the tumult over the language question, the Conservative campaign failed to convince the electorate, and the Liberals were returned with an increased majority. The results of the June 26 election, however, could not be regarded as a referendum on educational issues. There was, within the Anglo-Saxon population, a zealous nativist element which was not satisfied with the verdict and which was not prepared to let the matter rest until satisfaction had been obtained. The day following the election, the Regina *Daily Post* had already informed W. M. Martin, who had succeeded Scott as Premier, that the people were looking to him to make English the sole language of instruction "by whatever means are found possible and most expeditious."

By 1918, the cry "English only in schools" had become a panacea for all of Saskatchewan's ills. The principle of English only became much more than simply a problem affecting education as nativists argued that the maintenance of democracy, the Canadian nation, and the Empire all necessitated that English be the only language of instruction in schools. In its editorial of January 9, the independent Saskatoon *Daily Star* stated that while Canada was condemned in perpetuity to bilingualism, no sanction should be given to the teaching of foreign languages in Saskatchewan. If English were not the only language of instruction, it would be impossible to build the Canadian nation or to make the privileges of Canadianism "clear and compelling" to all.

In February, the matter was brought before the 3,000 delegates attending the Trustees' Convention in Saskatoon, and it was evident that extremist English-speaking trustees were controlling the proceedings. A resolution calling for English as the only language of instruction was introduced and supported on the grounds that it was necessary to forge the cosmopolitan population into a unified whole. An attempt to amend the motion to make a distinction between the teaching of French and the teaching of other languages was greeted by cries of "No!, No difference." The original motion was carried almost unanimously "to the accompaniment of loud cheering and sustained applause."[27]

These proceedings acted as a catalyst on an already seething issue. The resolutions of the Trustees were fortified by the subsequent support of the Orange Lodge, the Association of Rural Municipalities, the Baptist Conference, and the Anglican Synod of Saskatchewan.[28] In September, the Joint Legislation Committee of the Sons of England and the Orange Order in Saskatoon sent out thousands of circulars urging the public to demand a "satisfactory settlement" to the language question.[29] The agitation, which was now province-wide, was producing tangible results. In November and December, Martin's office was buried under an avalanche of petitions demanding the termination of foreign language instruction in schools.[30]

Sympathetic as the Liberals might be towards the non-Anglo-Saxon population, they were not about to totally disregard general public opinion on issues as politically volatile as schools and language. On December 27, the Premier responded to public pressure by introducing an amendment to the School Act abrogating the provisions which previously had permitted instruction in languages other than English. English, henceforth, would be the sole language of instruction with the exception of French, which could be used as a language of instruction in the first grade and which could be taught as a subject of study for one hour a day in subsequent grades.[31]

This concession did not meet with the approval of the nativist press, which maintained that Saskatchewan's salvation lay in the establishment of one language — English — in the schools.[32] From Calgary, the Reverend M. MacKinnon, serving as a Chaplain in Military District No. 13, condemned the amendment for not going far enough and declared:

> French must go, Quebec failed us during the war. We do not want Quebec reproduced in Saskatchewan.... Let all enlightened citizens speak, write and wire until French goes with German.... Favoritism and compromise today means contention and endless strife tomorrow.[33]

In the Assembly, Donald MacLean, the Conservative leader, declared that the schools must serve as a means of unifying the people of Saskatchewan into one "harmonious whole." He argued that the present bill was merely a compromise and he unsuccessfully moved an amendment to make English the only language of instruction.[34] When the legislature re-convened in January 1919, MacLean reiterated his opposition to the amendment and argued that in Saskatchewan, there was no pedagogical argument, no "sane argument" in favor of compromise on the language question. A Conservative motion to refer the bill to Committee of the Whole was defeated and it was given third reading.[35]

With the enactment of this lesiglation nativists rejoiced that the teaching of foreign languages had been abolished, but their vision of cultural conformity clashed with the exception made in favor of the French language. The school question, the language issue, the foreign menace to British institutions were all carried over into the intolerant decade of the twenties where they merged with the fear that Quebec was attempting to force bilingualism on the rest of the nation. This paranoiac amalgam excited emotions, inflamed passions and provided fertile ground for the Invisible Empire of the Knights of the Ku Klux Klan which invigorated patriotic and nativist sentiment and led concerned individuals on a crusade to make Saskatchewan a better place for Anglo-Saxons to live.

The campaign to make the Saskatchewan public school an instrument of cultural conformity in the period from 1913 to 1918 was indicative of a keenly felt anxiety on the part of individuals concerned with the essence of the province's character and institutions. The socio-cultural confrontation that occurred was in reality a microcosm of the polarization of views at the national level concerning the nature of the Canadian identity and character.

Anti-Catholicism, Francophobia and xenophobia were latent sentiments within the Anglo-Saxon community and they were capable of being intensified when a suitable occasion arose — for example, Scott's amendments to the School Act. The intensity of the nativist response can be attributed to the fact that, in an atmosphere of hysteria, accentuated by war-time appeals to passion and patriotism, nativists in Saskatchewan envisaged a total collapse of their conceptual world unless steps were taken immediately to restore Anglo-Saxon norms and values to a dominant status. The educational process was regarded as the most important means of selecting, preserving and enhancing the distinctive characteristics of the dominant elite in an attempt to maintain social solidarity and cultural homogeneity. The non-sectarian public school and English language instruction would usher in the Anglo-Protestant millennium in Saskatchewan.

FOOTNOTES

[1] R. England, *The Central European Immigrant in Canada* (Toronto, 1929), 211.

[2] J. T. M. Anderson, *The Education of the New Canadian* (Toronto, 1918), 114.

[3] C. C. Lingard, Territorial Government in Canada. The Autonomy Question in the Old North-West Territories (Toronto, 1946), 159-60. *Statutes of Canada,* 4-5 Ed. VII, chapt. 42, sec. 17, sub-sec. 3.

[4] D. Bocking, "Saskatchewan's First Provincial Election," *Saskatchewan History,* 17 (1964), 41-54.

[5] It was the intent of the School Act that members of a religious minority constituting a separate school district were legally compelled to support that school but the legislation was not explicit in this respect. In 1911, Judge McLorg of Saskatoon, in a decision involving the assessment of separate school supporters, ruled that each ratepayer exercised the option of supporting either the public or separate school. Archives of Saskatchewan [hereafter cited as AS], Papers of the Hon. W. Scott [hereafter cited as Scott Papers], 35193-194. Scott introduced his amendment to prevent ratepayers from jeopardizing the financial stability of school districts by opting to support the district that had the lowest rate of assessment.

[6] AS, Scott Papers, MacKinnon to Scott, December 30, 1912, 35271-273.

[7] *Ibid.,* January 6, 1913, 35276-284.

[8] *Daily Province,* January 10, 1913.

[9] AS, Scott Papers, MacKinnon to Scott, January 19, 1913, 25299-309.

[10] *Daily Province,* May 25, 1914. Reproduced *in extenso.*

[11] *Evening Province and Standard,* May 26, 1915.

[12] *Ibid.*

[13] *Ibid.,* June 3, 1915.

[14] Saskatchewan Public Education League, *Saskatchewan's Great Campaign for Better Schools* (Regina, 1916), 5-11.

[15] E. H. Oliver, *The Country School in Non-English Speaking Communities in Saskatchewan* (Saskatoon, n.d.), 9.

[16] *Ibid.,* 7, 10.

[17] *Evening Province and Standard,* December 27, 1915. Reproduced *in extenso.*

[18] *Ibid.,* January 24, 1916. Reproduced *in extenso.*

[19] AS, Scott Papers, 78510-513. The decision stated that the religious minority was compelled to support its separate school.

[20] *Evening Province and Standard,* January 20, 1916.

[21] *Morning Leader,* March 3, 1916.

[22] *Daily Star,* March 4, 1916.

[23] *Daily Post,* February 28, 1917.

[24] *Daily Star,* June 12, 1917.

[25] *Daily Post,* June 16, 1917.

[26] *Morning Leader,* June 12, 1917; *Canadian Annual Review,* 1917, 771.

[27] *Daily Post,* February 22, 1918.

[28] *Daily Star,* March 8, 1918; *Morning Leader,* June 17, 1918.

[29] *Daily Star,* September 14, 1918.

[30] AS, Papers of the Hon. W. M. Martin [hereafter cited as Martin Papers], 53 Ed., *passim.*

[31] *Statutes of Saskatchewan,* 1918-19, chap. 48.

[32] *Daily Star, Daily Post,* December 18, 1918.
[33] *Daily Post,* December 18, 1918.
[34] AS, Martin Papers, 18549-558.
[35] *Ibid.,* 18684-692.

LANGUAGE CONFLICT AND SCHOOLS IN NEW BRUNSWICK

NANCIELLEN SEALY
MOUNT ALLISON UNIVERSITY, SACKVILLE, N.B.

This paper stems from my interest in Acadian ethnic persistence in the Maritime Provinces and particularly on New Brunswick's North Shore, bordered by the Bay of Chaleur and the Gulf of St. Lawrence. I initially did research in a North Shore Acadian village[1] where schools supported French language maintenance and cultural persistence: teachers were usually from the village or the ecclesiastical parish; the French language was the medium of instruction; and symbols, pictures, and other reminders of the children's and teachers' Roman Catholicism were displayed.

Historical and contemporary examples from the North Shore indicate that the relationship between schools, language, and culture has not always been harmonious. In this paper I discuss language planning, schools and conflict. As will be described below, nineteenth-century Bathurst and Caraquet, as well as contemporary Campbellton,[2] have been scenes of conflict related to schools and language. A secondary aim of the paper is to suggest through the data possible future directions for sociolinguistic research in Canada, a field neglected by both sociologists and anthropologists.

Language Planning: A Global Concern

With a few notable exceptions[3] sociolinguists have only recently been concerned with problems of language planning, and many of their studies focus on the Third World.[4] However most, if not all, nations are characterized by linguistic pluralism which necessarily demands language planning or "decision-making about language."[5] Developing nations must select official and/or national languages, and thus the languages to be standardized, modernized, and taught in school. Giving special status to a language also gives special status to its native speakers, and the language selection may say as much about intranational ethnic and political relations as it does about a language's utility in industrialized and modern contexts.

Language is inherently linked to personal, social, and cultural identity, and language change is usually resisted. Although developing nations may become contexts for newly generated conflicts, some developed nations have a legacy of conflict which makes solution of language-based problems none the less difficult. In developed nations also, choice of language for school and government may be made for political rather than practical or pedagogically sound reasons. For example, the restoration of the Irish language occurred in a period of rising nationalism in Ireland,[6] and tentative findings suggest that the use of Irish as a medium of instruction for anglophone children is detrimental to their educational advancement.[7]

Various historical and sociocultural factors contribute to the need for, and influence the outcome of, language planning. In this paper I focus on the relationship of schools to language planning in New Brunswick. I attempt to indicate that schools are not limited to passive roles vis-à-vis language policy, but also affect that policy and its implementation.

Nineteenth Century New Brunswick: Mosaic or Melting Pot?

In the latter part of the nineteenth and early part of the twentieth centuries, the future of Canada's various ethnic and language groups was uncertain. In describing part of this period Hatfield writes:

> Throughout the 1890s the secular institutional expressions of Canada's cultural and religious duality came under severe attack by substantial elements of its British Protestant majority. The activities of the Equal Rights Association in Ontario, the abolition of the dual school system in Manitoba and the removal of French as an official language of the Northwest Territories all manifested a desire for a culturally homogeneous state on the American model.[8]

I would add that both "Canada's cultural and religious duality" and the continued heterogeneity of immigrant populations were under attack, as illustrated in Manitoba at that time.[9]

Minority group rights in schools were contentious issues. Education was a provincial matter, and though federal institutions were appealed to in several disputes, decisions were usually reserved for the province, the 1896-1897 Laurier-Greenway compromise on the Manitoba school question being an exception. The British North America Act did not spell out the nature of school rights for minority groups outside of Quebec,[10] and MacNaughton remarks in reference to the New Brunswick school crisis of the 1870s that

> there was nothing in the Constitution which obliged the provincial authorities to accord to the French language any rights and privileges in the legislature or in the schools, nor were they placed under any compulsion to restrict the use of French as the language of communication and study in the schools of Acadian districts.[11]

However, the provinces tended to restrict special school provisions for religious and language minorities. The events in New Brunswick were not unlike those occurring elsewhere in Canada as groups sought either to extend and protect their rights and privileges in schools or to deny those held by others.[12]

Today New Brunswickers of French origin make up 37 per cent of the province's population.[13] This representation was not always so strong,[14] and some nineteenth-century anglophones attempted to prevent Acadian ethnic persistence and expansion in the province. Before considering these attempts to acculturate Acadians via educational policy and school organization, let us briefly examine the history of Acadian culture to that time.

On returning from the Expulsion of the mid-1750s, Acadians had settled along New Brunswick's northern and eastern coasts and riverways, in the least accessible and agriculturally least productive areas, where anglophone settlers were few. Acadians engaged in fishing, farming, and woods-related work which provided little more than a subsistence living for most.

Though living in predominantly Acadian areas, Acadians did not control these areas in an economic or political sense, nor did they constitute an institutionally complete minority. The Roman Catholic Church was served by English-speaking bishops, and several francophone parishes had Irish rather than Acadian priests. In provincial elections between 1870 and 1896, francophones had won about ten per cent of the legislative seats;[15] only six seats in the Canadian Parliament had been won by New Brunswick francophones (out of 125 New Brunswick seats in a total of eight elections).[16]

New Brunswickers of French origin constituted 17.6 per cent of the population in 1881;[17] however, they were almost an invisible people to anglophones in the southern part of the province. Acadians figure little in historical accounts of the time,[18] and McNaughton remarks that references to Acadian schools were scant in government documents before approximately 1870.[19]

The New Brunswick legislature and populace as a whole are described as being little concerned with provincial schools in the mid-nineteenth century.[20] In 1871, however, the legislature passed the Common Schools Act which was designed to improve school conditions and overcome local apathy to education. "In brief, the Act established free, tax-supported, non-sectarian schools and made provision for the efficient operation, support, and supervision, of such schools."[21] A feature designed to contribute to better local school management was the division of the province "into local school districts containing no more than fifty resident children between the ages of five and sixteen years of age, unless the area embraced four square miles, or were a town, village or populous locality."[22]

Roman Catholics and thus Acadians opposed the Act which denied them customary religious privileges in the schools — e.g., members of religious orders were essentially prohibited from teaching in the non-sectarian schools. However, language and cultural (or "racial") differences were also involved — more involved, perhaps, than is generally recognized.[23]

Hatfield notes that "although the schools question of the 1870s was one of religion rather than ethnicity, the issue of language rights was intimately involved in the Acadian minority's opposition to the Common Schools Act."[24] French would remain the medium of instruction in the elementary grades of Acadian schools but English was to be used beyond this level, including at the provincial teacher training school in Fredericton.[25] Few text books in French were available, and "catechisms and a few other religious books formed nearly the whole literature of the French schools."[26] Hence, education in the French language with adequate texts and well-trained teachers was not supported, and instead seems to have received "benign neglect" from those empowered to improve the schools.

Among the arguments used to justify the provisions of the Act was that children of all denominations should be educated together so that bonds of friendship and co-operation might be created;[27] the schools were to be used to build harmony between groups. There was no mention made of the language to be used in building these harmonious relationships.

The Act of 1871 was resisted in various school districts by withholding of taxes; nearly all French-language schools had closed in protest in 1872.[28] In 1875, riots in Caraquet over the school issue resulted in the death of two men, a local Acadian and an anglophone constable.[29]

Following the violence in Caraquet and continued opposition to the Act, the Compromise of 1875 was made: students could be taught religion after class hours in school buildings, members of religious orders were permitted to teach provided they obtained a provincially approved teaching licence, and in populous areas Catholic children could be grouped together in the same school or schools,[30] all of which "legalized within the non-sectarian system of the province schools of a sectarian bias."[31]

The school tax was still held in little favour by many Acadians for whom education was a luxury ill-afforded; tax assessments were frequently not paid, and districts went without schools or maintained very poor ones. Few Acadians obtained any but the most rudimentary of education;[32] however, those that received some schooling were usually taught by Catholics and in the French language.

The 1880's was a period of Acadian cultural and political awakening; an Acadian nationalistic organization (*la société Nationale l'Assomption*) was formed, and efforts were stepped up to obtain Acadian bishops and priests to serve the increasing number of francophone Catholics in the province, which had risen to 51.9 percent of the Catholic population in 1881.[33]

Although Irish and Acadians jostled for power within the Church, outside they joined in opposing a further assault on their school privileges. In 1890 the Protestant minority in Bathurst charged that the Catholic-dominated board of school trustees was not acting according to the 1875 Compromise.[34] Issues thought to have been resolved in the Compromise threatened to split the province once more.

In 1894 a report made at the request of the provincial government could find the Bathurst school board guilty of no more than "grave mismanagement." Judge J. J. Fraser of the provincial Supreme Court and author of the report concluded that "the local board had sought to operate the conventional school under the schools act."[35] Nonetheless, from 1890 to 1895, the issue was hotly debated in the English-language newspapers and political forums in the province.

The Bathurst Protestants' cause had been championed by H. H. Pitts, a newspaper editor, staunch imperialist, and Grand Master of the New

Brunswick Loyal Orange Association. Pitts argued for a unilingual and culturally uniform Canada. Minority group privileges supporting languages other than English and denominations other than Protestant were to be swept away by a "new reform party." "This new party, he [Pitts] believed, would win the bloc vote of New Brunswick's British Protestant majority and impose its values on the province by force of law."[36] In the provincial election of 1892 Pitts campaigned on the Bathurst crisis and non-sectarian school issue, and won the legislative seat of Premier Blair. This was perhaps the high point of Pitts' political career, for though he won the election, he could muster little legislative support for curtailing, if not denying, minority privileges in the schools.

Hatfield suggests (62-64) that Pitts misjudged the New Brunswick scene; Acadians and English Canadians were accustomed to politics of consensus and accommodation, and neither group wished to become embroiled in sectarianism as it had been experienced during the 1870's. A combination of Blair's political acumen, Pitts' misreading of the New Brunswick political climate, and Acadian restraint and co-operation with Irish Catholics denied Pitts' bid to bring cultural and linguistic uniformity to New Brunswick schools.

I suggest as well that the local school districts had considerable power within their own domains and had become an effective unit for resisting provincial policy, as witnessed in opposition to the 1871 Act. In the establishing of smaller school districts, the Act had created its own undoing with regard to enforcement of other of the Act's regulations. Employing schools as acculturative tools, implicitly or explicitly, could be resisted locally by simply closing the school, and the ethnically homogeneous nature of New Brunswick regions and of many school districts ensured a certain uniformity of opinion regarding such action. It may be noted that school conflicts occurred in ethnically mixed, or somewhat mixed, communities like Caraquet and Bathurst.

In 1928 Acadians again attempted to legalize rights to education in the French language; this was achieved in "the so-called 'Regulation 32,' which permitted local school boards to adopt a truly bilingual programme of studies." However, strong anglophone reaction to the regulation resulted in its revoking soon after passage.[37]

Over the years religion has ceased to be an issue in New Brunswick schools, but language use and learning have continued as sources of contention. In 1969 the New Brunswick Official Languages Act spelled out the rights of minority groups to an education in their mother tongue. What had been de facto privileges for Acadians for nearly 100 years became rights; as we shall see in the section below, this did not prevent future inter-ethnic group conflict over language and schools, but instead reshaped conflict issues.[38]

New Brunswick's Present: Bilingualism and School Conflict

According to current federal policy Canada is to be a cultural mosaic rather than a melting pot, and language planning encourages language differences and expansion of bilingualism in the official languages of French and English.[39] Though education remains a provincial responsibility, the federal government encourages the realization of national goals through the schools; for example, funds are given the provinces to help defray costs of second-language teaching.

I have suggested above that the nineteenth-century New Brunswick school district was an organizational unit which permitted local Acadians to maintain French as the medium of instruction in circumstances which were other than strictly according to provincial policy. Here I discuss an example from twentieth century New Brunswick which illustrates that school organization today may similarly work against official language policy. The example is drawn from Campbellton, a northern New Brunswick community experiencing language change. But first it is important to clarify the sociolinguistic perspective towards these findings.

Conflict and Sociolinguistic Settings

Sociolinguistics has been defined as "the study of the relationship between the linguistic repertoire and its range, compartmentalization and fluidity, on the one hand, and the social role repertoire and its range, compartmentalization and fluidity within speech communities, on the other hand."[40] Perhaps to oversimplify, the sociolinguist is concerned with who speaks what language variety (language or dialect) and in what contexts. The study of the relationship between the linguistic and social variables becomes particularly relevant in contexts where language change is planned. For example, change of a speech variety's range may entail change of relative status of the variety and its speakers.[41] If the latter change is negatively perceived by the speaker, opposition and conflict may result. With these observations in mind we can proceed to our discussion of the Canadian material.

Campbellton is situated on the New Brunswick-Quebec border and has some 10,000 inhabitants, about half of whom are anglophone, half francophone. Residents work in pulp and paper mills in nearby towns and in service institutions, such as hospitals and schools.

Large numbers of Irish Catholics settled in Campbellton in the latter part of the nineteenth century, and about half of the town's anglophones are Roman Catholic.[42] Although the two language groups shared a Roman Catholic church until the mid-1940s, today each has its own "national" church.

The language-based conflict experienced in Campbellton relates to, and is reflected in, not only the school, but the larger sociolinguistic settings as well. Some brief comment on this larger context is appropriate as the sociolinguistic setting is, I suggest, probably typical of many Canadian communities where conflict continues between the two major language groups. The setting is characterized by what may be termed "language status reversal."

In Canada less than 5 per cent of the anglophones speak French; about 30 per cent of the francophones speak English.[43] English has an extensive range of contexts in which it is used, and if anglophones and francophones communicate it is usually in English. This is so not only in formal encounters in shopping, transacting business, and dealing with strangers, but in domestic and informal contexts as well. (For example, English is often the home language in francophone-anglophone marriages.) Attitudes explain and reinforce the language use arrangement; English is said to be easier to learn than French and it is thus "natural" for francophones to become bilingual and to speak English to anglophones.

Planned language change in Canada has altered this traditional arrangement; francophones no longer use English in contexts where it was once required. For example, bilingual posts in the federal public service ensure services in either official language. Legislation does not alter language use arrangements in local-level non-federal government domains, but pressures from community francophone associations are said to have been applied on Campbellton anglophone businessmen for such changes; services are requested in French as well as English. In stores where ten years ago clerks were unilingual anglophones, today they are bilingual or even unilingual francophones, and it is the unilingual anglophone customer who occasionally experiences difficulty being understood and served.

I suggest that in situations where the individual is obliged to speak a second language in which he is less than fluent, the individual is accorded and feels less status than the individual speaking his first language. Both anglophones and francophones express embarrassment and reluctance to use a language only weakly controlled, and systematic study of reactions in such interactions is clearly called for. Some anglophones newly experiencing this language status reversal and the position of being unable to communicate with the unilingual francophone express not only embarrassment, but stronger negative reaction, perhaps most commonly voiced as an anti-bilingualism and opposition to French as an official language.

Related to the above language change has been the alteration of the relationship between language skills and social mobility. Inglehart and Woodward have persuasively argued that the relationship between linguistic pluralism and political separatism is "dependent on two related situational factors:

1. The level of economic and political development attained by the country in question.

2. The degree to which social mobility is blocked because of membership in a given language group."[44]

I suggest that conflict between language groups (other than that specifically involving political separatism) may also be related to social mobility. Many Campbellton anglophones believe that jobs and job mobility are tied to language skills. Within schools, for example, certain administrative positions are bilingual posts; bilingual francophones do tend to get these higher paying and more prestigious positions, and anglophones generalize that all job opportunities for unilingual anglophones are restricted.

In areas like Campbellton where unemployment is high (about 30 per cent in the summer of 1975), threats of any kind to jobs and job advancement are taken seriously. Sociolinguistic research which might have foreseen problems resulting from language change affecting job mobility, or more importantly, language change which gives the impression of affecting job mobility, might usefully have produced suggestions for reducing anglophone negative reaction to current language policy.

Conflict and School Organizations

In addition to these changes in the sociolinguistic setting which potentially lead to conflict, more particular events unfolded in the community which contributed to tension between language groups. It was argued in the local school board that Campbellton could become an example to the rest of Canada by making its secondary school bilingual, with "bilingual" meaning that anglophone and francophone students would share buildings and facilities, though each language group would be segregated according to classroom where they would be taught in their mother tongue. Dual teaching systems would be maintained side by side. Furthermore, by association and participation in extra-curricular activities each group would learn the language of the other.

In the nineteenth century, the strategy of bringing the two groups together was to result in the acculturation of New Brunswick francophones; now the same strategy was framed to maintain and expand bilingualism. However, I suggest that neither unilingualism nor bilingualism could have been determined by this school organization. Most nineteenth-century Acadians received little education, and making English the medium of instruction, and housing anglophones and francophones in the same school probably had little effect on language retention of Acadians as a whole. Rather than having large numbers of francophones who went to school and who learned and adopted the English language, there were large numbers of francophones who simply never went to school. Some francophones who attended school and learned English did go on to adopt that language. I suggest, however, that more important than school organization in encouraging language loss and acculturation were factors which brought members of the two groups together in varied, frequent and direct contact, such as settlement patterns, intermarriage, and work relations.

Language learning also requires more than limited school association with speakers of the target language; language skills do not necessarily "rub off," but often must be taught. Furthermore, attitudes towards bilingualism and biculturalism influence the success of second language learning,[45] and schools probably tend to mirror community attitudes. As suggested above, anglophone attitudes towards bilingualism are mixed at best in Campbellton.

Opposition to the sharing of facilities from within both school and community has resulted in the beginning of construction of separate facilities for anglophone secondary students in Campbellton. In the meantime, students of both language groups share facilities by attending class in split shifts. If harmonious relationships are to be built among the school-age generation, it will not be on the basis of school associations; schools will not solve problems of interethnic group relations in the community, and they may exacerbate them. Schools may reflect the national language and cultural goals, but they cannot ensure their success, and in some cases, as in Campbellton, may undermine them.

Summary and Future Study Suggestions

I have suggested that sociolinguistic study of planned language change is needed in developed nations like Canada, where language problems may be as troublesome as those in developing nations. Particularly appropriate are studies in communities like Campbellton which might evaluate the sociocultural implications of recent national language policy on intergroup relations; the focus would be on bilingualism and biculturalism as a policy affecting and being affected by communities and specific vulnerable institutions with communities such as schools and churches.

In countries like Canada a wealth of historical material can be used in uncovering the development of inter-ethnic and inter-language group relations in local contexts. For the sociolinguist *cum* ethnohistorian the research possibilities are considerable. For example, study is needed of the development of "national" Roman Catholic churches, and the changing diglottic demands of each language group implicit in that development.

Sociolinguistics is poorly developed in Canada, as indicated by the small number of sociologists (8) and anthropologists (23) who identified themselves as having interest and/or expertise in language-related studies in 1973.[46] Significant Canadian research problems involve ethnic and language groups, intergroup relations, and thus the nature of Canadian society. Sociolinguistics is a research field which calls for development in this decade.

FOOTNOTES

[1] For a description of the village, see Nanciellen Sealy, "Ethnicity and Ethnic Group Persistence in an Acadian Village in Maritime Canada," Diss. Southern Illinois, 1974.

[2] Research of a preliminary nature was done largely with Campbellton anglophones from May to August, 1975; additional research is planned.

[3] See, for example, Einar Haugen, *Language Conflict and Language Planning: The Case of Modern Norwegian* (Cambridge, 1966).

[4] See, for example, Joshua A. Fishman, Charles A. Ferguson, and Jyotirindra Das Gupta, eds., *Language Problems of Developing Nations* (New York, 1968).

[5] Joan Rubin and Björn H. Jernudd, eds., "Introduction: Language Planning as an Element in Modernization," in *Can Language Be Planned?* (Honolulu, 1975), xiii.

[6] John Macnamara, "Successes and Failures in the Movement for the Restoration of Irish," in *Can Language Be Planned?* 65-94.

[7] John Macnamara, in *Bilingualism and Primary Education, A Study of Irish Experience* (Edinburgh, 1966), 136, reports that "there is a balance effect in language learning, at least where the time devoted to the second language is so extensive that the time available for the

mother tongue is reduced. Native-speakers of English in Ireland who have spent 42 per cent of their school time learning Irish do not achieve the same standard in written English as British children who have not learned a second language (estimated difference in standard, 17 months of English age). Neither do they achieve the same standard in written Irish as native-speakers of Irish (estimated difference, 16 months of Irish age). Further the English attainments of native-speakers of Irish fall behind those of native-speakers of English both in Ireland (13 months of English age) and in Britain (30 months of English age) . . .''

The influence of second-language learning and use on students' proficiency in the mother tongue and other school subjects is by no means decided; for findings which differ from those of Macnamara, see Wallace E. Lambert, "Measuring the Cognitive Consequences of Attending Elementary School in a Second Language," in *Language, Psychology and Culture, Essays by Wallace E. Lambert* (Stanford, 1972), 331-37.

[8]Michael Hatfield, "H. H. Pitts and Race and Religion in New Brunswick," *Acadiensis,* 4 (1975), 46.

[9]W. L. Morton, "Manitoba Schools and Canadian Nationality, 1890-1923," in *Minorities, Schools, and Politics,* Essays by D. G. Creighton, *et al.* (Toronto, 1969), 10-18.

[10]Lovell Clark, ed., "Introduction," in *The Manitoba School Question: Majority Rule or Minority Rights?* (Toronto, 1968), 1.

[11]Katherine F. C. MacNaughton, *The Development of the Theory and Practice of Education in New Brunswick, 1784-1900,* University of New Brunswick Historical Studies, No. 1 (Fredericton, 1947), 231.

[12]For discussion of similar events taking place elsewhere in Canada, see D. G. Creighton, *et al., Minorities, Schools and Politics* (Toronto, 1969). Also, Royal Commission on Bilingualism and Biculturalism, *Report, Book II: Education* (Ottawa, 1968).

[13]*Canada Year Book* (Ottawa: Information Canada, 1974).

[14]

TABLE

Population of New Brunswick
by Ethnic Origin (Percentages)

	British Isles	French
1871	79.2	15.7
1881	76.6	17.6
1901	71.7	24.2
1911	65.3	28.0
1921	65.2	31.2
1971	57.6	37.0

Source: Census of Canada

[15]Hugh G. Thorburn, *Politics in New Brunswick* (Toronto, 1961), 201.

[16]*Ibid.,* 189.

[17]See footnote 14.

[18]See, for example, W. S. MacNutt, *The Atlantic Provinces, The Emergence of Colonial Society* (Toronto, 1965).

[19]MacNaughton, 230.

[20]*Ibid.,* 161-66.

[21]*Ibid.,* 197.

[22]*Ibid.*

[23]*Ibid.,* 228-29.

[24]Hatfield, 47.

[25]*Ibid.*

[26]MacNaughton, 182.

[27]*Ibid.,* 196.

[28]M. H. Hody, "The Development of the Bilingual Schools of New Brunswick, 1874-1960," Ed.E. Thesis, Ontario College of Education, University of Toronto, 1964, 112.

[29]George F. G. Stanley, "The Caraquet Riots of 1875," *Acadiensis,* 2 (1972), 21-38.

[30]MacNaughton, 220-21.

[31]*Ibid.,* 221.

[32]Hody, 117-19.

[33]Hatfield, 65.

[34]For this description of the Bathurst school crisis I have drawn heavily from Hatfield, 49-57.

[35]*Ibid.,* 55.

[36]*Ibid.,* 49.

[37]Thorburn, 33.

[38]It should be noted that the de facto privileges were insufficient to provide French-language children with quality education; predominantly francophone counties customarily have had higher rates of illiteracy than predominantly anglophone counties. For further discussion, see M. H. Hody, 119-20.

[39]For description of federal language policy and programs, see the *Annual Reports* of the Commissioner of Official Languages (Ottawa: Information Canada).

[40]Joshua A. Fishman, "Sociolinguistics and the Language Problems of the Developing Countries," *International Social Science Journal*, 20 (1968), 213.

[41]Simon has made a similar point in suggesting that "compromise solutions in language conflicts do not merely equalize the status of the conflicting groups but actually reverse the order of dominance." For further discussion, see W. B. Simon, "A Sociological Analysis of Multilingualism," in *Sounds Canadian: Languages and Cultures in Multi-Ethnic Society*, ed. Paul M. Migus (Toronto, 1975), 3-22.

[42]I assume that francophones are Roman Catholic; the percentage of anglophone Roman Catholics is approximated by subtracting the number of Francophones (5,075) from the number of Roman Catholics (7,665); the difference (2,590) represents 50.2 per cent of the total number of anglophones (5,160). Source: *Census of Canada*, 1971.

[43]Royal Commission on Bilingualism and Biculturalism, *Report, Book I: The Official Languages* (Ottawa, 1967), 38.

[44]R. F. Inglehart and M. Woodward, "Language Conflicts and Political Community," in *Language and Social Context*, ed. Pier Paolo Giglioli (Penguin Education, 1972), 359.

[45]Wallace E. Lambert, "A Social Psychology of Bilingualism," in *Language, Psychology, and Culture, Essays by Wallace E. Lambert* (Stanford, 1972), 212-35.

[46]James E. Curtis and Ronald D. Lambert, *Directory of Sociologists and Anthropologists in Canada and Their Current Research* (Montreal, 1973), 114, 130.

THE MANITOBA SCHOOL QUESTION: AN ETHNIC INTERPRETATION

CORNELIUS J. JAENEN

UNIVERSITY OF OTTAWA

The Manitoba School Question is for most historians a threadbare issue: this is because it has been the subject of numerous polemical works, as well as of more dispassionate scholarly investigation.[1] The question might well be asked if there is anything further to be said on the subject, if there remain any aspects of the question which have not been investigated and reported upon. The reader will have to judge whether the present approach and interpretation have merit and validity. This paper is presented in the belief that the ethnic aspects of the controversy have long been overshadowed by the religious factors to the extent that the former have been virtually ignored.

Manitoba's public school system, created by a provincial statute of 1871, which the local legislature framed in accordance with the dual confessional and bilingual practice of Red River colony, made only indirect reference to language(s) of instruction and to ethnic communities. The Act of 1871 created a bifurcated Board of Education which would "select books, maps and globes to be used in the Common Schools, due regard being had in such selections to the choice of English books, maps and globes for the English Schools and French for the French Schools . . ."[2] The regulations of the Protestant and Catholic sections of the Board did indicate that some schools operated in French and others in English. When collegiate departments were established in 1885, the legislative amendment stated that the objective was "laying the foundations of a thorough education in the English or French language and literature." Since French textbooks were prescribed by the Catholic section of the Board, and English textbooks by the Protestant section, it would appear that linguistic and confessional differentiation were linked together.[3]

The Catholic schools, however, were not taught exclusively in French because there was a recognition on the part of the clergy that immigration, and especially migration from Eastern Canada, was altering the demographic balance, which had existed in Manitoba at the time of Union, in favour of Anglo-Celtic peoples and Protestants.[4] As early as 1877, *Le Métis* sounded the alarm, calling on all francophones to unite "to resist tyranny and to defend liberty of conscience and the rights of the minority on the school questions, as well as on all other questions."[5] There was no hostility to English settlement *per se,* only fear that the bicultural character of the West would be undermined. In that same year (1877), Father Lacombe, in correspondence with Bishop Taché concerning the colonization of the West with francophones, deplored the difficulty in obtaining bilingual teachers for Catholic schools. He went to Europe to recruit because Quebec was a very unfruitful source of bilingual teachers. In 1883, thanks in good measure to Lacombe's efforts, a French (Breton) order of teaching sisters which operated schools in England sent five bilingual teachers to Brandon, five to Prince Albert and four to the Métis settlement of St. Laurent. In rural homogeneously French settlements such as Ste. Anne or St. Pierre, Taché could continue to send unilingual teachers.[6]

As criticism of the dual confessional school system grew, in large measure because the system no longer comfortably fitted the socio-cultural contours, there developed an ethnic tension. Father Lewis Drummond, a French-Irish priest told the Manitoba Historical Society in 1886: "Thirty years ago, we who speak French were called by every one purely and simply 'Canadians'; others were known as English, Scotch or Irish. Lately the fashion has grown up of calling others Canadians and distinguishing us as French."[7] Superintendent T. A. Bernier of the Catholic schools warned in his annual report for 1886 that immigration was threatening dualism and therefore francophones would have to mount an "eternal vigilance."[8] Electioneering politicians sometimes called for the abolition of the official use of French. One widely circulated pamphlet of 1887 called for the exclusion of French "from our legislature, from our courts, from our statutes, and from our public schools."[9] The francophone community, at least its clerical leaders, seemed to place faith in the alleged visit of Messrs. Alloway and Greenway to the Archiepiscopal palace in St. Boniface in 1888 to deliver a Liberal pledge to Rev. Father Joachim Allard, Vicar General, that the official status of French and the dual school system were not in danger.[10]

There would develop the hypothesis that the federal and provincial Liberals — Mowat, Laurier, Greenway — deliberately provoked the Manitoba School Question in 1890 in order to break the basis of Conservative power, i.e., the alliance between tolerant Ontario Toryism and the conservative Quebec Bleus. According to this conspiracy thesis, which Rev. Father Gonthier expounded in a letter to *abbé* Lindsay, and which was sent on to the Vatican secretary of State on the occasion of Prime Minister Laurier's visit to Rome in August, 1897, the Manitoba Liberals undertook to restore or retain the rights of French instruction under a centralized non-sectarian school system.[11]

Whereas demographic changes forced the Catholic schools to move towards bilingualism these same changes influenced the Protestant public schools away from a predominantly Anglican character to a denominational bias and eventually to a common non-sectarian brand of Protestantism. The arrival of Mennonites and Icelanders in the 1870s had given rise to the assumption that these ethnic bloc settlements would eventually have their schools incorporated into the Protestant/English school system. There was little in the austere pietistic religion of the Mennonites or the Lutheranism of the Icelanders to indicate any affinity with the Catholic brand of public schooling. Furthermore, many of the Ontario migrants to Manitoba were of Clear Grit persuasion, adherents for the most part of the Methodist or

Presbyterian churches. It was not unusual for them to spearhead fundamental changes in the Manitoba constitution: the abolition of the Legislative Council; changes in the system of representation, substitution of the municipal for the parish system of local government; abrogation of the official status of French in the provincial courts, legislature and official records. All these were matters which altered the bicultural basis of Manitoba, which moved it away from the Quebec model to the Ontario model.

In 1874 contingents of Kleine Gemeinde and Bergthaler Mennonites settled on the East Reserve and the following year Old Colony (Fuerstenland) Mennonites settled on the West Reserve. All of these communities established church schools as they felt they were entitled to do, according to the tenth clause of the Lowe Memorandum setting forth the terms of agreement of emigration. It read: "The fullest privilege of exercising their religious principles is by law afforded to the Mennonites without any kind of molestation or restriction whatever, and the same privilege extends to the education of their children in schools."[12] The Mennonites in general assumed they would neither be required to support nor be required to have their children attend the public schools. The Protestant community, however, saw them as white Anglo-Saxon evangelical Protestants who would soon abandon their pietist Anabaptist position (which stressed pacifism and separation from the "world") to join in supporting those public schools which were under the jurisdiction of the Protestant section of the Board of Education.

By 1878 ten Mennonite schools in the East Reserve had registered with the Protestant section and had qualified for the legislative grant, although they continued to operate with their own non-professional teachers, following their own curriculum, and teaching in German. Great debates ensued among the Mennonites whether by accepting state schools they were not abandoning their original agreement with the Dominion government and undermining their own basic guarantees. Four schools withdrew from the public school system by 1880, and Bishop Gerhard Wiebe of the Bergthaler community informed the authorities that they believed "that all matters in connection with schools should be left to our own decision," also that there was merit "not to act in these matters different than our brethren of the Western Reserve who have never yet accepted the grant."[13]

William Hespeler, the honorary German consul in Winnipeg who had acted as immigration agent in Europe, was appointed to inspect Mennonite schools with a view to encouraging them to abandon the traditional church school system developed by Johann Cornies in South Russia. Hespeler resigned after two unsuccessful years. What he had failed to obtain through persuasion was achieved in some measure by the relocation of approximately 300 Bergthaler families from the swampy lands of the East Reserve to the agriculturally productive West Reserve. When they abandoned their closed village plan in favour of individual farms, the provincial authorities urged them to accept Protestant public schools. The Provincial Secretary went so far as to suggest to certain liberal-minded Mennonites that if they organized public schools they would be empowered to levy school rates on all property owners, including their more conservative brethren. Consequently, some conservatives declared that acceptance of the provincial grant was the equivalent of renouncing the privileges and guarantees of the Lowe Memorandum. A few school districts returned their legislative grants rather than be bound, according to their interpretation, to comply with provincial school regulations.

Wilhelm Rempel sought to reassure troubled parents and trustees in the twenty-two Mennonite public schools operating in 1886 over which he was assigned inspectoral jurisdiction. Also, the Protestant section of the Board of Education strengthened its prescribed religious exercises and its provisions for religious (i.e., Biblical) instruction, in such a manner as to enable Mennonites to put their own sectarian stamp on their local public schools. Still, many Mennonites remained aloof from the provincial system.

Then, in 1888, a Mr. W. Thiem-White was appointed inspector-instructor with the responsibility of visiting the schools, giving model lessons, providing teachers with some pedagogical information, and organizing new school districts. He informed the central educational authorities of "the nature of the difficulties to be overcome in providing for the education of the Mennonite people."[14] Thiem-White's reports were quite negative: fewer than half the school-age population attended provincially supported schools; the teachers were "illiterate and without ambition toward improvement, their work in the school room is useless or nearly so;" the course of study was extremely inadequate and consisted in good measure of religious indoctrination; the teachers were accorded very low status and were paid accordingly. The Protestant section of the Board decided, at its meeting of 7 March 1889, to notify all Mennonite schools that unless they complied with all the articles of the School Act and the regulations of the Board concerning instruction in English, use of authorized textbooks, conformity with standard curriculum, and the professional training of teachers, no financial assistance would be forthcoming.[15]

Five Bergthaler ministers organized a School Association which had among its objectives the creation of a Normal School in Gretna. Dr. George Bryce, chairman of the Board of Education, assisted them in obtaining the services of Heinrich Ewert, the son of one of the twelve Mennonite delegates who had "spied out the land" in 1873, a graduate of the Kansas State Normal School in Emporia and professor at the Halstead Seminary, as Principal. On the eve of the school crisis of 1890 there were only eight Mennonite schools operating under the Protestant section of the Board of Education and at least 150 private church-operated schools.

The Icelandic immigration which began in 1875, by contrast, was marked by a strong attachment to public schooling and a steadfast determination to learn English and to become assimilated. This was all the more remarkable because they had founded their ethnic reserve, New

Iceland, on the west shore of Lake Winnipeg in the territory of Keewatin just north of the Manitoba provincial boundary.[16] Swedes and Russian Jews also trickled into the province but they did not acquire reserves of land and they, like the Icelanders, did not attempt to establish their own school system. In other words, in 1890 there were immigrant groups which did not challenge the model of Anglo-conformity or the institution of common non-sectarian public schools.

It is significant that when Manitoba passed an act creating a centralized Department of Education, to replace the dual confessional Board of Education, and an act to abolish Catholic public schools, much of the rhetoric revolved about the concept of "national" schools. It was not only the French, but also Mennonites, Icelanders, Germans, Poles, Swedes and Jews who had to be channelled into the assimilating experiences of the public school, somewhat on the model of the American public school. Archbishops Taché and Langevin responded to the abolition of the dual confessional system by opening "free schools" (écoles libres) in opposition to "national schools" in areas of heterogeneous settlement and by encouraging taxpayers, trustees and teachers to retain the essential religious and ethnic qualities in areas of homogeneous settlement. The school legislation was still silent on the matter of language(s) of instruction, so that French could be employed with equal justification in the public school system as in the private and parochial schools.

Although francophone colonizing agents, especially the colonizing clergy, redoubled their efforts to find suitable teachers as well as settlers, Langevin's resistance movement ran into problems. Firstly, the Manitoba government brought down further legislation in 1894 requiring that "any school not operating according to the Act shall not be called a Public School and therefore shall not qualify for the legislative grant." Municipalities could no longer grant money to, or levy and collect taxes for the support of, schools operating as francophone écoles libres or Mennonite church schools. Secondly, the European immigrants did not always see eye to eye with their French-Canadian coreligionists on matters of public schooling; they often required what Dom Benoit of Notre-Dame de Lourdes called re-educating.[17] Thirdly, many teaching orders in Quebec and continental Europe which were approached with a view to staffing schools in Manitoba and the North-West Territories showed little interest in the Canadian West. The immediate result was that a number of schools in francophone districts — e.g., St. Claude, St. Alphonse, St. Eustache — decided to come under the public school umbrella. Finally, although most Mennonite elders had as strong objections to the school legislation as had Archbishop Langevin, they failed to form a common front.

Most Mennonites found it impossible to operate their local schools according to their principles and still qualify for public support. Catholic efforts to have the legislation of 1890 and 1894 rescinded or amended intensified the debate which raged within the Mennonite communities over the relative merits of church and state schools. By 1891, approximately three-quarters of the Bergthalers on the West Reserve led by Bishop Abraham Doerksen formed a separate communion at Sommerfeld committed to church-controlled schooling. The Bergthalers on the East Reserve reorganized formally as the Chortitz Community and continued to oppose public schools. On the West Reserve the most conservative group, the Old Colony or Fuerstenland people, not only opposed surrendering their charter right to church schools but also insisted upon the use of the German language.

The majority of Manitobans appeared to accept the concept of "national schools." The daily press argued that if public schooling had been found necessary in a country like Britain, then its necessity was even greater in a new community like Manitoba which had a heterogeneous and polyglot population. At a public meeting in Gladstone, for example, a speaker supported the school legislation on the following grounds: "Where we have so many different nationalities, it is necessary to have some time to bind them together and blend all their characteristics in one nationality."[18] Dr. George Boyce told the Manitoba College Literary Society that the "Canadian national spirit declared the unity of the people to be essential. Mennonites, Icelanders, Hungarians, Jews and others will not be Canadians unless they are educated into the spirit of our land. Out of this grew our great public school movement of 1891."[19]

By 1896, Mgr. A. Langevin had become preoccupied with the question of the professional qualifications of "his" teachers. He insisted on them being effectively bilingual in order to meet certification requirements and to satisfy the school inspectors and a growing proportion of parents. Also, the Catholic hierarchy in Western Canada was conscious that the flow of European Catholic immigrants could redress the proportional decline of Catholic strength in the West. Furthermore, an emphasis on languages of instruction rather than on confessional "separate" schools could result in a new regrouping of forces within the public school system. Mgr. Albert Pascal expressed these sentiments most succinctly in a memorandum to Prime Minister Wilfrid Laurier:

> The want of schools is also greatly to be regretted. The government should furnish a teacher gratuitously during the next two or three years in each new centre of settlement where there are 20 or 25 children of school age. These teachers should be qualified to teach the two official languages, French and English, to children of French origin, English and German to German children, English and Polish to Polish children, &c., &c. The teacher should also speak not only the English language but the language of the people amongst whom he is living, so as to be understood. If they hold good certificates from foreign countries or from other Provinces, they should be accepted at least for a year, or for always if they speak English, until we have teachers in sufficient numbers who have passed the examinations prescribed by the Government.[20]

By this time, the aggrieved minority had attempted unsuccessfully to obtain satisfaction through disallowance, appeals to the courts, remedial order-in-council and remedial legislation.

The defeat of the federal Conservative government in 1896 and the assuming of power by the Laurier Liberals made possible the famous Laurier-Greenway Compromise (more accurately it was a Tarte-Sifton agreement) which was announced on November 19, 1896 and which was incorporated into the new School Act of 1897. Clause 10 of the agreement read: "Where ten of the pupils in any school speak the French language (or any language other than English) as their native tongue, the teaching of such pupils shall be conducted in French (or such other language) and English upon the bi-lingual system."[21]

For the first time, Manitoba legislation laid down specific provisions for language(s) of instruction. Although each school district could have only a single bilingual character (e.g., English-German, English-Ruthenian), the province could have an unspecified variety of bilingual systems according to the ethnic communities which petitioned the authorities. The legislation invited the development of inspection services, teacher training programmes, curriculum, centralized examinations and authorized textbooks for each of these bilingual fragments. The Icelanders openly declared in favour of English public schools, but the "French" (Canadiens), "Germans" (mostly Mennonites) and "Ruthenians" (Ukrainians) organized their own teachers' associations and conventions and their own school trustees' associations and conventions.

Recognition had been accorded also to the social reality that if the public schools were to be employed as one of the chief agencies of cultural assimilation, then it was necessary to induce the children of the ethnic communities to attend these schools. There were grave legal reservations about the validity of any proposed compulsory attendance legislation. Therefore, if Dr. George Bryce's plan for assimilating the immigrants were to be achieved, the schools would have to be made more attractive to these ethnic groups.

The Compromise of 1897 could be interpreted as shifting the emphasis from confessionalism to ethnicity. The *Manitoba Free Press* was later to publish the following explanation of this bilingual provision:

> In order to avoid exciting anti-French prejudices in Ontario and elsewhere, the concession as to bilingual teaching was not limited to the French, but was made general to all non-English residents in the Province of Manitoba in the expectation that it would be taken advantage of only by the French and by them in a limited degree and by a few and diminishing number of Mennonite communities.[22]

The Catholic hierarchy, at least its Ultramontane bishops, had not been a party to this compromise. On the contrary, the negotiations carried on with Manitoba Liberal officials by Israel Tarte and Henri Bourassa did not satisfy Archbishop Langevin, largely because he was excluded from their confidence. Langevin attacked the language clause which placed Franco-Manitobans "on the same basis as the coming hordes of the future that Sifton saw." In a sermon delivered in his cathedral church, he protested:

... we who came as the pioneers into the country, who discovered it, have not more than the last arrivals, we whose rights are guaranteed by the constitution, are placed on the same footing as those who came from Ireland or the depths of Russia, we are not better apportioned than the Chinese and Japanese.[23]

Henceforth, bilingualism would mean English and any second language and would not be restricted to French-English dualism that historically had preceded the flow of foreign immigration.

But this did not necessarily work to the disadvantage of the francophone communities. Whereas in 1896 there had been only 25 French schools in the public system, by 1900 there were 84 schools under the jurisdiction of Rober Goulet "inspector of French-English schools". Two years later, there were 105 such schools and only six *écoles libres* in Manitoba. In the provincial election of 1899 the Conservatives called for the defeat of the Greenway government and *règlement défectueux,* i.e., a "defective, imperfect, insufficient" remedy as Leo XIII's encyclical *Affari Vos* called it.[24] But the Liberals argued that a vote for them was a vote for the certainty of preserving their present concessions and the hope of obtaining further ones. The provincial trend was for the Conservatives but the three predominantly French-Canadian constituencies of St. Boniface, La Vérendrye and Carillon all returned Liberal members.

The French-English bilingual schools continued to experience problems in finding qualified teachers as those who were eager to leave France because they viewed the secularization of education there as persecution, knew no English, and Quebec teachers seemed increasingly unwilling to learn English or come West. Moreover, the bilingual teachers in the system were not always fully qualified and it became increasingly difficult to obtain provisional authorizations or to dissimulate their true professional status. In 1902, for example, one-third of the teachers in the French-English bilingual schools had no diplomas. Moreover, Mgr. Langevin acknowledged in 1908 that he sometimes had to employ threats to persuade parents and trustees in francophone districts to maintain French instruction.[25]

Meanwhile, among the Mennonites Heinrich Ewert struggled to overcome conservative religious opposition to state schools with their centralized bureaucratic control and their emphasis on English and civic indoctrination. The experience of the Swiss-origin Mennonites of Ontario with bilingual schools in the nineteenth century was known. By 1899, Ewert had only 34 schools under his inspection; he increased this to 41 by 1902. That the quality of instruction and the qualifications of the teachers were below standard is apparent from Ewert's reports, although their tone was generally laudatory and optimistic. Ewert did succeed in making many Mennonites conscious of their German culture and their place among the German *Volk.* In an era of Anglo-Saxon racism and admiration of German scientific advancement these qualities were respected by the host society.

The greatest source of contention was the fact that when more liberal-minded Mennonites (usually Bergthalers) organized a public school district on Ewert's advice all the ratepayers, including a large number of conservative-minded Mennonites who opposed state schools in principle, were required by law to pay school rates.[26] In the election campaign of 1903, the provincial Conservatives were able to convince these aggrieved conservative Mennonites to break with their traditional abstention of exercising their franchise. They voted for the Conservative candidate and after the elections the Department of Education dismissed H. H. Ewert. The loss of his inspector's salary was not sufficient however to induce him to resign as principal of the Gretna teacher training institute because some liberal Bergthalers rallied to his support.[27]

Henry Graff was charged with inspecting Mennonite schools pending more permanent arrangements. He reported an undue resort to "permit teachers," irregular school attendance, few teacher candidates, but also zealous employment of the religious exercises and religious instruction clauses in the school legislation, and good quality instruction in German.[28]

With the appointment of J. M. Friesen as special inspector the provincial authorities hoped to bring all the Mennonite schools into the German-English bilingual system. However, the flag debate of 1907 marred the plan. The official report gave the essential results: no new school districts organized, objection to compulsory flying of the Union Jack on schools as a violation of the pacifist guarantees made by the Dominion government in 1873, fear that schools were being used to break down Mennonite fundamental beliefs and to force conformity to the "world" on the youth.[29] British views of "Germans" were changing also as the naval race and the colonial rivalry intensified between Germany and Great Britain. The Mennonites were now divided along sectarian progressive/reactionary lines, and also on such issues as the role of German in schooling, the support to be given to competing School Associations and their associated teachers' and trustees' conventions, and the support to be given either to the Gretna institute, or to the Altona institute, or to the provincial Normal courses in Morden. The Department of Education solicited written complaints to be employed at an opportune moment for the dismissal of J. M. Friesen.[30] Patronage and political intrigue were being employed in the ethnic community to forestall the efforts of "survivalist" elements to manipulate provincial school provisions to the achievement of their group objectives. What the provincial bureaucrats expected from the bilingual system was ethnic social disintegration and assimilation, not cultural transmission of group values and ethnic perpetuation.

The beginning of a wave of Ukrainian and Polish immigrants in 1897, ostensibly to engage in farming but forced by circumstances to turn also to the railways, mines and lumber camps, gave the bilingual system a new dimension. Those who settled in rural Manitoba, east of the Red River in marginal farm lands, in the Interlake country, and in the parkland belt west from Clan William along the south of the Riding Mountains and around Dauphin could be expected to make some demand for bilingual schools.

326

The parents, although largely of peasant origins with little formal education, gave the impression of being sufficiently motivated to realize the benefits of schooling for their children. A typical inspectoral report read:

> The large number of Galicians who have lately settled in the vicinity of Stuartburn has increased the school population of this district to a considerable extent. The children are bright, intelligent and most anxious to acquire a knowledge of the English language. They are well-behaved in school and easily managed.[31]

As the Ukrainians became aware of the possibility of organizing bilingual schools they naturally favoured these. The provincial authorities were faced with the immediate problem of finding qualified teachers to staff such schools, also with the long range problem of ascertaining the results of an expansion of the bilingual system to encompass an undetermined number of ethnic groups.

However much Archbishop Langevin had deplored the granting of equal school rights to all ethnic minorities, he very soon rallied to the concept and sought to exploit it to Catholic advantage. He obtained from Premier R. Roblin in 1901 a promise for support of Ukrainian, Polish and German schools.[32] In public addresses he strongly defended the teaching of the mother tongues of the immigrant communities, telling Catholic audiences in particular that in preserving the Ukrainian, Polish and German tongues the faith was being preserved.

> Schools must be established among them in which the English language will be taught according to the requirements of the law, but since the law concedes bilingual instruction, that is to say instruction of another tongue besides English for those who do not speak the latter, these strangers have the right to have their children taught in their own language, and that is their most ardent wish. But if all admit that English must be taught in Manitoba schools, not all are also of the opinion that one must teach also the mother tongue of the Galicians; a few even have proclaimed very loudly that it would be better to teach only English everywhere! An exorbitant, unjust and dangerous pretention which endangers the peace of our country.[33]

This was an extension of the traditional French-Canadian Ultramontane ideology of the inseparable relationship between language and religion.

Similarily, the Anglo-Celtic Protestants were not unaware of the advantages to be gained through support of the ethnic minorities. The Presbyterians in particular promoted an interest that had developed in 1898 when two young "Galicians" called on the Principal of Manitoba College requesting entrance in order to obtain "an English education." Dr. James Robertson, Superintendent of Home Missions in Western Canada, indicated in a public interview that the Ukrainians "should be put into the great Anglo-Saxon mill and be ground up" because "in the grinding they lose their foreign prejudices and characteristics."[34]

It was only a matter of time before the Archdiocese of St. Boniface and the Home Missions Board of the Presbyterian Church found themselves in open competition for the souls of Slavic immigrants and for the control of their schools, including control of the teacher training institutions and the inspection services which were natural bureaucratic outgrowths of the legislative provisions of 1897. In 1901, Archdeacon Fortin and Dr. Reid, a medical missionary at Sifton, called a closed meeting to discuss the possibility of bringing all Ruthenian-English bilingual schools under the direction of Manitoba College; Archbishop Langevin called a mass meeting of Catholic educators on January 5, 1902 to publicize his opposition to this segment of public schools coming under sectarian Protestant control. On January 16th a joint meeting of Catholic and Protestant representatives was held at the Winnipeg City Hall to discuss the question of education of immigrant children. No new solutions were proposed, but at least the Fortin-Reid plan had been blocked.

Then, in 1903, there arrived in Manitoba a self-styled Archbishop Seraphim, *alias* Stefan Ustvolski, who was under both interdict and excommunication of the Russian Orthodox Church following his incarceration at the monastery of Suzdalski for presumed insanity. He had come at the invitation of two Ukrainians favourable to Presbyterian missionary work — the editor of *Kanadijski Farmar* (Canadian Farmer) which followed the Liberal party line, and an immigration agent stationed in Winnipeg. Within a few months he had gathered a number of adherents, a number of whom he "ordained" as priests; within a year, the pastors of this schismatic sect organized the Independent Greek Church with John Bodrug as its senior minister.[35] This sectarian movement, tacitly supported by the Presbyterians who hoped to eventually absorb its adherents, very rapidly made its influence felt in school affairs.

In 1903, the Department of Education appointed John Baderski, a Polish Catholic, "organizer of schools."[36] The Independent Greek Church alerted the Protestant community against the allegedly undue influence of the Archdiocese of Saint-Boniface in the matter, while the Orthodox community feared another thinly disguised Polish and Magyar move to assimilate Ukrainians. Eventually the opposition lobby prevailed on the Conservative government and Baderski was replaced by a Ukrainian who also preached for the Independent Greek Church. Theodore Stefanik, the new school organizer, was much attached to his ethnic community, despite his Protestant leanings, and he made several recommendations for the expansion and improvement of the bilingual system. The insistence on bilingual "Ruthenian-English" readers, for example, drew the comment from the Deputy Minister that "under the bi-lingual system the teacher shall use his knowledge of Ruthenian as a medium of explanation, and do his teaching in English."[37]

The adoption of the democratic system of local school government resulted in Ukrainian parents and trustees demanding teachers of ther own ethnic group to staff their bilingual schools. The provincial authorities faced a dilemma. They had little inclination to recognize East European teaching certificates or to employ members of Catholic religious orders.[38] The alternative was to open a teacher-training institute, although there was always the possibility that this could encourage the expansion of the bilingual system.

In February 1905, the Roblin Conservative government opened a Ruthenian Training School in Winnipeg for the preparation of Ukrainian and Polish young men who would teach in the bilingual schools. The school was headed by a Yorkshireman who initially viewed the enterprise as "an act of self-preservation on the part of the state" but who came to view his task as one of great national service in character building, civilizing and Christianizing teacher-candidates. The school was soon relocated in Brandon, near an English Normal School, away from the seat of Catholic strength, and in the Minister of Education's predominantly Anglo-Celtic riding. The few Ukrainian instructors associated with the institute were of known Protestant leanings.

Archbishop Langevin protested vigorously and extracted the promise that a training school for Polish teachers would be organized in Winnipeg. But he was filled with bitterness when a Protestant was proposed as Principal of this second institute. He wrote confidentially to Premier Roblin:

> If things are such, and if you cannot see your way through granting us a Normal School for Galicians with a principal and, perhaps, an assistant, that we can trust, my idea is that we better leave aside the scheme; but the feeling of our Galicians, Poles and Ruthenians in Winnipeg and outside, and the feelings of other Catholics will be bitter against the Government and I will not blame them. Why did Mr. Rogers promise me so positively a Normal School for *our* Galicians if this school falls in the hands of our adversaries as it was the case with the first normal school now in Brandon and when Catholic pupils are under a Presbyterian ruling.[39]

The assumption of the chief officials in the Department of Education was that Manitoba would be an English-speaking and British province. Bilingual schools were a stage in the achievement of this ideal and were not conceived as being a permanent feature of the multilingual and multicultural province.

The bilingual school provision which was introduced in 1897 to assist in the reduction of ethno-religious tensions in Manitoba and throughout Canada did not have the desired effect in Manitoba. It may be argued that the Manitoba School Question became a less volatile political issue in Ontario and Quebec; however, in Manitoba, the raising of the ethnic problem tended to perpetuate old rivalries and to create new tensions.

The delicate balance between French and English-speaking Manitobans, upon which the provincial constitution and the first school legislation reposed, was quickly altered in the 1870s. Immigration and migration which included but a mere trickle of francophones altered the demographic base of the charter groups. The arrival of Mennonites and Icelanders accentuated revisions in favour of the Anglo-Celtic host society. The Mennonites long remained aloof of public schools but they had little in common with the Franco-Manitobans. The Icelanders were anxious to become integrated rapidly into the English-speaking Protestant-oriented world of the dominant society. The Manitoba School Question was the outcome, in some measure at least, of this readjustment in ethnic relations. The Mennonites were as disturbed by the imposition of a common non-sectarian public school system with overtones of political indoctrination as were the Franco-Manitobans, although not for precisely the same reasons.

The Compromise of 1897 opened the door to the possibility of ethnic group perpetuation through the bilingual school system. Designed as a measure of relief from the legislation of 1890-94 for Franco-Manitobans, whose Catholicism was sometimes said to be more repugnant to Anglo-Celtic Protestants than their French character, the legislation could not be restricted to them. The Mennonites would only slowly and reluctantly come to the viewpoint that the system offered them advantages. The Ukrainians and Poles, on the other hand, soon saw advantages in the bilingual compromise. The development of their bilingual schools, together with the necessary trained teachers, bilingual textbooks, special curriculum and separate inspection service aroused and perpetuated the kind of ethno-religious rivalries which the Compromise had been designed to remedy.

Archbishop Langevin and his clergy, by seeking to unite all Catholic ethnic minorities in order to obtain a recovery of the school rights enjoyed prior to 1890, failed to counterbalance the Anglo-Celtic dominant group. More important, they failed to obtain parity between francophone and anglophone communities. Indeed, through identification of the Franco-Manitoban cause with that of the immigrant groups, they paved the way for a permanent identification of Franco-Manitobans as just another fragment of the multiethnic mosaic.

FOOTNOTES

[1]The polemical works include: George Bryce, "The Manitoba School Question," *Canadian Magazine,* Vol. I, No. 7 (September, 1893), pp. 511-516; John S. Ewart, *The Manitoba School Question* (Toronto, 1894); J. Fisher, *The Manitoba School Question: A Series of Four Letters* (Winnipeg, 1895); Louis P. Kribs, *The Manitoba School Question* (Toronto, 1895); D'Alton McCarthy, "The Manitoba School Laws," *Canadian Magazine,* Vol. I, No. 5 (July, 1893), pp. 1-4; G. Smith, "The Manitoba School Question," *Forum,* Vol. 21 (March, 1896), pp. 65-73; F. C. Wade, *The Manitoba School Question* (Winnipeg, 1895); G. M. Weir, *The Separate Schools Question in Canada* (Toronto, 1934). More scholarly treatments are given in: Lovell Clark, *The Manitoba School Question: Majority Rule or Minority Rights?* (Toronto, 1968); L. Clark & W. L. Morton, "David Mills and the Remedial Bill of 1896," *Journal of Canadian Studies,* Vol. I, No. 3 (November, 1966), pp. 50-53; Gilbert Comeault, "Archbishop Langevin, Schools, and Politics in Manitoba, 1895-1915," (Unpublished Honours essay, University of Manitoba, 1970); J. R. Miller, "D'Alton McCarthy, Equal Rights, and the Origins of the Manitoba School Question," *Canadian Historical Review,* Vol. LIV, No. 4 (December, 1973), pp. 369-392; W. L. Morton, "Manitoba Schools and Canadian Nationality, 1890-1932," *Canadian Historical Association Annual Report* (Ottawa, 1951), pp. 51-59; D. A. Schmeiser, *Civil Liberties in Canada* (Oxford, 1964); C. B. Sissons, *Church and State in Canadian Education* (Toronto, 1959).

[2]*P.A.M.,* Education Box I, An Act to Establish a System of Education in Manitoba, 1871, clause 7.

[3]For a more complete account of French instruction in Manitoba public schools, especially the "legal vacuum" which existed from 1871 to 1897 and from 1916 to 1965, see my "French Public Education in Manitoba, 1818-1965," *Revue de l'Université d'Ottawa,* Vol. 38 (janvier-mars, 1968), 19-34.

⁴The decennial census of 1891 indicated that out of a population of 108,017 in Manitoba, only 7,555 had been born in Quebec, while 46,630 had been born in Ontario. The total number of Roman Catholics was 20,571, or less than one-fifth of the total population.
⁵*Le Métis*, January 18, 1877.
⁶I am much indebted to Professor Robert Painchaud of the University of Winnipeg who has generously shared information relating to schools. For an authoritative study of francophone emigration and migration to the West we must await his doctoral thesis.
⁷L. Drummond, "The French Element in the Canadian North-West," *Transactions of the Historical and Scientific Society of Manitoba,* No. 28 (1887), 14.
⁸*P.A.M.,* PR 10/7, Department of Education, Letterbook of Superintendent of Catholic Schools, Report for 1886.
⁹P. H. Attwood, *A Jubilee Essay on Imperial Confederation as affecting Manitoba and the Northwest* (Winnipeg, 1887), p. 15. I differ with Lovell Clark and others who maintain there was little or no dissatisfaction with the school system prior to 1889 and that D'Alton McCarthy's intervention provoked a sudden assault on the system. W. L. Morton puts it into its correct historical context: ". . . the feeling was there. The grievance existed. The people's mind had only to be directed to it, and the moment attention was drawn to it, the province of Manitoba rose as one man and said, 'We want no dual language — and away with separate schools as well'." W. L. Morton, *Manitoba: A History* (Toronto, 1957), 244.
¹⁰Jean Des Prairies, *Une Visite dans les Ecoles du Manitoba* (Montreal, 1897), pp. 10-12. I am much indebted to M. Gilbert Comeault of the Provincial Archives of Manitoba for bringing to my attention important documents on this subject.
¹¹"Mémoire sur la question des Ecoles de Manitoba," *Revue d'historie de l'Amérique Française,* Vol. VI, No. 3 (décembre 1952), Gonthier to Lindsay, 3 July 1897, 440-2.
¹²*P.A.C.,* RG 17, Series 1-2, Department of Agriculture, Letterbook 1873, Vol. 18, John Lowe to David Klassen *et al.,* 26 July 1873, pp. 167-9. The Order-in-Council of 13 August 1873 differed substantially from the original wording because the law officers of the Crown recognized that education was largely within provincial jurisdiction. It read: "That the Mennonites will have the fullest privilege of exercising their religious principles and educating their children in schools, as provided by law, without any kind of molestation or restriction whatever." Report of the Committee of the Privy Council, 13 August 1873, together with Secret Memorandum of 28 July 1873, copies in the possession of the author.
¹³*P.A.M.,* Education Box I, Minute Book "C" of Protestant Section of Board of Education, 1880-1886, Gerhard Wiebe to Rev. Pinkham, May 11, 1881, 37-38.
¹⁴*P.A.M.* PR 10/7, J. B. Somerset Correspondence, Memorandums, Statistics Book, 1886-1889, J. B. Somerset to Provincial Secretary, February 13, 1889, 81-82.
¹⁵*Ibid.,* Circular letter of March 22, 1889, 97.
¹⁶F. H. Schofield, *The Story of Manitoba* (Winnipeg, 1913), Vol. I, pp. 380-382; James A. Jackson, *The Centennial History of Manitoba* (Winnipeg, 1970), 118-119, 151.
¹⁷*A.A.S.B.,* Fonds Langevin, Dom Benoit to Mgr. A. Langevin, October 1, 1896.
¹⁸*Gladstone Age,* April 17, 1895.
¹⁹Rev. George Bryce, *The New Canadianism,* Inaugural address of the Manitoba College Literary Society, November, 1898 (Winnipeg, 1898), 9.
²⁰*P.A.C.,* RG 15, Vol. 736, No. 420 689, Mgr. Albert Pascal to Hon. Wilfrid Laurier, November 18, 1896.
²¹*P.A.M.,* RG2, D1, Executive Council, "Memorandum of Settlement of School Question," Ottawa, 16 November 1896.
²²*Manitoba Free Press,* January 13, 1916.
²³*Winnipeg Tribune,* November 23, 1896.
²⁴*Le Manitoba,* October 25, 1899. The text of the encyclical is given in the *American Catholic Quarterly Review,* Vol. XXIII, No. 2(April 1897), 189-195.
²⁵*A.A.S.B.,* Fonds Langevin, Mgr. Langevin to Armand Lavergne, n.d., 1908.
²⁶*Manitoba: Sessional Papers, 1903,* No. 22, Report of H. H. Ewert for 1902, 598-600.
²⁷Further internal divisions somewhat undermined the Collegiate Institute in Gretna. In 1905 a majority of the Bergthaler supporters voted to move the institute to Altona, the centre of their religious and cultural activities. The School Association split over the issue and by 1908 part of the community was supporting the Mennonite Educational Institute in Altona, directed by J. J. Balzer, and part was supporting the Mennonite Collegiate Institute in Gretna, directed by H. H. Ewert. Religiously the Mennonites were fragmented more than ever as American-based evangelistic groups made successful inroads into their communities.
²⁸*Manitoba: Sessional Papers, 1906,* No. 7, Inspector Henry Graff's report for 1905, 411-13.
²⁹*Manitoba: Sessional Papers, 1908,* No. 8, Inspector J. M. Friesen's report for Mennonite Schools, 498-501.
³⁰*P.A.M.,* PR 10/7, Robert Fletcher Letterbook, 1905-1911, R. Fletcher to J. S. Wolkof, February 5, 1909, 659.
³¹Manitoba, *Report of the Department of Education, 1897* (Winnipeg, 1898), Inspector A. L. Young's report, 35.
³²*A.A.S.B.,* Fonds Langevin, Langevin to R. Roblin, January 28, 1901; also, Memorandum to Hon. Roblin, 1901, Letterbook 1900-1901, 646.

[33] *Les Clôches de Saint-Boniface,* Vol. I (January 1902), p. 8. Langevin had already obtained the promise of Belgian Redemptorists to serve as priests in Ukrainian parishes. The clearest statement from Archbishop Langevin concerning the policy of linking the School Question, European Catholic immigration, and Franco-American repatriation is contained in a letter to a colonizing priest in 1898. Cf. *A.A.S.B.,* Fonds Langevin, Letter Book I, Mgr. Langevin to abbé Jean Gaire, April 5, 1898. Clarification of the question of francophone immigration to the West and the role of the Catholic Church will have to wait the completion of the doctoral thesis of Professor Robert Painchaud, University of Winnipeg, to whom I am grateful for the above reference. In a memorandum to the Canadian hierarchy and to two East European cardinals, Langevin maintained that a common front would force a favourable settlement of the School Question. *A.A.S.B.,* Fonds Langevin, Memorandum to the Canadian episcopate and to Cardinals Rampalla and Ledowchowski, September 27, 1901.

[34] *Manitoba Free Press,* November 15, 1898.

[35] The Independent Greek Church survived for a decade before being absorbed by the Presbyterians. Bodrug was given an appointment as school organizer by the Saskatchewan Department of Education.

[36] *P.A.M.,* PR 10/7, Robert Fletcher Letterbook, 1905-1911, R. Fletcher to Inspector H. Graff, December 8, 1906, 236.

[37] *Ibid.,* R. Fletcher to D. P. McColl, November 24, 1908, 808.

[38] Archbishop A. Langevin had appealed to Count Goluchowski, Austrian Minister of External Affairs, in 1899 and to the Emperor Franz Josef, in 1904, for teachers and clergy. These appeals had met with no positive response.

[39] *A.A.S.B.,* Fonds Langevin, Mgr. Langevin to R. Roblin, February 6, 1909, 331.33.

THE HUNGARIAN SCHOOL QUESTION
MARTIN L. KOVACS
UNIVERSITY OF REGINA

The School Question in the West

At the risk of gross oversimplification it is assumed that the original School Question, whether in its Manitoban or North-West Territories-Saskatchewan versions, tended to centre not only on the preservation of established rights but also on the problem of the comparative relation between the numerical weight of the French-speaking element in the respective populations and the proportion and, therefore, the power and influence of the French Canadian clergy within the Catholic church of the West. One may argue that the clergy was clinging to its executive authority apart from reasons of simple seniority in order to be able to undertake measures for the expansion of the French population, or that it was bent on increasing the number of the French-speakers in an instinctive anticipation of a "Parkinson's Law," not yet verbalized. Whatever the motives that initially prevailed, the French Canadian clergy of the West seemed persistently to contest, for a number of years at first, a controlling interest then a gradually decreasing share in the direction of the educational efforts of the area.

Notwithstanding the resolute counter measures, the French clergy of St. Boniface achieved little else in this struggle, besides retaining relative control in Manitoban rural public school districts with French majority populations, than time for dignified yet certain retreats in its attempts to recover educational "rights" and the principle of "duality" lost in Manitoba and the former North-West Territories.[1] Behind the tough resistance Mgr. Adelard Langevin, the Archbishop of St. Boniface, tended to act as the diplomat, the politician, the strategist, the tactician, the directing general, in sum, as the mind responsible for many newsworthy items in Canadian history between 1895 and 1915. One of his most momentous conceptions and definitely the most relevant to the argument of this paper was constituted by his beginning after 1905 to regard immigrants from Eastern Central Europe, particularly Ukrainians and Hungarians, provided under French-speaking clerical leadership, as potential associates in the support of further attempts to accomplish the coveted aims.[2]

The real or imagined adversaries in this struggle included not only Protestants, liberals, freemasons, socialists but also English and French-speaking Catholics, and, at times, even the Vatican. It is perhaps not generally known that, in later years, the Catholic Hungarian settlers mainly of Saskatchewan became involved in the controversy under the leadership of a small group consisting chiefly of a Catholic priest, a Presbyterian minister, and the Catholic editor of the Winnipeg Hungarian paper owing to their disapproval of French clerical leadership and its alleged de-ethnicising tendencies. The only visible protagonist in this portion of the drama, representative of the views and interests of the Primate of St. Boniface, was the Rev. Jules Pirot, ably assisted by two other French-speaking priests named Vorst and Conter. It is contended that it was the Archbishop's policies, plans and instructions rather than Pirot's own initiatives, which were dutifully and energetically carried out by the Parish priest of Kaposvar (near Esterhazy, Saskatchewan). The most spectacular phase of the Hungarian controversy took place in 1910. Since that year proved unusually significant also concerning the conflict in Manitoba and the East of Canada it can be hypothesized that also the eruption before the general public of the "Hungarian Question" not widely known up to this stage, was due in a great measure to the clash of the same political forces as in the rest of the country. It is quite possible that the Hungarians had received prompting for their entry into the fray from liberal party quarters.[3] The confrontation between the French-speaking clergy and the Hungarian group tended to take place along three lines which although appearing different yet constituted a coherent unity. Thus the problems of whether to obtain Hungarian-speaking or native Hungarian priests, of forming Hungarian bilingual schools, and the existence and program of the Canadian Hungarian Brotherhood Association constituted what was called by Pirot the "Hungarian Question," or more explicit, the Question whether the Hungarian identity of the settlers should and could survive.

The Origins of the Problem

One important event preliminary to the flaring up of the demand and agitation for "Hungarian schools" was constituted by the visit of the Rev. Lajos Kovács, the parochial priest in New York, among the Hungarians of such places in the prairie provinces as Winnipeg and Woodridge in Manitoba, and Esterhazy, Kaposvar, and Stockholm in Saskatchewan. The visit, which took place in the middle of August, 1908, seems to have created considerable interest as expressed in some emotion-laden scenes according to a report in the Hungarian paper. The description also reveals some of the features of the life at that stage of the Hungarian farmers as well as their apparent and unrequited desire for listening to sermons or even plain speaking in the Hungarian language. Thus, for instance, Kovács' sermon in Stockholm proved so attractive for Hungarians in the area that they converged on the church from distant places and in their endeavour to be present not only did they use carts and buggies but also undertook quite long trips on foot as in the case of three women who, carrying food bundled in kerchiefs, walked fifteen miles to be able to listen to the words of the Hungarian priest. "A whole camp of horse drawn vehicles was staying in front of the church." Under the impact of the clergyman's sermon "the whole audience in the church all of a sudden began to cry."[4]

It is very likely that part of the discussions which the American Hungarian priest had with his Canadian compatriots referred to the existence and practices of schools in the United States which catered to the

pertinent linguistic and cultural needs of Hungarians residing in the
industrial cities and rural settlements of the United States. That such was
the case and that further contact existed between the Magyars of the
Canadian West and the Rev. L. Kovács is indicated by an item in the prairie
Hungarian paper disclosing the availability in New York City of an
"excellent certificated female teacher speaking Hungarian, English, French
and German with the same fluency," together with the remark that "A great
service would be done to the Hungarian cause if she could be attracted to
take up teaching" in Canada. The Rev. L. Kovács was quoted as able to
give further information.[5]

There is of course temptation to inquire into the New York priest's
motives and the source of funds for the tedious and long journey from the
American metropolis to the modest and little known Hungarian communities of the Canadian plains. It appears that in addition to his undoubted
interest in them both as Magyars and Catholics, Kovács was drawn to
Canada by the prospect of the establishment of a new ecclesiastical entity
possibly incorporating all the Hungarian Catholics of the prairie region in
connection with the special project of various socio-cultural agencies of
Hungary, the *Amerikai Akció* ("Operation America").[6]

The actual event which brought the question of Hungarian school and
instruction to public notice was the consecration of the Kaposvar church on
November 8, 1908.[7] The speeches made and the words uttered on this
occasion by the principal actors of the later controversy could hardly have
been friendlier and more indicative of reciprocal respect. Archbishop
Langevin was reported to have held the Hungarians up as a worthwhile
example for all Christian peoples to follow, and gone to the extent of
claiming that "for Canada Hungarian immigration was more beneficial
than the English or American." This opinion, of course, did not fail mightily
to please the Hungarian settlers and, from the viewpoint of the French
clergy, could at that stage scarcely be faulted. Pirot's request to the
Archbishop that a Hungarian priest be assigned to assist him in his work in
the Hungarian settlements of Saskatchewan must have been received with
approval by the Magyars who could understandably take it for granted that
the person of the Rev. Menyhért Érdujhelyi was meant. Besides, the Belgian
priest's desire expressed on the same occasion for church support towards
the creation of a Hungarian Catholic press seemed at that time innocent
enough not to draw comments.

On the other side Peter Németh, the editor of the Hungarian paper and
later one of the main anti-Pirot polemists, indulged in heaping praise upon
Woodcutter, Conter and Pirot as

> priests who all three had taught themselves to speak Hungarian and
> thus could carry on work among Hungarians like veritable apostles.[8]

As to Pirot, he confided in Németh, as claimed by the latter, to the
extent of revealing to him that

> the Hungarian people in Kaposvar, Esterhazy and Stockholm had in
> previous elections voted for the Liberal candidates, but would not do so

any more, because His Grace Archbishop Langevin proposed establishing a strong Catholic political party with the purpose that every
good Catholic voter would support this clerical party in opposition to
the Liberal government.[9]

Still, the later contentious issues were foreshadowed in Németh's
exhortation to his countrymen in the course of the festivities connected with
the consecration, to be not only good Catholics but also good Hungarians
and how essential it was for the greater prosperity of the western Canadian
Magyar community of the future to provide the younger generation with
schooling also in the Hungarian language. No matter how he really felt,
Pirot did not at that stage openly contradict Németh's ideas. In fact, two
months later the Hungarian paper was in a position to report as one of the
results of the Kaposvar consecration and concomitant discussions that
Németh's initiative to obtain a Hungarian teacher for Esterhazy was

> Not only adopted by the Rev. Jules Pirot ... but he has also taken steps
> in this direction with the government. ... The teacher's position will be
> advertised and applications should be submitted to the Rev. Jules Pirot,
> parochial priest of Kaposvar. The teacher's salary is six hundred dollars
> per year ($600.00). The teacher must be fluent in spoken and written
> English.[10]

There is no documentary evidence where, if ever, this advertisement
was published. Apart from the above reference one of Pirot's statements
indicates that he had advertised to no avail in American and Canadian
papers.[11]

The Pirot-Érdujhelyi Debate

Major deterioration in the relations between the parties to the
Pirot-Hungarian controversy occurred and the actual polemics began with
Érdujhelyi's article about the need for, and the possibility of, Hungarian
schools in Saskatchewan. While the inevitable importance of the study of
the English language and culture was not only admitted but clearly stressed
in his paper, Érdujhelyi briefly explained the available alternatives. He
drew attention to the feasibility of a separate school in contradistinction to
the setting up of a public school as   privately recommended to him by
Archbishop Langevin.[12]

Érdujhelyi's article contained a number of indications both of his own
and of the Hungarian peasant farmers' attitudes towards the problem of the
language. He identified the school question as "the most urgent and at the
same time the most difficult problem of the Canadian Hungarians." He
predicted "the Hungarians of Canada will shortly disappear without
[appropriate] schools." The Hungarian priest was among the first to observe
and comment upon the worries of many later Hungarian parents as well,
often repeated in a self-justifying manner, that "children will not be able to
learn perfect English from a Hungarian teacher." Érdujhelyi assumed that
the "indifference and apathy on the part of Hungarian farmers was largely
due to their continual anxiety lest the children learn proper English."[13] Of

course, he sensibly admitted the necessity for the youngsters of obtaining the best possible command of the English language but he emphasized, more emotionally and instinctively than through any rational arguments, the importance of the retention of the native language and culture for the group as a whole. The prospect in Saskatchewan of instruction in Hungarian language and culture appeared to him less than promising. He pointed out rather sweepingly and indiscretely that

> the state of affairs is different here [in Saskatchewan] from that in Hungary where the Slovaks, Roumanians, Serbians, and other sundry people could live for centuries without learning the Hungarian language ... [but here schools] in which children do not acquire the English language will be banned by the government without pity.[14]

In his estimation there would be some eight or ten significant Hungarian colonies in [western] Canada requiring Hungarian teachers, but it was difficult to acquire even an English teacher — as the Dunaföldvár School District[15] near Wakaw had discovered. Moreover, the school building for the Buda School District in the same neighbourhood stood already completed yet without a teacher.[16] The schools of the larger Hungarian colonies were all run by English [speaking] teachers. One of the difficulties of attracting Hungarian speaking teachers must have been the non-cooperation of Hungarians who, when asked for information about general conditions in the colonies, "frightened" away would-be applicants, as had actually happened in the case of Érdujhelyi himself when he had almost persuaded a female teacher to accept the position offered by him to her.[17]

Érdujhelyi's practical suggestions for the solution of the problem were based on publications of the Department of Education, Regina, as well as on discussions with Archbishop Langevin, who recommended, as has been shown above, the utilization for the purpose of the existing public school system where two-thirds of the teacher's salary was provided by the government. The Hungarian priest saw the merit of the fact that the government's contribution was in proportion with the level of qualifications of the teacher. Accordingly, Érdujhelyi became aware of the possibility that a highly qualified teacher could be given a very good salary which in turn would induce the person to stay in his position permanently. Such an individual would be allowed to teach the Hungarian language both prior to and after the regular school hours; however, he or she need not only be highly qualified, but also very proficient in the English language and capable both of teaching English and of passing the prescribed provincial examination. The fact that such Hungarian teachers were most difficult to find militated against schools of this kind.[18]

The only alternative to the public school arrangement Érdujhelyi saw in what he called in Hungarian, "private school," and in English, "separate school." In his opinion the school district could employ, in such a "separate school," a teacher without any teaching certificates [any teacher's training] provided he had the proper cultural background. In such a case the quality of the school building could correspond to the pecuniary means of the district. As to the language, religious instruction, the Magyar language, history and geography were to be taught in Hungarian, the rest of the subjects in English. The pupils were expected to receive thorough grounding in both languages. Since such a school was not subject to government supervision and consequently did not receive any state support the farmers had to contribute towards the maintenance of the school, but they were not obliged, Érdujhelyi asserted, to share the costs of a public school.[19]

However, much of the Hungarian priest's projection of an English-Hungarian bilingual school to which his "separate" school seems to have amounted was based more on wishful thinking than on dependable examination of the realities of the educational scene of the Province of Saskatchewan of the era. First of all his command of English was not yet sufficient to enable him to appreciate the *nuances* in the text of the publications of the Department of Education. In fact, he had to ask Pirot to translate for him the pertinent regulations in the latter's broken and not quite adequate Hungarian.[20]

Pirot regarded it as important to correct the inaccuracies in Érdujhelyi's article perhaps not anticipating that, as it were, an intellectual "avalanche" was being precipitated. But, on the other hand, he might have been working towards a showdown intentionally. First of all he pointed out that the term "separate school" only referred to a religious and not ethnic institute. In other words, such a school was attended by children of the same denomination rather than of the same ethnicity. Consequently Érdujhelyi's Magyar school would be a "free school" neither supervised, nor supported by the Education Department and as such not mentioned in the School Ordinance.[21] Furthermore, in districts inhabited by denominationally mixed populations the only type of school permissible was the public school.[22] Significantly, the Hungarian priest's worst factual error, in alleging that the supporters of a "separate school" were not obliged to contribute towards the maintenance of public schools, was highlighted as such by his Belgian confrere. Apparently Pirot did not feel content with the mere correction of Érdujhelyi's factual slips and introduced a measure of personal innuendo and reproach.[23]

Érdujhelyi having, in the best of circumstances, a very high capacity for emotional impression could not let Pirot's article go unanswered. The Hungarian priest revealed his sources of specific information, in the persons of two German Benedictines who had disclosed to him that the main subjects at the "German school" of Munster were instructed in German and the others in English, and that no governmental objection had been forthcoming to German as the language of instruction.[24] Therefore, Érdujhelyi claimed, his main error was only semantic when he mistranslated the German name *Pfarschule* ("parochial school") as "separate school." This is how he had given an opportunity to Pirot to misunderstand him:

I do not want to brood over words therefore if the term means so much let us name the Hungarian schools free schools or parochial schools. The name does not matter to me ... and if the Canadian German children are allowed to learn in German and in English at the parochial schools then also the Hungarian children may learn in Hungarian and in English at parochial schools ... consequently in contradiction to Pirot's assertion that it is impossible to organize Hungarian schools in Canada according to my desire: I most decidedly adhere to my assertion and repeatedly recommend to my Hungarian compatriots the organization of Hungarian parochial schools after the pattern of the Canadian German schools. . . .[25]

In yet another article entitled "The Hungarian School Question,"[26] Pirot took it upon himself both to reply to Érdujhelyi's second article in the polemics and to sum up the essential features of the controversy in what he called "the final word about the Hungarian schools." In addition to repeatedly commenting upon the erroneous portions of the Hungarian priest's first article, he once again emphasized the fact that there was no possibility for the Hungarian settlements to establish "free or parochial" schools without being obliged to pay contributions towards public education since, unlike the German settlements referred to in Érdujhelyi's second polemic article, they everywhere constituted ethnically mixed colonies. In any case it was not an easy thing to organize an ethnic school. Also a teacher must comprehend and weigh his words carefully if he wanted to benefit the people with his instruction, that is, the proper comprehension and judicious interpretation of words [contrary to Érdujhelyi's position that they did not matter], the proper command of the language and, by implication, that of the official English language, were most essential. Besides, Pirot also added — this time more cuttingly:

I also have to repeat that we strangers, though not native Hungarians, love the Hungarian language and have gladly done what was possible for the retention of the Hungarian language and it pains us [to hear], short of having been publicized in newspapers, that we have not assisted the Hungarian people. Let Hungarian priests come then, or let them not depart from Canada and they will be able to see whether they can achieve more than we! ... [27]

The Concerns of St. Boniface

Indeed, Pirot's second statement became the "final word" in the polemics, at least for a while, since Érdujhelyi left his position at Wakaw for the United States. Pirot was somewhat surprised to find that Érdujhelyi was "angry" with him in view of the fact that the polemics up to that stage had been "gentle."[28] But the Pirot-Érdujhelyi debate in fact was part of what Pirot came to call the "fight" in his pamphlet. Indeed, Pirot and no doubt Archbishop Langevin were able to discern certain upsetting developments in Winnipeg and in the comparatively large Calvinist Hungarian colony of Bekevar up to and in the first quarter of 1910. There had been signs which had suggested particularly to the French priests that "Presbyterians were conducting a general campaign against Catholics of foreign origin all over Canada."[29]

There were a number of events which tended to create foreboding in the minds of the French-speaking priests. Events that were necessarily looked upon as part of a general "evangelical," liberal and Hungarian nationalist plot directed against the French Catholic hierarchy of the West.[30] The Rev. Kálmán Kovachy had already been well known in Kaposvar as the missionary visiting the small group of Protestants of that colony from his manse at Bekevar and as one of the contributors to P. O. Esterhazy's pamphlet.[31] It was he who sent for his younger brother Lajos ("Louis") to Hungary, employed there as a teacher. Lajos on becoming a "missionary" of the Canadian Presbyterian Church, was instrumental in the setting up of the first Hungarian Presbyterian congregation in Winnipeg. Both he and his older brother had literary ambition and made contact with the Hungarian paper of the Manitoba capital. Kálmán Kovachy having been deeply impressed with spiritism during his visit to Hungary in 1907 returned as a convert to that creed and before long established a thriving spiritist association at Bekevar, the members of which in many cases were to regard him highly until their deaths in some cases half a century later. A nucleus of the adherents of the creed kept on following him also politically in the support of the Canadian Liberal Party as well as in the organization of the Canadian Hungarian Brotherhood Society.[32]

Pirot made references to spiritism[33] at Bekevar and also remarks on "mesmerism." However, this latter practice does not seem to have been connected with either of the Kovachys but there was one member of the Christian Spiritists' Association of Bekevar — a resident of the Whitewood area — who discovered in himself a gift for hypnotism which he then later cultivated and began to advertise as a hypnotist healer also in the Hungarian paper of Winnipeg.[34] As to Lajos E. Kovachy, there has been no indication so far that he believed in or was connected with spiritism apart from his having been a most loyal supporter of his older brother. As also a determined follower of Kálmán in his liberalism of the Hungarian Kossuthist kind, he too was ready somewhat superficially to identify it with the Canadian liberalism of Clifford Sifton and his friends.[35]

In January 1910, Peter Németh made up his mind to leave the *Canadian Hungarians* newspaper for the *Canadian Farmer* and thereby to weaken the position of the former and strengthen that of the latter. On the actual taking over, Németh became the editor of the *Canadian Hungarian Farmer,*[36] which fact of course did not escape Pirot's attention. The priest warned him against joining the enemies of the Church and pointed out that he (Pirot) would fight what he described as "a Calvinist-Spiritist paper." Nevertheless, the advice was not heeded by the editor. Believing in the truth of the *dictum* that attack was the best defence the Belgian priest promptly declared the new Hungarian paper an "anti-Catholic" publication. The reasoning that resulted in this dramatic action was based on the premise that the paper had a leaning towards spiritism and Calvinism and that "gross intentional untruths regarding the Catholic faith were spread by it."[37] The fact that Peter Németh was born a Catholic and had been brought up at a Catholic school was hardly taken into consideration in Pirot's and, no doubt, the Archbishop's assessment of the value of the Hungarian paper.[38] In fact, the *Canadian Hungarian Farmer* became a major objective for attack in their planning, as was the Canadian Hungarian Brotherhood Society which had been established on the initiative of the Kovachy brothers, after the pattern of a similar association of Hungarian settlers in the United States, with the co-operation of Hungarian intellectuals of the Canadian West. The circumstance that the central president of the Association in 1910 was the Hungarian Calvinist minister of Winnipeg marked him out as a most important and most vulnerable person amongst the Hungarian intellectuals.

The vision of the Association hovering before the eyes of its founders included a number of things. It was expected to work for Hungarian schools but first of all it was meant to provide the antidote against the supposedly age-old curse of discord prevailing among Hungarians: the elimination of division along religious, cultural, social and political lines. It was to provide for the possibility of bargaining before elections through the concerted action of all Hungarians.[39] However, because of this integrating activity on the basis of the principle of ethnicity, it immediately became a potential threat and danger to the similar activity, for the same practical purpose but on the "horizontal" level of religious cosmopolitanism, of some of the French clergy of Archbishop Langevin. Expressed differently, while the French-speaking priests of St. Boniface warmly embraced and intently supported the principle of the retention on the prairies of the French Catholic culture[40] with the help of the Catholic voters of other ethnic groups, Archbishop Langevin and some of his subordinates seemed less inclined to endorse efforts for the maintenance of the identity in similar terms of such other ethnic groups as the Ukrainians and the Hungarians. It was perhaps felt that the French Catholics' political power of bargaining in the West would be less effective after the release of other ethnic groups from under the influence exerted upon them by certain members of the French speaking clergy. Therefore, the Hungarian Association, pursuing aims less than favourable to the Archbishop's purposes had to be opposed vigorously; so Pirot "condemned the society without any restriction" on the somewhat hollow-sounding reason that its activities were taking place "under the direction and auspices of irresponsible men."[41]

The Consul Intervenes

Until the beginning of May 1910, no "fighting" publications, apart from the Pirot-Érdujhelyi debate on the school question, appeared in newspapers. But then the initiative was taken up by the anti-Pirot group, when on the same day, May 3rd, two important actions were undertaken by L. E. Kovachy and P. Németh. The more spectacular of the two was an article in the Hungarian paper in which objections were publicly raised to those "priests of foreign origin" who only spoke broken Hungarian, who tended physically to abandon the Hungarian Catholics by not visiting them regularly and, owing to difficulties in oral communication, also intellectually. Because of their alienness towards the manner of thinking and feeling of the Magyars, the foreign priests did not, because they could not, establish *rapport* with them through references to the old country, through the observation of Hungarian religious or national festivities. These priests proved indifferent, nay, hostile towards the evolving unity of the Hungarian people of the West.[42]

The other and less conspicuous measure undertaken by L. E. Kovachy and Németh was one of much more serious nature. It was on May 3, 1910 that Dr. John Schwegel, the consul for Austria-Hungary, recently[43] appointed to Winnipeg, submitted a brief, drawn up by the two Hungarian intellectuals, to his superiors in the Ministry for Foreign Affairs in Vienna.[44] The document was signed by Peter Németh in his capacity as Secretary of the Roman Catholic parish, St. Stephen, Winnipeg, and by the Rev. L. E. Kovachy, as President of the Canadian-Hungarian Brotherhood Association. The purpose of the brief was to direct the attention of the Hungarian authorities to, and thereby hinder, Pirot's probable effort to collect donations among the clergy of Hungary ostensibly for the needs of his parishioners, but in reality, for the setting up of a French Catholic newspaper in Hungarian. His projected trip to Hungary was described as imminent. That this charge was not without foundation can be seen from Pirot's certain statements in which he promoted the idea of establishing a Hungarian Catholic newspaper with a clear purpose of eliminating the Winnipeg Hungarian paper from among the readings of the Magyar Catholics. Furthermore, he admitted his intention to make a trip to Hungary with the remark that it had to be abandoned owing to the non-availability of a substitute clergyman for the Belgian priest's parish and missions.[45]

Consul Schwegel's covering letter to the Kovachy-Németh brief is very relevant also because it contains his succinct and somewhat sweeping description and assessment of the position and aims of the French Catholic clergy and its relations with the Irish Catholic colleagues. According to the undisclosed sources of information of the consul, Mgr. Bruchesi in Montreal and Archbishop Langevin of St. Boniface were known to be enthusiastic defenders of the power of the Canadian French clergy, even if "the predominance appeared at that stage already completely out of date." Schwegel stressed his opinion that the admission of priests other than French speakers would be refused by the French hierarchy out of hand. In the consul's view, not only power was their aim but also the defence of "the long-lost cause of the French nation in North America, which is becoming weaker even in Quebec. . . ."[46] Dr. Schwegel, a former commercial *attaché*, drew attention to the fact that owing to their long national struggle the French in Canada did "not participate in the economic prosperity of the country." Then he identified Archbishop McEvay as the head of the powerful Irish clergy also in its sharp conflict with the French Catholic hierarchy.[47] From the viewpoint of Austria-Hungary, Schwegel's interpretation described the Irish as "more progressive than the French" and he mistakenly assumed that this was the reason for the greater understanding and fairness which the English speaking Catholics displayed "towards the endeavours of our compatriots."

As to the motives of supporting the Hungarians in their demands for Catholic Hungarian clergymen the consul made reference to an economic explanation: "one must not forget that problems, national, religious and of other types are today economic problems. . . ."[48] In view of the fact that economic success, expansion and the total integration of national resources interact, the augmentation of the potential of ethnic groups as factors in the life of the American Canadian Commonwealth is very important. The consul's support for the cause of the Hungarians derived from this insight regarded by him as the sole guiding principle for action on the matter. However, it is more than likely that the reason for the Prime Minister of Hungary of the time, to adopt the course of action recommended by the Winnipeg consul was hardly the latter's economic awareness, but the former's sensitivity to growing criticism in Hungary concerning the government's inability or unwillingness to solve the country's social and economic problems as well as to initiate more effective measures and reverse the tide of emigration from the country through the encouragement of the return of Magyars from the American continent.[49]

No doubt, the action of the Hungarian government or, in fact on its behalf, of the Ministry of Foreign Affairs of the Austro-Hungarian monarchy which still possessed the reputation and prestige of a major power, must have had some influence upon the actions undertaken or rather contemplated at that stage by the Vatican. It is not claimed that the initiative to separate the Saskatchewan portion from the diocese of Archbishop Langevin had anything to do with the diplomatic representations originally requested by Consul Schwegel, but the process commenced within the Catholic church administration at the beginning of 1910 was probably accelerated by the same.[50]

Priests and the School Question

As has been seen above, resolute action from May 3, 1910 onwards on the part of the Hungarian newspaper of Winnipeg and the intellectuals grouped around it could be discerned quite distinctly. From this time on their attack against their opponents was taking place in two different yet interdependent areas: the question of Hungarian schools (or rather English-Hungarian bilingual schools) and the more recent problem of the securing of Hungarian priests. The interdependence of the two regions of the campaigns was more clearly stressed later in the same month.[51] It was pointed out in the related newspaper article that the Hungarians of Canada required not just leaders but well educated, honest and patriotic leaders. Clergymen, as Hungarian leaders, must come up to this same specification with the added duty of instructing the people not only in religion and morals but also in patriotism — that is to say, by keeping them and their children good Hungarians and at the same time making them and their children good Canadian citizens. The reason for some of the Catholic Hungarian groups not holding such national days as March 15 or October 6[52] was squarely attributed to the desire of some of the non-Hungarian Catholic priests to keep their Hungarian parishioners aloof from such expressions of patriotism. To make their case clearer the writers of the article[53] brought up the example of the Hungarian Catholic clergy of the United States who personally conducted the celebration and commemoration of the national days. Furthermore, the priests there accepted, as a rule, the chairmanship of the local sections of the American Hungarian Association whose aims did not differ much from those of the Canadian Hungarian Brotherhood Association. The American Hungarian priest, in addition to fostering religion, practised the important task of implanting in his charges "pure Hungarian ethics" without which they could not promote the well-being of the receiving country. In the light of all this a priest working against the Association must be condemned and the obvious task of the Catholic Hungarians of Canada must lie in the endeavour to obtain Hungarian Catholic priests who could become competent leaders towards "the land of promise" where "the Magyars will become brethren to the Magyars." In their campaign for the same, the Hungarians should apply to members of the high Church hierarchy not only in Canada but in Hungary and the United States as well. Also the diplomatic representatives of Austria-Hungary should be approached with the same request.

Pirot's reply to this article,[54] in which he alleged that it was the Hungarians of Kaposvar who refused to agree to the Belgian priest's proposition to celebrate the Fifteenth of March, looks less than watertight in the light of subsequent events in the parish and its vicinity even if there could have been some members of the parish, perhaps of Slovakian or Bohemian extraction, who did not particularly favour the mentioning of Kossuth or the celebration of March the 15th at that comparatively early stage. Pirot's other argument as well that March the 15th, falling in Lent, could not be celebrated since "Catholics are not disposed to dance and amuse themselves in that season" and that Hungary's "sad situation" at that time was no cause for dancing or merry making, looks less than convincing. On the one hand there was no compelling reason why not to celebrate without dancing and, on the other, the later Hungarian Catholic priests of the parish as, for instance, Mgr. P. Santha regularly arranged for the celebration of the Fifteenth of March and other nationally festive days as a matter of course.

Attempts to Form Magyar Schools

The other prong of the attack on the part of Hungarians gathered round the *Canadian Hungarian Farmer,* concerned itself with the actual formation of "Magyar schools." It is well to remember that the local school district was mainly responsible for its own organization, for the election of trustees preferably from among the taxpayers of the same district as well as for the setting up of the school and the hiring of the teacher. The Department of Education with its headquarters in Regina carried out its advisory and supervisory functions through its inspectors in the course of their rather infrequent visits to the school districts and in other cases through correspondence. It also provided funds towards the pay of the teachers and, in the initial stages, assisted in the securing of loans for the erection and equipping of the school building. As the Hungarians had invariably settled in townships with mixed populations, the functioning and administration of the school districts, particularly in the beginning, were often accompanied by friction and instances of ethnocentric behavior. Frequent occurrences of such nature tended to stem from the question of where the school should be located implying the desire to have it in one particular person's or group's neighborhood rather than close to the geographical centre of the school district. The tendency to yield to this human weakness often resulted in petitions for the re-formation of the area of adjacent school districts or for the formation of new ones often inspired by considerations deriving from denominational or ethnic interests. In other cases the actual moving of the school house to another location was fought about.[55] Obviously it was very important, in fact decisive in this respect as well, whether the area possessed effective Hungarian leadership, who the trustees (the executive officers of the school district) were, and in which groups they belonged. The fact that comparatively frequent correspondence with the Department of Education was unavoidable necessitated the presence on the school board of at least a secretary-treasurer who had a reasonable command of spoken and written English. In the first few years of their existence it was not unusual for districts of Hungarian majority to have all or most trustees of Anglo-Celtic background.[56]

The struggle for potentially bilingual English-Hungarian schools tended to manifest itself at the local level in more or less successful attempts to take over the control of school districts with a Hungarian majority through the election of Hungarian trustees[57] and the subsequent hiring of Hungarian teachers or persons willing to undergo training to become such. The campaign for a Hungarian teacher — begun late in 1908, and also inspired by the visit of the Rev. L. Kovács, the parish priest of New York — did not lead to practical results until the spring of 1909. It was in May that A. Miklosy, a Hungarian, who as has been seen above, had teaching experience of three years in the United States, had left Louisiana and arrived in the Wakaw region of which the part inhabited by Hungarians at that stage was called *Mátyásföld*. The Hungarian paper stressed the rejoicing in the midst of the Hungarians there over their eventual success in finding a Hungarian teacher. It is not without interest to read that Miklosy on his way to take up his new position stopped over in Howell (the present-day Prudhomme) in the home of L. Fias, one of the influential settlers of the district, as in a year's time it became Howell's turn to advertise

for another Hungarian teacher.[58] By the beginning of the following year the
Hungarian paper was glad to report the success of the Hungarian teacher of
Wakaw, A. Miklosy, in completing his teacher-training course. In fact his
result was not only a pass but apparently he stood out among the 33
candidates by alone having been able to obtain a Class 1 certificate.[59] This
achievement must also have been due to the circumstance that Miklosy had
a university degree as well. But he proved himself also as an impressive
classroom teacher according to the account of the first public examination
which he conducted for his pupils in the Buda School District on May 6,
1910. Apparently the examination was so spectacularly successful that

> in the present case not even the customary Hungarian discord was
> capable of disturbing the feeling of genuine pleasure with the results
> achieved.[60]

The next development in this context did not occur until the September
of 1910 when the arrival in Winnipeg of Elek Perényi, "an outstanding
Hungarian printer," was reported. Attention was drawn to Perényi's close
relationship to L. Perényi, the former Hungarian Catholic parish priest in
New York, and to B. Perényi, the flag manufacturer. E. Perényi also
disclosed his intention to take up a homestead at Mátyásföld (Wakaw) and
settle there permanently. It was in the same issue of the Hungarian paper
that an advertisement appeared for a Hungarian teacher also fluent in
English to apply for a position in the Houghton Lake School District (No.
2544), Howell, Saskatchewan.[61] After the advertisement had been published
several more times, it was disclosed that E. Perényi became successful in
obtaining the teaching position. In fact, he had already begun teaching on
the 3rd of October. The Hungarian paper remarked with satisfaction:
"behold, already two schools, Wakaw and Howell, possess Hungarian
teachers."[62] In spite of the fact that no indication was given of Perényi's
intention to undertake a teacher-training course, according to the *Canadian
Hungarian Farmer* Perényi was acquitting himself "beneficially" for the
Howell area. Indeed, he initiated an evening course in English for adults. It
was reported that

> the numerous students make quick progress and, only after three and a
> half weeks the better learners already write and read English fairly
> well.[63]

As to attempts to take over the boards of school districts with
Hungarian population, there were occasions much less spectacular than in
the case of Dunaföldvár School District No. 1922.[64] The ratepayers, who
included Magyar and German speakers resident in the Wakaw area,
attended nearly in full number. Despite the presence of two interpreters for
the two groups, the meeting got out of hand almost right from the
beginning. It appears that Mr. Lukacsffy[65] wished to take the chair at the
call of several others without the usual formalities of adopting an agenda
and approving of the minutes of the previous meeting. Also the fact that the
Chairman of the Board of Trustees should act as chairman of the meeting

was ignored. Attempts by the Secretary and the Chairman of the Board of Trustees to assert themselves were of no avail:

> little success was met in this part of the proceedings and the chairman was not able to keep order. Nearly everyone talked at once, and whenever the Chairman attempted to speak he was interrupted.[66]

Once the nominations for trustees had taken place no attention was paid to the Secretary's warning as to the need that ten minutes had to pass before the voting. When Mr. Lukacsffy denied that it was necessary, someone else than the Chairman called for a show of hands. The Secretary and the Chairman proved unable to influence the events of the meeting. Not only did people begin talking without permission but the results of the voting were counted by people without any reference to the Secretary or the Chairman. Also at least two non-resident ratepayers were present, one being the father of a Hungarian and the other the teacher of the Buda School District, A. Miklosy. After the Secretary pointed out that the election of the trustees had not taken place according to the law the noise and shouting grew so great that the Secretary left the meeting even if most of the people stayed on.[67]

St. Boniface Launches an Offensive

It was almost unavoidable that at annual meetings of early school boards difficulties in communication should arise owing to lack of fluency or sheer ignorance of any more advanced level of English than the most basic staccato vocabulary. When under the pressure of excitement over their inability to state what they would regard as the truth of a situation or matter, Hungarians and members of other ethnic groups were apt suddenly to change over to discussion in their respective native languages, people of Anglo-Celtic background would view the state of affairs with alarm and suspicion. A good example of such a case occurs in the statement drafted by one of the friends of Pirot in the course of and in connection with the "Hungarian Question" polemics.

Apparently the Irishman, also a school trustee in the Esterhazy area, was asked as to the provisions of the Saskatchewan School Ordinance with reference to Érdujhelyi's allegations at a meeting of a school district at Benchonzie on August 28, 1910.[68] The author of the letter objected to Érdujhelyi's assertions among the Hungarians with regard to the setting up of Hungarian schools and the employment in them of Hungarian teachers and to his exhortations that such objectives were capable of attainment. He condemned the Hungarian priest as a troublemaker who would put Hungarian farmers not sufficiently educated into "a state of turmoil" by blaming the government for not authorising Hungarian schools which are not permissible by law. Furthermore, the letter implied that Érdujhelyi did not want to include the teaching of English at schools recommended by him, and was counteracting the beneficial influence in this respect of Woodcutter and Pirot. Finally the writer of the letter alleged that in promoting the cause of a Hungarian school Érdujhelyi was inciting people against the laws. He found the Hungarian priest guilty of the charge at once and meted out the punishment as well:

> ex-priests and others who will not work, and who seek to make an easy living by preying upon the credulity of their countrymen, to the detriment of the land of their adoption, are not good citizens, and should be deported at once.

Why should Érdujhelyi and others soliciting favour to Hungarian schools be treated with severity? Well, the meeting addressed by Érdujhelyi

> was held in a public school in a settlement composed principally of Hungarians and possibly two or three trustees of that nationality. Suppose they follow the advice of this sower of discord, what would be the result? ... Settlers rebelling against our laws; and while they are in this state we cannot expect to make good Canadians of them.[69]

The ever handy phobia of foreigners overruning the West, who not only refuse to assimilate but even plot against the laws of the country, was skilfully applied to the case of Érdujhelyi and his supporters in connection with the Hungarian Question, not only by the Irish letter-writer but also Father Pirot himself. Indeed, he seemed to have found the Achilles heel of his opponents in the sensitivity of the general public at that time to the apparently wilful non-conformity of East-Central European immigrants. So Pirot in his letters to the editor of the *Manitoba Free Press* kept on elaborating this very point.[70]

In spite of strongly worded counter-attacks from L. E. Kovachy and Peter Németh, Érdujhelyi remained, being a Catholic priest, the potentially most dangerous opponent for Pirot. The views he was defending, even if he made only one very short public statement against Pirot, could have been damaging. First he gave as the reasons for his declaration the fact that Pirot had sent a letter to the Hungarian Catholics of Székelyföld[71] (close to Arbury) calling Érdujhelyi "a Judas and a renegade," and that both Pirot and Vorst[72] had spoken to the Hungarian priest's parishioners prior to worship in a manner which Érdujhelyi regarded as "slanderously abusive." There can be but little doubt that the two priests made an announcement about the Hungarian priest's standing within the church. Thus they probably described him, as on other occasions, as a "schismatic and renegade" ex-priest who had rebelled against his bishop in Hungary and who was carrying out pastoral work in Székelyföld without the authority of Archbishop Langevin. Under the circumstances Érdujhelyi could not respond effectively concerning the claims about him to his French-speaking colleagues in any other way than through voicing his "contempt." Then the essential portion of his declaration that he regarded Pirot and Vorst as "the most dangerous enemies of the Canadian Hungarian ethnic group ['people'],'' since amongst others they failed to establish Hungarian [bilingual] schools at Kaposvar and Benchonzie respectively,[73] amounted to a sweeping generalization, to the avoiding of the consideration of an issue most sensitive for him through the application of the device of evasion also well tried in the Pirot pamphlet. The Belgian priest objected to lack of courtesy in not being named in the declaration by the title "reverend" and extended, with the application of some hyperbolic dramatization, the absence of a sense of politeness observed in the one priest also to the other Hungarian polemists and called them for good measure "anti-Catholics."[74] Apart from the expression of indignation Pirot himself could do little since the Szekelys failed to respond and ask for any action against Érdujhelyi. So the only means that was left in this connection — that is, appeal to the Archbishop for personal intervention — became Pirot's next move.

Mgr. Langevin and the Controversy

As to Archbishop Langevin's role in the controversy, Pirot in his preface to his pamphlet does not really desire to enhance the importance of his own contributions to the same by stating:

> There followed a battle royal, because our enemies had everything in their own hands: money, a weekly paper, the advantage of numbers, combined with the prestige of their nationality; while I was alone, though always well seconded by Rev. Father Vorst. . . .[75]

But rather he tried to create a more impressive contrast by exaggerating the resources of his opponents and at the same time presenting himself in the guise of an isolated country priest fighting almost single-handedly a plot directed against the Catholic Church as a whole. However, in the concluding chapter of the same publication — perhaps no longer recalling his previous statement — he expressed his gratitude "to all those who previously did help us by donations, words or prayers." That Pirot's work and struggle was not without interest to people in the East is further indicated when he writes that whenever he felt uncertain and dispirited psychological support arrived in the shape of "a charming letter . . . from Ontario or from Quebec." Moreover, it may be an understatement on the Belgian priest's part that "Archbishop Langevin never failed to support us in those days of struggle. . . ."[76] The Archiepiscopal support was not limited only to lending money for the development in parishes but there can be little doubt that Mgr. Langevin was not more parsimonious with his guidance either, and when it came to action in the struggle he did not fail Pirot when disciplinary intervention was required. In perhaps the most serious and most significant effort to destroy the two most important "weapons" of the Hungarian adversaries, the Archbishop went to the extent of taking advantage of the ultimate sanctions of the Church to destroy at one blow both the Hungarian priest and the Hungarian paper. The Archiepiscopal circular excommunicating those who received the [Canadian] Hungarian Farmer was issued by the Archbishop on September 22, 1910, and read from the pulpits in all Hungarian churches in the Archdiocese and "especially in the church in Benchonzie."[77] It was not published until the time thought tactically the most effective; so it appeared at the end of October.[78]

Confident that he would dispose of Érdujhelyi and reduce his flock to obedience to St. Boniface, Mgr. Langevin called what amounted to a meeting of the French-speaking priests most closely related to Hungarian settlements at Benchonzie (Lestock, Saskatchewan) on October 16, 1910. The size of the group of clerics attending the meeting seems to indicate its importance to the Primate, but it was probably also calculated to create evidence of archiepiscopal strength and authority. In addition to the Archbishop, the Rev. Conter, a Redemptorist from Otthon (near Yorkton), The Oblate Fathers Cahill and Planet and, of course, Pirot appeared together with Vorst as the host.[79] Also the people of Székelyföld were invited to come to Benchonzie, no doubt, somewhat inconvenienced by the strange place and by the absence of Érdujhelyi. The surviving accounts of the meeting tend to clash in the wording and some of the details, yet it is clear that the Székelys in essence stood up for the Hungarian priest in spite of the concerted endeavour to the contrary of the Archbishop and his retinue. Much of the effectiveness of the Primate's polished and logical speech to the parishioners was lost through the fact that the Székelys, being still rather new immigrants, did not understand much English, and the interpretation of the speeches in broken Hungarian by the Rev. Father Conter also reduced the speed of the proceedings.[80] As to the results of the discussion with the Székelys after the mass, they were told that their Hungarian priest, while he was suspended, could not be approved by the Archbishop. Concerning their reply that unless "any other Hungarian good Catholic priest" could be provided for them by the Archdiocese, they would keep Érdujhelyi, Pirot added piously,

> unfortunately no priest has been at hand so far. May God have mercy on those unfortunate people, as well as on this still more unfortunate suspended priest![81]

Translated into plain language the Archiepiscopal visit did not prove a success. On the contrary, Érdujhelyi was retained by his parishioners in open defiance of archiepiscopal authority purely on the merits of his personal qualities and particularly his ability to communicate with them in a way which helped to reinforce, rather than abruptly undermine, their values and identity. Viewed from another angle, the occasion was a reverse for the Archbishop because it constituted not only a serious loss of face but also a precedent soon to be followed by other Hungarian groups in demanding Hungarians priests. Thus it gradually became obvious that the Hungarian Catholics, or for that matter, many other Catholics with Eastern-Central European background, would not be amenable to the control of French-speaking clergy inspired with the ideals of Archbishop Langevin.[82] However, it took some further time and struggle to reach and accept this insight.

Indeed, Father Pirot at the end of 1910 failed to notice the significance of Érdujhelyi's and his parishioners' refusal to yield to ecclesiastical authority; he made one great final effort — probably at the request, but in any case with the approval of Archbishop Langevin. The Belgian priest took upon himself to write up the main events, the interpretation in the "appropriate" light; in short, the history of what he regarded as a controversy finished and for him victorious. The final page of the pamphlet was completed on January 1st, 1911 at Kaposvar, when the author could not yet know how wrong his prediction pronounced in the last paragraph of his booklet would turn out:

> ... Calvinist ministers, a schismatic priest, a consul and renegades, with their satellites ... when I consider how all these were led to commit fatal blunders, which wrought their ruin forever ... God has blinded those whom He would let perish....[83]

Postscript

How could Pirot have foreseen that other Hungarian priests would come before long to replace amongst others himself at Kaposvar[84] and that, before the new year (1911) was over, the Saskatchewan portion of the Archdiocese of St. Boniface would effectively be exempted from the immediate jurisdiction of Mgr. Langevin[85] and that in the same new year the twenty-fifth anniversary celebration of the Hungarian colony known by then as *Kaposvar* would take place without an active role for himself but marked with the speeches of almost all of those opponents whom he had denounced so vehemently a short while before.[86] Finally, it would have taken a real prophet to see the future necrological list of the later Archdiocese of Regina where his own name is alphabetically and peacefully registered together with those of his one-time assistant, Father Vorst, and his former adversary the Rev. Menyhert Érdujhelyi.[87]

Also for the Hungarians the new year began with strong claims of triumphs; also they failed to see the Pyrrhic nature of their "victory." How could they have anticipated that in no Hungarian settlement would anything emerge resembling a "Magyar school" or a "parochial school" of the type suggested by Érdujhelyi, that the few Hungarian teachers recruited for the imparting of instruction that approximated the bilingual type would soon drift to other occupations and other places owing to their inability to obtain non-provisional teaching certificates. Neither the organizers of the Canadian Hungarian Brotherhood Association, the editors of the *Canadian Hungarian Farmer,* nor the Hungarian settlers were aware that the greatly decreased vitality of the organization and the paper caused by the numerous members' and subscribers' refusal to have anything to do with them after the pronouncement of the Archiepiscopal ban and the "Presbyterian-Spiritist" epithet, would become a lasting feature.

Yet a durable achievement from the Hungarian viewpoint of the controversy was to lie in the changing of the French clerical attitude for the better towards the Catholic Hungarian communities with the resultant arrival and authorization of Hungarian priests to take the places of their French-speaking colleagues at Kaposvar and other controversial parishes and missions. Owing to this circumstance consciousness of the need for Hungarian language instruction as well was to grow deeper: Hungarian priests to arrive in the next few years and Protestant ministers were to provide this instruction after school hours and at Sunday and summer schools.

A major loser in the controversy, Archbishop Langevin could not but register another disappointment with a concomitant reduction of his authority to Manitoba. Even there his position in St. Boniface began to assume the appearance of an intellectual fortress under siege from all sides. Nevertheless, in 1911 it would have been impossible to anticipate his premature passing away four years later, soon to be followed by the abolition of bilingual schools of all types in his archdiocese. Irrespective of the circumstances, there is always something tragic in a collapse against overwhelming odds after a protracted and largely unsuccessful struggle.

FOOTNOTES

[1]For the events leading up to the Laurier-Greenway Compromise and the subsequent amendment of the Schools Act, 1890 by Manitoba in 1897, see P. Crunican, *Priests and Politicians: Manitoba schools and the election of 1896* (Toronto, 1974). Related developments to 1905 in connection with the North-West School Question, which were to determine the type of schooling also in Saskatchewan for a number of years, are very well dealt with in M. R. Lupul, *The Roman Catholic Church and the North-West School Question* (Toronto, 1974). See also fn. 12 below.

[2]In respect of the qualities attributed to the Archbishop, see the numerous letters to the Editor and other polemical items in the *Manitoba Free Press (MFP)*, for instance, in 1910. A relevant example of his leadership and gift of taking advantage even of poor positions is constituted by his turning to good use the initially horrifying number of non-French-speaking Continental immigrants. See the Archbishop's speech on the occasion of the twenty-fifth anniversary celebration of the establishment of the Academy of the Oblates, his stoutest supporters toward the end of August, 1910: ". . . We will not demand of them [different ethnic groups] to give up their language . . . but tell them 'Come to us, we will give you priests who speak German, Ruthenian, English and French like you do." R. R. Morice, *Vie de Mgr. Langevin* (St. Boniface, 1916), 260-261 and also 182-183.

[3]Both the Kovachys, *Kálmán*, the Minister of Bekevar (not far from present-day Kipling) his younger brother *Lajos*, the minister of the Presbyterian church of Winnipeg, and the managing editor of the *Canadai Magyar Farmer (CMF = 'Canadian Hungarian Farmer')*, and Peter Németh the editor of the same paper confessed to be convinced liberal supporters. It was with liberal assistance that the previous two papers, the *Kanadai Magyarság (KM =* Canadian Hungarians) and the *Canadai Farmer (CF* - Canadian Farmer), could be merged into the *CMF*. One of the reasons why the Rev. Menyhért Érdujhelyi experienced difficulties with his superiors and left Hungary was his ardent liberalism. See footnotes 32 and 35 below. As to the dispute and its political background in Manitoba and Ontario in and about 1910 see R. Cook, "Church, Schools, and Politics in Manitoba" and Marilyn Barber, "The Ontario Bilingual Schools Issue," in C. Brown, ed., *Minorities, Schools, and Politics* (Toronto, 1969), 34-37, 74-84.

[4]*KM,* August 21, 1908.

[5]*KM,* January 29, 1909.

[6]This operation envisaged the integration of immigrants to the United States from Hungary into the ecclesiastic-organizational structure of the old country according to denominational lines. While the initiative and the funds originated from the Prime Minister's office, the immediate prompting, the personal contact and necessary administration were provided through the agency of the respective denominations. The Rev. L. Kovács was one of the priests connected with this operation. See, for instance, Prime Minister (Count István Tisza) of Budapest, to the Minister of Foreign Affairs, Vienna, December 6, 1904, Office of the Prime Minister, ME 3958, Item XVI, Hungarian National Archives, Budapest.

[7]The church building built of field stone is a memorial to the perseverance and industry of the Rev. Jules Pirot who persuaded his parishioners to contribute funds and physical labor and provided, in the persons of his brothers, the skilled masons necessary for the project. Cf. *Leader-Post*, July 11, 1953.

[8]*KM,* November 18, 1908.

[9]*MFP,* October 25, 1910. In this context also see R. R. Morice, *op. cit.,* 181-183, and "Angry with 'Liberal Catholic' " by the Catholic Federation of Gretna, Man., *MFP,* August 29, 1910.

[10]*KM*, January 15, 1909.

[11]*KM*, March 5, 1909.

[12]The Hungarian priest took the trouble of interviewing the Archbishop, whose main argument in favor of the public school was the fact that two-thirds of the teacher's pay came from the government. *KM*, February 19, 1909. Concerning the "denominational" public schools of Manitoba, of which many actually functioned as *de facto* bilingual schools, see C. B. Sissons, *Bi-lingual Schools in Canada* (London, 1917), 140-156.

[13]This attitude reflected not only parental traumas in not being able to communicate satisfactorily with the English-speaking environment but also the parents' ambition for their children's social advancement.

[14]*KM*, February 19, 1909.

[15]The minutes of the Dunaföldvár S.D., No. 1922, January 23, 1909 are revealing: "As there was no teacher last year in the school there was no teacher's report. . . ." Records of the Department of Education, Saskatchewan Provincial Archives, Regina (hereafter: *RDE SPA*).

[16]The Hungarian settlers in the Wakaw area, although the settlement there had started about 1903, were not confident enough — owing to bad crops — to undertake the building of a school in 1907. The school was completed in the summer of 1908 but was without a teacher early in 1909 (cf. *KM*, February 19, 1909.) It was not until May 21, 1909 that the engagement of A. Miklosy, a Hungarian who had already been employed as a teacher in Louisiana for three years, was reported both by the Hungarian paper (*KM*, May 21, 1909) and in the minutes of the same date of Buda S.D. No. 1722, *RDE SPA*, Regina.

[17]*KM*, February 19, 1909. It is very likely that the female teacher referred to by the Hungarian priest was the same person recommended above by the Rev. L. Kovács, New York,. Cf. *KM*, January 29, 1909.

[18]*Loc. cit.*

[19]*KM*, January 20, 1909.

[20]Reverend Father Pirot, *One Year's Fight for the True Faith in Saskatchewan: Or The Hungarian Question in Canada in 1910* (Toronto, 1911), 6. "When he was at Kaposvar, the Hungarian priest, who was not able to read English, asked me to translate for him the School Ordinance relating to the language to be used in the schools of Saskatchewan." This fact combined with Pirot's "basic" Hungarian, far from enabling him to provide even a makeshift translation of the departmental regulation could have been an important contributory factor to Érdujhelyi's confusion in his interpretation of the same.

[21]If an accurate translation of the regulation had been available to Érdujhelyi, it would have been quite unlikely that the author of numerous scholarly historical studies would have committed the serious factual errors pointed out by Pirot. The related portions of "An Ordinance Respecting Schools," *The General Ordinances of the North-West Territories*, in Force September 1, 1905 (Regina, 1907):" 41 The minority of the ratepayers in any district whether protestant or roman catholic may establish a Separate school therein . . . [p. 1018] . . . 45 (2). Any person who is legally assessed or assessable for a public school shall not be liable to assessment for any separate school established therein. 1901, c. 29, S. 45" [p. 1019].

[22]*Ibid.*, 41.

[23]"The Rev. Menyhért Érdujhelyi expresses sorrow for the Hungarian people, yet the position of other ethnic groups in Canada is not better either. We are in an English dominion and he is fortunate who knows English and as to the others we will instruct them as much as possible. Even with no Hungarian Catholic priests in Canada, there have existed priests looking after the Hungarians, acquiring their language. With many a person who had not known the language of their native country, neither could they read and write it was here in this "wild" Canada that they have accomplished these skills. After all, also we would like everyone to know his own [parental] tongue but we are in a foreign country where the law is the same for all peoples of all kinds.. . ." *KM*, March 5, 1909.

[24]He was taken into the school during a lesson by Bruno Doerfler, the Prior of the local Benedictine monastery, according to whom their school "fully satisfied" the requirements of the Germans of Canada. Matthias Steger, the parochial priest of nearby Leofeld, who possessed intimate knowledge of the life of the Leofeld "German school," provided most of Érdujhelyi's information about their school practice. Cf. M. Érdujhelyi, "Hungarian Schools in Canada," *KM*, March 19, 1909.

[25]*KM*, March 19, 1909. Little did Érdujhelyi know the history of the "Ordinance 29 of the year 1901" and its impact on the Saskatchewan School legislation after 1905. Nor was he aware of the tiny number of parochial and, in fact, separate schools that were in existence in Saskatchewan at that time. Cf. C. B. Sissons, *Church and State in Canadian Education* (Toronto, 1959), 257-59 and 272-73.

[26]*KM*, April 2, 1909.

[27]This statement published in the April 2, 1909 issue of the *Canadian Hungarians* constituted an unveiled reference to Érdujhelyi, who had moved to Buffalo, New York at the beginning of the year. Cf. *KM*, January 29, 1909.

[28]Pirot, *op. cit.*, 6.

²⁹*Loc. cit.* Pirot's observation seems to be a reference to the activities initiated by Dr. James Robertson who as a missionary superintendent in Western Canada had been responsible for the related work on the part of the Presbyterian Church of Canada between 1881 and 1902. During his time of office 393 churches and 82 manses were built in the Canadian West. He was followed as superintendent by Dr. John A. Carmichael in 1903. He is identical with the Dr. Carmichael mentioned by Pirot as one of the "six men united to bring trouble and apostasy ..." (*op. cit.,* p. 5; see also p. 23). Cf. J. T. McNeil, *The Presbyterian Church in Canada 1875-1925* (Toronto, 1925), 107-110.

³⁰Note the introductory theme in Pirot's pamphlet: "The Hungarians of Canada soon recognized in the so-called 'Hungarian Leaders' wolves in sheep's clothing, and refused to have anything to do with them. The Evangelists sought vengeance in wholesale calumny against the Catholic clergy." Pirot, *op. cit.,* 2.

³¹Cf, M. L. Kovacs, *Esterhazy and Early Hungarian Immigration to Canada* (Regina, Saskatchewan, 1974), 42-46; 81-84.

³²The present writer is in possession of extensive material on the Kovachys, the other Hungarian polemists, and their roles in Canadian and U.S.A. history which he intends to publish separately.

³³"Spiritism" is an infrequent version of the Hungarian-neo-Latin noun "spiritizmus", just as "spiritist" derives from "spiritista," being equivalent to the English "spiritualism" and "spiritualist" respectively. Not only does spiritism — spiritualism — imply the existence of spirit as distinct from matter, but also the belief that communication can be established by departed spirits by means of phenomena through the agency of a *medium.* After early attacks by outsiders on spiritism, the adherents in Bekevar incorporated themselves as the "Christian Spiritists' Association of Bekevar, Saskatchewan." See their advertisement for instance, *CMF,* March 15, 1910.

³⁴János Szathmáry, *CMF,* September 27, 1910.

³⁵There is evidence that the younger Kovachy could persuade not only Kalman and his spiritist friends to contribute towards the founding of a *second* Hungarian newspaper *(Canadian Farmer)* in Winnipeg and towards the acquisition of the *first (Canadian Hungarians)* to be followed by the amalgamation of the two into the *Canadian Hungarian Farmer,* but also members of the Liberal Party of Manitoba or perhaps Canada, to invest heavily in his literary business venture. Cf. Rev. L. Kovachy's "Confidential" Statement to G. Szakacs and Gy. Izsak of Bekevar, dated Winnipeg, March 23, 1912. See also footnote 3 above.

³⁶The subscribers of the *Canadian Farmer* and the *Canadian Hungarians* received in February, 1910 — instead of the papers subscribed to — the first issue of the *Canadian Hungarian Farmer* which, however, carried on with the numbering of the *Canadian Hungarians.* Thus the reference of this *first* issue reads: *CMF,* February 8, 1910, Vol. VI, No. 6.

³⁷*Pirot, op. cit.,* 6.

³⁸In the strict hierarchial organization of the Archdiocese it would have been most improbable for a priest to enter into a confrontation, however minor, within the context of the Primate's struggle for the preservation of the French-speaking clergy's authority and the French language, without the knowledge and approval of the Archbishop.

³⁹*The Canadian Hungarian Brotherhood Association* (contemporary translation for "Kanadai Magyar Testveri Szovetseg") was founded in Winnipeg on February 8, 1908. The Rev. L. E. Kovachy was secretary among the first office bearers. Within a few days, the first branch of the Association came into being at Bekevar with the Rev. M. Kovachy as president and 43 persons as members. Cf. *KM,* February 14, 1908. As to the Association's program, see *CMF,* June 14 and September 6, 1910.

⁴⁰It is revealing to read the Rev. Pirot's warm feelings in his book towards the end of his life, concerning his own French-Walloon ethnicity. *Contes dau lon èt did près* (Gembloux: 1950): "Le wallon est pour moi la plus belle de toutes les langues, parce que ce fut la langue de ma mère, de mon père, de toute ma famille depuis des siècles, pour ne pas dire depuis toujours.... Je sens que je ne serais pas moi sans la langue de ma mère, de mon village, de mon pays.... Tant il est vrai qu'après la connaissance de Dieu, la langue est la plus doux trésor que nous tenons de nos parents ..." (p. 9.).

⁴¹Pirot, *op. cit.,* 6.

⁴²*CMF,* May 3, 1910. Cf., also Pirot, *op. cit.,* 7.

⁴³Dr. Schwegel, the former commercial *attachè* of the New York embassy, took up his position in Winnipeg, on February 12, 1910. *CMF,* February 15, 1910.

⁴⁴The whole matter was submitted by the Ministry of Foreign Affairs to the Office of the Prime Minister of Hungary for consideration with the request that the Prime Minister draw the attention of the clergy to the matter through the Prince-Primate of Hungary, the Archbishop of Esztergom. On the basis of this submission the Prime Minister of Hungary did request the Prince-Primate to inform the clergy of Hungary about Pirot's intentions and also arranged that the Austro-Hungarian Ambassador to the Vatican be instructed about the difficulties that Austro-Hungarian immigrants to Canada had to face on the part of the French Clergy, with a view to informing the Holy See along the same lines. ME III, ME K26, 1914, Item XVI: May 21, 1910, Hungarian National Archives, Budapest.

[45]"To deal a death-blow to the agonizing 'Hungarian-Calvinist Spiritist Farmer', we must have a Catholic paper.. . . Is it not a pity that the Hungarian Catholics, who are nine-tenths of the whole Hungarian population, must be taught through a paper founded and published by a Calvinist preacher? It is not only a pity, it is a shame to everyone of us." Pirot, *op. cit.*, 24. — In his reference to his journey to Hungary Pirot stated two objectives of the trip ". . . to get Hungarian priests and to discuss Hungarian matters with the Hierarchy." He further asserted "Dr. Schwegel and Co. wrote to the Hungarian government and to Hungarian papers, saying that I would go there now to collect money for French people!" *Ibid.*, 18. — Of course, as has been noted above, Schwegel and the others never claimed that Pirot's collection would be "for French people," but rather for a Catholic Hungarian paper in the interest of Archbishop Langevin's ultra-conservative clergy.

[46]Hungarian National Archives, *ibid.*

[47]As a matter of interest, the pamphlet of the Rev. Pirot bears on it the *Imprimatur* by Fergus Patrick McEvay, the Archbishop of Toronto, along with the permit of publication by Mgr. Langevin. See Pirot, *op. cit.*, 3.

[48]Hungarian National Archives, *ibid.*

[49]Thus the successive prime ministers after 1903 gave increasing support to "Operation America," the endeavor to involve the American Hungarian churches in the ecclesiastical organization of the old country with a view to governing them and influencing them from the Hungarian capital. Count Istvan Tisza, the lay head of the Reformed Church of Hungary, seemed, in addition, to have closer emotional ties with his co-religionists, the Calvinists, in the USA and Canada. It was Tisza who during the time of his first cabinet (November 3, 1903 — June 18, 1905) had seen the initial growth of the project and, again, as head of the cabinet between mid-1913 and mid-1917, took personal interest in the Operation. Count Karoly Khuen Hedervary served as Prime Minister in the sixteen months from January 1910.

[50]The Suffragan See of Regina became elevated to a full bishopric and filled with the person of Mgr. Olivier Elzear Mathieu on July 21, 1911, who displayed a much more conciliatory and in fact positive attitude towards the Hungarians of Saskatchewan, with particular reference to the question of Hungarian priests. Note the emphasis laid by the Vatican on the opinions of the major ethnic groups of the Province in the selection process of the new bishop and Archbishop Langevin's manoeuvring with consummate diplomacy to secure a French Canadian candidate. Cf. *La Presse,* Montréal, October 27, 1910 as cited in Pierre Morisette, "La Carrière Politique de W. F. A. Turgeon, 1907-1921," M.A. thesis (University of Regina, Regina, 1975), 137-39.

[51]*CMF,* May 17, 1910. Perhaps it was not particularly wise, on the part of the editor, to introduce the article with the stressing of the achievements of the Hungarian Calvinists in the organization according to ethno-national considerations. The mentioning of the leadership of Presbyterian ministers in the retention of Hungarian patriotism and in the establishment of the Canadian Hungarian Brotherhood Association seemed to have provided strong ammunition for the other side in describing the *Canadian Hungarian Farmer* and its supporters as a Protestant conspiratorial group. See, for instance, Pirot, *op. cit.*, 24. The projection of the image of a *bilingual* Hungarian school also in Saskatchewan, seems related to the residence in Winnipeg of the *CMF* editors.

[52]Both dates serve for the commemoration of the Hungarian War of Independence fought against the Habsburg dynasty's domination in 1848-49 under the leadership of Louis Kossuth. March 15, 1848 has been regarded as the first of a chain of events leading to the war while it was on October 6, 1849 that 13 of the generals conducting the war on the Hungarian side were executed in retribution by the Austrian authorities. The reference "Kossuth's Day" to March 15 by Pirot (*op. cit.*, 7) is inaccurate even if Kossuth's name and role in connection with the War of Independence would usually be commented upon in depth and breadth on the occasion of the yearly celebration, for instance, in Bekevar, Saskatchewan; the term Kossuth's Day has not been used among Hungarians to describe the event, nor did Kossuth play any major role in the activities of the first "Fifteenth of March."

[53]*CMF,* May 17, 1910.

[54]Pirot, *op. cit.*, 7-8.

[55]Thus, Marr Hall School District in the vicinity of Arbury, with a majority of Hungarian Catholic ratepayers, was the scene of protracted struggle with the English Protestant minority over such issues. Among the arguments used by the minority were the habits and customs of the "foreign pupils," which were "not congenial to the English" only to be disproved by an actual inspection. The spokesman of the group also brought up that "the Hungarian priests have in the past interfeared [*sic*] too much with the work of the school." (May 26 and August 16, 1911, Marr Hall S.D. No. 1879, *RDE SPA,* Regina.) The priests mentioned above were M. Érdujhelyi, who on his return at the invitation of the Székelys to Canada took up a homestead near Arbury, and O. Solymos, who as a result of the Hungarian campaign of 1910, was appointed to the Benchonzie parish in March 1911 (*CMF,* March 10, 1911). A copy of the Letter to the Editor concerning Érdujhelyi signed by "Canadian" in the course of the controversy (*MFP,* September 22, 1910) is incorporated in the same file.

[56]In some cases, prior to the establishment of the first Hungarian newspaper the ratepayers of some areas failed to show much confidence or willingness for the setting up, let alone the administration, of a school district. Thus the *Otthon* area near Yorkton, did not possess a school in the first seven years of its existence. It was a "commissioner" (C. J. Macfarlin) who saw to the setting up of a school district and a school house at the beginning of 1899. The district still was under official trusteeship in 1909. It was not until August, 1910 — perhaps under the impact of the "Hungarian School" campaign — that the ratepayers expressed desire for conducting their school under a board of trustees. See, April 14, 1899 and August 4, 1910, East Otthon S.D. 462, *RDE SPA*, Regina. Note also that one of the first branches of the Canadian Hungarian Brotherhood Association was formed at Otthon early in 1910. (*CMF*, March 1, 1910.)

[57]It was probably the presence of the Rev. Melchior Érdujhelyi who was listed as a ratepayer residing on the SW quarter of Section 32 Township 25 Range 17 and publicity in connection with the School Question that led to the formation of the Mathyas School District among the Szekely Hungarians who had already been settled for four or five years in the Arbury area when they undertook, at the beginning of January 1911, the first step towards the organization of a school district. It is of interest that some 80 children of school age resided in the area. However, soon afterwards a certain W. M. Brice submitted a counter-petition for the formation of Queen Mary S.D. of which he wished to be the official trustee. It is essential to note that Louis Nagy of Esterhazy, the leader of the pro-Hungarian-priest group at Kaposvar, was asked to be the spokesman for the ratepayers. Later on the Rev. Melchior Érdujhelyi became the Secretary-Treasurer for the district. See January 6 and April 24, 1911; April 24, June 27, and November 17, 1912, Mathyas S.D., No. 3141, *RDE SPA*, Regina.

[58]*KM*, May 21, 1909.

[59]*CMF*, February 8, 1910.

[60]*CMF*, May 17, 1910. "Miklossey," 32 years of age, naturalized American, had college education from Budapest, could speak, read and write English, French, German, Hungarian and "Galician" [Ukrainian]; therefore he was in a position "to impart instruction in the children's own language. None of the children would be able to communicate with a teacher speaking only English." Document, No. 12562, Buda S.D., No. 1722, May 21, 1909, *RDE SPA*, Regina. In a strange way, the School District still requested the Department of Education for a renewal of "Miklossey's" *provisional* certificate almost two years later. Document No. 5716, February 1, 1911, *ibid.*, *CMF*, September 20, 1910.

[61]The name of the place was later changed to Prud'homme and now it is known as Prudhomme. Howell had been the first parish in Saskatchewan of the Rev. Melchior Érdujhelyi, which he left for Buffalo, U.S.A. in January 1909. Cf. *KM*, January 29, 1909.

[62]*CMF*, October 18, 1910.

[63]*CMF*, December 23, 1910. The campaign for a Hungarian teacher in the Howell area seems to have been connected with the gradual emergence of support in this community for the Canadian Hungarian Brotherhood Association, which, however, in this instance involved the application of a precautionary device. Not a Branch but a "Hungarian Civil Circle" with simultaneous membership in the Association was formed on January 5, 1911. Among the names of 24 members appear those of Mr. and Mrs. E. Perenyi. Cf. *CMF*, January 13, 1911.

[64]The minutes of the annual meeting, January 14, 1911 were kept by J. C. Milliken, Secretary, who also functioned as the teacher of the district.

[65]Kristof Lukacsffy was a successful merchant and general businessman of the area and a supporter of what the *Canadian Hungarian Farmer* was standing for. Nonetheless, according to the minutes he seemed to possess little knowledge of or experience in the rules of committee procedures. His forceful participation in the meeting may be attributed to his recent (November 21, 1910) elevation to the Chairmanship of the Wakaw Branch, Canadian Hungarian Brotherhood Association. This assumption is supported by the presence at the same meeting of A. Miklosy, the Secretary of the same Association. Cf. *CMF*, December 2, 1910.

[66]Minutes of Annual Meeting, January 4, 1911, Dunaföldvár S.D. No. 1922. *RDE SPA*, Regina.

[67]*Ibid.*

[68]The letter to the editor, *MFP*, September 22, 1910, dated September 16, 1910 and signed by "Canadian," mentions Érdujhelyi as "living north of Cupar." In fact M. Érdujhelyi was listed as residing on Section SW 32, Township 25, Range 16 as a ratepayer within the Mathyas School District No. 3141 close to Arbury, Saskatchewan. However, he gave the above address at a meeting utilising the school house of Granatier S.D. [No. 1497] at Benchonzie [now known as Lestock]. In addition to stressing the need for Hungarian schools and Hungarian teachers, he denied that the Brotherhood Association stood for spiritism. Its purpose, he argued, was self-protection for Hungarians. Érdujhelyi also called for Hungarian priests. *CMF*, September 6, 1910. There is no mention of the meeting in the records of the School District.

[69]*Ibid.*

[70]For instance, "but the Hungarian farmers are intelligent, and the old settlers have experience of this country. They know that the schools must be Canadian; and in the new Hungarian settlements where they are not aware of Canadian law, experience shall soon teach them the advisability of respecting Canadian laws." *MFP*, October 3, 1910. "Rev. Kovachy and Co., all your work is anti-Canadian. You misrepresent the Canadian law to the new settlers; you want these to be not familiarized with Canadian life; you excite them every week against other people German, French or Slavic . . . but Canadian people are too straight to not see your anti-Canadian work." *MFP*, November 1, 1910.

[71]Although the usual reference to the Hungarians of *Szekelyfold* and *Mariavolgy* is usually "*Magyar*" the settlers of these two localities largely situated between the present-day towns of Cupar and Punnichy would call themselves *Székelys* as also suggested by the name of the first of the above-named settlements: Szekelyfold, meaning "the land of the Székelys." The Székelys had originally constituted a tribe of the Hungarians, the memory of which fact they retain and speak a distinctive dialect of the language. The main body of Székelys, more than two million, live in that portion of present-day Romania which prior to the end of the first World War constituted part of Hungary and, at an earlier stage, an independent principality — under the name *Erdély* or in Latin (and in English) *Transylvania*. A few hundred of the Székelys left their villages in their country which was known to them as *Szekelyfold* and settled in Bukovina whence their later offspring emigrated mainly to the above two places of Saskatchewan in 1906-1907.

[72]The name of the Rev. J. P. G. Vorst was spelt in the Hungarian newspaper as "Worst" — perhaps an intentional alteration to express an opinion about him. Érdujhelyi refers to the two priests in his declaration, inaccurately, as Frenchmen. No doubt it would have been better for him to be more specific and use the term "French-speaking." Vorst was Pirot's only assistant who was willing and persistent enough to learn Hungarian. He was the priest at Benchonzie (close to Cupar) in the fall of 1910.

[73]*CMF*, September 13, 1910. See also Pirot, *op. cit.,* 20.

[74]"They look at us from high; they would treat us as slaves. Before their association was formed, they crawled at our feet inspiring us with disgust and astonishment.. . ." Pirot, *op. cit.,* 20. The impact upon the main actors in the polemics of their one-time study of the great orators of antiquity at their respective classical grammar schools can be noticed distinctively in their written attempts to sway the emotion of the readers through the use of various rhetorical devices.

[75]Pirot, *op. cit.,* 3.

[76]*Ibid.,* 23.

[77]No doubt being in the midst of the Székelys and not far from Érdujhelyi's parish.

[78]*The Manitoba Free Press* did not publish the circular in its entirety; however, it gave the essential summary of it. For the full text see Pirot, *op. cit.,* 16.

[79]*CMF*, October 25, 1910.

[80]In Pirot's account ". . . his Grace addressed the people outside, his words being translated by Father Conter. His Grace explained thoroughly the points pertaining to the authority of the Church, and the Catholic policy with regard to the appointment of priests, to neutral or anti-Catholic papers or associations. It was a sermon truly apostolic; it made a deep impression on hesitating souls and also on some four or five rebels who left the ground.. . ." Pirot, *op. cit.,* 21. In the *CMF's* (October 25, 1910) words, a correspondent from Benchonzie reported a "very cold reception" owing to Father Vorst's "unworthy actions"; then he went on, saying "after the mass the Archbishop was speaking in English in the open air. His speech translated by the parish priest of Yorkton was hardly comprehended by anyone, being expressed in such twisted Hungarian. Also biblical phrases were freely mixed with such expressions as fool, stupid, pig and the like relating to those who long for Hungarian priests as well as to the only Magyar priest living in Canada.. . . There were people who began muttering with discontent and turned their backs angrily on the priests, who instead of preaching Christ's message, were stuttering such unkindly things."

[81]The Székelys of Benchonzie had been reported as being very enthusiastic about the CMTSZ (Hungarian Canadian Brotherhood Association). Apparently its meeting on August 28, 1910 was very well attended (*CMF*, September 6, 1910). The local membership of the CMTSZ obviously representing the majority of the Székely farmers of Benchonzie "declared with one voice that they would not accept a French priest, not even if he were to pay and that they would do their best to obtain a Hungarian priest before long."

[82]It is relevant in this context to mention the fact that the largest portion of the *Manitoba Free Press* article about the interview with Consul Schwegel (August 30, 1910) discussed above dealt with the desire of the Ukrainians (Ruthenians) to have priests "of the Ruthenian rite and nationality." The consul stressed that "What the Ruthenians chiefly object to is that the French bishop wants to force French priests upon them." None the less, St. Boniface apparently thought it wiser to take notice of only the Hungarian section of Schwegel's statement. Yet one of the Ukrainian intellectuals, William (Vladimir) Zaphorzan, chose to enter into the polemics on the Consul's side: "I wrote many times to His Grace Archbishop

Langevin asking him to secure for us from the old country a good secular priest . . . of our own nationality.. . . I think Dr. Schwegel has good reason in what he says because they are trying to force us to keep such priests, who can barely speak our language and sometimes need an interpreter.. . ." *MFP,* September 29, 1910. Of course, it should not be forgotten that there were many more "Ruthenians" in the Archdiocese than Hungarians and a greater proportion of them were willing to co-operate with the Archbishop. Cf. "S. E. Mgr. Adelard Langevin, Archevêque de St.-Boniface, et les Ukrainiens," *Rapport 1944-45, La Societe Canadienne d'Histoire de l'Eglise Catholique* (n.p., 1945), 109.

[83]Pirot, *op. cit.* 24

[84]In connection with the actual publication of Pirot's pamphlet (*op. cit.),* the *Canadian Hungarian Farmer* (June 30, 1911) had reason to state — among many unfavourable comments on the booklet and its author — that "Jules Pirot has been given notice by the people; the Parish of Kaposvar declared that they did not want French priests any more. Also Pirot . . . agreed to go. Why does he not go quietly?" Then see *CME,* August 4, 1911: "Jules Pirot . . . after having been turned out from Kaposvar has now cast his eyes on his Stockholm parishioners.. . . We would pay what we can to our spiritual father, but not to one who is undermining the reputation of the Hungarians, who changes the dogmas without authority . . . We have asked Our Lord Archbishop to suspend the Rev. Jules Pirot, Parish Priest from his office at Kaposvar and Stockholm." Signed by 36 Stockholm parishioners. The Rev. Pirot was finally transferred to Esterházy whose Hungarian parishioners at that time all belonged in Kaposvar Parish.

[85]The Most Rev. Olivier Elzear Mathieu, Rector of Laval University, Quebec, having been nominated on July 21 was installed as Bishop of Regina on November 23, 1911. Frank Gerein, Right Rev., *Outline History of the Archdiocese of Regina,* Golden Jubilee Year 1961 (Regina: 1961), 38-39. One of the first efforts of the new Bishop, to bring about more cordial relations with the Hungarians of his Diocese, proved successful. Thus the Rev. Melchior Érdujhelyi was placed in charge (according to *CMF,* March 16, 1912) of the Székely parishes (Magyar, Benchonzie, Székelyföld and Máriavölgy) and asked by the Bishop to search for a suitable priest in Hungary. Mgr. Mathieu's great part in bringing out Hungarian priests was acknowledged in *CMF,* May 15, 1914.

[86]"Esterhazy [properly Kaposvar] Jubilee . . . Those present included . . . L. E. Kovachy, Peter Németh, K. Lukacsffy.. . . Kálmán Kovachy recited a poem esp. composed for the occasion.. . ." *Regina Leader,* August 16, 1911.

[87]A note added to the necrology explains: "This is the list of Bishops and Priests, now deceased, who laboured in the Archdiocese from the earliest days." Gerein, *op. cit.,* 266, 267 and 263.

HOW TO TEACH A UKRAINIAN
SAVELIA CURNISKY

I

The period 1880 to 1915 saw a rapid influx of settlers into western Canada — Mennonites, Jews, Icelanders, Doukhobours and Ukrainians.[1] With this influx of "New Canadians," the number of school-age children increased with a corresponding growth in the complexity of educational problems.

The first major Ukrainian immigration into Saskatchewan took place near the turn of the century. The vast majority of those who did immigrate to Canada were poorly educated in general, as illustrated by their high rate of illiteracy, but highly trained in the practice of farming.

Before embarking on the specific Ukrainian experience in Saskatchewan, it is necessary briefly to overview the characteristics of the educational system to which the Ukrainian population had been exposed prior to emigration.

The strong religious orientation almost ubiquitous in peasant cultures was also evident in the educational systems of these areas which at the end of the first World War came to be incorporated for a short time in an independent Ukraine.[2] It can be generalized with only a slight risk of "sweepingness" that the Ukrainian type of education available in the peasant communities did not exceed, as a rule, some slight acquaintance with basic skills, biblical stories, church rites and hymns. As to the intelligentsia, the main elements of their education derived from the study of classical humanities and theology.[3] Thus higher education was restricted to a few, as only the relatively wealthy could afford it. The Orthodox Church, which was primarily responsible for education, gradually expanded schooling and also made the more advanced levels increasingly accessible.

In the course of their history Ukrainians had been exposed to three main cultures; accordingly the higher schools promoted a *"trilingual lyceum"*[4] — whereby Slavonic, Latin and Greek were to be learned. With alternating political domination of the Ukraine by Poland, Austria and Russia, their languages were also introduced into the curricula.

Opposition to the imposition of "foreign languages" rose markedly in time, and more and more subjects were taught in Ukrainian.

By 1868 the Prosvita Society or Society for Enlightenment had begun its activities in the Ukraine. This literary society regarded as its most important task the education of the peasants in Galicia through a network of local libraries and reading rooms.[5]

It is on record that their foreign governments viewed the Ukrainians as backward and ignorant and that they prohibited the publication of books in the Ukrainian language. The consequent struggle for the maintenance of cultural identity late in the nineteenth and early in the twentieth century kept the national spirit alive in the Ukraine and developed methods with which the people learned how to safeguard their rights and culture.

For the Ukrainian people throughout the world, 1918 marked the beginning of the establishment of the independent Ukrainian Republic. For a relatively short time, they even experienced a degree of freedom under the Russians for the publication of their books and newspapers. This advancement also effected a strong resurgence of nationalistic feelings among the settlers in Canada.

The absence of political and social structures for the enculturation of the New Canadians at the beginning of the Eastern European immigration is pointed out with dramatic frankness in J. A. Calder's speech to the House of Commons in 1919:

> We invited those people here: we sent across the seas our agents and explained the possibilities of this country of ours: how they would be welcome here, how well they could get along and all that sort of thing. And when we brought them here, and scattered them throughout Canada, we left them entirely on their own. Our policy in that regard has been nothing short of tragedy. We have done little to familiarize them with our laws; we have no policy in our country to Canadianize them; we have simply left them adrift.[6]

Of course, government action in this and many other respects was no part of the liberalism of the age. Therefore the education of the non-English was left to those of missionary spirit and incomplete teacher training, and it was they who made the prairie school the centre of culture and enlightenment.

The educational policy towards Ukrainians contained assimilationist and enculturative techniques combined with what may be called imperialistic and hegemonic elements. All these factors can be identified when one studies the Ukrainian experience in Saskatchewan. It is essential to take notice of the existence of a relationship between their former pattern of education and the manner in which Ukrainians were to react to certain aspects of the Saskatchewan system.

II

The Ukrainians on leaving culturally rich Eastern Europe, an area with highly developed folklore, complex popular music and long history, were to discover on arrival on the Prairies that their traditions and aspirations aroused little else than suspicion and censure. Their entry in search of quick material advancement into a country only recently established as a political and economic unit, yet bent on a national policy of assimilative intent, revealed an immediate contrast in purpose.

The Anglo-Canadians in western Canada, for example, continually raised the issue of Ukrainian "contribution" to the development of Canada, at the same time expressing the fear that since these immigrants were illiterate, they would raise their children without the benefit of schooling. If left unassimilated, these children — so the argument ran — would undermine the Canadian standards. An editorial in the *Regina Post* clearly expressed this fear:

> We invite their parents to Saskatchewan knowing them to be a vulnerable part in our national life and depending on the public school to remove that weakness at least in the second generation. The vast majority of the European immigrants are simple, industrious illiterate folk but amongst them are to be found dangerous demagogues who desire to remain indefinitely a distinct and unassimilated element.[7]

It is significant that in an historically bicultural nation, there should be little inclination to extend tolerance for cultural development to new and different ethnic groups. The determination of Ukrainians to hold on to their old customs was taken as an instance of primitivism and, more importantly, as a potentially divisive factor in national development. It was this concern over the putative dangers of ethnic separation which prompted the more zealous members of the host society not only to express their welcome and appreciation to newly arrived immigrants, but also sternly to warn them about their duty to respect the laws, to send their children to English-language schools and switch attachment from their native country to Canada.[8] References to the "cultural impoverishment" of Ukrainians often occurred in the writings of the day, especially in those of Gibbon, a writer in the twenties who maintained, however, that if the immigrants were given good housing and "their souls," they would act as decent citizens.[9]

The efforts to inculcate Anglo-Canadian values in the immigrants operated on many levels, but schools soon assumed prime importance. Schools, of course, in every country serve as instruments of cultural transmission and thus possess facilities and inducements to achieve their purpose, enculturation. In undertaking to teach Ukrainians civics and the English language, schools were very careful to offer correct guidance and proper methodology, to select particular teachers and appropriate textbooks and to encourage secondary ideological associations.

In the educational systems of Britain of the time, as in almost all other civilized countries, the school was held an agency of citizenship, with the difference that it was *not* to "teach" patriotism, even if *good education* also implied patriotism. In this context it is relevant to stress that much of the factual and emotional contents of the British curricula were connected with Britain's imperial status. The diffusion of British educational ideals in its imperial era[10] helped create that unique atmosphere in which the "colonials" were encouraged to become "proper British gentlemen" and "good citizens." In Canada (Quebec excepted), the British educational ideals unequivocally prevailed. In western Canada, however, where the immigration of disparate groups began to present a challenge, schools, and especially elementary schools, became crucial instruments of assimilation. An article appearing in the *Saskatoon Phoenix* summarized the role schools were expected to play: "Every school in Canada is to be a training ground for Canadian citizenship with the added bonus of a greater citizenship of the Empire."[11]

The institution primarily responsible for executing the educational policy of cultural assimilation was the provincial Board of Education. The Board's prerogative consisted of rigid control of examinations, licensing of teachers, selection and authorization of teachers, formulation of curriculum, and supervision and inspection of schools. To appreciate the prevailing desire for cultural conformity, one merely need note some of the lobbying measures directed at the provincial government and the Board. In a letter to Premier Scott (also Minister of Education), H. S. Doubleday of Asquith, Saskatchewan, emphatically expressed his attitude towards immigrants and education: "Let us have no cowardly reactionary measures to foreigners who came to this province . . . ; let them learn our languages, settle in our province if they will, but make them Canadian citizens."[12]

While Scott found himself acceding to such appeals, J. A. Calder, a later Minister of Education, was more sympathetic to the Ukrainians when he suggested that special attention should be given to the educational requirements of foreign settlements.[13] Although Calder sought the assistance of Manitoba officials[14] in matters of Ukrainian education, he experienced opposition from some Anglo-Canadian quarters demanding assimilation. In response to these pressures, Calder was forced to establish a general enquiry into education, especially to report on the educational conditions in foreign colonies with particular reference to the effectiveness of English language training.[15]

Language was not, however, the only issue in the struggle for cultural hegemony. National chauvinism, which had attained alarming levels immediately prior to World War I also in other countries, continued to be used to promote cultural assimilation in Saskatchewan for several decades. Appeals to patriotism had become an implicit and essential part of education, as indicated by the following correspondence. In a letter written to Premier Latta (again, Minister of Education), the Canadian Legion of the British Empire Service League, following their provincial convention at North Battleford, informed the Premier of the "careful examination of the teaching of the children particularly the immigrant children in the schools."[16] In a second letter to Premier Latta from R. M. Morris, Secretary-Treasurer of the Ontario School Trustees, this interest in appropriate training for the Canadian youth was reiterated: "We can't afford to lose the opportunity of instilling into the youth of today a sincere loyalty for Canada and for the British Empire."[17]

These twin elements, language and loyalty also for the British Empire, were being pressed in the schools on a Ukrainian population often hesitant but unable to resist them effectively. While representations in this respect did begin to reach the provincial government level, real power in education lay with the school inspectors and "Normal School" principals, who were nearly always Canadians of British descent. What became increasingly apparent, however, was that although Ukrainians were beginning to adopt English as a means of communication, their personal culture and outlook failed to change correspondingly.

The Saskatchewan provincial school system, true to its avowed function of perpetuating through transmitted Anglo-Canadian values, traditions and conduct, was geared to achieve its purpose with consistent diligent work. Anglo-conformity as an educational objective received special emphasis in Saskatchewan owing perhaps to the high relative density and great ethnic variety of its immigrant population.

The promotion of Anglo-conformity often went beyond the curriculum, which itself was already well steeped in British history. It was felt that the display of the Union Jack symbolizing Britain and Britain's place in history was an important instrument in developing pride in Commonwealth citizenship. When Premier Scott agreed, all schools were supplied with the Union Jack.[18]

It is interesting to note in this context the appointment of the only Canadian Director of the New Canadians, J. T. M. Anderson, who was charged with educational work in non-English communities. His commitment to Anglo-conformity was clearly evidenced in a report to the Deputy Minister of Education in 1921, suggesting field days to encourage "Canadian" games in the "Canadian" tradition in the "Canadian" language.[19] It can be assumed that to Dr. Anderson's "Canadian" could be quite easily interpreted "British" according to the need. Further, he felt the need for the presence both of English publications and of the Boy Scout and Girl Guide movements in the school as examples of sound social institutions for children.

In a letter to Anderson of January 1922, S. J. Latta suggested the use of films in a campaign designed to develop better Canadian citizenship.[20] A portion of the campaign sought to acquaint the Anglo-Canadians with other ethnic communities in the province and also to arouse a receptive attitude among the non-English towards citizenship. The more backward non-English community was to be given a glimpse of educational activities recommended by more progressive countrymen, presumably from the English community.

Compulsory attendance and its enforcement, a topic alluded to in reports to the Minister by Foght,[21] Woodsworth,[22] and Anderson,[23] emphasized the need to control as far as possible the educational processes to which the children of non-English Canadians were exposed.

In the process of involving all of the English-speaking community in the assimilation effort, community agencies and organizations adopted schools in the non-English areas. They provided these schools with language instruction books and propaganda designed to develop knowledge and a sense of pride of Britain and the British identity amongst the New Canadians.[24] The same community effort also led to the setting aside of a day called Better Schools Day[25] intended to allow every *citizen* the opportunity to examine the school system. Discussion at meetings held throughout the province centred on means by which the non-English could be induced to recognize and adopt standards and values acceptable to the English-speaking community. One reaction — interesting, though far from typical — came from an E. O. Thomas of Ettington, Saskatchewan,[26] who pointed out the difficulty of arriving at a response with no suggestions of alternatives or improvements.

W. H. Foght's *Educational Survey* published in 1918 suggested the development of larger school units. However, this suggestion was then not accepted owing to a variety of reasons, including other attempts at achieving uniformity in educational standards and practices — and consequently conformity amongst all young Canadians. At the Educational Conference of 1943[27] another bid made for larger school units was apparently based on the assumption that the stand-alone schoolhouse was now a left-over relic of a no longer existent pioneer lifestyle. It should, however, be noted that even at this time, besides other advantages of the larger units, such features as greater ease in establishing or continuing conformity and uniformity as a consequence of a greater degree of mixing of nationalities were casually mentioned as additional benefits. Remembering that the little red schoolhouse continued to function as before with the exception of being part of a larger school unit administrative structure, we can deduce that the "additional benefits" were perhaps not as secondary as they were made to appear.

Returning to the curriculum, the claim made above that it was steeped in British history, can be tested through a brief examination of statements on curriculum policy and textbooks of the time. A good starting point is item # 6 of a memorandum for the Inspector of Schools issued by the Department of Education in 1926:

> ... dealing with schools of foreign birth: attention should be chiefly directed to reading, spelling and writing, composition and civics. Teachers in such schools should be advised not to attempt to teach all subjects on the program of studies.[28]

Emphasis on English as the only language and foremost subject of instruction is typified by the following single, and technically valid, statement of J. A. Brown, Principal of a Normal School, that "the best pedagogical practice in teaching English to the non-English calls for the exclusive use of English as the language of instruction from the beginning of a child's attendance."[29] Further specific intent was incorporated into the material used for instruction. Any books in "foreign tongues" were acceptable only if, at the same time as they fulfilled the purpose of educating the foreign born, they instructed them along lines which would reinforce the ideas for which the British Empire stood. Other views of history, including the ones that derived from the past of these "foreign peoples," were regarded as inadmissible. The clearest statement as to the nature of history to be taught at school was compiled at the North Battleford Empire Convention:

> All teachers of British and Canadian History and kindred subjects *are to be* sympathetic to the ideals of our origin insofar as they relate to the perpetuation of the British traditions and the development of a true Canadian nationality along these lines.[30]

The closing phrase "along these lines," left little doubt as to the direction and consequently the limitations placed on educational content in this province.

In accordance with the stated policy of the Department of Education that teachers from Great Britain were of "inestimable value" to the foreign community,[31] every effort was made by both government and privately supported "community organizations" to encourage immigration of such teachers.[32] Inducements included financial incentives, as well as allowances, even if inadequate, for training. Evidently only teachers of British background were considered good enough. This tendency is further documented by the Deputy Minister of Education's request for an inspection report on Ukrainian teachers.[33] Inadequacies reported consisted mostly of varying levels of incompetency in the speaking and teaching of English — suspicion that Ukrainian was being taught during a large part of the school day rated high as a sign of unfitness.[34]

It would appear from statements of educational leaders of the time that the occurrence of behaviour patterns suggestive of a degree of adjustment and conformity on the part of members of non-British ethnic groups was externally welcomed and praised as achievement. However, in reality this act would amount to little else but a gesture, a mere pretence — just like the social acceptance of these "foreigners."

Such occurrences as concerts (in the English language), membership and participation in English-language community associations, the singing of God Save the King, educational advancement, apparent signs of loyalty to the crown, and visible material prosperity all were cited as tangible proofs of the benefits and success of the theory and implementation of assimilation. A letter from Norman McKay to Dr. Anderson read: ". . . you would consider yourself repaid if you would have been at the concert to draw into your soul the material proof. . . ."[35] Robert England reported on similar types of success he perceived while studying the Europeans of western Canada: "At the end of great community gatherings, here in the West, amongst these New Canadians, a singing of God Save the King with unquestioned loyalty in eye and heart. . . ."[36]

III

The response of the Ukrainian community to the campaign for Anglo-conformity proved little different from their response to similar assimilation campaigns conducted against them by the Poles and the Russians in Eastern Europe. Their homesteads in the bloc settlements permitted of easy isolation from English-speaking neighbours. With the building of their own churches and community halls, they provided focal points for the satisfaction of their spiritual, cultural, and educational needs within their own communities.[37] Their view of life directed them to seek an aesthetic and pleasant existence. They did not desire compulsory education, especially if it was designed to transfer their youth from the rural to the urban milieu.[38] Their culture prohibited conformity with the English-type civilization in particular because it encompassed a wide sphere of activity with primarily monetary or "get-ahead" rewards.

The Ukrainians did, however, feel an intense urge for education both for themselves and for their children.[39] They had understood and were willing to accept the necessity for the adoption of the English language. But, at the same time, they refused to abandon the right to use and teach their own language within their communities, since it was felt to be central to their continued cultural enrichment. On noticing that their special cultural needs found no favour among English-speaking Canadians, they sought to educate people from their own midst to become teachers. A letter from the Reverend N. Sikora of Radisson, Saskatchewan, dated March 31, 1908, contained a petition requesting the establishment of a Ukrainian Teaching Centre and funding for its operation.[40] It was made clear to the Department of Education that the centre would pay particular attention to the English language and good citizenship. The Department acceded to the request, and the first session commenced on October 13, 1909 with Joseph Greer as the Department-appointed principal. The Ukrainians found Greer to be arrogant and uncompromising in his position as principal, and the Ukrainian Teachers' Convention at Rosthern of 1913 unanimously requested his replacement.[41] Departmental response was to close the training centre a few years later.

Ukrainians sought approval of textbook material in the Ukrainian language to be applied in teaching both children and adults.[42] They wished to teach their children Ukrainian and hoped to take advantage of their better knowledge of their own language in learning about their new homeland. The Department never approved such requests, and although provision was made for the teaching of Ukrainian in the school up to a maximum of one hour daily, after school hours, no teaching materials were ever made available.

With the advent of larger school units, Ukrainians again feared loss of their rural way of life and the protection for their traditional culture afforded by it. The Ukrainians came to accept the necessity to adapt and adjust to the limitations put upon them by the community at large. They continued to await the opportunity to develop according to their own desire. In Rudnitsky's opinion, the Ukrainian withdrew during this time and preferred stagnation since it was felt that no development could take place on the existing terms.[43]

IV

The analysis here attempted not only relates the role of schooling in the endeavour to adjust the Ukrainians into British structures, but also deals with the manner in which the related methods and experiences were reached whether accepted or rejected. The incorporation of the foreign element in the British content made both of them more efficient producers than when they had functioned in their traditional cultures.

The Honorable Joseph Thorson could hardly be congratulated on the accuracy of his insight in the matter of Canadian development as evidenced by part of his address to the Men's Canadian Club in Regina entitled "The Shape of Canada in its Second Century":

> ... we have learned better than any other country the value and importance of leaving one another alone with each individual in our society free to develop the talents with which he or she has been endowed. *We have not made any attempt to press our people into a common or a particular mould.*[44]

Some idealists of the early twentieth century agreed that immigrants posed a national problem, but were unable to suggest an effective solution apart from the assimilationist approach. But the related educational experience in Canada seems to have created an identity crisis even for British immigrants as illustrated by the complaints of some contemporary Anglo-Canadians:

> We have become strangers in our own land. Our flag, our national anthem, the crown, all the tiny symbols, once a treasured part of our national heritage are taken from us and destroyed as symbols of a past, once glorified in, but now suddenly become shameful.[45]

Of late, enlightened authors propose that Canada should adopt a higher degree of tolerance for ethno-cultural differences. Canada, they argue, should not exalt one culture with its set values to the disregard and rejection of the values of the other contributing cultures. Not cultural monopoly and conformity are needed but variety and individuality, which, though exceedingly important, continue to be threatened, primarily by the school system.

Schools being tied to the function of transmitting knowledge, intellectual skills and attitudes based on Western Civilization, have ended up imparting elements of a common culture rather than creating an environment conducive to the study, recognition and acceptance of individual differences. One may hope that it has now become clearer, through the material presented, that cultural differences tend only to be tolerated and respected until they intrude on the values of the mainstream of society, when pressures for conformity begin.

It is argued that schools should have as a primary goal the creation of a learning environment in which all cultures may contribute towards enhancing the experiences and thereby the personal growth of all young people. If, within the present mode of operation, such a plan lacks feasibility, the fact perhaps may be regarded as a sign of the timeliness of appropriate reform.

It is true, a multicultural policy has emerged more as a portion, it appears, of political rhetoric than anything else, with limited influence on existing practice in the schools. The content of social studies courses, for example, at the elementary levels in Saskatchewan can be taken as an indication of the urgent need for critical analysis. The following example is drawn from the current authorized Grade VIII Social Studies textbook:

> Everything around us is our heritage . . . ; especially has our heritage been shaped by the influence of three nations — France, Britain and the United States of America. The histories of these three countries hold the key to true understanding of many of the things we prize in our inheritance.[46]

Eastern Europe and all other regions except Western Europe are largely ignored by the curriculum, which remains restrictive and not quite suitable for a large portion of our school population.

The ethnic communities if they are to maintain any significant level of cultural awareness — beyond token expressions of culture such as folk dancing and cuisine — must receive support from within the educational system. If schools are unable to be instrumental in safeguarding the contributions of other cultures, the call for the transformation of the present system seems justified. It is not the formalities like attendance for required number of times, graded-curriculum and teacher-supervision classrooms which are the essentials of education. Perhaps we should try to identify and benefit by some of the practices of the East Europeans — like that of self-directed education. Realizing that our school system tends to contain and perpetuate conformity and mediocrity, we must seek alternatives.

FOOTNOTES

[1]Early data referred to the Ukrainian population as Ruthenians, Bukovinans, Galicians and Austrians. The various names reflected geographic and former political conditions in Europe. As people came to Canada, they identified themselves according to the political rather than ethnic boundaries. This paper will refer to them only as Ukrainians.

[2]M. Hryshevsky, *A History of Ukraine* (London, 1941), 117.

[3]*Ibid.,* 414.

[4]*Ibid.,* 199.

[5]P. Markowsky, "A Preliminary Study of Ukrainians in Canada 1894-1957," Unpublished paper, University of Saskatchewan (Saskatoon, 1976), 5.

[6]*Debates of the House of Commons,* Dominion of Canada (Ottawa, 1919), vol. 2, 1870, April 29, 1919.

[7]Archives of Saskatchewan, *Newspaper Clippings* X3A, *The Post,* "School Attendance," February 2, 1917.

[8]J. Murray Gibbon, "The Foreign Born," *Queen's Quarterly,* 27 (1920), 335.

[9]*Ibid.,* 348.

[10]Promotion of cultural diffusion through education was not, of course, strictly a British phenomenon in the age of imperialism. France promoted a "Cartesian" educational ethic in its African and Asian colonies while Belgium developed its "Platonic" schools in Africa.

[11]Archives of Saskatchewan. *Newspaper Clippings,* X3A *Saskatoon Phoenix,* "The Educational Problem," September 25, 1915.

[12]A.S. *Scott Papers,* H. S. Doubleday to Scott, August 30, 1915, #34384.

[13]A.S. *Calder Papers.* 18a. J. Bodrug to Hon. Thos. McNutt, April 10, 1906; 18b. Calder to Bodrug, April 17, 1906, p. 2869; 18c. Calder to O. Smith, Commissioner of Immigration in Winnipeg, July 3, 1906.

[14]Unlike Saskatchewan, Manitoba for a time approached ethnic education with greater sensitivity by accepting Ukrainian teachers and allowing them to instruct in predominantly Ukrainian areas.

[15]A.S. *Calder Papers.* File 18, Education: New Canadians. Calder to A. Ball, March 21, 1912.

[16]A.S. *Latta Papers.* Letter from the Canadian Legion of the British Empire Service League, June 27, 1927.

[17]A.S. *Latta Papers.* File 32; General I-M. W. M. Morris to S. J. Latta.

[18]A.S. *Scott Papers.* File IV: Education: General. Scott to B. Cumberland, #33974.

[19] A.S. *Latta Papers.* File 18; Anderson, J. T. M. Dr. Anderson's Annual Report to Deputy Minister, January 1, 1921.

[20] A.S. *Latta Papers.* File 18; Anderson, J. T. M. J. T. M. Anderson to S. Latta, January 31, 1922.

[21] W. H. Foght, *Educational Survey* (Regina, 1918).

[22] Public Archives of Canada. *Woodsworth Papers.* Cote, M. G. 27, III, C7 Vol. 19, "A Report on the Social Conditions in Rural Communities."

[23] A.S. *Latta Papers.* File 18; Anderson, J.T.M. Dr. Anderson's Annual Report to Deputy Minister, January 1, 1921.

[24] A.S. *Martin Papers.* File 56; Education: New Canadians. A. Motherwell to Anderson, June 2, 1920.

[25] A.S. *Department of Education.* File 23; Better Schools Day, Proclamation by R. S. Lake, Lieutenant Governor, May 25, 1916.

[26] A.S. *Department of Education.* File 23; Better Schools Day, E. O. Thomas to Department of Education, July 28, 1916.

[27] A.S. X15 *Saskatchewan Education Conference.* J. Lewis' speech "Inequality of Opportunity."

[28] A.S. *Latta Papers.* File 32; General I-M. Memorandum from Department of Education to Inspector of Schools.

[29] A.S. *Department of Education.* File 106; Provincial Normal Schools, J. A. Brown's form "Report of Practice Teaching in Rural Schools," 1931.

[30] A.S. *Latta Papers.* File 32; General B-D. Letter from the Canadian Legion of the British Empire Service League, June 17, 1927 (my italics).

[31] A.S. *Department of Education.* File 8; Teacher Training School for Foreign Language Communities, Letter to A. Ball, May 31, 1913.

[32] A.S. *Department of Education.* File 138; Motion Pictures in Saskatchewan Schools. Lloyd to Ball, September 10, 1919.

[33] A.S. *Department of Education.* File 8d; Teacher Training School for Foreign Language Communities, A. Ball to Saskatchewan School Inspectors, August 16, 1912.

[34] A.S. *Department of Education.* File 8d; Teacher Training School for Foreign Language Communities, Howard A. Everts, Inspector of Schools, Canora to A. Ball, October 11, 1913.

[35] A.S. *Martin Papers.* File 56; Education: New Canadians, 1919-1922. N. McKay to Anderson, December 24, 1920.

[36] Robert England, "Glimpses of Europeans in Western Canada," *Canadian Geographical Journal,* 5 (1932), 10.

[37] A.S. *Calder Papers.* File 18; Education: New Canadians, Address to Department of Education delivered by J. Syrnick at the Ruthenian Teachers Convention, July 1917.

[38] A.S. *Department of Education.* File —; "Better Schools Day," Wm. Heivson to Department of Education.

[39] V. Lysenko, *Men In Sheepskin Coats: A Study in Assimilation* (Toronto, 1947), 87.

[40] A.S. *Department of Education.* File 12c; Foreign Community and Private Schools, A Report to the Department of Education from Hepburn School District.

[41] A.S. *Department of Education.* File 8a; Teacher Training School for Foreign Language Communities, Rev. N. Sikora to Department of Education.

[42] A.S. *Scott Papers.* File 18c; Education: Foreign Schools, Ruthenian Teachers Convention Resolution sent to W. Scott, July 31, 1913. #34628. Another example from the same file came from I. Gabrichm of Aberdeen, Saskatchewan, April, 1913.

[43] S. Rudnitsky, *Ukraine: The Land and Its People* (New York, 1918).

[44] A.S. *Gordon Papers.* File; Bilingualism & Biculturalism, Address by Hon. J. T. Thorson, February 23, 1967 (my italics).

[45] A.S. *Gordon Papers.* File; Bilingualism & Biculturalism.

[46] A. A. Cameron, *Canada's Heritage,* (Toronto, 1955), vii.

ETHNIC STUDIES AND THE SASKATCHEWAN COMMUNITY COLLEGE SYSTEM

ALLAN W. WALKER
PROVINCE OF SASKATCHEWAN,
DEPARTMENT OF CONTINUING EDUCATION,
RESEARCH AND PLANNING BRANCH

Introduction

Since Saskatchewan is a country-based province with the majority of its population living in small communities or on farms, the Saskatchewan government introduced, some four years ago, the community college system, the basic task of which is to facilitate the distribution of adult educational activities throughout the province. The fifteen regional community colleges recently implemented throughout the province provide educational opportunities associated in the past usually with urban centres. Through the establishment of contact committees in nearly every recognizable community, emphasis has been placed on local participation in deciding what adult education activities will be offered when and in which localities.

The ethno-demographic composition of Saskatchewan is distinctly heterogeneous. Although persons from the British Isles constitute the most dominant ethnic groups, these groups incorporate less than half of the population. Other major ethnic groups include Germans, Ukrainians, Scandinavians, French, and Native Indians. Some regions, and in particular some communities, exhibit a high concentration of persons from one or more particular ethnic groups.

Given the community college mechanism and mandate as well as the ethnic heterogeneity of the province's population, the first two and in the present context the most relevant questions that come to mind must necessarily relate on the one hand to the degree and type of interest expressed in *ethnic content studies* through the college system, and then, on the other, to the effects of that interest as shown in the number and kinds of activities with ethnic content initiated by the colleges. It is the intent of this paper to explore and interpret the trends in connection with these questions.

Procedure

In attacking the above problems, three sources of information were examined. Aspects of community college philosophy and organization were identified through the reading of ministerial committee and department reports. These data were supplemented by interviews with persons directly involved in the actual implementation of the college model. Next, the ethnic composition of the province was determined with the help of 1971 Census data on ethnic descent, mother tongue, and language most often spoken at home. And finally interest in ethnic content education activities was gauged on the basis of college participation as well as other pertinent data collected through community surveys.

The analysis of participation in ethnic content activities was based on the registration records of the three community colleges longest established: Cypress Hills, Parkland, and Carlton Trail. Most of the other twelve colleges have only recently advanced from a developmental to an operational stage.

For the purposes of this study there are two possible definitions of *ethnic studies:* 1) "those educational activities which focus on elements of the culture and history of an identifiable ethnic group," and 2) "studies designed for the need of, and delivered for, an identifiable ethnic audience." Owing to lack of data on the ethnic composition of course participants, only the first of these could be employed here. There were difficulties, moreover, in putting in operation a definition according to content, since some activities have an ethnic content element only in the sense that the skill, such as native crafts, is associated with a particular ethnic group; or the course may focus on transferring a skill, and its ethnic association may be merely coincidental. Only a detailed analysis of each course would come close to satisfying more rigid definitions of ethnic content. Since neither time enough nor data were available to conduct a thorough investigation, in the present context only those ethnic content courses were included which could be identified by course name as offering a skill associated with one or more ethnic groups.

Community Colleges

When the community college concept was first introduced in 1972, three pilot regions in the southern part and one in the northern part of the province were designated. Then after a year of developmental work, educational activities were offered and over the next four years another eleven college regions, covering the entire province, were developed.

The basic assumptions underlying the college system may be stated as follows: 1) adults know what they want to learn, 2) communities should fully participate in decisions concerning what, how, and where activities will be offered, 3) local facilities and resources should be used wherever possible, 4) adults whether dwelling in rural or in urban areas should enjoy as much as possible the same educational opportunities, and 5) colleges should assist existing delivery agencies and fill gaps in this respect where necessary.[1]

To put these concepts in operation the community colleges have developed an organizational structure which is unusual in adult education. In each college region — ranging in population from 40,000 to 80,000 in the rural regions, and numbering more than 160,000 in urban-centred regions — a large number of contact committees have been organized.[2] Each contact committee, averaging about six members, is largely responsible for identifying what activities are to be delivered in its community. In one established college region with a population of 80,000 there are nearly 100 such committees with close to 600 active members.

The colleges have avoided hiring permanent, full-time instructional staff. In order to maintain a high degree of responsiveness to changing community demands, the colleges contract with existing educational institutions (e.g., school boards, universities, technical institutes) and private individuals to deliver activities to meet community interests. Most college staff, employed by a provincially appointed board, perform program co-ordinator roles. The board, consisting of local persons, receives an annual grant and operates within the general guidelines of the governing act.[3]

Initial results would indicate that the college system has been very successful in delivering or assisting the delivery of adult education activities. Registrations for the 1975-76 college year totalled 73,000.[4] Registrations in the three longest established colleges totalled nearly over 24,000, representing a 20 per cent increase from the previous year. The total adult population of these three college regions is 151,000 (taking into account only those persons 15 years of age and older).[5] Thus, the participation rate in these three regions was about 16 per cent of the adult population.[6]

About 80 per cent of the registrations were in social demand or personal interest courses. These non-credit courses are usually about 20 hours in duration, and have an average class enrolment of 13 persons. A likely contributing reason for the popularity of these activities is the low cost: average tuition fees cover roughly 20 per cent of the course costs, the rest being provided in the form of subsidies.

Thus, there appears to be considerable interest among the people of Saskatchewan in adult education, and the college sytem has been responsive to the prevailing expectations. Most of the activities offered to date have been of the non-credit personal interest nature.

Ethnic Composition

As mentioned above, the ethnic composition of Saskatchewan is heterogeneous. Although persons from the British Isles constitute the largest component (42 per cent), other ethnic groups figure prominently, including Germans (19 per cent), Ukrainians (9 per cent), Scandinavians (6 per cent), French (6 per cent), Native Indians (4 per cent), and Poles (3 per cent).[7] Thus, these latter six groups make up nearly 50 per cent of the population.

The provincial ethnic descent breakdown cited above indicates considerable variation from region to region, as well as from community to community. This phenomenon, of course, is a result of the way in which Saskatchewan was settled. Persons from the British Isles compose 54 per cent of the population in the southeast corner, but only 20 per cent in the northern part of the province. Similarly, Germans constitute 34 per cent of the population in the middle western part, but only 11 per cent in the middle eastern part of the province.[8] Ukrainians make up 41 per cent of the population of the middle eastern part, compared to only 2 per cent in the southwestern corner of the province.[9]

The assertion that although Saskatchewan exhibits a heterogeneous ethnic composition, the population tends to be much more homogeneous in terms of mother tongue and language most often spoken at home is supported by statistical data. The large majority, 74 per cent, of the population indicated that English was their mother tongue (language first spoken and still remembered).[10] This is nearly twice the proportion of those who claimed their ethnic descent as being British. In the cases of all non-British groups the percentages related to non-English mother tongues were considerably lower than the percentages pertaining to corresponding ethnic descent. For instance, while 19 per cent of the Saskatchewan population called their ethnic descent German, only 8 per cent gave their mother tongue as German.[11]

This domination of the English language is even more pronounced if one looks at statistics on "language most often spoken at home": ninety per cent of the population falls into this category.[12] The table below illustrates the striking dominance of English when ethnic descent, mother tongue, and language most often spoken at home are tabulated.

Group	Ethnic[13] Group	Mother[14] Tongue	Home[15] Language
British Isles (English)	41.1%	74.1%	89.9%
German	19.4%	8.2%	2.0%
Ukrainian	9.3%	5.8%	2.7%
Scandinavian	6.4%	1.3%	0.1%
French	6.1%	3.4%	1.7%
Native Indian	4.4%	2.8%	2.3%

However, it must be stressed that ten per cent of the population continue using a language at home other than English, and 26 per cent profess a mother tongue other than English. Furthermore, the prominence of non-English groups, in terms of ethnicity, mother tongue, and language most often spoken, varies considerably from region to region.

Ethnic Content Activities

The paper has so far dealt with community college concepts and operations as well as the ethnic composition of the province. Now participation in community college courses having an ethnic content will be discussed. Ethnic-related activities which focus on cultural or historical traits of an identifiable ethnic group, include second languages, such as French, German, English, Norwegian, Ukrainian, and Russian as well as other pursuits, e.g., Easter Egg Painting, Native Crafts, Norwegian Rosemaling. It is, of course, open to debate as to what courses should be considered ethnic-related. Some of the above activities perhaps should not be considered ethnic-related at all, while courses with more ethnic content may be omitted from the following discussion because an ethnic content is not readily indicated by the course titles.

In 1974-75, the three established colleges delivered 30 ethnic-related activities with a total enrolment of 300.[16] Most of these courses (80 per cent) were in the second language area, namely French, Ukrainian, Norwegian and German. Other subjects included Easter Egg Painting and Native Crafts. Preliminary analysis of 1975-76 enrolment data for the three colleges indicates a similar participation pattern. A total of 27 ethnic-related courses with a total enrolment of 270 was recorded. About three quarters of these activities were in the second language area.[17]

Looking at 1975-76 enrolment statistics for the entire college region, about 1,400 registrations were in ethnic-related activities.[18] Here again, as with the participation pattern experienced in the three established colleges, 80 per cent of the enrolment was in second language courses, the most popular of those being French, Norwegian, German, Ukrainian, and Spanish. Other ethnic-related pursuits included Ethnic Dancing, Easter Egg Painting, Native Crafts, Norwegian Rosemaling, Ukrainian Embroidery, Ethnic Cooking, and Tole Painting.

The number of registrations in ethnic-related activities compared to total college registrations was low: they only constituted between one and two per cent of the total college enrolment.[19] This proportion remains relatively constant whether one looks at 1974-75 or 1975-76 enrolments.

If the definition of "ethnic-related" activities were expanded to include activities such as Chinese Cooking, Sausage Making, and Square Dancing, the above one to two per cent proportion would rise considerably. But emphasis in these courses being on the imparting of the skills, any reference to "ethnic" seems coincidental.

Part of the college mandate is to identify the adult education needs or at least interests of communities. One method used in this respect has been door-to-door surveys of rural communities, conducted by local contact committees.

During the 1974-75 college year, a total of 17 rural communities were surveyed in the southwest corner of Saskatchewan. The surveys covered a total of 2,425 informants. Questions were directed toward finding out what adult education activities people would like to see offered. A total of 59 individual requests for ethnic-related activities were received. Over half, 53 per cent, of the requests were for second language courses, two-thirds of which were for French. The other pursuits in which interest was expressed were Ethnic Dancing and Native Crafts.[20]

The above 1974-75 trends tended also to prevail in community surveys conducted in 1975-76. Out of 18 community surveys, with a total of 2,300 respondents, there were 19 requests for ethnic-related activities. Most of these requests (83 per cent) were in the second language area.[21]

In the 35 community surveys, only one to two per cent of the respondents indicated an interest in ethnic-related activities. This ratio is very similar to that between the number of registrations in ethnic-related college activities and the total college enrolment.

In summary, it appears the community college system has aroused very minor interest in ethnic-related activities. This seems to be the case whether one examines actual participation or interest expressed through community surveys.

Conclusions

The tasks and activities of the Saskatchewan community college system, the ethnic composition of the province's population, and the interest in ethnic-related educational activities as manifested through the college system have been examined. The paucity of courses in ethnic-related studies requested or delivered through the colleges to date is indeed striking. One reason for the limited interest in such courses may be the function of other agencies, as for instance the Department of Culture and Youth, to provide individuals and communities with opportunities to stage events with ethnic orientation. Similar related activities of other agencies, both government and service, probably lessen the demand on the college system, owing especially to the very recent arrival of the colleges.

A second probable reason is that the type of ethnic-related activity usually in demand will not readily lend itself to delivery through a public education system. A good example is the festival type function which is well suited to staging through other private or public agencies and institutions. Ethnic activities involving a classroom setting or instructional components may be relatively unattractive owing to their very nature.

A third potential reason is that some ethnic groups may neither wish to, nor perceive the need to, use public institutions such as the colleges to preserve and transmit their cultures. They may prefer less formal methods than those available through an educational institution, even though the colleges are less structured than the more traditional agencies. Furthermore, the colleges may be seen as yet another assimilation mechanism by some strong ethnic communities, such as Hutterites or German Mennonites.

Another likely cause for the relatively few ethnic-related college activities lies in the colleges' conscious avoidance of a close association with any particular groups, be they ethnic, religious, economic, or political. Such a policy was seen as crucial to the long-term development of the community college system. Thus, it is possible that this approach, while strengthening college autonomy and likely promoting broad community credibility, may have weakened both working relations with various groups and the prospect of more extensive ethnic-related activities.

The final possible factor worth considering in this context may be the most important. The assumption that the relatively small interest expressed in ethnic-related activities may be a reflection of generally diminishing ethnic ties appears to be supported by the fact that, despite Saskatchewan's considerable heterogeneity in ethnic descent, three of four persons claim English as their mother tongue and nine of ten as the language most often spoken at home.

However, once the college system has been placed on more solid foundations, different groups may see the colleges as an effective channel for activities connected with ethnic interests. Also the fact that one in four persons in the province professes to a mother tongue other than English, could be interpreted as an indication of considerable potential interest in ethnic studies. Thus, there could develop a tendency to require the colleges to institute activities enabling persons interested to acquaint themselves with their own heritage as well as with the traditions of others. This trend will appear particularly relevant if the colleges maintain their present orientation of delivering personal interest learning activities.

FOOTNOTES

[1]Saskatchewan Department of Continuing Education, *Report of the Minister's Advisory Committee on Community Colleges* (Regina, 1972) and *Harper Committee Report on Community College Development* (Regina, 1975).

[2]Saskatchewan Department of Continuing Education, Research and Planning Branch, *Population Distribution for Saskatchewan Community College Regions* (Regina, 1974).

[3]Province of Saskatchewan, *The Community College Act,* 1973.

[4]Saskatchewan Department of Continuing Education, *Community Colleges: 1975-76 Participation Statistics,* September, 1976.

[5]*Ibid.*

[6]*Ibid.*

[7]Statistics Canada, *1971 Census of Canada* (Catalogue 92-723 Vol: 1-Part: 3, Bulletin, 1.302, Table 4), (Ottawa, 1973).

[8]*Ibid.* (Catalogue 92-723, Vol: 1-Part: 3, Bulletin 1.3-2, Table 4).

[9]*Ibid.* (Catalogue 92-723, Vol: 1-Part: 3, Bulletin 1.3-2, Table 4). "Regions" refer to the 18 Census Divisions in Saskatchewan. Unfortunately, neither Census Divisions nor the 13 Electoral Districts share coterminous boundaries with the 15 college regions.

[10]*Ibid.* (Catalogue 92-725, Vol: 1-Part: 3, Bulletin 1.3-4, Table 20).

[11]*Ibid.* (Catalogue 92-725, Vol: 1-Part: 3, Bulletin 1.3-4, Table 20).

[12]*Ibid.* (Catalogue 92-726, Vol: 1-Part: 3, Bulletin 1.3-5, Table 28).

[13]*Ibid.* (Catalogue 92-723, Vol: 1-Part: 3, Bulletin 1.3-2, Table 4).

[14]*Ibid.* (Catalogue 92-725, Vol: 1-Part: 3, Bulletin 1.3-4, Table 20).

[15]*Ibid.* (Catalogue 92-726, Vol: 1-Part: 3, Bulletin 1.3-5, Table 28), 1973.

[16]Saskatchewan Department of Continuing Education, Research and Planning Branch, Unpublished enrolment statistics from the Student Information System, August 1975.

[17]*Ibid.* Unpublished enrolment statistics from the Student Information System, June 1976.

[18]*Ibid.* Unpublished enrolment statistics from the Student Information System, June 1976.

[19]*Ibid.* Unpublished enrolment statistics from the Student Information System, June 1976.

[20]*Ibid.* "Report on 1974-75 Surveys", December 1975.

[21]*Ibid.* Unpublished statistics from adult interest community surveys, November 1975 to May 1976.

IDENTITY AND ALIENATION

SPEARHEAD ANCHORAGES AND INITIATION OF NETWORKS, WITH SPECIAL REFERENCE TO THE PORTUGUESE CASE

GRACE M. ANDERSON
WILFRID LAURIER UNIVERSITY

For some years now we have been using the term "chain migration" when discussing the formation of ethnic neighbourhoods. The first phase of chain migration begins when early pioneers of a particular ethnic group pass along information about economic opportunities, arrange means of transportation, accommodation and sometimes jobs for their compatriots in the native country — usually kin or hometown friends.[1] This process naturally leads to the formation of residential ethnic enclaves and also to occupational specialization. A good example of this is the concentration of Portuguese immigrants in the area around the Kensington Market district of Toronto. They are employed in the construction industry, semi-skilled jobs in medical services and in the cleaning services trades. If this process is expressed graphically, as in Figure 1 below, person A helps B, later B assists C, when C is established he lends a hand to D, and so the process continues through chain formation.

Figure 1

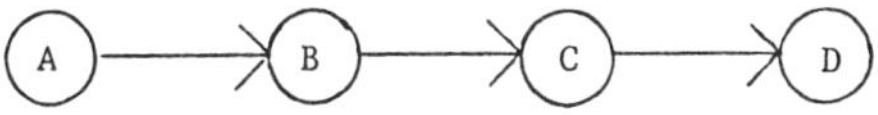

$A \longrightarrow B \longrightarrow C \longrightarrow D$

Figure 2

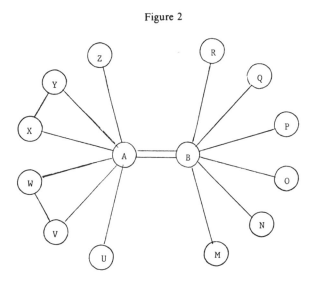

Figure 3

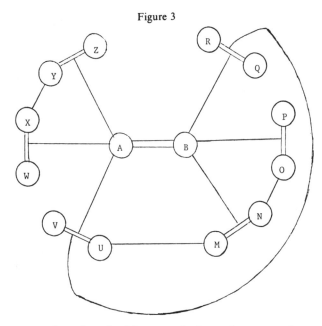

More recently, when looking at ethnic enclaves, we have spoken of "networks." Don Aronson calls networks "a new tool"[2] — that is, a new methodology. But networks can also be regarded in their theoretical aspects, as Bott has demonstrated, and she has used networks to explain social interaction.[3] A network differs from a chain, in that the interaction is viewed at one stage removed. In figure 2 the network is loose-knit the members of interaction set of A are isolated from the interaction set of B, whereas in figure 3 the interaction sets of A and B are interrelated either through ties of kinship or friendship or neighbourhood and social proximity.

Boissevain has referred to the interconnectedness very aptly as "friends of friends."[4] Bott has distinguished very carefully between the characteristics of a network as contrasted with a group. "In a network," she writes, "the component external units do not make up a larger social whole: they are not surrounded by a common boundary."[5] One friend's network touches that of another at the point of their mutual interaction and so on through the contacts of friends of friends of friends — or kin for that matter — so that no neat boundaries are to be found in networks. In fact Tilly has envisioned the world covered by networks and has likened it to a melon in a string bag.[6] Craven and Wellman have described the city as a highly organized "network of networks" by contrast to Wirth or Thomas and Znaniecki, who tend to see the arrival of large numbers of immigrants in the city as a disorganized mass of people.[7]

The idea of chains of communication and assistance can therefore be extended to the concept of networks of communication and contact. Both chains and networks differ from groups in that the latter are usually considered as a whole entity, whereas chains and networks are usually traced from ego-centric beginnings.[8]

Granovetter has found in his research that a very wide range of weak links of casual acquaintances was more productive in the job search leading to upward mobility than a smaller group of very intensive relationships.[9] This phenonomenon may help to account for the slower upward pace in society of some ethnic groups as compared with others. Moreover, certain groups have more interconnections with adjacent ethnic groups than do other ethnic, linguistic, or national communities.[10]

In my studies of Portuguese immigrants in Canada it seems relevant to use the concept of networks in describing how these immigrants have come to this country and how their subsequent settlement patterns have evolved. There are approximately 200,000 persons of Portuguese background in Canada at the present time, at a conservative estimate. They are found in major metropolitan centres such as Montreal and Toronto (92,000 in 1975) and Vancouver. They are also to be found in regional cities like Calgary, Edmonton, and Winnipeg. They have also spread into many smaller cities and small towns, as well as into some rural areas. In the cities many of these immigrants are frequently engaged in the construction industry and in the cleaning services trades. In rural regions they own fruit farms in the Okanagan Valley and are seasonal fishermen on Lake Erie where they are residing in Leamington and Wheatley.

Recently my interest has been focused on how these networks were initiated. Who arrived first to form the first anchorage?[11] I shall refer to the first pioneers in an area as "spearhead anchorage" since these persons entered a new area, became established and then aided other members of the same ethnic group to follow them and also to become established in the same region. Between 1972 and 1975 the author interviewed several of the initial pioneers in each settlement of 2,000 or more Portuguese immigrants between Vancouver and Kingston, Ontario.[12] Several interesting examples of spearhead anchorage come to mind.

Manuel Cabral was the pioneer who aided and directed the settlement of Portuguese in Galt-Cambridge, Hamilton, Oakville and Kitchener areas, and Captain Antonio Quintal assisted immigrants into the Vancouver and Kitimat areas of British Columbia. Cabral is a Portuguese American, completely bilingual, and a second generation immigrant. He settled in Southern Ontario in the late 1920s. He eventually established a mink feed business and travelled throughout the province on sales tours. Everywhere he went he attempted to find a Portuguese-speaking person. It was not until 1953 that he was successful in this quest, when an American-Portuguese business acquaintance alerted him to the fact that a relative of his would soon be arriving in Montreal. Upon hearing this news he contacted immigration officials and was able to meet the newcomer and many of his compatriots. Thereafter the immigration personnel informed Manuel Cabral whenever they had Portuguese-speaking persons in the area in search of work. Cabral therefore had the opportunity to assist many immigrants from the Azores Islands and continental Portugal to find jobs and accommodation. Much of this work was done on a voluntary basis.

Captain Quintal was only 21 when he joined a yacht crew to replace a sick seaman at Funchal in Madeira. After a prolonged journey he arrived at the port of Vancouver in 1940. He then joined the crew of coastal vessels and alternated practical experience with further studies until he eventually became fully qualified as a pilot guiding ships into Vancouver Harbour. In this capacity he had frequent contact with immigration officials. Commencing in 1954 men from Portugal, and more particularly from the Azores Islands, began arriving in Vancouver and the Captain's services were in much demand as a translator. Quintal suggested that some of the men who were having difficulty locating work should go to the northern town of Kitimat, where construction had been commenced on a smelter. Many Portuguese immigrants can trace their residency in Vancouver or Kitimat to the initial assistance given by Captain Quintal.

It is noteworthy that both of these pioneers arrived as young men, they were bilingual at an early age, and they were thus able to establish themselves long before the waves of recent Portuguese immigrants began arriving in 1953.[13]

In the case of Winnipeg, early immigrants, who were usually unskilled labourers, were sent to work as section hands on the railways. They came to Winnipeg to do their banking and more especially to send money home to their families who had been left behind in Portugal. It was natural that some should settle in Winnipeg after their year of contract labour was finished. Early immigrants who had learnt some English became "crucial gate-keepers" to jobs for later arrivals.[14]

A few of the immigrants were married before coming to Canada with their families. Some of these families insisted on being located in a large city. Calgary received its first Portuguese family in this way. The first permanent settlement of Portuguese immigrants in Kingston, Ontario, was also by a family group. The first arrivals in a location, as a rule a family, became central to the attraction and settlement of other Portuguese immigrants. Often they were the originators of a pattern of residency, being usually the first among the Portuguese in the area to purchase a home they could therefore offer accommodation to single men or the marrieds who had left a young family in the homeland until they could establish themselves. The family home often became the centre of social events for the burgeoning community, and the single men gravitated to it. Often several of them boarded with a pioneer Portuguese family.

In some cases a Manpower official directed immigrants to a job in a town where there were severe labour shortages. Oshawa, for example, became an area of Portuguese location in this manner through the sending of an immigrant to work in the area as a gardener. When he arrived he felt very isolated without friends with whom he could converse in his own language. He invited a friend to join him and the process of reaching out to others had begun. Networks extended to other areas and aggregation of immigrants accelerated.

Usually those early immigrants with the greatest linguistic ability and with jobs which permitted them to learn English became the first interpreters; later they often became foremen, or else they initiated entry into the better-paid jobs in other sectors of the economy such as the automobile assembly business. In some cases their wives commenced a local variety store which also handled imported foods such as octopus and sardines from the homeland. When the store business grew to the stage where extra help was required, the man usually left his wage-earning job and became a self-employed store owner. As the children became old enough to be helpful they frequently joined their parents in giving additional assistance in the store after school and in vacation periods.

Usually it was not until a few years after the first immigrants arrived as labourers that the better-educated Portuguese persons came to Canada. These commenced ethnic businesses such as travel agencies, real estate offices, and Portuguese clubs and newspapers. It was a frequent occurrence for these persons to arrive with some knowledge of English or French. They were able to make their own arrangements for transit here and were able to establish themselves without much need for local assistance.

Some of the entrepreneurs have been heartily disliked in the local ethnic community for exploitation of their compatriots. (For example, exorbitant fees may be charged for filling out forms for which free assistance is available through governmental or voluntary agencies.) Other members of the community have freely given a large amount of time to their fellow countrymen who were in need of assistance.

Communication about jobs and housing flows along interaction networks through kin, hometown friends, and local Portuguese neighbours. Because of these networks stretching to the hometowns of the immigrants, occupational specializations are often organized according to region of origin of the first entrants. For example, in Leamington and Wheatley on the shores of Lake Erie, men from the fishing town of Nazaré in Continental Portugal are engaged in fishing; from the Azores Islands men work in the saw mills; and from Aveiro, a market town in Mainland Portugal, they go into the local construction industry.

Networks of communication frequently present a problem to industry, for when one person moves, often a large proportion of the workforce also moves. At times they leave suddenly to go to a better paying job in the same industry, and often go without waiting for wages due, departing at a moment's notice. Networks can extend both horizontally to a person of similar status or else vertically — that is, to a person of higher socio-economic class, who may also be a sponsor for them.[15] However, in the Portuguese case, vertical sponsorship occurred rarely. Information may occasionally pass between the sexes: for example, a mother in the homeland may be requested by letter to locate someone in the village who has a son in Vancouver who may be contacted in that city for advice in the job hunt.

The evidence from other studies of ethnic groups in Canada suggests that networks may not be open-ended, for in some cases there are no *social* connections between two ethnic groups. Stymiest in his study of inter-ethnic relations in a Northwestern Ontario town found that the relationship between Indians and white ethnic groups, both immigrant and native born, was characterized by a rift with regard to the communication about job and housing vacancies.[16] Their social networks of communication never made contact. Similarly, in the study of Africville (a black settlement on the outskirts of Halifax, Nova Scotia) Clairmont and Magill found that the African Baptist Churches provided a channel of communication for blacks with each other, but that initially there were no contacts with City Hall except through white "caretakers," and the latter were not regarded as spokesmen for the Africville residents.[17] In a study of national elites Wallace Clement's research suggests that usually only the white Anglo-Saxon Protestants are included in the social network of the core elite where many important decisions are made and business is conducted privately, and that therefore persons of other ethnic groups seldom were upwardly mobile into the core group.[18]

Ethnic networks of communication and assistance frequently lead to the growth of regional ethnic enclaves. These are functional for the adjustment of the immigrant. Complete isolation from the ethnic community in the period of settlement may lead to emotional breakdown. These networks are sometimes functional for the community. In the case of the Portuguese settlement in Winnipeg, the moving of these immigrants into a blighted area of the downtown core resulted in physical upgrading of the area. Workers, many of them employed in the construction industry, assist their kin — Portuguese friends and neighbours — in restoration of the houses. This phenomenon has also been observed elsewhere and has been labelled a "freelance slum clearance movement."[19]

In conclusion it should be noted that networks of contact not only facilitate location in a specific area but lack of contact in a particular city or region may prevent settlement of a particular ethnic group in a specific locality. We have all too little knowledge about immigrants who knew of opportunities in a location which would be entirely new to their own ethnic group and where the opportunity was declined, although there are hints of this hiatus in the literature.[20]

FOOTNOTES

[1]John S. MacDonald and Leatrice C. MacDonald, "Chain Migration, Ethnic Neighbourhood Formation and Social Networks," *Milbank Memorial Fund Quarterly*, 42 (1964), 82.
[2]Dan R. Aronson, "Social Networks: Towards Structure or Process?", *Canadian Review of Sociology and Anthropology*, 7 (1970), 221.
[3]Elizabeth Bott, *Family and Social Network: Roles, Norms and External Relationships in Ordinary Urban Families*, second edn. (New York, 1971).
[4]Jeremy Boissevan, *Friends of Friends: Networks, Manipulators and Coalitions* (Oxford, 1974).
[5]Bott, 58.
[6]Charles Tilly, "Foreword" in Grace M. Anderson, *Networks of Contact: The Portuguese and Toronto* (Waterloo, 1974).

[7]Paul Craven and Barry Wellman, "The Network City," Research paper no. 59 (Toronto, Centre for Urban and Community Studies, University of Toronto, July 1974); Louis Wirth, "Urbanism as a Way of Life," *American Journal of Sociology,* 44 (1938); William I. Thomas and Florian Znaniecki, *The Polish Peasant in Europe and America* (New York, 1927).

[8]It is possible to consider networks as interconnected wholes if advanced computerized techniques are used, but it is seldom that large scale funding and high-powered analysis are brought together.

[9]Mark Granovetter, "The Strength of Weak Ties," *American Journal of Sociology,* 78 (1972-73), 1360-80.

[10]See Raymond Breton, "Institutional Completeness of Ethnic Communities and the Personal Relations of Immigrants," in Bernard R. Blishen *et al., Canadian Society: Sociological Perspectives,* 3rd. edn., abridged (Toronto, 1971) and Edward O. Laumann, *Bonds of Pluralism: The Form and Substance of Urban Social Networks* (New York, 1973).

[11]Clyde Mitchell, *Social Networks in Urban Situations* (Manchester, 1969).

[12]David Higgs interviewed pioneers in Quebec and the Atlantic Provinces. We were both assisted by graduate students Domenico Raimondo and Maria de Sousa.

[13]For more complete details see Grace M. Anderson and David Higgs, *A Future to Inherit: Portuguese Communities in Canada* (Toronto, 1976). Further aspects of immigration settlement patterns and a typology are outlined in the introduction to Part II of the above, "Patterns of Settlement."

[14]See Grace M. Anderson, *Networks of Contact: The Portuguese and Toronto* (Waterloo, 1974).

[15]See Wallace Clement, *The Canadian Corporate Elite: An Analysis of Economic Power* (Toronto, 1975), 207 ff. see especially "Ethnicity and Inequality of Access," 231 ff. in above. My appreciation is expressed to Laird Christie for suggestions in regard to this section.

[16]David H. Stymiest, *Ethnic and Indians: Social Relations in a Northwestern Ontario Town* (Toronto, 1975), especially "Patterns of Exclusion," 77-78.

[17]Dennis Wm. Magill and Donald H. Clairmont, *Africville: The Life and Death of a Canadian Black Community* (Toronto, 1974).

[18]Clement, *op. cit.* See also Merrijoy Kelner, "Ethnic Penetration in Toronto's Elite Structure," in Craig L. Boydell *et al., Critical Issues in Canadian Society* (Toronto, 1971).

[19]Villiers quoted in Brigette Neumann, Richard Mezoff and Anthony H. Richmond, *Immigrant Integration and Urban Renewal in Toronto* (Toronto, 1973), 90.

[20]See for example Raymond Breton and Howard Roseborough, "Ethnic Differences In Status," in B. R. Blishen *et al., Canadian Society: Sociological Perspectives,* third edn. (Toronto, 1968).

SOCIAL ADJUSTMENT PROBLEMS AND ETHNIC GROUP MEMBERSHIP

A. J. CROPLEY
UNIVERSITY OF REGINA, CANADA

Argyle (1967), Kelvin (1970) and other writers in the area have conceptualized social behaviour as involving the acquisition and practice of special sets of social skills. These include ability to recognize social cues, knowledge of appropriate responses to other people's actions, and similar attributes. People who fail to master the abstract principles or rules underlying interpersonal behaviour, experience difficulties in conforming to the ways of a particular society and, as a consequence, are sometimes socially maladjusted. A recent study by Kovacs and Cropley (1975) has applied this point of view to understanding adjustment problems experienced by members of ethnic minority groups. At the same time, Davis and Cropley (1976) have also used a similar approach in the study of juvenile delinquency. The purpose of the present paper is to bring together these two lines of thought in order to gain some insights into majority-minority ethnic group relations.

The Concept of Socialization

An important concept in the analysis of social adjustment is that of *socialization*. This has been defined by Kelvin (1970) as the process through which individuals learn how to live harmoniously with each other as members of a society. As a result of the socialization process, developing children acquire understanding of the environment in which they live, especially the social environment, and acquire the capacity to respond smoothly and readily to the various situations they encounter in their lives. They learn who and what they are, what their rights, privileges and duties are, what they mean to other people and other people to them, how to express feelings and wishes, and many similar principles for guiding behaviour. When their patterns of socialized responses to the various situations of life conform to the norms and expectations of other members of a society, people are said to be well socialized. As a result, they are able to function smoothly within the society, and to experience a good deal of ease in conforming, at least to its broader forms. Their social environment is relatively easy to interpret, and other people become understandable and even predictable.

All people experience this process of socialization, of course, not just immigrants or members of ethnic minority groups. Merely in the process of growing up, children are assimilated more or less successfully into society. Indeed, children growing up share some of the problems of immigrants. As Hartley and Hartley (1966) have pointed out, they are required to abandon roles and values that were appropriate in the past, and to adopt those of the new society (that of adults). During adjustment to the adult social order, children may become alienated from their societies as they abandon the ways of childhood but fail to find full acceptance into the world of adults. This is the phenomenon that Keniston has labelled "developmental estrangement" (1965, p. 456). A failure to "learn the rules" of the society may result in the appearance of behaviours that society disapproves of or proscribes because they are regarded as odd, delinquent or even criminal.

Failures in socialization — delinquency

All children, then, are involved in a process of social adjustment as they grow up in a given society. However, some do not make the transition as smoothly as others, and experience conflicts with established standards. When these conflicts result in socially proscribed behaviours the children may be labelled delinquent, especially if the behaviours concerned are highly visible and annoying to other people, and the children are members of groups with low social status (such as some ethnic minorities).

Explanations of delinquency are not invariably couched in terms of defects in social development, however. Review of the literature reveals that many different explanations have been advanced on the basis of widely differing theoretical approaches. For example, Eysenck (1964) argued that delinquency is related to psychobiological deficiencies such as underactivity of the central nervous system. Empey and Lubec (1971) conceptualized delinquency as a manifestation of membership in outgroups such as low socio-economic status groups or minority racial groups, or other disadvantaged segments of society. More recently, however, several writers such as Hunt and Hardt (1965) and Warren (1969) have attempted to explain juvenile delinquency in terms more directly related to the present paper, by conceptualizing it in terms of defective or arrested social development. Warren (1971) and Cross and Tracy (1971) have recently carried out research based on this general perspective, and have concluded that it provides a useful framework for the analysis of real-life delinquent behaviour.

Davis and Cropley (1976) followed this line of attack and regarded the delinquent as a person who is marked by being poorly socialized. The particular aspect of the idea of social maturity used by these writers was the notion of "interpersonal maturity" originally advanced by Sullivan, Grant and Grant (1957). Persons operating at a high level of interpersonal maturity are able to understand not only the recurring regularities of interpersonal behaviour so that, for example, they can predict what will happen next, but they are aware of the abstract laws or principles out of which other people's behaviour arises. They can, for example, understand their motives, and are aware of the basic canons that guide behaviour within a society. By contrast, persons of low interpersonal maturity may be aware of the concrete consequences of their actions, but they do not understand the organizing principles that make behaviour consistent and lawful, either within individuals or within a society.

Sullivan and his associates postulated that the developmental sequence leading to interpersonal maturity can be described in terms of seven sequential stages or levels of personality integration. However, for practical purposes juvenile delinquents may be regarded as functioning at levels II to V exclusively. These levels have the following chief characteristics.

Maturity Level II: (Integration of Non-Self Differences)

At this stage, the individual is able to distinguish self from non-self. In addition, the ability to make rudimentary distinctions among the aspects of the external world is also present. Level II individuals are cognitively concrete. Consequently, they are unable to organize their experiences in terms of abstract concepts such as time, morality, etc.

Maturity Level III: (Integration of Rules)

At Level III, the individual's ability to predict events and interpersonal responses in the external world is based on a few concrete, "rule of thumb" procedures. However, Level III individuals lack the conceptual ability to account for and understand the abstract principles which underlly relationships among people and events. Consequently, they are confined to dealing with the concrete properties of the world, without understanding the abstract rules out of which those concrete relationships arise.

Maturity Level IV: (Integration of Conflict and Response)

At Level IV the perception of the influence and psychological force of others occurs. Individuals whose understanding and behaviour are integrated at this level have internalized a set of standards by which they judge their own and others' behaviour. They can perceive a level of interpersonal interaction in which individuals have expectations of each other and can influence each other. The relationships of past to present and present to future begin to take on meaning. Level IV individuals show ability to understand reasons for behaviour, and also possess a limited capacity to relate to people emotionally and on a long-term basis. They are concerned about status and respect, and are strongly influenced by people they admire.

Maturity Level V: (Integration of Continuity)

At Level V the perception of stable action patterns of self and others is found. People who function at this level are able to comprehend patterns of behaviour. They understand that they themselves and others behave in the same way in different situations. They see a continuity in past, present and future. They begin to see others as complex, flexible systems that cannot be dealt with on the basis of a few simple rules or procedures. They are aware of the existence of many points of view, and of different roles in different situations. Temporal relations become fully integrated at this level, and as a result, the Level V individual is capable of establishing and carrying through longer-range plans than persons fixated at lower levels.

392   A. J. CROPLEY

The various I-Level stages are not mutually exclusive. A given person may display some characteristics of all four levels, perhaps showing few Level II traits; strong evidence of Level III, or predominance of Level IV features, and virtually no development of Level V characteristics, and so on. Thus, each person displays a profile or pattern of levels.

Davis and Cropley (1976) showed that, among juvenile delinquent boys who committed repeated offences despite intervention by juvenile authorities in the form of apprehension and confinement within an institution for young offenders, there was a significantly lower level of interpersonal maturity than among non-recidivists. Repeated offenders showed, in fact, less well-developed understanding of the "rules of the game" according to which interactions among the members of society are organized. These boys could not discern the principles out of which interpersonal behaviours arose. Other people tended to be unpredictable except in terms of concrete reactions to specific behaviours, and consequently to be viewed primarily as relatively capricious givers or withholders of gratifications. Thus, these authors regarded delinquency as a problem centring on failure to acquire familiarity with the accepted way of doing things within a given society.

Adjustment Problems in Ethnic Children*

Interestingly, although their appearance is by no means universal, a wide range of adjustment problems is also seen among ethnic children. These range from mere rebelliousness to juvenile delinquency, and even to "personal disorganization" (Zubrzycki in Stoller, 1966). Studies in several countries have also referred to conflicts between ethnic children and their parents, including those of Derbyshire (1970) in the United States, Eisenstadt (e.g., Eisenstadt and Ben-David, 1956) in Israel, Zubrzycki (1964) in Australia, and Glass (1960) in the United Kingdom. More overt antisocial behaviour has been described by Harris (1962) and Derbyshire (1970) in their references to street gangs of minority youths in Australia and the United States respectively. Although there is apparently no general or overwhelming tendency for ethnic children to engage in delinquent behaviour, writers in several countries have pointed out that it is not infrequently seen. In Canada for example, Kidd (1958) referred to antisocial behaviour among ethnic children, while Stoller (1966) mentioned its occurrence in Australia and Eisenstadt (1951) in Great Britain. In the United States, there is a substantial literature dating back many years and including studies by Child (1943), Smith (1937) and von Hentig (1945). More recently, Derbyshire (1970) has commented on delinquency among Mexican-Americans.

---

*Ethnic minority groups very frequently owe their existence to some kind of immigration. As a result, many concepts in the discussion of ethnic groups in this paper derive from the literature on immigration.

However, delinquency is not simply a response to immigration. Koenig (1952), for example, concluded that it is three and one-half times more common in the children of immigrants than among their parents. Consequently, an explanation in terms of the dynamics of social adjustment is called for. Kovacs and Cropley (1975) have attempted to develop such an explanation. They explain the psychodynamics of antisocial behaviour among ethnic children using a model similar to that employed by Davis and Cropley (1976) in discussing juvenile delinquency among the population at large, and based upon the idea of inadequate or defective socialization. In particular their explanation depends heavily upon the problem of detachment of minority group children from the ways of the old country. As they grow up in a society children acquire both roles and identity (Derbyshire, 1970). The culture provides a familiar context within which developing children become aware of what is expected of them by other people, and what they may expect in return. They learn, in fact, the rules of the culture.

However, in the case of ethnic children, there may be a number of special problems. One major source of cultural learning is the child's parents, while another is influential agencies in the community at large such as peers, teachers, mass media and popular heroes (sport stars, for example). It is well known that there are often discrepancies between the values espoused by parents and the behaviours they endorse, and those valued by their children. In the case of ethnic children, this phenomenon (the so-called "generation gap") may be seen in an exacerbated form. Parents belonging to the majority ethnic group are usually well adjusted to the culture in which the family lives. They speak its language, know its basic customs and are familiar with the day-to-day way of doing things. They may even be among the society's better-established members and be the ones who set the standards. In the case of children of minority ethnic groups, by contrast, the parents may be unfamiliar with the dominant society's ways of functioning. They may be unskilled in the majority culture's language and otherwise lacking in the means to communicate clear expectations and credible models to their children. The parents may even subscribe to social mores appropriate to a geographically remote society (that of the old country). Furthermore, they may attempt to pass on to their children a version of the original ethnic folkways which is doubly out-of-date because of the fact that they have been resident in the new society for a long period of time. They may, for example, attempt to raise their children to conform to an idealized memory of the old country's culture in the form in which they now recall it from their residence there many years earlier.

A further problem arises from the fact that, in the case of children of recent immigrants, it is not uncommon for the parents to have joined forces in a struggle to succeed, so that both mother and father may be working long hours with the result that they lack the time or the determination to keep in touch with their children. Not uncommonly, in addition, immigrant parents may be of only moderate educational and cultural sophistication, so that they may lack insight even into the ways of the original society, not to mention those of the receiving society. As a result, the values and lifeways espoused by the parents may seem inappropriate or even absurd to the children.

This latter problem is made more severe by the fact that children usually perform the necessary socio-cultural adjustment to new societies at a much faster rate than adults (e.g., Borrie, 1959; Listwan, 1960). The children may be familiar with many of the ways of the majority ethnic group while the parents may be content to look back upon the values of the old country. As a result, children are exposed to two socializing agencies, one found within the home and represented by the parents, the other within the community and represented by teachers, ethnic majority group peers, sports heroes, T.V. stars and the like. This means that children of ethnic minority groups may be exposed to two powerful, but conflicting, sources of influence (e.g., Zubrzycki, 1964). Finally, rejection of the parental value system may even be advantageous to minority group children. For example, if their parents display habits and behaviours which are considered odd to members of the dominant ethnic group, acceptance for the minority group children may be conditional upon rejecting their own parents. The result may be that minority group children are "in a vacuum between two cultures" (Harris, 1962, p. 61), or "torn between two cultures" (Jupp, 1966, p. 74).

Although the concept of faulty acquisition of the "rules of the game" as it is played by the dominant society seems to lead to some similarities in the conceptualizations of juvenile delinquency on the one hand and problems of adjustment in ethnic minority group children on the other, it is clear that the parallel is far from perfect. For example, Sullivan and his associates conceptualized delinquency as resulting from arrested social development; a state of immaturity or fixation in a lower developmental stage. In the case of ethnic children, by contrast, the problem is conceptualized as one of conflict between value systems rather than one of failure to develop. Indeed, Kovacs and Cropley (1975) have gone further to suggest that, in the case of ethnic group members the problem may not be one of failure to acquire the ways of the dominant society, but rather a process of shedding, estrangement or loss, as a result of a kind of regression. This is because it may be necessary for ethnic children, and adults too, to reject portions of the value systems of the ethnic society in favour of the relevant portions of the belief systems of the dominant ethnic group. Thus, they have argued that the problem is essentially one of *alienation*. The concept of alienation has a wide variety of meanings and uses. However, it is always used in a sense implying loss or estrangement. In the present context, it refers to a process of detachment of an individual from the beliefs, values, attitudes, habits and, indeed, the identity that has been formed as a result of growing up in a particular society, or of being exposed to the ways of a particular ethnic group.

In discussing this condition of being torn between two cultures, that of the majority society and that of the minority groups of which ethnics are members, Kovacs and Cropley (1975) argued that emphasis has conventionally been on the absorption of ethnic children into the dominant society. As a result, inadequate emphasis has been given to the simultaneous process of their detachment from the ways of their ethnic group. In other words, insufficient attention is frequently paid to the fact that assimilation into the dominant society requires a process of alienation from the minority group. Most discussions of relations between ethnic minority children and the dominant society emphasize only the problems of attachment, and neglect those of detachment. However, the vacuum occupied by children exposed simultaneously to two cultural traditions is the result of the simultaneous experience of two pressures — movement towards the dominant culture, it is true, but accompanied by movement away from the minority culture.

This problem is exacerbated by the fact that the majority society's views about relationships with minority groups often emphasize speedy acceptance of the majority way of doing things and of majority values. This insistence on "unconditional surrender" (Kavass, 1967, p. 64) to the majority ways may include suspicion of organizations that provide models of the ethnic lifeways for minority group children, such as ethnic organizations or foreign language newspapers, and may even extend to hostility towards those who are detected in public speaking a foreign language (Harris, 1962, p. 56). As a result, ethnic group members run the risk of experiencing a state of *dual* desocialization or alienation. On the one hand, they may be alienated from the ethnic society because of the movement towards the majority ways, but at the same time, they may retain sufficient of the old ways to remain alienated from the majority group. This is the state of being in a vacuum already referred to.

Alienation from the old values that have made life seem ordered and meaningful may result in a sense of loss of purpose, a feeling of not belonging, a loss of meaning and dignity, and similar subjective reactions. These have movingly been described by Cirtautas (1957) as being like the fate of a tree that has had its roots destoyed; unlike the tree, however, the human being is aware of being uprooted. Alienation from the ways of the old society may result in loss of status and self-esteem, in the "interruption and frustration of natural life expectations" (David, 1970, p. 79), and thus in eventual *desocialization* (Eisenstadt, 1954), with its associated disruption of self-image, loss of acquired roles, and similar negative effects. In extreme cases, these effects may result in severe pathology such as mental illness, criminal behaviour, alcoholism, and other destructive reactions, including suicide (Kovacs and Cropley, 1975).

Alienation from the majority culture takes many forms. For example minority group members may experience occupational alienation, as a result of which they are expected to take the lowest-paid and the most unpleasant jobs, residential alienation in which they are forced by various pressures (including low incomes resulting from occupational alienation) to live in undesirable or inconvenient locations, often involving the poorest levels of public amenities, the lowest standards of upkeep of streets and utilities, and so on, and even legal alienation as a result of which they may have fewer rights and less protection before the law, either through deliberate or unintentional discrimination. Again, these kinds of alienation have the effect of desocializing the ethnic minority group members, with exacerbation of the kinds of effects already described as resulting from desocialization.

Avoiding The Negative Consequences Of Alienation

This line of argument has led Kovacs and Cropley to the view that adjustment problems in ethnic groups can be dealt with in a helpful and humane manner by measures that attempt to counter the effects of their simultaneous alienation from both old and new societies. In particular, they argue for the importance of multiculturalism as a model for relations among minority and majority cultures. The particular feature of multiculturalism that is of relevance is that it does not demand abandonment of ethnic group ways as a precondition for acceptance into the majority culture. Consequently, acceptance of the majority society's ways does not require a violent process of alienation from the ethnic group. Multiculturalism avoids imposing severe pressures favourable to the development of alienation among minority group children. They are permitted to retain substantial portions of their ethnic background which thus act as a "buffer mechanism" (Brody, 1970, p. 19) mediating their successful integration into the dominant culture's ways. Indeed, it may well be that the occurrence of alienation and the associated risk of socially maladjusted behaviour of the kind that has been sketched out earlier is determined by the way in which the dominant society handles the question of existence within its midst of minority groups. Where there are intense pressures for rapid and total assimilation, the conflict between cultures that has been described may be expected to occur. On the other hand, where a policy of multiculturalism is pursued, alienation may be reduced and the negative consequences eliminated.

However, Smolicz and Secombe (1975) have argued that the adoption of multiculturation as a model for relations between majority and minority cultures, as envisaged by Kovacs and Cropley, is simply a modified form of the older assimilationism model, seen in its most inhumane form in the "melting pot" model adopted in the United States of America in the early days of immigration to that country. This is because the multiculturalism approach still seems to envisage eventual amalgamation of ethnic and majority cultures. Smolicz and Secombe advocate a non-assimilationist approach centring on "ethnic co-existence" (p. 291). In societies functioning according to such a policy, alienation would presumably not occur, because the ethnic lifeways would enjoy status equal to those of the majority group, and would not have to be discarded by minority group members. However, it is difficult to see how in practical terms, a kind of "drift" of ethnics towards the values and ways of the dominant group could be avoided as long as this group dominated business, professions and mass media. Thus, ethnic co-existence would probably require a reorganization of society of a kind likely to be resisted by the majority group, even without any conscious hostility on the part of its members, since they would otherwise experience alienation themselves, as their society changed. Ethnic co-existence would also require penetration of the whole structure of a society by ethnics who were able to achieve prestigious positions without adopting the dominant group's ways as a prerequisite for success. Whether the dynamics of group functioning and socialization would permit this to occur is questionable.

A somewhat similar criticism of the Kovacs-Cropley model for avoiding the negative consequences of alienation has been made by Putnins (1976). He argued that their model is linear or unidimensional, with assimilation to the majority group and assimilation to the minority group seen as opposite ends of a single continuum. Thus, as a person becomes more assimilated to one group, he is necessarily more alienated from the other. Putnins suggests, by contrast, that the continuum of alienation-assimilation can be applied to the degree of identification with both cultures. In this conceptualization, it would be possible for a person to be assimilated to both cultures, or for that matter, alienated from both. This model seems to permit a situation in which a particular person could be well integrated into both majority and ethnic cultures, and seems to offer a way of conceptualizing what Smolicz and Secombe had in mind when they referred to ethnic co-existence. For this reason, although Kovacs and Cropley may have correctly identified the problem that they referred to as "alienation," it seems likely that they did not sufficiently emphasize the importance of ethnic co-existence in the conceptualization of multiculturalism.

REFERENCES

M. Argyle, *The Psychology of Interpersonal Behaviour* (Harmondsworth, Middlesex, 1967).

W. D. Borrie, *The Cultural Integration of Immigrants* (Paris, 1959).

E. B. Brody, "Migration and Adaptation: The Nature of the Problem," in E. B. Brody (ed.), *Behaviour in New Environments: Adaptation of Migrant Populations* (Beverly Hills, California, 1970).

I. L. Child, *Italian or American: The Second Generation in Conflict* (New Haven, Connecticut, 1943).

K. Cirtautas, *The Refugee: A Psychological Study* (Boston, 1957).

H. J. Cross, and J. J. Tracy, "Personality Factors in Dilinquent Boys. Differences between Blacks and Whites," *Journal of Research in Crime and Delinquency,* 1971, 8, 10-22.

H. P. David, "Involuntary International Migration," in E. B. Brody (ed.), *Behaviour in New Environments: Adaptation of Migrant Populations* (Beverly Hills, California, 1970).

J. C. Davis, and A. J. Cropley, "Psychological Factors in Juvenile Delinquency," *Canadian Journal of Behavioural Science,* 1976, 8, 68-77.

R. L. Derbyshire, "Adjustment of Adolescent Mexican Americans to United States Society," in E. B. Brody (ed.), *Behaviour in New Environments: Adaptation of Migrant Populations* (Beverly Hills, California, 1970).

S. N. Eisenstadt, "Delinquent Group Formation among Immigrant Youth," *British Journal of Delinquency,* 1951, 2, 34-45.

S. N. Eisenstadt, *The Absorption of Immigrants* (London, 1954).

S. N. Eisenstadt and J. Ben-David, "Intergeneration Tension in Israel," *International Social Science Bulletin,* 1956, 8, 54-75.

L. T. Empey and S. G. Lubec, *The Silverlake Experiment: Testing Delinquency Theory and Community Intervention* (Chicago, 1971).

H. J. Eysenck, *Crime and Personality* (Boston, 1964).

R. Glass, *Newcomers: The West Indians in London* (London, 1960).

M. Harris, "Morals and Manners," in P. Coleman (ed.), *Australian Civilization: A Symposium* (Melbourne, 1962).

E. Hartley and R. E. Hartley, "Foreword," in R. Taft, *From Stranger to Citizen* (London, 1966).

W. Hunt and J. Hardt, "Developmental Stage, Delinquency and Differential Treatment," *Journal of Research in Crime and Delinquency*, 1965, 2, 20-31.

J. Jupp, *Arrivals and Departures* (Melbourne, 1966).

I. I. Kavass, "Migrant Assimilation," *Australian Quarterly*, 1962, 34, 54-66.

P. Kelvin, *The Bases of Social Behaviour* (London, 1970).

K. Keniston, *The Uncommitted: Alienated Youth in American Society* (New York, 1965).

J. P. Kidd, *New Roots in Canadian Soil* (Ottawa, 1958).

S. Koenig, "Second- and Third-Generation Americans," in F. J. Brown and J. S. Roucek (eds.), *One America: The History, Contributions and Present Problems of our Racial and National Minorities* (New York, 1952).

M. L. Kovacs, and A. J. Cropley, *Immigrants and Society: Alienation and Assimilation* (Sydney, Australia, 1975).

I. A. Listwan, "Mental Disorders in Immigrants: Further Study," *World Mental Health*, 1960, 12, 38-45.

A. L. Putnins, "Immigrant Adjustment: A Note on Kovacs and Cropley's Model," *Australian Journal of Social Issues*, 1976, 11, 209-12.

W. C. Smith, *Americans in Process: A Study of our Citizens of Oriental Ancestry* (Ann Arbor, 1937).

J. J. Smolicz and M. J. Secombe, Review of "Immigrants and Society," *Australian Journal of Education*, 1975, 19, 290-92.

A. Stoller, (ed.), *New Faces: Immigration and Family Life in Australia* (Melbourne, 1966).

C. Sullivan, M. Grant and J. Grant, "The Development of Interpersonal Maturity: Applications to Delinquency," *Psychiatry*, 1957, 20, 273-85.

H. von Hentig, "The First Generation and a Half: Notes on the Delinquency of the Native White of Mixed Parentage," *American Sociological Review*, 1945, 10, 792-98.

M. Q. Warren, "The Case for Different Treatment of Delinquents," *Annals of the American Academy of Political and Social Sciences*, 1969, 381, 47-59.

M. Q. Warren, "Classification of Offenders as an Aid to Efficient Management and Effective Treatment," *The Journal of Criminal Law, Criminology and Police Science*, 1972, 62, 239-58.

J. Zubrzycki, *Settlers of the Latrobe Valley: A Sociological Study of Immigrants in the Brown Coal Industry in Australia* (Canberra, 1964).

SOUTH SLAVS ON A NORTHERN MARGIN: THE FRONTIER EXPERIENCE OF CROATIAN MIGRANTS DURING CANADA'S GREAT DEPRESSION

A. W. RASPORICH
UNIVERSITY OF CALGARY

In certain circumstances, some of the most dynamic social change is observed at the margin, and not at the centre, of a newly emerging civilization. This hypothesis coincides with the somewhat outmoded frontier interpretation of history, which has held for some time that some of the greatest changes in North American society have often been wrought first upon its frontiers, before being adopted at its civilized urban core. Recent ethnic historiography has quite properly ignored this conventional wisdom as a sole guiding principle, but has swung to the other extreme of concentrating almost solely upon the urban ethnic ghetto as its paradigm of social analysis.[1] What, however, of the great number of immigrants who seldom saw a city beyond their first entry into the country, and lived away from its centre for much of their lives? The "new" ethnic history has often neglected the frontier migrants, perhaps for reasons of documentary scarcity, and perhaps because they also defied social classification, being neither rural nor urban. It might then be instructive, in view of this bias in recent ethnic scholarship, to leave behind what W. L. Morton has typed "the pavement mentality" of the modern urban historian.[2] Let us look instead at social change and ethnic identity among a segment of the Croats in Canada during the Great Depression, a group of marginal men on the frontiers of Canadian society, cut off from the mainstream of Canadian society and more settled communities of Croatian Canadians.

The instructiveness of these observations for the Croatian experience in Canada during the nineteen-thirties is that the Croats had devolved from one social periphery in south-central Europe to another on the northern Canadian frontier. Yugoslavia was certainly at the economic borderland of Europe from its inception as a nation after World War I with the break-up of the Austro-Hungarian empire. As E. H. Carr has acutely observed in his *Twenty Years Crisis,* the newly created nations of southern and central Europe remained industrially underdeveloped agrarian economies in the inter-war period.[3] Even the wealthier regions of Yugoslavia such as Slovenia were chronically short of currency and continued in the traditional practices of self-subsistent peasant agriculture. The poorer regions of Croatia, Bosnia and Herzegovina were still in the throes of agrarian crisis, characterized by overpopulation and excessive partition of the land which had beset them since the late nineteenth century.[4] High rates of outward migration had been characteristic of these regions ever since the 1880s, and the flow continued unabated from Yugoslavia during the 1920s. By the latter half of that decade, emigration totalled 117,000 for the twenties, despite the closing of American doors to Yugoslav immigrants after 1924. And by far the largest number of these (67,000, or 57%) were from traditional Croatian areas of migration such as Dalmatia, Slavonia and pockets of Bosnia and Herzegovina.[5]

The already limited choices which confronted the marginal agriculturalist and unskilled worker were still further restricted when the United States virtually closed its door to immigrants from Yugoslavia in the Johnson-Reed legislation of 1924, which effectively reduced the quota to 671 per year. The net result was to shift the flow of emigrants to their second and third preferences, Latin America and the Commonwealth countries. Canada, which had barely 2000 Croats, Slovenes and Serbians in 1921, began to receive some four to five thousand Yugoslav citizens per year after 1925. And, by 1929, they ranked fourth in order of all continental Europeans coming to Canada. Of the nearly 28,000 citizens of Yugoslavia who came in the period before 1930 over half (52%) were Croats.

Table

Croatian Immigrants to Canada, 1921-31
as a Percentage of Total Yugoslav Migration to Canada, 1921-31

Estimated figures appear in parentheses () where statistics are unavailable. Estimates are taken as average actual figures in that category for the decade.

Year	Yugo-slavs	Croats	% C/Y	Returnees Y/C		Net Y/C	
1921	87	—	—	—	—	—	—
1922	179	(93)	(51.7)	—	—	179	(93)
1923	717	(371)	(51.7)	31	(21)	686	(350)
1924	1976	(1021)	(51.7)	130	(88)	1846	(933)
1925	2487	(1286)	(51.7)	106	(72)	2381	(1214)
1926	4998	2719	55.2	253	(172)	4745	(2466)
1927	4656	2142	46.1	418	(284)	4238	(1858)
1928	5921	3423	57.8	673	(458)	5428	(2965)
1929	4030	1682	41.7	783	(532)	3247	(1150)
1930	2745	1576	57.8	1115	771	1630	805
1931	604	(315)	51.7	1265	861	-661	(-546)
Totals 1921-31	28400	(14628)	(51.7)	4774	(3259)	25041	(12380)

Source: Annual Returns reported to Canada, Department of Immigration from Iseljenički Komesariat, Zagreb; contained in P.A.C., R.G. 76, vol. 623, ff. 938332, Parts II and III.

Footnote: The number of Croatians who remained in Canada by 1931 with the effective closing of Canadian doors to migrants from "non-preferred" countries is open to some question given the figures presented in the 1931 census. The total number of Yugoslavs declared in that census were 17,110 of whom 12,674 were males and 4,436 were females. Given the net migration of some 25,000 Yugoslavs in the decennial period since 1921, and adding to these the approximately 2,000 Yugoslavs listed in 1921, there were theoretically 27,000 Yugoslavs in 1931 in Canada, some 10,000 more than the actual number declared. Leaving the disappearing third for a moment, it appears at minimum that Croats could be counted at 52% of the total 17,110 or 8,845. If one were to count as Croats the number of Roman Catholics declared in the 1931 census, the percentage of Croats would be much higher at 77% of 17,110 or 13,141 Croats, a figure which closely approximates the above projection of Croatian immigrants entering in the ten-year period prior to 1931. Source: Canada, *Dominion Census* (Ottawa: King's Printer, 1936), vol. I.

Discounting the approximately 1700 returnees to Yugoslavia during this period, there were then over twelve thousand Croatian immigrants to Canada just as the country entered the Great Depression of the nineteen-thirties. It was approximately this number which became the effective population base of this ethnic group for the next decade, as the door soon closed to immigrants of "non-preferred countries" in 1931.

Spatially, the vast majority of Croats were spread across central and western Canada. Half were located in Ontario, seventeen per cent in British Columbia, another seventeen per cent in Alberta and Saskatchewan, and ten per cent in Quebec. Relatively few located in the large metropolitan areas; and Canada's four major urban centres, Toronto, Montreal, Winnipeg and Vancouver, only contained twenty per cent of the entire group. Indeed, it was the smaller, more specialized manufacturing centres with high proportions of industrial labour such as Hamilton, Kitchener and Windsor which contained nearly as many as the major cities of Canada. Further, it appears that, in many cases the total number of Croats increased in inverse proportion to the decreasing size of Canada's towns, cities and villages of 1,000 or over. Although statistics are not readily available for small urban communities, it is clear that relatively northern, resource-based communities such as Timmins-Schumacher and Rouyn-Noranda in northern Ontario and Quebec, the Coal Branch in northern Alberta, and the mining towns of British Columbia such as Princeton and Anyox contained much higher concentrations of Croats per capita than did larger metropolitan centres.[6]

Demographically, the group was predominantly masculine (74%) as was its larger Yugoslav counterpart, and predominantly within the age group from 25-34 (58%).[7] Although many indicated that they were married (72%), which represented a significant increase from the pre-World War I migrant, many had left a wife and possibly one or two children in their native land, and might not retrieve them, if at all, for another decade. Overall, the proportion of males to females in the community was 2:1 in urban areas and 3:1 in rural areas.

Leaving aside the settled communities established prior to World War I, and those immigrants who had settled in urban manufacturing centres, one is left with the residual migrant culture which had arrived since 1926. The core group in this masculine culture were the approximately two thousand to twenty-five hundred single-male migrant workers, who roamed the country in search of work during the hungry thirties. Variously employed by the railroads, mines, logging camps and construction companies, they are elusive entities to find in the historical record. Some evidence of this nomadic group does however remain beyond the oral record of individual Croats, and is recorded in the papers of Frontier College. Its peripatetic schoolhouses on wheels were organized during the thirties by Principal Edmund C. Bradwin, whose sociological monograph upon the *Bunkhouse Man* in 1928 was a pioneering work upon the history of immigration before 1914. The careful primary record which the College continued to keep of its immigrant pupils remains an equally valuable parallel source for the social history of depression migrants.

It appears from these accounts that Croatians made up the vast majority of the single male workers who were nominally entered as Yugoslavs by their instructors.[8] The instructors' records also indicate that the Yugoslavs and Croats numbered from ten to twenty per cent of the camp population which they visited. Occasionally, the concentrations were much higher, as indicated by a young Dr. Benjamin Spock, who went as a student from Yale to join a railway extra-gang in Northern Ontario during the late twenties. He was confronted by a track crew which was almost entirely Croatian — and which, therefore, had little inclination to learn English from its beleaguered teacher.[9] Reports by the Croats themselves often indicate that their absolute numbers ran very high, and one oral account places their number as high as 1000 out of 1400 workers upon a highway project near Smith Falls in the early thirties.

The Croat migrant labourers were a highly mobile group, and organized themselves into work-gangs which suddenly would pull out of camp to take employment on another project. Very often such informal work parties were organized in quasi-military fashion under a natural leader, often one who could speak English with some fluency, and would secure work for an entire gang of otherwise inarticulate labourers.[10] They naturally tended to be drawn from the same village, town or region in their homeland, in the same way that the Irish railway navvies of the nineteenth-century banded together for self-protection.[11] Their strong internal discipline and capacity to move suddenly upon a day's notice for a job which promised higher wages and better conditions was the object of admiration by one of the College instructors who observed, "It is interesting to see how the Yugoslavs leave in bunches and arrive together. In July (1932) eight left school and camp — in Aug. ten arrived and five joined my class." In the same year another instructor lamented, "About a dozen Polish and Yugoslavs are going to-day. Think they will make more money out West. Well — it's up to them. I have 'the good old Finns' left anyway."[12]

The crucial determinants in such decisions were the declining prospects of work and wages as the depression began to settle in. Wages which had been as high as six or seven dollars a day for construction workers, navvies, and lumberjacks in the late nineteen-twenties dropped rapidly with the decline in industrial activity during the early thirties. By 1932, if work was available at all, the choice would often be between the federal relief camps established by the Bennett administration which paid 20¢ per day or $5.00 per month, or the more limited private sector where contract work netted the labourer 35-40¢ per hour minus board, or $1.50 per diem.[13]

A rather typical odyssey for a Croatian day-labourer in the early thirties was provided by one respondent who himself emerged as the leader of construction gang labour by the mid-thirties.[14] Before the depression began he had worked in isolated railway construction camps in British Columbia, Alberta and Manitoba. After 1930, he moved eastward in search of work, to Nova Scotia (New Glasgow and Antigonish), New Brunswick (Moncton), Quebec (Laval, Montreal), and then to Northern Ontario (James Bay, Cochrane, Timmins). After a brief sojourn upon a power project at Masson, Quebec, he gravitated to more lucrative Ontario highways projects in 1932. Interim work was provided by the federal air-base construction at Trenton in 1933, and for the next fifteen months he was able to earn very little but was also enabled *faut de mieux* to concentrate upon learning English at the Frontier College facility.[15] Then, with little notice, he and several compatriots from his native city of Mostar in Herzegovina departed for a new highways project in the Muskoka district. It was probably this group that another Frontier College instructor at Bracebridge commented upon in 1934 — "On arrival I was assigned to this hut and have seven Croatians as roommates. They are very fine bright fellows anxious to improve their English."[16]

The tenor of this comment points up the tendency of the highly mobile immigrants in an isolated environment and their apparent willingness to assimilate to the host society, at least in the learning of the English language and in applications for citizenship.[17] The numbers of Croats and/or Yugoslavs who took an active interest in the English language instruction offered by the College were generally above average according to instructors' accounts. Many were mature men in their thirties, and many were married with wives and children in the old country. Often one of these Croats would emerge as a "brilliant" or "star" pupil, and was consequently asked to inscribe his comments in the teacher's ledger either in his native or adopted language.

In general, these comments reveal an eager predisposition to learn English as *the* language of Canada and North America, and a considerable deference to their mentors. One of the comments is particularly revealing of their universal preference for English over French: "Kao dobar Hrvat, gubim Hrvatsku, postivam Canadu, a osobite se intersam za Engleski jezik kao svjetski, jer isti mi je potrebam u mojoj buducnosti (Like a good Croatian, I am losing Croatia and acquiring Canada, and am particularly interested in the English language as a universal language, for it will also be useful to me in my future)." One Charlie Majhanovich, a naturalized Croat, wrote quietly but exultantly in his newly acquired language, on the same theme, "I am glad to have learned the language of my new country." And yet others were deeply appreciative of the particular efforts made by the College's instructors, as was one John Perich, who worked on road construction north of Port Arthur. He fervently proclaimed, "With my teacher's help, I have learned more English in five months than I have in six years without help."[18]

The perspective of assimilation and the acculturation process from the immigrant's perspective is more difficult to ascertain. Some immigrants upon the frontier were of course never exposed to Frontier College nor to formal schooling of any kind. Yet they did learn the English language through contact with their fellow workers of other nationalities or through reading daily newspapers which were passed from hand to hand in the frontier work camps. Equally it seems from the high level of political consciousness among the Croats that they must have had a great deal of exposure to an active ethnic press as well as to Canadian dailies.[19] This certainly appears to have been the case in at least one of the northern Ontario road camps serviced by the College, for the instructor commented, "We had: "The Toronto Daily Star" — "The Montreal Star" — "Port Arthur News Chronicle" — "Fort William Daily Times Journal" — "Winnipeg Prairie [sic] Farmer" and a few Finnish and Yugoslavian papers."[20]

The new Croatian migrant was also exposed, and sometimes willingly so, to a welter of competing interests and ideologies. Each could and did offer under different circumstances vital service and information to the immigrant. The official Yugoslav network of consular officials and news service were important intermediaries in the process of immigration and settlement, particularly in the deciphering of immigration regulations and laws emerging from the major centres such as Montreal, Toronto, Ottawa and Vancouver.[21] The small-town connection was provided by the patriotic Peasant Party to which the settled Croats on the small urban frontier responded positively to the local news and information provided by Peter Stankovič, the energetic editor of the Winnipeg-based Hrvatski Glas, the first Croatian language newspaper in the British Commonwealth. Dependent upon generating news, subscriptions by local solicitation and advertising from small northern communities such as Schumacher, Port Arthur and Sudbury, Stankovič and the Peasant Party generated a readership of four or five thousand by the mid-thirties.[22] For those of no fixed address, the male migrant workers, the more clandestine network of the Communist Party appeared to provide yet another level of continuous information through their newspaper Borba (The Struggle) founded in 1930.

One of the most active in its formation was Tomo Cačič, a native of Lika who had been involved in the radical miners' unions of the western American frontier prior to World War I and in the syndicalist agitation of the International Workers of the World (I.W.W.). Cačič returned to Canada in 1924, after a brief sojourn in Soviet Russia and a Yugoslav concentration camp, and became involved in the Communist Party and the organization of miners and lumberworkers in western Canada. His propagandist activities formally began with the editing of "Bilten Nezaposleni," a mimeographed bulletin for the unemployed in Vancouver, and in 1930 he began a more ambitious fortnightly newspaper, Borba, which was based in Toronto. This radical newspaper would result in his arrest under Section 98 as a Communist agitator in 1932 with two years' imprisonment in Kingston Penitentiary, and finally ended with his deportation from Canada late in 1933.[23]

The radicalism of the frontier Croats and Yugoslavs was most evident in the minetowns and milltowns of Canada's northern frontier. Militancy and radicalism had in fact been a longstanding tradition in western Canada, which had seen the growth and decline of several radical unions, such as the Western Federation of Miners, the I.W.W., the O.B.U. and the Mineworkers' Union of Canada, from 1900-1930.[24] The penetration of the latter into the Coal Branch region of northwestern Alberta radicalized the Croats and south Slavs of that region into an uncharacteristic outburst of violence in 1930. It was vividly remembered for the police reaction and deportations that it engendered, by one of the Croatian participants:

> In 1930 there was trouble at Mercoal. The majority of men joined the Mineworkers of Canada, but the company favoured the United Mineworkers of America. The local union was asked to send miners to Mercoal to protest and picket. One day we were on the ridge facing south to the mine entrance. Some RCMP were escorting some men, about ten or twelve to work. We were shouting Scabs go back. One man by the name of Peter Maticevich and another in a brown leather coat jumped between the police and the scabs. A commotion started and we thundered "Hura-Hura" and started pushing, fist fighting, throwing rocks. Even some of our men got hurt. How we got separated I do not know but they did not start work for some time. One day we got news from Coalspur. Two passenger cars arrived with RCMP and Alberta Police and Special Police. They sent a section man from Coalspur to go ahead of the train because somebody was told the Communists set dynamite on the railway. We were told to go home to our camps. In a few days the police started to round up the suspects. They arrested Pete Meticevich, Jack Tomicich, Tony Botrkof and Louis Matonovich. Meticevich and Tomicich were deported and Matonovich and Botrkof served prison and were released. Funny thing is, Matonovich was not in this last push, but someone else was wearing his brown leather coat. If Matonovich told who was wearing his coat he would only put another man in the same spot.[25]

The acute political consciousness of the radical left resulted in the deportation of seven more Yugoslavs from 1930-1934, and over two hundred were deported ostensibly for health reasons or legal technicalities which contravened immigration department regulations.[26]

Two strikes of the mid-depression years suffice to demonstrate both the sustained and militant quality of radical protest among the south Slavs and the harsh response of the mineowners to a radicalized work force. These were the Anyox strike in northern British Columbia in 1933 and the Rouyn-Noranda strike of 1935. Both additionally revealed the degree to which the communist Mineworkers' Union of Canada had penetrated labour and ethnic groups abandoned by the international unions or the management-inspired company unions.

The Anyox copper mine, located some ninety miles up the Portland Canal from Prince Rupert, was operated by the American-owned Granby Consolidated Mining Company for some thirty years prior to the depression. It had attracted even prior to World War I many southern Slavs, and among those who came to Anyox were particularly heavy concentrations of miners from Lika, Herzegovina and Montenegro.[27] Working through the war as suspect Austrian aliens, their numbers were increased by the migration of the twenties, and by 1930 they probably counted in total some 170 out of a total labour force of 1000. In February of 1933, the Mineworkers' local went out on strike for increased wages of fifty cents per day and a reduction in living costs charged by the mineowners. An extremely bitter confrontation ensued, complete with police action against the militant miners, many of whom left for Vancouver. Several were, however, bound over for trial upon charges of unlawful assembly in Prince Rupert, and among these were several south Slavs including Joe Servich, Matt Yurgevich (Jergovich) and John Rodoman. When these were successfully acquitted, the Workers' Unity League carried the battle to the docks of Vancouver, where they forcibly attempted to prevent strikebreakers from boarding the steamer "Catala" bound for Prince Rupert. Although the Communists appear to have won the battle for increased wages by 1934, they and the miners lost the war when the Granby interests sold the mine to C.P.R. Consolidated of Trail. The mine was gradually dismantled for scrap metal from 1935 to 1942, despite a reputed fifty million pounds of extractable copper still in the ground.[28]

Radical Croats were the more direct object of discrimination in the case of the Rouyn-Noranda strike of 1935. Here, the Workers' Unity League made a particular effort to organize the Croatians, who numbered about four hundred strong in the labour force in the Noranda district. Radicalized by the decline in wages and by deteriorating working conditions, they were at the forefront of the miners' unions for improved conditions. Nine members of the mineworkers' negotiating committee of twelve which precipitated the strike of 1935 were in fact Croats. However, their attempts to achieve a ten per cent wage hike and a "dry house" for the muckers as well as recognition for the Workers' Unity League met with strong resistance from management.[29]

After a violent confrontation between the militia and the strikers in June of 1935, sixteen Croatians were arrested and charged with unlawful assembly and inciting riot. They were subsequently sentenced to prison for two years, and were later transferred to St. Vincent de Paul prison in Montreal, where further investigations were conducted by the Department of Labour and Immigration into their possible deportation. While none of the Canadian leaders of the Workers' League were imprisoned, the ethnic elite and rank and file suffered heavily. Some three hundred and fifty of the Croatians lost their jobs immediately, and approximately another one hundred were deported to Yugoslavia for their part in the strike.[30]

Ironically, the sixteen leaders who had been imprisoned were the belated object of a concerted effort for their liberation by the American-based Croatian Fraternal Union, itself heavily supported by Pennsylvania coal-miners. After several visits by its executive officers to prison officials, to the Minister of Justice and to the newly elected prime minister, Mackenzie King, the sixteen were eventually freed by June of 1936.[31] The wholesale deportation of hundreds of ethnic radicals during the early thirties had thus come to an official end with the Liberal victory of 1935.

Mackenzie King, unlike R. B. Bennett, was more inclined to listen to the voices of industry and labour from south of the border, and the more substantial voice of ethnic groups in the A.F.L. and C.I.O. had sharply reduced the forced exodus of labour radicals.

The next displacement of radical Yugoslavs from Canada in the late thirties was to be the voluntary exile of a few in support of the Republican cause in the Spanish Civil War. When the Canadian Spanish Aid Committee began to agitate for funds in 1936, it found physical and moral support among Canada's radical ethnic communities. Yugoslavs, many of Croatian background, would play an important role, both in the leadership and in the rank and file of the International Brigade raised for the assistance of the Republicans. The expatriate newspaper editors, Tomo Cačić and Peter Zapkar, who had both been deported from Canada in 1933-34 for their Communist activities, continued to wage an international propaganda effort against dictatorship and fascism in their native Yugoslavia and in Europe.[32] Another to join was the Mineworkers' organizer, Edo Jardas, who had participated actively in the Anyox strike and later in the radicalization of the gold miners in the Timmins-Schumacher and Rouyn-Noranda fields. Jardas was one of the first to enlist in the George Washington Battalion raised in the United States early in 1937, and he actively promoted the idea of a distinctly Canadian unit, the "Mackenzie-Papineaus."[33]

By late 1937, approximately thirteen hundred Yugoslavs from Europe and from North America had joined the brigade and its national units, and of these some seventy were from Canada. Of the Canadian Mackenzie-Papineau battalion, ten chose to list their nationality as Croatian on their identity cards, the only ethnic group apart from the Ukrainians to do so.[34] Those Croats from Canada who served in Spain might be identified more closely, for at least eighteen of them who served in the larger brigade were from the province of Lika, a rugged intermountain karstland region which bordered on the northern Adriatic coast. Occupationally, most were miners in Canada, although many were originally of rural and semi-rural background around the two towns of Gospić and Perušić in Lika.[35] What distinguished them from their contemporaries who had emigrated to northern Europe and to Latin America was that most of the Canadian Croatians had been resident in their adopted country for a longer period of time, many for as long as ten years. This commitment was reflected in the fact that many also chose to return to Canada when the opportunity for repatriation came in 1939 for those who were already naturalized citizens.[36]

The relatively small number of Croats who served in Spain does not however imply a similar degree of radical commitment by the remainder of the Croat community. The vast majority stayed in Canada, and of these only a small minority were political activists. But the Spanish volunteers were symbolic of the tenuous position which the Croats had held at the bottom of the social order in Canada since the onset of the depression. The uncertain prospects of service in a cause for which many had no lasting commitment must be balanced against the prospect of deportation or death in an industrial accident. The alternative choices in the latter regard might be summed up in two grim examples taken from the year 1930. In June of that year, thirteen natives of Hrvatsko Primorje in northwestern Croatia were killed aboard a drilling scow near Brockville on the St. Lawrence River, and thirty others, mainly Croats, were injured in the blast. Two months later, eight Croats and nine Serbs and Slovenes were killed in a mine explosion which trapped forty-six miners in Princeton, British Columbia.[37]

The universal appreciation of their marginal existence may be observed in a poignant poem which appeared in 1930, not in the press of the radical left, but in the more conservative "Croatian Voice." Here is the translation of the words in Croatian of a virtually unknown but eloquent poet from the gold-mining district of Schumacher, in northern Ontario, lamenting the lot of the immigrant miner:

And now let your thoughts go,
And let them see the sights
Of the underground, where in holes stir
Human beings, amidst chunks and caverns.
Like worms through tunnels they crawl
And heavy rocks pull up to the daily sun.
During their life they dig their grave,
Passing their entire life in darkness.

No one cares for the poor people,
Especially when they are miners.
Only when someone loses his life,
The newspapers make a little noise.
But everything subsides, and so does this lament,
As does anything human pertaining to the poor.
And when crying widows
Count the bodies lifted from dark caverns
For this no one's head aches
And the world sleeps quietly as before.[38]

Under such harsh and compelling circumstances, militancy was a condition of survival, and radicalism offered but one means towards securing it. Desperate men in desperate circumstances, some chose to revolt, others to endure and yet others to leave. The responses were limited in scope, and often resulted in bitter recriminations between one faction and another upon the best programme for group survival. Yet it is constantly surprising to note the degree to which ranks were closed when assisting a fatally injured worker's family, or when building a home, church or cultural centre through co-operative effort. Each group ultimately recognized the precariousness of their existence as a marginal group on the very edge of Canadian society, and this recognition served often to blunt internecine conflict under the desperate conditions of the great depression.

FOOTNOTES

[1]This trend is particularly evident in recent American ethnic historiography, *viz*, David Ward, *Cities and Immigrants* (Boston: 1971), and Rudolph Vecoli, "Contadini in Chicago: A Critique of the Uprooted," *Journal of American History*, 50 (December, 1964), 404-17. A recent Canadian example is Robert Harney and Harold Troper, *Immigrants: A Portrait of an Urban Experience, 1890-1930* (Toronto: Van Nostrand, 1975).

[2]The author is indebted to Professor W. L. Morton for his insightful reference to social change on the margins of society. His own views of the urban bias of modern historiography are contained in his "Reflections on an Unliterary Landscape," *Mosaic*, 5 (1971), and upon the immigrant experience in Canada, "The Historical Phenomenon of Minorities: The Canadian Experience," XIV International Congress of Historical Sciences, San Francisco, August, 1975.

[3]E. H. Carr, *The Twenty Years' Crisis, 1919-39* (London, 1961), 57-58. See also, Louis Adamic, *The Native's Return: An American Immigrant Visits Yugoslavia and Discovers His Old Country* (New York, 1934).

[4]Rudolf Bičanić, *Agrarna kriza u Hrvatskoj, 1873-1895* (Zagreb: 1937).

[5]Specific statistics for Canada are contained in P.A.C., R.G. 76, vol. 623, ff. 938332, Parts II and III. "Tables of Overseas Migration of the Kingdom of Serbs, Croats and Slovenes, 1926-30." Prepared by the Chief of the Commisariat of Emigration, Dr. Fedor Aranički, Zagreb. See table, p. 17.

[6]See *Seventh Census of Canada, 1931* (Ottawa, 1943), XIII, monograph on "Racial Origins and Nativity of the Canadian People," chapter on rural-urban distribution, 624-33.

[7]*Seventh Census of Canada, 1931* (Ottawa, 1936), vol. 1, "Population."

[8]*P.A.C.,* MG 28, I, 124, Frontier College Papers, Instructors' Registers, vol. 152, Toronto and Northern Railway Extension, Moose Factory, July, 1931. The instructor, J. C. Fair, lists 130-165 men of whom 25% were Yugoslavs, and of these a high proportion were identifiable by surname as Croats. The preponderance of Croats among Yugoslav workers in this period is verified also by Robert England, author of *The Central European Immigrant in Canada*, in an interview with Dr. H. Palmer, University of Calgary, in Calgary, in Victoria, B.C., July, 1976, reprinted in *Canadian Ethnic Studies*, 8 (1976), 18-33.

[9]Toronto *Globe and Mail*, Oct. 3, 1973, p. 16. Copy provided to the author by H. Herman of the University of Toronto, who is currently preparing a doctoral thesis on migrant workers of Croat and Macedonian background upon the northern Ontario frontier.

[10]An admirable, first-hand account of one such group leader is contained in S. Bradica, "Odkriče Kanada," in S. Gazi, ed., "Spomenica na dvadeset godina Hrvatski Seljačkih Organizacija u Kanadi" (Winnipeg, 1952), 34-42, translated and reprinted in *Canadian Ethnic Studies*, 8(1976), 95-102.

[11]See Kenneth Duncan, "Irish Famine Immigration and the Social Structure of Canada West," *Canadian Review of Sociology and Anthropology*, 2(1965), 19-40.

[12]*P.A.C.* MG 28, 1, 124, vol. 62, Frontier College, Instructors' Correspondence, George Lantz to Dr. E. Bradwin, Ouimet, Ontario, August 31, 1932. See also Lantz to Bradwin, August 1, 1932.

[13]*P.A.C.,* MG 28, I, 124, vol. 198. Frontier College Papers, Federal Relief Camps, questionnaires prepared by instructors for the Department of National Defence, January, 1936.

[14]Anonymous to author, March 30, 1975. These details are confirmed in several other interviews conducted by the author, most recently, Milan Rasporich, Thunder Bay, July, 1976.

[15]*P.A.C.,* MG 28, I, 124, vol. 64, Instructors' Registers, Frontier College, A. H. Fraser, Trenton Air Camp, May, 1933.

[16]*P.A.C.,* MG 28, I, 124, vol. 67, R. Russell Gordon to E. Bradwin, Bracebridge, May, 1934.

[17]Linguistically, the levels of illiteracy for Yugoslav arrivals was below that for southern and eastern Europeans at 9.8% for immigrants ten years of age or over (Poles, 13%; Czechs, 9.6%; Italians, 11%). Most would continue to declare Serbo-Croatian as their mother tongue (62%) by 1941, but a substantial number of the first generation declared English as a major language of usage in addition to the mother tongue (83%). *Canada Census, 1931*, vol. IV, p. 1010. The number of illiterates in the male population was somewhat less than among females, 11% vs. 23%, although larger numerically at 1190 vs. 714. *Ibid.*, IV, 984.

[18]*P.A.C.,* MG 28, I, 124, vol. 152, F. Kinnaird, Hydro Ontario, July, 1929. Entry by Croatian pupil, E. Ruckmeyer. *Ibid.,* vol. 155, Camp Dorset, R. R. Gordon, instructor, entry by C. Majhanovich. *Ibid.,* vol. 62, Kenora, Ontario, D. S. Wood, instructor; student, M. Kotovich.

[19]*Vide*, P.A.C., MG 28, I, 124, Instructors' Registers, vol. 64, H. Fraser, Trenton Air Base Camp, May, 1933; vol. 152, J.C.S. Fair, Moose Factory, July, 1931.

[20]*P.A.C.,* MG 28, I, 124, vol. 153, ff. 1932. Frontier College, Instructors' Registers, George Lantz, Ouimet Camp, April 12, 1933.

[21]The official organ of the Yugoslav government was *Glas Kanada* (1934-43), which the National Library in Ottawa lists as a "Serbian" newspaper. It also contained information in

the Latin alphabet for Croatian and Slovene readers. "National Library Holdings of Newspapers of Canadian Cultural Communities," October, 1973.

[22]The paper which first appeared under the title *Kanadski Glas (Canadian Voice)* in 1929 changed to *Hrvatski Glas (Croatian Voice)* in 1931. Interview with Peter Stanković, Aug. 14, 1974, and ms. supplied to author by P. Stanković, re: "Croatian Voice." See also *Hrvatski Glas*, March 14, 1939, "Kratki Historijat Hrvatskog Glasa."

[23]See "Razgovor sa Tomo Čačičem," in *Jedinstvo*, Jan. 8, 1957. See also *20 Godina Kratki Pregled Historije Naprednog Pokreta Jugoslavenskih Iseljenika U Kanadi* (Toronto, 1950), microfiche, Mclaren micropublishing, Toronto.

[24]The two terms "radicalism" and "militancy" have been defined with reference to the labour movement in western Canada during the early twentieth century in a penetrating paper by David J. Bercuson to a History Department Colloquium, University of Calgary, March, 1975, and to appear in printed form in a forthcoming *Canadian Historical Review*. D. J. Bercuson, "Labour Radicalism and the Western Industrial Frontier, 1896-1919." See also A. R. McCormack, "The Industrial Workers of the World in Western Canada: 1905-14," *Can. Hist. Assoc'n Ann. Report*, 1975, 167-191.

[25]Reminiscence by Mike Krypan in Toni Ross, *Oh! The Coal Branch* (Edmonton: D. W. Freisen & Sons, 1974), pp. 286-7. Principal Bradwin himself cautioned his instructors not to sponsor "C.C.F., Communism or any other untried social experiment." *P.A.C.*, MG 28, I, 124, vol. 71, Bradwin to Allan McColl at D.N.D. project #13 at Kowkash, Ontario, 1935.

[26]*P.A.C.*, RG 76, vol. 16, File re: Communist Agitators Deported from Canada, 1931-37.

[27]A. B. Grado, *Migraciona Enciklopedia*, vol. 1, "Kanada" (Zagreb: 1930), p. 217. See also S. Raymer article of Apr. 9, 1930 in *Pučka Prosvjeta* clipping, located at the Zavod za Migracije ..., in Zagreb, vol. 138, ff. II 14 2c. "British Columbia, 1928-30."

[28]See Oswald Hutchings, "History of Anyox (Hidden Creek) Mining District" (n.p. 1966, typescript by author), contained in U.B.C. Special Collections, University of British Columbia.

[29]*Zajedničar* (Pittsburgh), Dec. 4, 1935.

[30]Typical deportation entered for Croatians in immigration files for this period read: "S. P., Jugoslav, arrived in Canada, July 4, 1926 ... deported aboard Ansonia, Oct. 28, 1933 from Quebec, convicted of unlawful assembly, Royn [sic], Quebec." P.A.C., RG 76, vol. 16.

[31]*Zajedničar*, July 15, October 21, 1936.

[32]*Jedinstvo*, Oct. 26, 1956. Petar Erdeljač, "25-Godisnjica Jedinstva I 20 Godišnjiča Internaciolnih Brigada u Spaniji."

[33]*Hrvatski Narodni Kalendar* (Toronto, 1938), 63-99.

[34]Victor Hoar, *The Mackenzie-Papineau Battalion* (Toronto, 1969), 32.

[35]Branimir Gusić, *Lika u Prošlosti i Sadašnjosti* (Karlovać, 1973), 259-63.

[36]*Jedinstvo*, May 15, 1970, Ivan Stimac, "Sječanja iz Spanije." It is interesting to note that in 1931 eighty per cent of the "Yugoslavs" listed in the Dominion Census remained unnaturalized, the highest of all Slavic groups except the Czechs. But, by 1941, fully two-thirds of all "Yugoslavs" had received citizenship. *Eighth Census of Canada, 1941* (Ottawa, 1946), vol. 1, 744.

[37]*Hrvatski Glas*, July 7, Aug. 26, 1930.

[38]*Hrvatski Glas*, Aug. 25, 1930. Poem "Seljak i Radnik" by S. Mahovlić, Schumacher, Ontario.

DECLINE OF THE WASP? DOMINANT GROUP IDENTITY IN THE ETHNIC PLURAL SOCIETY

LINDA BELL DEUTSCHMANN
UNIVERSITY OF TORONTO

The purpose of this paper is to begin the task of filling in a vacuum; a vacuum created by the virtually complete absence of research information concerning what has been happening to, and happening within, the "dominant group" in Canada. This paper reports the results, to date, of a continuing three-pronged investigation into the components of Wasp (White Anglo-Saxon Protestant) identity in Canada. The Wasp subjects were all Canadian-born, of British (English, Irish, Scottish or Welsh) ancestry, and Protestant background.[1] The first part of the investigation concerned the observation of ethnically homogeneous Wasp and Ukrainian small groups videotaped under laboratory conditions.[2] The second part involved the use of a structured self-administered questionnaire designed to compare Wasp-Canadians' personal and group identity features with those of Ukrainian-Canadians.[3] The third phase, just begun, involves in-depth, semi-structured interviews with native-born Wasps only.[4] It is hoped that these studies, along with research into the historical position of the group, will help to give the "dominant group" its rightful place in the study of race and ethnic relations in Canada.

The literature on race and ethnic relations, on self-concept and ethnic identity, and on ethnic cultures (i.e., the literature of sociology, social psychology, and anthropology) has avoided serious investigation of "ordinary" Wasps. There are studies of the extremes — the very weak and the very strong, the "poor whites" and the political, economic, and social elites.[5] Such works emphasize class and thus unintentionally distort ethnicity. Although they rarely claim to deal with the Wasp group as a whole, or even a major part of it, the overall impression that they convey is that every Wasp is born at least middle or upper-middle class — an impression hardly supported by the evidence.[6] There are also, of course, many studies of group prejudice and discrimination.[7] These focus mainly on the valence of "dominant group" attitudes toward particular other groups, the "accuracy" of beliefs about these other groups, and the consequences for these others and for society as a whole. The emphasis is thus placed on the "others" rather than the dominant group. The absence of other kinds of studies about the Wasps, along with the relative absence of studies of minority group forms of prejudice, seems to imply that prejudice and discrimination are the unique and important distinguishing characteristics of the group.[8] Finally, there are studies of the "ethnic" or "national" minorities within the Wasp group.[9] The studies of the Scottish, Irish, Welsh and English in Canada are useful in a limited way. They tend to be almost purely historical, and ignore the extent to which assimilation and intermarriage have blurred the lines between the groups and have produced a general Wasp or "Anglo" category which is not strongly connected with a particular British homeland (nor completely submerged in an undifferentiated "Canadian" identity).[10]

Thus, with only one notable exception, we find only journalistic accounts (often tongue-in-cheek) which deal with the changing position of the Wasp in the Canadian or North American setting.[11] This neglect of the dominant group as a legitimate subject matter for research is surprising in view of the importance of this group. Even more surprising is the frequency with which observers have objected that Wasps are not worth studying, that we already know all that is interesting about them, or that they *have* no special characteristics.[12] Although Wasp superiority in numbers and positions of influence may be eroded in some places and challenged in others, Wasps still enjoy power and influence in society such that their problems are likely to have society-wide implications.[13] Some experts seem to feel that the Wasp way of life and the mainstream society are virtually the same, so that specific studies are not necessary.[14] It is, however, increasingly possible to distinguish between the unique institutions of the Wasp cultural tradition and those of the more eclectic Canadian mainstream.[15] The process of separation can be illustrated with reference of the "national" flag. The early "Ensign" flag, clearly British in inspiration, was replaced by a new design which, apparently quite deliberately, did not relate to the heritage of any particular group or groups within the society but drew instead on the natural environment (presumably shared by all.)[16] The new flag, then, is "mainstream" or common domain, and exists outside the Wasp cultural context. It is not surprising that a large proportion of the Wasps interviewed so far have expressed a lack of identification with the new flag.[17]

Not only does the mainstream reflect increasing cultural input from many new groups other than the Wasp group, but other types of cultural change are occurring as well.

> The rationalizing technological, "advanced" culture which establishes so many of the present conditions of contemporary life is as hostile to some British-American values as it is to those of other ethnic groups. Many British-Americans are as upset about the new pressures of super-culture as others are.[18]

This is often not recognized by observers of "minority cultures" who see their members facing what appears to be a single "dominant culture" which is both Wasp and "modern" at the same time. There are signs then, that the frequently heard argument that Wasps are not distinguishable from "society as a whole" should be reconsidered.

Similarly, it has been stated that the important parameters of the Wasp group are already known. Since there are no general studies of Wasps, this assertion needs factual support. Much of what passes for information about Wasps seems to be based on minority group perceptions of them, on the investigator's personal experiences, or on overgeneralizations derived from elite studies.

Thus, the purpose of this paper is to begin the task of filling in the vacuum, showing what has been happening to the Wasp group in Canada, and how the group has responded.

The Historical Transition to Ethnic Pluralism

We can define ethnic pluralism at this point as the "sharing of social space and its control by three or more ethnically differentiated groups."[19] At the opposite end of a continuum (one based on degree of sharing) we would find "uniculturalism" or "the control of social space by a single ethnic group or category." Thus, a fully "unicultural" society (pure, hypothetical case) would have only one culturally acceptable means of access to societal resources: all facilities would be the exclusive preserve of the members of the dominant group and those fully assimilated to it.[20] The recognized social roles and their organization in society would reflect the norms of the dominant group and the societal goals would correspond to the cultural priorities of that one group. This would make assimilation a prerequisite to any kind of participation or sharing in the resources of the society, and it would mean that identity differences would be based on intra-cultural distinctions, that is, ethnicity would be an unanalysed, taken-for-granted aspect of life. In such a society, the ethnic consciousness of the dominant group would be either co-extensive with the national consciousness of the society or would replace it. The unassimilated outsider would be at best a "guest," denied the right to participate or enjoy a socially-validated identity within the structure.[21]

At the opposite end of the continuum we would find the hypothetical "pure" case of the pluralistic society. In this society all facilities would be available in such a way that members of different cultural groups could gain access to them without conforming to the ways of any other groups. Thus, each group or category would be *able* to participate fully in any or all areas of the society, although there might be a variation of participation levels within groups. No single group could monopolize or dominate in any organizational area or at any level in the social system. The ethnic consciousness of members of cultural groups (ethnic identity) would be distinct from their consciousness of membership in the society (national identity).

While a totally unicultural society is conceivable (the assumptions underlying the model do not contradict each other, and we can find some "primitive" societies which have closely approximated this form), the totally pluralistic society remains an unknown configuration.[22] In all known societies, there are many unicultural aspects, and even in areas in which extensive sharing of control takes place, the sharing is rarely fully equal. In Canada, we can document a transition from a relatively unicultural society, one of clear Wasp dominance, toward a more pluralistic one, but one still in most respects a long way from the completely pluralistic end of the continuum.

Since the 1770s the British have been the major national origin group in Canada, first predominant because of institutional power alone (conquest) and then on wide numerical dominance as well. Those of British origin established the cultural patterns that, in interaction with the realities of developing a new land, the only gradually diminishing influence of the mother-country, the ever-present example of the United States, and some minor adjustments for minorities, eventually developed into the "mainstream" or "Canadian" way of life. Given this origin and developmental pattern, it is not surprising that the mainstream reflects the British cultural input even now. But it is a hang-over of the past.

The increasingly effective challenge to the continuation of Wasp dominance of the mainstream of Canadian society occurs on many levels. Some of the factors can be listed here, such as the decline in Wasp numerical superiority,[23] the decline of British prestige in the world (and in Canada), the decline in the relative importance of British connections for political purposes and for trade, the rise of "bilingualism" and the "new ethnicity,"[24] and the steady undermining of the ideologies that have legitimated Wasp dominance in the past — the ideologies of race and conquest.[25]

To the extent that the transition to pluralism and the development of a more ethnically diverse or neutral mainstream occurs, the Anglo-Protestant category faces significant changes that affect its position. For example, at the facilities level of the social system, pluralism means loss of power in the nation's major institutions. Those which remain part of the mainstream will become more and more "integrated," while those which remain strictly Anglo will become less and less important to the society as a whole.[26] Similarly, at the value level, increasing pluralism means that much of the legitimacy formerly accorded to Wasp dominance is eroded.

The three phases of this research have each helped to shed light on the consequences of these changes for the Wasp group in Canada. The following paragraphs summarize some of the most important findings.

Both Wasps and Ukrainians maintain ethnic boundaries.[27] The Wasp boundary is composed of class, lifestyle and friendship distinctions which add up to an effective ethnic boundary but which are not often recognized (by the Wasps) as such. The Ukrainian boundary is openly and explicitly ethnic — issues of class, lifestyle and friendship tend to be consciously subordinated to it.[28] Ukrainians and Wasps tend to choose most of their friends from their own group,[29] to recognize common features that they share with others from their own background,[30] and to realize that they have values, traditions and orientations that set them apart. The Wasps are more likely to attribute their sense of common understanding to things other than ethnicity, such as type of family or school background, while Ukrainians see family and school experiences as framed by ethnicity. Both groups see religion, or religious background as bound up with their cultural values and identity, even if they have lapsed from actual participation.[31]

Demographically, both groups show relatively high rates of ethnic endogamy and some degree of residential segregation.[32]

Both groups recognize that there are threats to the preservation of their ways in Canadian society. The Ukrainians point consistently toward the overwhelming influence of the Canadian and North American mainstream. The Wasps point at various aspects of the current erosion of their position relative to others in the society, and lack of recognition of their values in the new society.[33]

Unlike the Ukrainians, the Wasps show no sign of meeting the challenge by recognizing or supporting any *overt* ethnic boundary maintenance mechanisms. They insist that there is not, and should not be, a Wasp group (in the organizational sense) for them to be responsible to or for them to rely on.[34] While rejecting the idea of ethnic group formation for themselves, they are divided over their attitudes toward the organization of other ethnic groups.

Our initial interviews in the third phase of the research seem to indicate that Wasps control their perception of ethnic pluralism by redefining their personal horizons. There is very little difference in the amount of meaningful interethnic contact experienced by Wasps living in a mixed residential area compared with those in a more segregated one.[35] It was found, however, that there was a tendency for those exposed to the greatest degree of ethnic pluralism in their lives to express ambivalence toward it, fatalism about changing the pluralist trend, negative attitudes toward themselves and their cultural group, and lack of interest in neighbourhood and political organizations. Those who experienced less pluralism in their daily lives tend to be opposed to increasing it, more likely to mention that the changes should be controlled (without specifying how it should be done), more positive toward themselves and their cultural group (although somewhat defensively) and slightly more likely to favour neighbourhood and political participation.[36]

Although it is too early to regard these findings as more than a rough indication, they do suggest that the transition toward ethnic pluralism, slight though it may seem, has already had considerable effect on many members of the Wasp group. As a former dominant group it lacks the mechanisms for ethnic maintenance that characterize successful minority groups, and it is prevented by both its own values (especially individualism) and by human rights legislation, from developing ethnically exclusive organizations. Thus, Wasps are entering a period of history when they can no longer count on their access to government and other major institutions to protect their way of life, but are unable or unwilling to develop new means of coping with the changing society around them.

FOOTNOTES

[1]The term Wasp is less than satisfactory. The other terms in use, such as Anglo-Protestant, Anglo-Saxon, or the recent governmentaleze "Anglo-Celt" share the same problem of racial connotation as opposed to cultural identification. It is assumed, in this paper that the

native-born, of British ancestry and Protestant background constitute the core of the "dominant group." The short term Wasp seems to cover this as well as any of the later terms.

[2]This part of the study was directed by Dr. Wsevelod Isajiw in the excellent small groups facilities at Scarborough College, University of Toronto.

[3]An early report on this investigation, "Different Ways of Being Ethnic: the Ukrainians and the Wasps in Canada" by Wsevelod W. Isajiw and Linda Bell Deutschmann was presented at the CSAA Annual Meetings in Quebec, Spring 1976.

[4]Fifty interviews of the "pilot study" for this phase of the research had been completed at the time of writing. Another 200 interviews with a systematically selected sample of Wasps was completed by September 1976, but not yet processed.

[5]Canadian studies include John Porter, *The Vertical Mosaic* (Toronto, 1965) and Wallace Clement, *The Canadian Corporate Elite: An Analysis of Economic Power* (Toronto, 1975). The same types of studies are characteristic in the United States as well.

[6]Even if the Wasp predominates in some parts of the prestige, wealth and power systems, it does not follow that a majority of Wasps are privileged. Because of the numerical size of the group, Wasps may be predominant in *both* the upper and lower ranges of the society, while the average Wasp is found in the middle.

[7]The books referred to are those which, like Jean Leonard Elliott (editor), *Immigrant Groups* (Minority Canadians) Volume 2, *define* the minority in terms of its vulnerability to dominant group prejudice and discrimination.

[8]We not only need more studies about other aspects of Wasps, but studies of *minority* group prejudice and discrimination would be valuable too.

[9]While the term "ethnic" might seem more accurate, I have sensed a strong resistance to both "ethnic" and "minority" in these groups. It is a topic for further research to find out whether the term "national minority," as used in European studies, would be more accurately descriptive.

[10]In the course of our interviews, few respondents expressed special interest in, or attachment to, any part of the British Isles. (For example, in response to the question "Are you especially interested in what goes on in Britain, that is, more than you are interested in most other countries?" thirty-one per cent of a sample of 200 expressed no interest at all, and only 16.5% of them expressed real interest. When asked "Do you think of any part of the British Isles as a homeland?" sixty per cent of the same sample answered "not at all." At the same time a majority felt that their British background made some difference to the kind of "Canadian" they were.)

[11]The exception is Charles H. Anderson, *White Protestant Americans; From National Origins to Religious Group* (Englewood Cliffs, N.J., 1970). There is only one chapter on Wasps, however, and little data to support it. An example of the tongue-in-cheek approach is as follows:

> They are the only group which did not encounter in the New World an established Western culture and thus were denied the character-forming experiences of discrimination and economic exploitation. Deprived of the wholesome loneliness of the newly arrived stranger, never having been called dirty, sub-human or different, this underprivileged group even had to wait until a war and the arrival of strangers made it possible to form its equivalent of the Sons of Italy, the D.A.R. One wonders whether we will ever succeed in assimilating it into the texture of American society.
>
> (Quoted in a student essay; original source unknown.)

[12]The objections cited were voiced so many times when this study was discussed (especially with respect to funding) that I have made a special point of dealing with them here.

[13]In fact a case could be made that the large part of the Canadian identity search has been precipitated by a Wasp identity crisis.

[14]Much of the standard material for teaching race and ethnic relations is characterized by constant running together of "dominant group," "dominant society," "majority," "mainstream," etc., as if these terms all meant the same thing.

[15]The mainstream increasingly reflects borrowings from all of the cultural groups, although not equally or in all areas. The impact of human rights legislation has pushed some Wasp institutions into the mainstream and side-lined others. For example, the businessmen's clubs that have remained Wasp have lost importance in the commercial life of Toronto, while those which have stayed in the mainstream have become less Wasp.

[16]As noted by a Westerner, the assumption shows an Eastern bias in the assessment of the Canadian natural environment. In this case, avoiding ethnic bias has not resolved Canada's symbolic contradictions.

[17]In the pretest of the interview instruments, 50 Wasps were exposed to several questions about the flag and their feelings toward it. Of the 50, more than ninety per cent (96%) reported that they were originally opposed to, or strictly neutral toward the new design, and more than 60 per cent (63%) were still opposed to it, or resigned to it at the time of the interview.

"A few years ago, the Canadian flag was changed from the un-official British version to the present red maple leaf design. Were you in favour of the new flag?" "How do you feel about it now?"

Many respondents qualified their answers, stating that they wanted a new *Canadian* flag, but felt that the design chosen was "empty," "meaningless," and without "emotional significance". It was not necessary for the whole flag to be British, but some part of it should have been.

[18]Michael Novak, "Letter to the Editor," *Commentary,* October 1972.

[19]One group means uniculture, two groups means the possibility of biculture, and three or more raises the possibility of pluralism.

[20]Societal resources is a generalized term for all the material and nonmaterial goods of the society (e.g., money and weapons, prestigious memberships, skill and knowledge).

[21]That is, the unassimilated would have only a limited guest or intruder role that would make long-term survival precarious. The "guest worker" problem illustrates this well.

[22]In fact, some of the premises appear to contradict each other. Unequal participation can be predicted, if each culture responds according to its own priorities, but unequal participation almost always leads to unequal distribution of power and influence.

[23]The extent to which this has occurred varies from province to province. The 1971 Census figures show the following proportions of persons claiming British Isles ancestry.

    93.8% in Newfoundland
    82.7 in Prince Edward Island
    77.5 in Nova Scotia
    57.6 in New Brunswick
    10.6 in Quebec
    59.4 in Ontario
    41.9 in Manitoba
    42.1 in Saskatchewan
    46.7 in Alberta
    57.9 in British Columbia
    48.6 in the Yukon
    25.2 in the NorthWest Territories

These percentages were calculated on the basis of figures provided in the 1971 *Census of Canada,* volume 1 Part 3, Bulletin 1.3-2 Population by Ethnic Groups.

In Toronto, where this research was begun, the percentage claiming British ancestry dropped from 72.7% in 1951 to 60.7% in 1961, and to 56.9% in 1971. Based on *Census of Canada* 1971 Volume I Part 3 Bulletin 1.3-2 Table 6; 1961 Volume I Part 2 Bulletin 1.2-7 Table 39; and 1951 Volume I Table 36.

[24]The "new ethnicity" often billed as a revival of ethnicity actually seems to be something new. It is linked to the affective vacuum left by the loss of British pre-eminence and the rise of the affectively neutral technological "superculture," as well as to the ability of ethnic minorities to mobilize societal resources for ethnic purposes. This ability has been increased by ideological positions such as multiculturalism and by the fact that most of these groups are no longer strangers in a new land but citizens of the second and third generation.

[25]None of the Wasps interviewed expressed a racial justification for the privileged position that Wasps have held, although many admitted they were unhappy about the racial dimension of "third World" immigration. The claim is more in the nature of "We got here first," than "We're inherently better." Conquest was not mentioned, although it might have come up if the interview had concerned itself with the French-English relation.

[26]For example, social-business clubs, often highly prestigious in the previous generation, will either cease to be ethnically exclusive or they will lose their importance in the mainstream of the business world. (This seems to be the fate of Toronto's exclusive Granite Club, among others.)

[27]The term "ethnic boundaries" is derived from Fredrik Barth (editor), *Ethnic Groups and Boundaries: The Social Organization of Culture Difference* (Boston, 1969).

[28]Throughout the interviews, it seemed clear that many Wasps were verbalizing these ideas for the first time, whereas the Ukrainians were dealing with familiar (though not necessarily settled or consistent) ideas. For the Wasp, the ethnic dimension is usually latent, in contrast to the highly overt and verbal ethnic component presented by the Ukrainian group.

[29]When asked to think about their best friend, and then identify whether the friend was of their own ethnic background or not, most either did not know or thought they were the same. Among the Wasps, however, having a best friend from another group seemed to be much more a matter of open pride than it was for the Ukrainians.

[30]This conclusion derives mainly from the small groups observation. It was clear that the Wasp group had a "we-they" boundary with respect to the other groups in their environment. But this boundary was not recognized (by them) as ethnic, except insofar as the others created it by their exclusiveness. It was found that Wasps needed to "test out" many sources they thought might explain their sense of commonality. They sometimes attributed this feeling to growing up in small town Ontario, sometimes to having similar family life styles, or similar reactions to others who were not Wasp.

[31]It seems preferable to regard "religious background" (as distinct from current religious belief or participation) as a part of the *ethnic* dimension. Even where there has been no religious

participation for two generations, cultural values associated with religious background tend to remain.

[32]See, for example, Warren E. Kalbach, "Propensities for Inter-Marriage in Canada as Reflected in the Ethnic Origins of Native-Born Husbands and their Wives: 1961 and 1971," a paper presented to the annual meeting of the Canadian Sociology and Anthropology Association, August 24, 1974, Toronto. Even when the different sizes of the groups are controlled for, the British origin group has a relatively high rate of endogamy. A finding which should qualify the assertions of those in our samples who so emphatically denied caring about whether or not their spouse was from their own group, and denied trying to influence their children's choices of friends and partners.

[33]When asked what they would change about Canada, if they could, both groups strongly attacked the present government ("get rid of Trudeau"), but for different reasons. Economic policies were attacked first, then ethnic ones. The Ukrainians attacked the failure to live up to multi-cultural ideals and promises, while the Wasps protested uncontrolled and unselective immigration.

[34]There were several questions in the survey which related to "ethnic group." Wasps, unlike Ukrainians, often skipped these questions, or indicated that they did not apply to them. When asked about obligations to the group, Wasps were much less likely to admit to any than were Ukrainians. For example:

"Do you feel obliged to vote for candidates of the same background?
    Ukrainians agreeing   33.0% (total N = 100)
    Wasps agreeing   12.0%
"Do you feel obliged to protect the interests of the group when new laws or practices threaten it?"
    Ukrainians agreeing   82.0% (N = 100)
    Wasps agreeing   40.0%
"Do you feel obliged to support organizations that bring group members together?"
    Ukrainians agreeing   77.0% (N = 100)
    Wasps agreeing   34.0%
"Do you feel obliged to help other members of your group?"
    Ukrainians agreeing   89.0% (N = 100)
    Wasps agreeing   34.0%
"Do you feel obliged to patronize businesses run by people of the same group as yourself?"
    Ukrainians agreeing   67.0% (N = 100)
    Wasps agreeing   12.0%

Wasp rejection of group solutions was consistent throughout all three phases of the study. When faced with problems, their response was either apathy ("What can be done about it, anyway?") or *individual* action such as a letter to a politician. There was some evidence that there is extensive reliance on family or close friends, but never an attempt to organize a group to represent Wasp interests.

[35]The distinction between meaningful and superficial contact should be further developed. It appears that our Toronto Wasps have extensive and frequent contact with members of other groups, but these are often extremely superficial, having little apparent (measurable) effect on them.

[36]The sample size on which these final assertions are based is only 50 respondents, all adults, but not selected systematically. Therefore, it is best to regard these ideas as hypotheses for further testing rather than conclusions.

THE CANADIAN IDENTITY AND MULTICULTURALISM: THE IMPLICATIONS FOR STUDENTS AT THE ELEMENTARY LEVEL

MARGUERITE BURKE
BRUNSKILL SCHOOL, SASKATOON

Margaret Atwood has this to say about the importance of teaching Canadian literature in our schools:

> A piece of art, as well as being a creation to be enjoyed, can also be ... a mirror. The reader looks at the mirror and sees not the writer but himself; and behind his own image in the foreground, a reflection of the world he lives in. If a country or a culture lacks such mirrors it has no way of knowing what it looks like; it must travel blind. If, as has long been the case in this country, the viewer is given a mirror that reflects not him but someone else, and told at the same time that the reflection he sees is himself, he will get a very distorted idea of what he is really like. He will also get a distorted idea of what other people are like: it's hard to find out who anyone else is until you have found out who *you* are. Self-knowledge, of course, can be painful, and the extent to which Canadian literature has been neglected in its home territory suggests, among other things, a fear on the part of Canadians of knowing who they are; while the large number of mirror and reflection images contained within that literature suggest a society engaged in a vain search for an image. ...[1]

Canadians are struggling to define a unique Canadian identity; the concept is elusive, it escapes definition.

Atwood points out that this search for identity is a middle-class struggle and is characteristic of the middle class throughout the western world. Daniel Levine maintains that the struggle for identity is directly related to the trend towards urbanization. He says that the destruction of rural community life, as we knew it in the late 1800s and in the early part of this century, has directly contributed to the identity crisis faced by all North Americans.[2]

Undoubtedly the transition of our society from rural to urban in the last fifty years has contributed to identity confusion among Canadians. A person living in rural Canada fifty years ago made a limited number of contacts which tended to be very intense. His friends knew about his family, his work, his interests, his ethnic background, his religion, his prejudices, and his early experiences.

In the city, society is more impersonal. An individual meets many people, but his contacts are not as intense. He may be identified as an employee of a specific firm or as a member of a specific club. The total picture of his identity does not emerge through these superficial contacts. His associates are not aware of his personal life. He may be stereotyped as a member of a particular socio-religious or ethnic subgroup — he is an Indian, a Mennonite, or a French Canadian. He may, also, be stereotyped according to his age or his profession — he is a senior citizen or a teenager; or he is a teacher, a lawyer, an accountant or a laborer. The individual is dependent upon society to reflect his identity; when this fails he is fragmented and does not see himself whole.

Many factors, then, contribute to our need to define the Canadian identity — the impersonal urban society, an emerging middle class, the search for a meaningful folklore and folk heroes, and the need for dependable cultural boundaries.

It seems to me that Canadians must ask themselves two questions: "Do we have a national identity?" and "Is it possible to define it?" We must also ask ourselves "What are the implications for our young people if we do not define it?"

Arnold Edinborough, the former editor of *Saturday Night,* points out the problem of the Canadian teacher. He questions whether there is a unique Canadian identity and suggests that it is impossible for the school to come to grips with a concept that sophisticated writers have not been able to describe.[3]

Solange Chaput Rolland, following a six months' tour of Canada, observes that French- and English-speaking Canadians lack a common denominator.[4]

If adults in this country have difficulty in recognizing the Canadian identity, then it is to be expected that our young people will suffer from identity confusion.

Some ten years ago, Governor General Georges P. Vanier noted in his New Year message to the Canadian people that concern about a unique Canadian identity is a problem only at home, never abroad. He maintained that Canadian soldiers engaged in combat during the First and Second World Wars were secure in the knowledge of their Canadian identity.[5]

W. L. Morton, in his efforts to define the Canadian identity, notes the northern character of Canada and our need for a metropolitan culture to serve as a baseland. Historically, he says, our economy has been built on products of the north — fish, furs, timber, and wheat. More recently the natural resources of the Shield have played an important role in our economic development. Economic necessity has produced a "wilderness" people surviving in a rigorous climate. The Canadian identity, Morton observes, is bound up with the northern character of our country.[6]

In varying degrees throughout our history we have been dependent on foreign powers to provide us with a metropolitan culture and an economic baseland. First France, then Britain, and during the last half of this century, the United States has served as this baseland. Does Canada still feel the need for an external baseland? This appears to be a question that we are asking ourselves at this time. Is our approach to national and international politics changing because we are rejecting the influence of an external baseland?

Regionalism and our policy of multiculturalism are factors which have played important roles in the development of our identity. Canada is divided by her heritage and her geography into a number of distinct regions which have acted as obstacles to communication among Canadians. Historically each region in Canada has had its own unique pattern of settlement. The early French settlements along the St. Lawrence River Valley determined the nature of Quebec. The influx of the United Empire Loyalists into southern Ontario and the Atlantic Provinces contributed to the character of these regions. During the late 19th century the immigration of Europeans to western Canada was responsible for determining the character of the West. The various regions in Canada have been separated from one another by the sheer size of Canada as well as by natural barriers. The economic growth of each region has influenced the occupational pursuits, the political interests, and the values of the people, and has been responsible for the emergence of cultural differences within the nation.

Moreover, Canada has been marked by the dual nature of her population from her inception as a nation. First there is the historic dualism between French and English Canada. Then, there is the dualism of the individual who identifies himself with two cultural traditions — that is, with an emerging Canadian culture as well as the culture of his forefathers.

Authorities in Canadian studies identify the diverse nature of the Canadian population as the most distinctive single characteristic of Canada. Canadians, they point out, have adopted values that emphasize both their cultural and religious differences.

The late Edward McCourt, former Professor of English at the University of Saskatchewan, describes a Canadian in these terms:

> Canada is my country. I have lived here nearly all my life and I am a Canadian.
> A Canadian is a man whose people have lived in Canada for several generations; he is an Irishman newly arrived from Cork and an Ulsterman from Derry; he is a Japanese from Kyoto, a Scot from the Outer Hebrides and a Slav from Central Europe; he is a Laplander, an Icelander, an Indian, an Eskimo, a laborer from Manchester and a peer from the Home Counties. A Canadian is any man who chooses to spend his life within that part of the globe bounded by Cape Race and the 49th parallel and Nootka Sound and the North Pole.[7]

Peter C. Newman identifies the pluralism of Canada as unique in North America. "The traditional difference," he writes, "between the American melting pot and the Canadian mosaic probably remains the single most important strand in the fabric of our national identity."[8]

To the "new Canadian," says Newman,

> What makes Canada such a special place is the unwritten contract between the people of various backgrounds living here, that bigotry will never be condoned, that instead of abusing each other, we will talk out our differences. ...
> It's vital that we never lose hold of the mystique of Canada; the way everyone is allowed "to be" — allowed to curse the winter, love the land, endlessly debate the meaning of our national existence. ... It's good to be tribal and ethnocentric. ...[9]

Ramsay Cook recognizes the ethnic and regional nature of Canada when he discusses the Canadian identity:

> Perhaps instead of constantly deploring our lack of identity, we should attempt to understand and explain the regional, ethnic and class identities that we do have. It might just be that it is in the limited identities that "Canadianism" is found, and that except for our over-heated nationalist intellectuals, Canadians find this situation quite satisfactory.[10]

The central theme then of Canadian history has been one that recognizes the pluralism of her people and has resulted in many lifestyles. In each region we have responded to the land in different ways; and our response has given rise, not to a homogeneous but to a heterogeneous population. Canada has related to the land and history with many strong variants. What are the implications of this for the elementary schools in Canada? Are we reflecting in classrooms the richness of the many cultures that we have inherited?

In the last decade, Canadian universities, as a result of the revived interest of ethnic groups in their cultural roots, have incorporated in their curricula programs concerned with the Canadian subcultures. Anthropology and Sociology departments, in particular, have encouraged research in the lifestyles of Canadians associated with various ethnic groups.

Both the elementary and high schools, on the other hand, have been slower to recognize the importance of teaching students about their cultural heritage. Canadian Studies in the public schools are still largely concerned with Canadians of British and French origin. Students whose forefathers belonged to one of these major groups learn about and identify with the history and cultural traditions of their ancestors. Students whose ancestors came here from other parts of the world are denied similar experiences. If the student is to develop a positive self-image, he must have the opportunity to identify with his own cultural group. Psychologists have observed that this identification tends to strengthen family ties. The public school should, therefore, be prepared to present a more comprehensive study of Canadian ethnic groups.

Both the schools and the public must take responsibility for the use of Canadian materials in our schools. We must pressure school boards and departments of education to buy Canadian materials. Canadian publishers must receive public support so that the curriculum materials used in our schools will be Canadian in origin. We must support the arts in Canada, then make sure that the child is introduced to them at a very early age.

A Canadian Studies curriculum, derived from Canada's many cultural groups, does not teach narrow nationalism. The student who is encouraged to learn about the differing lifestyles of Canadians is better prepared to develop an understanding of other people at the international level. In our movement back to the basics, let us be sure that we include courses in the social sciences concerned with our own cultural variations. Surely we must believe that this is basic! Let us remember that the child who is led to recognize that the social, religious, and political institutions of a people are their response to their physical environment and to their historical experience is more capable of appreciating the needs and aspirations of other groups.

FOOTNOTES

[1]Margaret Atwood, *Survival* (Toronto, 1972), 15-16.

[2]Daniel U. Levine, "The Unfinished Identity of Metropolitan Man," in Richard Wisniewishi, ed., *Teaching About Life in the City,* National Council for the Social Studies, 1972, 33.

[3]Cited by Dr. F. J. Gathercole, in an address to the Saskatoon Teachers' Convention, Saskatoon, Saskatchewan, February 24, 1967.

[4]Sollange Chaput Rolland, *My Country, Canada or Quebec?* (Toronto, 1966).

[5]Governor General Vanier, New Year's message to the Canadian people, January 1, 1966.

[6]W. L. Morton, *The Canadian Identity* (Toronto, 1962), 93.

[7]E. McCourt, "My Canada," *Maclean's* (February, 1972), 17.

[8]Peter C. Newman, "Curse the Winter, Love the Land: Enjoying the Canadian Dream," *Maclean's* (April 1973), 3.

[9]*Ibid.*

[10]Ramsay Cook, "Canadian Centennial Celebrations," *International Journal,* XXII (Autumn 1967), 663.

V ETHNIC RESEARCH: RESOURCES AND METHODOLOGY

AN ORAL METHODOLOGY FOR ETHNIC STUDIES FROM THE JUNIOR SECONDARY TO THE GRADUATE SCHOOL

STANLEY H. SCOTT
NOTRE DAME UNIVERSITY, NELSON, B.C.

"If any wan comes along with a history iv Greece or Rome," Finley Peter Dunne's Irish immigrant philosopher, Mr. Dooley, once recounted, "that'll show me th' people fightin', gettin' dhrunk, makin' love, gettin' married, owin' the grocery man and bein' without hard-coal, I'll believe they was a Greece or Rome, but not before."[1] Unfortunately for Mr. Dooley, much history written today — particularly detailing immigrant and ethnic groups in Canada — reflects two distinct positions of historical literature. The first viewpoint notes the names, dates, and accomplishments of the great ethnic individuals of our country; in short, these biographical sketchbooks primarily show how successful — and how Waspish — some of our immigrants have become. The second grouping of historical literature has produced voluminous statistical work that numerically establishes the significance — or insignificance — of Canadian minorities.

But how valid, how significant, how revealing are these attempts at social history? What often seems to be missing from these traditional and not-so-traditional accounts is the human quality of the past. Quantitative and purely descriptive methods certainly can contribute to the deciphering of events, but what of the day-to-day activities of immigrants awash in a new land, with old customs, a strange language, and little hope but hope itself? Only in developing the climate of success, rather than establishing the fact of success, can the historian understand the complexities of Canadian society. Where, in short, is the history of the undistinguished?

Perhaps one of the most effective research tools in the expanding ethnic research programmes has been the refinement and expansion of oral history. With the publication of Professor Oscar Lewis' *Children of Sanchez* in 1961, the development of the taped interview, a most important instrument of oral history, has created a controversial and interesting discussion among students of society. Often the debate has centred on reliability and accuracy, bias of the interviewee, and intent and inflection of the interviewer. Since the 1940s, however, many of these potential shortcomings and advantages have been recognized and publicized by oral historians, and, besides, they have developed and refined the method to a higher level of sophistication and acceptability. The recent works of Barry Broadfoot *(Ten Lost Years,* and *Six War Years),* as well as other books by Lewis, and the biography *Huey Long* by T. Harry Williams illustrate this process.[2] Oral methodology, despite some legitimate criticisms, has obviously begun to play an important role in historical investigation and the creation of a more life-related literature.[3]

While the exact nature of oral research has been as varied as the topics investigated, I would like to propose a technique that was developed and tested specifically with the co-operation of immigrants and ethnic groups. Under consideration were the West Kootenays of British Columbia, a rural community based primarily on resource extraction and exploitation industries of the interior. Isolated from the urban centres to the west and from the prairies to the east, the Kootenays provided a most suitable area for examination. For there, almost side by side, existed large numbers of Russian, Italian, and English immigrants.[4] Intermingled with Scandinavians and Americans, these three groups apparently had reached an unusually high level of co-operation and peaceful coexistence typical of the popularized version of the "Canadian mosaic." Although Russian Doukhobors (primarily agrarian-communal-religious idealists), Italians, industrial labourers recruited by the Canadian Pacific Railway for its Cominco smelter at Trail, and English, usually affluent fruit ranchers sustained in part by remittance monies, had independently begun immigrating to the area prior to 1900, they were transformed by 1975 into a veritable multi-cultural society.[5]

Funded by a Multicultural Project Travel and Equipment Grant, from the Department of the Secretary of State, and a "Professions for Tomorrow" Personnel Grant from the Government of British Columbia, a five-person team began developing a research plan in February 1975 to study social and cultural relationships within the West Kootenays.[6] This team employed a combination of international, national, and local history techniques, as well as a modified version of Oscar Lewis' methodology. Aware of the need of advance preparation, the team first conducted extensive background investigations locally and at the Provincial Archives of British Columbia, which resulted in five basic position papers. The first three of these papers were, in the main, socio-economic studies of conditions in Italy, Russia, and England between 1870 and 1910. The essays revealed a number of kinds and conditions of alienation — real and imagined — that led to emigration. The fourth paper sketched a narrative history of the West Kootenays in a provincial and national setting, while the final one discussed printed secondary sources relating to the development of ethnic attitudes in Canada, 1900-1940. Although preliminary to the project proper, these investigations uncovered much valuable information, led to a better understanding of local and international developments, and provided data which would prove invaluable during the actual interview sessions.

Next the team spent approximately two weeks establishing a hypothesis for the study. Now knowledgeable of the secondary literature on ethnic studies in Canada, first they questioned several areas of interest. Did the popularized Canadian mosaic exist?[7] Was the Americanized "melting pot" more applicable?[8] What were the linguistic, economic, social, and cultural ramifications of assimilation? What were the interactions of the Russians, Italians, and English? How did the three groups view their own past? The Canadian past? Many questions, the team eventually agreed, could not be answered. Emerging instead was a generalized series of queries: a) how did individuals within each group view their past? b) how did they relate to social change? c) how did they recall and react to institutional change? and d) how did the family as a social unit change through three generations?

From these questions evolved an *a priori* research plan — the investigators would divide into three groups and, using extended interviews, examine three generations of a single family within each immigrant group. The historical relations of time, place, and social change would emerge, they hoped, with the seventy-year development of the families. The total taped sample therefore would involve only nine people. After considerable consultation, each ethnic community would select a sample family group. Seeking neither averages, generalizations, nor a sweeping ethnic history of the communities of the West Kootenays, the teams would allow nine members of three families to recall their memories for the record. The researchers assumed that vertical comparisons would emerge within each family group; they also expected horizontal comparisons and contrasts to develop within the same generation of the three family groups. And they hoped that expansive insights into the Kootenay past as well as the historic relationship of immigrant and ethnic families would become known.

While the teams perceived the interviews as partially unstructured, they were also aware of the pitfalls of informal sessions. A *Guide* was therefore created as the next procedural step. To serve as a general outline, the *Guide* was a checkoff sheet to be compiled after each interview session, allowing for continuity from generation to generation and from family to family. Never intended to be all-inclusive, the outline simply identified certain broadly related subject areas.

The first of seven subdivisions of the *Guide* was a section detailing family and personal relationships. Biographical information such as date and place of birth, family size, number of brothers and sisters, and general family recollections came within this area. Other reminiscences — the actual immigration, family discipline, in-laws (if any), and personal feelings such as loneliness, discrimination, elation — also were listed here. Linguistic patterns (in the home and school), family holidays, special events and occasions, artifacts, heirlooms, the manner of storing the past, and humour, as well as family financial patterns — major purchases, crises, decision-making — were also included in family relationships.

Another section developed occupational relationships. Included were recollections by members of each generation of the occupational roles of their fathers and mothers. Education, training, advancement, seeking jobs, losing jobs, language at work, relationship with the boss, attitudes toward other ethnic workers were discussed. Other more specific factors — time clocks, benefits, retirement, attitude toward professionalism, unionism, comparisons between the new and the old country (known or idealized) — also took up a significant part of the outline. Each point (unionization, for example) was placed in a historical perspective from family to family and generation to generation.

Varying aspects of socialization also became the bases of two other sections. The first, relationships with the ethnic community, stressed the functions of such culture-retaining factors as ethnic schools, churches, jokes, holidays, and organizations, as well as ethnic marriages, mores, and folkways. Each participant, for example, was asked to relate the contributions of his or her ethnic group. Neither accuracy nor universals were sought; rather, the researchers wanted a personal opinion. The second community-related section examined such culture-diminishing contact with the larger society as interaction, slang, myths, non-ethnic schools, churches, clubs, games, music and food.

Finally, three sections traced the world as perceived by the interviewers of the families. One section was designed to discuss values and beliefs, including the definition of self, morality, change, success, and failure; another to identify institutional changes such as schools, religion, government, language, and communications. Then the third section sought to explore the recreational activities of the generations and their involvement in team and individual games, land use, television, radio, and theatre.

To establish a built-in check on recollections, many questions, in slightly revised form, resurfaced in all seven subdivisions. Language, for example, was not only considered as a means of communication at schools, in the churches, on the job, within the community, but also as an institution. Often a key question from a previous interview would open the next session. None of these descriptions have done more than hastily trace a detailed and well developed outline. For the more than cursory observer, the entire *Guide* has been attached as an appendix to the present paper.[9]

By June 1975, the team was ready to select the sample families from each of the three groups.[10] First the members contacted local ethnic organizations and held meetings with both the executive and general memberships. Then they also met with interested community leaders. Careful not to define the families, the team cautiously avoided such terms as "successful," "typical," "representative," and "example," preferring instead that the local ethnic community make those distinctions (if necessary) in selecting their participants. Families of three available generations (the first being the immigrant) were the only requirements; English skills were not necessary, since additional monies were available for translators.

Numerous interesting and potentially exciting comparisons became obvious once the sample families had been selected. The first generation had been youthful immigrants, ranging from six to thirteen at passage. Now between seventy-six and eighty-seven, they had come to Canada between 1902 and 1904. Despite their advanced ages, they proved remarkably alert, attentive, and anxious to commence the project. The Italian and Russian immigrants were male; the English, female. The second generations were all male, pleased with their personal and ethnic group successes. All businessmen, they ranged in age between forty-five and fifty-one. Three women formed the third generational participants, aged twenty-four, twenty-five, and twenty-six. Significantly (location within the West

Kootenays had not been a predetermined factor) the families were from the centres of their own particular immigrant community — the Italian family, three generations in Trail, the Russian, three generations in the Castlegar and Slocan Valley, and the English, three generations in Crawford Bay on the east shore of Kootenay Lake. Separated then by distances between thirty and ninety miles, the families could not only develop interesting family histories, but offer invaluable insights into the diverse regional history of the Kootenays.

Once the ethnic communities had selected the three families, the team arranged a series of preliminary meetings. Completely informal, these gatherings normally included the three generations, friends, and other members of the larger family. No taping was done, and after the original introductions and explanations, these sessions generally developed into social occasions, since the primary purpose of these meetings was to allow both parties to become accustomed to one another.[11] Following several three- to four-hour meetings, the research teams met collectively to discuss observations, insights, and potential problems.[12]

By the middle of June, all the advance preparation was complete, the families selected, and the schedules established. Only the interviews remained. The time budgeted for each individual was approximately ten taped hours, spanning a period of about two weeks — for a total of thirty hours per family. The estimates proved inadequate. All individuals recorded more than sixteen hours; four exceeded twenty hours, and one talked for almost thirty. The teams had originally planned five two-hour sessions; in practice, most meetings ran at least three hours — at the participant's insistence.[13] In each case, the first interview was the most crucial. At that time, common misconceptions about history ("I don't know anything about history — I've seldom been out of the Kootenays and only voted once") and individual shyness forced the teams to alter their strategy. Instead of directing the opening session toward personal development, they encouraged the interviewees to begin with a biographical narrative.[14] Then after listening to the tape, the researchers had ample avenues back to the *Guide.* Moreover, the participants, after the original "ordeal" always were most willing discussants during the second and following sessions, often remembering numerous additional stories, activities, and relationships. Once into the process, they apparently thought of little but the project for the next several weeks; each individual was sincerely disappointed when the interviews ended.[15]

The two researchers acted as a team throughout the procedure. In almost every study, the same two interviewers worked with the three generations of the same family; in any case, at least one person participated in all three levels, thereby establishing links between interviewer and interviewee. For each three-hour taped session, the teams spent another ten to twelve hours diagnosing the information, eliminating the completed sections of the *Guide,* and detailing the remaining areas. Yet invariably the *Guide* proved simply an organizational outline. Since each generation presented new insights, many hours were spent developing question areas between tapings. During the sessions, the teams also alternated roles in directing the discussions because the researchers quickly realized that participant enthusiasm required matching listener interests. Seldom were the elderly interviewees as exhausted at the end of three or four hours as the interviewers.[16]

Perhaps a few brief examples will amplify the findings and illuminate the methodology. The vertical differences between the three generations of the same family, of course, were the most obvious. Allowing the participants to define as much of their past as possible, the teams queried them about ethnicity. The Italians, for example, clearly had varied viewpoints — the first generation informant claimed that he was an Italian-Canadian; the second, a Canadian-Italian; the third, simply a Canadian. The English family also revealed some striking comparisons. The first generation informant insisted on tea at three, the second drank nothing but coffee, and the third took neither, preferring instead Coca-Cola. Naturally similarities also developed — some apparent to the participants, other not. The first and third generation Italians defined the family in remarkably similar fashions; the first and third generation Russians, both communalists and living in common-law marriage, found no relationship between their similar life styles and ethnic heritage. The second generations of all the families had surprisingly comparable definitions of work, success, and morality. Marriages outside the ethnic group occurred throughout the groups of the study. While the members of the first and second generations were markedly defensive about their choices of mates, the informants of the third only expressed unanimous surprise at the question. The three third generation women also exhibited comparable attitudes in defining friendship, success, ambition, and careers; their linguistic patterns included most of the western Canadianisms; their dress was equally contemporary, and their homes were typically North American West. Surprisingly, most recollections of history — local and otherwise — remained much the same from generation to generation and family to family.

Striking dissimilarities, however, also emerged. Only the first generation Russian seemed to understand contemporary society; only the first generation English retained substantial customs and mannerisms of the Old Country. The heavy physical demands on all the first generations gave way to feelings of affluence in the second and to significant symptoms of boredom in the third. Political awareness declined noticeably within the English family, rose sharply within the Italian, fluctuated wildly within the Russian. As an avenue for social mobility, educational expectations declined most conspicuously with the English, increased with the Italians, and remained stable with the Russians. Naturally views on such widely diverse subjects as abortion, violence, national and provincial politics, ecology, and social change varied far too greatly to be generalized into any specific categorization. While historical recollections of events were generally uniform, the interpretations also reflected substantial deviations within the families and across generational lines.[17]

Once collected, the data have numerous public, educational, and scholarly applications. Depending on the resources, the team had several options for presenting the materials to the public of the Kootenays. Since an interested drama department existed at Notre Dame University, a series of radio plays from the tapes were devised; without such a group, the team could have edited a series through the capable facilities of the Kootenay Cultural Society, an organization that has recorded local artists (including the Doukhobor Women's Choir) for commercial and civic productions. Neither summations nor changes were contemplated, but rather three comparative and contrasting one-hour sequences. To reach as many localities as possible, the team also developed a collection of newspaper articles. Both presentations — radio and newspaper — were advertised with the assistance of posters drafted by resident artists at the Kootenay School of Art.[18]

Educational uses of the project, of course, were equally diversified. A packaged presentation of the techniques (stressing the strengths, as well as the problems) was developed for the elementary and secondary schools of the region. Coupled with slides, the examples clearly stimulated student interests in the local ethnic past, and also provided the teachers with new field project ideas. Scholarly potentials also abounded. Once transcribed, the interviews provided excellent primary data for professional behavioral scientists, and other research projects also emerged; since 1975, for example, an extensive examination of the Cominco work force (primarily Italian) has been underway. The original concept of that scholarship came from the Italian interviews. An edited manuscript will allow scholars throughout Canada to examine the findings of the project, thereby expanding the scholarly understanding of our immigrant/ethnic heritage.[19]

Several potential pitfalls, however, must be recognized before the methodology can be widely applied. Advance preparation is absolutely essential for successful sessions. The interviewer must be knowledgeable about the local, regional, and national past; otherwise, often the interviews will hopelessly break down. The team must also establish rapport with the participant, thereby creating an amicable atmosphere. Yet the researchers still must not intimidate the participant, since recall, in any case, is never 100 percent. The first generation Italian, for example, insisted that the Cominco strike had only involved fifty workers, none of whom were Italians, when in fact the stoppage had concerned approximately forty percent of the workers (400 men), who were *mostly* Italian. Gently the team developed the question at three sessions, but the participant remained resolute. But in his recollection, he interpreted an important event of his own past. Another potential problem can be transcription. Our project, for example, when typed out covered 3,000 pages. Some secondary projects, of course, will derive real and greater benefits from retaining or reducing the tapes. The sound of the voices will make the testimony more personal, and some scholars such as linguists, will also prefer voice editions.[20] Most importantly, the interviewers must remember that the data represent raw sources of the past, not history as developed by historians.

Thus oral history, like all other methods, does not provide all the answers to the past. But it does offer significant insights into the nature of immigrant/ethnic groups conspicuously lacking in conventional historical sources. When properly applied, the methodology can be useful at every level of intellectual inquiry — from the junior secondary to the graduate school. While still new, oral history has forced historians to reconsider the past. For no longer can they practise their profession using only the printed recollections and records of the elite. Now the recollections of the undistinguished can become an important part of the record of the past.

FOOTNOTES

[1]Much of the research leading to this paper was aided by grants from the Canadian Government, Department of the Secretary of State, Multicultural Research Project, and the British Columbia Professions for Tomorrow Project. Without these grants, the two-year project would still be in the early stages. Assistance provided by Celi Scott, Dan Grant, Margaret Murphy, and Andy Shadrack proved invaluable to the author; to them, many thanks are due. The project involved background research and extensive (15-30 hours per occasion) participant observer interviews. English, Italian, and Russian three generation families were selected and taped at individual sessions between May and September, 1975.

[2]Barry Broadfoot, *Ten Lost Years* (Toronto, 1974), and *Six War Years* (Toronto, 1975); Oscar Lewis, *Children of Sanchez* (New York, 1961), and *Five Families* (Toronto, 1959); T. Harry Williams, *Huey Long* (New York, 1970).

[3]For a comprehensive discussion on oral history see the Notes on the Canadian Aural/Oral History Conference in *Sound Heritage*, 5 (Winter, 1975).

[4]For more on the Kootenay Society, see Stanley Scott, "Assimilation or Multiculturalism — The Origins of Kootenay Society," in *The Pacific Northwest*, eds., G. Love and E. Bingham (Eugene, 1977).

[5]The author, by using the term "popularized vertical mosaic," does not attempt to mislead the academic community. An equal society (rather than John Porter's pyramiding stratification) is implied.

[6]The author and Celi Scott began in February, and the other team members joined the project in May, 1975.

[7]See John Porter, *The Vertical Mosaic: An Analysis of Social and Class Power in Canada* (Toronto, 1965) and James L. Heap, ed., *Everybody's Canada: The Vertical Mosaic Reviewed and Re-examined* (Toronto, 1974).

[8]See Daniel Patrick Moynihan, *Beyond the Melting Pot* (Cambridge, 1963).

[9]See Appendix.

[10]The groups were the Doukhobor Historical Society (Castlegar), the Columbo Lodge (Trail), and the IODE (Nelson).

[11]One informal meeting was a surprise party for the second generation Italian's twenty-fifth wedding anniversary, while another was a Sunday morning pancake dinner by the second generation Russian for all his family.

[12]Some revamping was necessary. Since the other two third generation participants were women, a request was made (and granted) that the Russian family allow the second child, a woman, to be the participant.

[13]The researchers simply miscalculated the participant interest. The second generation English, for example, insisted in the beginning that he had little to offer. Then he talked over thirty hours!

[14]Normally the narrative would run two sessions, or approximately six hours.

[15]Six months after the sessions ended, the second generation Russian requested another interview, recalling forgotten information.

[16]Ongoing preparations were essential. The first generation English, for example, had worked in the wheat fields of Saskatchewan during World War I, been involved in the One Big Union movement in Vancouver, and had hopped freights during the depression. Few of these areas are extensively covered in the *Guide*.

[17]No detailed comparisons were made. These statements should not be viewed as absolute conclusions, but rather as observations.

[18]This research project was endorsed by Notre Dame University, the Kootenay School of Art, the Nelson and District Historical Society, and the Kootenay Cultural Society. All provided excellent support and encouragement.

[19]An edited manuscript of the interviews, tentatively entitled *Kootenay Diary,* will simply allow the immigrant/ethnic participants to speak for themselves.

[20]Numerous research ideas inevitably emerge. The Cominco work force, for example, is now under examination. Funded by a Canada Council Grant, a new research team is developing those themes. The tapes and transcripts are in the holdings of Notre Dame University. For some of the applications of oral history, see Murray R. Nelson and H. Wells Singleton, "Using Oral History in the Social Studies Classroom," *Clearing House,* 49 (October 1975), 89-93; and B. K. MacMaster, "Oral History Speaks for the Other America," *America,* 128 (May, 1973), 411-13.

Appendix

GUIDE
Three-Generational Interview Series
(Relate, when possible, intergenerational)

I.   *Family and Personal Relationships*
Birthplace
Date of Birth — Father/Mother
Remembrances — ambitions, occupation, happy, easy going, disciplinarian?
           — Family — size, what was your position and relation in the family?
What did your father/mother remember most about_____?
What did he miss the most?
Whom did he miss the most?
When did you/your family emigrate? Why?
Age at migration?
        Vehicle of immigration — passage (rates) boat?
                          — conditions
                          — agents
        Route of migration in Canada — circumstances that caused you to move?
First Recollections — remember your first view of Canada?
           — what was it like on the boat?
           — how did Canada appear to you?
           — immigration processing?
           — what do you remember about the climate?
           — did you feel lonely?
           — did you take the train across the country?
        First recollections of B.C. What was the countryside like? Did you apply for Citizenship? Why not?
Family Do you have recollections of your parents' house?
    Have you ever returned? Change in views?
    Was your family close?
        Relations of gender — father to oldest son
                          — father to daughter
                          — mother to daughter
                          — relations to older members of the family
        Who ran the household?
        Who handled finances?
        Who had what household duties? What were yours?
Did your parents have any myths about immigration — Wild West
                                                 — Promised Land
Did you come as a family, a community, or as individuals?
        Chain migration of individuals
        What was your class position in_____before you emigrated?
        Did you send money home? Why?
        Did you have a job to come to in Canada? Who got it for you?
        Would you have come if you didn't have one?
Did you speak English at home? at school? at work?
What language are you most comfortable with?
Should Canada adopt_____as a national language (French)
What language would you prefer your children spoke?
Did you have any language problems at school?
What were the special family occasions — important *family* dates?

Did your parents ever prepare a special meal for you? What?
What did you do on those days?

Special social occasions — church, baptisms, confirmations, first communions
Did your family keep photos?
Did they keep family artifacts and souvenirs?
Were there family heirlooms?

Did you like school? What was fun about school?
Did you skip school often? Why?
Did you consider it important?
What were your teachers like?
What's the funniest thing you remember about school?

Was your family very wealthy?
Do you remember any financial crisis? Did you ever go hungry?
Could you save money? For what?
    What was a major purchase?
    Would you borrow money?
Can you remember ordering through catalogues? Was there anything special you remember waiting for?

What was the first electrical device you remember your family owning?

What do you remember about your parents' methods of child raising?
Did you fight with your parents? Ever leave home? Was discipline strict?
Would your parents swear?
What was punishment like?
Did you get an allowance?
Parents views on smoking and drinking? Your views:

When you emigrated did you bring private possessions? Furniture?
    Possessions — yours or the families? How important was private ownership?

In growing up what was your favorite object or article?

Did you have any hobbies?
Did you have any pets?

What was dinner like? Family occasion? Any rules? Grace?
What kind of activity was there after dinner?
Were there games?
Did you play cards? Gambling?
Who would you talk to if you were in trouble?
Did you ever go visiting? Entertain visitors?

Did your family ever go on a holiday? How far? How often?
How many? How much?

If there was sickness in the family who would you go to?
    Doctors? Hospitals? What were medicines like?
In the case of a non-medical emergency who would you go to:
    a) emotional problems
    b) financial emergency
    c) crime
    d) accident
What would you do on a Sunday? Picnic?

At the time of Emigration
    How would you view your personal appearance?
    How many changes of clothes did you have?
    Did you need glasses? Did you have them?
    Were you able to bathe often?

What was your first experience with death?
How were births viewed? Celebrations?
Was there ever any family planning?
What was thought of as an ideal family size?

Did you value independence:
Extended families?
Privacy — with family, with brothers and sisters.
    If you wanted privacy where did you go?
Do you remember your first girl friend?
What did you do on a date?
How did you learn about sex?
What do you remember about your wedding?

After immigration, what was the first custom that you dropped?

Do you remember any diet changes:
    — did you buy at a market or a supermarket?
Did you grow any of your own food?
Did you eat fresh food or canned food?

Did you participate in sports? Do you enjoy watching?
Were you fond of athletics?
What are your favorite sports?
Do you read newspapers?
Which parts do you read (local, sports, politics, international, women's section, comics,
    editorials, letters, business)
Which magazines do you read?

How often do you watch T.V.?
Do you go to movies? What kind?
Do you read many books? What kind? In what language?

Were you different from your friends or were they different from you?
What was/is your perception of your nationality? What does that mean?
Were you ever jealous of anyone? Why?
What achievement in your life are you most proud of?
How did your father view other ethnic groups? You?
Was your father satisfied with his work?

Did you ever work with your dad?
When were you considered an adult?
Did you have any fantasies — what did you dream of?

Did you ever quarrel?
Who quarreled? Between who?

Christian names?
Family customs and habits?
Who did you want your sister/daughter to marry?
Your in-laws?
What did/do you think of your son-in-law
                    daughter-in-law?

Remittances?
Scandals in the family?
Prearranged marriages?
Childhood —
Teenage years —
                    What do you remember about
                    these periods in your life?
Adolescence —
Young adult —
Protest

Describe the furniture — physical baggage that you brought? What was left? What
    jettisoned on route? Why did you bring what you did? Abandon what you
    did?
How does the family decide on who gets what in terms of family possessions?
Wills?

Who do you identify with — Identification? Reference Group:
Historical Tradition in family — how is it maintained?
        What is history for you?
RELATE QUESTIONS BETWEEN ALL GENERATIONS!!!!
Home ownership or rental? House size and satisfaction?
Social mobility? Railway propaganda?
Old country myths — as perceived by 2nd and 3rd generations?
New country myths — as perceived by 1st generation?
At what age were you considered an adult?
At what age did you consider yourself independent?
At what age do/did you consider your children independent?

II.   *Occupational Relationships*

    (This is a brief sample; identify occupations(s) in interview #1 and prepare detailed
    preempt)
    Father's job
    Did your mother work (Woman's role)?
    Training, License, Tickets?
    Education — occupation (Correlation????)

Describe a day of work at the plant/mill.
Attitude toward bosses?
Opportunity for promotion and advancement?
Rates of pay — adequate? Was there a minimum wage?
Hours? Time clocks?
Production quotas?
Security?
What did you do at lunch time?
Coffee breaks?

Relations with company?
Company recreation?
Company benefits — UIC — anything of the like?
Company town? Houses?
Retirement plans? How you handled it?
The big bosses? Feeling? Their place in town?
Company teams and picnics?
Hospitalization? First Aid — plant?
          Profit sharing or exploiting you for profit???

Age at start of first job?
          — sons follow father?
          — occupational change through generations?
Were you ever fired? Why?
How did you get to work?
What did you wear?
Safety practices and equipment?
Shiftwork?
Sick days — company policy?
Holidays — Statutory and yearly?
Layoffs?
Seniority? Who was laid off first — ethnic workers?

Relations with other workers? Did you talk amongst each other?
Employee solidarity — ethnic, otherwise.
Social relationships with other workers: bosses? foremen?
Bosses — racist
          — Italian, etc.

Language at work — boss — peers
Did you work with oriental labor?
SCABS?
What would you think of Vietnamese immigrants coming to Trail to work in the
          plants.
Strikes — what do you think about them?
Do you remember any radical unionists?
Union meetings — did you join a union? Are unions of value?
How did established unions treat the immigrant?
Political pressure in the plant?

Did you work out of necessity?
Were you proud of your work?
Did you view yourself as an artisan or as a laborer?
          Service Occupation — vital occupation?
Alienation and Boredom?
What do you see as the future of your occupational group?
Job satisfaction?

Do you remember any bad years?
Recessions?
Job pressures affect faculty?
Wage cuts in the depression?
Purchasing power?
What was the most important external thing that affected your job?
Do you remember any company disasters?
Did you feel that you were contributing to the war effort?
          (Heavy water plant — Italians)
Do you remember any industrial sabotage?
Did you ever feel that your work was contributing to pollution?
If it were possible, what, with respect to your occupational role, would you change or do
          differently?
Agricultural techniques

          Production quotas
          Crop production
          Secondary Skills and their uses.
          (See economic preps in preliminary papers)

III.   *Ethnic Community Relationships*

          What community organizations were in existence?
                Ethnic schools?
                Ethnic clubs?
                Ethnic church? — unifying force?
                Ethnic gangs — Street corner society?
          Was there an attempt within the group to teach and to learn a new language?
          Were you accepted, upon arrival, by the established immigrants of your own race?
          Was there an ethnic hierarchy?
          Who was the leader? How was he chosen?
          Were you ever exploited by members of your own race?
                — unscrupulous members of the ethnic community?
                (Italians — "padrone system" — pay for a job.)
          Who dealt with such individuals — internal matter?
                            — R.C.M.P.?
          Ethnic newspapers and entertainment?
          Did you celebrate ethnic holidays?
          Pubs and drinking — ethnic diversity?
          Was your community "institutionally complete" — could it function completely
                independent of a larger society?
          Did you deal only with people of your ethnic descent?
          Does the ethnic community buy goods at one place?
          Did your community pull together in times of trouble?
          Who is a success story in your community? Why?
          Who are the failures? Why?
          Is there pressure within the group to retain ethnicity?
          From who?
          Is there an ethnic community pressure on ethnic marriages?
          Unspoken community myths and laws, social mores and folkways?
          Has there been a breakdown of_____culture? When? How? Why?
                How do you feel about that?
          Has North American life diminished or amplified the_____way?
          How has the community changed? Why? What went wrong/right?
          How has the younger generation helped/destroyed the ethnic group?
          How did your group feel about other ethnic groups? How did they feel about you?
                Concentration camps — Japanese. Did you ever feel that you may be treated si-
                milarly?
          Regionalism — how would you accept a(n)_____from another area? (Italians
          —   Calabrians, Sicilians, Piedmontese).
                What is the chief contribution your ethnic group made to the Canadian society?
          What would you do if you could do it all over again? What would you change? What
          would you retain?

IV.   *Larger Community Relationships*

          How were you treated by Canadians when you arrived?
          Processing — medical checks etc.
          How were you treated by — customs officials?
                             — immigration officials?
                             — transport officials?
                Treated as individuals/community?
          Discriminated against — slang? Your feelings at the time?
          How did you feel about Canadians? How did you view yourself?
          How were you assigned settlements or an initial place to sleep?
          Did you ever encounter varied rates in stores etc.?
          Were you treated fairly by the receiving society?
          How did you feel when you went into town? Different?
          Were you ever refused entrance on the basis of nationality?
          Did you ever encounter segregation?
          Do you ever remember fights or brawls — what caused them — ethnic issues?
          Non-ethnic friends?
          Who was your first Canadian non_____friend?
          What did you like about him/her?
          Were you ridiculed or encouraged by your family for having non-ethnic friends?

Did your inability/ability to communicate inhibit/facilitate the making of friends?
Did you date outside your ethnic group?
Did you ever consider marriage outside your ethnic group?
Did you feel superior, equal or inferior to other ethnic groups?
Did you feel that the larger community had more opportunities?
How did you feel about Orientals? Russians? Hindus? Italians?
Were you ever aware of any common myths about how other groups lived? Did you
share any myths about North American Indians?
    What did you perceive to be other groups' ambitions?
    Did they seem to be different? Why?
    What did other groups do that you didn't?
    What did you do that they didn't?
    Eating habits of other ethnic groups?
    Did the other groups dress differently?
    Did you adopt the clothing of any group?
    What is the first other-group characteristic that you adopted?
Did you perceive any other group as an occupational threat?
Did they work in any similar occupations and trades? Higher/Lower?
What did you admire most in other groups?
What did you resent most?
Did you ever feel a "keeping up with the _____ " syndrome?
Did you ever belong to another ethnic group's club?
Non-ethnic clubs — Kiwanis? Kinsmen? Knights of Columbus? Rotary? Lions?
Legion? Veterans of Foreign Wars?
Drinking habits, pubs — leveling influence?
Did you feel secure in Canada — as a group?
                              — as an individual outside the group?
How did you view the law: for other groups/your group/against you/equitable?
    Relations with law enforcement officials?
Was there ever, in either talk or practice, an ethnic vigilante movement "to protect our
own?" From what?
Did you ever prefer other ethnic food?
                      other ethnic music?
Do you remember any controversial issues in which your group opposed the majority?
Do you remember any scandals in which you or your group may have been caught in
the middle? How did the larger community react? Group feeling at the time?
Protest — group feeling with respect to it?
        — against the larger community?
        — with the larger community against specific issues?
        Is it a levelling influence with respect to the larger community?
            — Anti-Chinese riots in Vancouver (1906)
            — Amchitka protests
Were you allowed to vote?
Who did you support in elections — block voting?
Personal Habits — Relate to other groups, to the core group (the larger community),
and to other generations within the family.
        — hair styles
        — shaving legs, etc.
        — slacks vs. skirts
        — beards, long hair — discrimination: towards? Against?
        — shoes
        — cosmetics

V.   *Recreation (Overt) And Entertainment* (What is done in A Performing Way)
    (This section should develop in narrative pre-empt)
    What did your parents relate as recreation/entertainment habits of the old country?
    Recreation
    Music
    Sports — Hockey
            — Bicycling
            — Soccer
            — Wrestling
            — Curling (Canadian)
            — Boxing
            Who would you cheer for at an Olympic event?
            Who, in your opinion, is the ideal athlete?

Picnics
Church — what recreation facilities did the church provide?
Gardening
Fall Fairs
Holidays — When? Where?
Local and National festivals and holidays
Indigenous camping activities
      — swimming
      — camping
      — fishing
      — hunting
      — skiing
Contemporary activities
      — kite flying
      — drag racing
      — pinball
      — pool
      — gambling

Bowling	Bingo
Tennis	Bridge
Golf	Do you own a boat? Camper? Why? Why not?
Chess	Hobbies — recreation

Team sports at school?
Where is the furthest you have ever been from the Kootenies? Scenic changes in Kootenies? For better or worse?

Entertainment

Music — ideal entertainer?
Sports — contact sports? Do you regularly watch T.V. sports?
Plays — favorite dramatist?
Concerts. Singing. Choirs.
Television — How much do you watch? Favorite show? Favorite type of programming?
Newspapers — Which ones? Which parts?
Books — favorite author? Areas in which you are interested — reading areas? Last book read?
Movies — Specific types? Last movie seen? Favorite Star?
Records — How much do you spend on records?
Opera. Youth Groups. Photography.
What magazines do you subscribe to?
Games in family (unisexual and bisexual)?
Holidays — Decorating the Christmas tree, Easter, Thanksgiving. What is the most fun thing you have ever done?

VI.   *Values and Beliefs*

     (Seek views indirectly — forceful or direct approach will provoke answers designed to please interviewer)

     What in your mind are the basic values of life?
          — definition of values?
          — morality?
     What are your parents' values?
     What do you think of them?
     How are yours different?

     What values were carried to Canada from the old country?
     What were the first values lost or abandoned?
     What were the first values absorbed?
          What do you think of other people's values?
          Have your ethnic group values been changed for the better or the worse?
          What is the most important thing your ethnic group has lost?
          What customs or values would you like to see resurrected?

     What do/did you want for your children?
     If you had a lot of money what would you do?
     What change would you work to make the world more utopian to make the good life better?
     Do you have the good life here?
     What is the most important thing you have learned in your life?
     How do you regard laws?

Conformity — what is it to you?
            — are you an individual?
Describe a good citizen?
How do you judge success?
Do you consider yourself successful?

Do you consider yourself/your generation optimistic or pessimistic?
Do you consider yourself a pragmatist — end justifies the means?
Do you believe that man is basically good?

    What does social change mean to you?
    Do you welcome change?
    Are times better now than before?

Responsibilities and roles in a marriage — man?
                                            — woman?

Should there be a change?
Relationships toward the old?

Are all men created equal?
Are some inferior — if so how?

Best form of political control?
How do you view politicians — their values?
Is there such a thing as too much government? Too little?
Are there inalienable rights?
Do you believe all men and women should have the right to vote?
Participatory democracy?
What do you think about unemployment, UIC, pensions, etc.

Morality and Manner — sex education in school or at home?
Prohibition
Censorship
Military conscription
War
Gun control

How do you interpret the Bible — liberal? figurative?
Funerals — Habits? Beliefs? Traditions?
Wakes?
Afterlife?

Materialism vs. Functionalism

Do/did you go to church?
What does church/religion mean to you?
Does it instill values?

Views on — divorce
         — abortion
         — contraception
         — homosexuality
         — women's lib
         — drugs and alcohol
         — prostitution
         — gambling
Matters of individual choice or should laws legislate them?
Superstitions?

VII.   *Institutions*
    (Changing attitudes between the generations. How the institutions changed.)
    Monarchy
        Nobility — class distinction?
             — at home?
             — in Canada?
        Titles? Hierarchy?
        Your feelings?
    Holidays
        What you did?
        What was celebrated — traditional?
                    — national?
                    — neo-national?
        Dress? Drink? Food? Customs? Habits?

Schools
> — ethnic schools?
> — institutionalized for the purpose of assimilation?
> — force schooling?
> — Separate or Public? — Russian experience
>   — Free schools — Slocan today.

How do you feel about free schools today when others have been denied that liberty? (Doukhobors)

Art and Music
> Concerts?
> Poetry?
> School bands?
> Music and religion?
> Musical selections?
> Musical ethnocentrism?

Ethnic vs. non-ethnic art appreciation?

Religion and the Church

Priests etc. — ethnic group members?
Other religions of the area?
Religious toleration — the Ashram?
Non-ethnic missionaries?
Orthodox vs. non-orthodoxy?
Marriage customs?
Religion in your daily life?
Define sin?
Spiritual experiences?
Afterlife?
Family Bible?
Doctrine?
Theology and Dogma?
Circumcision?

Catholicism
> — christenings
> — tithes
> — confirmation
> — confession
> — abandonment of the use of Latin
> — meat on Friday
> — rosaries
> — scapula
> — church symbolism — statues
> — Lent — giving things up
> — fasting
> — Italian saints

Politics, Parties and Philosophy
> Nationalism vs. Internationalism vs. Imperialism vs. Colonialism vs. Regionalism?
>
> Party preference?
> How do you relate to various philosophies:
> > Social Credit?
> > N.D.P.?
> > Liberal?
> > Conservative?
> > Campaign participation?
> > Anarchy?
> > Third International?
> > Suffrage?
> > Patronage?
> > Block voting?
> > Prohibition?

Government Institutions and Services
> Law and Police?
> Bureaucracy?
> Local Civil servants — licensing agents?
>   — bureau of statistics?

Criminal penal certificates?
Taxes and land ownership?
Postal service?
Sanitation services?
Equality before institutions — your dealings with?
Any unpleasant incidents with government agents or officials?

Language   *Humour*
— cliches?   Jokes? Comic strips?
— idioms?   Whose expense?
Ethnic poetry and writings?
Historical scholarship — your feelings?
                    — Simma Holt?
Historical publications about your group?
Physical use of the language?
Written use of the language? Correspondence?

Medicine
— clinics?
— hospitals?
— family doctor?
— home cures?
— midwives?
— births and deaths?
— transfusions?

Communication
Newspapers? Radio? T.V.? Word of mouth?
How was vital information passed? Rumour?

Financial Institutions
— usury?
— pawning?
— credit?
— pragmatism?
— banks?
— credit cards?
— personal loans?
— bankruptcy?
— borrowing?
— mortgages?
— debt?
— collectors?

THE CANADIAN INSTITUTE OF UKRAINIAN STUDIES
MANOLY LUPUL
UNIVERSITY OF ALBERTA

If the main criterion of a scholarly paper is the number and/or kind of footnotes it contains, then this will have to be judged a non-scholarly paper about a scholarly matter of great significance to anyone seriously interested in "Culture, Education, and Ethnic Canadians," the theme of this conference. On 19 June 1976 the Board of Governors of the University of Alberta approved the establishment of the Canadian Institute of Ukrainian Studies on the Edmonton campus — an institution to serve the academic needs of Ukrainians in Canada as a whole.

Bearing in mind that the Institute's budget of at least $350,000 per year will be forthcoming out of public funds, this is a significant development in two all-important ways. First, the large government commitment gives the Institute the kind of "official" status which no other institution pursuing Ukrainian academic studies exclusively has hitherto enjoyed. The Institute, in short, is a public rather than a private institution — the first of its kind outside the Soviet Union. Secondly, the Alberta grant is the largest sum of public monies ever given to any Ukrainian project anywhere in the Free World.

The government funds are granted without term; that is, they are for no stipulated fixed period such as three, five, or ten years. They are permanent and monies unspent in any academic year will remain in the Institute's account. Moreover, the government has agreed to commit annually to the Institute that percentage of funds which $350,000 bears to the total University operating grant for the academic year 1976-77. The arrangement could only be upset by the Institute failing to meet its own purposes or objectives.

Purposes or Objectives

The objectives of the Institute are six in number:

1) To encourage program development in Ukrainian-Canadian and Ukrainian studies at the undergraduate and graduate levels;
2) To serve as a resource centre for English-Ukrainian bilingual education, improving such immersion programs as that in Edmonton (the preparation of teachers included) and encouraging their development elsewhere;
3) To encourage research on Ukrainian-Canadian and Ukrainian subjects by graduate students, university academic staff, other scholars with a respectable record of publications, and research workers on contract to the Institute;
4) To encourage publication of three types of works:
   a) research on Ukrainian-Canadian and Ukrainian subjects
   b) paperback reprints of out-of-print and other books
   c) paperback editions of notable master's and doctoral theses;

5) To serve as a national, inter-university clearing house for Ukrainian Studies in Canada to facilitate coordination in program development (especially at the graduate level) and to avoid duplication in research and publications;

6) To assist in the establishment of creative contacts among professors, scholars, writers, scientists, and librarians by promoting and organizing meetings, seminars, lectures, conferences, and tours.

Program Development

The Institute will offer no courses or degree programs. In program development, the Institute's main concern will be to expand and strengthen department-based programs of Ukrainian studies at all Canadian universities at the undergraduate level especially, and to avoid wasteful duplication at the graduate level, and especially where research and publication are concerned.

The main thrust of the Institute in evolving its program *outside the University of Alberta* will be to help the development of undergraduate courses in Ukrainian language, literature, history, sovietology (i.e., post-revolutionary political and ideological developments in Ukraine), the history of Ukrainians in Canada, and of Ukrainian curriculum and instruction (methods) courses *wherever the demographic base and local interest and initiative warrant it.*

At the University of Alberta, the above will be supplemented by efforts to secure the appointment in the Faculty of Education of a specialist who knows Ukrainian well to help prepare future teachers and Ukrainian teaching materials, and generally to provide leadership for effective English-Ukrainian bilingual education in and outside Alberta. The Institute will also furnish visiting professorships to personnel knowledgeable in the changing social patterns among Ukrainians in Canada, in Ukrainian church history, rite, and traditions, in Ukrainian ethnography, arts, and customs, and in the economics of Soviet Ukraine.

The Institute's own particular specialization at the University of Alberta will be the study of Ukrainian Canadians, with particular emphasis on the preparation of personnel knowledgeable in Ukrainian studies complemented by East European, Soviet, and/or Canadian studies, and capable of meeting the growing needs of school systems, *ridni shkoly* (supplementary schools), faculties of education, university departments, departments of education, other government departments (e.g., culture, secretary of state), and the Ukrainian-Canadian community as a whole.

As part of its program-development function, the Institute will provide annually ten undergraduate scholarships worth $1,500 each for an eight-month period of study at *any* Canadian university to deserving (i.e., able) students living away from home and interested in an undergraduate degree with concentration in Ukrainian studies (at least five full courses in Ukrainian language and literature, eastern European, Soviet, and/or Canadian studies in a three-year program and eight in a four-year Arts or

Education program). Scholarships of $500 to students residing at home will increase the number of scholarships available.

Research and Publications

The Institute will further research and publications in four main ways:

1) by providing five thesis fellowships annually worth $3,500 each for master's students (M.A. and M.Ed.) and three dissertation fellowships annually worth $5,000 each for doctoral students (Ph.D.);

2) by awarding research grants to academics and other qualified scholars;

3) by initiating an "Alberta Library in Ukrainian-Canadian Studies" — a series of paperback works (monographs, theses, collections of documents, memoirs) dealing with all aspects of Ukrainian life in Canada, past and present;

4) by initiating a "Canadian Library of Ukrainian Studies" — a series in which the main emphasis will be on nineteenth and twentieth century Ukrainian philosophers, political thinkers, social and literary critics and publicists, and analytical studies in general.

In its first year, the Institute will undertake a detailed survey of the instructors, students, and non-academics in Ukrainian studies, including the research underway, the research which has been completed (both published and unpublished), and the special interests and competencies of interested scholars in Canada. The comprehensive survey, updated annually, will constitute an integral part of the Institute's inter-university, clearing-house function to prevent duplication and encourage research and publication in a systematic and disciplined manner to meet the most pressing needs.

Other notable publication projects will include that conceived by Professor George Luckyj of the University of Toronto's Department of Slavic Languages and Literatures to improve the teaching of Ukrainian literature and language at the university level; a four-volume alphabetical encyclopedia of Ukraine in English edited by Professor Luckyj and based on the several volumes already available in Ukrainian edited by Professor Kubijovyc of Sarcelles (near Paris); and the first comprehensive and analytical history of Ukrainians in Canada (perhaps in several volumes) based on numerous monographs utilizing hitherto largely untapped sources, many (such as the newspapers) in the Ukrainian language.

Other planned activities include a newsletter, workshops on the state of Ukrainian-Canadian and Ukrainian studies, conferences on Ukrainian Canadians and Ukrainians, library acquisitions at the University of Alberta ($15,000 annually), "Symposium," a semi-annual journal of Ukrainian *graduate* studies edited by Professor Luckyj and containing notable seminar papers, dissertation abstracts and parts of theses, and student travel bursaries for study in Ukraine or research in European centres related to Ukrainian-Canadian or Ukrainian life.

Structure

Besides the director, there will be two associate directors, an advisory council, and, to give force to the Institute's inter-university function, a national body known as Associates of the Institute (all full professors or the most senior personnel engaged in Ukrainian studies at a particular university). The national or all-Canadian character of the Institute needs to be emphasized. The Institute is not Alberta's nor is it an Alberta Institute just because it happens to be located in Edmonton. The associates will meet annually at the Learned Societies in conjunction with the Conference on Ukrainian Studies of the Canadian Association of Slavists, or more frequently at the discretion of the director.

Ultimate Significance

But what, you might ask, is really the ultimate significance of what has been achieved? Perhaps the answer is self-evident in a culturally pluralistic society which recently entered the multicultural era. In any case, Ukrainian Canadians, who are without meaningful contacts with Ukraine and whose predicament as a minority facing the twin perils of Russification abroad and Anglo-Americanization at home is well known, must shore up their defences. They can no longer afford to settle for slogans and clichés on the crucial question of survival as an ethnocultural group.

Moreover, the encouragement of Ukrainian studies through the Institute might well be the severest test for multiculturalism itself, for if the survival-conscious Ukrainian Canadians fail to exploit the numerous opportunities offered by the Institute, then multiculturalism might indeed be confined to the quaint and frequently exotic folkloric dimension — the so-called "ethnic thing." On the other hand, should the response be sufficiently enthusiastic to encourage even other ethnocultural groups to seek similar institutes, then Canada's identity could certainly change considerably. We could find ourselves in the midst of a cultural and linguistic renaissance — and why should anyone be opposed to that?

Finally, it does appear that the Ukrainian community in Canada is rapidly approaching its fourth major crisis in leadership. The first crisis took place before the first world war and was met by the special teacher-training schools for "Ruthenians" or "foreigners" established by the governments of the three prairie provinces. The second crisis emerged by 1918 after the training schools were closed and it was met by the establishment of Ukrainian residential institutes by the Ukrainians themselves. The third crisis was clearly evident by 1950 and it was met by the fortuitous immigration of over 30,000 Ukrainians to Canada between 1948 and 1952. We are now on the brink of the fourth crisis.

The characteristics of each crisis have been similar: increased wealth followed by increased mobility, increased urbanization and increased assimilation, resulting in an increased rate of language loss, a hazy and fragmented knowledge of Ukrainian history, literature, arts and customs, and an overall indifference to the Ukrainian predicament at home and abroad. That predicament today is what it has always been, namely, survival.

To survive Anglo-Americanization at home and Russification abroad, a new source of leaders is needed — leaders who are fluent in English and Ukrainian, and, wherever possible, French; leaders who are aware of the history of Ukrainians in Canada and in Ukraine; who are familiar with Ukrainian literature; who are at home with Ukrainian arts and customs; and who are fully conversant with the state of Ukrainian life in Canada and abroad. If Ukrainians truly are not a minority like most other minorities in Canada; if like the French, the Native peoples, the Baltic peoples, and the Métis, Ukrainians cannot afford to immerse themselves fully in the Anglo-American melting pot for fear of disappearing, then articulate leaders will be needed at all levels of society and in all forums that count. This the projected Institute will try to provide. Like the teacher-training schools, the residential institutes, and the third immigration, the Institute as the cap on the Ukrainian educational ladder with its first rung in kindergarten will hopefully carry the Ukrainians through the next crisis and perhaps even avert future ones. If it does not, perhaps nothing else will — and it is quite possible that all those who prize multi-culturalism will be the poorer as a result.

SOURCES FOR ETHNIC STUDIES IN HISTORICAL FEDERAL GOVERNMENT RECORDS
BRYAN CORBETT
PUBLIC ARCHIVES OF CANADA, OTTAWA

Documentary information for Ethnic Studies in Canada, until recent years, has been difficult to locate in major Canadian archival repositories. There have been many reasons for this lack of material, including lack of demand for this information by the research community, improper funding of archives and other similar institutions, thus inhibiting any systematic acquisitions activity, unwillingness on the part of ethnic organizations and individual members of ethnic communities to make their correspondence, reports, and other information available to researchers through archival repositories, and the failure on the part of archival repositories to recognize the value of and need for such material. Though some archival repositories, including the Public Archives of Canada, are moving to remedy this situation, much remains to be done. However, though there is a notable lack of private material available, government records contain a wealth of information for Ethnic Studies.

The Canadian experience has been such that government has always played an enormously important and fundamental role in our society. From the arrival of the first European settlers in this country, governments at all levels have been more or less actively involved in our social, economic and political life. Though many people may question the need or desirability of such actions, researchers, at least, should be thankful for such involvement. The records created, used and maintained by government departments and agencies in the course of their day-to-day activities form a rich source of information on the Canadian past.

For Ethnic Studies this is especially important. The amount of information in government records on the history and developments of ethnic communities in Canada is quite extensive and reasonably comprehensive. This is especially true in the historical records of the federal government housed in the Public Archives of Canada in Ottawa.

The British North America Act of 1867 made immigration the concurrent responsibility of both the federal and provincial governments. In the first years after Confederation, some provincial governments maintained immigration agents at home and abroad. However, after a series of meetings between federal and provincial officials beginning in 1868, the federal government assumed almost total responsibility for government immigration activities. Though all Canadian governments realized the need to encourage immigrants to come to Canada, this became more imperative with the acquisition of the Hudson's Bay Company's territory in the North-West in 1870.

By the transfer agreement, Canada acquired a vast empire of extensive resources and a relatively sparse population. It became a recognized responsibility of every federal government from 1870 to the First World War to exploit the resources and fill the land with immigrants. To meet these challenges, Canada turned to Europe and other continents to provide the necessary financial and human elements. The history of immigration to Canada and land settlement in what is now the three prairie provinces constitutes a unique chapter in Nineteenth and Twentieth Century Canadian government involvement in the social and economic lives of its people, for it was by and large total involvement and commitment. The federal government assumed responsibility for encouraging and on occasion selecting immigrants for Canada. At various times the national government provided assisted passages for the prospective new Canadian. Once he was in Canada, the government became more involved by providing information and assistance to the new settler. Once the immigrant was settled, the government was often called upon to provide new or expanded services from Post Offices to seed grain relief. Once he was firmly established in the new country, federal government activity declined but never ceased. This record of activity on the part of the federal government, first apparent in 1867, continues to this day.

For the scholar, researcher, or layman interested in Ethnic Studies, the record of this federal government activity and responsibility is vitally important. The record is essential for the genealogist tracing a family tree. The record is invaluable for those interested in the history and development of their community and in comparing that community with others. The record is necessary in understanding the forces of integration, assimilation, preservation and survival. The record provides essential information, on the development of agriculture and industry and the relationship between labour and capital. Though of less importance for religious or educational studies, the record is not without value. Needless to say, the record is not without its shortcomings and failures, but it is vital to the field of Ethnic Studies.

The Public Records Division of the Public Archives of Canada has as its major responsibilities the acquisition and preservation of material documenting the activities of the federal government and making this material available to the Canadian public for research purposes. In the course of fulfilling these responsibilities, the Division has acquired much of the documentation which details federal government activity in the areas of immigration and land settlement. Although this documentation is not the only material in the Division which is of value for Ethnic Studies, it constitutes a major source of information.

At Confederation, the Department of Agriculture was assigned responsibility for the immigration activities of the federal government, indicating the basic intention of the Dominion to induce agricultural workers and farmers to come to Canada and develop her agricultural lands. This basic intention remained unaltered, at least in theory if not always in practice, well into the 1920s and, indeed, until after the Second World War. Agriculturalists and domestic servants during this period were always considered to be the most desirable class of immigrants. It was only after 1945 that the Canadian government officially began to encourage the immigration of other classes or groups.

By and large, this changed emphasis is reflected in the administrative structure which was established for the implementation of immigration policy. The Department of Agriculture continued to be responsible for immigration until 1892, when the rapidly growing Department of Interior assumed responsibility for this activity. This further emphasizes the determination of the government to settle stout and sturdy farmers on western lands, for it placed the two agencies most directly responsible for immigration and land settlement under one Department. Though the Immigration Branch in effect received departmental status in 1917, with the creation of the Department of Immigration and Colonization, the "basic intention" of the government remained the same, as it did in 1936 when the Immigration service was placed under the Department of Mines and Resources. Only after western lands had been occupied and the Great Depression had made farming seem less attractive did the "basic intention" of the government change. With the end of the Second World War and the resulting immigration of thousands of refugees, the government created the Citizenship and Immigration Department in 1949 to provide the new immigrant with an easier transition into Canadian society. This "basic intention" was further changed in 1966, when Canadian manpower, occupational, and labour needs were more closely tied together with the creation of the new and present Department of Manpower and Immigration.

The records of these departments and agencies are located in Record Groups 17 and 76 in the Public Records Division. The records of the Department of Agriculture relating to the immigration activities of the Federal Government are both extensive and detailed. The General Correspondence Series,[1] consisting of incoming letters, reports and memoranda arranged numerically by date of receipt, contains information from immigration agents, companies and individuals interested in promoting immigration and land settlement enterprises, public health and quarantine officers, individual immigrants and group leaders, and others interested or involved in immigration. Outgoing letters in reply to those received are arranged in several series of letterbooks written by senior officials, including the Secretary, the Deputy Minister, and on occasion, the Minister of Agriculture.[2] These series provide a chronicle of the day-to-day activities of the Department in inducing immigration to Canada. They are remarkably complete and detailed. Contemporary indices and registers, as well as more current finding aids, facilitate access to the material.

A wealth of information on governmental immigration activities prior to 1892 is contained in these records. The immigration and migration of the Icelanders to Gimli, Manitoba and the surrounding area is detailed. The thorough and lengthy reports of John Taylor, Icelandic Agent, on the journey west, on the settlement of the region and the development of the colony, leave a vivid picture of the community, its problems and its successes. The correspondence and reports of men like Jacob Shantz, Mennonite Agent, and William Hespeler, Immigration Agent at Winnipeg, enable the researcher to investigate the movement and settlement of the Mennonites, including their situation in Russia, their transportation to and within Canada, the settlement of the land, the Mennonite loan, the problems with squatters and other aspects of their lives in Canada.[3] Other, but perhaps not as well known, settlements, such as the Danes at New Denmark, New Brunswick, the Germans at Langenburg, Saskatchewan, and the Swedes at New Stockholm, Saskatchewan, are also documented in these records. These few examples indicate the extensive nature of the records and serve to illustrate their value for Ethnic Studies.

The second major source of material on immigration is found in the records of the Immigration Branch.[4] In 1892 responsibility for immigration was transferred from Agriculture to the Department of the Interior. The Immigration Branch was established in 1896 to work in conjunction with the Dominion Lands Branch in expediting settlement on prairie lands. Though the Branch has changed departments several times since then, its basic organization has remained the same until the present time. The records of this Branch are vital to many areas of Ethnic Studies.

The records of the Branch cover a variety of areas. There are administrative files on advertising Canada as a place for immigrants, the internal operations of the immigration service including agent's files, the evolution of the Immigration Act and Regulations, as well as the payment of bonuses and assisted passages. Files of correspondence, reports, and memoranda relating to each national group, often including lists of immigrants, are included in these records. In addition, there are extensive files on a wide range of subject areas not easily identified with any particular Ethnic group. These files include such subjects as the immigration of railway and other workers, enemy aliens, internment, communists and so-called agitators, employment agencies, colonization societies and companies, the railway companies, the activities of religious organizations, inspection of immigrants, the immigration of women and children, as well as occupational groups such as teachers, nurses, and engineers, the reaction of individuals, trade unions and businesses to immigration, deportations, refugees, and Citizenship regulations. Included in the records of the Immigration Branch are microfilm copies of the passenger manifests for vessels arriving at Quebec City from 1865 to 1899 and at Halifax from 1881 to 1900, and Registers of Chinese immigrants entering Canada between 1885 and 1903 under the terms of the Chinese Immigration Act. The last two sources give extensive information on individual immigrants of value to genealogists, researchers interested in quantitative analysis, and others. This outline of available material from the Immigration Branch is by no means inclusive, but it does illustrate the value of these records for Ethnic Studies.

The land records of the federal government relating to western Canada constitute another major source for Ethnic Studies. With the transfer of Rupert's Land to Canada in 1870, the Dominion Government became responsible for the land and resources of this vast territory. In 1873, the Department of the Interior was established to administer the land and its resources. This Department was responsible for timber reserves, irrigation, mining lands, and many other areas besides land settlement, but it is the latter records which have the greatest significance for Ethnic Studies.

The Dominion Lands Branch was first established in the Department of the Secretary of State, but with the creation of the Department of the Interior in 1873 the Branch became the nucleus of this new agency. As surveys were made and land was opened for settlement, and the number of migrants and immigrants increased, the Dominion Lands Branch grew in size and importance. It was, in effect, the largest land owner in Canada with responsibility for settling the newcomers, exploiting the resources and securing orderly growth and development of the Canadian West. Not without difficulties this agency succeeded in its difficult task. As a large percentage of the settlers who occupied these lands were immigrants from Europe, the importance of the records of the Dominion Lands Branch for Ethnic Studies is obvious.

The correspondence, reports and other documentary material of the Dominion Lands Branch[5] contain considerable information on the policy of the government in disposing of these lands, the administrative structure which was established to implement these decisions, and the effects of these policies on individuals and communities in western Canada. The evolution of the Dominion Lands Act and Regulations under which so many settlers acquired land is also documented. The records of the day-to-day operations of land offices across the prairie West give a reasonably comprehensive picture of development, growth and failures. The activities of railway, colonization, and land companies in their settlement and financial activities are well documented. The records contain reasonably detailed information on major immigrant group settlements and the development, and growth of hamlets, villages, towns, and other communities throughout the West.

In addition to these policy and general administrative files, the Dominion Lands Branch created files on each individual settler and his or her homestead and pre-emption. These records contain considerable personal information on each settler, such as place and date of birth; date of immigration and naturalization, as well as documentation on the development of the land. Although the files do not contain information on land transfers after the original land grant was issued, they do contain information of considerable importance for Ethnic Studies. These records, and the accompanying Township Registers, were sent to the governments of the three prairie provinces in order to assist them in the administration of the lands after the transfer of resources under the Natural Resources Transfer Agreements of 1930. The Public Records Division has a card index to the Letters Patent for each homestead arranged by section, township, and range within each meridian which provides access to these files. In addition, an alphabetical index to the names of patentees arranged in general chronological order also greatly facilitates access to this material. These files and the corresponding indices enable researchers to study community settlement patterns and to locate information on the individual home-steader.

The immigration and land settlement records constitute the two most extensive and comprehensive sources of information for Ethnic Studies to be located in the historical records of the federal government. Many other, though less comprehensive and extensive records are of interest to researchers in this field of study. A few examples will illustrate the range of additional information available.

The records of the Canadian National Railways[6] and its predecessors contain documentation on the real estate and land transactions of the companies, on their colonization and immigration schemes, and on labour relations, including nominal payrolls for employees during the construction phase. The records of the Royal Canadian Mounted Police[7] contain the correspondence of the Comptrollers' and Commissioners' Offices, the files of Divisions and detachments, and other documentation pertaining to the settlement of prairie lands and the administration of civil and criminal laws. In a similar vein, the records of the Department of Justice[8] contain considerable information on the settlement of land claims and disputes, internment of enemy aliens, the incidence of crimes, and many other subject areas. The Department of Agriculture after 1892 concerned itself more with agricultural development than with immigration. The records of this agency[9] contain information on the development of the agricultural industry across the country and are of value in the study of the economics of the prairie region. The Department of Labour records[10] contain consider-able correspondence of interest to researchers studying ethnic groups, including files of the National Selective Service administration, the Unemployment Relief Branch, the Women's Bureau, the Japanese Divi-sion, the Fair Employment Practices Branch, as well as material on the immigrant in the work force, strikes and lockouts, collective agreements and conciliation and arbitration. The Governor General's Numbered Corre-spondence,[11] consisting of despatches, correspondence, and reports to and from the Governors-General, reveal considerable documentation on early Canadian external and imperial affairs, including material on the immigra-tion of many European and Asiatic groups. Similarly, the records of the External Affairs Department[12] contain extensive documentation on foreign affairs, immigration, refugees, trade relations, and many other subjects. Finally the records of various Royal Commissions, including those on the National Development in the Arts, Letters, and Sciences,[13] on Broadcast-ing,[14] on charges that the Japanese Black Dragon Society was operating in British Columbia,[15] on Japanese Property Losses,[16] and on Bilingualism and Biculturalism[17] provide considerable information on and analysis of education, culture and ethnic groups.

Many other records of federal government Departments and agencies contain information for use in studying Ethnic groups. Unfortunately, it is impossible to list them all in this paper. However, these few examples provide an indication of the extent and importance of federal government historical records.

Although the sources in these records are extensive and relatively comprehensive in the areas they cover, there are major gaps in the information they contain. Researchers interested in studying more recent conditions affecting ethnic minorities in Canada are greatly handicapped in their endeavours. Records are created and maintained by government departments for administrative purposes. The length of time a record is retained by a department varies with the value of the record for those purposes. The Public Records Division, as part of the records management process, receives these records for permanent retention when they are no longer required by the departments for their day-to-day activities. In general, material over thirty years old is readily available for research at the Public Archives. However, material less than thirty years old is less comprehensive, with access often controlled by the departments. This does not mean that no material is accessible but rather that the complete record is not available for research at the Public Archives.

There is a serious gap in the historical records of the federal government relating to the field of urban affairs. Primarily because of constitutional and political limitations, historically the federal government has not played an overly large role in the urban community. Thus records needed for the study of culture, assimilation, adaptation, and education in the urban setting are lacking. Information in this field must be sought in provincial and municipal archives.

There is often a lack of follow-up information on individuals and communities after the initial immigration and successful settlement. After the Mennonites had immigrated and successfully settled on farms in western Canada in the Nineteenth Century, documentary evidence of their activities at the federal level disappears. More information is available on Mennonite activities during the First World War and on post-war immigration. Thus federal records often lack continuity and this makes study on the post-immigration period difficult.

For the most part, the historical records of the Dominion Government contain little information on the lives of individuals. Few case files are retained in the Public Records Division. Concern for the right of privacy of the individual partly explains the lack of this material. In addition, most case files tend to be similar in nature. Files on the repayment of loans under assisted passage schemes are basically routine. Consequently, little attempt has been made to preserve such records. Cost is always a factor in any repository. The cost in storage facilities alone makes any comprehensive acquisition activity for paper records of this nature an impossibility. However, many departments are microfilming this type of record or are placing the information in computer format. These and other measures will make it possible to preserve case files and make them available for research purposes within the limits of the right of personal privacy.

Finally, the very nature of these historical records in some ways limits their usefulness for the study of ethnic affairs. For the most part, these records contain information on the administration and to a limited extent on the formulation of policy. These records frequently do not contain the political, social or economic reasons for these policies, nor do they provide a complete story of their administration. For the most part, the records are not the correspondence of the Ministers of the Crown or even the Deputy Ministers, but rather those of senior and junior departmental officials implementing previously agreed policies. This is especially true of the more modern records. In addition, because these records are those of government departments and officials, created, maintained and used for their day-to-day activities, the correspondence to and from individuals, groups and communities is limited. The vast majority of people have few if any dealings with the government beyond the paying of taxes. Though this may only seem to state the obvious, it should always be borne in mind.

Even with these drawbacks and shortcomings, the historical records of the federal government form a major and, indeed, essential body of information for many aspects of Ethnic Studies in Canada. The significance and importance of this material for scholarly research has been recognized by the Public Records Division. Three programmes are being undertaken to identify and disseminate these records to the research community.

Microfilming of the records of the Immigration Branch was begun approximately two years ago as a joint endeavour with the provincial archives of the three prairie provinces. Since then the Public Records Division has assumed the full cost of the project and under the auspices of the Diffusion Programme of the Public Archives has given copies of this material and its accompanying funding aid to these respositories. The filming of this collection will be completed during the current year and will be available on Interlibrary Loan to researchers across the country.

With financial assistance from the Multi-cultural Programme of the Federal Government, in 1973 the Public Records Division began the preparation of a "Guide to Immigration and Land Settlement Sources" in its holdings. The project involves a file-by-file and, in some cases, a document-by-document listing of sources from most government departments pertinent to these broad subject areas. Some form of computerized subject and nominal index either for the total selected holdings or for the sources from each department or agency will be produced. In addition, a brief analytical introduction to the records of each department will be written which will outline the role played by that department in the area of immigration and land settlement. It is anticipated that the index and the introductions will be microfilmed and made available either for purchase or for borrowing on Interlibrary Loan. This project, when completed, should greatly facilitate research in many areas of Ethnic Studies. Though the current financial and staff situation makes the early completion of this project uncertain, most of the identification and listing of sources has been completed. The lists in their unfinished form are available for consultation in the Public Records Division.

A third programme of some interest to researchers in Ethnic Studies is the Department of the Interior Project. With the transfer of the natural resources to the prairie provinces from the federal government in 1930 and the consequent dissolution of the Interior Department in 1936, the historical and administrative records of that department were scattered to successor departments and agencies, and to other governments. The need to locate, identify, inventory, and arrange these records has been recognized. In addition, the need to produce a good administrative history of a department which played such an enormously important and fundamental role in the settlement and development of western Canada has also been recognized. After a brief preliminary survey of Interior Department records in Canada, four staff members were assigned, on a part time basis, the task of locating and identifying the Interior records and preparing the administrative history of the Department and its Branches. Unfortunately, staff transfers and financial exigencies have forced the project to be limited to the identification and description of records in the National Capital Region. It is expected that the programme will continue, but on a much-reduced scale. This project and those outlined above should assist researchers and the general public in the area of Ethnic Studies.

This paper is only a brief discussion of the major and some of the minor sources of documentation available in the historical records of the Federal Government. In spite of their limitations, these records form a unique body of information and documentation for the study of the individual and the collective past of ethnic groups. It is only through the study of records such as these that a full understanding of the past can be achieved.

FOOTNOTES

[1] Public Archives of Canada, Records of the Department of Agriculture, RG 17 AI-I, 1852-1920, 142m.
[2] *Ibid.*, RG 17 A1-2, 5, 6, 8, 10, and 12, 1852-1916, 12.3m.
[3] *Ibid.*
[4] P.A.C., Records of the Immigration Branch, RG 76, 1872-1972, 138m.
[5] P.A.C., Records of the Department of Interior, Dominion Lands Branch, RG 15, CI(a), 1871-1946, 213.6m.
[6] P.A.C., Records of the Canadian National Railways, RG 30, 1834-1975, 1350m.
[7] P.A.C., Records of the Royal Canadian Mounted Police, RG 18, 1868-1965, 300m. The inventory for this Record Group has been published and is available free of charge from the Public Archives of Canada.
[8] P.A.C., Records of the Justice Department, RG 13, 1838-1967, 285m.
[9] P.A.C., Records of the Department of Agriculture, RG 17 BII-1, 1920-1959, 211.5m.
[10] P.A.C., Records of the Department of Labour, RG 27, 1890-1973, 840m.
[11] P.A.C., Governor General's Numbered Correspondence, RG 7, G 21, 1867-1941, 54m.
[12] P.A.C., Records of the Department of External Affairs, RG 25, 1876-1965, 416m.
[13] P.A.C., Records of the Royal Commission on National Development in the Arts, Letters, and Sciences (Massey). RG 33/28, 1949-1951, 6m.
[14] P.A.C., Records of the Royal Commission on Broadcasting (Fowler), RG 33/36, 1955-1957, 3.9m.

[15]P.A.C., Records of the Royal Commission to investigate charges that the Japanese Black Dragon Society was operating in British Columbia (Cameron), RG 33/60, 1942, 8.2m.

[16]P.A.C., Records of the Royal Commission on Japanese Property Losses (Bird), RG 33/69, 1947-1949, 7.8m.

[17]P.A.C., Records of the Royal Commission on Bilingualism and Biculturalism (Laurendeau-Dunton), RG 33/80, 1963-1971, 588m.

A PRELIMINARY GUIDE TO SOURCES FOR ETHNIC STUDIES IN THE ARCHIVES OF SASKATCHEWAN

SASKATCHEWAN ARCHIVES BOARD, REGINA

Introduction

Over the past three decades, the Archives of Saskatchewan has been actively engaged in documenting all aspects of the development of the province. These activities have resulted in extensive collections in both Saskatoon and Regina of official records of provincial government departments, private papers of residents of Saskatchewan prominent in all walks of life, the records of organizations and voluntary associations, business records, photographs, maps, architectural drawings, pamphlets, published local histories, and oral history interviews. Each of these documentary forms contributes to the understanding of the social development of Saskatchewan; and, given the nature of Saskatchewan society, virtually each collection reflects and documents the multicultural heritage of the province.

The following general guide has been prepared as a preliminary and necessarily tentative attempt to examine the provincial archives collections from the viewpoint of those working on the history of the ethnic communities in Saskatchewan. Each collection has been examined from this point of view and brief notes prepared. These notes are meant to be suggestive rather than definitive and serve only to highlight the variety of source material which must be examined by those conducting research in this field.

For each collection mentioned, the Archives of Saskatchewan has prepared a descriptive guide or card index. The guides are supplemented by a variety of indexes, helping to pin-point references to specific individuals, subjects and communities. For example, in 1974, an index to source materials on ethnic groups in the clippings and pamphlets files in the Archives' Regina office was completed. These guides and indexes and our collections may be consulted by visiting or writing either of our offices; and, when necessary, source materials can be transferred from one office to the other.

Beyond providing assistance to researchers, the preparation of this preliminary guide has served to focus the attention of the archivists on the gaps in our historical documentation. While extensive resources have been preserved, much remains to be done to ensure the preservation of the complete archives of Saskatchewan's ethnic communities. The staff of the Provincial Archives is actively seeking relevant materials either for deposit or to borrow for microfilming. The cooperation and advice of researchers and community leaders will be of considerable assistance in Saskatchewan's efforts to document its multi-cultural past.

Ian E. Wilson,
Provincial Archivist.

Saskatchewan Archives Office,   Saskatchewan Archives Office,
University of Regina,   Murray Memorial Library Building,
Regina, Saskatchewan.   University of Saskatchewan,
S4S 0A2.   Saskatoon, Saskatchewan.
                                    S7N 0W0.

Phone: 565-4067   Phone: 343-3686

Newspapers and Newspaper Indexes

The Regina office has a microfilm copy of each issue of each weekly newspaper published in Saskatchewan since 1943. In addition, the Saskatchewan Archives has originals and/or microfilm copies in either or both of its offices in Regina and Saskatoon of the

Regina Leader and Leader Post 1883-1976
Saskatoon Daily Star, Phoenix and Star Phoenix 1902-06; 1921-71
Prince Albert Daily Herald 1943-1971
Moose Jaw Times Herald 1921-1971

and early runs of a number of weeklies including

Saskatchewan Herald (Battleford) 1878-1925
Alameda Dispatch 1901-1942
Indian Head Vidette 1884-1899
Kindersley Clarion 1910-1942
Lloydminster Times 1905-1942
Melfort Moon 1904-1936
Moosomin Courier 1884-1892
Prince Albert Times 1882-1899
Qu'Appelle Progress 1885-1927
Shaunavon Standard 1913-1942
Watson Witness 1907-1942
Yorkton Enterprise 1902-1909; 1911-1928

We have also runs of a number of publications printed either in a foreign language, or to appeal to a particular ethnic or cultural group. These include

L'Etoile de Gravelbourg 1927-1947
Le Voix Catholique (Gravelbourg) 1935-1937
Patriote de l'Ouest (Prince Albert) 1910-1941
Der Courier (in German) 1907-1925
St. Peter's Bote (in German) 1904-1947
Le Métis (in French) 1878-1881
Svoboda (in Ukrainian) 1893-1923
Canadian Ruthenian (in Ukrainian) 1911-1930
Ukrainian Voice (Saskatoon: in Ukrainian) 1925, 1935-1942
Ukrainian News (Saskatoon: in Ukrainian) 1943-1945; 1949-1973
Vistnyk (Ukrainian) 1929-1967
Canadian Hungarian News 1925-1976
Future of the Nation (Yorkton: in Ukrainian and English) 1933-44, 1946-51

These dailies, weeklies, and monthlies will, to some extent, reflect the interests, activities, and objectives of various ethnic groups and the prevailing attitudes towards such matters as the immigration of members of those groups, the clash between various ethnic groups and the government over such matters as education, Canadian participation in World Wars I and II, and conscription.

These attitudes are reflected further by such important prairie publications as the *Grain Growers' Guide* and the *Western Producer.*

Newspaper indexes to the Regina Leader-Post for the period 1883-1973 have been prepared by staff members of the Legislative Library and Saskatchewan Archives. Through use of summer help, newspaper indexes have also been compiled to the Saskatoon *Phoenix,* 1902-1908, *Western Producer,* 1925-1940 and *Le Patriote de l'Ouest,* 1910-1917 and 1929-1932. Entries with respect to ethnic groups, organizations, prominent individuals and settlements may be found in these indexes.

Theses

Over the years the Saskatchewan Archives has collected on microfilm or in the original a number of post-graduate dissertations relating to the history of Saskatchewan and to the Territorial period prior to 1905. Some of these theses, or parts thereof, are concerned with immigration and settlement, attitudes towards minority group(s), assimilation and so on. "Old Colony Mennonite Settlements in Saskatchewan: A Study of Settlement Change," by R. J. Friesen, "L'Association Catholique Franco-Canadienne de la Saskatchewan: A Response to Cultural Assimilation, 1912-1934," by R. J. Huel, and "Yorkton during the Territorial Period, 1882-1905," by J. W. McCracken are examples from this collection.

Photographs

At present the photograph collection houses approximately 70,000-80,000 photographs catalogued under a variety of names and subjects. For entries, researchers may look at the alphabetical card index under names of ethnic groups, individuals and organizations or under subject headings such as frontier and pioneer life, immigration, schools and so on.

Tape Recorded Interviews

Under the "Towards a New Past" oral history programme, the Saskatchewan Archives and the Department of Culture and Youth have co-operated in collecting approximately 1000 tape recorded interviews with native people, Métis and early settlers of the province. Oral history projects have been conducted among the following ethnic or religious groups: Americans (52), Blacks (6), Chinese (2), Doukhobors (43), East Indians (59), French (115), Hungarians (35), Italians (32), Jews (11), Mennonites (25), Métis (47), Native People (41), Norwegians (8), Poles (180), Roumanians (7), Scandinavians (9), and Ukrainians (82). (Number in parentheses denotes number of interviews conducted.)

Immigration Pamphlet Collection

Pamphlets and brochures issued by government, land and railway companies to promote settlement in Western Canada, including one pamphlet in German language about New Elsass colony (Strasbourg, Saskatchewan area).

Department of Education, School District Files

The Saskatchewan Archives has Department of Education files for 5260 school districts in its holdings. These files provide names of original families, correspondence and documentation about the petitioning, erection and operation of the school district. For those interested in Black settlement, the Eldon School District No. 3613 file should be of value, for Jewish settlement, the Hoffer School District No. 4735 file, and for Welsh settlement, the Llewellyn School District No. 807 file.

Political Pamphlet Collection

Pamphlets and brochures distributed by various Canadian political parties, including some printed in German and Ukrainian languages.

Private Papers

Personal papers and correspondence may contain information of value to ethnic study and research. Through guides or finding aids, the researcher may locate files of relevant material in the following collections:

Scott, Walter (1867-1938), Regina, Sask., Journalist, Premier of Sask.

Motherwell, William Richard (1860-1943), Regina, Sask., Cabinet minister, Sask.

Makaroff, Peter George (c.1898-1970), Saskatoon, Sask., Lawyer.

Martin, William Melville (b.1876), Regina, Sask. Judge, Premier of Sask.

Calder, James Alexander (1868-1956), Sask., Politician.

Douglas, Thomas Clement (b.1904), Regina, Sask. and Ottawa, Ontario, Premier of Sask.

Latta, Samuel John (1886-1946), Regina, Sask., Politician.

Lepage, Dumont (-1974), Gravelbourg, Sask., manager of French language radio station, and President of L'A.C.F.C.

McNaughton, Violet Clara (1879-1968), Saskatoon, Sask., Editor.

Lavoie, Phillipe E. (1886-1953), Ile à la Crosse, Sask., Physician.

Gardiner, James Garfield (1883-1962), Premier of Sask.

Lloyd, Woodrow Stanley (1913-1972), Regina, Sask., Premier of Sask.

Hamilton, Charles McGill (1878-1952), Regina, Sask., Cabinet minister, Sask.

Stechishin, Michael (1900-1950), Wynyard, Sask., Judge.

Turgeon, William Ferdinand Alphonse (1877-1969), Prince Albert, Sask., lawyer, politician, jurist, diplomat.

Records of Businesses and Organizations

Records of businesses and ethno-cultural organizations can be useful sources for those engaged in ethnic study and research. Originals or microfilm copies of records from the following businesses and organizations have been acquired by the Saskatchewan Archives thus far.

Radio-Gravelbourg Limitée (CFRG-CFGR), Gravelbourg.

Radio-Prairies-Nord Limitée (CFNS), Saskatoon.

St. David's Society of Regina, 1940-1973.

L'Association Culturelle Franco-Canadienne de la Saskatchewan, 1913-1936.

Saskatoon Jewish Community.

Zion Evangelical Lutheran Church at Hague and Rosthern.

Saskatoon Hellenic Orthodox Community.

Daughters of Penelope, Royal Canadian District #24.

Daughters of Penelope, Telemachus Chapter #69, Saskatoon.

Volksverein, 1905-1938.

La Caisse Populaire d'Albertville, 1916-1936.

St. Jean Baptiste Society, Gravelbourg, 1912-1932.

Pioneer Organizations

Since 1955, several pioneer history projects have been conducted by the Saskatchewan Archives and OFY groups in the province. Many of the people contacted had immigrated to Canada and recalled their experiences as homesteaders. Questionnaires covering such aspects as religious life, pioneer diet, social and recreational activities, and tape-recorded interviews resulting from these surveys have been deposited at the Saskatoon and Regina offices of the Saskatchewan Archives.

Directories

A small collection of directories which is useful in providing some information relating to ethnic groups includes:

McPhillips Saskatchewan Directory, 1888.

Henderson's Manitoba and Northwest Territories Gazeteer and Directory, 1899, 1900, 1904.

Henderson's North-West Territories Gazeteer and Directory, 1905, 1906, 1907.

Wrigley's Saskatchewan Directory, 1921-1922.

Other directories include runs of the Regina, Saskatoon, Moose Jaw, and Prince Albert City Directories c.1910-1965, and regional telephone directories c.1955-1965.

Saskatchewan Sessional Papers (Unpublished) 1888-1944

(See Journals of the N.W.T. and Legislative Assemblies for lists of Sessional Papers tabled in the House.)

Includes a number of unpublished annual reports, but chiefly returns tabled in the Territories or Saskatchewan Legislature to questions relating to such matters as separate schools, instruction in foreign languages, group settlement such as Hutterite Colonies. Two examples of returns relating to ethnic groups are those re payment for flour advanced to the Métis of the Qu'Appelle Valley in 1892, and the Memorial adopted by the Legislative Assembly on May 10, 1906, concerning Professor Mavor's report on the Canadian West, Doukhobors, etc., and related correspondence.

Statutes of Saskatchewan and Ordinances of the North West Territories
(private and local, and public Acts of the Territorial
    and Provincial Legislatures)

Includes Acts of incorporation passed in response to petitions of various denominational-supported charitable organizations such as the Catholic orphanage at Prince Albert and St. Paul's Hospital in Saskatoon, theological and Bible Colleges such as the Lutheran Seminary in Saskatoon and the Mennonite College at Rosthern, and Acts of incorporation of villages, towns and cities whose districts were/are populated chiefly by a particular ethnic group such as the Hungarians at Esterhazy, the Mennonites at Herbert, the French at Gravelbourg, the Ukrainians at Yorkton.

Includes also legislative provisions respecting foreign language instruction in the provincial school system, and public aid to separate schools.

An early example of legislation aimed at assisting a particular ethnic group was that providing for the protection of buffalo in 1877. An example of prejudicial legislation was the Act passed in the early 20th century prohibiting the employment of white women in businesses operated by Orientals.

Orders-in-Council 1892-1939

Indexes have been prepared to these documents. Examples of entries are:

French in Saskatchewan
    — R. D. Coutts makes special survey of schools in French settlements — 1920.
Immigration
    — H. M. Hennequin to conduct lectures in Holland to promote immigration — 1925.
Indians
    — Indians prohibited from entering a pool room, billiard room, or bowling alley — 1913.
Doukhobors
    — provisions for civil marriages — 1922.
Esterhazy
    — establishment of a Mechanics and Literary Institute — 1932.
Mennonites
    — appointment of F. Ford and D. P. McColl to enquire into private schools in Mennonite settlements in the Hague, Osler, and Warman districts — 1908;
    — educational provisions — 1930.

Ruthenians
— appointment of John Kuhn to assist J. Megas as Inspector of School Districts in Ruthenian settlements — 1912.
Education
— appointment of J. T. M. Anderson as Director of Education among the new Canadians — 1918.

Public Records

These files, which include photo or microfilm copies of selected Department of the Interior files, and microfilm copies of Immigration Branch records in the Public Archives of Canada, Ottawa, include also records of Territorial and Saskatchewan Government departments and agencies of which the school district files are perhaps the most fruitful single source for ethnic studies.

A guide has been prepared to approximately 150 reels of the Immigration Branch files, and file titles are available for the scores of reels yet to be fully described. Guides have also been prepared to other useful records created at Ottawa. These include the files of Dominion Land Surveyors, and a selected group of Dept. of the Interior files which are particularly informative with respect to group settlement and the activities of various land and colonization companies.

Another important group of public records is that created by various Saskatchewan Royal Commissions and Special Committees. Representative of those of value to ethnic researchers are the Commissions regarding the Practices of the Old Colony Mennonite Church (1906), Immigration and Settlement (1930), the Estevan Coal Miners' Strike and Riot (1931-32), the Regina Riot (1935-36), and the Saskatchewan Committee on Instruction in Languages other than English (1966).

Two further examples are the Relief files relating to the Re-establishment of Saskatchewan Mennonites in the Vanderhoof and Burns Lake districts of British Columbia, and the Department of Agriculture's Farm Labour Divisions post W.W. II records concerning the placement of Displaced Persons including Mennonites, Dutch, German Baptists, Japanese Canadians, and Polish Veterans.

Local Histories

The Archives holds scores of both published and unpublished local histories in the original, or in photocopy or microfilm form. A few examples are:
"History of Krydor" (Ukrainians)
"Southey Seen" (Germans and others)
"Homesteading to Homecoming" (St. Gregor district, Germans, Yugoslavians and others)
"The Spy Hill Story" (Icelanders and others)
"Land of Hope" (Jewish settlements)
"Stockholm and District" (Swedish and Hungarians)

"Sketches of Hafford and District" (Ukrainians and others)
"They Came to Wood Mountain" (Serbians, Yugoslavians and others)
— a number of histories prepared by students of schools on Indian reserves.

Maps

A series of Cummins' Rural Directory Maps c.1917-1930 in bound volumes or separate sheets, which show the names of the occupants of rural lands in Saskatchewan, as well as the location of urban communities, schools, and post offices. A further collection of approximately 3,000 maps include those showing land use patterns, electoral, municipal, and school district and school unit boundaries.

Petitions: 1888-1944

(See Journals of the Territorial and Saskatchewan Legislative Assemblies for lists of petitions.)

Petitions include those submitted by various ethnic and religious groups requesting incorporation of a variety of organizations and institutions such as the Sisters of Charity Providence Hospital, Moose Jaw, the Ruthenian Greek Catholic Parishes and Missions in Saskatchewan, the Russo-Greek Catholic Orthodox Church in Saskatchewan, the Saskatchewan Norwegian Lutheran College Association, the Finnish Lutheran Church, the German-English Academy at Rosthern, the Mennonite Union Waisenmant (re care of orphaned children), the English Club at Medicine Hat, the Order of St. Benedict in Saskatchewan. Includes also petitions such as the four submitted in 1901 requesting permission to teach the German language in public schools.

Homestead Records

Homestead records are files for each quarter-section of land homesteaded under the provisions of the Dominion Lands Act and Saskatchewan homestead regulations. The file usually includes an application for entry showing the birthplace and country of origin of the homesteader, and an application for patent showing the work done during the first few years of occupancy to meet homestead requirements. Many files are for homesteaders belonging to ethnic groups.

Reminiscences

K. P. Landine — Swedish, 1905-1917.
C. E. Kieper — German, Langenburg, 1887-1950.
Mrs. W. Taphorn — German, St. Gregor, 1906-1955.
Mrs. S. Friesen — German, Rosthern, 1899-1960.
Mr. F. Eliason — Swedish, 1905 —.
Mr. J. Bonas — German, Muenster, 1905.
Rev. A. K. Maximchuk — Ukrainian.

F. F. Boechler — German, 1903-1960's.
R. Barrie — French, Duck Lake.
A. Kolden — Norwegian, 1903.
H. Molbrud — Norwegian, 1903.
Mrs. L. Derdall — Norwegian, 1902.
W. Welke — German, 1884.
W. N. Lozowchuk — Ukrainian, 1928.

ETHNIC CANADIANS

ETHNIC CANADIANS: SYNOPTIC COMMENTS
MARTIN L. KOVACS

It is not very often nowadays that ethnics are encountered in actual face-to-face groups, apart from brief, occasional organizational meetings. This fact is reflected in the application by research workers of such terms as *category, collectivity,* or *community,* complete with the adjective to refer to what others, mainly sociologists and historians, term *ethnic group.* In accordance with the traditions of British sociology and anthropology there is a strong tendency to explain the ethnic group-community in terms of rationally organized networks and hierarchies of roles, structures, institutions, values, and boundaries largely actuated by competition for classes of resources. The birth, or perhaps rebirth of the concept *ethnicity* a few years ago took place just in time to witness the resurrection of interest in *ethnic groups.* To the more symbol-directed researcher there might be a measure of temptation to see in this "resurrection" and accompanying aspirational upheaval some similarity to the *rites de passage* and the *liminality* of the "rituals of status elevation" and the "rituals of status reversal." These processes appear characterized by the aspiration of "the structurally inferior" to "symbolic structural superiority," while for the "structurally superior" the object of striving consists in the achievement of "symbolic communitas" even at the price of undergoing "penance."[1]

But returning to the consideration of the term *ethnic group,* it may be asserted that, since ethnic research is a multidisciplinary endeavour, one of the difficulties facing it is connected with terminology. Indeed, uncertainty reflected in this respect is instanced in the case of both of the terms *ethnic* and *group.* The adjective deriving from the noun *ethnos* has been applied as a verbal vehicle for the expression both of "people" and of "nation." In the former sense, it came to be connected with the description of primitive cultures and societies. Perhaps, the pejorative sense attached to the term, when relating to non-Anglo-Celtic immigrants, might have sprung from this circumstance. In more modern sociological usage, the term *ethnos* has transcended its original narrower meaning and now tends to refer to the characteristic traits and complexes of a culture that set it aside from other cultures. Therefore, the definitional qualifications of *ethnic group* include a *common cultural tradition,* and "a sense of identity which exists as a subgroup of a larger society;" a distinguishing language or religion is seen as an optional trait.[2] Consequently, it is not unusual to refer to religious, racial, aboriginal and even dominant groups as *ethnic.*

With a broad enough categorization all Canadians may belong in one or even several ethnic groups. However, in the papers constituting this volume the term *ethnic* often refers to groups, processes, institutions, and structures connected with ethnicity, categories, and phenomena other than Anglo-Celtic. So, in the context of this book the concept *ethnic Canadian* is usually meant to imply Canadians with ethnic backgrounds substantially other than Anglo-Celtic.

Ethnicity and Rights

The more recent years have witnessed a greater tendency toward referring to group solidarity and threatened or actual militancy in the building up or reinforcement of "rights." The upsurge of broader and stronger waves of social assertion has led to a steady growth in demands for a fuller share of socio-economic rewards also on the part of the ethnic categories. Owing to overall social pressure for this objective an "aspirational" revolution seems to be going on in many segments of the Canadian society. Its impact can be detected in a variety of social phenomena.

As to the Indians,[3] opportunity has been given to them to evolve claims on the basis of: a) aboriginal rights, b) treaty rights, and c) specific band claims. Lloyd Barber explains that negotiation — that is, formal social bargaining — has constituted the method used in attempting to reach a proper settlement of the aboriginal claims. Such groups as the non-Status Indians, the Inuit and the Metis do not fall under the direct responsibility of the Federal Government. It is a long and time-consuming process to bring about just and lasting settlements of the claims, owing partly to the Natives' different conception of legal terms such as "the surrendering of their sovereignty," and partly to their viewing land not as a commodity, but as a component of "the total life experience."

The consideration of treaties made many years ago in different economic, social and political circumstances to reinterpret and reassess their meaning from the viewpoint of the present and the acceptance of expressive arguments as legal or instrumental evidence may establish precedents for other contexts as well. However, the compilation, presentation and negotiation of the claims, including the Native demand for a "citizenship plus" special status and *not* for the equal standing of the other ethnic groups as posited for a multicultural democracy, can be regarded as an effective attempt of the Native groups to create self-help.[4] Their mobilization of commitment is seen to aim at the regeneration of a cultural identity, gradually lost in the past, and at the gaining of greater control of resources connected with prestige and power.

School, the instrument of formal education, can be regarded as one of the major cultural resources of the society. The non-provision of teachers and schoolhouses promised in some treaties is brought up by Lloyd Barber as an example of the failure of successive administrations of Indian affairs to fulfil treaty promises explicit or implicit. For this reason, and because of the tendency of the education system of the past not to appreciate the basic cultural values of the Natives, the Indians insist on Indian control of Indian education.

In such circumstances, special attention has been paid in the last decades to the education of the Indians (as shown by June Wyatt). whose *rights* have been interpreted to include not only provision for secondary and tertiary education, but also their involvement in the crystallization of a curriculum and teaching methods suitable to the needs of Indian students. The training of native teachers who then could act as *cultural brokers*,[5] equipped to bring about and keep up meaningful communication between the two discrepant cultures, that of the Natives and that of the school, through the articulation of the respective learning styles, is Wyatt's major recommendation resulting from the observation over three years of the Mount Currie School and community. This approach is seen as aiming at the utilization of local Indian community-centred experiences both of the Native instructors and of their students towards the gradual development of school-based skills with a view to better realizing the latter's right to education, and, presumably, to reduce thereby the speed of cultural alienation and its potentially disorganizing effects.

Ethnics and Ethnic Groups

At times it is no easy task properly to comprehend the arguments of some sociological or anthropological studies owing to the tendency to introduce and use technical terms, either newly-coined, or applied with a greater or smaller degree of difference from their *established* meanings (if a consensus in this regard exists at all). Thus, Joseph Manyoni observes, the terms *ethnicity* and *ethnic group* may have been defined and utilized without due attention to their conceptual contents at various analytical levels. Therefore, he argues, *ethnicity* can be conceived of at the *cognitive* level as *ethnic identity* possessing psycho-socio-cultural attributes, while at the *structural* level as indicative of *ethnic groups.* The latter is the transformation of the former, resulting through "consciously organized action of the participants." Manyoni suggests that the excessive inclusiveness or exclusiveness of the term *ethnic group* could be remedied by the judicious application, instead, of the terms *racial minority, cultural minority, religious minority,* and *linguistic minority.* Yet, actually, the terms suggested may point at successive stages in the socio-cultural adjustmental development of the ethnic group and would apparently preclude the *majority* from the chance of possessing *ethnicity* and forming or constituting *ethnic categories.* Of course, the application of *group* may be doubtful and contain, on occasion, connotations for the rendering of which the word *category* or *community* would be more appropriate.

Also Patrick Baker draws attention to terminological difficulties. In his exposition "the ideal Canadian model of a 'harmonious' mosaic ... is inadequate to capture the social reality." The example used for the corroboration of his proposition, a report on "The Black Presence in the Canadian Mosaic," is seen to be content to remain "at the level of perception to the exclusion of structural consideration." Its recommendations are deemed to have lost contact with social reality, since they have not been based on the assessment of the efforts of the elements of power, stratification and vested interests upon the putative consensus of attitudes and values which one would expect to be characteristic of the equilibrium of the *Canadian Mosaic,* an ideal model of society. These shortcomings of the report and the numerous contradictions in its text are traced by Baker to the inadequacy of an *ideal* model applied to the *practical* task of coping with structural-attitudinal problems. As a further argument to support Baker's proposition, the inequality of the term *mosaic* to carrying its intellectual burden might be stressed. As a unidimensional metaphor with strictly fixed components *mosaic* fails to reflect the endless variety and uninterrupted dynamism of the elements that constitute the tridimensional society.

Ethnicity and Folklore

Folklore may be regarded as one of the auxiliary disciplines of ethnic research, since its scope includes the study of folk culture along ethnic lines. Folk culture, in its turn, constitutes a portion of the potentially primordial culture characteristic of nomadic and peasant societies of the past. Therefore, it can be conceived in a certain sense as attempts at explanation in symbols of the environment, physical and socio-cultural. With the dominant culture increasingly tending towards expression in *signs,* the collection and interpretation of the surviving remnants of the cultural traditions, including legends, of cultural minorities is conducive to the building up in a larger measure of a Canadian cultural identity in the context of multiculturalism, as illustrated by Klaus Burmeister through the examination of the Native legend of the Qu'Appelle Valley in southern Saskatchewan, as well as in its several versions embedded in ethnic cultures.

Ethnicity and Languages

A statistical analysis by Alan Anderson of trends in the ethnic population of Saskatchewan as a whole, reveals a rapid and steep decline between 1961 and 1971 in the percentage of those still able to converse in their traditional mother tongues. While a large majority in 18 ethno-religious bloc settlements in north central Saskatchewan still could speak the traditional language, the proportion of those still using it fairly often was about 60% on an average among the ethnic groups. The inclination to prefer English as a means of communication seemed to be in an inverse ratio with the age of the speakers; the lower the age the higher the tendency to use English. The length of the period since immigration, as one would expect, tended to be in direct proportion with the number of ethnics with preference for the use of English.

Five factors (inter-ethnic marriages, school policies, the breakdown of the institutions and segregation of ethnic communities, secularization, rural depopulation coupled with rapid urbanization) have been singled out as significant processes of change contributing to the further progress of assimilation despite the recent re-emphasis of multiculturalism.

While, undoubtedly, such cultural factors as the low literacy of the Ukrainian-Polish immigrants and the decline in status among Catholic Germans[6] of German scholarship and culture could have been greatly conducive to the striking variation between the rates of language retention in the two categories, the investigation of the potential correlation in this regard between ethnicity and the rate of language retention will probably constitute a rewarding research topic.

Ethnicity and the Image Makers

Perhaps the best known of the crusading image makers in the 1920s and through the 1950s, Watson Kirkconnell, became not only a spokesman but also a transplanter of the best literary products of central and eastern European cultures. He tended to denounce the initial reactions of the receiving society to foreign immigrants as "ignorant and discreditable phases," when referring to the "European coolies" role ascribed to them and when pointing out the superficial nature of the folk costumes and folk dances as being only "picturesque incidentals." He carried out his work of liaison among different cultures not only by means of his translations and prose writings, but also through his contribution to the development of the concept of a multi-ethnic Canadian society. It may be added that Kirkconnell was creating an image for the ethnic groups that was unknown at the time when the schools were concentrating on a type of history based on political events and interpretations.[7] Needless to say his approach was instrumental in improving the social standing of members of non-Anglo-Celtic and non-French categories, since status is often ascribed in the light of information made available in the printed and other media. While Fred Dreisziger's presentation of Kirkconnell's role mainly in the inter-war period can be looked upon as a good example of an Anglo-Celtic literary scholar's achievements in respect of creating a truer image of ethnic groups, Jorgen Dahlie provides an instance of the work of an ethnic intellectual in the same direction.

Perhaps owing to the pre-occupation of anthropology and sociology with groups rather than individuals, studies have tended to overlook the influence of Canadian and Ethnic-Canadian leaders, intellectual, communal or political, who writing in their respective languages exerted a great impact in the shaping of the outlook and reciprocal attitudes both of the members of the receiving society and those of the ethnic groups. The story of Ole Hjelt, a radical, reveals to what extent this homesteader-intellectual of Norwegian origin acted as leaven in development of social and political thought in the midst of Norwegian and Swedish immigrants. Since his writings transcended the prevailing political values of most of his contemporaries and fellow Norwegians, he got into innumerable clashes with them, yet he managed to keep his readers alert both culturally and intellectually.

Image makers of another kind are introduced by Victor Buyniak. Supplied by the teacher training institutions of western Canada, it was first the Ukrainian[8] teacher-intellectuals, then the university graduates, who, in addition to scholars specially invited from the old country, provided socio-cultural and political leadership for their compatriots and undertook the practical task of educating them. Also a veritable network of Ukrainian societies, clubs and other institutions sprang up to provide wide cultural-intellectual enrichment for the group. After 1921 the arrival of more educated immigrants, combined with an increasing number of graduates from Canadian universities and with the impact of Ukrainian periodicals and books, resulted in new strong Ukrainian consciousness.

This process may be seen as a telling example of how ethnically related peasant categories of disparate pasts equipped themselves under the leadership of image makers with the ideology of a nation.

Ethnicity and Nation Building

The immigrants who later on became known as Ukrainians were originally divided into several groups according to territorial descent, denominational membership, and political leaning. Many Ruthenians and Galicians fell into five general categories according to their respective degrees of Anglo-Celtic conformity and also a dual loyalty tended to prevail among them in 1914. Local patriotism to various parts of Austria-Hungary grew into a Ukrainian nationalism through the expectation of the establishment of an independent Ukraine in case of the potential defeat of Russia, an ally of Britain and, therefore, of Canada.

The government controls of the war years between 1914 and 1919, like press censorship, the stigma of being set aside as "enemy aliens," and internment, did not aim at finding solutions for fundamental issues, but at dampening political dissent. On the other hand the Ukrainian leadership of the time was too dogmatic and rigid to be articulated through compromise into the Canadian context, although the desire for the creation of a thriving and unified Canadian nation was well rooted in their midst. The examination of three Ukrainian newspapers by Nadia Kazymyra also revealed the editors' (and, probably, the readers') preoccupation with the question of the English-Ukrainian bilingual schools. Even if the issue of language often overshadowed the war itself in the papers, neither the editors nor the readers could help the abolition in the West of the bilingual school system. In fact, utterances not only in respect of the war and the independence of the Ukraine, but also on the school question, came almost to be regarded as indicative of disloyalty.

The difficulties which were facing nation states, not unlike the one that Canada desired to become, had not gone unnoticed in earlier days. In this context Lord Acton in Joel Novek's view has a message for our era. "The effort to force everyone to live the same way can be far more divisive than the acceptance of whatever differences do exist." Pressure for universalism and conformity will be countered by growing demand on the part of particularism for local autonomy and political decentralization. Modern nation-states have great difficulty, owing to their failure to deliver in accordance with promise, in retaining the loyalty of ethnic minorities, since majorities have learned "to use democratic methods to subjugate minorities." Novek's presentation of a topical illustration of the point almost recalls Darwinian features:

> Thus, English speaking majorities in various parts of Canada have used their voting strength to deny educational rights to French-Canadians who are trying to do the same thing in Quebec where they are the majority.

As to the future, the prognostication is for increasing tendencies to confront centralized power through resorting to cultural dualism and political decentralization — perhaps, as envisaged by Acton, leading to less ideological influence on social life and to greater tolerance with regard to cultural differences.

ETHNICITY AND SOLIDARITY

The measure of *solidarity* would be the extent of the *loyalty* of the individual members to a group. In the case of ethnic groups the loyalty is likely to be in respect of the *ethnicity,* of which one aspect is *identity.*

Ukrainians

The Ukrainians in the Northend of Winnipeg are one of the minorities of Manitoba ecologically, demographically, politically and economically. *Ethnic boundaries* constitute a most important factor in the maintenance of the ancestral culture, but, according to the view of Leo Driedger, they can be maintained only by the direction of macro-social structures. Ukrainians have maintained microstructures in the Northend characteristic of rural ethnic enclaves. Residential segregation, institutional completeness, cultural identity and social distance as well as social psychological factors, such as religious ideology, charismatic leaders from their status elite, historical symbols (memory of independence, etc.), writers, institutions and newspapers must reinforce enclavic elements to keep the enclave dynamic.

The failure of the Winnipeg Ukrainians to control macro-social structures is seen to a great extent to be balanced by their maintenance of important microstructures. Consequently, it cannot be stated with certainty whether they will assume "new forms of identity" or whether the process is actually indicative of assimilation. In any case, there are signs suggesting a strong ability of the Ukrainians to compete in their urban environment as a result of the combination of enclavic with social-psychological factors. The analytical tools applied in Driedger's study appear helpful also for other types of studies.

Esterhazy Area

The changes that have accompanied the development of Esterhazy, originally a village in the middle of farming settlements in eastern Saskatchewan, into a mining town of some three thousand inhabitants have caught the attention of Donald Willmott. These changes have included a major weakening of ethnic solidarity in the area.[9] Expressed briefly, the Hungarian Canadians of Esterhazy have maintained a higher degree of residential segregation and for a longer time than the Czech Canadians of the same area. On the other hand the members of the latter group have had a better opportunity for the developing of their social and psychological states. While the institutional strength of the former group would lie in their Kaposvar parish, that of the Czechs is centred in the Bohemian Hall. However, their microstructures proved equally insufficient for a continued survival of the groups' respective ethnic solidarity after 1945, despite the traumatic experiences of some of the Hungarian Canadians of Esterhazy during the two wars.

The Indians

The Indians are exposed in varying measures to the impact of the same social and economic forces as other ethnic groups. One of Carmen Lambert's findings is that the Native people tried to offset the impact of the debilitation of their ethnic identity, consequent upon their rural urban shift, through the projection of a new interest focus, Pan-Indianism. This neo-Indian identity has been probably designed to create the cultural moorings for a new Indian solidarity on the basis of such symbolic identifications as (in the case of the White Horse Indians) racial descent, territorial origins, Indian status, cultural traits and cultural values. However, the term *Indian* also originally a misnomer, a mistaken categorization by the whites, has been used by the Indians only in communication with the outside world. As a result, preference to *Indianness* would take the second place behind tribal loyalty which is based on valid historic symbols. The measure of Indian solidarity to be achieved is seen to depend not only on the commonality or diversity of symbolic identifications, but also on the commonality of the political objectives adopted, e.g., land claims. Since, however, the tribal differences of the Indians include differential expections and norms of behaviour, group attitudes and responses vary from tribe to tribe and from situation to situation resulting in what might be termed a type of situational solidarity.

Saskatchewan

The major hypothesis of Zenon Pohorecky's paper seems to be that there is a positive correlation — other variables being equal — between the numerical ratio of the ethno-cultural organizations of ethnic groups and the extent of their respective ethnic solidarity. The major assertions are based on a comparatively recent and panoramic categorization of pertinent quantitative and qualitative relationships in respect of the majority of such organizations in Saskatchewan. The striking contrast in this regard, as, for instance, between the German Catholics and the Ukrainians, is assumed to have derived from the circumstance that the two principal roles of an ethno-cultural organization, that of mediation towards the general Canadian milieu and that of the maintenance of the group's unique cultural identity, have been tempered differently by both "the apparent decline in discriminatory practices against minority groups" and the variance in the groups' traditional methods and devices to achieve their objectives. It is of interest to notice the claim that the longer exposure of the one-time Galicians, Ruthenians and Ukrainians to the oppression of the dominant majorities of the day has led for the Ukrainian settlers of Canada to greater experience and resourcefulness in the maintenance of their ancestral culture, than was the case with other ethnic groups. A significant portion of the paper, the Appendix, contains a categorized listing of most of the ethnic organizations of Saskatchewan.

ETHNICITY AND EDUCATION

Aspirations

There can be little doubt that ethnicity, as a rule, is influenced by the type, quality and length of education. But does ethnicity as such contribute to differences in levels of education? Investigation in this respect by Ann Denis appears to indicate that inequalities observed in educational attainment in terms of ethnicity, social class and "differential access to salient societal resources" do derive, in a certain measure, from ethnic origin in itself. A positive relationship is seen to exist between ethnicity and the aspiration to complete university studies, but ethnic categories often exhibit attitudinal variables in diverse ways, as to both sexes. Further research in this respect will be designed to learn the degree of intensity of an association that links ethnic origin and ethnic identity, as well as to discover the extent of the persistence of ethnic differences with socio-economic status under control.

It requires further research to decide whether the positive correlation observed by Ann Denis between ethnicity and educational aspirations in respect of certain selected groups of university students would prevail also in other circumstances. Is it possible that differences in attitudes to special treatment in education may partly stem from differences in ethnicity?

Black Students

While the general trend in the Canadian West has been toward the mingling of students of various ethnic backgrounds in the classroom, Michel Laferriere points out a contrasting tendency in this respect with regard to blacks in Nova Scotia. In the case of Ontario, non-acceptance is cited as the main issue for them. On the other hand, it is claimed that the blacks of Quebec have hardly ever caused institutional or language problems, nor have their educational results differed from those of their white fellow students. As to the Haitians of Montreal, those under the Protestant school board — mostly English speakers — were exposed to special treatment as special cases. In the instance of the Francophone School Board, no motivation existed for a 'problem definer' to emphasize the blackness of students as their main common denominator. Laferriere identifies the absence from education of self-fulfilling categorization in Montreal Catholic schools as the major factor for the lack so far of the emergence of black radicalism.

The Native People

The 'educational revolution' among the Indians and the Inuit of the Yukon and the Northwest Territories has turned out, in James Frideres' opinion, to be less than an overall blessing. It resulted in their modernization largely in less than a generation's time and in concomitant and widespread alienation. The uneven distribution of educational opportunities for the Natives derived from the fact that a proportion of the whites within the total population was regarded as a measuring device for the process. The introduction of curricula of the southern type to Native schools and classes, another distinct case of educational alienation, can be traced back to the same cause: since the Indians and Inuits have seldom possessed a vocational training required by the industries of the North, their schooling is not reflected in their income or the extent of their socio-economic mobility. Yet another natural outcome of a higher educational attainment for the Natives was the expectation of higher rise in the occupational hierarchy. Family alienation ensued after the setting up of distant boarding schools for Native children through their removal from their kin and, as a result, the familiarity with their ancestral culture practically ceased to exist. Of the favourable consequences, the emergence of a small but vocal "Native Euro-Canadian educated" leadership is mentioned, which should bring about the coalescing of the Natives into a self-assertive political group.

ETHNICITY AND CULTURAL RESOURCES

The School As an Issue

The school controversy, which originally began in Manitoba and the Northwest Territories has become best known as the Manitoba School Question; the controversy has been going on with shorter or longer intervals right up to our own time, and may be conceived of as a type of competition for cultural resources. The English speaking majority's view in this respect is presented in Marilyn Barber's chapter. The non-Anglo-Celtic settlers of the prairies often succeeded on inferior soil and in circumstances which were not acceptable to others. The expectation of the receiving society that these foreign immigrants should take over the institutions, language, traditions, values and way of life of the Anglo-Canadians, mainly through the agency of the public elementary school, was promptly challenged by the separate school system of the Roman Catholic minority, and the issue of the language of teaching soon evolved into a centre of controversy on the plains. Owing to demographic, territorial and historical circumstances, the respective proportions of the francophone element in the three prairie provinces after 1905 are seen to have been the decisive factor for the extent of the retention of the ancestral language in the school. The success of the French Roman Catholics under the direction of Archbishop Langevin to retain a definite degree of bilingualism in Manitoba favourably affected other ethnic groups, but in particular the Galicians' and the Ruthenians' (the later Ukrainians') desire also to set up bilingual schools. The subsequent establishment of Ruthenian training schools was destined greatly to influence the future history of the Ukrainian ethnic group. Saskatchewan followed Manitoba's example to the extent of founding training schools for "foreign language communities" — without permitting bilingual schools. Soon the direct method of learning English through actual speaking was discovered and applied, resulting in the elimination of the need for non-Anglo-Celtic teachers as linguistic intermediaries between the Anglo-Celtic and other ancestral cultures. With the gradual approach of the First World War greater and greater emphasis was placed in the school on Canadianization and loyalty to Canada and the British Empire, until "the coming of war translated the pressure for education reform into a hostile demand for immediate and total conformity."

Conflict in New Brunswick

The school controversy spread over to New Brunswick at an early stage. The New Brunswick religio-cultural attitudes are seen by Nanciellen Sealy to resemble tendencies all over the country. It was as early as the 1890s that determined attacks were launched on the Roman Catholic separate schools by the Anglo-Protestant majority. The provinces were but slightly inclined to grant special provisions for the schools of the minorities, whether religious or ethnic. The New Brunswick variant of the school question originated from opposition to the Common Schools Act, 1871. Moves in the 1890s to curtail minority privileges failed owing to co-operation between the Irish and the French Catholics. In more recent years the controversial issue was generated only by the demand for the use of the ancestral tongue as the language of education, which objective was realized in the New Brunswick Official Languages Act 1969. One of the consequences of the measure has been what is termed "language status reversal," leading, in some places, to the exchange of unilingual anglophone for bilingual francophone and to a much wider use of French in service situations. The resultant embarrassment of the unilingual anglophone may have taken the form of anti-bilingualism and opposition to French as an official language. So a legacy of conflict tends to make solution of language-based problems of the present more complex.

The Manitoba School Question

While the circumstances in New Brunswick and certain other parts of the East favoured the co-operation of Francophone and Irish Catholics the situation on the prairies was different. Even before the opening up of the West on a large scale, a steady shift took place in favour of the non-French element in the population of the area. How and why this change occurred with particular reference to the ethnic groups is discussed by Cornelius Jaenen. By the time of Archbishop Langevin in the 1890s provincial legislation made it impossible for both the francophone *free schools* and the Mennonite private schools to receive municipal monetary support. The French Canadian prelate intended to meet the new situation with the building of European immigrants into the St. Boniface Diocese, in which, however, the francophone supremacy was to be preserved through the acquisition and training of dependable priests.

This he hoped to achieve through the Government's providing bilingual teachers — that is, teachers who spoke both English and the language of the ethnic group in question. The School Act of 1897, based to a large extent on the same idea, furnished Manitoba with what may be called a "multi-bilingual" system, which in practice, amounted to no more than three participants: The French, the Mennonites, and the "Ruthenians." In

Langevin's view, the new arrangement had the serious flaw of not according the pioneering French element any greater say than the latest-coming immigrants, yet the number of the *French-English* schools quickly increased after 1896. But properly qualified francophone teachers were not easy to find and in some cases only the intervention of the Archbishop supported by threatened sanctions would persuade the people of francophone districts to retain instruction in French.

When the occasion arose with the arrival of the first waves of Galician, Ruthenian, and Polish immigrants Langevin succeeded in obtaining support for bilingual schools for these immigrants from the Manitoba government in 1901 and, in the spirit of his ultramontane views, championed the cause of providing instruction in the mother tongue. Soon, an open contest followed between the Catholics and Presbyterians for the membership of the Ukrainian settlers. As has already been seen, the opening of a Ruthenian Training School by the Manitoba government in 1905 proved to be of great significance for the retention of the Ukraininan culture. The identification by Langevin of the francophone cause with that of the European immigrants significantly contributed to the survival of the latter. However, the Prelate did not succeed in the recovery of the French Catholic school rights lost in 1890, nor could he secure the perpetuation of the bilingual system. On the contrary, the French-Canadian minority came to be regarded as just another ethnic group.

The Hungarian Question

The Hungarian controversy essentially belongs in the framework of the long struggle mainly between French- and Anglo-Canadians for the control of cultural, political, and economic resources. In the present writer's interpretation, Archbishop Langevin and his assistants attempted to weaken part of the socio-cultural *boundaries* of the non-francophone Catholic ethnic groups, including the Hungarian Canadians, with particular reference to the control of the twin communal microstructures, the church and the school. In this context Langevin well realised that he should oppose any type of instruction in Hungarian that would strengthen enculturation in Magyar traditions and culture and would impede his grand project of maintaining French Catholic political power sufficient to ensure the retention of English-French bilingual schools.

In other words he set out to build up the macrostructural control of the political behaviour of the Catholic regions of Saskatchewan and Manitoba to ensure the institutional fortification of bilingual education in the whole area of the overwhelmingly French settlement. Apparently, the Hungarian Canadian participants of the conflict also had the intention of achieving some degree of macrostructural control over the totality of the Hungarian Canadian settlement of the prairies through the securing of the only Hungarian language paper and the organization of a comprehensive, non-confessional, supra-regional Hungarian Brotherhood Association to act ultimately as an instrument in the competition for economic and cultural resources through political pressure, brought about by the possible election to the legislature of Hungarian Canadians. Such objectives were, of course, to say the least, unacceptable to the prelate; therefore both the Hungarian paper and the Association had to be discredited, or their credibility undermined. There is some evidence to indicate that the socio-cultural intransigence of the Hungarian Canadians (and, for that matter, of the Ukrainians and some other ethnic groups) on the prairies well suited the related objectives and strategy of the federal and provincial Liberals of the time, who, therefore, provided appreciable moral and financial support to the Hungarian Canadian leaders, and that this also contributed to a reasonably satisfactory termination for them of the *Hungarian Question* conflict.

However, the Magyar settlers, not having had experience, on the whole, of minority roles in their country of origin, failed to attach much importance to compatriot teachers for the maintenance of their ancestral culture. Since the parents felt confident that the enculturation of their children in the usually multifilial families would take place easily, they were inclined to assign priority for their children to the mastering of the language of the receiving society, the obvious key to economic and social mobility. On the other hand, the unsophisticated peasant farmers, having been deeply rooted in their folk culture, greatly felt the need for such priests who not only did speak some Hungarian, but possessed sensitivity to their flock's ways of thinking and could establish *rapport* in *their* language.

Although in this context the Hungarian effort to eliminate a francophone control in parishes with large Magyar population and to obtain Hungarian priests and, to a lesser extent, Hungarian teachers for their schools is seen in retrospect as a minor event, yet it might have advanced at the time the cessation of the ultramontane domination of the Roman Catholic Church of Saskatchewan. Furthermore, the examination of the material reveals, on the micro-historical level, the details of Archbishop Langevin's *front line* and the *skirmishes* undertaken for and against his *outposts,* some of which were the Hungarian Canadian parishes of Saskatchewan.

The Termination of the French Bilingual Education in Saskatchewan

Raymond Huel's interpretation of the school question reflects what adds up to the polarization between, on the one hand, the classical missionary stance of the British Empire (often verbalized from the reading of Vergil's *Aeneid*[10] in the Great Public Schools) with Canada contributing to its enlightening and civilizing efforts and, on the other, potential "menace" to this Anglo-Celtic endeavour, generated by the French and the other non-British ethnic groups through their attempts to maintain their language and culture.

Prime Minister Laurier's failure to secure federal provisions for confessional schools also in Saskatchewan and the refusal of the new provincial government in 1905 to act according to the constitutional guarantee in respect of the religious minority's right to set up and operate separate schools, were only the beginnings of a long process. A phase of this ended with legislation in 1919 to secure the public school as an instrument for the unification of the people of Saskatchewan into a 'harmonious whole' through the enactment of unilingual education (with some exceptions in favour of the francophones). Thus education became a most essential macrostructural instrument for the government to attempt in the interwar period the achieving and maintaining of British social solidarity and cultural homogeneity in Saskatchewan.

Huel's chapter can be considered also the account of some of the consequences for the French Canadian minority in the West of Archbishop Langevin's well-meaning but largely ill-assorted strategy in the rearguard actions in what was to become a gradual withdrawal of the French Canadian minority of the West to the status of *just another ethnic group* under the leadership of the francophone clergy.

The Assimilationist Model of Education

Of course the collapse of the French bilingual schools was not the only collapse; as seen in Nadia Kazymyra's paper, also the Ukrainian schools suffered the same fate. The chapter by Savelia Curnisky provides the description of the consequences of this development. The Saskatchewan system of education of the interwar period is seen as designed to achieve uniformity of education and conformity on the part of the non Anglo-Celtic population, irrespective of the deeply rooted national and peasant traditions of the Ukrainian immigrant. Not only their ancestral culture but also their knowledge of eastern Europe was neglected by the curriculum which was centred on the instruction of the English language, British history and pride in and loyalty to the British Empire. The present-day ethnic communities, Curnisky believes, must receive support from within the educational system if they are to maintain any significant level of cultural awareness, unless it is to be only a token expression of culture such as folk dancing and cuisine. In other words the schools should not limit their functions to those of assimilation but should also contribute to the enculturation of the ancestral culture.

Viewed in the context of its era, this system of education proved most effective in achieving its main objective: the creation of a cultural "common denominator" for the members of the many disparate ethnic categories of the province. In retrospect, it might be regarded as regrettable that a portion of the enculturative effort of the public school curriculum should not have been reserved for the ancestral culture. However, such an insight would have been truly remarkable and, indeed, unique at a time when most of the governments of the world were vying with one another in an attempt to assimilate their ethnic minorities.

Outcome of the School Question

It is helpful to recall in the present setting that Alan Anderson's investigation in 18 ethnic bloc settlements in Saskatchewan in 1968-71 was indicative of a surprisingly rapid decline between 1961 and 1971 in the proportion of those settlers still conversant with their (non-English) ancestral tongues. These findings signify a very high degree of linguistic assimilative effectiveness in the past of Saskatchewan as a part of the Canadian society.[11] The provincial legislation codifying the outcome of the School Question controversy and the education system translating the law into practice, have had a major share in this comparatively quick linguistic change.

Donald Willmott's finding as regards the considerable weakening of the *solidarity* of two Saskatchewan ethnic groups formerly strong in this respect, may also justify the proposing of the hypothesis that linguistic assimilation tends to be the external sign of far-reaching socio-cultural changes within a group.

The trend is further corroborated by the conclusion of Allan Walker's paper which points out that an important feature of the community college system in Saskatchewan is the weight that is given to local participation in determining types, contents, and times of adult education activities in a locality. Since persons of Anglo-Celtic origin constitute less than half of the population, a very high demand for ethnic-related and folkloric content within the curricula of the community colleges could be expected. Yet, in reality, the system seems to have aroused a very minor interest in ethnic-related activities. The most significant single contributory cause to this state of affairs, as identified by Walker, seems to lie in a vast shift in the ethno-linguistic structure[12] of the population of the province. This process is illustrated by the fact that, despite the statistical presence of a non-Anglo-Celtic population of almost 60% in 1971, nearly 70% claimed English as their native tongue and no fewer than 90% as "the language most often spoken at home."

At this stage, attention is drawn to Alan Anderson's assumption that the expected discontinuation in the near future of the use of non-English ancestral languages in Saskatchewan may not mean the simultaneous disappearance of the respective *ethnic identities,* but probably the gradual reinterpretation of the criteria for the same. No doubt, the role of the control of the school as a *microstructure* and of its *macrostructural* equivalent, education, proved most significant in the assimilative process. Yet, it was only one of several admittedly interacting factors, of which five are referred to in Anderson's paper. Perhaps future research will throw light on the functions and relative weight, in the context, of such factors.

The School of the Present

While the achievement of an ethno-cultural democracy among the numerous ethnic groups of Canada seems to be the ultimate purpose of *multiculturalism*[13] adopted by the federal government in 1971, this policy is very properly based on the simultaneous encouragement of a more distinct Canadian Identity. According to John Mallea, consensus at the local level is lacking as yet on what, if any, function the school in this context ought to have. To educational theoreticians it appears crystal-clear that the roots of the child's personality spring from his native culture. Yet the fact that sudden and complete severance from the ancestral ethnic culture of the individual often leads to other types of alienation as well is being recognized by the practitioners of education only very gradually. The circumstance that the consideration also of the other (than the Anglo-Celtic) ethnic backgrounds and contributions to Canadian life and culture, as an organic part of the general Canadian history in the school curriculum, still remains to be operationalized, apparently constitutes a sign of the cultural lag between theory and practice. But this lag may be regarded as a natural offspring of the unicultural and unitraditional policies of the educationists of not so long ago.

The school, not unlike many other aspects of the Canadian society, is being affected in a larger measure by the conflict between the universalizing tendencies of an ever-quickening process of modernization and the discrepant cultural norms of the ethnic groups, in which clash, rootedness in an ethnic culture as well may moderate the alienating influence of a technological mass society.[14] Despite a more cautious assessment today of the school's potential to reform the basic structures of society, the school can contribute very greatly to the promotion of social cohesion, and, at the same time, of the freedom of cultural maintenance including customs, values and languages.

IDENTITY AND ALIENATION

Social Network and Alienation

The formation of ethnic enclaves, an important phase in the life of an ethnic category, often derives from *chain migration*. Recent studies have directed attention to the essential role in this process of *social networks* which also seem to affect the occupation concentrations of members of ethnic groups. An examination of the immigration patterns of Portuguese speakers (a recent immigrant category) by Grace Anderson[15] tends to suggest a decisive part played by chain migration both in the initiation and in the developmental aspects of later Portuguese settlement patterns. Thus, many of the pre-1953 Portuguese immigrants became the *spearhead anchorages* of networks in respect of the later Portuguese arrivals. Contact, or lack of it, with social networks appears to constitute a significant factor not only in determining occupational and residential choice for newcomers, but also in the reduction of the rate of alienation through increased opportunities for ethnic in-group interaction.

Dual Alienation

The most important characteristic of *well socialized* people is smooth functioning within the society. They are capable of conforming to the *broader forms* of society and of interpreting their social environment with comparative ease. The actions of others will become more meaningful and predictable for them. Children, not unlike immigrants, go through the process of *assimilation* into society. In the course of their growing up they are expected to give up the roles and values of the previous stage in their development, and finally they must appropriate those of the society of adults. During the process of their adjustment to the adult social order children may become *alienated* from their social groups as they discard the modes of childhood but cannot achieve full identification as adults. The symptoms of this *developmental estrangement* may include types of behaviour socially disapproved or proscribed, because they may be looked upon as deviant or criminal. This case of "defective or arrested social development" may be, in Arthur Cropley's explanation, the consequence of the fact that parents may not have the skill or the means "to communicate clear expectations and credible models to their children." They may even transmit the folk ways (values) of aversion of a culture which is distant, not only spatially, but also temporally. As ethnic group children as well are exposed to the twin processes of assimilation (attachment to the new culture) and alienation (detachment from the ancestral culture) they may be exposed to *dual* alienation (desocialization). *Multicultural*[16] approach would reduce the negative consequences of alienation. This approach may envisage eventual assimilation to the dominant group, or *ethnic coexistence,* a state of relative and lasting balance between the dominant and the minority groups. This state of affairs would encompass the *structural* integration and the retention of socio-cultural segregation of the individual groups.

Marginal Identity

The life, in the depression, of the itinerant Croatian labourers in Anthony Rasporich's presentation constitutes a fair example of multiple alienation. The first variant of their alienation had occurred in their crisis-ridden native country, which circumstance apparently was then the reason for their immigration to Canada. Nonetheless, they tended to come through chain migration from the same village or region. No doubt their life in the camp and intermittent work in a greater or smaller distance, coupled with a feeling of uncertainty, provided another type of alienation for them. Moreover, they were *marginal men*[17] territorially living far away from the main centres of Canadian culture and civilization as well as socially hovering in a precarious manner between labouring and unemployment at the very bottom of society. It is not entirely surprising that some of them should have become radicalized, or that, when participating in miners' strikes, they attracted attention and concomitant discriminatory treatment which at times ended in their deportation. They may be deemed the prototypes of the unemployed, or partly employed, of the depression years drifting from one place to the other without any roots and without being able to form permanent groups, institutions, or microstructures.

The historical-analytical examination of the lifestyle and culture of rural groups of immigrants does not occur nearly so frequently as the social-analytic type based on the study of urban ethnic groups, despite the potentially sharper insight into social processes that the study of such a subject might yield.

The Alienation of the WASP

An unexpected candidate for ethnic alienation, the so-called WASP (White Anglo-Saxon Protestant) category, is offered by Linda Bell Deutschmann. Perhaps it is somewhat unusual to posit that also the dominant groups in a society constitute ethnic groups and are exposed to the same social processes as any other ethnic group is. Thus Deutschmann finds that the cultural boundary lines between the component groups of the WASP or "Anglo" are gradually disappearing owing to such processes as intermarriage or, simply, assimilation. These constituent groups, the Scottish, Irish, Welsh and English, are now seen to be located in a general category, members of which have already been largely alienated from their respective home lands in Britain, though on the other hand, they have not been completely absorbed in a Canadian identity. Of course, additional socio-cultural influence occurs from other ethnic groups as well through quite extensive intermarriage, we might add. Moreover, the Anglo-Celtic group is just as susceptible to all the various types of cultural change as the other groups are. In the wake of the modernizing influence of the technical urban culture, the values and mores are transformed in the same proportion as those of the other groups. It can almost be posited as a theorem that there is no integration without disintegration, precisely the same way as there is no assimilation without alienation.

Negative Self-Image

Attention is drawn by Marguerite Burke to the fact that Canadian studies in the public schools still seem to concentrate on Canadians of British and French origin; so students deriving from this sort of background attempt to learn about the history and cultural traditions of their ancestors and also identify with them. But students of different ancestry cannot have similar experiences. Without the opportunity for identification with one's own cultural group one cannot develop a positive self-image. On the other hand it might be remarked that negative self-image results in what we call alienation. To avoid this contingency it would be the task of the public school to undertake an equally inclusive and thorough study of the other ethnic groups of Canada.

ETHNIC RESEARCH: RESOURCES AND METHODOLOGY

Oral Research

Oral history constitutes a new technique for historical research. Its birth has been obviously connected with the availability of reasonably light tape-recording devices. The oral research method suggested by Stanley Scott contains a preliminary study of the cultural backgrounds of the respective ethnic groups to be investigated. The interviewing is restricted to one "knowledgeable" member from the three generations of each of the ethnic groups contained in the settlement to be studied. In the illustrative case, the West Kootenays region of British Columbia, one member from each of the three generations of Russian, Italian, and English families — that is, all told, nine persons — were interviewed. Each of them was questioned in depth with the help of extensive question sheets. A Guide was drawn up to serve as a check-off sheet to be completed as part of each interview session. A remarkable finding revealed the existence of "superficial" cultural traits, presumably indicative of the technological culture common to all groups. But, "surprisingly, most recollections of history — local or otherwise — remained much the same from generation to generation and family to family."

This observation may be interpreted as meaning the continuation of what may be termed *group memory*, likely forming part of individual ethnicity. Also occasion was found for the application in practice of the research results as exemplifying the techniques as well in a "packaged" form. In consequence, a project of a new type was introduced at the elementary and secondary schools and interest and sensitivity were created among the students as regards local history as well as the ethnic heritage.

Ethnic Institutes

The establishment of the Canadian Institute of Ukrainian Studies on the University of Alberta campus indicates just as great an achievement from the viewpoint of Ukrainian studies as the Saskatchewan Indian Federated College,[18] recently set up on the campus of the University of Regina, does for the sake of Indian studies. Both institutes may be looked upon as macrostructures, potentially expressive of a degree of cultural autonomy. At the time of the writing of these remarks (1977), both of them are going concerns, active in accordance with their respective programmes. As to the Institute of Ukrainian Studies, Director Manoly Lupul refers to the strengthening and expansion of department-based Ukrainian studies at all Canadian Universities with particular reference to the undergraduate level. The Institute itself specializes in the training of research personnel for Ukrainian and related studies. In Lupul's view "a new type of leaders" as well is envisaged, presumably, as a result of the work in the future of the Institute, who are not only familiar with as many aspects of Ukrainian culture and literature as possible, but who have a command of English and, possibly French in addition to Ukrainian. Indeed a hierarchy of leaders is visualised, distributed to all levels of society, to act probably as liaison persons with "all forums that count."

In this context an account of recent developments as regards Indian studies suggests that the Indian Federated College, University of Regina, has been striving toward similar ultimate objectives. For the time being, the College is seen as a macrostructural institution run by Indians for Indians with a view also to promoting the image of *Indianness,* possibly in contradistinction to tribal loyalties which still seem to prevail. Of course, the term *Indianness* is used for lack of a more appropriate one since, as has been noted above, the word *Indian,* in addition to being a misnomer, is not readily used by the Indians themselves. Nonetheless, there are some signs of an emerging Indian, or, rather, a *Dene* nationalism:

> We, the Dene of the Northwest Territories, insist on the right to be regarded by ourselves and the world as a nation. ... What we seek, then, is independence and self-determination within the country of Canada. This is what we mean when we call for a just land settlement for the Dene Nation.[19]

Ethnic Archives

The recent revival of concern for ethnicity, ethnic categories, and their contributions to Canadian culture and economy will most probably affect, in due course, the students of the general Canadian history as well. In anticipation of the emergence and quickening of such a trend, important innovations have taken place in the organization of great collections of archival records.

As a conspicuous example of this development, the newly established Ethnic Archives within the structure of the Public Archives of Canada, Ottawa, offer rich holdings in respect of ethnic-related materials. Bryan Corbett of the Public Archives enumerates and explains the types and respective research potential of various classes of archival records, referring to individual immigrants, to ethnic groups and their areas of settlement. Furthermore, the files of ethno-religious organizations, papers concerning the contributions of the railway companies to the peopling and development of the West, and many other topics are contained in the Public Archives. Similar categories of materials are kept in the custody of the Provincial Archives of Saskatchewan (Regina and Saskatoon), though naturally in smaller quantities. Particularly interesting, and in many cases unique, are collections of private papers, records of businesses, socio-cultural organizations, as well as Saskatchewan newspapers and newspaper indices. The newly appointed Provincial Archivist, Ian Wilson, has initiated measures to facilitate ethnic research through the appointment of a staff archivist with particular responsibilities in connection with the research and documentation of the history of the ethno-cultural communities of the Province.

Greater emphasis has been placed on the collection of ethnic-related records, and guides will be provided for the location of material of this type among the multifarious holdings of the Archives.

This trend, paralleled in many other archives, reflects a gradual shift of research to a new and important field and, by the same token, manifests the rising status of the ethnic categories within the framework of Canadian society.

Concluding Propositions

Although the authors of the papers derive from a variety of cultural backgrounds and disciplines and write on seemingly disparate topics, the propositions that could serve as an integrative element for the volume might be worded *tentatively* as follows:

a. The studies which make up this volume represent a cross-section of opinion, more or less valid, concerning the state and outlook of ethnic research in this country in 1976.

b. Despite the spate of recent conceptual studies on the nature, effects, and implications of *ethnicity,* there is room for further discussion of this concept particularly in the Canadian context.

c. The School Question, the macrostructural competition for the control of education, schools, and related cultural resources between the English- and French-speaking Canadians, cannot be limited *territorially* — for instance, only to Manitoba — or *timewise* to any one date, or *ethnically* to the francophones and the anglophones. On the contrary, the controversy flared up in many places in Canada, including Saskatchewan. It has continued, at least in its ethno-cultural consequences, ever since its inception and has been *publicly* reopened more recently. Numerous ethnic categories have participated in it, either actively or, more frequently, passively, at times intended as political instruments for the major contestants.

d. The results so far of the School Question controversy have relevance for the present and the future. They may be summed up very briefly as the provision — notwithstanding unfortunate traumatic experiences of ethnic groups — of a common denominator for a very large portion of the Canadian society in a quickly emerging Canadian culture, with the English (and lately also the French) language as a means of interethnic and supraethnic communication.

e. In view of this development and the growing consciousness also in this country of the socio-economic and cultural input of members of the numerous smaller ethnic categories, it might be timely for the school to acknowledge this fact in its curriculum and its teaching as well.

f. Multicultural Canadian society may be regarded as an association of dynamic ethnic categories (with ethnicity being subject to periodical reinterpretation) ranging from the dominant groups through those aspiring to cultural autonomy right to the ones tending to seek socio-economic advancement by assimilating with the dominant groups.

g. Both assimilation and alienation are processes and the results (sums) of the same processes, which impinge on all ethnic categories or, for that matter, on all social groups.

h. Subjective factors, often overlooked, play an essential part in the shaping and life of ethnic phenomena; thus, *alienation* would often be the consequence of subjective impressions, and it may refer to a subjective state of the individual or the group mind, brought about by change felt excessive or unwelcome by persons and the group affected. Furthermore, self-esteem is based in a great degree on one's pride in one's work and cultural background, including ethnicity. However, self-esteem in most cases needs social recognition and support also through the allotment of commensurate socio-economic resources, expressed in financial terms and social status. Self-esteem, work-pride, and cultural-ethnic pride may be conceived each as a *continuum* between the parameters of maximal and minimal achievements. Indeed, attainment may decline into minus values which may be construed again as signs of *alienation* of varying severity. It may then be hypothesized that one important aspect of *Canadianism* ("striving for Canadianness"), *Canadian unity* (non-politically perhaps "consensus for and pride in Canadianness") might be looked upon as a function of the self-esteem, work-pride, and cultural-ethnic pride of the persons forming the constituent ethnic categories.[20]

FOOTNOTES

[1] Victor W. Turner, *The Ritual Process* (Chicago, 1969), 167, 203.

[2] *Modern Dictionary of Sociology,* ed. by G. A. and A. G. Theodorson (New York, 1969), 135, 136.

[3] For the discussion of other Indian-related topics, see *Ethnicity and Folklore, The Indians, The Native People,* and *Ethnic Institutes* below.

[4] John Parker is critical about the enhancement of the self-concept through ethnic identification. Compensation for insufficient status achievement without actually promoting achievement does not serve its purpose. He points at the paradox, facing many low-status ethnic groups, of having to pay the price for culture retention in reduced chances of competition in the modern technological society. John Parker, "Ethnic Pluralism in Canadian Perspective," in N. Glazer and D. P. Moynihan, *Ethnicity: Theory and Experience* (Cambridge, Mass., 1975).

[5] The *cultural brokers* of the present appear very similar to the *bilingual teachers,* appointed or voluntary, in Manitoba and Saskatchewan earlier this century. See *The Manitoba School Question* below.

[6] Note Zenon Pohorecky's related observations and cf. *Saskatchewan* below.

[7] An additional and characteristic instance of Kirkconnell's image making, or more accurately, transmitting activity is the anthology *The Magyar Muse* (Winnipeg, 1933) which set out his interpretation of the Hungarian image through the translation of selected poetry.

[8] For the consideration of other Ukrainian-related topics, see *Ethnicity and Nation Building, Ukrainians, Saskatchewan, The Manitoba School Question, The Assimilationist Model of Education,* and *Ethnic Institutes* below.

[9] See Talcott Parsons' view on the relationship between *solidarity* and *loyalty;* "Some Theoretical Considerations on the Nature and Trends of Change of Ethnicity," in N. Glazer and D. P. Moynihan, *Ethnicity: Theory and Experience* (Cambridge, Mass., 1975), 59 ff.

[10] Vergil, *Aeneid,* VI, 1782-1784.

[11] Up to about the Second World War "anglo-conformity" was the prevailing pattern of assimilation in the English-speaking part of Canada. Howard Palmer, "Reluctant Hosts: Anglo-Canadian Views of Multiculturalism in the Twentieth Century," in Canadian Consultative Council on Multiculturalism, *Multiculturalism as State Policy* (Ottawa, 1976), 85.

[12] In connection with language loss it is relevant to call attention to Carmen Lambert's remark in her paper that language may function as a "barrier to complete cultural assimilation" and as a tool of the maintenance of a "philosophy and a mode of thought" particular to an ethnicity.

Furthermore, it would be useful also to ponder the implications of the positive correlations between the status of language and the status of its speakers, as well as of the inherent "linkage of the language" to personal, social, and cultural identity, as attested in Nanciellen Sealy's study.

[13] Of course, much depends on the interpretation in practice of the concept *Multiculturalism.* For some relevant questions in this context, see Palmer, *op. cit.,* 104-105. Also see footnote 16 below.

[14] See, also, Wsevolod W. Isajiw, "Olga in Wonderland: Ethnicity in Technological Society," *Canadian Ethnic Studies,* 9 (1977), 77-85. The article contains useful observations on ethnicity and multiculturalism as well.

[15] For further information see Grace M. Anderson and David Higgs, *A Future to Inherit* (Toronto, 1976), for instance, 42-43.

[16] *Multiculturalism* refers to a recent federal policy designed to interpret and evaluate the relationships, in the first place between the two principal categories (popularly described as "charter groups") and, then, between these two and the other ethnic categories, with a view to formulating practical measures. There seem to have been certain difficulties experienced in the proper understanding of the term on the part of the general public. Neither the resort

to the metaphor *mosaic,* nor the wording of some of the official explanations appears to have contributed sufficiently to the better comprehension of the meaning of multiculturalism, even for sophisticated observers. The *mosaic,* only suggesting a one-dimensional, rigidly-fixed and static variegation, tends to suggest a surface and, therefore, superficiality and, more importantly, appearances rather than the essential features of Canadian society, which a symbol would be expected to convey.

Would it not be more expressive and relevant to adopt the *maple tree* in this symbolic role, adding at the same time greater force to the mystery of the *Maple Leaf?* The branches and the leaves of the tree would figuratively show the visible ramifications and complexity of the existing society, into which, in addition to the ethnic colouring, it is divided. The trunk, with its innumerable cells, fibres, and filaments, may well be seen as symbolic representation of the Canadian culture, with the roots signifying the parent and component ethnic cultures. The thought of the lateral and vertical growth of the tree, together with the periodical loss and renewal of the leaves, would adequately exhibit the dynamism of multicultural Canada.

This metaphoric use of the maple tree would also be expressive of some of the findings of the studies in this volume which seem to imply that the behaviour of both individuals and groups is greatly subject to affective stimulation, often in direct contradiction to the expectations of scholarly logic, leading to an ever-broadening and intensifying interethnic interaction.

For recent variegated discussion of *Multiculturalism,* see "The Francophone Viewpoint" and "The Anglophone Viewpoint," in Canadian Consultative Council on Multiculturalism, *Multiculturalism As State Policy* (Ottawa, 1976), 27-57, 59-118.

[17] *Marginality* may be regarded as a group of symptoms characteristic of a certain type of *alienation.* For a concise discussion of *marginality* itself, see J. W. Vander Zanden, *American Minority Relations* (New York, 1966), 313-19.

[18] The Saskatchewan Indian Cultural College entered into federation with the University of Regina in May, 1976. Its objectives were "1. To have direct control and administration of an institution of education by the Indian peoples of Saskatchewan, 2. To research, develop, and implement methods and programmes to make relevant the educational process to the Indian peoples of Saskatchewan, and 3. To maintain and promote the various Indian cultures of Saskatchewan in terms of histories, beliefs, and values." Programme of the *Saskatchewan Indian Federated College, University of Regina* (Regina, Saskatchewan, 1977), 5.

[19] Excerpts from the *Dene Declaration, Statement of Rights,* passed at the second Joint General Assembly of the Indian Brotherhood of the Northwest Territories and the Metis Association of the Northwest Territories on July 19, 1975. See Mel Watkins, *Dene Nation — the Colony Within* (Toronto and Buffalo, 1977), 3-4.

[20] The contributions of the present writer to this volume have been made possible through the Canada Council Research Grant S75-0408, which fact is gratefully acknowledged herewith. The present writer also wishes to express his appreciation to Dr. L. G. Crossman for helpful comments.

Views and opinions expressed by individual authors are not necessarily shared by the editor.